"Anyone interested in what Hank Rosso calls 'the joy of giving' will find value in this carefully edited book. Its comprehensive coverage and thought-provoking content provides numerous opportunities for reflection on what is required and what it means to be an effective and ethical fundraiser. In this fourth edition of a now classic text, the authors continue to advance the profession of fundraising. We are treated to updated information, findings from recent scholarship, and an instructor's guide to further enhance learning."

> —**Mary Tschirhart,** Professor, The Ohio State University; co-author of *Managing Nonprofit Organizations*

"Achieving excellence in fundraising is an important goal for CASE members worldwide who have chosen a career in the field. There is much debate as to the extent to which fundraising is an art or a science. The reality is that to be excellent, it has to be a combination of both, delivered with commitment, passion and integrity. New ideas and innovation continue to develop in the rapidly changing world of community and connectivity. Valuable, therefore, to have this fourth edition of *Achieving Excellence in Fundraising* which not only reminds us of the essentials of fundraising principles, but also covers new ground. The chapter on the opportunities availed in the 21st century through fast evolving social media is timely. As is the chapter on the joys imbued in philanthropic support including evidence both of the contagiousness of giving and its life enhancing and extending qualities! For those coming fresh to a career in fundraising there is much to discover here. For those who have made a career in this life transforming profession, this book provides helpful reminders and considerable food for thought."

> —**Sue Cunningham,** President, Council for Advancement and Support of Education

"Achieving excellence in fundraising is a major goal of the best nonprofit CEOs and development professionals. This fully updated and comprehensive volume covers everything from developing the right philosophical approach to fundraising to understanding how to establish and execute both old and new fundraising strategies, as well as how to create and manage a development office. This book will be invaluable to both emerging and seasoned fund development professionals."

> —**Emmett D. Carson, Ph.D.,** Chief Executive Officer, Silicon Valley Community Foundation

"Philanthropy is uniquely invaluable to the well-being of culture and community, and *Achieving Excellence in Fundraising* remains uniquely invaluable to the advancement of philanthropy. The Fund Raising School has relied on all previous editions of this knowledge-filled book to deliver highly impactful training to fundraising professionals around the world. This 4th edition combines timeless wisdom with the latest research-based strategies that are essential for fundraising success in the 21st Century economy."

> —**Bill Stanczykiewicz,** Director, The Fund Raising School and Senior Lecturer, Philanthropic Studies, Indiana University Lilly Family School of Philanthropy

"It is fitting that this fourth edition of *Achieving Excellence in Fundraising* marks the transition from what was once a center on philanthropy to now the Indiana University Lilly Family School of Philanthropy. Yet, more importantly, this edition reaffirms the principles of the former center's visionary, Henry A. 'Hank' Rosso, whose voice and ideas reverberate and are woven within each essay, particularly, Gene Tempel's introduction who further inscribes, etches and connects Rosso's legacy to the IU Lilly Family School's present and future."

> —**Brian Johnson, Ph.D.,** President, Tuskegee University

"It's hard to imagine a more useful addition to the bookshelves of nonprofit professionals. But this book won't just sit on the shelf-fundraisers, board members and nonprofit executives will find it to be a handy and astute reference guide to building a comprehensive giving program. I've kept this book close at hand in every nonprofit job I've had. The new edition is based on many decades of research and professional experience from some of the top experts in the field, and is a useful reference guide for building stronger relationships between grantmakers and fundraisers."

> —**Caroline Altman Smith,** Senior Program Officer, The Kresge Foundation

"This book is an indispensable resource for both the fundraising novice and the seasoned professional. It is a current and comprehensive collection of essays written by highly respected professionals and touches every dimension of philanthropy. I strongly recommend it for everyone working in the philanthropic sector."

> —**Rodney P. Kirsch,** Senior Vice President for Development and Alumni Relations, The Pennsylvania State University

Essential Texts for Nonprofit and Public Leadership and Management

The Handbook of Nonprofit Governance, by BoardSource

Strategic Planning for Public and Nonprofit Organizations, 3rd edition, by John M. Bryson

The Effective Public Manager, 4th edition, by Steven Cohen et al.

Handbook of Human Resources Management in Government, 3rd edition, by Stephen E. Condrey (Ed.)

The Responsible Administrator, 5th edition, by Terry L. Cooper

Conducting a Successful Capital Campaign, revised and expanded edition, by Kent E. Dove

The Public Relations Handbook for Nonprofits, by Arthur Feinglass

The Jossey-Bass Handbook of Nonprofit Leadership and Management, 3rd edition, by David O. Renz, Robert D. Herman, & Associates (Eds.)

Benchmarking in the Public and Nonprofit Sectors, 2nd edition, by Patricia Keehley et al.

Museum Marketing and Strategy, 2nd edition, by Neil Kotler et al.

The Ethics Challenge in Public Service, 2nd edition, by Carol W. Lewis et al.

Leading Across Boundaries, by Russell M. Linden

Designing and Planning Programs for Nonprofit and Government Organizations, by Edward J. Pawlak

Measuring Performance in Public and Nonprofit Organizations, by Theodore H. Poister

Human Resources Management for Public and Nonprofit Organizations: A Strategic Approach, 3rd edition, by Joan E. Pynes

Understanding and Managing Public Organizations, 4th edition, by Hal G. Rainey

Designing and Conducting Survey Research, 3rd edition, by Louis M. Rea et al.

Fundraising Principles and Practice, by Adrian Sargeant, Jen Shang, & Associates

Making Critical Decisions, by Roberta M. Snow et al.

Handbook of Practical Program Evaluation, 3rd edition, by Joseph S. Wholey, Harry P. Hatry, & Kathryn E. Newcomer (Eds.)

The Instructor's Guide for the fourth edition of *Achieving Excellence in Fundraising* includes syllabi and supporting materials for semester-long undergraduate and semester-long graduate versions of the course. The Instructor's Guide is available free online. If you would like to download and print a copy of the guide, please visit:
www.wiley.com/college/tempel

IUPUI

LILLY FAMILY
SCHOOL OF PHILANTHROPY

INDIANA UNIVERSITY
Indianapolis

The Indiana University Lilly Family School of Philanthropy is the world's first school dedicated solely to education and research about philanthropy. Established in 2012, the school was inaugurated in 2013 and named for one of America's great philanthropic families in honor of their generations of generosity and leadership.

Indiana University has been at the vanguard of philanthropy education since the Center on Philanthropy at Indiana University was founded at Indiana University—Purdue University Indianapolis (IUPUI) in 1987. Led by the center, Indiana University (IU) established the field of philanthropic studies; established the nation's first bachelor's, master's, and Ph.D. degrees in the field; and created the nation's first endowed chair in philanthropy.

The Lilly Family School of Philanthropy prepares students, philanthropy professionals, donors and volunteers to be thoughtful innovators and leaders who create positive and lasting change. Alumni of its programs lead national nonprofits and foundations, serve international relief organizations, and lead hands-on neighborhood human services centers.

As the pioneer of the unique, liberal arts-based field of philanthropic studies, the school and its world-class faculty offer unparalleled academic degree programs and rigorous, objective research that sets the standard for the field and provides a crucial resource for philanthropy and nonprofits. Through global partnerships, teaching and learning experiences on six continents, and an international student body, the school increases understanding of philanthropy within and across cultures.

The Lilly Family School of Philanthropy integrates innovative academic, research, international and training programs with groundbreaking resources such as The Fund Raising School, the Women's Philanthropy Institute, and Lake Institute on Faith & Giving.

The Fund Raising School, which Hank Rosso moved to Indiana University in 1987 to form the centerpiece for the founding of the Center on Philanthropy, continues today as the premier international, university, and curriculum-based fundraising education program. For the more than 40 years since its founding in 1974, The Fund Raising School has taught successful, ethical, systematic, mission-focused fundraising, volunteer board leadership, and nonprofit management practices to more than 43,000 people in more than 40 countries. Experienced fundraising professionals comprise The Fund Raising School's faculty, offering multiple online and in-person sessions of 15 different regularly scheduled courses in Indianapolis and in cities around the nation as well as sponsored, customized courses in locations around the globe.

As a hub for philanthropic thought and research, the Lilly Family School of Philanthropy regularly convenes innovators, scholars, philanthropists, fundraisers, nonprofit and foundation professionals, and researchers to share their diverse perspectives, exchange ideas, and develop insights that anticipate trends, address pressing issues, and shape the future of philanthropy.

For more information, please visit: philanthropy.iupui.edu.

ACHIEVING EXCELLENCE IN FUNDRAISING

FOURTH EDITION

Eugene R. Tempel, Timothy L. Seiler,
and Dwight F. Burlingame,
Editors

WILEY

Published by John Wiley & Sons, Inc., Hoboken, New Jersey
Published simultaneously in Canada

For general information about our other products and services, please contact our Customer Care Department within the United States at (800) 762-2974 and outside the United States at (317) 572-3993 or fax (317) 572-4002.

Wiley publishes in a variety of print and electronic formats and by print-on-demand. Some material included with standard print versions of this book may not be included in e-books or in print-on-demand. If this book refers to media such as a CD or DVD that is not included in the version you purchased, you may download this material at http://booksupport.wiley.com. For more information about Wiley products, visit www.wiley.com.

Library of Congress Cataloging-in-Publication Data:

Names: Tempel, Eugene R., editor. | Seiler, Timothy L., editor. |
    Burlingame, Dwight, editor.
Title: Achieving excellence in fundraising / Eugene R. Tempel, Timothy L.
    Seiler, and Dwight F. Burlingame, editors.
Description: 4th edition. | Hoboken, New Jersey : John Wiley & Sons, Inc.,
    [2016] Includes bibliographical references and index.
Identifiers: LCCN 2015038322 | ISBN 9781118853825 (cloth)
Subjects: LCSH: Fund raising.
Classification: LCC HG177 .R67 2016 | DDC 658.15/224–dc23 LC record available at
http://lccn.loc.gov/2015038322

Printed in the United States of America

10 9 8 7 6 5 4 3 2

This book is dedicated to the Trustees of Indiana University, University and campus leadership, donors and funders, faculty and staff who believed in the potential of, and took the bold steps to create, the Indiana University Lilly Family School of Philanthropy.

CONTENTS

PART ONE: A PHILANTHROPIC CONTEXT FOR FUNDRAISING   1

PART FIVE: THE ART OF SOLICITATION   361

PART SIX: INVOLVING VOLUNTEERS   429

PART SEVEN: ETHICS AND ACCOUNTABILITY   465

PART EIGHT: YOUR CAREER IN FUNDRAISING   501

LIST OF TABLES, FIGURES, AND EXHIBITS

Tables

Figures

Exhibits

FOREWORD

The mark of a vital institution is that it renews its traditions to stay in tune with the times. A mark of a great institution is that is spawns other institutions and traditions, celebrating their multiplicity as they thrive. Such is an institution that is being renewed in the 4th edition of *Achieving Excellence in Fundraising*.

The book contains new research and fresh voices that update and complement the lasting wisdom as formulated by Hank Rosso, the editor of the first edition. Hank's vision of an ethical, joy-inducing, and dignified profession has come to guide many who practice and study philanthropy. The Fund Raising School he brought to Indianapolis served as the seed of the Center on Philanthropy, now the Lilly Family School of Philanthropy at Indiana University. The four decades of instruction in the curriculum he crafted thrived on a creative tension between the research findings of academics and practical feedback from those in the field. This creative collaboration is in evidence in the current volume, which succeeds in that rare accomplishment – integrating the insights of professors and practitioners.

Just as the legacies of Hank Rosso, Robert Payton, Charles Johnson, and others of their time are seen in these pages, so is the institution building work of our current editors. Tim Seiler has been at the helm of The Fund Raising School for two decades and has inducted legions of passionate students into the ranks of the globally expanding fundraising profession. He extended the brand and impact of

The Fund Raising School with a dogged focus on integrity and attention to what is actually known, and known to work.

Gene Tempel was involved in the founding of the Center, and after a quarter century of nurturing Indiana's role at the epicenter of serious philanthropic deliberations, he achieved the launch of the world's first School of Philanthropy and served as its founding Dean. A "pracademic" (a word I learned from him), in the sense of successfully straddling the divide between research and practice, Gene has stewarded this book over the years as a reflection of the work being done in Indiana.

Dwight Burlingame is the academic soul of the book and of the School that has risen in tandem with it. He has written key works on philanthropy, mentored current leaders in the field, edited seminal series of publications, and established venues for researchers to explore questions about the once much more mysterious practices of giving and asking.

Together Tim, Gene, and Dwight have constituted a singularly important node for multiple networks of practitioners, institution builders, and academics in the philanthropic sector worldwide. Ask anyone you respect in the world of philanthropy, be they donors, fundraisers, or academics, and ask them to examine the tapestry of their professional relationships. It won't take too long for them to identify the threads that lead back to our editors and the work they have pioneered in Indiana.

If you do not yet have your own thread to connect you to Indiana, you are about to have one.

As with the original edition, this volume "has integrity as a holistic work." However, there are different pathways you can take through the volume. It can be used as a textbook or a reference source when particular issues arise, or even as an aid when some inspiration is needed in the midst of an operational or moral conundrum.

Novices will find essential concepts explained clearly and located within a context that gives them meaning and relevance. The experienced professional can delve into contemporary research such as work on empathy that informs the joy of giving, while also brushing up on fundamentals of relationship building that have withstood the test of time. Those who lead organizations will find descriptions of proven operational structures and guidelines for managing the variety of processes that make up a comprehensive fundraising effort. Trustees and volunteers can understand how they can be most useful to their organization, and how they can allow themselves to be most usefully managed by staff leadership. All of us will benefit from wrestling with the difficult issues when we need be sure that we stand on solid ethical ground. In addition, readers from inside and outside professional philanthropy will be keen to read about the changing professional identities and career paths of fundraisers.

Finally, the book is a collaborative effort of faculty and practitioners who have poured their knowledge and dedication to philanthropy into its pages. By reading *Achieving Excellence in Fundraising* you join an institution that flourishes by enabling others to succeed in their passion to improve the world.

Amir Pasic
Dean
Indiana University Lilly Family School of Philanthropy
May 2015

PREFACE

The fourth edition of *Achieving Excellence in Fundraising* has its foundation in the lifetime of work by Henry A. "Hank" Rosso. He had a dream that colleges and universities would provide research education and training to help build the foundation for professionalizing fundraising. He published *Achieving Excellence in Fund Raising* in 1991, bringing scholars and practitioners together to help fundraisers better understand and do their work. In the foreword to the first edition, Bob Payton projected that the book would become a classic. The fourth edition being published 15 years later is evidence that it has. It is also a reflection of how farsighted Hank was in his work. Many of the principles that he espoused have been confirmed or modified by research. The longevity of The Fund Raising School, the continuing validity of many of the principles taught originally in The Fund Raising School, and the modification of others through time are further evidence.

The first three editions of *Achieving Excellence in Fund Raising* were supported by the Indiana University Center on Philanthropy that housed The Fund Raising School founded by Hank in 1974. In 2012 the programs and the institutes of the Center, including The Fund Raising School, became part of the Indiana University Lilly Family School of Philanthropy. The publication of the fourth edition marks the transition from the Center on Philanthropy to the Lilly Family School of

Philanthropy. One of the milestones in that transition is the School's continued commitment to do research and offer education and training related to Hank's work in the founding of The Fund Raising School.

The first challenge of a nonprofit organization is to survive its founder. The Fund Raising School has survived its founder. The Fund Raising School has now existed as an integral part of the Lilly Family School of Philanthropy longer than it existed as a separate independent organization. Hank and his wife Dottie founded The School in 1974 and it celebrated its 40th anniversary in 2014. It became part of the Center on Philanthropy in 1987. Hank served as an advisor and mentor to all of us until his death in 1999. Tim Seiler has been the Director of The Fund Raising School for 20 years, from 1996 to 2015. The current Director, Bill Stanczykiewicz, began serving as Director on June 29, 2015.

The fourth edition reflects a commitment to the original principles and philosophy that are the hallmark of achieving excellence. It also reflects the changing environment for philanthropy and fundraising, new developments in the way fundraising work is done, and the increasing understanding and knowledge about philanthropy and fundraising developed by the Lilly Family School of Philanthropy, other colleges and universities, and research organizations across the United States and around the world.

The editors of this volume knew Hank Rosso personally. They interacted with Hank, served on panels with Hank at conferences and symposia, and they understood Hank's philosophy. The fourth edition is transitional in another sense. If *Achieving Excellence in Fundraising* is to continue to be the classic that Bob Payton predicted, it must not only reflect the growing body of knowledge about fundraising and philanthropy but it must also be embraced by a new generation of scholars and practitioners. The fourth edition is a step in that direction. All the authors in the fourth edition are philanthropic studies faculty members at the Lilly Family School of Philanthropy, alumni of the School, or current faculty members of The Fund Raising School. Most of them did not know Hank.

The first edition was promoted primarily as a way to help provide knowledge for a rapidly growing fundraising corps. The number of members of the Association of Fundraising Professionals (then NSFRE) grew significantly from 1980 to 1990. The third edition is being used as a textbook by faculty members teaching fundraising, philanthropy, and nonprofit management courses in colleges and universities today, so the fourth edition was written and edited with its being used as a textbook in mind.

The work of philanthropy is about the work of public purposes and causes – the public good. Philanthropy rests on the power of the case for support. It also reflects the interest and desires of donors to accomplish something beyond themselves. The work of fundraising is about substituting pride for apology. The fourth edition focuses on respect for the process of fundraising, respect for the donor, and respect for the individuals being served by the nonprofit organizations that fundraisers represent. It focuses on the importance of language in conveying that respect. We do not "get" gifts. Hank taught us that fundraising is the work of teaching people the joy of giving. Sara Konrath's research, as she writes in Chapter 2, substantiates this concept. Fundraisers do not make "the ask," which implies a confrontational situation between volunteers and fundraisers and the donors from whom they seek gifts. They solicit gifts by inviting donors to join them in supporting worthy causes. Although demographics and psychodemographics are important in understanding donors and engaging them with organizations based on their own interests, fundraisers do not "target" donors, and they do not "move" them toward desired ends. It is important for us to understand these concepts today with the sophistication of donors, with the interest of donors following up on their gifts at smaller levels, and with the new generation of philanthropists committed to making things happen today.

Organization of the Fourth Edition

The fourth edition of *Achieving Excellence in Fundraising* has been reorganized to bring more chapters more closely together around key fundraising execution. Some chapters from the third edition have been combined. Chapters have been updated and edited. New chapters have been added to reflect important new areas of knowledge and changing dynamics in philanthropy.

The fourth edition has been developed as a textbook for academic courses in fundraising, philanthropy, and nonprofit management. An instructor's guide is available from the publisher at www.wiley.com/college/tempel. It can also be used by practitioners as a reference in their own work and to help them prepare for the CFRE exam.

The 37 chapters of the fourth edition are grouped into eight parts. Part One consists of five chapters that form the essential context for understanding and engaging in philanthropic fundraising.

Part Two consists of eleven chapters that prepare fundraisers to understand philanthropy from various perspectives of donors, not only individual donors but also foundations and corporations as donors.

Part Three includes four chapters that focus on the structural aspects of a total development program. The total development program ranges from the annual fund program to the planned giving program. This section helps fundraisers understand how the various programs support one another and how they interconnect.

Part Four consists of five chapters dedicated to the management of the total development program. This includes organizational readiness for fundraising and using consultants for special purposes.

Part Five includes five chapters that discuss the different ways fundraisers and their organizations can engage donors and invite them to make gifts at different levels. It outlines how different approaches are appropriate for different levels of gifts and gifts for different purposes.

The three chapters in Part Six focus on the external nature of fundraising and philanthropy and include the current call for greater transparency and accountability by an organization's various constituents.

The two chapters of Part Seven deal with the ethical and legal framework for fundraising.

Finally, Part Eight is about professionalism, with one chapter on building a career and the other on the resources available to assist in that development.

Reflections on the Fourth Edition

As mentioned in the Acknowledgments, we have transitioned from administrative roles to faculty positions and look forward to how the fourth edition is embraced by university faculty as well as by fundraising practitioners. In dispatching our contribution to the academic study and the practice of fundraising, we look forward to the fourth edition adding to and enriching the discourse surrounding philanthropic studies and philanthropic fundraising.

We note that our work was previously supported by the Indiana University Center on Philanthropy. We are grateful to have the continued support of the Indiana University Lilly Family School of Philanthropy.

We fervently hope that the addition of more research-based chapters, others supported by research, along with the chapters that reprise time-tested, nearly universal principles of effective fundraising practice, if successful, will serve not only as an overview of current philanthropic fundraising but will also prepare the upcoming generation of scholars and practitioners to produce in its time the fifth edition of *Achieving Excellence in Fundraising*.

ACKNOWLEDGEMENTS

The fourth edition of *Achieving Excellence in Fundraising* would not have been possible without the first three volumes. We are again acknowledging Hank Rosso who founded The Fund Raising School in 1974, and in 1991 accepted the challenge to share his knowledge and experience with a larger audience by editing the first edition of this book. We also acknowledge The Fund Raising School which has grown and developed from the day when Hank Rosso transferred it to Indiana University to help establish the Center of Philanthropy in 1987 to its current status as a key part of the Lilly Family School of Philanthropy. This book also owes deep gratitude to the Lilly Family School of Philanthropy for its sponsorship and for the role it has played in the development of Philanthropic Studies as a field, for its research dedicated to philanthropy and fundraising through the years, and for the contributions it has made to the development of The Fund Raising School, the Women's Philanthropy Institute, the Lake Institute on Faith and Giving, the development of baccalaureate-, master's-, and doctoral-level programs at Indiana University. These assets all help shape the fourth edition of *Achieving Excellence in Fundraising*.

A word of thanks to Hank's wife, Dottie Rosso, one of the founders of The Fund Raising School. Her encouragement for the continuation of Hank's legacy and her affirmation that the programs of The Fund Raising School and the Lilly

Family School of Philanthropy fulfill Hank's vision for the study of philanthropy and fundraising have been a source of support.

Thanks to all the authors who contributed to the first three editions of *Achieving Excellence in Fund Raising*. Special thanks to all the authors and contributors to the fourth edition of *Achieving Excellence of Fundraising* as well. They include Philanthropic Studies faculty members, faculty of The Fund Raising School, staff of the Lilly Family School of Philanthropy, and alumni. All have contributed to the ongoing development of knowledge for this book and for the field. We are grateful for the research developed through the Lilly Family School of Philanthropy by the Indiana University Philanthropic Studies faculty and faculty and researchers around the globe who have contributed to the development of knowledge these past 25 years.

Thanks to Lilly Endowment for support of the fourth edition of *Achieving Excellence in Fundraising* as part of a transition Grant to the Lilly Family School of Philanthropy. The editors themselves have gone through transitions. Each has stepped down from long-term time service in administrative and leadership roles in building philanthropic studies and The Fund Raising School to become members of the Philanthropic Studies faculty at the Lilly Family School of Philanthropy, for the version of this book marks their transition as well.

The Lilly Family School of Philanthropy and Wiley have initiated many projects together. This is as true now as it was when the first three editions were published. We owe gratitude to Wiley for continuing to publish books that help strengthen the nonprofit sector especially fundraising and philanthropy. And special thanks to our editor at Wiley, Matthew Davis, who encouraged the development of this fourth edition.

Each of us has a special word of thanks to our staff and colleagues who supported our involvement in this project and covered for us in other ways from time to time. To our families we send heartfelt thanks for their unending support and sacrifice throughout our administrative careers and during the development of this book.

Thanks to Elisabeth Lesem, the Hartsook Fellow at the IU Lilly Family School of Philanthropy and Gene Tempel's graduate assistant. She did heavy lifting on this project. Not only did she help coordinate the solicitation of chapters and the application of unified standards with all the offers, but she also contributed research and co-authored several chapters as well. We all owe Elisabeth a debt of gratitude for her work on this edition until she graduated with an MA in Philanthropic Studies and became the Foundation Officer at the Indiana Repertory Theatre. We hope her work on this volume serves her well in her career.

Special thanks also to Sarah Nathan, a Lilly Family School of Philanthropy alum and faculty member at Bay Path University, who managed the production of the manuscript for the third edition of *Achieving Excellence in Fundraising*. We were fortunate to have her experience help us complete the fourth edition. She spent five weeks working on uniform standards, editing the text from beginning to end, and assisting the editors with their various responsibilities. We are grateful for her assistance and we hope her work on this volume contributes to continued development as a scholar and teacher in the field.

THE EDITORS

Dwight F. Burlingame is Professor of Philanthropic Studies and holds the Glenn Family Chair in Philanthropy. Dr. Burlingame holds degrees from Moorhead State University, the University of Illinois and Florida State University. He received the Certified Fund Raising Executive (CFRE) credential in 1989. He has been active over the last 25 years in developing philanthropic education at Indiana University and for the field of civil society education globally. He also serves as an active member of the national Association of Fundraising Professionals' Research Council, the Association for Research on Nonprofit Organizations and Voluntary Action (ARNOVA) where he is currently the Treasurer, a board member of Learning to Give, and the International Society for Third-Sector Research. Burlingame is an expert in the field of philanthropy and fundraising and spent six years as editor of the *Nonprofit and Voluntary Sector Quarterly*, the official journal of ARNOVA. He is also the co-editor of the *Philanthropic and Nonprofit Studies* book series for Indiana University Press, and has written or co-written 10 books, nearly 60 articles and more than 100 book reviews. Dr. Burlingame is also the editor of *Philanthropy in America: A Comprehensive Historical Encyclopedia*, published in 2004. He is active in the nonprofit community as a board member and volunteer, a frequent speaker, consultant, and author on topics relating to philanthropy, corporate citizenship, nonprofit organizations, and development. In 2013 he received the Rosso Medal for lifetime achievement in fundraising.

Timothy L. Seiler is the inaugural Rosso Fellow in Philanthropic Fundraising and Clinical Professor of Philanthropic Studies at The Lilly Family School of Philanthropy. In June 2015, he transitioned from being the Director of The Fund Raising School, a position he held for 20 years. During that time The Fund Raising School expanded its service through in-person and online courses domestically and internationally. In November 2014 he was named Outstanding Professional Fundraising Executive by the Association of Fundraising Professionals Indiana Chapter, and in December 2014 he received the Henry A. Rosso Medal for Lifetime Achievement in Ethical Fundraising from the Indiana University Lilly Family School of Philanthropy. Seiler teaches core curriculum courses and customized programs for The Fund Raising School and regularly makes conference and seminar presentations locally, nationally, and internationally. He is an author and editor and was editor-in-chief of the *Excellence in Fundraising Workbook Series*, author of the workbook *Developing Your Case for Support*, and co-editor of *Achieving Excellence in Fundraising*, Third Edition. Formerly vice president of the Indiana University Foundation, Seiler was a major gifts officer for university development and coordinated the constituency development program for the schools and programs on the Indianapolis campus. Seiler serves the nonprofit sector not only as a fundraiser, author, and teacher but also as a volunteer and board member and serves as a mentor to young professional fundraisers. He earned a B.A. degree in English from Saint Joseph's College, Rensselaer, Indiana, and M.A. and Ph.D. degrees in English from Indiana University. He also holds the Certified Fund Raising Executive professional designation.

Eugene R. Tempel is Founding Dean Emeritus of The Indiana University Lilly Family School of Philanthropy and a Professor of Philanthropic Studies. He led the world's first school devoted to research and teaching about philanthropy. An internationally recognized expert on the philanthropic sector, he has four decades of leadership and fundraising experience. He helped found the School's precursor, the Center on Philanthropy, and was its executive director for 11 years, transforming it into a leading national resource. Generous donors recently established the Eugene R. Tempel Endowed Deanship – Indiana University's first named, endowed deanship – at the School. A member of several nonprofit boards, Professor Tempel is a past chair of the national Association of Fundraising Professionals' Ethics Committee. An early leader in creating the field of philanthropic studies, he was the first elected president of the Nonprofit Academic Centers Council and a member of Independent Sector's Expert Advisory Panel that helped create national guidelines for nonprofit governance and ethical behavior. The author of several works in the field, he has won numerous awards and has been named among the

50 most influential nonprofit sector leaders 13 times by *The NonProfit Times*, which also named him the sector's first "Influencer of the Year" in 2013. He earned a B.A. in English from St. Benedict College and an M.A. in English and an Ed.D. in Higher Education from Indiana University and is a Certified Fund Raising Executive.

AUTHOR BIOS

Eva E. Aldrich, M.A., CFRE, is President and CEO of CFRE International, the globally acknowledged voluntary certification for fundraising professionals. Prior to joining CFRE International, Aldrich was Associate Director of Public Service and The Fund Raising School at the Indiana University Lilly Family School of Philanthropy. Before that, she was a member of the consulting team at Johnson Grossnickle & Associates, a firm committed to strengthening the field of philanthropy and to empowering nonprofit organizations to make the world a better place. Aldrich has been widely published in fundraising journals and is one of the editors of *Achieving Excellence in Fundraising*, 3rd Edition. She serves on the Advisory Committee of the Nonprofit Leadership Studies Program at Murray State University and is a doctoral candidate in Philanthropic Studies at Indiana University.

Lehn Benjamin is an Associate Professor of Philanthropic Studies. Her research examines how nonprofit organizations challenge and reinforce the marginalization of poor communities and the consequences for democratic citizenship. She has focused specifically on how performance and accountability requirements of funders shape the work of nonprofits. Her recent research seeks to shed light on these questions by looking at the daily work of frontline staff and the experience of the people they serve. Prior to joining the faculty at IU, she worked in South Africa during the democratic transition, on the Senate Banking Committee,

Subcommittee for Housing and Urban Affairs, and for the U.S. Department of the Treasury's Community Development Financial Institutions Fund.

Melissa S. Brown helps charities turn knowledge into action. Consulting services include surveys, program evaluation, and background research. She staffs the Nonprofit Research Collaborative, which surveys charities to assess what works in fundraising. She teaches regularly for The Fund Raising School. As a volunteer, she serves the AFP Research Council, Association of Philanthropic Counsel, and Giving USA Advisory Council on Methodology. Before founding Melissa S. Brown & Associates in 2011, Melissa worked at the Indiana University Lilly Family School of Philanthropy, including 10 years as managing editor of *Giving USA*. She studied at Reed College and the University of Pennsylvania.

Aaron Conley is a practitioner and scholar of philanthropy, fundraising and volunteerism. He earned an Ed.D. in higher education and philanthropic studies from Indiana University. He is now a faculty member of The Fund Raising School, teaching the course on campaigns. Dr. Conley's professional experience extends nearly 25 years. He has served as vice chancellor for advancement at the University of Colorado where he oversaw all academic and athletic fundraising, parent giving and the CU Alumni Association. He also served as vice president for development and alumni relations at the University of Texas at Dallas where he led that institution's first comprehensive campaign. He has also held advancement roles with the University of Pittsburgh, Florida State University and Purdue University.

Elizabeth J. Dale is an assistant professor in the Master of Nonprofit Leadership Program at Seattle University and a Ph.D. candidate in Philanthropic Studies at the Indiana University Lilly Family School of Philanthropy. Her research focuses on the philanthropic practices of lesbian, gay, bisexual, and transgender (LGBT) individuals and couples, women's giving, and the intersection of gender and philanthropy. She teaches in the areas of philanthropy, governance, fundraising, and marketing and communications. A former fundraiser who achieved CFRE designation, Ms. Dale holds an M.A. in Women's Studies from The Ohio State University and a B.A. in Journalism and Women's and Gender Studies from Ohio Wesleyan University.

Pat Danahey Janin is a doctoral candidate in philanthropic studies at the Lilly Family School of Philanthropy at Indiana University. A native of Colorado, she has studied, volunteered, and worked in the United States and Europe in the cultural and educational fields, most recently for the Fulbright Commission in Paris. She continues to steward the summer Hallock awards for bicultural youth for the American Women's organization AAWE. Her current research focuses on the changing landscape and purpose of international volunteering, including government, higher education, and INGO programs. She received her MBA from ESCP Paris, her Magistère from the Sorbonne Paris IV, and her B.A. from Colorado State University.

Caitie Deranek Stewart is an Assistant Director of Development at The Indiana University School of Medicine, a nationally recognized medical education and research institution. She will complete her Masters of Arts in Philanthropic Studies from the IU Lilly Family School of Philanthropy and Masters of Public Affairs in Nonprofit Management from the School of Public and Environmental Affairs-IUPUI in 2016. Caitie joined the staff of the Lilly Family School of Philanthropy in 2011 and has experience managing fundraising events ranging from intimate major gift donor gatherings to large gala-style events in addition to an annual fund portfolio.

Roberta L. Donahue has over 25 years of experience in the nonprofit sector managing all areas of fundraising, as well as marketing, volunteers, and fiscal management. Currently, Ms. Donahue is Senior Development Officer for Indiana State University Foundation and serves on the faculty of The Fund Raising School of the Lilly School on Philanthropy at Indiana University. Ms. Donahue is a Certified Fund Raising Executive (CFRE), a past president of the Indiana Chapter of AFP and was selected as Outstanding Fund Raising Executive of the year in 2005. She earned a B.A. from Marian University, Indianapolis, and an M.B.A. from the State University of New York at Binghamton.

Sean Dunlavy serves as the Director of Fundraising and Institutional Advancement at the Indiana University Lilly Family School of Philanthropy. He is responsible for developing, cultivating, and soliciting support from a diversified portfolio of foundations, corporations, and individual donors to the School. Mr. Dunlavy has over 25 years of experience managing complex and comprehensive development and marketing programs including as Vice President for Development at the Indianapolis Symphony Orchestra and Executive Director for the Catholic Schools Foundation/Inner City Scholarship Fund in Boston, Massachusetts. He earned his B.S. in Business Administration at The University of Dayton and a Certificate in Fundraising Principles and Techniques from The Fund Raising School at the Indiana University Lilly Family School of Philanthropy.

Elizabeth A. Elkas, Associate Dean for Development with the Indiana University School of Medicine, has more than 30 years of development experience in the nonprofit sector. She started her career with the Indiana University Foundation and then helped grow the medical school development team from three people to over 30 professionals. Now leading a fourth capital campaign, she has presented at the Association of American Medical Colleges and the Association for Healthcare Philanthropy. She has served on the faculty of The Fund Raising School of the Lilly Family School of Philanthropy since 1991. Ms. Elkas holds a B.A. from Bucknell University and an M.F.A. from Indiana University.

Deborah Eschenbacher is president of Eschenbacher & Associates, Philanthropic Consulting, located in Columbus, Ohio. With over 30 years' experience in the nonprofit sector, she has served in lead development positions and as executive director of several state affiliates of national nonprofit organizations. Her higher education development experience includes major gifts officer at The Ohio State University and director of corporate and foundation relations at Ohio University. As a faculty member of The Fund Raising School, she began teaching courses in 1997. She was the second student to receive an M.A. in philanthropic studies from Indiana University and also holds a B.S. from Ohio University. Active in her community, she serves on several nonprofit boards.

Derrick Feldmann is president of Achieve, a creative research and campaigns agency, and a sought-after speaker, researcher, and advisor for cause engagement. He is a recognized thought leader in helping the cause and corporate industry understand the next generation donors, activists, and employees who are redefining causes. Derrick is the lead researcher and creator of the Millennial Impact Project, an oft-cited, multiyear study of how the next generation supports causes, and the producer of MCON, a national annual conference of more than 15,000 viewers that explores whether and how organizations are taking advantage of today's heightened interest in causes to create movements.

Tyrone McKinley Freeman, Ph.D., is Assistant Professor of Philanthropic Studies and Director of Undergraduate Programs at the Indiana University Lilly Family School of Philanthropy, where he teaches undergraduate and graduate students and directs the B.A. degree program in Philanthropic Studies. For 15 years he worked in fundraising, holding leadership positions in community development, youth and family social service, and higher education organizations, where he engaged in annual and major gift fundraising. His writings have appeared in academic and practitioner publications including *Advancing Philanthropy* and *The International Journal for Educational Advancement*. He is co-author of *Race, Gender, and Leadership in Nonprofit Organizations*. As a scholar, Tyrone's research focuses on the history of American philanthropy and fundraising, African American philanthropy, and philanthropy and higher education.

James M. Greenfield, ACFRE, FAHP, has served since 1962 as a national fundraising executive to three universities and five hospitals. He retired from Hoag Memorial Presbyterian Hospital in February 2001 after 14 years as Senior Vice President, Resource Development and Executive Director, Hoag Hospital Foundation, where more than $120 million was raised during his tenure. He is the author and editor of 10 books and more than 40 articles and chapters on fundraising management. Most recently, he is the author of *Fundraising Responsibilities of Nonprofit Boards* (2009), part of the BoardSource Governance Series.

Elena Hermanson earned a B.A. degree in Philanthropic Studies from the Indiana University Lilly Family School of Philanthropy with honors in 2015, and was recognized as the Chancellor's Scholar for her academic excellence. She has worked as a research and editorial assistant for *Giving USA* and co-authored *Giving USA Spotlight: Giving Tuesday: A Planned Day of Spontaneous Giving* and *Giving USA Spotlight: The Next Generation of Alumni Giving*. Additionally, she has researched and made an academic conference presentation about social impact bonds as innovative financing tools for social change. She is dedicated to her family and giving back to the community. Elena hopes to follow in the footsteps of her grandfather, who has dedicated his life to others as a mentor, community leader, and philanthropist.

James M. Hodge has worked with philanthropists at Bowling Green State University, Mayo Clinic, and the University of Colorado for more than 35 years. Focusing on gifts of significance, Jim has worked primarily with benefactors who have given more than one million dollars to the institutions he has served. He has been labeled a reflective practitioner, an individual who not only inspires philanthropy but also seeks to advance best practices for the profession. Jim has been a long-standing faculty member at Indiana University–Purdue University Indianapolis, an instructor for The Fund Raising School, a distinguished lecturer at the Lake Institute on Faith and Giving, and a frequent keynote speaker on the topics of value-based philanthropy, transformational philanthropy, and working with entrepreneurs as philanthropists.

Frances Huehls is Associate Librarian for the Joseph and Matthew Payton Philanthropic Studies Library at Indiana University–Purdue University Indianapolis. She holds Master's degrees in Philanthropic Studies and Library and Information Science, as well as a Ph.D. in Higher Education from Indiana University. Dr. Huehls is editor of *Philanthropic Studies Index* and *PRO: Philanthropy Resources Online*.

David P. King is the Karen Lake Buttrey Director of the Lake Institute on Faith and Giving as well as Assistant Professor of Philanthropic Studies within the Indiana University Lilly Family School of Philanthropy. He is a graduate of Samford University and Duke Divinity School. His Ph.D. in Religion is from Emory University. Having served local churches and national faith-based organizations, he is also fueled by facilitating conversations with faith leaders, donors, and fundraisers (of all generations) around the intersections of faith and giving. Trained as an American religious historian, his research interests include investigating how the religious identity of faith-based nonprofits shapes their motivations, rhetoric, and practice.

Sarah King is pursuing a Master of Arts in Philanthropic Studies at the Indiana University Lilly Family School of Philanthropy. She completed her undergraduate studies in Biology with a concentration in Neurobiology and Physiology at Purdue University. Sarah's background motivates her to focus on social and biological foundations of philanthropic behavior. She is also an active participant in her community, serving as a board member for several nonprofit organizations, including her leadership role as president for the nonprofit organization Project Sweet Peas.

Sara Konrath is an Assistant Professor of Philanthropic Studies at the Indiana University Lilly Family School of Philanthropy. She received her Ph.D. in Social Psychology from the University of Michigan. Konrath is the director of the *Interdisciplinary Program on Empathy and Altruism Research* (iPEAR), a research lab with a primary focus on motivations, traits, and behaviors relevant to philanthropic giving, volunteering, and other prosocial behaviors. Her work has been published in top scientific journals and has been featured in national media outlets. See www.iPEARlab.org for more information.

Elisabeth Lesem holds a Master's in Philanthropic Studies from the Lilly Family School of Philanthropy. She had the privilege of serving as Graduate Assistant to Founding Dean Emeritus of the Lilly Family School of Philanthropy, Gene Tempel, for two years. Now, she is the Foundations Officer at the Indiana Repertory Theatre. During her master's coursework, she had the opportunity to help the Board of Directors at a family foundation build their grantmaking program. She is honored to contribute to the 4th edition of *Achieving Excellence in Fundraising*.

Margaret M. Maxwell, CEO of Maxwell Associates, works with nonprofit organizations throughout the country in the areas of strategic planning, governance, marketing, and fund development planning. She also is a faculty member of The Fund Raising School, a program of the Lilly Family School of Philanthropy at Indiana

University. Prior to her work as a consultant, she was Vice President for The Children's Museum of Indianapolis, one of the nation's premier cultural institutions, where she led the fundraising, marketing, strategic planning, and earned income programs. She received both a B.A. in journalism and an MBA in marketing from Indiana University.

Debra Mesch is Director of the Women's Philanthropy Institute (WPI) at the Indiana University Lilly Family School of Philanthropy. She holds the Eileen Lamb O'Gara Endowed Chair in Women's Philanthropy at the Lilly Family School, the first such endowed chair in the world. Dr. Mesch's primary responsibility at WPI is to guide the research agenda on the role of gender in philanthropy. She and her colleagues have written several reports for the *Women Give* series examining the effects of age, marital status, and income of gender differences in the likelihood and amount of giving to charity. In addition to the translational reports for the *Women Give* series, Dr. Mesch is author or co-author of many articles for academic journals.

Sarah K. Nathan is Assistant Professor of Nonprofit Management and Philanthropy at Bay Path University in Longmeadow, Massachusetts. She holds a Ph.D. in philanthropic studies from the Indiana University Lilly Family School of Philanthropy. She began her career in philanthropy as a 19 year old student, calling alumni at her alma mater, Concordia College in Moorhead, MN, where she later became Associate Director of the Annual Fund. Today, her research interests include the fundraising profession, membership organizations, women in the nonprofit sector, and philanthropy education.

Una Osili is Professor of Philanthropic Studies and Director of Research at the Lilly Family School of Philanthropy. Dr. Osili leads the School's extensive research program on household financial behavior and charitable giving. Dr. Osili provides guidance for the research for *Giving USA* and directs the School's signature research project, the Philanthropy Panel Study (PPS), the largest and most comprehensive study of giving and volunteering of American families over time. Dr. Osili is a prolific researcher with an extensive body of published research. She earned her B.A. in Economics at Harvard University and her M.A., and Ph.D. in Economics from Northwestern University.

Andrea Pactor is Associate Director of the Women's Philanthropy Institute. In this role, Andrea is responsible for program and curriculum development and implementation, marketing, social media, and operations. She has organized four national symposia on women and philanthropy, co-authored several book chapters, and co-developed the first-ever online course about women and philanthropy for *The New York Times* Knowledge Network and the online conference, SHEMAKESCHANGE, about the intersection of women, money, and philanthropy. Andrea has served arts, education, and faith-based organizations as a professional and volunteer. She has a BA from The American University, an MA from the University of Michigan, and an MA in Philanthropic Studies from Indiana University.

Katie Prine graduated from Hanover College and has served the nonprofit community in Indianapolis for more than a decade through her work in development. Her experiences at Noble of Indiana, the Indianapolis Symphony Orchestra, and currently at the Indiana University Lilly Family School of Philanthropy as the Associate Director of Development have offered her the opportunity to raise funds for unique and diverse organizations as well as helped her acquire skills in building the annual fund, prospect management and solicitation, database management, strategic planning, and planned giving.

Philip M. Purcell is Vice-President for Planned Giving at Ball State University Foundation. He received his B.A. degree (*magna cum laude*) from Wabash College and his J.D. and M.P.A. degrees (with honors) from Indiana University. Phil currently serves as a volunteer on the Tax Exempt Organizations Advisory Council for the Internal Revenue Service. He teaches Law and Philanthropy, Nonprofit Organization Law, and Planned Giving as adjunct faculty for the Indiana University Maurer School of Law and the Lilly Family School of Philanthropy. Phil has served on the boards for the Partnership for Philanthropic Planning and Association of Fundraising Professionals (Indiana Chapter). He is a member of the Indiana and American Bar Associations.

Dean Regenovich is Assistant Vice President for Development at the University of South Florida Foundation. He previously served as the Assistant Dean for Advancement at the Indiana University Maurer School of Law, Executive Director of Development for the Office of the Vice President at Indiana University, and Director of Planned Giving for the Indiana University Foundation. Dean has 20+ years of experience in major gift and planned gift fundraising. He is a faculty member at The Fund Raising School at the Indiana University Lilly Family School of Philanthropy where he teaches planned giving and major gift fundraising. Dean has an LLM in Taxation from Georgetown University Law School, a JD from The John Marshall Law School, and a BS in Accounting from Indiana University.

Patrick Rooney is Professor of Economics and Philanthropy and the Associate Dean for Research and Academic Affairs at the IU Lilly Family School of Philanthropy. Previously, he served as the ED of the Center on Philanthropy and its Director of Research, which he built into one of the nation's premier philanthropy research organizations, leading research projects for organizations such as Giving USA Foundation, Bank of America, American Express, Google, The Aspen Institute, and United Way Worldwide. He has served on the boards and advisory committees of many nonprofits. He earned his BA, MA, and Ph.D. in Economics at Notre Dame.

Genevieve G. Shaker, Ph.D., is one of the few academicians who is also a practicing advancement officer. She is on the faculty at Indiana University–Purdue University Indianapolis where she serves as associate dean for development and external affairs in the IU School of Liberal Arts and assistant professor of philanthropic studies in the Lilly Family School of Philanthropy. Her research focuses on higher education advancement and she has a particular interest in faculty and staff philanthropic giving. In 2015, she was recognized nationally by the Association of Fundraising Professionals, which named her as its Emerging Scholar.

Jeff Stanger is a nonprofit consultant and a member of the faculty of The Fund Raising School at the Lilly Family School of Philanthropy at Indiana University. He has taught international fundraising professionals via the Community Solutions Program, part of IREX and the U.S. State Department. He has worked in the fundraising field for nearly 20 years, including 10 with The Salvation Army and six as the Indiana Divisional Development Director. His consulting firm is Cause Geek and specializes in digital fundraising, annual campaigns, and grants.

Amy N. Thayer is Director of Research at Achieve where she is responsible for identifying and devising appropriate methodologies and data-collection strategies for projects like the Millennial Impact Report and the Millennial Running Study. Amy's research integrates cross-disciplinary scholarship with mixed-methodological inquiry in an attempt to uncover specific mechanisms responsible for individuals' behaviors. Amy has conducted examinations of youth philanthropy, philanthropy education, and the charitable giving of high net worth donors, as well as projects devoted to the understanding and promotion of generosity. She has a vast history working in the nonprofit sector, previously leading research projects in a university setting, a major HMO, municipal government; and for organizations serving girls and at-risk youth.

Lilya Wagner is director of Philanthropic Service for Institutions and is on the faculty of The Fund Raising School and The School of Philanthropy at Indiana University as well as St. Mary's University in Minnesota. Previously Lilya was Vice President for Philanthropy at Counterpart International in Washington, D.C., an international development organization. During 14 years of association with the Center on Philanthropy at Indiana University she served as associate director of The Fund Raising School and director of the Women's Philanthropy Institute. She is a frequent speaker and workshop presenter in North America and also internationally. Her published writings include articles and book chapters on philanthropy, fundraising, and the nonprofit sector.

PART ONE

A PHILANTHROPIC CONTEXT
FOR FUNDRAISING

CHAPTER ONE

A PHILOSOPHY OF FUNDRAISING

By Henry A. Rosso

Introduction by Eugene R. Tempel

Twenty-five years have passed since Henry "Hank" Rosso undertook the development of *Achieving Excellence in Fund Raising*. The original edition won the prestigious Staley Robeson Prize from the National Society of Fund Raising Executives – now the Association of Fundraising Professionals. Fundraising was still two words then. Hank was a superstar among fundraisers. Many of us are privileged to call him our mentor.

Hank founded The Fund Raising School in 1974, 40 years prior to the time we began work on the fourth edition of *Achieving Excellence in Fundraising*. The work Hank started has grown and prospered with The Fund Raising School as an integral part of the new Indiana University Lilly Family School of Philanthropy. However, we continue to feel his influence through the IU Lilly Family School of Philanthropy's Rosso Medal for Lifetime Achievement in Ethical Philanthropic Fundraising, through The Fund Raising School, through *Achieving Excellence in Fundraising*, fourth edition, and especially through this chapter.

In this chapter Hank offers his philosophy on fundraising, a philosophy developed over a lifetime of work as a fundraiser, consultant, and teacher. The principles upon which he founded The Fund Raising School in 1974 have stood the test of time and culture with adaptations and modifications rather than replacement, and so has his philosophy of fundraising. Both his principles and his philosophy have been substantiated by research on philanthropy, donor behavior, and fundraising available today. This is why we have continued to include Hank's Chapter, A Philosophy of Fundraising.

This chapter covers some of Hank's basic tenets, including:

- The importance of mission in fundraising.
- Why you exist is more important than what you do.
- The importance of integrating fundraising into an organization.
- Substituting pride for apology in fundraising.

Hank's original chapter, "A Philosophy of Fund Raising," in subsequent additions, including this fourth edition, is included unaltered and in its entirety. The fourth edition is being published 25 years after Hank developed his original chapter. It is a tribute to all he contributed to the profession of fundraising and the development of philanthropy.

A central theme in Hank's philosophy and in the way he approached his work was "fundraising is the servant of philanthropy." He opened and closed the first chapter of his book with that theme. Fundraising is not an end in itself. When it becomes that, both the organization and philanthropy are diminished and fundraising becomes a mere technical application of skills. Fundraising in Hank's view was only a means to an end that rested on organizational mission. We know today that donors are motivated to give primarily because they believe in the cause. The pillars that support Hank's central theme are as relevant today as they were in 1991. For example, research shows that high net worth donors depend on professional fundraisers and colleagues to help them make decisions about their giving (Indiana University Lilly Family School of Philanthropy, 2014).

The most significant of these pillars is "why do you exist?" This question enables an organization to articulate its mission in terms of the societal values it is fulfilling. Mission is what gives us the privilege to ask for philanthropic support. Mission is particularly important in an era where nonprofit organizations are encouraged to develop new income sources, undertake market-based activities, focus on social enterprise, form collaborations and partnerships, and approach venture philanthropists with confidence.

Hank's philosophy also rested on the role of the governing board. He saw governing boards as not only being responsible for fundraising but also for stewardship of the organization's mission and resources. The governing board today must ensure the public trust of the organization if fundraising is to be successful. Heightened calls for transparency and accountability make the role of the governing board even more important today than it was in 1991. Trust is the bedrock upon which philanthropy rests.

Fundraising as the servant of philanthropy must be part of an organization's management system. This is a pillar of Hank's philosophy of fundraising that is also critical today. Fundraising cannot be a separate, isolated, activity. Ensuring trust means conducting fundraising that is based on mission by staff and volunteers who are committed to the organization and who represent the organization with integrity. Staff and volunteers of an organization who embrace a culture of philanthropy enable fundraising by accepting philanthropy as a legitimate and important source of income to support a worthy cause.

Hank believed that philanthropy must be voluntary. Today this pillar of Hank's philosophy is more important than it was in 1991. The interest in self-expression through philanthropy calls for a more open approach by organizations. Pluralism becomes an important tenant. Another of Hank's beliefs is applicable here: "Fundraising is the gentle art of teaching people the joy of giving." To ensure long-term donor engagement and donor satisfaction that lead to increased philanthropy, fundraisers must remember that giving is voluntary. As we will see in Chapter 2, contemporary research demonstrates that there is a joy in giving.

Perhaps the greatest contribution Hank made was to teach the substitution of pride for apology in fundraising. As the number of people engaged in fundraising has grown, and fundraisers have sought a more professional approach, recognizing that fundraising is a noble activity based on organizational mission has been central to professional development. Another of Hank's statements about soliciting a gift is applicable here: "Set yourself aside and let the case walk in." The case for support as discussed in Chapter 4 gets back to the main reason why individuals give.

The last two paragraphs of this chapter carry the same subtitle as the opening line, with a slight variation: "Fundraising as Servant to Philanthropy." Hank explained the role of fundraising in terms that foreshadow the models currently needed to assist wealth holders in determining their philanthropy. He wrote of fundraising: "It is justified when it is used as a responsible invitation guiding contributors to make the kind of gift that will meet their own special needs and add greater meaning to their lives."

Today more than ever fundraisers need a philosophy of fundraising. The call for accountability, the need to inspire trust, the leadership of volunteers, the involvement of donors in their philanthropy, and the new approaches to philanthropy discussed in the following chapters all call for fundraisers to be reflective practitioners who can center themselves with a philosophy of fundraising. Hank's philosophy provides an excellent beginning for us to develop our own philosophy.

A PHILOSOPHY OF FUNDRAISING

Fundraising is the servant of philanthropy and has been so since the seventeenth century, when Puritans brought the concept to the new continent. The early experience of fundraising was simple in form, obviously devoid of the multifaceted practices that characterize its nature in the contemporary United States. These practices now make fundraising more diversified and more complex than ever before.

The American spirit of giving is known and respected in other nations. American fundraising methods are equally known and admired abroad, as foreign citizens who have attended classes taught by The Fund Raising School will attest. Ironically, the practice of resource development that is so much a part of the culture, necessity, and tradition of not-for-profit organizations in the United States is not sufficiently understood, often misrepresented, and too often viewed with suspicion and apprehension by a broad section of our own population, particularly by regulatory bodies. Few still argue with the observation that fundraising has never been considered the most popular practice in this country.

Dean Schooler of Boulder, Colorado, a scholar and student of fundraising, takes the teleological view of a vitalist philosophy that phenomena are not only guided by mechanical forces but also move toward certain goals of self-realization. Indeed, fundraising is never an end in itself; it is purposive. It draws both its meaning and essence from the ends that are served: caring, helping, healing, nurturing, guiding, uplifting, teaching, creating, preventing, advancing a cause, preserving values, and so forth. Fundraising is values-based; values must guide the process. Fundraising should never be undertaken simply to raise funds; it must serve the large cause.

Organizations and Their Reasons for Existing

Organizations of the independent sector come into existence for the purpose of responding to some facet of human or societal needs. The need or opportunity for service provides the organization with a reason for being, as well as a right to design and execute programs or strategies that respond to the need. This becomes the cause that is central to the concern of the organization. The cause provides justification for more intervention, and this provides justification for fundraising.

The organization may *claim* a right to raise money by asking for the tax-deductible gift. It must *earn* the privilege to ask for gift support by its management's responsiveness to needs, by the worthiness of its programs, and by the stewardship of its governing board. An organization may assume the right to ask. The prospective donor is under no obligation to give. The prospect reserves the right to a "yes" or a "no" response to any request. Either response is valid and must be respected.

Each organization that uses the privilege of soliciting for gifts should be prepared to respond to many questions, perhaps unasked and yet implicit in the prospect's mind. These may be characterized as such: "Why do you exist?", "What is distinctive about you?", "Why do you feel that you merit this support?", "What is it that you want to accomplish and how do you intend to go about doing it?", and "How will you hold yourself accountable?"

The response to "Who are you and why do you exist?" is couched in the words of the organization's mission statement. This statement expresses more than justification for existence and more than just a definition of goals and objectives. It defines the value system that will guide program strategies. The mission is the magnet that will attract and hold the interests of trustees, volunteers, staff, and contributors.

The answer to "What is distinctive about us?" is apparent in the array of goals, objective, and programs that have been devised to address the needs of the value system as well as serve as symbols of fidelity to it.

"How do we hold ourselves accountable?" is the primary question. It is a continuing call for allegiance to the mission. It acknowledges the sacredness of the trust that is inherent in the relationship with both the constituency and the larger community. The organization is the steward of the resources entrusted to its care.

It is axiomatic that change is a constant. Shifting forces within the environment quicken the pace of change, thus posing a new constant. Not-for-profit organizations must always be prepared to function in the center of whirling pressure.

Organizations cannot afford to be oblivious to the environment that surrounds, and indeed engulfs, them. Forces within the environment such as demographics, technology, economics, political and cultural values, and changing social patterns affect daily business performance, whether this performance pertains to governance, program administration, fiscal responsibility, or fundraising.

To Govern or Not to Govern

Governance is an exercise in authority and control. Trustees, directors, or regents – the interchangeable nomenclature that identifies the actors in governance – are the primary stewards of the spirit of philanthropy. As stewards, they are the legendary "keepers of the hall." They hold the not-for-profit organization in trust to ensure that it will continue to function according to the dictates of its mission.

The trustees must bear the responsibility to define and interpret the mission and ensure that the organization will remain faithful to its mission. Board members should accept the charge that trusteeship concerns itself with the proper deployment of resources and with the accompanying action, the securing of resources. Deploying resources is difficult if the required resources are not secured through effective fundraising practices. It stands to reason that trustees as advocates of and stewards to the mission must attend to the task of pressing the resources development program on to success.

Institutionalizing Fundraising

Fundraising projects the values of the total organization into the community whenever it seeks gift support. All aspects of governance – administration, program, and resources development – are part of the whole. As such, these elements must be part of the representation when gifts are sought. Fundraising cannot function apart from the organization; apart from its mission, goals, objective, and programs; apart from a willingness to be held accountable for all of its actions.

Fundraising is and must always be the lengthened shadow of the not-for-profit entity, reflecting the organization's dignity, its pride of accomplishment, and its commitment to service. Fundraising by itself and apart from the institution has no substance in the eyes and heart of the potential contributor.

Gift Making as Voluntary Exchange

Gift making is based on a voluntary exchange. Gifts secured through coercion, through any means other than persuasion, are not gifts freely given. They do not have the meaning of philanthropy. Rarely will gifts obtained under pressure or through any form of intimidation be repeated. These gifts lose their meaning.

In the process of giving, the contributor offers a value to the not-for-profit organization. This gift is made without any expectation of a material return, apart from the tax deductibility authorized by government. The reasons for making a gift are manifold.

In accepting the gift, it is incumbent upon the organization to return a value to the donor in a form other than material value. Such a value may be social recognition, the satisfaction of supporting a worthy cause, a feeling of importance, a feeling of making a difference in resolving a problem, a sense of belonging, or a sense of "ownership" in a program dedicated to serving the public good.

Trustees, administrators, or fundraising practitioners so often misconstrue the true meaning of this exchange relationship, and they violate the acknowledgement process by offering a return of substantive value. This alters the exchange, reduces the meaning of philanthropy, and diminishes the gift in its commitment to the mission. The transaction is one of a material exchange, a self-centered quid pro quo with none of the spirit of philanthropy in the exchange.

Substituting Pride for Apology

Giving is a privilege, not a nuisance or a burden. Stewardship nourishes the belief that people draw a creative energy, a sense of self-worth, a capacity to function productively from sources beyond themselves. This is a deep personal belief or a religious conviction. Thoughtful philanthropists see themselves as responsible stewards of life's gifts to them. What they have they hold in trust, in their belief, and they accept the responsibility to share their treasures effectively through their philanthropy. Giving is an expression of thankfulness for the blessings that they have received during their lifetime.

The person seeking the gift should never demean the asking by clothing it in apology. Solicitation gives the prospect the opportunity to respond with a "yes" or a "no." The solicitation should be so executed as to demonstrate to the prospective contributor that there can be a joy to giving, whether the gift measures up to the asking properly and in a manner that puts the potential contributor at ease.

The first task of the solicitor is to help the potential contributor understand the organization's case, especially its statement of mission. When a person commits to contribute to a cause and does so because of an acceptance of and a belief in the mission, then that person becomes a "stakeholder" in the organization and that for which it stands. This emphasizes that philanthropy is moral action, and the contributor is an integral part of that action.

Fundraising as a Servant to Philanthropy

Philanthropy is voluntary action for the public good through voluntary action, voluntary association, and voluntary giving (Payton, 1988). Fundraising has been servant to philanthropy across the millennia. Through the procession of the centuries, the thesis has been established that people want and have a need to give. People want to give to causes that serve the entire gamut of human and societal needs. They will give when they can be assured that these causes can demonstrate their worthiness and accountability in using the gift funds that they receive.

Ethical fundraising is the prod, the enabler, the activator to gift making. It must also be the conscience to the process. Fundraising is at its best when it strives to match the needs of the not-for-profit organization with the contributor's need and desire to give. The practice of gift seeking is justified when it exalts the contributor, not the gift seeker. It is justified when it is used as a responsible invitation, guiding contributors to make the kind of gift that will meet their own special needs and add greater meaning to their lives.

CHAPTER TWO

THE JOY OF GIVING

By Sara Konrath

According to the Corporation for National & Community Service, 62.6 million Americans devoted nearly 7.7 billion hours to unpaid volunteer work in 2014, which was valued at an estimated US$173 billion. Moreover, Giving USA has found that over $358.38 billion was donated to charitable organizations in 2014. Eighty percent of this came from individuals and bequests. Fundraising professionals likely helped to bring a significant portion of individual donations into nonprofit organizations. Development staff are integral to the success of nonprofit organizations.

And yet, development staff have high turnover. A recent national study of development directors found that 50% of them planned on leaving their current job in the next 2 years, and 40% of them planned on leaving the field of fundraising altogether (Bell and Cornelius, 2013). While there are many organizational characteristics that likely feed into fundraisers' levels of job satisfaction, one factor that should not be ignored is fundraisers' *perceptions of themselves*. Therefore, this chapter covers:

- Fundraisers' role in facilitating the joy of giving
- The psychological benefits of giving
- The social benefits of giving
- The physical health benefits
- Ways to maximize the benefits of giving.

Fundraisers are Givers, Not Takers

Although fundraisers participate in a number of complex day-to-day activities, most of these are focused in some way on raising money for a nonprofit organization. In other words, their job is to ask people for money. Fundraisers are often seen as salespeople. But the salesperson role is not fully accurate, because salespeople are perceived as being money-oriented and driven by profits. The fundraiser-as-salesperson analogy may make fundraisers see themselves as *takers*—taking hard-earned money and valuable time from those who often do not have much of either. Indeed, a 2014 Gallup Poll found that salespeople are among the least trusted professions in the United States, comparable to politicians.

But in more ways, fundraisers are actually *givers*. Without fundraisers, nonprofits could not follow their important missions. Donors and volunteers could not be as effective in actualizing their personal values. Fundraisers are the high priests of giving. Most donors cannot directly help people in the most effective way possible. For example, someone who feels genuinely concerned about the plight of homeless people can certainly give money directly to homeless people they encounter. But this is likely to address the problem in a limited and temporary way. Giving to a long-term shelter that also has education and job-training programs may be a better investment in terms of what the donor wants to accomplish. Fundraisers help to match people's values with opportunities to give, and in doing so, they are helping to feed the hungry, take care of the sick, share musical and cultural experiences, and educate generations of students.

Besides the obvious social good this accomplishes, there has been a lot of research recently on the potential benefits that happen to givers themselves. As Hank Rosso, founder of The Fund Raising School at the Indiana University Lilly Family School of Philanthropy wrote *"Fundraising is the gentle art of teaching the joy of giving."* This chapter summarizes the research on the health and well-being benefits of giving money (charitable donations) and time (volunteering). When fundraisers help givers to give, they may not realize that they are bringing these givers more happiness and better health. By being mindful of these health and well-being benefits of giving, I hope that fundraisers can see themselves as serving an important giving role, so that they can also personally experience the joy of giving.

Psychological Benefits of Giving

Many of us believe that if we only had more time and money, we would be happier. In fact, there is much research finding that *giving away* our time and money makes us happier, even though after giving we have less for ourselves.

There have been many studies examining volunteering and well-being, with the vast majority of them finding that people who regularly volunteer have higher happiness, life satisfaction, and psychological well-being than those who do not volunteer. Of course, volunteers are different than non-volunteers in a number of ways that could explain why they are happier. For example, they tend to have higher incomes and have more social and psychological resources than non-volunteers. But there has been a lot of research finding that these differences do not fully explain the happiness effects of giving time. Even when scholars statistically control for these variables, the results remain similar.

In addition, a few studies have used a method that is also used to test to see if a new drug works, a randomized control trial. Researchers start with a group of people who are pretty similar at the beginning, and then ask half of these people to volunteer for a period of time, and the other half to be on a waiting list. These studies have found that volunteering actually *causes* people to have higher self-esteem and feel less depressed (Li and Ferraro, 2005). Other studies find that helping others does not need to be done in the context of a nonprofit organization to increase people's well-being (Tkach, 2005; Otake, et. al., 2006). Being kind to others feels pretty good.

Does giving away money also make people happier? Before answering this question, it is important to note that there is often overlap between the people who volunteer and who donate their money. Givers tend to give generously in a variety of ways, so fundraisers should be mindful that sometimes their next big donors are literally right under their nose volunteering for their events and programs. In fact, the "time-ask effect" finds that if people are first asked to give their time to an organization, and then only later asked to make a financial donation, they will give more of both (Liu and Aaker, 2008). When people are first asked to make a financial donation, they give less time and money. This is because thinking about money automatically activates concepts of individualism and self-focus (Vohs, Mead, and Goode, 2006).

There are far fewer studies on the psychological effects of giving money compared to giving time, however, the results in these studies are pretty consistent. Most of these studies find that giving money to others, including charities, is associated with more happiness than spending it on oneself. For example, one study asked participants to spend a small amount of money (either $5 or $20) on themselves versus another person, and then the researchers measured participants' mood at the end of the day. People who spent their money on someone else were happier than those who spent it on themselves, regardless of the amount of money spent (Dunn, Aknin, and Norton, 2008). Other research has found that simply *recalling* spending on others has similar mood boosting effects. These positive emotions, in turn, inspire even more giving behavior (Aknin, Dunn, and Norton, 2012). So, giving feels good, even if we are just recalling a time when we gave, and these good feelings could pay off in terms of increased donations.

Donating money in the specific context of the workplace not only makes people happier, but it has been shown to increase job satisfaction and make people work better on teams (Norton, et. al., 2010). This implies that corporate giving programs should be channeled directly through employees in addition to being handled by corporate development directors. Giving employees a chance to choose where corporate charitable dollars should be spent may have implications for employee retention and productivity.

Fundraisers need not worry that they might erase these benefits of giving by sharing the news with potential donors. Even when people are aware of the potential happiness effects of giving, this does not diminish the psychological rewards (Anik, et. al., 2009). Indeed, one study found that donors gave *more* when they learned of the potential happiness-building effects of giving (Benson and Catt, 1978).

Nor should fundraisers worry that these psychological rewards will necessarily be fleeting. Several studies demonstrate that giving is associated with long-lasting good feelings. For example, people who are asked to regularly and frequently do *small kind acts for others* feel happier up to 2 months later (Tkach, 2005). There are similar findings when it comes to *giving money to others*. For example, one study found that people who chose to spend more of their employment bonus on others felt happier up to 2 months later (Dunn et. al., 2008), while another study found that participants who donated more money to charity at one time point were happier up to 9 years later (Choi and Kim, 2011).

Even more incredible is that these happiness boosts seem to be noticeable by outside observers (Aknin, Fleerackers, and Hamlin, 2014). It is not just that people think they are happier after they give, but it seems as though they are genuinely experiencing more positive emotion.

These effects are pretty strong and have been found in many studies. And yet, when people are asked to guess which one will make them happier, spending money on themselves versus spending it on others, they have no clue about the powerful effects of giving on their own happiness. Instead, they think they will be happier when spending on themselves (Dunn et. al., 2008). This, in part, could help to explain why people so desperately chase after the latest gadgets and fashion, but it also reveals an opportunity for fundraisers to fill in a knowledge gap.

Not only can giving money make people happier, but it also makes them feel richer. A recent study gave some participants the opportunity to make a donation to a needy child, while other participants were not given this opportunity (Chance and Norton, 2015). Donating money made people feel as though they were doing better financially than average. This is despite the fact that objectively they had less money because they just gave some away.

Giving time to others can lead to similar feelings of abundance (Mogilner, Chance, and Norton, 2012). A recent paper gave some participants the opportunity to give their time to help others (e.g. write a letter to a sick child) while other participants either spent time on their own or were allowed to leave the experiment early, thus buying them time. Across four studies, the authors found that giving time to others led to more feelings of "time affluence," the subjective feeling of having a lot of free time available. Amazingly, people feel like their schedules are less rushed after giving away time to others, despite the fact that objectively they have less time because they just gave some away.

The psychological benefits of giving and volunteering go beyond the increased experience of positive emotions among psychologically healthy populations. Giving is also associated with fewer symptoms of depression and anxiety (Hunter and Linn, 1980; Musick and Wilson, 2003), which, if untreated, could become full blown psychological disorders. Among those who have ongoing psychological problems, such as post-traumatic stress disorder or social anxiety, giving can help to manage their symptoms (Alden and Trew, 2013).

Social Benefits of Giving

The joy of giving and volunteering can also spread to others.

First, there is research finding that giving is literally contagious. People's giving behavior spreads into their closest friendships and family members, and into their broader social networks (Tsvetkoa and Macy, 2014). This is because when people are the recipients of generosity or see someone else give, this inspires us to give as well. For example, parents can influence their children by not only giving, but by directly talking about their giving behaviors with their children (Wilhelm, Brown, Rooney and Steinberg, 2008). Parents also have an influential role in the development of giving-related traits in their children. Research has found that there are certain parenting styles that predict more empathic and giving children. Highly involved fathers and parents whose discipline focuses on others' feelings have more empathic children (Koestner, Franz and Weinberger, 1990).

On the flip side, parents also have an influence on their children's narcissistic self-focus. Narcissism is a personality trait that involves an inflated sense of self-esteem and entitlement. Just as parents can encourage their children to be more aware of others' needs, they can help to create self-centered and miserly children. All they need to do is indulge their children's every whim, reminding their children of how superior and special they are (Brummelman, et. al., 2015).

Not only is giving socially learned and spread, but it also enriches people's social relationships, both in quantity and quality. Kind people are likeable, and others want to be around them. For example, the number one trait that both men and women are looking for in a romantic partner is kindness (Sprecher and Regan, 2002). One randomized control trial asked one group of preadolescents to do 3 small kind acts for others each week for four weeks, and another group to visit 3 new places each week. The researchers found that the teens in the kindness group became more popular with their peers by the end of the study (Layous, et. al., 2012).

Volunteering and donating money to important causes can help people to meet others who share similar passions, and more deeply enmeshes people within their local communities. For example, one study found that older adults who were assigned to volunteer had more social connections over a period of 4 to 8 months, while those in the wait-list control group had a decline in their number of social connections. Volunteers also experienced a 16.7% increase that others would support them if they needed it, while people in the control group experienced a 25.3% decline in perceived social support (Fried, et. al., 2004).

Among older adults, volunteering helps people who are dealing with shifting roles, for example, as older adults retire and their children become more independent of them (Greenfield and Marks, 2004). It can help to give people a sense that they are important and needed, which can help to buffer them from the potential stresses of aging, including losing important social relationships and experiencing declining health.

Physical Benefits of Giving

There has been a lot of research examining the physical health implications of volunteering and giving. For example, interesting new work has been examining what happens in the brain while people make charitable donations. This research finds that when donating money, the pleasure / reward centers of the brain light up as much as when receiving money (Harbaugh, et. al., 2007; Moll, et. al., 2006). These physiological effects mirror the psychological effects discussed earlier in this chapter.

However, there is only limited research examining the immediate physiological consequences of giving. Our research has found that people who are highly empathic have lower levels of the stress hormone cortisol after stressful events (Reinhard, et. al., 2012; Ho, et. al., 2014). Other research confirms that shifting one's focus away from the self and toward others can buffer oneself from stressors (Ableson, et. al., 2014), and that giving money to others is directly associated with lower cortisol (Dunn, et. al., 2010). In addition, volunteering has been shown to be associated with better cardiovascular health in a number of studies.

Taken together, increased positive emotions and decreased stress hormones are likely to have implications for physical health. Indeed, volunteers self-report being healthier than non-volunteers (Kumar, et. al., 2012). And our research has found that volunteering is associated with good health especially for religious people (McDougle, et. al., 2013). Perhaps by volunteering, religious people are affirming their most cherished beliefs to help and serve others.

Giving can also make people physically stronger, at least temporarily. In one study researchers asked people who were waiting for a subway to hold a 5 pound weight with their arms stretched horizontally for as long as they could. They were then given a $1 payment and half of them were asked to donate it to UNICEF (they all did), while the other half just kept it. People who donated the money were able to hold the 5 pound weight for a longer period of time than those who did not donate the money. Two other studies confirmed that giving literally made people physically stronger (Gray, 2010). That feeling of "I can make a difference" is literally energizing.

The Joy of Giving Across the Lifespan

Given all of the benefits of giving described so far, it should perhaps no longer be surprising that volunteering is associated with longevity. An analysis of over a dozen studies across a 25-year period found that volunteering is associated with a 47% reduced risk of dying overall, and a 24% reduction in the risk of dying when statistically adjusting for demographic variables. There are no known studies on whether giving money is associated with a reduced mortality risk, or whether volunteering is associated with certain causes of mortality more than others (e.g. cancer, heart disease, injuries).

Most of the research so far on the effects of giving time and money been conducted on older adults, because they tend to have more time to volunteer for non-profits and to be in studies. Studies have generally found that the health and well-being benefits of giving tend to be stronger as people age (Van Willigen, 2000). This might be because of different types of volunteer jobs across different age groups, or different motives for volunteering as people age. Yet, giving time and money is also associated with more psychological well-being and better health in middle-age adults, adolescents, and even children.

The joy of giving around the world

Similarly, most of the research on the effects of giving time and money have been conducted on people from North America and Western Europe. However, there is an emerging cross-cultural literature that suggests people from many cultures around the world experience the joy of giving and volunteering.

There are a number of large cross-national studies that take advantage of the Gallup World Poll, which conducts regular large surveys that represent approximately 95% of the world's population. These studies have examined between 136 to 142 countries worldwide, and confirmed that in most cultures, volunteering is associated with higher well-being (86% of cultures studied) and better health (88% of cultures studied), and donating to charity is associated with higher well-being (90% of cultures). These results are similar even in poor countries where resources are scarcer, and are not explained by the fact that volunteers and donors may differ in demographic factors such as gender, age, religiosity, and income.

Taken together, all of this research shows that even though of course giving away money and time means that there is less left for the self, it does not feel that way. The *paradox of generosity* is that people feel happier, richer, and healthier after giving their money and time to others. Having money in itself does not make people happier, but the way people spend it can affect their happiness.

The Importance of Motives

So should we give in order to experience these benefits? No, there is evidence that "nobody can reap the personal rewards that generous practices tend to produce by going through the motions of generosity simply in order to reap those desired rewards" (Smith and Davidson, 2014, p. 7).

There are many different reasons to volunteer. Some of these reasons are more focused on others' needs, such as wanting to help others or joining in with loved ones on causes that are important to them. Others are more focused on how one might personally benefit from helping, such as learning new things, feeling better about oneself, escaping one's troubles, and helping to promote one's career.

One study examined whether the motives of 4,085 Australian volunteers were associated with a number of well-being indicators. The researchers found that people who volunteered for other-oriented reasons had higher self-esteem, psychological well-being, and self-efficacy, which is a sense of oneself as competent (Stukas, et. al., 2014). These other-oriented volunteers also felt more socially connected. People with the more self-oriented motives of escaping their troubles or promoting their career scored lower on these well-being indicators. One potential personal benefit of volunteering is learning new things, and in this study, having this motive was associated with better well-being.

One of our studies used the Wisconsin Longitudinal Study to examine whether motives for volunteering among a sample of 3,376 older adults predicted their risk of dying four years later. We found that older adults who volunteered for reasons related to others' needs had a lower chance of dying four years later (Konrath, et. al., 2102). Those who said that they volunteered because they could personally benefit had a slightly *higher* chance of dying four years later. In our study we statistically controlled for a number of different potential explanations for these results, such as their previous mental and physical health and their socioeconomic status. So we know that these results are not because other-oriented volunteers were healthier or richer than more self-oriented volunteers.

When it comes to the reasons that people choose to donate money, there is much less research. So far, scholars have identified several reasons for making donations, without examining the implications for health and well-being. Similar to volunteering, many people donate money because they are aware of the need and they care about the recipients. They also donate because they trust that organizations will use their money appropriately and productively. There are also a number of less prosocial motives for giving: to avoid being embarrassed when publicly asked to donate or to fit in with others, to gain power or recognition for their gifts, to enjoy tax incentives for giving, to avoid feeling guilty, or to feel good about themselves. One additional major reason that people give is simply because they are asked. Studies find that the vast majority of charitable donations (between 85-86%) come after being directly asked to give.

Based on the findings that other-oriented motives for volunteering are better for health and well-being, it is likely that other-oriented motives for charitable donations are associated with similar benefits. However, future research will provide more insight on this question.

Maximizing the joy of giving

Besides having other-focused motives, there are a number of practices that seem to maximize the joy of giving.

First, the social aspects of giving seem to contribute to their happiness. For example, when scholars examined a set of 37 studies on the relationship between volunteering and well-being, they found that volunteering was associated with double the amount of happiness when the volunteering activities involved directly interacting with others, versus a more indirect type of helping (Wheeler, Gorey and Greenblatt, 1998). There are no known studies that examine similar questions with respect to charitable donations, but I would expect that giving in person (e.g. directly to a fundraiser or at a charity event) would make people happier than giving in other ways (e.g. mail, online, automatic payroll deductions).

Next, there are specific ways to give that can maximize the joy of giving. Framing the giving instruction as more concrete (e.g. make someone smile) instead of more abstract (e.g. make someone happy) increases the happiness of giving to others (Rudd, Aaker, and Norton, 2014). So, fundraisers should consider designing their donation appeals to elicit simple concrete behaviors, rather than higher level conceptual ones.

Giving in a variety of different ways and to different types of people also makes people happier than giving the same way and to the same people over and over again (Tkach, 2005). This suggests that, just like a healthy diet of food, a healthy giving diet should involve variety to avoid the acts becoming routine. Since some of the joy of giving comes from its novelty, fundraisers should think about how to encourage a variety of giving experiences among their constituents.

At times, it is not even necessary to actually give in order to experience the joy of giving! As in the case of motives, the psychological aspects of giving and donating are at least as important as the behaviors themselves. For example, simply counting the number of kind acts that one performs can make people happier (Otake, et. al., 2006). People who became more aware of their kind acts by counting them ended up feeling happier and more grateful compared to control participants. Altruistic attitudes also matter, such as saying that you enjoy helping others, or that you try to help even if others can't return the favor. In fact, altruistic attitudes at one time point had a larger independent effect on positive emotions than prosocial behaviors such as volunteering for a nonprofit organization or helping friends (Kahana, et. al., 2013). It is the thought that counts – being ready to serve and help matters, even if actual opportunities for helping do not present themselves.

Why is giving good for people?

Why is giving good for people's health? The ultimate why, in terms of why *as a species* we should find giving so rewarding, is that we are hard-wired for face-to-face contact that includes lots of mutual touch, eye contact, and smiles. Such interactions activate a complex bonding and stress regulation system that originates in parental caregiving, but generalizes beyond infants and to any distressed person (Preston, 2013). Ultimately, I believe that giving is good for us because when giving to others we are acting in accordance with our deepest nature.

But we can also analyze specific processes that happen *in the moment* when someone is giving, versus *over time*, after repeated practices of giving.

The immediate act of giving causes people to shift their focus of attention away from themselves and toward others. Focusing on the self can be quite toxic for mental health, while shifting one's focus of attention toward others can reduce anxiety and stress. Indeed, one study found that volunteering helped people to take their mind off their work during leisure time, and create new psychosocial resources to cope with stress (Mojza, et. al., 2010). Other leisure activities did not seem to have such benefits.

When giving people also tend to make comparative judgements about the situations of the recipients versus their own situations. Giving helps people to feel more gratitude for their own situations; "*It could be worse.*" In one study that provides some initial support for this idea, people felt higher life satisfaction after giving to a charity that helped poor people than after giving to a charity that did not involve a downward comparison (Huang, 2014). However, this might be because giving to people directly is more pleasurable than more indirect giving.

As reviewed in this chapter, giving leads to more positive emotion in the moment, which helps to repair and restore one's mind and body from stressors. Positive emotion in itself predicts healthier and longer lives (Danner, Snowdon, and Friesen, 2001), so the "joy of giving" in itself may be a critical explanation for the physical health benefits of giving.

It is also worth underscoring the increases in physical activity that come with giving. For example, one study found that volunteers had a 31% increase in the distance walked each week, while control group participants declined 9% (Freid, et. al., 2004). Volunteering means getting off the couch and out of the house, and physical activity in itself is associated with better health and well-being and greater longevity.

Next, what happens *after* repeated giving interactions? Over time, giving makes people see that they have an important role to play in relieving others' suffering and making others happy. In other words, giving increases givers' sense of meaning and purpose in life (Musick and Wilson, 2003). Studies have found that people with a defined sense of purpose in life live longer and healthier lives than those with a less defined sense of purpose (Reker, Peacock and Wong, 1987).

Over repeated giving interactions, people start to meet like-minded others, feel more connected and less lonely, and increase their sense that others are there for them. In themselves, social connections predict healthier and longer lives. Repeated giving interactions are like deposits into a resilience bank account with compound interest. All of the potential explanations of why giving is associated with better health have something in common: they help people to deal with unanticipated negative life events and stressors. For example, studies have found that volunteering helps people to deal with changing roles and provides a sense of stability in unstable situations (Schwartz and Sendor, 1999; Meier and Stutzer, 2008). Giving to others functions as a social insurance policy, that if something bad happens, everything will be okay. Again, this is as long as the giving comes from a true spirit of generosity.

Is there such thing as giving too much?

Of course, it is possible for people to give beyond their means in terms of time and money, but I suspect that joyful givers know their limits.

When it comes to volunteering, studies have found that volunteering between 1 and 15 hours per week is associated with optimal health and well-being (Choi and Kim, 2011). Volunteering less than 1 hour per week is not beneficial, perhaps because this represents more intermittent volunteering, rather than regular weekly practices of giving.

As for charitable donations, one recent study found that Americans who donated 10% of their money were happier than those who donated less than 10% of their money (Smith and Davidson, 2014). The authors used 10% as a cutoff point since some religions encourage this amount of giving, however, they did not explore whether there a point at which giving was no longer associated with increased happiness. This could be because it was highly unusual for people to give this much away—only 2.7% of their participants did so. Another study found that the more money people gave, the higher their psychological well-being, and the authors did not find any cutoff point after which there were fewer benefits of giving (Choi and Kim, 2011). In fact, spending money on others is associated with increased well-being even in relatively poor countries (Aknin, et. al., 2013). However, it seems reasonable to assume that at a certain point, donating to charity might be bad for well-being, especially if people give to the point that they cannot take care of their own needs. Such over-giving is rare, and the more common problem is *under*-giving.

In general, it seems best for people to give from their surplus resources. For example, it might be better for lower income people to give their time than their money, since researchers have found that volunteering predicts higher happiness in low income people compared to high income people (Dulin, et. al., 2012). This might have to do with available resources of lower income people, who may have more surplus time than money.

Finally, when it comes to other acts of kindness, the more people give, and the more they make giving part of the practice of their everyday life, the more joy they experience from giving. For example, performing nine acts of kindness per week leads to more happiness than performing three acts per week (Tkach, 2005).

A daily dose of "Vitamin G"

Doctors regularly recommend that their patients make healthy eating choices, get lots of physical activity, and refrain from smoking. Yet at this point in time, it is hard to imagine that doctors would recommend a daily dose of Vitamin G (giving) to their patients. However, as more research on the links between altruism and health emerges, perhaps one day giving will be included in the list of healthy lifestyle behaviors (Hirschfelder and Reilly, 2007). Until then, development professionals play an important role in disseminating this information. By helping others to give by keeping up with the latest research on the health effects of givers, fundraisers are giving as much (or even more) than the donors that they cultivate.

Conclusion: A Recipe for Giving

It seems appropriate for a chapter title that refers to a famous cookbook to end with a recipe for giving. These measurements and ingredients are taken from previous research summarized in this chapter, but expert givers (like expert cooks), will make changes to suit their lifestyle and preferences. These are just guidelines, and there is still a lot left to know about how to optimize giving for our health and well-being.

When using this recipe givers must understand that there are many ways to be generous. Overall, I recommend creating *practices of generosity* since research finds that such regular practices are what seem to drive the psychological benefits of giving (Smith & Davidson, 2014). Whether you are a marathon runner, a concert pianist, or learning a new language, the best way to become an expert at a new skill is to break it down into smaller repeated pieces that can be practiced regularly, typically at least once per day. The recipe for "Giving Goulash" is as follows:

- Slice and dice your schedule and budget so that you can give your time and money to nonprofit organizations. This will create regular times to practice and prioritize generosity.
- Add specific concrete giving goals (e.g. make someone smile, feed a child).
- Reduce your focus on the self, and increase your focus on others when giving. Let your self-focus simply evaporate as others' needs become central.
- Measure your kind acts: pay attention to the ways that you give to others, whether it's opening a door for a stranger, letting a neighbor borrow a tool, listening to others, or volunteering and donating to charities.
- Add a pinch of gratitude for the resources that allow you to give.
- Mix with social interactions: give together with other people to maximize the benefits.
- Season with a willingness to be the recipient of others' giving. Allowing others to give to you not only benefits them in all the ways described in this chapter, but helps you to avoid compassion fatigue.
- Variety is the spice of giving. Give in many different ways to maximize flavor.

- Simmer the different ingredients of giving in oxytocin, the bonding and stress regulation hormone.
- Be ready to serve whenever needed, with a caring attitude toward others.
- Savor the pleasure of making a difference in others' lives.
- Repeat often, whenever you see someone hungry for kindness.

Discussion Questions

1) Compare and contrast the effects of giving money versus giving time on givers' health and well-being. Is there more research on one area or the other? Is giving money or time better for health and well-being?
2) Do you think that there some people or circumstances for which giving might be harmful, rather than helpful, for health or well-being?
3) If someone feels good after donating their money or time to a charitable organization, does this mean that their actions were not altruistic?
4) How can fundraisers apply these findings to their own professional practice?
   a. How might this information be used to help them feel more satisfaction with their jobs?
   b. How might this information be used to help them achieve their fundraising goals?

Key References/Further Reading

Aknin, L., Barrington-Leigh, C. P., Dunn, E. W., Helliwell, J. F., Biswas-Diener, R., Kemeza, I., Norton, M. I. (2013). Prosocial Spending and Well-Being: Cross-Cultural Evidence for a Psychological Universal. *Journal of Personality and Social Psychology*, 104(4), 635-652.

Anderson, N. D., Damianakis, T., Kröger, E., Wagner, L. M., Dawson, D. R., Binns, M. A., Cook, S. L. (2014). The benefits associated with volunteering among seniors: A critical review and recommendations for future research. *Psychological Bulletin*, 140(6), 1505-1533.

Bekkers, R., Konrath, S., & Smith, D. H. (2014, in press). Conducive biological influences (genetics, physiology, neurology, and health). In D. H. Smith, R. Stebbins & J. Grotz (Eds.), *The Palgrave Research Handbook of Volunteering and Nonprofit Associations*.

Bekkers, R., & Wiepking, P. (2010). A literature review of empirical studies of philanthropy: Eight mechanisms that drive charitable giving. *Nonprofit and Voluntary Sector Quarterly*.

Calvo, R., Zheng, Y., Kumar, S., Olgiati, A., & Berkman, L. (2012). Well-being and social capital on planet earth: cross-national evidence from 142 countries. *PLoS ONE*, 7(8), e42793.

Dunn, E., & Norton, M. (2013). *Happy money: The science of smarter spending.* New York, NY: Simon and Schuster.

Fried, L., Carlson, M., Freedman, M., Frick, K., Glass, T., Hill, J., Zeger, S. (2004). A social model for health promotion for an aging population: Initial evidence on the experience corps model. *Journal of Urban Health*, 81(1), 64-78. doi: 10.1093/jurban/jth094

Harbaugh, W. T., Mayr, U., & Burghart, D. R. (2007). Neural responses to taxation and voluntary giving reveal motives for charitable donations. *Science*, 316(5831), 1622-1625.

Holt-Lunstad, J., Smith, T. B., & Layton, J. B. (2010). Social Relationships and Mortality Risk: A Meta-analytic Review. *PLoS Med, 7*(7), e1000316. doi: 10.1371/journal.pmed.1000316

House, J., Landis, K., & Umberson, D. (1988). Social relationships and health. *Science*, 241(4865), 540-545. doi: 10.1126/science.3399889

Kumar, S., Calvo, R., Avendano, M., Sivaramakrishnan, K., & Berkman, L. F. (2012). Social support, volunteering and health around the world: Cross-national evidence from 139 countries. *Social Science & Medicine*, 74(5), 696-706.

Konrath, S. (2014). The power of philanthropy and volunteering. In F. Huppert & C. L. Cooper (Eds.), *Wellbeing: A Complete Reference Guide. Interventions and Policies to Enhance Wellbeing* (Vol. VI, pp. 387-426). West Sussex, UK: John Wiley & Sons Ltd.

Konrath, S., & Brown, S. L. (2012). The effects of giving on givers. In N. Roberts & M. Newman (Eds.), *Handbook of Health and Social Relationships*: American Psychological Association.

Leary, M. R. (2004). *The curse of the self: Self-awareness, egotism, and the quality of human life.* New York, NY: Oxford University Press.

Moll, J., Krueger, F., Zahn, R., Pardini, M., de Oliveira-Souza, R., & Grafman, J. (2006). Human fronto–mesolimbic networks guide decisions about charitable donation. *Proceedings of the National Academy of Sciences*, 103(42), 15623-15628.

Okun, M. A., Yeung, E., & Brown, S. (2013). Volunteering by Older Adults and Risk of Mortality: A Meta-Analysis. *Psychology and Aging* 28(2), 564-577.

Schreier, H. M., Schonert-Reichl, K. A., & Chen, E. (2013). Effect of Volunteering on Risk Factors for Cardiovascular Disease in Adolescents: A Randomized Controlled Trial. *JAMA pediatrics*, 167(4), 327-332.

Smith, C., & Davidson, H. (2014). *The Paradox of Generosity: Giving We Receive, Grasping We Lose.* New York, NY: Oxford University Press.

Wheeler, J. A., Gorey, K. M., & Greenblatt, B. (1998). The beneficial effects of volunteering for older volunteers and the people they serve: a meta-analysis. *International journal of aging & human development*, 47(1), 69-79.

CHAPTER THREE

PLAN TO SUCCEED

By Timothy L. Seiler

After completing this chapter you will be able to:

1. Recognize the multi-step process of the fundraising cycle.
2. Assess your organization's strengths and weaknesses in fundraising planning and execution.
3. Evaluate your role as the staff person who oversees the fundraising process.
4. Instruct others, staff and volunteers, how they can be helpful in fundraising planning and in the execution of the plan.

This chapter is about the importance of planning for fundraising. Experience shows that fundraising success comes from effective planning. Organizations with a fundraising plan are likely to raise more money than organizations without a plan (Nonprofit Research Collaborative, 2014). Typically, the more effective the plan, the more effective the fundraising. Using a planning model called the fundraising cycle, this chapter describes a multi-step process that begins with an awareness of what donors seek in their gift-giving and ends with developing a relationship of repeated giving. While the fundraising cycle can be used also for evaluation, the chapter does not address evaluation because that topic is covered in subsequent chapters in this book (see Chapter 22, "Organizational Development for Fundraising," and Chapter 23, "Budgeting for Fundraising and Evaluating Performance").

The first thing to note about the fundraising cycle is its name: cycle. The fundraising process is continuous. The ongoing nature is illustrated by the continuing arrows inside the steps of the model. These arrows represent the loop formed by the interrelated steps of the fundraising process. The complexity of the fundraising process lies in part in the reality that various constituencies from whom gifts are sought will be at different stages in the process. The fundraising manager must coordinate the various activities necessary for moving the constituencies through the phases in the cycle.

The second thing to note about the fundraising cycle is the number of discrete steps constituting the whole. Starting with the step labeled "Planning Checkpoint: Examine the Case," and proceeding clockwise around the cycle, there are fourteen steps. Soliciting a gift comes at step thirteen. Planning to solicit a gift involves twelve steps. Skipping or shortchanging any of the steps leading to the solicitation will end in less than desirable results. Soliciting the gift (step thirteen) does not stop the process; it begins it anew. Thus, the fundraising cycle is a continuous process of planning for and asking for charitable gifts, practicing good stewardship, and establishing ongoing relationships with donors (see Chapter 31, "Stewardship and Accountability").

Prior to the first step in the fundraising cycle is the nonprofit's need to understand marketing principles and how they apply to the fundraising process. Such awareness requires the nonprofit to develop feedback systems to measure and monitor the needs, perceptions, wants, and values of prospective donors. What do prospective donors seek for their own lives that they can find through involvement with the nonprofit? The better the nonprofit understands that exchange, the better it will manage its fundraising cycle. A growing body of research demonstrates that a primary motivator of giving is the "warm glow" that comes from charitable giving (see Chapter 2, "The Joy of Giving").

The first step in the fundraising cycle (Figure 3.1), a planning checkpoint, is the examination of the nonprofit's case for support. The case is the sum of all the reasons why anyone should give charitable gifts to the organization. Each nonprofit must develop its own compelling case based on how it meets clearly defined and understood community needs. The case illustrates how the nonprofit serves the community, providing benefits and adding value.

The case must provide persuasive responses to these questions:

1. Why does the organization exist? The answer lies in the human/social problem or need addressed by the nonprofit. This is the organization's mission, its *raison d'etre.*

FIGURE 3.1. THE FUNDRAISING CYCLE.

Awareness of Marketing Principles

Strategic Checkpoint:
Demonstrate Stewardship and Renew the Gift

Planning Checkpoint:
Examine the Case

Planning Checkpoint:
Analyze Market Requirements

Action Checkpoint:
Solicit the Gift

Planning Checkpoint:
Prepare Needs Statement

Action Checkpoint:
Activate Volunteer Corps

Planning Checkpoint:
Define Objectives

Planning Checkpoint:
Prepare Communications Plan

Action Checkpoint:
Involve Volunteers

Planning Checkpoint:
Prepare Fundraising Plan

Planning/Action Checkpoint:
Validate Needs Statement

Planning Checkpoint:
Identify Potential Giving Sources

Planning Checkpoint:
Select Fundraising Vehicle

Planning Checkpoint:
Evaluate Gift Markets

Source: Adapted from Henry A. Rosso and Associates, *Achieving Excellence in Fund Raising* (2nd ed.), p. 24. Copyright © 2003 Jossey-Bass inc., Publisher. Reprinted by permission of Jossey-Bass inc., a subsidiary of john Wiley & Sons, inc.

2. What services or programs does the nonprofit provide to meet the need or solve the problem?
3. Why should prospective donors (individuals, corporations, foundations) provide gifts and what benefits accrue to donors who make gifts?

These answers form the basis of the organization's mission. The next step is to analyze market requirements. The nonprofit must test its mission as articulated through its case against the wants and needs of the market or gift sources from which it seeks charitable gifts. Only the marketplace is a true test of the validity of the nonprofit's proposed solution to the human, social problems it addresses. Such market validation is critical to successful fundraising. If the organization seeks funding from several markets – individuals, corporations, and foundations, for example – it must test its mission in each market.

If the markets do not understand or accept the importance of the needs being addressed by the nonprofit, fundraising faces a serious obstacle. Worse, if the markets do not even know of the nonprofit or the needs it addresses, fundraising is not possible. Donors will give to those organizations they care about which addresses the needs they care about.

In meeting clearly identified community needs understood to be of value to the potential donors the nonprofit can formulate compelling arguments for why its work merits philanthropic gifts.

Next comes the preparation of a needs statement. This is the organization's plan for carrying out its work towards mission fulfillment. Program plans are projected for annual needs and for longer-term needs. Financial planning follows program planning and defines the resources required for carrying out programs and delivering services. This includes descriptions of sources of revenue needed to support the program plan. This is the justification for fundraising.

The preparation of this needs statement involves the volunteer leadership of the nonprofit, especially board members, selected major donors, and other volunteers who can affect the organization and its fundraising. The needs statement shapes future fundraising goals and objectives and must include not only ongoing programmatic needs but also longer-term needs for capital improvements and financial stability, such as an endowment.

The next planning checkpoint is the definition of objectives. The programs for fulfilling the mission must be translated into specific, measurable action plans for how the organization intends to provide solutions to problems it addresses. If the mission statement explains "Why," goal statements answer "What," and objectives provide an answer to "How." To be credible to the market sources objectives must be realistic and achievable within the resources available to the organization.

The acrostic **SMART** helps clarify what objectives are:

Specific

Measurable

Achievable

Results-oriented

Time-determined

An example of a fundraising objective might read something like this: "By expanding our social media presence combined with direct mail, we will increase by 10% the number of new donors to the annual fund within the next fiscal year." In short, objectives are specific illustrations of how the organization will execute its fundraising plan.

Next comes the first action step in the fundraising cycle: involvement of volunteers. While earlier steps involved board members and selected other volunteers in planning, this step calls for action in developing and carrying out effective fundraising strategies. Because an effective gift solicitor is one who believes in and is committed to the cause, the earlier involvement steps prepare the volunteers to be effective solicitors of their peers. Historically, and still today, the most effective gift solicitation is that of a peer volunteer asking for gifts in a face-to-face solicitation (Schervish and Havens 1997, p. 241).

One of the most effective ways to involve volunteers is in the validation of the organization's needs statement. Philanthropic support requires constant validation not only by the board but also by other volunteers. For volunteers to give and solicit philanthropic gifts they must reaffirm the needs statement through continued involvement in analyzing the nonprofit's plans. Such involvement is critical before launching the fundraising program or campaign.

The next step in the cycle is an evaluation of gift markets to determine their ability and perceived willingness to fund the nonprofit's programs through charitable gifts. This step includes making informed judgments about which markets to approach and the gift amounts to be sought.

The most likely sources of gifts are individuals, corporations, foundations, associations, and government agencies. Historically, the most generous source has been individuals, about 80% of total philanthropy in recent years. Much individual wealth has gone into family foundations and community foundations in recent years, and thus foundations have been the fastest-growing source of gift funds. Combined with outright giving and bequest giving, giving to family foundations in recent years brings the total of philanthropic support from individuals to 87% (Giving USA, 2014).

Many nonprofits, however, will not experience such a high percentage of gift support from individuals and even from individuals combined with foundations. They may have larger percentages of support from corporations and foundations. The focus of market evaluation, then, should be on building and sustaining as diverse a funding base as possible. The more diverse the funding base, the more likely the nonprofit can sustain itself in a volatile fundraising environment and can be more responsive to the needs of its market constituencies.

Planning continues with careful selection of fundraising vehicles (strategies). With the gift market evaluation completed, the fundraising staff and volunteers must now determine which fundraising techniques will be most effective within each market. Fundraising strategies or methods include direct mail, special events or benefits (often called fundraisers), grant-seeking, personal solicitations, donor recognition groups (or gift clubs), and a growing method, e-mail and social media. Just as market evaluation calls for diversity of funding, so selection of fundraising methods should explore every opportunity for raising gift funds to carry out the organization's mission.

Fundraising programs include the annual fund, special or major gifts, capital campaigns, and endowment programs. The latter two often rely heavily on planned giving as a way for donors to make larger gifts than they typically make through annual funds or special gifts programs (see Chapter 19, "Capital Campaigns" and Chapter 20, "Establishing a Planned Giving Program").

The successful fundraising program will analyze all the methods, test various ones, and evaluate their effectiveness through cost-benefit ratios and other measures of success. Long-term sustained fundraising effectiveness will match the various methods to the different gift sources to identify what works best in which markets.

Identifying potential gift sources is the next planning step in the cycle. This step distills and refines the gift market evaluation into lists of specific prospective donors. The prospective donors will be present in each market: individuals, corporations, and foundations. Each prospective donor is identified and qualified by three criteria:

> **Linkage** to the organization, a meaningful connection, such as benefiting directly from the work of the nonprofit organization, or geographical proximity, or a personal connection to someone involved with the organization, including a board member or other donor
>
> **Ability** to give gifts at the level being sought, determined by formal and informal research into the financial capacity of donors/funders
>
> **Interest** in the work of the organization, that is, why the work matters to the donor/funder.

While many exercises in finding prospective donors begin with identifying individuals (and corporations and foundations) with the most money (ability), such exercises are futile unless followed with efforts to determine donors'/funders' interests in the nonprofit and their capacity to make contributions or grants. Lacking interest in the work and linkage to the nonprofit – often through a committed, involved volunteer – the wealthiest funder will not give just because of the ability to so.

Volunteer involvement through a prospective donor development committee builds a priority list of specific giving sources. Furthermore, this type of volunteer involvement builds ownership of the fundraising plan and process among the volunteers.

The tenth step in the cycle is the preparation of the fundraising plan. The previous nine steps focused on analysis, or fact-gathering, and planning.

Preparation of the fundraising plan is a call to action. Fundraising staff drafts the plan and involves volunteer leaders in refining and validating the plan. The plan should account for proper execution by allocating the resources necessary for implementing the plan. The plan should also include the management steps of monitoring and evaluating to provide for modification if needed.

The fundraising plan needs to spell out how much money will be raised for what programs in what time frame using which methods. The plan should include roles for volunteers and staff.

Understanding of the organization's mission and its fundraising plan by those prospective donors who will be asked to make gifts is essential to successful fundraising. People give money to causes they know about and care about. Thus, the next planning step is the preparation of a communications plan. For effective fundraising communications must go beyond the dissemination of information. Communications must stir the emotions and the intellects of those from whom gifts are sought. Effective fundraising communications touch the heart and the head.

The goal of fundraising communications is to lead prospective donors to an understanding and acceptance of the nonprofit and its purposes and create a desire to share in seeing that the mission is fulfilled. Effective fundraising communications are a two-way interaction providing a means for donors to express concerns. Effective communications create an opportunity for the exchange of values which is fundamental for successful fundraising.

Fundraising is about relationships built on mutual interests and concerns. One of the saws of fundraising is that people give to people with causes. The next action step in the cycle is to activate a volunteer corps of solicitors.

Fundraising in the United States has been largely a volunteer activity, action taken by people so committed to a cause that they make their own gifts and then eagerly invite others to join the cause. Still today no solicitation is more compelling than one done by a volunteer advocate who personally solicits gifts to support a nonprofit to which she is passionately devoted.

While volunteerism in fundraising remains strong today, there is a growing trend, especially among large organizations, to rely more and more on highly trained fundraising staff to solicit, especially major gifts. Among universities and colleges, and to some degree among hospitals and medical centers, major gifts fundraising is becoming more the purview of paid staff than of volunteers. In fact, this trend to rely more on paid professional staff has become pervasive (Walker, 2006, p. 64). Nevertheless, the effective nonprofit will renew and expand its volunteer corps of fundraisers to expand the base of donors. It is a generally accepted norm that one volunteer is needed for every five personal solicitations.

With twelve steps now completed it is time to solicit the gift. Some gifts, from the board, the staff, and certain volunteers, will probably already have been part of earlier stages in the process. This step represents the carrying out of the fundraising plan among the broader constituency and is the culmination of all that has been done so far.

The solicitation step calls for already committed donors to visit personally those from whom gifts will be sought. The current donor makes the case for the organization, explains his own level of commitment, and invites the prospective donor to join in the fulfillment of the mission by making her own charitable gift. The solicitation step is a dignified process of asking with pride for a philanthropic gift to help carry out the important work of the nonprofit.

Soliciting and receiving the gift is not the end of the process. In fact, it is only the beginning of a deepening relationship between the donor and the nonprofit. Proper gratitude for and acknowledgement of the gift must be expressed by the nonprofit. Additionally, the nonprofit must also disclose how the gift is used and demonstrate the highest level of accountability and stewardship in the appropriate, wise use of the gift.

Properly thanking donors, reporting the use of gifts, and demonstrating wise stewardship of contributed funds makes possible the renewal of the gift. The renewal process, step fourteen, leads to the beginning of the cycle anew. The case must be renewed by testing it again among the constituency. Renewal requires ongoing analysis of how effectively the nonprofit meets the requirements and fulfills the needs of its gift markets. The needs statement must be checked and re-checked to demonstrate the continuing effectiveness and worthiness of the nonprofit.

Conclusion

Fundraising is simple: the right person or persons asking the right prospective donor for the right gift for the right program at the right time in the right way. It is not, however, easy. Fundraising is a multi-disciplined process requiring extensive involvement of staff and volunteers in a series of interrelated steps described in the fundraising cycle. The fundraising cycle is a complex process that when properly managed leads to the successful alignment of all the "rights" described above. The main responsibility of the professional fundraising executive is to manage the process, serving as catalyst and coach for all involved in the planning and the execution of the fundraising process.

Discussion Questions

1) In which of the steps in the fundraising cycle is your organization the strongest? In which do you need to improve?
2) What is your organization's approach to engaging volunteers in the fundraising process?
3) How can the application of the fundraising cycle improve your fundraising planning?

CHAPTER FOUR

DEVELOPING AND ARTICULATING A CASE FOR SUPPORT

By Timothy L. Seiler

A fter completing this chapter, you will be able to:

1. Explain how the case for support is the justification for fundraising.
2. Identify the components that make up a case resources file.
3. Recognize how the case resources file are the building blocks for a case statement.
4. Distinguish between an internal and an external case statement.
5. Enumerate the key elements in a fundraising expression of the case for support.

Nonprofit organizations know intuitively that their work merits philanthropic gift support. If they assume that their potential donors or funders share this intuitive knowledge, they are mistaken. A case for support is a *sine qua non* for nonprofits. A case for support is the rationale underlying fundraising; it is the reason nonprofit organizations deserve philanthropic support. Without a case for support, a nonprofit does not have a right to seek philanthropic support, to raise money.

The case for support at the most general level is the general argument for why a nonprofit deserves gift support. The case is bigger than the organization and relates to a cause being served. The case for support is an encyclopedic accumulation of information, parts of which are used to argue that the organization deserves gift support for doing its work.

A case statement is a particular expression of the case. A case statement is not as big as the case. That is, a case statement is a specific illustration of some of the elements making up the case. While the case is made up of numerous reasons why the organization deserves gift support, not every reason is included in a case statement. A case statement focuses on or highlights critical factors important in arguing for gift support. A case statement selects and articulates specific points from the overall case (Seiler, 2001; The Fund Raising School, 2009).

This chapter moves from the development of the general case for support to the expression of the case, distinguishing between the internal case and the external case. The chapter also describes the role of staff and volunteers in doing the work of case preparation.

The preparation of the case begins with an understanding that nonprofit organizations raise money to meet larger community needs. Unmet social needs lead to the creation of nonprofit organizations, and the case for support is built on how well the organization meets those needs. The effectiveness of the case depends on how well the cause is served.

The case is the bedrock upon which philanthropic fundraising is built. It is the urgent call for a solution to a problem, the meeting of a need. The persuasiveness of the case relates directly to the nonprofit's ability to solve problems and to adjust to meet changing market or societal needs. The case for support is the expression of the cause, addressing why anyone should contribute to the advancement of the cause. The case is larger than the organization's financial needs; it is larger than the organization.

Preparation, development, and validation of the case begin with staff. If the organization has on staff a development director, she should be the catalyst in the preparation and development of the case. The development professional typically serves as an interpreter of the concerns, interests, and needs of the external constituencies while also articulating the needs statement of the organization. The development staff not only knows the organization internally but also interacts regularly with external constituencies. The staff must be able and willing to bring back inside the organization what the perceptions of the organization are among the constituencies where gift support will be sought.

It is not uncommon for development staff to discover that not everything is perfect among the constituencies. Occasionally constituents are misinformed or uninformed. Sometimes there are perceptions that the organization is not effective. Perhaps constituents lack confidence that gifts are needed or that they really make a difference. Finding out how to address these concerns will strengthen the case for support. Development staff must know the organization inside and out and must represent the constituency outside in (see Figure 4.1).

FIGURE 4.1. STAFF AND CONSTITUENCY PARTICIPATION IN CASE DEVELOPMENT.

Source: The Fund Raising School.

Getting others involved, though, in the development of the case is important. Seeking the ideas of key constituents – board members, volunteers, donors, and potential donors – is particularly effective in enlisting volunteer leadership for articulation of the case in fundraising. Having a role in developing and validating the case increases the enthusiasm of those who will articulate this case in their own words. They will question what puzzles them or challenge what disturbs them. If they are representative of others from whom gifts will be sought, their questions and challenges will strengthen the case for support.

Where to Start with Case Resources?

The development of the case begins with compiling information elements which provide the background for everything a potential donor might want to know about the nonprofit organization. These components are case resources and might be already existing documents within the organization. Case resources provide information upon which the case statement is built. Case resources are a database, an information bank, from which case statements are drawn. Case resources are the elements that develop a statement of the case. This initial statement of the case is likely an internal document that provides the starting point for the development of case statements for informational purposes and for fundraising.

Case resources consist of the following information elements:

Mission statement

Goals

Objectives

Programs, Services

Finances

Governance

Staffing

Facilities, Service Delivery

Planning, Evaluation

History

Information about all these elements must be in ready form in the nonprofit organization's office, and the information must be available, accessible, and retrievable when needed for fundraising. Let's take a closer look at each of the case resources, which are summarized in Table 4.1.

Mission Statement

A mission statement is a philosophical statement of the human, societal needs being met by the nonprofit organization; it explains why the nonprofit exists. A mission statement is an expression of the value or values in which the organization believes and around which it does its work. By stating an organization's values and beliefs, a mission statement gives insight into the organization's core values.

A common misconception is that mission statements express what an organization does, as exemplified by statements such as "It is the mission of the agency to provide after-school care." This is a goal statement, not a mission statement.

Any statement containing an infinitive phrase – to deliver, to serve, to provide – is a goal or purpose statement, telling what the organization does. A mission statement, on the other hand, explains why the organization does what it does. An effective mission statement provides a base for identifying beliefs and values. A good mission statement often begins with the words "We believe" or "We value."

TABLE 4.1. ARTICULATING A CASE TO ATTRACT DONORS.

	Case Components	Must Articulate
1.	Mission statement	An awareness of the cause; insight into the problem addressed by the nonprofit.
2.	Goals	The desired achievement that is expected to solve the problem.
3.	Objectives	What will be accomplished by reaching the goals.
4.	Programs and services	The nonprofit's service to people (including stories of how people benefit).
5.	Finances	The expenses of providing programs and services, as a validation of the need for philanthropy.
6.	Governance	The character and quality of the organization as shown in its volunteer leadership and governance structure.
7.	Staffing	The qualifications and strengths of staff.
8.	Service delivery	The advantages, strengths, and effectiveness of the mechanics of program and service delivery.
9.	Planning and evaluation	Program and fundraising plans and evaluation processes that demonstrate service commitments, strengths, and impact.
10.	History	The heroic saga of founders, staff, and others, and the credibility established by success over time.

For example, a shelter for animals might use the following as its mission statement: *"Concern for Animals believes that all animals deserve humane treatment. Because we care about all animals, Concern for Animals provides shelter and food for abandoned and unwanted animals."*

Here is another example of a statement that is more of a goal (or purpose) statement than a mission statement:

The Support Life Center is dedicated to providing life-affirming choices to meet the needs of women affected by unplanned pregnancies.

This sentence describes what the Support Life Center does, but it does not state why it does it.

Here is a revision of the statement that articulates the core value that the organization believes in and is therefore a more effective mission statement:

Women facing unplanned or unwanted pregnancies deserve compassion and support. Often they do not know where to turn for life-affirming alternatives, assistance, and information. The Support Life Center is dedicated to meeting the physical, emotional, and spiritual needs of women facing unplanned or unwanted pregnancies *(Seiler, 2001, p. 22-23).*

The following steps are suggestions for how to develop and write an effective mission statement that clearly states the organization's values and beliefs:

1. Assert the dominant value the organization believes in.
2. Describe briefly the conditions preventing fulfillment of that value.
3. State briefly what needs to be done to alleviate the conditions in Step 2.
4. Affirm that your organization challenges the conditions described in Step 2 and can carry out what is outlined in Step 3.

The mission statement gives donors and potential donors an opportunity to find the shared values between them and the nonprofit organization. Because people give charitable contributions to organizations with values they share, it is important for organizations to express their values clearly. Because the first step in the fundraising cycle is to examine the case for support, and the first element in the case is the mission statement, it is critical that the mission statement be a statement of values.

Goals

Goals answer the question "What does the organization do?" Goal statements are general expressions explaining what the organization wants to accomplish as it seeks to meet the needs or resolve the problems described in the mission statement. Goals are usually stated in ambitious terms not easily measured. Goal statements guide the organization towards fulfilling the beliefs expressed in the mission statement. Because organizations typically have multiple programs, goals will also be multiple. That is, the organization will have several program-related goals, some of which require funding, and funding the program goals leads to the formulation of fundraising goals.

Objectives

Objectives differ from goals in degree of specificity. Objectives are more precise than goals and explain how the organization expects to reach its goals.

A goal statement might be "To increase annual fund income." Objectives illustrating how to reach that goal are "We will increase annual giving from individuals by 5% in the next fiscal year" and "We will increase corporate giving and corporate sponsorship by 15% in the next fiscal year."

Programs and Services

The programs and services component of the file should include descriptions of how the organization provides service to its clients. Stories of how recipients of services have benefited are an effective means for showing who benefits from the programs and services provided by the organization. Potential donors and funders are more likely to be responsive to fundraising appeals when they recognize that real people are benefiting from the nonprofit's work.

One of the best ways to build this part of the file is to collect testimonials from clients and beneficiaries telling their own stories about how the organization helped them, how they as recipients received benefit from the organization's programs and services.

Finances

Financial information about the organization links budgeting with objectives and program descriptions. Information about finances gives a clear picture of how the organization acquires and spends financial resources. This financial overview establishes and validates the need for philanthropic gift support and justifies fundraising. The financial overview offers as well the opportunity to demonstrate fiscal responsibility and accountability for prudent use of funds. In short, the fundraising plan needs to be based on the organization's full financial plan. Making a case for philanthropic support requires the ability to show a clear picture of all income and expenses for the organization.

Governance

The issue of governance of nonprofits is critical in attracting charitable gifts. The governance structure of nonprofits indicates the character and quality of the institution. This part of the case resources file should contain relevant information about how the board is composed and how it functions. Complete dossiers of each board member and organizational material such as by-laws and conflict-of-interest statements should be part of the case resources file.

This element of the case file should not be taken lightly. Governance is often a litmus test for potential contributors. The quality and integrity of the governing body indicate the strength of the nonprofit. Potential contributors have more confidence in nonprofits with boards who are serious about their commitment to governance and who hold the organization accountable to the public.

Staffing

As the governance of nonprofits is a matter of integrity and quality, staffing indicates competence and professionalism. This part of the file should illustrate the credentials and qualifications of staff, paid and volunteer. Staffing patterns reveal how the organization delivers programs and services effectively. This part of the file should contain résumés of the staff.

Competent, skilled staff members, together with dedicated, energetic board members, offer a persuasive case for potential contributors to make charitable gifts. It is essential to keep this element of the file current. Staff should review their résumés at least annually, updating continuing education and professional development they participate in to improve professional competence.

Facilities and Service Delivery

The next component in the case file is a description of facilities and service delivery. This should explain how people access programs and services. Occasionally facilities are distinguishing factors: visibility, accessibility, convenience are advantages for program and services delivery.

This section might also include plans for renovation, expansion, or new construction and will help make the case for capital fundraising.

Planning and Evaluation

Information about planning and evaluation should describe the process used for planning and the measures taken for evaluation. Program plans precede fundraising plans; program plans validate the need for service. So the very first step in beginning to develop a case for support originates in the organization's strategic plan. The organizational plan articulates where the organization is going and what it takes to get there. Fundraising plans demonstrate the need for philanthropic support for the organization to carry out its strategic plan.

Evaluation provides a means for demonstrating effectiveness and efficiency in programs and accountability and stewardship of philanthropic resources.

Planning and evaluation documents show that the organization takes its work seriously and holds itself accountable. This inspires confidence in donors and potential donors.

History

In talking about its history a nonprofit should focus on its accomplishments in terms of service to its constituencies. The history should capture the spirit of the people, both service providers and beneficiaries. The focus should be on the organization's heroes. History is the heroic saga of the organization.

Internal Case and External Case and the Difference Between Them

With these elements in place the case resources file, or internal case, is ready. An operational case resources file (internal case) prepares the organization to develop expressions, external case statements, for fundraising. The external case statement tells the story to the constituencies.

While the internal case is a database of information and knowledge, the external case statement orders and presents the information for communications, public relations, and fundraising. External case statements take the form of brochures, foundation (and corporation) proposals, direct mail letters, Web-site development, campaign prospectuses, news releases, newsletters, speeches, and face-to-face solicitations. It might be helpful to think of an external case statement as "the case at work" (Rosso, 1991).

In making the transition from building the internal case to developing external case statements, the focus is on answering these questions:

1. What is the problem or social need that is central to our concern?
2. What special service or programs do we offer to respond to this need?
3. Why are the problem and service important?
4. What constitutes the market for our services?
5. Are others doing what we are doing to serve our service market, and perhaps doing it better?
6. Do we have a written plan with a statement of philosophy, objectives, and a program?

7. What are the specific financial needs against which private gift support will be sought?
8. Is the organization competent to carry out the defined program?
9. Who are the people associated with the organization: staff, key volunteers, trustees or directors?
10. Who should support the organization?

In writing external statements of the case, it is helpful to remember that the purpose is to stimulate a potential donor to take a series of steps, ultimately ending in the decision to make a gift. The qualities that must exist in the writing and be present in case statements to stimulate this sequence of reactions on the part of potential donors are excitement, proximity, immediacy, a sense of the future, meaning, and relevance.

Case statements need to excite the reader (or listener). Much of philanthropy begins with an emotional response to the external need as defined in the case for support. Proximity to the problem creates a sense of emotional awareness as well as a geographic proximity. How real is the problem in the potential donor's life? How important, even urgent, is it that the potential donor take action to help solve the problem? This is a sense of immediacy. What happens if the donor delays in responding to this need? In addition to immediacy, the need to act now, there should also be a sense of the future. This is not a one-time action but an ongoing process. It is unlikely that all problems can be solved now, so what does the future hold as a promise to address the ongoing problems? What is the meaning to the donor? Case statements should communicate to the donor the values and benefits of participating which are of importance to her. The mission expressed in the case should connect to the donor's values.

Qualities such as these in the expression of the case achieve the desired sequence of responses by the donor (see Table 4.2). Relevance grabs the attention

TABLE 4.2. QUALITIES AND RESPONSES.

Case Expression Qualities	Sequence of Response
Relevance	Attention
Proximity	Interest
Sense of the Future	Confidence
Immediacy	Conviction
Excitement	Desire
Importance	Action

Source: The Fund Raising School, 2002.

of the donor and focuses on the importance of the problem or need the nonprofit addresses. A sense of nearness will interest the donor, building a sense of concern on the donor's part. The immediacy of the problem and the sense of the future instill in the donor the confidence that the nonprofit has defined the problem accurately and offered a compelling solution. This trust leads to a conviction on the part of the donor that the nonprofit will produce the desired results in addressing the problem. Excitement about what can be done will lead to the donor's desire to be part of the program because it will bring satisfaction and enjoyment. Finally, the importance of this project or program will move the donor to take action, to become a participant by making a gift to the nonprofit.

Putting the Case to Work: Creating Case Expressions

The process of developing a case for support moves from creating or collating the key components that comprise a case resources file to the development of statements of the case finally to expressions of the case for information, education, and fundraising. To distinguish between internal and external case statements, it might be helpful to think of externally oriented case statements as case expressions.

Expressions of the case for support must fit the interests and needs of donors and funders, such as individuals, corporations, foundations, and other funders. Case expressions, then, are tailored to the audience—recipients of direct mail, new donors and donors who are renewing gifts or even increasing their gifts; recipients of email blasts; corporations or foundations receiving formal proposals; donors being solicited in a personal, face-to-face meeting. While the iteration of the case is specific in each instance, what all the case expressions have in common is the mission of the organization: all fundraising supports the mission.

Effective case expressions for fundraising must do the following:

1. State a need: this is a community need, the "cause" being served
2. Document the need: what external evidence exists to confirm that this is a problem
3. Propose strategies to alleviate the need: organizational goals, objectives, programs
4. Identify who benefits: recipients, beneficiaries, community as a whole
5. Demonstrate organizational competence: governance, staffing, facilities
6. Specify resources required: philanthropic support
7. Tell how to make gifts: checks, credit/debit cards, mobile devices, online
8. Explain benefits of giving: "what's in it for donors/funders"

Conclusion

In creating case expressions it is critical to keep the donor or funder uppermost in mind. Case expressions must be understandable to the audience; it is unsafe to assume the audience knows the organization at all, let alone as well as the creators of the case expressions know the organization. Case expressions should avoid "insider language" or jargon and must be written in the clear, precise language of the vernacular.

Developing a case for support is the first step in the fundraising process. Reviewing the case at least annually is a way to keep the case current and relevant. These questions can serve as an annual review of the case for support:

1. Who are we and why do we exist?
2. What do we want to accomplish?
3. How will we do it?
4. How do we hold ourselves accountable?
5. What distinguishes us from others doing similar work?

Answering these questions regularly validates the organization's case for support and prepares the organization to develop case expressions that articulate boldly and compellingly why it deserves philanthropic gift support.

Discussion Questions

1) How clearly are the core values of your organization articulated in your mission statement?
2) How complete is your organization's case resources file?
3) What are the major challenges you face in developing case expressions for financial support?
4) Who are the players you enlist in developing your organization's case for support?

CHAPTER FIVE

INDIVIDUALS AS A CONSTITUENCY FOR FUNDRAISNG

By Timothy L. Seiler

After completing this chapter, you will be able to:

1. Recognize the importance of individuals as a constituency for fundraising.
2. Describe the general principles of the constituency circles model.
3. Articulate the importance of the alignment of constituent segments.
4. Appreciate the impact on giving of individual life roles/responsibilities.

Effective fundraising requires an intimate knowledge of the nonprofit's constituency, a distinct group of people with actual or potential interest in the organization. Some organizations have "natural" constituencies readily identifiable and generally accessible. Schools, colleges, and universities, for example, have students and alumni. Many educational institutions expand their constituencies to include parents and grandparents of current students. Hospitals have patients, often referred to in fundraising circles as "grateful patients." Arts organizations have patrons, members, and audiences. Many organizations have "friends," formal groups identified as Friends of the Library, for example, or informal groups of people affiliated with the organization, and of course corporations, foundations, associations, and other types of donors/funders are constituencies for fundraising (see Chapter 8, "Corporate Giving and Fundraising," and Chapter 9, "Foundation Fundraising"). This chapter focuses on individuals as a constituency. The identification and development of individuals as a constituency are at the heart of sustainable fundraising.

Identifying the Individual Constituent

Organizations without such a natural constituency still have constituencies. The organization might need to work harder to identify and build its constituency, but every nonprofit organization has its own constituency. At the very least the constituency consists of people who need the services of the nonprofit, those who provide the services and direct the programs, those who govern the organization, and those who support the cause. In developing its constituency an organization should expend the resources necessary to identify, inform, involve, and bond the constituency to the organization. The energy, time, and money invested in constituency development will be returned in multiples by serving the nonprofit through volunteers, donors, and advocates. The bond for this philanthropic activity is the nonprofit's mission.

The constituency is a set of interested persons serving the cause with passion. A synonym for constituency is "interested parties." These interested parties include persons currently involved with the organization, those who have been previously involved, and those with the potential for future involvement. All constituencies also have active and inactive groups, interested and uninterested, close and distant. For fundraising purposes it is essential to know the interests, needs, and wants of the people in the constituency because their level of involvement helps or hinders the nonprofit as it seeks to accomplish its goals. The constituency is made up of stakeholders interested in the health of the nonprofit and willing to invest in it.

A Constituency Model

A helpful way to think about an organization's constituency is to visualize a set of concentric circles (see Figure 5.1). These widening circles represent the energy of an organization and the flow and dissipation of the energy moving outward from the center. An analogy is the action of a rock thrown into a body of water. Where the rock enters the water the action (energy) is highest. As the waves radiate outward from where the rock enters the water, they become wider but weaker; that is, the waves move farther away from the center of the action, but they are smaller and have less energy. This is how the constituency of a nonprofit interacts with the organization. The closer to the center of the action, the greater the energy,

FIGURE 5.1. THE CONSTITUENCY MODEL.

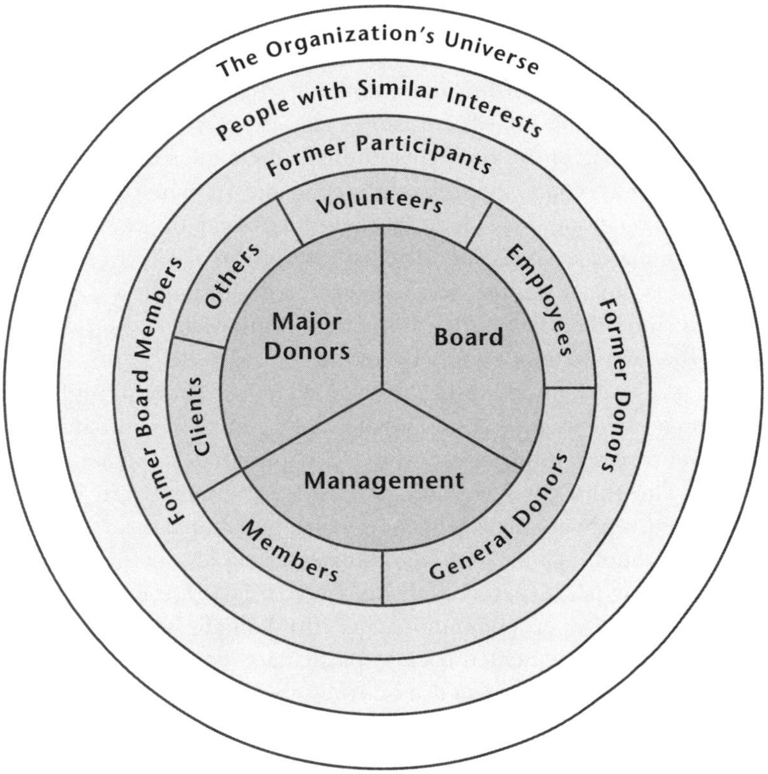

the stronger the bond. The core constituency, then, is at the center of the concentric circles. Those members of the constituency who are in the second, third, and fourth circles – moving away from the center – have a weaker bond with the organization. The farther away from the core the constituency segment lies, the lower the energy and the weaker the bond to the organization.

For the constituency model to affect fundraising positively, certain constituent groups should populate the inner circle, the core. The board of trustees, the senior management team, and major donors will ideally form the core of the organization. The trustees hold the organization in public trust and are responsible for the mission, vision, and policies of the organization. The senior management team carries out the organization's programs to meet the community needs articulated in the mission. Major donors demonstrate their commitment to the cause not only through their gifts of substance but also by serving as advocates for the cause. All three core components of the inner circle provide the energy for the organization and influence the direction of the organization. Fundraising begins here at the center.

While these three groups are the critical ones to be in the central circle, large organizations might include additional groups: alumni boards, visiting committees, foundation boards, advisory committees, and friends groups, for example, might be part of the core constituency for complex organizations.

In the second circle are volunteers, for program delivery and for fundraising; clients receiving the organization's services; employees, those who are not part of senior management; general donors, those who make gifts more modest than those made by major donors; members, if the organization is a membership organization; and others involved with the organization, such as vendors, who have a stake in the organization but are not in the central circle.

All the components in the second circle are important because they provide a broad base of support and a potential for greater future involvement, including more strategic volunteer activity and major gift development.

The third circle, former participants, former board members, and former donors, represents a drop in energy as these groups are farther from the core of the organization. While "former" indicates a state of what once was, and might imply something negative, this circle holds potential for reactivation and reinvolvement. Imaginative, open communication efforts might reveal that these groups would simply like to be invited back to participate more fully. If they once were participants, board members, or donors, they surely shared the values of the organization. Exploring how to win back their affections and their loyalty might move them back into the second circle and perhaps into the core circle.

The fourth circle, people with similar interests, is an ill-defined constituency segment. Constituents here are distant from the energy center. They typically know little of the organization, and the organization rarely knows much about them. This is the segment usually approached through direct mail or via social media or even special events in an attempt by the organization to acquire new donors. It is worth probing this segment, although the organization needs to recognize that returns from this segment are likely to be low for the time and energy expended.

The very last circle is the organization's universe. Every organization has such a constituency segment and often knows little about the giving potential. Involvement will be minimal and whatever gifts come from this circle will probably be modest in size, but the gifts might be regular and long-lasting. The donors in this segment might give year after year, and the cumulative giving becomes substantive over time. This circle, too, is worth attention and energy.

Several principles of the constituency circles model are important. First, because energy is at the center and flows outward, the bond is strongest at the center. Fundraising, then, begins at the center of the constituency circles and is taken to the outer circles by the board, management staff, and major donors in the inner circle. The constant challenge for the development program is to align the central players in the core circle. A dysfunctional fundraising program is one that finds the board and/or the management staff on the outer circles.

A second principle is fluidity in the circles. A major donor this year will be a general donor next year. Board members' terms expire and they become former board members. Other changes occur in the constituency for many reasons: people change residences or occupations, donors' interests change, donors' financial capacity changes. Patterns in constituency development show that a 20 to 25 percent change annually is to be expected. Effective constituency development requires consistent involvement with all the circles in the model.

Identifying and Attracting Likely Donors

One of the truisms of fundraising is that the best prospective donor is a current donor. Someone who has made a gift has demonstrated interest in and involvement with the organization. That donor is likely to consider another gift. Experienced fundraisers testify that every donor at one level is a prospective donor for a gift at a higher level. Working conscientiously with the constituency model will reveal the most likely candidates for renewed gifts and for increased gifts, leading ultimately to major gifts (including perhaps planned gifts).

The most likely donors are identified by three characteristics: Linkage, Ability, and Interest. Linkage is contact. Often such contact is person to person, a peer of the potential donor. The personal contact, the linkage, makes possible a personal visit to the potential donor for the organization to make its case for a gift. Linkage can also be geographic, emotional, or professional (more is discussed about this under Wheel of Roles and Responsibilities). Linkage is another term for the more commonly used concept "network." Linkage is determining who knows who and can arrange the visits necessary for successful gift solicitations.

Ability means the financial capacity of the gift source to give a gift at the level the nonprofit deems appropriate. Research by the nonprofit helps determine the capacity. Peer evaluations (linkage) of gift capacity are also effective in determining the ability factor.

Interest in the nonprofit and its work is essential. Even the most financially able gift source will not make a gift to an organization in which he or she has no interest. Interest follows information and precedes involvement.

All three of these characteristics, linkage, ability, and interest, are imperative for identifying the most qualified and most likely prospective donors. It is most likely that these characteristics will be in greater evidence in the inner circles of the constituency model. Surely it is important to test the principles across all the circles, but the most likely prospective donors will be found in the first two or three circles.

Some aspects of the constituency arise automatically. For instance, the client base becomes an immediate adjunct of the constituency because it acts in response to services offered. Trustees, management staff, and beginning program staff become an early part of an organization because they must make available the services that are needed by their clients. Contributors, volunteers, and advocates take longer to develop. They must be sought out and invited to become the philanthropic base that will augment and celebrate the organization's work. The fundraising person must be sensitive to the fact that there is constant interaction within and between the constituency circles and among the elements that make up each circle. Individuals gravitate toward the core circle as their interest is touched and then deepened; they drift away if their interest slackens, if they are ignored, or if their interests change or are neglected. A studied program of constituency involvement and thoughtful cultivation is necessary to maintain the vitality of the constituency base.

A responsible fundraising staff should assert itself continuously to develop an *awareness* within the constituency of the organization's mission, goals, and objectives; to foster an *understanding* of the service to that mission; and to invite constituency *commitment* to the organization through the process of making a gift. This gift-making process forges a strong bond of the constituency to the nonprofit organization and its mission.

An effective, externally oriented communication program is the first necessity. In developing any human relationship it is necessary to get the attention of the subject, the person who the organization wants to involve. The person must be made aware that the organization exists and that it exists for a purpose that may hold an interest to him or her. Awareness must be converted into understanding, first of the guiding mission that delineates the human or societal needs that must be addressed, and second of the programs that will respond to these needs. From awareness to understanding to acceptance is the direct path to involvement and the process that is so necessary for constituency development.

People will identify with an organization if they understand and can accept its reason for being, if they accept that the programs are valid and responsive, and if they strongly believe that the people associated with the organization are competent and trustworthy in their service to the mission.

Various techniques are applicable to this process of identifying and involving a constituency, particularly the segment that is likely to contribute funds and to volunteer time. One of the first and most effective instruments for constituency development is fundraising. The fundraising process is based on intelligent, purposeful communications with the amorphous and unidentified market, including prospective donors and donors. A sensitively managed communications program will invite interest in the organization, its mission, its goals, and its programs. The outreach or public relations effort should include periodic newsletters, both electronic and print, that contain information of interest to the reader. These publications too often are self-serving informational instruments that extol the accomplishments of staff members while neglecting the concerns, questions, and curiosity of the constituency. Periodic surveys of readers' interests and reactions to the value of the newsletter might well evoke the kind of response that will heal the myopia of an overly abundant self-interest.

Special events offer an opportunity to attract the attention of potential constituents. A special event may be defined as an activity that is designed to accomplish a variety of objectives, one of which is to invite possible constituents to become involved and to learn more about the organization. Events may include open houses, come-and-see tours, 10-K runs, leadership dinners, fashion shows, discussions, seminars, workshops, annual meetings, and book sales (see Chapter 30).

Properly staged events can serve purposes other than just raising money. They can encourage people to become part of the organization's expanding constituency base. Social media platforms are excellent methods for reaching a broad constituency of potential donors (see Chapter 29).

It is important to know and understand the concept of constituency circles, but this understanding must be translated into an understanding of each individual constituent in order to create and maintain the exchange relationship underlying effective fundraising and giving.

Roles and Responsibilities that Influence Giving

In identifying candidates for major gifts or for volunteer leadership positions fundraisers are well served by a model defined as the Wheel of Roles and Responsibilities (Figure 5.2). This model shows the many roles and responsibilities assumed by individuals. The roles and responsibilities can help determine the behavior of constituents in relating to the nonprofit organization.

The individual who is a prospective major gift donor or leadership candidate is in the center of the wheel. Each spoke represents a role or responsibility demanding a portion of the individual's time, energy, ability, and inclination to be involved with a fundraising program. The roles/responsibilities include family, career, religion, education, recreation, politics, and social.

FIGURE 5.2. THE WHEEL OF ROLES AND RESPONSIBILITIES.

Family is of central concern to most individuals. The family will often influence positively the gift-giving decision. However, family interests can also hinder the major gift process. The fundraising executive needs to determine how the family role influences the gift decision of each individual major gift donor in the constituency.

A career or profession will often influence a constituent's ability or inclination to help a nonprofit organization. Certain professions are conventionally viewed as most likely to be major givers: attorneys, doctors, investment managers, and in recent years technology investors and entrepreneurs. Other professions – educators, nurses, social workers – are generally viewed as having little capacity to give. Effective constituency development goes beyond conventional attitudes and explores each individual for capacity and inclination, ignoring convention as the sole determinant.

Religion has been and continues to be a bedrock of philanthropy. Historically, giving patterns reveal that religion influences generosity to secular causes. It is true, however, that commitments to church, temple, synagogue, or mosque can reduce financial capacity to give to other causes.

The role that education plays in an individual's life can be an important factor in major gift capacity. If a major gift prospective donor is paying tuition for family enrolled at private universities, his or her capacity to give to a nonprofit is likely limited for the duration of the educational process. If the person values education because of the stature he or she currently has, it can be a very important factor in determining interest in philanthropy in higher education.

Recreational interests can play an important role in the prospective donor's life. Some interests might be so costly as to reduce the potential for gift-giving. On the other hand, recreational interests provide a forum for involvement and interaction. The astute fundraising executive will determine how the nonprofit can meet the donor's interests through recreation.

Politics, or civic engagement, plays a role in most people's lives to the degree that it influences how people interact. Those constituents most actively engaged in communities of interest and shared values have wide-ranging connections, thereby expanding constituency circles.

Social roles are important to fundraising for how they build networks and make connections. A socially active, energetic constituency will extend itself widely, creating many opportunities for delivering the nonprofit's message. Broadening social contacts will assist in establishing helpful linkages.

These roles change many times during one's life. The fundraiser must recognize that some of these roles might be in conflict with the organization's fundraising needs and will therefore militate against the making of a major gift. On the other hand, the roles might be compatible with the organization's needs and will form a basis of linkage to the organization, thus facilitating a major gift. The more fulfillment a donor can realize for one or more of these roles, or interests, the greater the number of contact points the organization can have with the donor. The role of the fundraising executive, along with volunteers, is to identify those elements that provide a basis for the exchange relationship, focusing on the compatibility of shared values.

Conclusion

Constituency development is critical for long-term, sustainable fundraising success. Most organizations will have a larger constituency than they can interact with effectively. While it is true that an organization's constituencies include corporations, foundations, and associations, it is the individual as a constituency that likely provides the best opportunity for most organizations to experience sustainable fundraising. Organizations should spend the maximum time and energy identifying constituents, cultivating meaningful relationships with them, inviting them to move closer to the core of the organization, and bonding them to the organization. Sensitive attention to the needs, values, and motivations of the constituents will attract them more intimately to the mission of the organization. Recognizing changes in life stages (roles and responsibilities) and how those changes lessen or increase capacity and willingness to give will lead to more robust relationships with the constituents.

Discussion Questions

1) What does your organization's constituency circles look like, moving from the inner core circle to the outlying ones?
2) Select one segment and define how it can be developed in greater detail – for example, alumni from various decades or by gender, former board members by length of service, former donors by recency of gifts, etc.
3) Discuss with other leaders in your organization the importance of understanding individuals as constituents for philanthropic support.
4) Examine at least one major constituent segment and how the wheel of roles affects that segment's gift-giving capacity.

PART TWO

CONSTITUENTS: WHAT DONORS VALUE

CHAPTER SIX

CONTEMPORARY DYNAMICS OF PHILANTHROPY

By Dwight F. Burlingame and Pat Danahey Janin

Philanthropy and the world that fundraisers work in are constantly changing. Today we have witnessed a global recognition of the important role that private support in giving of time and/or money plays in the vast array of divergent cultures. Since the publication of the first edition of *Achieving Excellence in Fundraising* in 1991, both the nonprofit/philanthropic/civil society sector and the fundraising profession have been enhanced by research and education and both have grown tremendously. As the authors of this chapter noted in the third edition of this work (Rooney and Nathan, 2011): "Even recent popular culture has embraced philanthropy. *The Philanthropist* – NBC's short-lived television series … *Idol Gives Back*, *Oprah's Big Give*, and … *Hope for Haiti*, philanthropy is now an essential element of pop culture" (p. 117). The way that philanthropy has played out across the world is as diverse as the missions of the groups and organizations that make up the sector. To understand the contemporary environment in which fundraisers work, this chapter addresses:

- The roles of philanthropy and its cultural roots.
- The economic climate for fundraising.
- Opportunities for philanthropy today.

Roles of Philanthropy

The root of the word philanthropy comes from the Greek meaning love of human kind. A lexical history of the word uncovers a "multifaceted term, with many layers of meaning in both its historical and its contemporary usages" (Sulek, 2010). Indeed, there are many possible motivations for philanthropic activities, whether it be love of other persons, the beautiful, the good, the divine, or wisdom; personal excellence, civic virtue, or morality; rational understanding, moral sentiment, or goodwill; the pleasures of social interaction, etc. However, even if we use the most basic definition, love of others, as a simplified understanding of philanthropy today, it does not belie the inherent moral nature of philanthropic actions. This is why the Lilly Family School of Philanthropy at Indiana University uses Robert Payton's broad definition of philanthropy – voluntary action for the public good – as a foundation for its work. In this conception, philanthropy is purposeful in both action and intention. It is much bigger than the nonprofit or nongovernmental sector, which is the primary focus of this book, and, at the same time, encompasses the work that fundraisers do. Philanthropy is a tradition that manifests itself in various ways in virtually all cultures around the globe.

Philanthropy defines the field in a positive way, in terms of what this sort of action does and why. It affirms a value, a concern for the well-being of people beyond oneself, and a concern for the public good. It asserts that the most important aspect of action (formal and informal) in this so-called sector is the public purpose and mission of action (Payton and Moody, 2008, p. 36). In this context, the roles of philanthropy are generally defined as:

- Reduce human suffering. Through healthcare, human services, and international relief, nonprofit organizations seek to make life more comfortable for those who are injured or ill, to aid victims, and to assist those not able to sustain themselves. This is perhaps the oldest role of philanthropy, a role that has existed throughout recorded history.
- Enhance human potential. Nonprofit organizations enhance human potential through religion, education, the arts, culture and humanities, public and society benefit, the environment and international efforts.
- Promote equity and justice. Philanthropy promotes equity and justice through human services and advocacy on behalf of those who cannot speak for themselves by promoting structures and programs within the public, private, and nonprofit sectors. Through advocacy efforts, nonprofit organizations often give voice to the voiceless.

- Build community. Through organizations and voluntary associations, people come together, they belong, and make a contribution to their neighborhood, city, state, country, or world through community building.
- Provide human fulfillment. Philanthropy provides all people the opportunity to become that best image we have of ourselves. Through giving and sharing, humans express their ideas and values. Peter Drucker (1990, p. xvii) best captured this notion when he said, "To make contributors out of donors means that the American people can see what they want to see – or should want to see – when each of us looks at him or herself in the mirror in the morning: someone who as a citizen takes responsibility. Someone who as a neighbor cares."
- Support experimentation and change. Philanthropy supports experimentation and stimulates change by taking risks, exploring areas that the larger community or the market sector may be unwilling to enter, and often funds alternative or new solutions.
- Foster pluralism. Nonprofit organizations and participation in nonprofit organizations allow for multiple responses to an issue and, at its best, includes a wide variety of voices. In a society in which philanthropy flourishes, parallel power structures are allowed to carry out what the government will not or cannot do.

This understanding of philanthropy, that we care for those who need assistance in our community, is as old as the land upon which we live. Traditions of caring, sharing, and giving are ever present in Native American stories, many of which influenced early settlers in North America (Jackson, 2008). In 1630, aboard the ship *Arabella,* John Winthrop gave his sermon "Model of Christian Charity" as a guide for the colonists' actions at Massachusetts Bay. Among the rationales he provided for charity is the inherent connections between all people, rich and poor. Because of this connection, a reciprocal obligation to care for others binds people together. Almost a century and a half later, Benjamin Franklin, although a strong individualist, participated in many voluntary associations. He established the Junto, a civic club for young men, the first volunteer fire department, and the public library in Philadelphia. Franklin is also credited with "inventing" the matching gift. Historian Kathleen McCarthy (2003) reveals how generations of Americans have used philanthropy to gather, speak freely, and lobby for reform, comprising an "American Creed."

This tradition of voluntary association was documented in detail by French political writer Alex de Tocqueville a hundred years after Franklin. The history of philanthropy in the United States is rich and diverse and in the last 40 years we have seen a more scholarly treatment of the subject, which has been informative for the practice of philanthropy at home and abroad. In recent years, scholarship on the history of philanthropy and how we organize ourselves to get the common good done has resulted in many excellent resources for the fundraiser to avail him/herself.

American understanding of the sector as "nonprofit," "voluntary," "independent," or "third" is relatively new. First studied in great length and legitimized by the Commission on Private Philanthropy and Public Needs report published (commonly referred to as the Filer Commission) in 1975, the nonprofit sector was recognized as a powerful force in both the economy and society. The Commission's final report emphasized the close yet sometimes adversarial relationship between nonprofit organizations and government. In many ways, the Commission is credited for the subsequent "professionalization" of the sector. Perhaps its greatest legacy will be a sector grounded in research: research that today helps identify emerging trends, challenges conventional wisdom, and provides invaluable insights into philanthropic organizations and their practices.

History and Understanding of Philanthropy

The nonprofit sector has grown significantly since the Filer Commission's report, both within and outside the United States. The spread of community foundations, the global growth of the study of philanthropy and nonprofit organizations, and the increase in research and journal publications specifically devoted to philanthropic/nonprofit subjects has been notable.

In her recent essay on community foundations, historian E. Sacks notes that "Community foundations are the most identifiable form of structured community philanthropy" (Sacks, 2014, p. 3). They raise money in their communities, support local nonprofit organizations, and integrate local citizens on their board. Traditionally, community foundations served a geographical area; however, mobility and connectedness in today's global society are expanding the notion of community. Their numbers have more than doubled in the United States in the last 20 years. In 2014, there were an estimated 763 community foundations in the United States actively making grants. Sixteen community foundations are amongst the largest 100 grant-making foundations. Their development outside of the United States started in the 1970s and 1980s and has spread throughout the Americas, Europe, the Middle East, and Asia, resulting in a higher number of Community Foundations outside of the United States. This development attests to the flexibility of the concept and the ability to engage citizens in their communities (Sacks, 2014, pp. 2–3).

The size and scope of philanthropy education has increased significantly since the first study of programs in the United States in 1996 by Seton Hall University. The first survey indicated a total of 179 institutions and 284 programs covering undergraduate, graduate, noncredit, continuing education, and online courses in nonprofit management education (Mirabella, 2007, p. 13S). In 2015, there were 292 colleges and universities offering nonprofit management courses, which included 91 programs with noncredit courses, 73 continuing education programs, and 168 graduate degree programs (Mirabella, 2015).

A recent study of philanthropy education in the United Kingdom and Continental Europe reveals an "embryonic philanthropy education sector" across Europe, primarily at the postgraduate level in Western European countries (Keidan, Jung, and Pharaoh, 2014, p. 41). Although these programs are found in diverse social sciences disciplines, they are predominantly provided in business schools. A similar characterization of philanthropic education as "embryonic" is true for much of the rest of the world. As noted by Dr. Huehls in Chapter 37, there has been a significant growth in books and journal publications that provide research findings that advance the professional and thoughtful practice of philanthropy and fundraising.

Size and Scope

As noted, philanthropy and nonprofit organizations have always played a significant role in American society, but they play an even more significant role today. The nonprofit sector has grown to be a large part of the U.S. economy. According to the National Center for Charitable Statistics at the Urban Institute (McKeever and Pettijohn, 2014), approximately 1.44 million nonprofits were registered with the Internal Revenue Service in 2012. This number, however, is an understatement of the sector's true size because it does not capture nonregistered groups – namely religious organizations and churches, which are not required to register, as well as small, mostly informal groups. Between 2002 and 2012 the number of registered nonprofit organizations grew by 8.6 percent, from 1.32 million to 1.44 million organizations. Among those reporting public charities, human services comprise the largest subsector (35.5 percent), followed by education (17.1 percent), health (13 percent), public and social benefit (11.6 percent), and the arts (9.9 percent). Among the smaller subsectors, international and foreign affairs and environment and animals saw the largest growth rates in the number of organizations, increasing by 22.5 and 21.2 percent, respectively, from 2002 to 2012. The growing nonprofit sector means that there are more opportunities for volunteer involvement and gift giving.

Just as the number of organizations has increased, so too has Americans' generosity through charitable giving. Since 1955, the Giving USA Foundation has been calculating annual charitable giving. According to Giving USA: The Annual Report on Philanthropy for the Year 2014, total giving was estimated to be $358.38 billion, or 2.1% of GDP – a 7.1 percent increase in current dollars (5.4 percent increase in inflation adjusted dollars) over 2013 giving. Giving has steadily grown since the 2009 recession at an average of 3.6 percent between 2010 and 2014. Giving reached the pre-recession giving levels in 2014. One of the most useful things that these data reveal is that giving by individuals is *always* the largest slice of the giving pie. In 2014, individual giving and bequests was 80% of all giving, comparted to 87% in the early 1990s. This is why mastering the art and the science of fundraising is so critical to the health of the nonprofit sector: no longer can an organization rely on the generosity of one foundation or corporation.

To obtain a more complete picture of giving, one needs to examine the sources of giving by subsector. For example, giving to religious causes represents about one-third of all charitable giving annually. In 2014, specifically, it accounted for 32 percent of all giving. Although this number is declining, a recent study indicates the larger role religion plays if one considers donations to Religiously Identified Organizations (RIOs), such as Catholic Charities, Church World Service, Jewish Federations, the Zakat Foundation, or World Vision, in addition to giving to congregations (McKitrick et al., 2013). Educational causes, the second largest subsector, also receives the second largest number of contributions, 15 percent in 2014. In addition, whereas human services organizations significantly outnumber other charities, they receive only 12 percent of all gifts. These contributions include support for disaster relief efforts. It is worth noting that 12 percent of all donations go to foundations and 8 percent to the health subsector.

International giving is a more complex picture and requires some searching to compile informed data. Giving Korea, Giving Japan, Giving Mexico, Giving Puerto Rico, and Giving Europe are illustrative of the growing country and regional efforts to collect giving data. Perhaps the *2013 Index of Global Philanthropy and Remittances* published by The Center for Global Prosperity at Hudson Institute is the fundraisers' first stop to get a sense of the global giving picture.

Being informed of the data available from *Giving USA* and other sources **can** empower your work. While organizations within a subsector may experience changes based on their own unique circumstances, national data are always a useful benchmark. Furthermore, national averages by subsector can help fundraisers engage in meaningful conversations with staff and board members about key trends as well as greatly assisting in tracking and comparing the organization's rates of fundraising growth against the particular subsector as a whole. In 2015 the Lilly Family School of Philanthropy at Indiana University developed *The Philanthropy Outlook 2015 and 2016*, which provides data and analysis for predicting growth rates in U.S. giving. The first edition predicts giving to grow in 2015 and 2016 at about a 3.1 percent growth rate. The *Philanthropy Outlook* provides another resource for the informed fundraiser to utilize.

Fundraising and The Economic Climate

A chapter about the contemporary dynamics of philanthropy would be remiss if it did not address the financial climate and its effect on charitable giving. It is no secret that many nonprofit organizations have found fundraising a challenge, especially during recessions. The Great Recession of 2007–2009 in the United States resulted in the first decline in giving since 1987. Charitable contributions have climbed continuously since the recession lows of 2009, representing a 12.3 cumulative gain in inflation adjusted dollars over the past four years. Through an analysis of giving over forty years, it is clear that changes in giving are closely tied to economic changes, especially in household wealth, household income, and, for foundations, stock market performance. When adjusting for inflation, giving usually increases in non-recessionary years and slightly contracts in recession years.

Social venture philanthropy and social enterprise ventures have seen considerable growth and often serve as alternative revenue streams to traditional fundraising for nonprofits. Social enterprise is an attractive solution to operate in the marketplace as a business using revenues to advance social goals. This hybrid organizational form is developing across the globe and presents a new way to mobilize innovative ideas and resources to contribute to long-term societal challenges. However, a recent study in Canada demonstrated that the current legal forms available both for nonprofit and for-profit organizations limit either the opportunities to earn business income and raise financing or to pursue social ends (O'Connor, 2014). There is a resulting call to develop an agenda for the social enterprise system in Canada that is in the interests of all members of the nonprofit community including fundraisers.

The current economic climate is both a glass-half-full and glass-half-empty scenario. At the organizational level annual giving can have significant swings, such as a 10 percent swing from budgeted or expected revenue to actual (on average), viewed as a glass-half-empty. However, viewing the glass as half-full, giving fell *only* 5 percent following the worst recession since the Great Depression. Organizations adopting the glass-half-full attitude have generally been successful in emphasizing their proactive response to the economic climate in ways that donors indicate are most important to them. These include better stewardship, more frequent communication about the needs they are meeting, as well as making choices that result in greater organizational efficiency and impact. At the same time, successful fundraisers know to be sympathetic when talking to potential donors and acknowledging the situation the donors may be in at any particular time.

When faced with an uncertain economy, now or in the future, the importance of staying true to the best practices outlined in this book cannot be stressed enough. Fundraisers must remain faithful to the organization's mission, be creative, and keep engaging board members and asking for their help. Most of all, fundraisers must remain positive. Fundraising is an inherently optimistic profession that serves society well, especially in times of distress.

Opportunities for Philanthropy

Clearly, economic crisis requires creative responses by fundraisers. Other opportunities exist as well. Among the most promising is the use of electronic media outlets to fundraise, attract volunteers, and build community around an organization's mission. Both e-fundraising, social media, and the various marketing/challenge campaigns are given ample consideration in this volume. According to social media expert Chris Brogan (2010, p. 44), "Creativity, creation, communities of interest and culture itself are at the heart of what social media is equipped to enable." This is especially important for nonprofit organizations who may be able to reach a much broader audience for a fraction of the cost they once did. Just as making connections between people is an important part of a fundraiser's job, so too are quality connections at the heart of effective social media. A willingness to experiment with different tools of electronic communication can open up new pathways to build relationships with donors, volunteers, and clients. Corporate community engagement strategies around the world provide illustrative examples for fundraisers on how to navigate regional differences in our increasing interconnected philanthropic world.

Another opportunity in philanthropy is recognizing the importance of small organizations and small donations. While the research on donor behavior most often focuses on high net-worth individuals (see, for example, the "U.S. Trust, Bank of America Corporation Studies of High Net Worth Philanthropy" and Million Dollar Donor reports found at www.philanthropy.iupui.edu/research), analysis of long-term giving patterns show that two-thirds of Americans donate something in any given year. This is a greater portion of the population than those who vote, making giving and volunteering more democratic than even the political process. On the other hand, the top 3 percent of income earners account for half of all contributions, including through family foundations and bequests. While the small number of high net-worth donors are often the focus of fundraisers because of their ability to provide transformative gifts, annual donors, even if their gifts are "small," should never be overlooked. The two simply require different strategies. Fundraisers need to be careful not to devalue the generosity and potential of donors who make smaller gifts and the contributions made by small nonprofit organizations. In communities large and small, "small" gifts from many donors literally keep a community and its people going, providing services that are often invisible, but essential. Small gifts give people a voice and foster pluralism (Tempel, 2008). There are many opportunities for fundraisers to reach out and make connections among donors of all levels.

Conclusion

In the coming years, fundraisers will have to deal with a number of economic challenges, legal and political issues, technological changes, social and educational changes, and ethical issues as they seek to increase philanthropic support. Creative partnerships, engaging new types of volunteers and attracting a new generation of donors will be necessary for organizations to continue their significant role in a larger, more effective nonprofit/philanthropic sector. Philanthropy takes on society's most intractable problems: homelessness, abuse, hunger, and others. It gives voice to the voiceless, advocates for justice, and offers care, hope, and help. Nonprofit organizations often provide what government and business cannot or will not do to solve the toughest problems and champion the public good. No matter the challenges the sector faces, philanthropy will always fundamentally be about love, charity, hope, fresh starts, experimentation of new ideas to solve problems, and new beginnings. As the institutional stewards of philanthropy, it is up to fundraisers to bear this in mind as they fulfill their role in building a just and civil society.

Discussion Questions

1) How do you define the role of the philanthropic sector?
2) What significance does the sector play in your community?
3) What are the major sources of income for your organization?
4) In the future, what do you anticipate to be the most challenging issues facing philanthropic organizations – legal, political, economic, technological, social, and educational?

CHAPTER SEVEN

PROSPECTIVE DONOR AND DONOR RESEARCH AND DATABASE MANAGEMENT

By Katie Prine and Elisabeth Lesem

Information that organizations accumulate on their donors, volunteers, event attendees, and other constituents is the bridge to successful fundraising. This bridge allows us to reach out from behind our desks via letters, phone calls, and face-to-face meetings to raise money for our organization. However, what happens when the data are wrong? Or even worse, it is not there? It makes the job of the fundraiser increasingly difficult when the end of the bridge is not intact and the information needed is not at hand. Let us also consider the flipside of this equation when we have a strong bridge between donor and organization. How might we build upon that relationship and gain more insight to help us in our work? This chapter will address:

* Both the importance of the fundraising database and prospective donor management due to their interconnectedness,
* The basic elements of a data system,
* The various uses of a database,
* Approaches to prospective donor research,
* The ethics of prospective donor research.

Database 101

In its most basic form, the fundraising database is comprised of the information necessary to facilitate the development process. For some organizations, the need may be as simple as recording the name, contact information, and gift history of a small number of donors. This will facilitate a prompt gift receipt and a personalized thank-you letter and the information can be used to produce the annual honor roll of donors. In following years, that same data can be used to renew their generous support.

For others, the need for data has expanded to a comprehensive collection of data elements including an almost limitless number of attributes such as event attendance, volunteer activity, linkage indicators, wealth and asset information, predictive modeling data, marketing segments acquired from external vendors, contacts with the organization, online behavior, and more. If the information is available, it can be stored in a database, analyzed, and used to increase the effectiveness and efficiency of the organization.

While it has become easier to store, analyze, and use vast amounts of data, it is important to remember that fundraising is about people. Ultimately, the process of asking for money will determine the overall success of any fundraising program. Those who are most successful at database management leverage the data they have at their fingertips to more effectively manage both resource allocation and their personal relationships with others. Simply collecting data for the sake of doing so is a certain path to "analysis paralysis" for many fundraising professionals, not to mention time consuming for those doing the data entry.

Sample Data Elements

The data elements one could acquire and store are limited only by the imagination of those responsible for capturing them. For the purposes of this discussion, data are considered to be more fundamental in nature, captured for individual donors and prospective donors, and used for the purpose of increasing the effectiveness of the solicitation process.

The Basics

While nonprofit organizations may differ greatly in their ability to collect, maintain, and utilize data, certain core data elements are essential for all. All organizations must capture and maintain simple contact information such as name, address, phone number, email, employment information, and historical giving transactions.

These core data elements provide the ability to perform the main functions necessary to maintain a fundraising operation. Direct mail solicitations, telemarketing, email, personal solicitations, gift receipts, thank-you letters, honor rolls, invitations to special events, and more can be generated with this small amount of data. Employment information, in addition to assisting with matching gift procurement, also provides helpful information when determining a prospective donor's capacity to give.

Acquiring core data elements often takes place at the time of the first gift to an organization. Data are captured from pledge cards, information provided on a check, or from online giving forms. RSVPs to organizational events and volunteer opportunities also provide opportunities to capture data on new prospective donors and update those already in the database. Brokerage firms who specialize in renting or selling lists of potential donors help organizations acquire information based on criteria the nonprofit determines.

Solicitation History

In addition to the basic giving history of each donor, the database should contain a solicitation history for each prospective donor. This information is valuable on both a micro and macro level. For the individual, it is helpful to know which solicitations (both personal and mass) have been made, when they were made, and what the resulting outcome is. This information may be tracked by coding each appeal (and segment within each appeal) with a unique code. That tracking code is applied to the individual's record at the time of solicitation and again on the gift transaction.

On a macro level, these data allow the nonprofit the ability to analyze the success of each individual solicitation, watch for oversolicitation and undersolicitation, and monitor donor response to appeals at every level. As a management tool, this information is valuable to determine future solicitation activity and to allocate resources most effectively.

Event and Activity Data

As the organization begins to expand its data catalog beyond the basic data elements discussed above, the logical next step is to record interactions with the organization. Keeping a comprehensive record of these interactions begins with the recording of attendance at any functions held throughout the year. This may include an annual fundraising auction, attendance at board meetings, or participation in a volunteer activity. These interactions with the organization should be recorded, as these data are critical to build a historical account of each donor and prospective donor's relationship with the nonprofit entity. Tracking these data can indicate which individuals have the greatest linkage and interest to your organization.

To further enhance use of the data, event activity should record both those invited and who attended and the RSVP status of each invited guest. Those who respond in the affirmative but never show up are very different prospective donors than those who attend every event. These data can provide important insight into individual donor behavior as well as assist in the analysis of the effectiveness of each individual event.

Personal Interaction

In addition to events and activities involving many, a historical account of personal interactions with each individual should be recorded. The relationship between donors and organizations often outlasts the tenure of staff. Therefore, as members of the organization's team come and go, it is helpful to have detailed accounts of prior interactions recorded in the database, from phone calls or personal notes to face-to-face visits.

After each contact with donors or prospective donors, staff should be encouraged to document pertinent details of the discussion. This may include specific interests of the donor, funding opportunities, concerns, and more. As others currently on the staff or those who join the staff in the future begin to work with that same donor, the historical record will help them understand what has happened in the past and plan appropriately to continue the relationship.

Ideally, the nature of each contact will contain not only the substance of the discussion but also the type of interaction (phone, email, personal contact), circumstances, and next steps required to move the relationship forward.

Prospective Donor Research 101

Returning to the analogy of using information to build the bridge to donors, prospective donor research requires organizations to creatively look within their own data to determine the strongest bridges and then look externally for additional information to help fortify and build up those bridges. The end result can uncover prospective donors otherwise not considered for a more substantial gift.

Looking from Within

For more than 20 years, the field of prospective donor research has experienced tremendous growth in the number of individuals entering the field and in the scope of the field itself. The one thing that has remained constant, however, is the basic fundamentals of prospective donor research: the LAI principle (linkage, ability, interest). These fundamentals are the basis upon which quality, comprehensive research is performed. Linkage is one of the easiest, yet highly critical, principles to identify. *Linkage* is the direct connection of an individual to an organization, whether as a board member, volunteer, donor, etc. *Ability* refers to an individual's capability to make gifts at a designated level; interestingly, it is also the least reliable qualifier. Studies have shown that individuals with a lower giving capacity tend to give more based on percentage of income. *Interest* is one of the most important indicators of a prospect's likelihood to give. The level of a prospective donor's involvement with the organization, as well as their belief in the mission and vision, correlates directly with their level and frequency of giving.

Prospective donor research professionals provide thoroughly vetted prospect lists utilizing the Linkage Ability Interest principle as the foundation of the fundraising effort (see Chapter 3). The value of background preparation in terms of time saved and quality information is measureless for fundraising staff working directly with donors. Prospective donor research professionals recognize and utilize the appropriate reference materials for any given project, and not only identify and qualify viable prospective donors, but also know how to determine who is *not* a likely prospect and remove those individuals from working lists.

Prospective Donor Identification   The work of prospective donor research is to identify those individuals who have the closest connection to the organization, the ability to make a gift at a defined level, and are inclined to offer financial support. The best place to begin prospective donor identification is to analyze key segments of the organization's pool of current donors.

Major Gift Donors   Close relationships should already be established with major gift donors, allowing fundraisers to know when the donor is ready for the next step along the fundraising cycle. Research can provide additional information on any changes that may have taken place with the donor that will help fundraisers know when the time is right to begin cultivating for the next gift. Indicators may include increased annual giving, an empty nest situation and/or children who have graduated from college, a job promotion, sale of a business, or retirement.

Annual Donors   Analyzing the top annual donors of an organization is an excellent way to determine who may be ready for cultivation beyond their current gifts. Reviewing contact reports on these individuals should provide valid information as well. Ongoing communication with fundraisers working directly with donors, in concert with the research analysis, will aid in the development of a solid major gift prospective donor list.

EXHIBIT 7.1. PEER SCREENING FORM.

Prospect Identification, Evaluation, and validation		
Campaign or program:		
Evaluator:		
Date:		
Location:		
Names	Gift capability/probability	Comments

Source: The Fund Raising School, 2009b, p. VI-23.

Board of Directors   A potential major gift pool lies within the organization's board of directors. It may be surprising to learn that many who serve at a high level within a nonprofit organization have yet to make their own leadership gift. The financial involvement of an organization's board members sets the tone for the community-at-large, and it should be a priority for their involvement. Board members also offer a level of influence among their own social and business networks that help achieve the fundraising goals of the organization.

Peer Screening   Peer screening is an important tool for qualifying prospective donors, and utilizing the board and other high-level volunteers as peer screeners is a good way to engage them in the fundraising cycle. A valuable and inexpensive way to identify potential prospective donors is to ask these individuals to review lists of potential donors and then share, in a confidential manner, what they know about certain individuals' giving habits, interests, and ability. Also, these individuals may be able to provide an introduction to the prospective donors if there has not been a close relationship to the institution in the past. See Exhibit 7.1 for an example of a peer screening form.

Building Prospective Donor Profiles   Research profiles differ based on an organization's needs. A profile is not a biography but rather a concise document that highlights the donor's linkage, ability, and interest. Three basic pieces of information should be found in all profiles regardless of style. A good example of what a research profile may look like is provided by The Fund Raising School in Exhibit 7.2.

EXHIBIT 7.2. DONOR RESEARCH PROFILE.

Prospect Profile Form

Date prepared: Date revised:	Trustee	Donor	Friend	Mailing list	# of solicitations
Source(s):					
Card: donor _____ prospective _____					

Last name	Educational background
First/middle names	
Residence address/phone	Social/business activities
Business address/phone	
	Spouse name (maiden, if applicable)
Position/title	Marriage date
Directorship/business affilation (shares held)	Family history (children/parents/interests/ achievements/other information)
Foundation affiliations	
Community/philanthropic/social affiliations	Political affiliation
Professional memberships	Religious affiliation
Special interests	Military service
Awards/honors/and so on	Attorney
	Bank
	Trust officer
Close friends/relevant personal relationships	Tax adviser

Source: The Fund Raising School, 2009b, p. VI-21.

Verified Contact Information   This includes the donor's full name and home, business, and electronic contact information. It is very easy to depend on the information found in the database and not take the time to verify that there have been no changes in the prospective donor's contact information. Verifying contact information should be the first thing a researcher does when preparing materials for the profile.

Linkage   Any and all ties to the organization should be determined and documented in the profile. This includes not only the obvious ties (donor, graduate, board member, etc.) but also any close relationships to individuals within and/or close to the institution.

Background   Prospective donor researchers must collect and record information, such as current business information and career highlights; a brief, relevant family history; relation to family or private foundations; and civic activities (nonprofit board memberships, corporate board memberships, educational background, etc.).

Giving History   The profile should include all gifts to your organization, as well as other philanthropic giving (and any known political giving). A prime indicator of a donor's interest lies where an individual puts his or her money. This exercise should offer some insight and allow a researcher to offer more accurate suggestions about the direction to take with a prospective donor.

Wealth Indicators   One should approach researching an individual's wealth as it relates to his or her philanthropic potential using a sense of reality regarding what can be found publicly, what could be perceived to be intrusive, and what the limitations of research are. Unless a prospective donor divulges some of his or her private financial information, prospective donor researchers must rely on public information. This may consist of real estate holdings and market values; family foundations; some public stock holdings and options; compensation, if the prospective donor is a top officer of a public company; and in some instances, the percentage of ownership in a private business. Divorce settlements and inheritance could be found by searching court records, but the researcher should be aware that a prospective donor may perceive that as intrusive. It is important to be clear with fundraising staff that research can only provide indicators of a prospective donor's wealth rather than pinpointing precisely an individual's net worth.

Gift Capacity   There are multiple avenues to determine a valid solicitation amount. A skilled researcher will take into account both an individual's known

TABLE 7.1. INCOME/ASSET/GIFT RANGE GUIDELINES.

Income Level	Asset Accumulated	Suggested Gift Potential (to be given over 5 years or through a planned giving vehicle)	Rating
$5,000,000 or more	$200,000,000 or more	$10,000,000	$10 million
$2,000,000 to $5,000,000	$100,000,000 to $200,000,000	$5,000,000	$5 million
$2,000,000	$50,000,000 to $100,000,000	$2,000,000	$2 million
$1,000,000 to $2,000,000	$20,000,000 to $50,000,000	$1,000,000 to $2,000,000	$1 million
$500,000 to $1,000,000	$10,000,000 to $20,000,000	$500,000 to $1,000,000	$500,000
$100,000 to $500,000	$1,000,000 to $10,000,000	$250,000 to $500,000	$250,000
less than $100,000	$1,000,000 to $10,000,000	$100,000 to $250,000	$100,000
$100,000 to $250,000	Less than $1,000,000	$50,000 to $100,000	$50,000
$50,000 to $100,000	$500,000 to $1,000,000	$25,000 to $50,000	$25,000

assets and their inclination, based on interest and giving history, in order to determine an appropriate gift size. Some organizations develop guidelines that use known assets and prior giving to determine a prospect's level of philanthropic potential. It is important to consider that this identified potential relates to total philanthropy, and any one organization is only a part of a prospect's gift intentions. However, such guidelines can be useful as a quick determinant of gift potential and can be shared with volunteers who participate in peer screenings as well as utilized by research staff when a quick estimate is desired. Table 7.1 shows a set of sample guidelines. These sample guidelines can easily be adapted to any organization's giving levels.

The key is to find a formula that works best for a particular institution. Often, this is determined through trial and error. A researcher should devise gift capacity guidelines and test the results with fundraisers in the field to determine the method that is most comfortable and accurate for the organization.

Once gift capacity is determined, a rating code should be assigned. (See Table 7.2 for a sample rating chart scale.) Ideally, this rating will be entered into the organization's database, which allows one to pull prospective donors rated at

TABLE 7.2. SAMPLE RATING SCALE FOR MAJOR GIFT PROSPECTIVE DONORS.

Rating	Potential Gift Amount
10	$10 million +
9	$5 million to $9.99 million
8	$2 million to $4.99 million
7	$1 million to $1.99 million
6	$500,000 to $999,999
5	$250,000 to $499,999
4	$100,000 to $249,999
3	$50,000 to $99,999
2	$25,000 to $49,999
1	Less than $25,000

various levels. The rating should reflect the prospective donor's total capacity for giving (i.e., the dollar amount he or she is capable of giving to the organization outright over a five-year period, or through a planned gift vehicle such as a trust or bequest). Again, the rating scale can be adjusted to match the organization's prospective donor pool and their giving capacity.

The prospective donor researcher should enter the ratings assigned by peer screeners into the database as well. More ratings assigned from various resources allow for a more realistic determination of an individual's true potential. It is important to include a disclaimer within your prospective donor profile indicating that the rating assigned for giving capacity indicates total capacity, of which your institution may be part of a donor's overall philanthropic interests.

Tools for Prospective Donor Research

Much of today's prospective donor research is conducted online through a multitude of websites. However, it is important to remember that a single resource will not get the needed information on every prospective donor; while the Internet and fee-based resources have increased efficiency for the researcher, not all pertinent information is found there. Prospective researchers should remember to utilize the resources available at public and university libraries, as well as the expertise of librarians. Additionally, the community of prospective donor research professionals provides its take on informative and useful information sources, and many share this information on their research websites. Links to many of these sites can be found at the website of the Association of Prospect Researchers for Advancement (www.aprahome.org). Popular fee-based resources include WealthEngine, LexisNexis, iWave, Alumni Finder, and Hoovers; many fundraisers prefer free resources like Google, Zillow, GuideStar, newspapers, and magazines.

Prospective Donor Management

The primary objective of a prospective donor management program is to facilitate communication between all parties involved in the relationship with a prospective donor and track the activity leading to a gift. Ideally, fundraisers working directly with donors, pertinent research staff and/or prospective donor management staff, and development leadership engage in routine prospective donor review meetings. These discussions should include information about completed solicitations, progress in moving forward the relationship with a prospective donor, review of portfolio, and activity with newly identified prospective donors. Regardless of the size of an organization, a prospective donor management program will provide for a necessary flow of communication, goal setting based on portfolio activity, accountability, and tools for management that lead to strategic and focused fundraising.

Prospective donor research is necessary to achieve the best fundraising results for the organization by helping to build the best possible relationship with the prospective donor. A strong prospective donor management process emphasizes the care and attention that build a relationship with the prospective donor throughout the span of that individual's involvement with the organization. The engagement strategy for each prospective donor needs to be monitored, and significant interactions with the donor that move the relationship forward need to be documented so they become part of the organization's memory. This also allows for the fundraiser and the organization to establish and maintain efficiency and accountability in relationships with prospective donors. The resources used to provide quality prospective donor research (which include staff time and financial investment in resources) require that a system be in place to track the effectiveness of work done by research: to determine that fundraisers working with donors are utilizing the research provided by pursuing face-to-face visits and further qualifying the prospective donors, to ensure that the proper interactions are taking place with prospective donors in the pool so that relationships are consistently moved forward and to determine if additional resources are necessary, either in staff or resources. An effective prospective donor management program will ensure that prospective donors move along the fundraising cycle effectively. Typically, programs track and report dollars raised, proposals submitted, the number of prospective donors in each stage of cultivation, and the number of significant contacts the organization has with a prospective donor (defined as an interaction that moves the relationship with the prospective donor forward).

Ethics in Prospective Donor Research

It is critical that prospective donor research protects the integrity of organizations by closely following a code of ethics. This code of ethics may differ from organization to organization, but the underlying principles for all remain consistent. Two key documents related to ethics with which the prospective donor researcher should be familiar are *A Donor Bill of Rights*, developed by the Association of Fundraising Professionals (AFP) and several other organizations, and the *Ethics Statement*, developed by the Association of Prospect Researchers for Advancement (APRA).

Some of the key points of *A Donor Bill of Rights* assert the right of donors to be informed about the organization's mission and intended use of donations and to be confident that the board and staff of the organization are capable of carrying out the intended work. Also, it upholds the need for organizational accountability and transparency. AFP's *A Donor Bill of Rights* emphasizes the right of the donor to receive appropriate thanks and to be assured that their donation and confidential information are handled with all due care and respect by the organization.

APRA's *Ethics Statement* outlines the standards by which professional prospective donor research hold themselves and their work accountable. In addition to protecting both the confidential information of the individual and the institution and to abiding by all laws and institutional policies, prospective donor researchers are charged with abiding by fundamental ethical principles. These fundamental principles of the *Ethics Statement* include a commitment to confidentiality, accuracy, and relevance of information gathered on prospective donors; a responsibility to lead by example in creating and following policies that support ethical prospective donor research; honesty and truthfulness regarding their role as prospective donor researchers and the role of research at the organization; and avoidance of conflicts of interest.

The principles included in both *A Donor Bill of Rights* and the *Ethics Statement* insist on a method for protecting donor data within the organization, as well as within the research department. Sensitive information should be protected by the use of a secured database and through other controls on data, such as making sure that sensitive information is not sent via e-mail, restricting access to information only to those who have a need to know it, and educating staff and volunteers about the importance of confidentiality. Often, individuals close to an organization, like a board member or major donor, may ask for the personal information of a fellow board member. By putting in place clear policies, both for maintaining sensitive information and for consequences if those policies are violated, these uncomfortable situations can be avoided.

Conclusion

Today's donors have high expectations and want you to know who they are and remember their preferences. If a prospective donor tells you to only solicit them in the summer and they receive a renewal letter in December, they probably will not respond. It is vital to track information on prospective donors, listen to them, and use it as a bridge builder for a better relationship. Prospective donor research can help an organization quickly identify on which key individuals to focus attention, and prospect management ensures that all donors move through the fundraising cycle, receiving appropriate contacts along the way.

Discussion Questions

1) Name at least three ways accurate information is essential to fundraising.
2) How can readily available databases be helpful in prospective donor research?
3) Why is peer screening still a useful prospective donor research tool?
4) What are three of the basic elements of ethics related to prospective donor research?

CHAPTER EIGHT

CORPORATE GIVING AND FUNDRAISING

By Dwight F. Burlingame and Sean Dunlavy

Business engagement with philanthropy has been part of capitalism for a very long time. The overarching philosophical reason for why companies have supported nonprofit organizations has been to increase the environment for successful business to take place. The commonly noted argument that "the healthier the community, the more business one will be able to conduct," is globally espoused. In most countries the ability to start a company or corporation is given by the state; therefore, the company has an ultimate responsibility to provide for the social and economic well-being of citizens as it conducts its business. Primary responsibility rests first to employees and other stakeholders and, second, to the general public whether through philanthropic gifts, taxes, or other partnerships.

In this chapter you will learn about the recent history of corporate giving, the ways businesses engage with nonprofits, models of corporate giving, including an illustrative case study of a company's corporate social responsibility program, and the benefits for a company to participate in corporate "philanthropy."

During the first part of the twenty-first century, companies and nonprofits continued to address several major social and economic issues as they sought to articulate their relationships. High on the list of causes were basic human needs (including health and education), community impact causes, environmental sustainability, and more sensitivity to demands of shareholders and consumers. Especially because of the economy and the recession, companies are more focused on making their giving collaborative, strategic, and productive. Asking how the relationship benefits each party will continue to dominate the corporate–nonprofit relationship, whether the nonprofit or business is small or large. Within the current environment, the wisdom echoed by Hank Rosso years ago is especially relevant today: "In accepting the gift, it is incumbent upon the organization to return a value to the donor in a form other than material" (Rosso, 1991, p. 6).

In the past 35 years, the growth of cause-related marketing, sponsorships, and various other partnerships between business and nonprofits has been the fastest growing area of corporate financing of nonprofits. This growth represents a major swing of the pendulum of how corporations seek to engage with and articulate their relationship with the philanthropic sector. As many have noted, since the 1980s, there has been a significant movement in corporate giving from philanthropy to defined and more integrated relationships (Austin, 2000; Andreasen, 2009). The most famous cause-related marketing program that started this trend was the restoration of the Statue of Liberty in 1983. American Express partnered with the restoration committee and donated $0.1 cent for each transaction on its credit card for a three-month period. The program resulted in a $1.7 million "donation" to the Statue of Liberty fund and a reported 28 percent increase in the use of American Express credit cards over the previous year – truly doing well while doing good.

History

For all practical purposes, corporate support of charitable activities is a twentieth century invention. In the nineteenth century most court rulings rendered corporate giving for charitable purposes not appropriate unless such giving was business-related. Laissez-faire arguments of the time, not unlike the argument put forth by Milton Friedman (1970), were that company management could not give away stockholders' money since it was the "social responsibility of business … to increase its profits." Many point to business support of the YMCA by the railroads in the early twentieth century to provide "safe" housing for workers as the beginning of corporate philanthropy or perhaps more appropriately entitled strategic corporate giving or enlightened self-interest.

The majority of corporate support of nonprofit organizations over the last century could be characterized as self-interested rather than interest for others or for the public good. This is an important realization for anyone doing fundraising for nonprofits, for it provides the context for building a successful corporate development program – one that is built upon seeking gifts as well as other sources of revenue that benefits both parties.

The development of regular giving programs by companies began in 1936 with what Hayden Smith (1997) refers to as the modern era. It was in 1935 that the Internal Revenue Code was amended to allow for deductions by companies for charitable gifts supporting the promotion of business purposes. In 1936 the recorded figures of corporate giving on federal corporate income tax forms was around $30 million. By 2013 this figure had grown to an estimated $17.88 billion, excluding sponsorships and other forms of partnerships. According to *Giving USA 2014* (2014), most of the growth in corporate giving has taken place in the last 35 years and can be explained by the removal of certain historical legal obstacles and the growth of the size and number of companies. Most important of the legal cases was the 1953 case of A.P. Smith Mfg Co. v. Barlow, in which the New Jersey Supreme Court refused to overturn the decision of corporate management in regard to a gift made to a charity that had no known benefit to the business. This case reflected the growing importance placed on the role of business in society – both economic and social. Nevertheless, many companies elect to distribute profits to shareholders through dividends and leave giving to owners and about only a third of all companies claim philanthropic contributions on their federal corporate income tax. Smaller firms generally donate a larger share of their income to nonprofits.

Even with the growth in dollar amounts of corporate giving over the last 35 years, on average corporate profits have risen at a much faster rate than corporate giving. For example, from 1986 to 1996 corporate giving as a percentage of profits went from 2.3 to 1.3 percent. By 2013 corporate giving as a percentage of profits had declined even further to an estimated 0.8 percent (*Giving USA*, 2014). Several forms of corporate support, such as sponsorships, are not included in the *Giving USA 2014* figures. Several reasons for the various changes in what businesses give and to whom can be attributed to the changing philosophy, the CEO's role, the change of corporate culture, increased global competitiveness, the changes in the economic environment, and the way in which dollars move from companies to nonprofits.

Corporate Giving for Nonprofits

As noted earlier, in 2013 corporate giving was approximately 5 percent (or $17.88 billion) of total charitable giving in the United States (*Giving USA*, 2014) and it represented around 0.8 percent of corporate pre-tax income – down from a high point of 2 percent in 1986. Corporate foundations gave approximately a third of the total. The amount of giving by corporations is directly linked to corporate profits. What is surprising to many is that giving as a percentage of corporate pre-tax profits does not go up accordingly. In fact, it is the reverse. For example, in the banner year of 1986 corporate giving was $5.03 billion, corporate pre-tax profits were $246.0 billion, and giving as a percentage of pre-tax profits was 2 percent. In 2013 corporate giving was $17.88 billion, corporate pre-tax profits were $2,263.7

billion, and giving as a percentage of pre-tax profits was 0.8 percent. More than one-third of corporate philanthropic giving is through in-kind donations – often in the form of a company product – but in 2013 the ratio of corporate cash contributions increased over that in 2012, (*Giving USA*, 2014, p. 212).

As might be expected, the most commonly sought gift from companies is cash for special and new projects or for capital campaigns and sponsorships. However, businesses today shy away from large ticket item requests and prefer to focus on support activities that address community needs met in partnership with others, including government. Corporations are most interested in supporting causes that (1) form a link with the company and the nonprofit that will benefit the company economically and socially and (2) are relatively proactive and narrow in scope. Of course, many companies still do a considerable amount of reactive giving spread around to many different organizations.

It is important for the fundraiser to recognize that one of the major ways that companies support nonprofits is by supporting workplace charitable campaigns. Being listed as an agency in such workplace campaigns can engender more operating support as well as recognition for the nonprofit. Matching gifts for employee contributions are still present but in the last few years have been on the decline, especially in the dollar amount of the match. In-kind contributions of company product and employee time are still common in certain industry groups such as pharmaceuticals. Employee loan programs are available in many communities. Research and development support from corporations is limited to a few nonprofits, primarily in the health and education field.

A report by the Business Civic Leadership Center (2008) presented results of research on how companies invest in communities. The major motivation identified by respondents in the study was a desire to improve the "local competitive" environment for business, to improve the quality of life in the community, and finally to retain and recruit customers and employees.

As this report suggests, corporate engagement in the future with community nonprofits will be more about how they can create a more highly qualified workforce for their core operations, not corporate citizenship or giving activities. Thus it is no surprise that childhood education programs have taken on increasingly higher priorities for company engagement with nonprofits and using post-secondary education support to supply a competitive workforce remains a high priority.

For additional details on how companies engage in corporate giving by size, type of nonprofit supported, regional variation, industry variation, and what corporate departments have responsibility for community investments the reader is referred to the Business Civic Leadership Center's various reports. They can be found on the US Chamber's website at: http://www.uschamberfoundation.org/corporate-citizenship-center.

In addition, a study by -the Indiana University Center on Philanthropy (2007) reported on themes and practices of "exemplary" giving by major corporations. Some of the findings are:

- Increase linkages with nonprofits through employee–directed giving and volunteering; grants and gift-in-kind to local community needs; and customer-directed giving (cause-related marketing).
- Identify focus needs that match business goals with high social impact.
- Seek external long-term commitments for important societal needs.
- Build sustainable and more long-term partnerships with nonprofits that benefit both parties.
- Increase transparency in and among all stakeholders.
- Discontinue practices that aren't creating maximum benefit.
- Measure or at least try to measure the actual social impact of the company giving programs.

Fostering corporate relations is an ongoing process. Linkage, ability, and interest are important in any fundraising effort, as The Fund Raising School has advocated for decades. Determining the approach to the company will be determined by the case for support and the number of potential corporate givers. Certainly, a personal approach is the most often preferred method. The complexity of an issue tends to drive the approach, including the amount of fundraising resources an organization may have.

After a verbal or meeting contact, completing a contact report is crucial. This document should indicate the essence of the contact and serve as a record of the information shared and commitments, if any, made for future action. Only the necessary information that would not be embarrassing if the potential donor were to read the contact report should be included. Reviewing company corporate citizenship and sustainability reports is a good way to gain a greater understanding of your potential corporate partner. Knowing past corporate behavior is also important to avoid "felonious philanthropy" from a company to your nonprofit. Avoiding accepting gifts that are "tainted" from corporations is as equally relevant as it is from individuals.

Once a gift relationship is established the fundraiser needs to create a plan for managing that relationship. The first is the delivery of the quality of service or stewardship of the gift. The second component of a plan is considering what the future relationship will bring to the nonprofit. Both components of a relationship plan should be carefully integrated with an assessment of how outcomes are to be measured by both parties. In the long term, having a clear case and how it is assessed will render more beneficial and longer-term relationships.

Models of Corporate Giving

Much of the basis for this section is drawn from an earlier work by Dwight Burlingame and Dennis Young (Burlingame and Young, 1996) where four models were developed of how companies approach their giving and volunteering to nonprofits. The utilization of these models provides fundraisers with a context in which to approach businesses for support for their missions. The four major models are:

Corporate productivity or neoclassical model

Ethical or altruistic model

Political (external and internal) model

Stakeholder model

A summary of each with implications for fundraising follows.

Corporate Productivity Model

This model comes from the basic premise that corporate giving will help the company increase profits and return more value to shareholders. Corporate giving activities must therefore demonstrate in some way the increase in profits. This may be done directly by giving cash or a company product or indirectly by improving company morale or worker productivity. The notion of "enlightened self-interest" is very consistent with the neoclassical model as long as the focus remains on the long-term profitability of the company. It further suggests that the term "corporate philanthropy" is a bit of an oxymoron and that a more accurate phrase is "corporate citizenship" or "strategic philanthropy" to convey the purpose of the engagement between the company and the nonprofit. Types of giving that are clearly in line with this model are:

Projects that help market company products, like sponsorships, cause-related marketing, and other partnerships.

Projects that improve employee morale and thus increase productivity.

Projects that facilitate the improvement of the public image of the company.

Projects that lower corporate costs, such as grants for research by nonprofits that lower the company's internal expenditures for product development.

The opportunity for the fundraiser is to match organizational mission and activities with the company's desire for improved productivity along these lines noted. Fundraisers will want to facilitate the understanding of corporate giving personnel in how gifts of support to the nonprofits functions can contribute to the company's bottom line whether directly or indirectly.

Ethical or Altruistic Model

The classical notion of corporate philanthropy is based on the premise that businesses and their leaders have a responsibility to be good corporate citizens and corporate giving and volunteering is a way to demonstrate corporate social responsibility to society. It also assumes that corporations have discretionary resources. When a company is in difficult economic times one would not expect giving to be based upon this model. The giving program must have the capacity to be able to alert corporate leaders to community priorities and where the company might be a partner in seeking solutions. Types of giving consistent with this model are:

- Projects that address community need where the company operates or has markets.
- Projects that appeal to corporate leadership, individually or as citizens.
- Projects that engage employees in community efforts to address local issues.

Fundraisers need to be keenly aware of how gifts to their organizations will benefit the community through the engagement of employees and corporate leaders.

Political Model

The political model is played out both externally and internally in many businesses. The external form is based on the idea that corporations use giving to build relationships that protect corporate power and influence those limits that governments have over companies. Under this model, the corporate giving program serves as a liaison to community allies. Types of giving that are consistent with this model are projects that build closer bonds between the nonprofit and the company. Efforts that substitute for government initiative or more appropriately minimize government intervention and portray the corporation as a good public citizen are typical. Environmental or arts projects are good examples.

The internal paradigm is built upon the premise that the corporate giving officer or representative is an agent with the larger corporate game in which she or he needs to build internal allies and prove the benefit of giving to their respective areas in the company. Corporate giving programs must therefore facilitate the building of alliances with human resources, marketing, research, public relations, and like units so they can see the value of nonprofit support to their area. Giving that is consistent with this model includes employee volunteerism, sponsorships, cause-related marketing, partnerships, and educational programs for employees as well as social service projects, and research and development interest most often designed for a short-term return in today's corporate environment.

Fund raisers will want to be strategic in assessing how they engage with all units of the company, not just the corporate giving unit. Projects that are relevant and meet the needs of the nonprofit while meeting the needs of the company – both internal and external – become foremost. Building the case for support is crucial in maximizing this model.

Stakeholder Model

The stakeholder theory of corporate giving is based upon the idea that the corporation is a complex entity that must respond to the needs and pressures of a variety of key stakeholders, including shareholders, employees, suppliers, customers, community groups, and governmental officials. Under this framework, managing the company is best accomplished by managing the various stakeholder interests. Thus to be effective corporate giving activities need to help address stakeholder interests. Types of giving consistent with this model are:

Employee benefit or volunteerism projects

Community education or environmental projects

Projects that help consumers of company products or services

It does not take a major leap of faith to apply the stakeholder theory to small business owners as well. Whether in a large or small business, management interacts with a variety of interested parties. Fundraisers will concentrate their efforts on identification of key stakeholder groups and develop project proposals that will articulate the nonprofit mission that appeals to defined stakeholder interests of the company. An overall strategy on the part of the nonprofit will be to demonstrate how it is a community stakeholder championed by the corporate giving program.

The above-mentioned models provide a theoretical framework for understanding corporate engagement efforts and they can be used as a basis for doing more empirical research on the effectiveness of various approaches. Understanding how the company works can provide a more strategic corporate fundraising program on the part of the nonprofit. Each model attempts to bring a more nuanced understanding of corporate giving. At the same time, one should recognize that all or some of the models may be operating within any one particular corporation at any particular time. Within the current global and economic challenging times, political activities are more complex and the variety of stakeholders more diverse. Increased efforts to demonstrate how corporate giving affects the double bottom-line (that is, social return and financial return) is prevalent.

Other authors such as Sargeant and Jay (2004) have articulated a more simplistic approach by drawing a distinction only between self-interested giving and philanthropic giving, which does not directly benefit the company. The Committee Encouraging Corporate Philanthropy (CECP) lists three categories of why companies give:

- Charitable – where little or no business benefit is expected.
- Community investment – gifts that … support the long-term strategic goals of the business and meet a critical community need.
- Commercial – where benefit to the corporation is the primary motivation (CECP, 2008).

CECP also noted that among its members corporate giving is divided into three broad categories as Corporate Community Affairs (35 percent of overall giving), Corporate Foundation (37 percent of overall giving), and all other groups (28 percent of overall giving) which would include support from marketing, research, human resources, and regional offices. The reader is referred to the CECP website for up-to-date reports on corporate giving around the world (www.cecp.co).

Case Study

The following case study of Cummins Inc., "A Legacy of Corporate Philanthropy," is instructive on how many companies operating globally view their giving back to society.

The term "corporate social responsibility" is often used interchangeably with corporate responsibility, corporate citizenship, social enterprise, sustainability, sustainable development, triple bottom-line, corporate ethics, and in some cases corporate governance. Though these terms are different, they all point in the same direction. Throughout the industrialized world and in many developing countries there has been a sharp escalation in the social roles corporations are expected to play. Companies are facing new demands to engage in public–private partnerships and are under growing pressure to be accountable not only to shareholders but also to stakeholders such as employees, consumers, suppliers, local communities, policymakers, and society at large. The following is an examination of one company's efforts to define and implement an effective corporate responsibility plan.

Cummins Inc. is a Fortune 500 corporation that designs, manufactures, and distributes engines, filtration, and power generation products. Headquartered in

Columbus, Indiana, United States, Cummins products can be found in nearly every type of vehicle from heavy-duty trucks to tractors to passenger vans.

Cummins' strong tradition of corporate contributions and employee involvement originated from the belief that corporate responsibility will contribute directly to the health, growth, profitability, and sustainability of the company in the long run. Corporate responsibility is a form of enlightened self-interest, as noted by former CEO J. Irwin Miller: "While some still argue that business has no social responsibility, we believe that our survival in the very long run is as dependent upon responsible citizenship in our communities and in the society, as it is on responsible technological, financial and production performance" (Cummins, 2009, p. 10). Cummins wants to use its philanthropy to support employee efforts to build stronger communities. Giving dollars, however, is not a central component of the Company's Corporate Responsibility program. In 2013, Cummins invested more than $16.3 million in corporate responsibility efforts to support the 67 percent of employees participating in the Every Employee Every Community program. The Company's total investment includes about $7.4 million in grants from the Cummins Foundation (Cummins, 2014, p. 96).

Company leadership continues to evaluate how to sustain community impact given the myriad of challenges facing communities, the country, and the world. The Foundation focuses primarily on communities where Cummins facilities are located and in support of the Company's three global priorities:

> Environment – ensuring that everything they do leads to a cleaner, healthier and safer environment.
>
> Education – improving the quality of educational systems to ensure that the students of today are ready for the work forces of tomorrow.
>
> And social justice – ensuring economic and educational opportunities for those marginalized by poverty and discrimination.

In 2013, about 48 percent of the Foundation's spending went toward social justice/ equality of opportunity activities while 42 percent went toward education initiatives and 10 percent went to environmental efforts (Cummins, 2014, p. 96). The report can be viewed at: http://www.cummins.com/global-impact/sustainability/past-reports.

Leadership engagement is a crucial factor in the success of Cummins' community improvement projects, particularly those that aim to have a high impact with sustainable goals. Leaders play an essential role in encouraging employee engagement, providing business resources to support those efforts and championing key strategic projects that are linked to the business.

Employees are the key component to successful corporate responsibility. Employees are motivated and empowered to be engaged in improving their communities. Cummins implements this by creating and supporting community involvement teams at all Cummins locations to organize the skills, processes, and talents of employees to help serve their communities. Cummins also uses philanthropy to supplement the capabilities of Cummins employees. Engagement is the underpinning of responsibility to communities – employees around the globe using their skills to make their communities better places to live and work. Their aim is to use their global footprint and the strength of employees' skills to achieve impact and results.

Employees engage through a network of more than 200 Community Involvement Teams (CITs) around the world. CITs serve as liaisons to their communities and are the primary onsite coordinators for community involvement initiatives. Using tools such as a community needs assessment, as CITs determine how to use employees' skills and talents to tackle the biggest problems facing their communities.

The Every Employee Every Community (EEEC) program attempts to ensure that every employee is given the opportunity to contribute at least four hours on company time to his or her community. Many employees, particularly those engaged in skills-based projects, contribute more hours than that each year.

Employee engagement is also evidenced with Community Impact Six Sigma (CISS), which helps to solve community problems through skills-based volunteerism by joining with partners around the globe to leverage their Six Sigma skills and training. CISS projects use data to drive sustainable improvement through the use of business tools and skills.

Corporate responsibility is one of Cummins' six core values. Far more than just philanthropy, Cummins believes that corporate responsibility is not only making responsible business decisions but affirmatively reaching out to help communities and engage their workforce in addressing community needs.

In conclusion, by being "a good corporate citizen" Cummins believes that it has improved its competitive edge in respect to attracting and retaining investors, clients, and employees. Its strategies are carefully aligned to their core business strategy and contribute directly to the health, growth, profitability, and sustainability of the company in the long run.

Marketing, Sponsorships, and Partnerships

The dramatic growth in earned revenue as the major source for support of many nonprofits has meant that the way businesses engage in their philanthropic or social role has also changed. As noted at the beginning of this chapter, since 1982 there has been a major change away from corporate philanthropy to giving that is designed to build alliances and partnerships or downright commercial relationships. Partnerships with nonprofits can and should provide strategic payoffs for both parties. In addition to the financial benefits, more control of the funds, new marketing skills, and even new knowledge about products and services accrue to both parties.

It is worth noting that a fair amount of confusion exists in the terms used in what is broadly defined by Andreasen (2009) as cross-sector alliances: "any formal relationship between a for-profit and a nonprofit organization to pursue a social objective in ways that will yield strategic or tactical benefits to both parties" (p. 157). Thus, such alliances are designed to have the same goal of traditional corporate giving – a positive social impact as well as economic. Cause marketing has traditionally been defined as "a company's providing dollars to a nonprofit in direct proportion to the quantity of a product or service purchased by consumers during a particular period of time" (Burlingame, 2003, p. 185). When that period of engagement is extended over a longer time frame it is often referred to as "cause branding."

Sponsorships, on the other hand, are not directly tied to customer purchasing behavior, but it does mean company investments of cash or in-kind for a return of access to an activity, event, or cause represented by the nonprofit. Such activity is not a "gift" in the true meaning of philanthropic, but a strategic investment by the company with an expected return.

Galaskiewicz and Colman (2006) provide a useful framework by dividing the objectives of company engagement into philanthropic, strategic, commercial, and political, which are not very different from the models of corporate giving noted by Burlingame and Young earlier in this chapter. Another paradigm used to view the impact of the corporate–nonprofit alliance has been provided by Gourville and Rangan (2004). They divide benefits for both parties according to first-order and second-order benefits. First-order benefits for the nonprofit are the contribution of cash, volunteers, or in-kind services for the cause. Corporation first-order benefits are in the form of sales. Second-order benefits are expected benefits that will result for either side in the future. Sponsorship and cause marketing campaigns are illustrative examples.

Opportunities

Various studies have reported many advantages for corporations and nonprofits that engage in cross-sector activities. On the for-profit side, cause marketing or sponsorship may influence consumer behavior by increasing the perception of "goodness" of the firm or as a responsible corporate citizen. Employee morale may be improved and it may also build the pool of potential applicants to work with the company. Various socially conscious investors may be more likely to support the business. Cone Communications (www.conecomm.com) have found that good business practice acceptance rates that include cross-sector alliances have continued to increase and that as many as 8 out of 10 Americans have a more positive image of companies that support nonprofits or causes that they care about. Further, in their 2013 Social Impact Study they found that having a social impact has become the major emphasis of corporate social responsibility (CSR) programs.

According to IEG Sponsorship Report (2009) and others, managers of nonprofits and fundraisers report that companies seek the following second-order benefits from their sponsorship and cause marketing activities in addition to increasing profits and direct commercial benefit:

- Category exclusivity
- Credit on related materials
- Program naming
- Tickets and hospitality for the nonprofit events
- Access to the nonprofit's database

On the nonprofit side, cross-sector activities may have several advantages including:

- Increased revenue
- New volunteers
- Enhanced public awareness of the nonprofit's mission
- Connections to the company's network of employees and other contacts
- Diversified income streams
- Access to new audiences and potential donors
- Enhanced knowledge of marketing and other corporate experiences

Many examples have been reported in the press. Illustrative examples of the diverse forms of cross-sector marketing collaborations can be found in Andreasen (2009). Good contemporary sources to be consulted by the fundraiser include *Corporate Philanthropy Report*, the Committee Encouraging Corporate Philanthropy (CECP), and the Boston College Center for Corporate Citizenship web sites (including the annual publication of *The Corporate Citizen*).

Challenges

Potential negative effects of cross-sector activities need to be examined closely by nonprofit management. First and foremost should be a concern with how the collaboration with a for-profit will affect donor activity. Will the commercial nature of the activity decrease trust in the nonprofit mission? Will donors or potential donors think they have already contributed their fair share to the nonprofit through their participation in a cause-related marketing activity and thereby cause a decrease in gift income? Will potential gifts from other companies in the same industry group decrease if one company enjoys exclusivity to the nonprofit brand? Will the nonprofit actually waste resources if the alliance activity fails?

Sponsorship and cause-marketing activities may only cause temporary effects and not build donor loyalty over time. Ties to the nonprofit may be based on a special event activity and not in the mission of the organization. Traditional fundraising may be neglected because of the focus on earned income activities. Further, concern with the ability of the nonprofit to adjust to the business culture and be an "equal" partner in a cross-sector alliance is an issue. This is especially true when a business partner is selected. Joint promotion activities may be viewed as the nonprofit "selling out." The private-sector marketer may insist on more publicity for the relationship than the nonprofit would ordinarily do. Licensing agreements call for special attention and legal fees are not insignificant.

Marketing relationships with nonprofits can also be problematic for the corporation. The mission of the nonprofit may not be of interest to the consumer; more complicated accounting procedures need to be followed; and the commitment of time and energy from company personnel may not create expected financial payoffs. Some consumers may even view company support of cross-sector activities as exploitation. This is especially true when more money is spent for an ad campaign than what is actually donated to the cause.

Such concerns can inform the fundraiser on what to be aware of in building a partnership with a corporation. Developing a plan and procedures to prevent management error should be foremost in building a successful cross-sector venture that will be of benefit to both parties. Sponsorship and cause branding guidelines should be approved by the nonprofit board of directors. Whether part of the development office or not, effective coordination and communication with the development staff is imperative. Senior management needs also to take an active role is shaping business partnerships and assessing the benefits.

Measuring the impact of marketing alliances is probably the most important action in the current state of the art. Studies in the field often fail to apply rigorous standards in measuring effects on either or both parties.

Conclusion

Business engagement with philanthropic organizations for public purposes has been multifaceted and has had various degrees of change – back and forth –over the last 100 plus years. Once part of direct business activity, it turned toward more focused public purposes before returning to today's environment of being mainly business-driven. Fundraisers in today's environment will want to demonstrate how corporate support helps the overall revenue picture of the nonprofit and company giving and marketing personnel will want to demonstrate how their engagement with nonprofits helps the business to be a viable economic entity while also producing social good.

Since the 2008–2009 great recession in the United States, reports have shown that attitudes of CEO's support for corporate citizenship often remains strong during a recession, but some gaps between those beliefs and the practices do exist. Helping businesses and nonprofits meet societal needs – economic and social – makes for a challenging and rewarding partnership between the corporate giving officer and the fundraiser.

Discussion Questions

1) "The business of business is business" is a phase often cited on why public companies should leave charitable giving to shareholders. What is your perspective?
2) What type of corporate social responsibility model does Cummins Inc. represent? Why?
3) Why doesn't an increase in company pre-tax profits convert into an increase in giving as a percentage of corporate pre-tax profits?
4) How would you evaluate a potential corporate partner for your nonprofit?

CHAPTER NINE

FOUNDATION FUNDRAISING

By Sarah K. Nathan and Elisabeth Lesem

A philanthropic foundation is an organization created with designated funds from which the income is contributed as grants to nonprofit organizations or, in some cases, to support the defined mission of the grantor. Some foundations are pass-through foundations that do not have endowments. This chapter focuses on those foundations with endowments. Modern philanthropic foundations – just over a century old – are often heralded as a uniquely American approach to philanthropy (Fleishman, 2007). The relationship between a grantmaking foundation and a nonprofit is built on a mutual desire or interest in improving a civic or public good. Public charities are the mechanisms through which most foundations carry out their public responsibilities. In 2012, the year most recent data are available, there were 86,192 foundations in the United States with a combined $715 billion in assets (Foundation Center, 2014). Given the diversity of the foundation field, this chapter:

- Reviews the types, size, and scope of foundations.
- Examines trends in foundation giving.
- Recommends basic approaches to pursue foundation funding.

As a funding source, foundations (or grantmakers) are often attractive to nonprofit organizations because of their vast resources and interests. For nonprofits, such grants have the potential to provide significant monetary support for a program or operations during start-up or expansion. However, matching foundation interests with nonprofit missions requires research, planning, and on-going relationship building. Therefore, grant seeking and proposal writing are fundraising functions of a comprehensive development operation. Combining a culture that encourages appropriate relationships with grantmakers and appropriate investments in a foundation relations program will help establish systematic and measurable goals for foundation resources.

Size and Scope

Foundation assets (commonly referred to as endowments) and distributions from those assets continue to shape the public discussions around global issues. With a significant number of foundations passing the $10 billion level in endowments, according to reports compiled by the Foundation Center (2014), top tier foundations have the capacity to disperse funds regionally, nationally, and globally in an attempt to radically change social outcomes and enhance communities. Foundations provide a significant amount of support for the nonprofit sector, second only to individual support, and 15 percent ($53.97 billion) of the actual dollars of charitable giving in 2014 (*Giving USA*, 2015).

In addition to the numbers of foundations and totality of the grants awarded, the growth of independent and community foundation assets between 1995 and 1999 eclipsed any previous period of recorded growth. Many factors are believed to support the increase: impressive gains in the U.S. stock markets, increased gifts to all foundation types, and the rise of mega foundations in the western portion of the United States. Like many nonprofit organizations, foundation assets generally took a hit during the Great Recession. However, foundation giving is on the rise as endowments continue to recover (Foundation Center, 2014).

Traditionally, large foundations have been located in the East and Midwest, largely a result of the individual fortunes that established them during the Industrial Age. The gains in information technology, based largely in the West, helped fuel a geographical shift.

Program growth continues to be modest in corporate foundation grants in part because of more conservative transfers in cash and assets to foundation programs.

Types of Foundations

Because of the complexity of the foundation field, it is important to understand the characteristics of four types of foundations. There are four primary models: independent, corporate, community, and operating.

Independent Foundations   As defined by the Internal Revenue Service (IRS), independent foundations are private foundations established to provide support or distributions to tax-exempt organizations through grants. Assets of independent foundations are usually established through gifts from individuals or families and often carry the names of the original funders. Independent foundations are required by law to distribute a minimum five percent of their endowment annually.

During the years of wealth creation in the late 1990s, the expression "family foundation" became common to describe an independent foundation with noteworthy involvement and decision making by living family members, both immediate and extended. In 2012, 82 percent of all foundation giving came from independent foundations, which are established by individuals or families (Foundation Center, 2014). According to the Foundation Center, "overall foundation giving will continue to grow a few points ahead of inflation in 2014. Independent and family foundations will likely show an even higher rate of growth" (2014, p. 2). These independent family foundations have a large capacity for change, and thus an even greater responsibility for transparency and accountability.

Large, well-established independent foundations generally have a full-time staff, often in proportion to the size of assets. Smaller foundations may have only one full-time person dedicated to daily operations. Family foundations may include family members as needed. Independent foundations often define specific areas of interest for funding or limit grants to a specific geographical area. Independent foundations constitute the vast majority of all foundations in the United States; examples include the Bill and Melinda Gates Foundation, the W.K. Kellogg Foundation, and the Lilly Endowment.

Corporate Foundations   The corporate foundation is another type of independent foundation. A corporate foundation generally receives its assets from an associated for-profit company or business and often serves as a grantmaking vehicle for the company. Its mission and funding interests often mirror the business interests of the company and the foundation may work in concert with the company's community relations efforts. A corporate foundation often has a separate board of directors, usually comprised of employees and individuals related to the company. Giving by corporate foundations is considered a part of corporate philanthropy, which is covered in Chapter 8.

Most corporate foundation giving reflects the companion company's products, services, and consumers' interests, both current and potential. Corporate foundation decisions are often directly influenced by employee involvement and interest in the nonprofit organizations seeking support. The management of corporate foundations differs from one to the next. Many corporate foundations have staff dedicated to receiving, processing, and administering proposals and grants. Others may combine foundation responsibilities with other employee duties. The Wal-Mart Foundation and the AT&T Communications Foundation are examples of corporate foundations. There are approximately 2,629 corporate foundations in the United States (Foundation Center, 2014).

Community Foundations   Community foundation growth has slowed from the rapid expansion during the 1990s, but the popularity of the vehicle has permanently altered the philanthropic landscape. The increase in community foundation assets can be attributed to several factors, including the corresponding rise in individual donors' asset values and the seeding and incubation of small donor-advised funds. The sharing of costs, reduction in administrative duties, enhanced return on well-managed investments, and ability to remain involved in grantmaking decisions attracts donors to advised funds at community foundations. Although only 1 percent of all foundations, community foundations were responsible for $4.9 billion in grants in 2012 (Foundation Center, 2014).

Unlike other foundation structures, community foundations generally both receive gifts and make grants through special IRS provisions. As public charities, they must receive assets from a large pool of donors and consequently fund a wide range of community needs. Most community foundations limit their interests and grants to a particular geographical area and consider it a primary mission to support communitywide initiatives and develop unrestricted funds specifically for this purpose. Community foundations are exempt from the 5 percent minimum distribution requirement.

In addition to unrestricted fund, community foundations generally have several fund pools: unrestricted funds, donor-advised funds, and donor-designated funds. With a donor-advised fund, a donor retains the right to make suggestions to the community foundation as to which qualified 501(c)(3) organizations or causes should receive grant money. A donor-designated fund allows the donor to select the specific nonprofit organizations or causes that will receive grants based on the fund's income. Both funds are established with a permanent gift to the community foundation and allow the donor an immediate tax deduction under IRS rules. The community foundation usually specifies that the gift be combined and managed with other foundation investments.

Examples of community foundations include the Cleveland Foundation (the first community foundation established in the United States), the New York Community Trust, the Columbus (Ohio) Community Foundation, and the Silicon Valley Community Foundation. While the largest number of community foundations are in the state of Indiana, Michigan, and Ohio, community foundations are present throughout the United States.

Operating Foundations Comprising just 5 percent of all foundations, operating foundations seldom make grants to other nonprofit organizations. Operating foundations are preferred by donors who wish to be involved in the charitable work more directly rather than working through public charities. Because they are dedicated to conducting research and/or operating programs to support the work of the original charter or governing body, the IRS mandates that they spend at least 85 percent of their income in support of their own programs. Although operating foundations are not usually a source of cash grants, they are often a resource for nonprofits engaged in complementary research, work, and programs. In addition, operating foundations often serve as conveners in a particular body of knowledge and may provide opportunities for engagement with community practitioners and experts.

Examples of operating foundations are the Getty Trust and the Wilder Foundation. The Goodrich Foundation in Indianapolis operates its own educational programming related to the study of liberty. Another kind of operating foundation is The Lilly Cares Foundation, one of the philanthropic arms of Eli Lilly and Company. It distributes pharmaceuticals to ill and economically disadvantaged people who are not covered by medical insurance (Foundation Center, 2014). The Lilly Cares Foundation does not have any assets, but it distributed an equivalent of $697,004,928 in 2013 in Lilly medications (Foundation Center, 2014).

Trends in Foundation Support

Foundations are defining more clearly their interests and expectations of recipient organizations. They are also requiring more extensive evaluation of funded programs and organizations. Foundations continue to learn from past grants and use this information to make better and more effective grants for the future. Collaboration among foundations is a key trend in combating global issues and is an expected result of their grants to nonprofits. Foundations are also emphasizing effective governance and management of organizations in making grant decisions of any type. Several trends have emerged as new directions for foundation support.

Evaluation

Emphasis on evaluation of grantees and foundation activities continues. The literature on nonprofits indicates that early attempts at evaluation by foundations served two purposes: checking for accountability to grantor financial policies and expediting grantee renewal decisions. Foundations continue to evaluate grants using these criteria, but the scope of evaluation has grown to help foundations analyze the success of a programmatic field of interest and help shape future grants. In many foundations, these learning opportunities impact future grant recipients by focusing on particular segments of a program and providing helpful advice about past success and disappointments. For foundation grant recipients, more extensive post-grant evaluation, often by external evaluators, may be required at the conclusion of a program. An objective review of the progress of a particular grant and program is intended to help organizations focus on program results and impacts.

Collaboration

Collaboration is a mutually beneficial and well-defined relationship entered into by two or more organizations to achieve common goals. This relationship includes a commitment to a definition of authority within the mutual relationship; accountability for success; and a sharing of resources and rewards. In an attempt to avoid replication of services and funding of programs, foundations and their grantees are participating in more collaborative efforts than ever before. Foundations are also interested in seeing stronger and more inclusive programs based on the expertise and client bases of cooperative organizations. For the grantee organizations, the potential for more substantial financial support and the power of a larger group working on an identified need can have a substantial impact on a community problem.

Emphasis on Diversity

According to the U.S. Census Bureau, only half of the nation's population is expected to be non-Hispanic white by the year 2025. Foundations expect this diversity to be mirrored in the leadership of nonprofit institutions in the United States.

Increasingly, foundations are requesting that nonprofit boards of directors and staff reflect the diversity of the communities and populations they serve. Some foundations require that nonprofits actively recruit in a way that encourages diversity and some ask for evidence of board diversity composition. Simultaneously, the boards of community and private foundations are maturing and responding to this trend with their own commitment to diversity (Daniels, 2015).

Capacity Building

Campobasso and Davis, in *Reflections on Capacity-Building* (2001), define capacity building as the development of an organization's core skills and capabilities, such as leadership, management, finance and fundraising, programs, and evaluation, in order to build the organization's effectiveness and sustainability. It is the process of assisting a group to identify and address issues and gain the insights, knowledge, and experience needed to solve problems and implement change. Capacity building is facilitated through the provision of technical support activities, including coaching, training, operational assistance, and resource networking. As with any idea, capacity building is still broadly defined and working through several shifts in approach and application. Many foundation programs have begun to develop a focus on building internal and external resources to support nonprofit programs. Programs like the Organizational Impact Program at the David and Lucile Packard Foundation have devoted important resources to define and develop capacity building as an interest area.

Donor Advised Funds

Charitable gift funds at for-profit financial services firms, known as donor advised funds, have garnered increased attention and support over the last two decades. The premise of these gift funds, such as the Fidelity Charitable Gift Fund and the Vanguard Charitable Endowment Program, is to allow donors to make irrevocable gifts to the fund and recommendations on the future distribution of those funds. For the donor, the advantages are an immediate tax reduction, the opportunity for the corpus of the fund to increase in value with the help of professional money managers, and the ability to remain anonymous with potential grantees. There is an estimated $45 billion in donor advised funds, but unlike independent foundations, they are not subject to the annual 5 percent pay-out (Neyfakh, 2013).

Donor advised funds are increasingly attractive to donors who do not want to establish their own foundation but want to keep some control over their grantmaking. In the nonprofit community, concern is expressed over the fee structure of the funds and the control given to financial services professionals rather than community and nonprofit experts. Although these donor advised funds may not approach grantmaking as independent foundations, this is a trend to watch as the sector evolves.

Types of Support

Foundations commonly provide five types of support: operations or unrestricted, program, capital, pilot, and challenge or matching. Operations or unrestricted grants are made to support the ongoing operations of a nonprofit with no conditions for their use. Led by a major announcement from the Ford Foundation in June 2015, there is a new emphasis on operating or unrestricted support (Callahan, 2015). Program grants support a specific set of activities and plans. Capital grants generally provide support for building construction funds, large equipment purchases, and endowment growth. Pilot grants award start-up funding for new programs at an organization for a limited period of time. Challenge or matching grants support an effort to encourage philanthropic giving in a constituent segment.

As a potential funding source, foundations have several unique features, including a requirement for independent foundations to distribute a minimum percentage of their endowment through grants to qualified 501(c)(3) organizations. There are a number of excellent resources on the current scope and size of the foundation sector. The Foundation Center, publisher of the *Foundation Directory*, and its web site (www.foundationcenter.org) provide resources and publications on a range of topics from starting a foundation to measuring and evaluating programs supported by foundation grants.

Before Approaching a Foundation

Foundations are interested in funding nonprofits with diverse financial sources. It is important to consider a foundation grant as one component of a fully diversified fundraising program. Support from clients, friends, and community members is an important tool in demonstrating a clear mission, broad community support, and a solution-focused organization.

Preparation is key in submitting foundation requests, and the first step is researching the foundation to determine any linkages and interest. The specific strategies described here are general rules. Adaptations may be necessary, depending on the culture of the organization and foundation.

Foundations are approachable because of their clear guidelines and structured timelines, but foundation fundraising is similar to all fundraising in that the most successful partnerships are built on trusted relationships established over time.

A nonprofit with clearly established priorities from its governing board and executive staff will have fewer difficulties in determining appropriate foundations to contact than will organizations without clear operational mandates and strategic plans in place.

Making a Request

As with all fundraising, the written request or proposal is the final result of intensive and thorough preparation. In foundation fundraising, it includes a review of the requesting organization's mission, identified needs, and the foundation's preferred interests. The Fund Raising School (2009) suggests using the LAI principle (linkage, ability, interest) in qualifying foundation prospects. Using this principle, ask three sets of questions about each prospect:

1. Does the foundation have any previous relationships with my organization? Does my organization have any friends, staff, or constituents with connections or influence at the foundation? Determine any linkages that exist or should exist before approaching the foundation.
2. Does the foundation have the assets and make grants of the size necessary for my program? Review current and past grant information to determine the typical gift size.
3. Does the foundation have any interest in funding the type of program my organization is proposing? Has the foundation funded in this grant area previously? Review guidelines and funding interests.

Several tools are available to nonprofit organizations to find information on foundations. Many nonprofit and for-profit companies produce annual compilations of foundation information for a fee, but some of the best resources cost little or no money. Because the IRS governs foundations, each year they must make a Form 990-PF available to the public. Although this form has always been available to the public, in 1998 the IRS made obtaining the form easier and less time-consuming. Most foundations place Form 990-PF on their web sites for immediate viewing. Form 990-PF provides basic information, including board of directors, total grant amount distributed, grant recipients, and awards. Many independent, corporate, and community foundations publish a web-based annual report, listing much of the same information and providing more detailed descriptions of their support.

Foundation guidelines are an important piece of information to determine the suitability between a foundation and a potential program. Guidelines establish the current interests of the foundation, usually by program type or geographical area; give specific procedures for preparing grant proposal; provide typical funding parameters; and define deadlines for submitting a grant request. After reviewing the selected foundation information, the organization should carefully check the application for submission instructions and formatting.

Only after completing the preliminary research is the nonprofit ready to begin an initial conversation with a foundation. The next step, preferably, is an initial phone call to the prospective foundation to discuss the proposed program or project and the likelihood of funding in the current operational year. Nonprofits may also discover more specific information about a particular foundation's operations and interests. This initial conversation with a foundation representative does not ensure that a proposal will be funded, but it does provide more information for the nonprofit organization preparing a request.

Some foundations do not accept unsolicited phone calls. In these instances, it is useful for the nonprofit to prepare a brief letter of inquiry to the foundation, indicating the parameters of the program and how the program will benefit the larger community. Unless specifically requested, do not include any budget numbers in the initial inquiry and focus instead on the proposed project. Recently, there has been a shift to sending a letter of interest, briefly describing what the nonprofit intends to do with grant funds.

The Proposal

If an initial inquiry letter or phone call has been positively received and the foundation representative encourages continuing the funding discussion, the nonprofit should prepare a proposal package. The details of the package are variable and should follow the published guidelines of the foundation.

A complete proposal package may contain the following items:

1. Cover sheet, including appropriate contact information
2. Abstract or executive summary
3. Identification of needs statement
4. Case statement
5. Proposed solution
6. Expected outcomes
7. Evaluation tool
8. Governance and staffing
9. Budget and budget explanation
10. Project timeline

Much like a well-written story, the proposal should articulate the identified need and the solutions the organization will use to solve the problem.

After assembling the proposal package, provide a copy to your organization's leadership to review before submission to the foundation. The CEO should provide a cover letter (or the cover sheet mentioned earlier) to demonstrate the organization's commitment to the proposal.

At the Foundation

Once received by the foundation, your proposal will likely follow an internal review process. Information about the process is often published in the foundation's documents. Generally, the proposal is received and recorded in a central processing area. It is then reviewed to ensure that all necessary materials are included and that it generally fits within the foundation's guidelines. In small foundations, a single person often completes both tasks. Large foundations may have these steps completed separately.

A program staff person will review your proposal to determine its applicability to foundation priorities. If this review is successful, you may be contacted for further information or to arrange a site visit. Remember that the grant officer with whom you interacted now becomes your advocate or fundraiser for your idea. A site visit, or program visit, is an opportunity for foundation staff to leave with clear project plans and outcomes. It is also an opportunity for the nonprofit to articulate ideas, connections, and impacts that could not be included in the original proposal. While it is important to be prepared for the site visit, the nonprofit should not attempt to orchestrate or manipulate staff, participants, or outcomes.

The Grant Decision

If the organization has successfully received a grant from a foundation, the opportunity for an extended foundation relationship begins. Provide immediate and appropriate thanks and recognition to the foundation. Depending on the length of a program, the nonprofit may be required to submit intermediate reports, or the foundation may contact the nonprofit several times for updates on progress. Continue to remain in contact with the foundation. The program's success is important to the foundation, and its staff will provide support and guidance throughout the program's duration.

At a minimum, a nonprofit will be required to provide a post-grant evaluation at the conclusion of the program period. The level of evaluation proposed at the outset of the project will also determine the level of contact and reporting to the foundation. In addition, the relationship developed may provide future funding opportunities for new programs at the organization.

A proposal denial does not preclude a relationship with the foundation. A number of factors, including timing, the current foundation portfolio, and future commitments, may influence a decision. Thank the foundation for considering your request and accept your current denial letter. At the conclusion of the grant process, some foundations will discuss the reasons for denials and may offer advice for resubmitting a proposal.

Nonprofits should keep in mind that the number of foundation proposals sub-mitted is not an accurate measure of foundation fundraising performance. Strong relationships and focused proposals are keys to a strong track record with founda-tions.

Conclusion

Working with foundations can be an exciting and successful process for many nonprofit organizations. Clearly defined program and strategies of research and relationship building can lead to organized and appropriate grant proposals that may result in foundation support for an organization's ongoing operations and special program. If an organization is successful in receiving foundation support, the impact of a single grant can provide greatly needed funding to implement an important program or provide vital support for an organization. Successful foun-dation fundraising results from clear, specific research; a focus on similar interests; and a dedication by both the foundation and the nonprofit to support the com-munities and causes they serve.

Discussion Questions

1) Use the principle of Linkage, Ability, and Interest to identify one or two foun-dations whose funding priorities match your organization's mission.
2) What steps are involved in approaching a foundation for funding?
3) How can your organization incorporate grant seeking and proposal writing into its fundraising operations?

CHAPTER TEN

GENDER AND PHILANTHROPY

By Debra J. Mesch and Andrea Pactor

Gender matters in philanthropy. Research, demographics, and increased visibility by and for women in philanthropy attest to their growing influence and power. Yet, a 2014 poll in *The Chronicle of Philanthropy* found that 40 percent of women in nonprofits with assets greater than $25 million said their organizations were not attending to women as donors. Considering the dramatic pace at which women's roles in society have changed over the past 40 years, demographics that increasingly favor women in education, employment, and earnings, research documenting women's power and influence in charitable giving, and pressure from women themselves, what prevents more institutions from leveraging the resources women bring to philanthropy? This chapter seeks to explore some of the challenges and opportunities in working with women donors and encourages all to pay more attention to women as donors. It covers the following:

- Male orientation among nonprofits and changing demographics.
- Changing organizational culture to see women as donors.
- Understanding typical women philanthropists.
- Fundraising among women.

Context

Why more nonprofits do not attend to women as donors is likely in part a result of not recognizing and adapting to cultural shifts that have profoundly affected women's place in society. Institutions may not engage women as donors because of outdated perceptions about women; lack of awareness that gender matters in philanthropy; organizational culture and leadership; and fundraising strategies designed primarily for men. Just as biological, social, and cultural differences exist between men and women, so too do differences in philanthropy behavior. What works for men may not work for women.

Underlying some of the above are subtle and imperceptible factors. Social scientists have found that social behavior may not always be conscious. The concept of implicit bias – the unconscious stereotyping or attribution of certain qualities to a specific social group – is gaining traction as a cause of pervasive biases about age, gender, and race among others (Banaji and Greenwald, 2013). Researchers in the fields of psychology and sociology in particular have demonstrated empirically that most people hold implicit biases. New as a field of inquiry in fundraising, strong anecdotal signs suggest that fundraisers and institutional leaders may create strategies that favor a male pattern of charitable giving because they are unconsciously ascribing negative stereotypes to women as potential donors. Identifying and overcoming implicit bias requires intentional, deliberate, long-term strategies.

When a group of fundraisers at a conference was asked why organizations would not attend to women as donors they quickly identified five reasons: (1) organizational leadership is predominately male, (2) events are tailored for men, (3) databases list males as main prospects, (4) board recruitment is male-focused, and (5) women are dispersed to auxiliary boards or other entities perceived as less important. The extent to which these reasons are driven by implicit bias, business as usual, resistance to change, lack of awareness about women's changing role in society, or something else has yet to be explored empirically. What is clear, however, is that organizations that engage women fully in all facets of their fundraising strategy will raise more money, develop more loyal and satisfied donors, and create powerful advocates for the organization's mission. A paradigm shift in fundraising that fully engages men *and* women is necessary to ensure that the nonprofit can maximize revenue for its mission.

Demographics and data

The world and women's place within it have changed significantly over the past several decades. Demographics increasingly favor women in education, employment, and earnings. Increased education generally leads to higher paying jobs. More than half of all college students and higher education alumni are female. Moreover, many women are choosing not to marry, and there are three times as many female single-headed households as male-headed households (15 million versus 5 million as of 2011) (Vespa, Lewis, and Kreider, 2013). Women who do marry, often marry later and have fewer children than in generations past.

From an employment and earnings perspective, the traditional breadwinner–homemaker model is virtually nonexistent. Over half of women in married couple households are employed. In 40 percent of households, women are the primary breadwinner, a 29 percent increase since 1960 (Wang, Parker, and Taylor, 2013). According to Pew Research, "married mothers who out-earn their husbands are slightly older, disproportionately white and college educated." Additionally, "the share of married mothers who out-earn their husbands has gone up from 4 percent in 1960 to 15 percent in 2011, nearly a fourfold increase." Women now hold 51 percent of managerial and professional jobs in the workforce (Wang, Parker, and Taylor, 2013).

Women also have increasing access to wealth. As women live an average of 5 years longer than men, they often inherit twice, both from their parents and from their husbands. Women represent 42 percent of the nation's top wealth holders with gross assets of $2 million or more and 39 percent of the total wealth in that category, approximately $5.15 trillion (Internal Revenue Service, 2007).

Despite the overwhelming evidence of the potential and power of women in philanthropy, societal perceptions persist that suggest women are less philanthropic than men, that they defer to their husbands in charitable decision making, and that women do not make big gifts. Recent research counters these perceptions.

Women are not less philanthropic than men. In fact, the opposite is true. The Women's Philanthropy Institute's *Women Give* series provides empirical data affirming that women are as likely, and often more likely, as similarly-situated men to give to charity. *Women Give 2010* looked at giving by adult male- and female-headed households and found that single female households give more than comparable single male households across income and marital status (Mesch, 2010). The same is true for age. *Women Give 2012* found that Baby Boomer and older women are more likely to give and give more across all giving levels than their male counterparts (Mesch, 2012).

One reason the perception arises that women are less philanthropic than men is that women tend to spread their giving across more nonprofit organizations, making smaller gifts to more organizations (Andreoni, Brown, and Rischall, 2003). Fundraisers may be aware only of the contribution to their organization and not understand the full extent of the female donor's giving. This is an example of how women's giving patterns differ from those of men. It also demonstrates why fundraisers may need to adapt their conversations to learn about the donor's full giving story and motivations.

Research across several studies has found fairly consistently that women are deeply involved in household charitable decision making. Two studies of high net worth households found that in nine out of ten households, women are either the sole decision maker or at least an equal partner in charitable decision making (Indiana University, 2011). Further, when only one spouse decides, the wife decides twice as often as the husband (Brown, 2006). Specifically, in giving to education, the wife also decides twice as often as the husband (Rooney, Brown, and Mesch, 2007).

Women make big gifts. For example, Women Moving Millions, an initiative started by sisters Helen LaKelly Hunt and Swanee Hunt, raises million dollar gifts from women for women's and girls' causes. Despite fundraising during the 2008–2009 recession, the initial campaign raised about $180 million from 110 women over a three-year period, exceeding its goal by 20 percent. The Million Dollar List offers more evidence that women make big gifts. This searchable database, managed by the Indiana University Lilly Family School of Philanthropy, includes hundreds of publicly announced gifts of $1 million or more by women to all subsectors. For example, gifts by individual women from 2000 to 2013 to higher education alone totaled more than $4.5 billion.

Research affirms that men and women view philanthropy differently and that different strategies are required to engage the female donor. As a fundraiser who raises funds primarily from men indicated, it is not that one strategy is better than the other but rather that different strategies are needed to reach women. Fundraisers who are aware of the research will review their donor engagement strategies and adapt them to better meet women according to their preferred charitable giving patterns. They will seek to make the integrated approach part of the internal culture of their organization as well.

Organizational Culture and Leadership

When organizations are successful in meeting their fundraising goals, there may be little incentive to analyze the donor database, to address leadership equity by gender, or to adapt engagement strategies to ensure that they appeal to both men and women. Yet most nonprofits know that is easier and less expensive to retain current donors than it is to acquire new ones. Why would a nonprofit not wish to reach and leverage the strengths of all of its donors – male and female – to build capacity and ensure sustainability?

In some cases, when the organizational culture is male-led and male-dominated, fundraising follows traditionally male strategies because they are familiar and work for male donors. Such strategies include campaigns, a sense of urgency, peer recognition, deadlines, and a high-pressure, fast-paced, intense, and competitive environment. As an illustration, early in her new position at a predominantly male institution the first female chief development officer was asked repeatedly by the male trustees when the new campaign would start. She asked her predecessor why the trustees were so focused on a campaign. He responded, "Because that's when we are at our best. We love the competitiveness." While many women are competitive, when it comes to making philanthropic decisions, they tend to be much more focused on making an impact than on outshining a peer.

The presence of women in leadership positions across institutions increasingly matters. Many women donors take note of board diversity and the percentage of women in top staff positions. Preliminary results of the BoardSource 2014 *Leading with Intent* survey reveal a general increase in gender equity in board chairs (46 percent female/54 percent male) and board composition (48 percent female/52 percent male) (BoardSource, 2014). A more detailed analysis in the 2012 Board-Source study finds gender disparity by budget size and gender of the CEO (Board-Source, 2012b). Nonprofit organizations with budgets greater than $10 million average 37 percent female representation on boards. Those nonprofits with budgets of less than $1 million average 51 percent female representation on boards. In the same study, the gender of the CEO matters even more. Nonprofits with a female CEO averaged 50 percent female representation on boards while 77 percent of the nonprofits led by a male CEO had a majority male board (BoardSource, 2012b). Ample literature in management and leadership journals finds that greater diversity of boards and decision-making staff leadership generates better decisions and likely more money.

Savvy institutions should not only examine fundraising models but also related marketing, communications, special events, and stewardship practices to ensure that they appeal to men and to women. In general, women look for diversity in images, appreciate stories about the impact of their gift in addition to metrics, and want to understand the outcomes their philanthropy provides. By not using language and visuals that resonate with all donors, nonprofits lose the potential of increased revenue, networks that share the mission with new audiences, and they risk alienating the primary charitable decision-maker in the household.

Potential is in the database

Databases are consistently mentioned as an impediment to growing women's philanthropy and to accurately measuring women's giving. Most databases identify males as the main prospects in households. Careful examination of nonprofit databases by gender may yield a persuasive rationale for more deeply engaging women as donors.

Counting the number of individual male and female donors may reveal that more women than men support the nonprofit. Comparing donor categories may also be a useful exercise. When Duke University fundraisers analyzed average lifetime giving for three distinct groups of undergraduate alumni – men, women, and alumni couples – they found that women graduates were the only group since 1996 that showed improvement in giving (Cam, 2013).

Accurate and appropriate recognition of women donors is a thorny and persistent issue. More high net worth women than men (60.4 versus 52.1 percent) expect the nonprofit to send a thank you note for a gift of any amount (Indiana University, 2011). As important as sending the thank you note, it is, perhaps, even more important that the organization ensures that the acknowledgement is correctly addressed. Many female donors are appropriately offended when a thank you letter is addressed to her spouse or partner when she made the gift. Fixing this chronic database error requires organizational buy-in at all levels, but it is well worth the investment.

When the Indiana University Women's Philanthropy Council and the Indiana University Foundation surveyed departments across the university system, they learned of at least seven different ways to address correspondence to married households with "Mr. and Mrs. John Smith" the most frequently used 43 percent of the time. To standardize procedures and ensure that female donors receive appropriate recognition for gifts, Laurie Burns McRobbie, First Lady of Indiana University, and Dan Smith, President and CEO of the IU Foundation, sent a letter instructing units to use the default address block of "Mr. John F. Smith and Ms. Jane G. Smith" with the salutation "Dear Mr. and Ms. Smith, Dear Mr. and Mrs. Smith, or Dear John and Jane" (M. Boillotat, personal communication, January 15, 2015). Recognition of female donors is a deliberate and well thought-out feature of a new advancement database system at the university.

Today's Female Donors

Singer and actress Barbra Streisand is a strong example of today's woman philanthropist. When she learned that women and men exhibit symptoms of heart disease in different ways, that cardiology is focused on male-pattern heart disease, and that fewer women than men participate in heart-related clinical studies despite the fact that heart disease is the leading killer of women, she acted in perhaps her most powerful role. In 2012 Streisand contributed $10 million to create the Barbra Streisand

Women's Heart Center at Cedars-Sinai Medical Center in Los Angeles. Streisand had developed a strong relationship with the Center's medical director after the doctor treated one of her friends. The actress took an active role in raising additional funds for the Center including several million dollar gifts. She has become a staunch advocate for women's heart health, raising her voice for the cause at TEDx talks and supporting Fight the Ladykiller, a new campaign organized by the Women's Heart Alliance, which educates about gender differences in heart disease. Streisand knows her gift will have both immediate and long-term impact and will fill an important gap in medical research.

Like Streisand, today's female donors often prefer to engage with an organization or cause and to learn more about it before making a gift. They want to build relationships with staff, volunteers, board members, and other stakeholders. Then they will consider generous gifts. The nonprofit organization that provides them opportunities to deepen engagement, apprises them periodically of the impact of their gifts, and connects them regularly to the mission through effective storytelling will benefit in the long term by loyalty and likely increased giving over time. Just as Streisand reached out to her network to raise additional funds for the heart center, so, too, do today's female donors advocate for the causes about which they are passionate with their friends, family, and across their networks, including social media. The keys to working effectively with women donors are engagement, building relationships, sharing stories of impact, and regular stewardship. These may take longer than transactional fundraising, but the return on investment is priceless.

A *Chronicle of Philanthropy* (Berkshire, 2014) profile of a female donor to The Arc, a national nonprofit organization that serves and advocates for people with intellectual and developmental disabilities, underscores many of these traditionally female characteristics. As motivations for her support of The Arc, this donor cited the personal connection to the cause and direct exposure to the impact of the work as well as support for the mission and the "untapped potential for fulfilling it." She expressed the view that the interaction with the organization is a relationship that requires time to deepen. The donor also referred to the impact that collaboration would have on fulfilling the mission. Such characteristics tend to resonate more with women than with men. Women also pay attention to detail. The Arc donor commented that her "favorite kind of gift acknowledgment is one unaccompanied by a new appeal for money."

Reaching the female donor

Over time efforts to engage women as donors have emerged in the United States. They have originated with both institutions and individual women or groups of

women. In the late 1980s and 1990s several institutions recognized women's growing economic clout and sought ways to involve them in philanthropy. In 1988,
the University of Wisconsin established the first women's philanthropy initiative in
coeducational higher education – a model that has spread to several dozen other
institutions, mostly public universities – across the country. The early 2000s saw
both grassroots and top-down initiatives for women at a myriad of organizations.
Giving circles proliferated and democratized philanthropy; they attracted new philanthropists across income levels, races, ethnicities, and ages. National nonprofits
such as United Way World Wide and the American Red Cross established special
initiatives to attract and cultivate women donors. Although each of these models
has different characteristics, their common focus is to provide women with the
opportunities for philanthropy in ways that are well-suited to their values, passion,
and financial abilities.

As research demonstrates the power and influence of women in philanthropy,
attention is shifting from stand-alone women's philanthropy programs at institutions to development of intentional and deliberate plans to engage women across
the fundraising strategy – from an annual fund to major gifts, principal gifts, and
legacy gifts. Such programs are fully integrated and aligned with the institution's
overall development program. Stand-alone programs, especially in higher education, are difficult to sustain given competing interests and pressures in development offices along with constrained financial and human resources. Shifting the
fundraising strategy to be fully inclusive internalizes it within the organization's culture and develops shared ownership and responsibility across many departments.
Rather than placing one individual in charge of raising funds from women, the
entire development team makes sure that their portfolios are gender-balanced and
that they are asking women for gifts. In the long run, these more inclusive strategies are apt to positively affect institutional culture, generate additional revenue,
and enable all donors to flourish.

Building the momentum to change the culture of giving to a more inclusive
model is a long-term endeavor. Three preliminary steps can help. The first step is
to understand the current donor pool. Who are the institution's donors and what is
the breakdown by gender? In the case of couples' giving, what details are available
about who is actually making the charitable decisions in the household? What percentage of female donors have been consistent givers over time, including annual
gifts of $25? A women's college was surprised to receive a $750,000 bequest from
an alumna; she had supported the college with a $25 gift for many years. However,
because of the nominal size of her consistent gifts, this donor was not considered a
major prospect. Many institutions have stories like this and data demonstrate that
women who make consistent annual gifts to organizations often remember them
with estate gifts as well.

Once the analysis of the donor pool is complete, it is critical to build the foundation for measuring impact, again taking a long-term strategic view. A baseline is essential to be able to measure the difference women donors make to fulfill the nonprofit's mission. Finding the appropriate metrics to measure the goals the institution sets out to achieve can be challenging. Basic metrics such as the increase in the number of women giving, the amount of dollars raised, and the percent of women on boards may be useful, but may not tell the whole story. Metrics related to fundraising portfolios and communication tools are more instructive to gauge the shift to a more inclusive culture. Tracking the number of visits and solicitations, attendance at events, and distribution of photos and stories by gender keeps the entire team focused on the desired outcomes.

Indiana University First Lady Laurie Burns McRobbie (2013) addresses this challenge directly:

> We are in the process, however, of confronting what is possibly our most important task; developing measurable goals by which our financial success will be judged … how should we measure changes in the numbers of female donors to Indiana University and the aggregate amount of their gifts, and from what baseline? How should we measure the effectiveness of our outreach and partnership efforts in motivating new gifts and new donors? It is exceedingly difficult to develop tight criteria that fully and accurately capture the role women play in giving.

The final preliminary step is to learn more about the organization's core stakeholders. Some nonprofits survey their donors to learn about motivations for giving, preferred communication methods, and attitudes about philanthropy. When Duke University surveyed its alumnae prior to establishing a women's philanthropy program, it found the top two motivators were gratitude for education received (73 percent) and to support the university's mission (64 percent). The least popular motivators were responses to peer solicitation, qualification for board participation, desire to match other donors, and any form of recognition – all coming in at under a 4 percent response (Cam, 2013). The Duke survey responses support many research results about gender differences in philanthropy.

One advantage of the growing body of research about donors is that the individual institution can measure its results against nationally random samples such as the Lilly Family School of Philanthropy's high net worth studies. For example, the 2011 study found that women more than men cite personal experience with a nonprofit organization (81.9 percent versus 73 percent) and the organization's ability to communicate its impact (46.4 percent versus 32 percent) as factors that influence their charitable decision making. Another area of significant difference between women and men in the same study is the offer of involvement with the organization (15 percent versus 5.3 percent).

Other nonprofits hold focus groups with female donors or conduct qualitative interviews with select donors to learn how they wish to be engaged. Sometimes female donors will approach the nonprofit with ideas about creating a group of female supporters to build community, to expand networks, and to collectively support the organization's mission.

Analysis of the data collected from the database, surveys, focus groups, and interviews allows the nonprofit to pinpoint gaps and opportunities for donor engagement.

Her story

In *The She Spot* co-author Lisa Witter stated, "Women are not a niche audience. They are ***the*** audience" (Witter and Chen, 2008, p. xv). Witter has said that when you reach women, you reach men, too, emphasizing women's roles as chief financial officer and chief charitable decision-maker in many households.

Reaching out to women as donors does not mean nonprofits must start over with their fundraising strategies. Rather, it requires a recognition that men and women respond to different prompts. Then it requires a conscious, well-articulated, inclusive plan with strategies that will appeal to both men and women. A successful plan is based on awareness that the time spent building, nurturing, and stewarding the relationship with the female donor will lead to larger gifts over time. Fundraising based on female-giving patterns is not revolutionary. In fact, it is being practiced more and more because all donors – both male and female – are demanding it. It asks fundraisers to work smarter, not harder.

> ***Be there with her.*** For most women, philanthropy is about making a difference. Tell her about the organization's mission, vision, and impact. Show her what the organization does with her gift. Take her on a site visit to see a program in action. Focus on the donor's connection to the nonprofit and its mission. If possible and within rules about client confidentiality, find ways for donors to have meaningful and quality interaction with people the organization serves.
>
> ***Engage her.*** Recognize that many women are interested in building a relationship with the organization prior to giving to it. The Arc donor mentioned earlier "thinks of the charities she supports as relationships – and she likes to go slowly." Although this may lead to the perception that women don't give or are reluctant donors, the fact is that their giving pattern is

different. Once engaged, women tend to be more loyal donors and give more over time to the causes in which they are actively engaged.

Seek her opinion. Listen to her. Make sure her voice is heard when meeting with a couple. One husband told a fundraiser while his wife was out of the room, "I don't know why you are talking to me. My wife makes all the charitable decisions."

Collaboration is often cited as an example of how women and men differ in their philanthropic behavior and leadership. Many women value the power of collaboration in their philanthropy, as exemplified by the tag line of the giving circle Impact 100 of Greater Indianapolis, "the power of women giving as one." The Washington Women's Foundation describes their power of collective giving as "giving, learning, leading together." Bringing people together to solve problems and leveraging the power of collective giving for maximum impact is one of the strengths of the giving circle model.

Ask her. Asking for contributions from women donors means that fundraisers must schedule visits with women. Often women do not give because they are not asked. Recognize that female donors may be at different life stages; customize your appeals accordingly. Have conversations with loyal donors about the opportunity to leave a legacy. Be prepared to discuss how she can make a "planned gift" without jeopardizing her finances. One fundraiser reported that an 89 year old female donor she visited had 52 charitable remainder trusts. She used the income from the trusts to create more charitable remainder trusts. In this case, the donor leveraged deferred giving vehicles to enjoy her giving while living and at the same time ensuring her legacy.

Women's Giving Across the Generations

Most recent studies of Millennials (born 1980–2000) and giving examine the cohort as a generation, but scant research has examined generational differences in giving by gender. A 2008 Lilly Family School of Philanthropy study found that motivations vary by generation and that gender also affects motivations. The research found that Millennial women are more likely to be motivated by a message to improve the world while Boomer and older women are more likely to respond to the responsibility to help others (Brown and Rooney, 2008).

One 35 year old female donor's philanthropic journey highlights characteristics common to both Millennials and women. Katherine S. described how she "fell in love" with the mission of the children's hospital the first time she visited it under the auspices of her college sorority. Throughout her college years she raised funds for the hospital at dance marathons and became a leader of the collegiate chapter. The dance marathon experience influenced her career choice and she continues to support the organization as a donor. Her philanthropic journey fits the profile for both millennial and female donors – engagement, relationship, giving, loyalty, and impact. Now married, she is clear about her philanthropic priorities. "My husband has his nonprofits and I have mine. The children's hospital is at the top of my list."

Women Give 2014 found a significant generational difference among women donors when examining the nexus of women, religion, and giving. Younger single women (younger than 45) who are religiously unaffiliated give roughly two times larger amounts to charitable organizations than women who are affiliated but who infrequently attend religious services (Mesch and Osili, 2014). The study demonstrated that the religiosity-giving relationship, which has been assumed to be the same regardless of gender and age, is a more complex relationship than previously thought. It is likely that further research on gender, generation, and giving will reveal more nuances.

Conclusion

The paradigm shift that engages men and women as donors requires fundraisers to work smarter, not harder. While it is difficult to pinpoint exact figures, it is likely that women will control and allocate trillions of dollars of intergenerational wealth that will be transferred in coming decades. When fundraisers recognize that men's and women's attitudes about money and wealth differ – that for men money is often perceived as power, achievement, and prestige and for women money represents personal security and a way to achieve goals – they will understand that a large proportion of women's wealth will go to charity (Wilmington Trust/Campden Research Women and Wealth Survey, 2009; Levinson, 2011).

Creating intentional and inclusive fundraising strategies today to engage women will transform the fundraising culture, build long-term loyal donors, and generate more resources to help fulfill an organization's mission for the future.

Discussion Questions

1) How have women's roles changed in America over the past 50 years and how have those changes affected their involvement with philanthropy?

2) What are some of the differences between men's and women's charitable giving behaviors?

3) Databases are often cited as obstacles to growing women's philanthropy. What are some additional reasons why it might be difficult to properly acknowledge women for their gifts?

4) How does sharing stories about women donors grow women's philanthropy?

5) In an era of big data, metrics are key to demonstrating impact. What additional metrics can help nonprofits measure their effectiveness in changing the organizational culture to be more inclusive and engaging for all donors?

CHAPTER ELEVEN

INCLUSIVE PHILANTHROPY: GIVING IN THE LGBT COMMUNITY

By Elizabeth J. Dale

One of the most prominent social movements of the twenty-first century has been the activism and visibility of the lesbian, gay, bisexual, and transgender (LGBT) community. Not only has the LGBT community pushed for marriage equality, antidiscrimination laws based on sexual orientation and gender identity, and a repeal of the "Don't Ask, Don't Tell" policy in the military, but it also has been actively involved in creating a range of nonprofit and political advocacy organizations to address a wide variety of causes, from social services for LGBT youth and the elderly to organizations supporting individuals with HIV and/or AIDS. LGBT people are also vital members of communities across the country and are beginning to be recognized as a diverse and important donor base to a variety of causes, from animal welfare and the arts, to human services and higher education. While there is growing interest in understanding the diversity of donors within the philanthropic sector, research on LGBT donors is just beginning. Although more research is clearly needed before definitive conclusions can be drawn, fundraisers should understand the unique histories, concerns, and philanthropic motivations and practices of LGBT individuals in order to build successful, donor-centered relationships.

Lesbian, gay, bisexual, and transgender people are often considered together in popular discourse, which has important cultural and political significance.

LGBT individuals share "a common experience of not conforming to cultural norms regarding sexual orientation and gender identity or expression" (Institute of Medicine, 2011). Individuals who identify as lesbian, gay, or bisexual often express same-sex attractions and behaviors. Transgender individuals express their gender in ways that are different from their biological sex at birth. While LGBT individuals are often clustered together, each group within the LGBT community forms a distinct population. While this chapter often uses the combined acronym LGBT, it is important to recognize that many differences exist among and within these groups, and specific findings may only apply to a particular subset of the LGBT population.

One challenge in researching the LGBT community is that accurately surveying the LGBT population is difficult. According to the Williams Institute on Sexual Orientation Law and Public Policy at the UCLA School of Law, approximately 9 million adults in the United States openly identify as lesbian, gay, bisexual, or transgender, comprising 3.8 percent of all Americans (Gates, 2011). Surveys find that women, younger adults (aged 18–29), and people of color are more likely to identify as LGBT than men, older adults, and individuals who identify as non-Hispanic white, which may skew survey results (Gates and Newport, 2012)

The social, economic, legal, and policy environment for same-sex couples has changed and continues to change at a rapid pace in the U.S. In June 2015, the United States Supreme Court ruled 5 to 4 in *Obergefell v. Hodges* that same-sex couples have a constitutional right to legally marry in all 50 states and Puerto Rico. This ruling extended a range of benefits to married same-sex couples, including the ability to file joint state and federal tax returns, to receive Social Security survivor benefits, and to be treated as married for estate, gift, and transfer tax purposes. According to the U.S. Census Bureau, as of 2010, there were 131,729 same-sex married couple households and 514,735 same-sex unmarried partner households in the United States, which is likely an undercount given the Williams Institute's study (O'Connell and Feliz, 2011). Despite a changing legal environment that extended marriage rights to same-sex couples, the LGBT community continues to face social stigma, employment discrimination, higher poverty rates, youth homelessness, and an increasing need for senior services, resulting in important disparities from their heterosexual peers (Badgett, 2001; Quintana, Rosenthal, and Krehely, 2010; LGBT MAP and SAGE, 2010).

Even though LGBT people have a rich history of creating and participating in nonprofit organizations, they are an often overlooked segment of the donor population, and most philanthropic research fails to account for differences in sexual and gender identities (Garvey and Drezner, 2013b). Because people in minority communities understand and enact giving differently than individuals with majority identities (e.g., white, middle class, heterosexual, and male), fundraisers are well-served to recognize the unique motivations and reasons for giving among diverse donors. This chapter offers a review of existing studies on LGBT giving and provides suggestions for nonprofit organizations and fundraisers who wish to create a welcoming and inclusive environment for LGBT donors.

An Overview of LGBT Giving

Even with the recent progress in LGBT equality, there is no truly comprehensive study of LGBT individuals' philanthropic giving from a nationally representative sample. To date, most research has surveyed donors through partnerships with LGBT nonprofit organizations. As a result, survey results often reflect a more "out" or openly identified LGBT population, as well as a higher proportion of donors and volunteers. Existing studies also tend to focus on LGBT donors in large cities and have disproportionately focused on donors on the west coast, and in the San Francisco Bay Area, in particular. Finally, a significant amount of LGBT giving research has focused exclusively on giving to LGBT organizations, which is a subset of LGBT individuals' total giving. While this approach is important to understanding the growth and development of the LGBT philanthropic sector, it neglects the full picture of LGBT donors and the myriad causes they support. Clearly, more research is needed. However, despite these important limitations, existing studies show a relatively consistent picture of giving patterns among LGBT donors that can guide future fundraising efforts.

Like any individual donor, the decision to give for an LGBT person results from a complex combination of donor interests, ability, and knowledge. Research shows that, on average, LGBT donors contribute an equal or slightly greater amount of their personal income compared to donors in the general population. One study found LGBT donors gave 2.5 percent of their income ($1,194) to charitable causes compared to 2.2 percent ($1,017) in the overall donor population (Badgett and Cunningham, 1998). Importantly, despite the social and political issues the LGBT community faces, the majority of LGBT philanthropy is not directed to LGBT causes but to nonprofits with no affiliation to the LGBT community. Surveys estimate LGBT donors may contribute between 50 and 75 percent of their giving to non-LGBT organizations (Badgett and Cunningham, 1998; Rose, 1998).

Like donors generally, LGBT people give to a wide variety of causes, but they also show some interesting patterns that diverge from the general donor population. First, LGBT donors give to advocacy and civil rights efforts at a much higher rate than the general U.S. population (Badgett and Cunningham, 1998; Horizons Foundation, 2008; Rose, 1998). The Horizons Foundation (2008) reports that more than 86% of LGBT donors gave to an advocacy or civil rights organization, while another survey found LGBT donors gave 25 percent of their total contributions to LGBT advocacy organizations and 13 percent of their contributions to non-LGBT advocacy organizations (Badgett and Cunningham, 1998). This is vastly different from societal giving patterns where the average person in the United States gives only 2 percent of charitable contributions to advocacy groups. Second, LGBT donors are both less likely to give and give a lesser amount to religious organizations, whereas as many as 67 percent of U.S. households that contribute to charity give to religious organizations. The religious subsector receives the largest share of individual giving, but LGBT donors are half as likely to give to religion (Horizons Foundation, 2008). Finally, compared to all donors in the United States, LGBT donors are as much as four times more likely to support the arts and twice as likely to give to health-related nonprofits (Horizons Foundation, 2008).

Several surveys have focused specifically on LGBT donors' philanthropic giving to LGBT organizations; however, this is often proportionately less than many might expect. The Horizons Foundation (2008) study of donors in the San Francisco Bay Area estimated that just 5 percent of the area's LGBT population had made a contribution to a local or national LGBT organization. LGBT donors also support a variety of HIV/AIDS-related organizations through monetary gifts and volunteer time, and many people attach such giving to support the LGBT community. One study found as much as 14 percent of LGBT donations and 15 percent of volunteer time were directed to HIV organizations (Badgett and Cunningham, 1998); similarly, the Horizons Foundation study found that LGBT donors were almost twice as likely to have supported an HIV organization in comparison to an LGBT organization.

Research also shows that LGBT people volunteer at a significantly higher rate than the average American (Horizons Foundation, 2008). While the typical volunteer in the United States contributes 18 hours per month, one study found LGBT individuals volunteer 29 hours per month (Badgett and Cunningham, 1998). About half of this time was for LGBT organizations. This may be due, in part, to LGBT organizations' smaller sizes and heavy reliance on volunteer labor. Similar to other donor research, volunteering and giving are complementary and not mutually exclusive – LGBT people often did both. People who volunteered for LGBT organizations donated more money than those who did not volunteer, and donors to LGBT organizations gave more volunteer hours than non-donors (Badgett and Cunningham, 1998). While these summary statistics are helpful in understanding LGBT philanthropy, LGBT giving is evolving and continued research is needed to obtain generalizable survey results.

Giving and The LGBT Movement

The philanthropy of any community cannot be understood without a broader understanding of its historical, social, and political context. While the legal and social equality issues affecting LGBT people have been part of mainstream American political and cultural discussions since the 1990s, the LGBT community is still relatively young, and positive connotations of LGBT individuals are even more recent (Miller, 2006). Until recently, few LGBT issues or organizations received much corporate, foundation, or government funding, and their existence was largely based on the support of individual donors and volunteers who gave to support the growth and development of organizations that served their communities. As a result, many of these organizations face ongoing challenges in carrying out their respective missions and have not been able to attend to long-term institutional development.

The history of the LGBT movement in the United States demonstrates the community's philanthropic impulse and how advocacy played a central role in early philanthropic work. In the 1950s and 1960s, organizations like the Mattachine Society and Daughters of Bilitis formed to help develop the gay and lesbian community but maintained deliberately low profiles given McCarthyism and the enforcement of U.S. laws criminalizing homosexual sex between consenting adults. However, the 1960s ushered in a new era of social and political change as the African American civil rights movement, protests of the Vietnam War, and the burgeoning women's movement inspired more political and visible action.

A pivotal moment took place on Friday, June 28, 1969 when LGBT patrons stood up to a police raid at the Stonewall Inn, a Greenwich Village gay male establishment on Christopher Street in New York City. After the initial raid the first night, patrons and other onlookers who had gathered outside refused to disperse and barricaded the police inside. Both the police and rioters returned the next night. While the Inn reopened on Sunday night for business as usual, the riots served as a rallying point. Stonewall is considered a defining moment in the formation of LGBT organizations and the community's growing political action.

While LGBT philanthropy was activated in the 1970s, it strengthened and diversified in the 1980s as a response to the AIDS epidemic. Many gays and lesbians, who had never participated in LGBT organizations before, were motivated to press for public resources to fight AIDS, especially as they saw close friends die from the disease. Novelist and screenwriter Larry Kramer helped found the first AIDS-service organization, the Gay Men's Health Crisis, in New York City in 1981, which raised $150,000 in its first year from a community that had previously been reluctant to openly fund gay institutions (Miller, 2006). While the AIDS crisis had the effect of strengthening many gay male organizations, it also brought lesbians and gay men together. The response to AIDS also led to the creation of new social and recreational organizations, from twelve-step groups and sports leagues to gay churches and synagogues. By the late 1990s, the sense of urgency for HIV/AIDS funding had subsided and AIDS-service organizations reported decreases in funding. Although HIV and AIDS would continue to be a vital health concern, the AIDS crisis also positioned the LGBT community to take a greater role and press for equal rights in all areas of life.

As with many social movements, the LGBT community faced challenges and backlash in the 1990s and early 2000s. In spite of setbacks like the ban on openly gay military service members and the passage of the Defense of Marriage Act in the 1990s, equal rights initiatives were underway, including hate crime legislation, workforce discrimination, second-parent adoption policies, housing protections, gender identity freedom, youth protections, and same-sex marriage, all of which have experienced varying degrees of success. One of the most visible initiatives during this time was same-sex marriage. In 1999, Vermont's Supreme Court ruled unanimously that the state was obligated to extend the same common benefits and protections that flow from marriage under Vermont law to same-sex couples, and, beginning in April 2000, Vermont began granting civil unions. Four years later, in 2004, Massachusetts became the first U.S. state to offer marriage to same-sex couples. As additional states legalized marriage, other states instituted new prohibitions and bans. It was not until 2014 that a majority of U.S. states granted and/or recognized same-sex marriages and in 2015 that the Supreme Court ruled in favor of marriage equality, permitting same-sex marriage nationwide.

Many LGBT organizations that began as all-volunteer efforts have professionalized and grown over time. Despite such success, most LGBT organizations remain comparatively small and rely on annual support to a large degree. The 2008 recession had a profound effect on the nonprofit sector and LGBT organizations were particularly vulnerable (Movement Advancement Project, 2009). Over time, a number of LGBT foundations – both public and private – have been created to respond to community needs. Examples include the Astrea National Lesbian Action Foundation in 1977, one of the earliest women's foundations in the country, the OUT Fund for Gay and Lesbian Liberation established in 1990, the Gill Foundation and the Horizons Foundation, among others. These foundations not only raise funds from a broad base of individuals but also award grants to LGBT organizations as well as to LGBT programs within more mainstream nonprofits.

Donor Characteristics

LGBT individuals are members of every geographic, socioeconomic, cultural, religious, ethnic, racial, political, and other grouping one could consider. In fact, one political science scholar described LGBT individuals as being "born into a diaspora, spread across geographic communities and born into families where gender, race, or ethnic identities – but not a gay identity – may be instilled from the beginning" (Badgett and Cunningham, 1998, p. 13). The later development of an LGBT identity, often in one's teens or early adulthood, may be overshadowed by one's other identities, or it may become an identity of central importance. As a result, it is important to understand how characteristics of LGBT donors vary, such as gender, race, and ethnicity, as well as age, income level, education, level of "outness," employment status, and religious tradition, among others. There are also likely to be important generational differences as younger LGBT individuals are experiencing a more accepting society than their older counterparts.

In a survey of LGBT donors' giving to LGBT causes, researchers found that LGBT people who are open about their sexual orientation to most or all of their family members and co-workers volunteer more hours and donate more money than those who are not "out" to their families and colleagues (Badgett and Cunningham, 1998). The same survey found that donation amounts increased with the donor's age. LGBT people with lower incomes volunteered more hours than people with higher incomes and LGBT people with higher incomes donated more than people with lower incomes, though lower income donors often gave a larger proportion of their total income. There were some small differences among individuals of different races and ethnicities, finding that LGBT African Americans, Asian Americans, and Latinos reported volunteering more hours for all causes than whites, but that whites gave an average larger donation amount (Badgett and Cunningham, 1998).

Early research also found that giving patterns differ among lesbians and gay men, much like research on male and female donors generally. When comparing men and women with similar characteristics, gay men donated $245 more than lesbians to LGBT organizations and volunteered two hours more per month (Badgett and Cunningham, 1998). This finding, which is in contrast to other research showing women are more likely to give and give higher amounts (Mesch, 2010), could be due to a variety of factors. Many lesbians support women's organizations as well as LGBT organizations because there is relatively less support for these causes.

While women's organizations may present a competing cause for lesbian support, research has found that lesbians who contribute to women's organizations actually give more time and money to LGBT organizations (Badgett and Cunningham, 1998). A second factor may be related to the fact that lesbians are more likely to have children than gay men. Recent figures estimate that 27 percent of female same-sex couples and 8 percent of male same-sex couples are raising children under 18 (Gates, 2015). As a result, women may have a different set of financial and time demands that limits their involvement in LGBT organizations. Third, lesbians have not always felt welcome in the same organizations as gay men; therefore, lesbian donors may want to be certain an organization supports lesbians before giving. Finally, the feminist philanthropy movement is still educating women about the importance of giving time and money to organizations and is encouraging women to think about their philanthropy in a more strategic way (Kendell and Herring, 2001).

One challenge to understanding LGBT philanthropy is the myth of "queer affluence," particularly among gay men. Both in the LGBT and mainstream media, gay men have been portrayed as wealthy with a high level of disposable income and no children, and thus, not only more affluent but also not in need of philanthropic support (Cunningham, 2005) Further, because many of the existing surveys are based on convenience samples of current donors, research has often surveyed a population with above-average income and educational levels, which can obscure the very real needs of millions of LGBT people. The data present a complex picture. Recent U.S. Census data show that same-sex couples are more likely to be employed, have a higher household income, and are 55 percent less likely to have children under age 18 living at home than different-sex couples (Flandez, 2013). While there are certainly individuals who fit this description, it is important to recognize that they are not representative of all LGBT people, many of whom are particularly vulnerable and who experience multiple oppressions. The most recent statistics available show that single gay men earn between 10 and 32 percent less than heterosexual men and that transgender individuals are more likely to face employment discrimination and unemployment (Badgett et al., 2007). Nearly 20 percent of children raised by same-sex couples live in poverty, compared to 14 percent of children being raised by different-sex couples (Gates, 2015). Same-sex couples are also more likely to be raising adopted or foster children. One scholar wrote, "The myth of gay affluence is simply that – a myth. In reality LGBT people do not constitute an economic elite class and, indeed, experience oppression comparable with every other disenfranchised group in the United States. Furthermore, LGBT people of color and transgender people are particularly vulnerable and experience multiple oppressions" (Cunningham, 2005, p. 11). Fundraisers need to recognize that LGBT individuals are at all places on the economic spectrum and have different abilities and capacities to give.

Motivations to Give

In many ways, LGBT donors are just like members of the general giving population in terms of motivations and deterrents for giving. LGBT donors want to know that the organizations they support are professional and well run and that their gifts are used wisely; they want to be recognized for their support in a timely and accurate manner and feel connected to the organizations' work (Horizons Foundation, 2008). However, LGBT donors' unique societal experiences have created some specific motivations as well as barriers to giving. Understanding these motivations is essential to enlarging the base of donors and volunteers for LGBT-related and non-LGBT organizations alike.

Many LGBT people are motivated to give based on a desire for social change – for social and political change for LGBT people, as well as for other minority groups (Gallo, 2001). Given that many LGBT individuals have personal experiences with discrimination and still may not enjoy full social and legal equality, a majority of LGBT donors see advocacy and civil rights as an important cause in their giving. Instances of discrimination and anti-gay rhetoric may often motivate an LGBT individual to give or volunteer for an LGBT organization for the first time. This also extends to support for other minority groups. One study reports, "Because [LGBT donors] have been discriminated against or felt prejudice because of their sexual orientation, they want to give to organizations whose mission statements reflect anti-discriminatory causes (anti-homophobia, anti-racism) or whose mission is to primarily serve the disadvantaged" (Rose, 1998, p. 75). Therefore, organizations that address discrimination and advocate for minority interests would be well served to cultivate LGBT donors.

A related motivation for many LGBT donors is a sense of responsibility to build and take care of one's own community, often described as community uplift or support. While this motivation has been well-documented among African American donors, it is just beginning to be understood among LGBT donors (Garvey and Drezner, 2013b). For example, some LGBT alumni give to their alma mater to make institutions more welcoming and affirmative for LGBT students, as David Goodhand and his partner Vincent Griski did in giving $2 million to the LGBT Center at the University of Pennsylvania (Lewin, 2000). This "felt responsibility" applies to both LGBT and non-LGBT organizations. In one focus group, a female donor explained, "If the LGBT community doesn't support itself, no one else will" (Horizons Foundation, 2008). Many LGBT individuals report that they donate because they or someone they know has benefitted from the organization. Another reason many individuals get involved is to meet other LGBT people (Badgett and Cunningham, 1998). Fundraisers in organizations such as universities can create meaningful opportunities for their LGBT alumni to know one another, to support their values of inclusiveness, and to raise support for students who often need affirmation, encouragement, and financial assistance (Garvey and Drezner, 2013a).

Another unique motivation is the idea that LGBT individuals may give to non-LGBT organizations as a way of exerting an LGBT presence in mainstream society. One study found that many LGBT people do not consciously think about their giving in an LGBT/non-LGBT framework (Horizons Foundation, 2008). While there may be a propensity to consider giving to an LGBT organization based upon one's identity, it also speaks to how giving is interrelated to many aspects of one's identity. One donor said, "I don't put my giving in buckets. You need to be part of the mainstream – being part of other [non-LGBT] organizations advances us" (Horizons Foundation, 2008).

While most LGBT individuals do not cite tax motivations as a strong factor in deciding to give, same-sex couples who are married can now access the same tax benefits as different-sex married couples. These benefits also tend to apply to people with higher incomes who are more likely to claim deductions for charitable contributions. Similarly, some LGBT donors may have a higher planned gift capacity if they do not have children, though this also needs to be balanced with their increased challenges related to aging. Because of the historical patchwork nature of relationship recognition, many LGBT individuals have actively planned their estates through wills and trust documents. Established organizations are particularly attractive for planned giving, as they often have the capacity to handle more complex gifts. Still, organizations of all sizes are well served to have a planned giving program that includes simple bequests.

All of these motivations speak to the idea that current and potential donors must feel a connection to an organization's mission. While there are often many motivations for giving at play at any one time, fundraisers must help build the bridge for how the organization's work is relevant to the life of the donor. This brings us to our final section about awareness and sensitivity when fundraising in the LGBT community.

Awareness and Sensitivity in LGBT Donor Stewardship

At its core, fundraising within the LGBT community is no different than fundraising among any other group of individuals (Fender, 2011). Successful fundraising is driven by reciprocal relationships and face-to-face communication, whether from a development officer or a peer who is passionate about an organization. Many

LGBT donors report giving because they were asked, and missed opportunities often arise because a potential donor was not asked to support an organization. In fact, a significant portion of LGBT individuals report that the reason they have not given is because they have not been asked to contribute (Horizons Foundation, 2008).

Potential LGBT donors are often sensitive to an organization's overall policies of diversity and inclusion. For example, LGBT donors may want to know that the organization requesting their support has an employment nondiscrimination policy that includes sexual orientation and gender identity, that health care and other benefits are extended to same-sex domestic partners, and that the organization has a commitment to cultivating diversity on both its board and staff. All of these desires can further an organization's reputation for inclusivity. In contrast, donors often refuse to give to organizations that are known to discriminate against the LGBT community, whether in policy or practice, such as the Boy Scouts of America's ban on openly gay leaders, which ended in 2015, but exceptions for troops sponsored by religious organizations are still allowed.

Beyond such organizational commitments, fundraisers should cultivate LGBT donors with awareness and sensitivity. Fundraisers need to be able to speak with LGBT donors about relationship and family issues like any other donors. One piece of advice given at an Association of Fundraising Professionals International Conference was, "Be comfortable enough with yourself and with your own sexual orientation that having a conversation about sexual orientation with me as a donor is not a big deal" (Cohen and Red Wing, 2009). Fundraisers should engage potential donors in meaningful conversation and understand their interests and priorities. As one fundraiser said, "It means a lot to LGBT people to feel like somebody is speaking to them in a meaningful and authentic way, and that they're acknowledging who they are and celebrating who they are" (Flandez, 2013).

One clear expression of an organization's cultural competency comes in how LGBT donors are recognized, particularly same-sex couples. Organizations need to recognize the importance of salutations and use the correct language in print materials and solicitations. "If organizations want to get it right, they need to openly talk to their donors, queer or straight, about how they want to be recognized (or solicited, or communicated with for that matter)" (Fender, 2011). For some donors, it may mean acknowledging a gay man's spouse as his husband, keeping names together on a donor recognition wall, or addressing mail to a lesbian couple as "Ms. and Ms." or with no salutations at all. It is particularly important to note such preferences in donor database systems, as development officers may change and a reliance on manual edits can often lead to unintentional mistakes. Development staff need to address such data collection techniques at an organizational level.

Finally, a number of larger organizations, such as higher educational institutions, have established LGBT affinity groups, recognizing the importance of building a community from within. These groups can serve as a way for LGBT individuals to have a positive experience with their university, even if they may have experienced discrimination and/or marginalization as students, and can help build trust and reliability with a new donor group (Garvey and Drezner, 2013b). They also offer a way for institutions to gain input on policies and practices, in addition to raising financial support. As research shows that LGBT individuals may be more likely to volunteer, the social interactions an affinity group provides can help establish connections among LGBT donors and promote further engagement. An alternative to beginning an affinity group would be to partner or co-sponsor a program with an LGBT community organization.

Recommendations for Inclusive Fundraising

There are a number of steps organizations and fundraisers can take to increase donor support from the LGBT community to both LGBT and non-LGBT causes, many of which emulate fundraising best practices.

• *Recognize the multiple identities LGBT individuals hold.* Identifying as lesbian, gay, bisexual, or transgender may be an important aspect of someone's identity and rarely can be ignored; however, we all hold multiple identities that are likely related to our philanthropic interests. At the same time that LGBT identity is important, it may be equally or even more important for a lesbian to support feminist causes, a gay Latino man to support the local Hispanic community, or a same-sex couple to support their alma maters.
• *Include sexual orientation and gender identity in an organization's nondiscrimination policies.* Similarly, work to ensure personnel and benefits policies apply equally to LGBT and non-LGBT employees.
• *Diversify all levels of your organization.* Recruit LGBT staff, trustees, and advisory committee members, in addition to having gender and racial/ethnic diversity. Avoid having a "token" member who is expected to speak for an entire community (impossible to do!) and recruit in pairs when possible.
• *Engage in active outreach to the LGBT community and let the community know you welcome their involvement and participation.* This could include having LGBT-specific programming, establishing affinity groups, celebrating Gay Pride month in June, or aligning your organization with movements for LGBT equality. It also means highlighting the efforts of LGBT donors and volunteers in newsletters and other publications.

• *Publicize how your work contributes to issues of social justice.* Understand who among your clients identifies as LGBT and how your services reach vulnerable and marginalized populations, including people of color, low-income people, youth, the elderly, and transgender people.

• *Get to know potential donors and ask for their support.* As the National Center for Lesbian Rights' experience shows, if organizations want to increase donor support, they have to ask. The NCLR suggests, "Begin by asking people you know, then widen the circle of people you know, ask often and in many different ways, ask for well-defined needs, say thank you often, be accountable to the community you serve, spend donors' money wisely to further your mission" (Kendell and Herring, 2001, p. 102). As the research shows, potential donors need to be made aware of the importance of their support.

• *Demonstrate results, effectiveness, and institutional stability.* Like all donors, LGBT donors want to know that your organization is well run and that gifts are used for the purpose for which they are intended. Maintaining high-quality stewardship practices will enhance donor loyalty and may be essential for securing planned gifts. This includes accuracy in data management and highlighting the contributions of LGBT donors in fundraising communication.

Discussion Questions

1) Your organization wants to focus on expanding its fundraising to LGBT donors. What steps would you take to increase your fundraising in various vehicles (i.e., direct mail, special events, major gifts)? What do you think holds the most promise for your organization?

2) Given LGBT donors' increased desire to fund advocacy and support organizations that are welcoming and inclusive, evaluate a nonprofit organization to see how it may be perceived by an LBGT donor. What changes/improvement could be made?

CHAPTER TWELVE

FAITH AND GIVING

By David P. King

A fter completing this chapter, you will be able to:

1. Describe the significant role of religious giving in the philanthropic sector.
2. List the multiple ways in which religious giving has been defined.
3. Differentiate the foundations of giving in various religious traditions.
4. Explain the multiple religious motivations that inspire religious donors.
5. Describe the shift in religious giving and how it affects the cultivation of relationships with donors.

Exploring the intersections of faith and giving in the context of fundraising is a complicated task. On one hand, faith has undergirded much of philanthropy for centuries, for at the heart of most religious traditions is the "love of humanity." The Hebrew and Christian scriptures admonish followers to love one's neighbor as well as to care for the poor and for those with physical and spiritual needs within their communities. On the other hand, while many define giving as a central tenet of their faith tradition, they see this as somewhat distinct from philanthropy and professional fundraising.

Other complications for practitioners and researchers also emerge. Quantifying and categorizing religious giving is often difficult. How do you measure compassion or charity? What counts as religious giving? Are we attuned to faith as a motivation for giving or only concerned with donations to explicitly religious organizations?

Finally, faith and money can be taboo topics. Just like issues such as politics or sexuality, when faith is added to the mix of philanthropy, the topics can be difficult to discuss. Engaging faith in fundraising requires embracing a diversity of language, multiple expectations, and people's personal stories and religious experiences. Yet, understanding how to navigate the worlds of faith and giving should be a vital part of any successful fundraiser's work.

Making Sense of the Religious Giving Sector

Fundraising broadly defined is an aspect of all religious institutions. In reviewing historian Peter Brown's book on wealth in early western Christianity, G. W. Bowersock (2015) noted, "Faith and money lie at the core of all religious institutions; although faith can exist without money, religious institutions cannot." *Giving USA*, the most widely recognized annual report on charitable giving defines religious giving quite narrowly to a subset of religious institutions: religious congregations, denominations, missionary societies, religious media, and organizations formed for worship and evangelism. So, by *Giving USA's* standards, giving to a church, mosque, or religious broadcasting agency counts as religious giving. Donations to Catholic healthcare or religious higher education does not (*Giving USA*, 2015).

By the Numbers   Religious giving, even if defined narrowly to include only the religious institutions identified above, continues to dwarf all other subsectors. According to *Giving USA*, religious giving makes up 32% of all charitable giving. The next largest subsector is education at only 15%. In addition, giving to religion continues to grow. From 2012 to 2014, giving to religion increased 8.6% (5.4% adjusted for inflation) for an estimated all-time high total of $114.90 billion in contributions (*Giving USA*, 2015).

While religious giving has continued to grow, its growth has slowed dramatically from past decades. In 2014, religious giving increased 2.5% (basically a flat rate of change – only .9% adjusted for inflation). In addition, religious giving has decreased dramatically as a percentage of the share of overall giving. Even while dwarfing the other subsectors, religious giving has declined from a height of 57% of the total over the 1985-1989 period to roughly 33% of all charitable giving over the last five-year period.

Religious Congregations　By *Giving USA's* definition, local congregations and houses of worship stand out as making up the overwhelming majority of all religious giving. The majority of congregations in America are relatively small – 59% have less than 100 members. Yet, the largest 10% of congregations contain half of all church-going Americans. Most congregations are small, but most affiliated Americans are members of larger congregations. And while around a third of congregations have an endowment, 80% of all congregational gifts come from individuals. The religious sector more generally is less dependent on foundations, bequests, and corporate or governmental grant funding (Chaves, 1998). Therefore, the majority of religious giving and the correlating focus of researchers has been understanding individual donors to congregations.

Making Sense of the Shifts in Religious Giving　Yet, the world of religious giving in which many of us grew up is not the world of charitable giving today. While religious giving continues to grow slowly, it has declined drastically as a share of total giving. If the preponderance of religious giving is entrusted to congregations, then it would hold that significant changes in individuals' engagement with congregations has been a major factor affecting religious giving. These changes have become more evident in recent years.

Congregational Size, Attendance, and Affiliation　First, as in any organization, there is a percentage of members that are what economists refer to as "freeloaders" - those who do not pay their fair share. For instance, one in five American Christians give nothing to church or any religious organization (Smith, Emerson, & Snell, 2008). Social networks formed within communities remain one of the most important factors in encouraging giving (Putnam and Campbell, 2010). As more and more religious Americans associate with larger congregations, some scholars hypothesize that it is also easier to remain anonymous, less engaged, and less likely to give. While this may be the case in some instances, other researchers have demonstrated that large congregations are no more likely to leave attendees with fewer social networks than smaller faith communities. Religious congregations that are successful focus on cultivating these social networks, but they also explicitly discuss the need to give, and allow multiple opportunities to participate in giving. The size of the church alone is an inaccurate predictor of attendees' ability to form social networks. In the context of religious giving, it remains the case that larger congregations are growing larger while smaller congregations continue to have more difficulty keeping pace with their financial needs.

In addition to the skewing of religious Americans to larger congregations, attendance itself continues to fall. Attendance has always served as one of the best predictors of religious giving. There are numerous studies all showing that people who attend church, mosque or synagogue weekly (or two to three times a month) are between two and four times more generous in their charitable giving than those who attend less frequently or not at all. While studies differ, a recent survey by the Pew Research Center estimated that 37% of U.S. adults attend worship services weekly while another 33% attend monthly or yearly. Other studies have the weekly attendance percentage much lower. Attendance has been taken as one measure of an individual's religiosity, but it is less attendance itself, and the benefits of social networks actualized in regular attendance that lead to increased giving. As weekly or monthly attendance has fallen, religious institutions must reconsider how they communicate the need to give as well as how they form social relationships within the community in other ways (Lipka, 2013).

Along with average size and attendance patterns, religious affiliation has also changed drastically in recent years. The slowing growth of religious giving cannot help but be analyzed alongside the Pew Research Center's 2015 *America's Changing Religious Landscape* report. Between 2007 and 2014, the U.S. Christian population declined from 78.4% to 70.6% and the religiously unaffiliated has grown to 22.8% of the population (second only to evangelical Protestants at 25.4%). More than one in five Americans no longer affiliate with any religious tradition. The number rises to one in three among Americans under the age of 30. The Pew study offers us some important insights into the influence of religion and religious organizations in American society alongside the "rise of the nones" (nones are the unaffiliated – those checking none of the above on surveys). A declining interest in institutional affiliation across society has likewise grown even more so among religious institutions. Those nominally associated with religious traditions are now much more likely to report their absence of religious affiliation while the negative public influence of religion in political and social issues has pushed others to dissociate.

Yet, while attendance and affiliation are significant predictors of religious giving, we know that the large majority of the religious unaffiliated are not irreligious. The majority were reared in a religious tradition, continue to engage in forms of religious practice, and seek forms of spiritual community. Many identify as spiritual even if they do not affiliate with a religious tradition. What *Giving USA* or Pew do not measure is the religious or spiritual motivations of the unaffiliated. Religious organizations must not "write off" this population, but rather think creatively for ways to challenge and include them in their work.

Increased Competition   When religious giving is defined largely as religious congregations, denominations, and missionary societies, it is clear that the religious marketplace is changing and congregations are facing increased competition for the gifts of faithful donors. Particularly, the growth of parachurch organizations, also called religious special-purpose groups, have risen dramatically. Parachurch groups are 501(c)(3) organizations that were founded to work outside of congregations and across multiple denominations. They usually focus on a narrower mission than congregations. Local congregations must serve multiple functions (worship, education, social services, pastoral care, etc.). The ability of a parachurch to focus on a single purpose (such as alleviating child poverty in Africa, religious education among college students, or the publishing of religious literature) often allows for a more explicit and compelling mission to market to potential donors than the composite needs of a local congregation. These parachurch agencies are also often much better equipped with professional marketing and fundraisers to solicit support. From small grassroots agencies to multi-billion dollar industries, these special purpose groups are also expanding in number quite rapidly. Between 1995 through 2007, they grew at a rate of 190%, twice the rate of growth of congregations and well over twice the rate of non-religious public charities (Scheitle, 2010). If attendance and affiliation may be affecting giving to congregations, these changes do not necessarily preclude giving to these other faith-based nonprofits out of religious motivations.

Expanding the Definition of Religious Giving

The expansion of faith-based agencies beyond local congregations and their continual fundraising success should force us to consider the categorization of religious giving and what that might mean for the work of the professional fundraiser. An expanded view of religious giving forces us to pay increased attention to how institutions are religious as well as how donors see their faith as a part of their charitable giving.

When asking individual donors to determine the appropriate religious category of the organization benefiting from their giving, we see that 73% of all Americans' charitable giving goes to organizations with religious ties (see Figure 12.1). Congregations make up 41% of that giving, but another 32% is given to what scholars of the 2013 study, *Connected to Give: Faith Communities*, named as "religiously-identified organizations" or RIOs. While not included in *Giving USA's* religious giving numbers, these organizations with religious ties (such as Catholic Charities, World Vision, Jewish Federations, or the Zakat Foundation) have faith or a religious identity as a significant part of their mission. Maybe even more significant, however, is that donors were clear that they often gave to these organizations because they identified the organizations as religious. (McKitrick, Landrew, Ottoni-Wilhelm, & Hayat, 2013). Only 27% of all charitable giving went to organizations that donors saw as non-religiously identified organizations (NRIOs).

FIGURE 12.1. DISTRIBUTION OF GIVING TO CONGREGATIONS, RIOs, AND NRIOs.

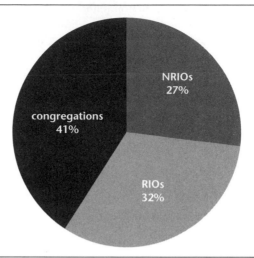

Source: McKitrick, Melanie, J. Shawn Landres, Mark Ottoni-Wilhelm and Amir Hayat. 2013. *Connected to Give: Faith Communities.* Los Angeles: Jumpstart.

An important contribution of the *Connected to Give* study was asking individual donors themselves how to classify the beneficiaries of their giving. With that framing, 55% of Americans give to organizations with religious ties (either a congregation or a RIO). Thirty-three percent give to both congregations and RIOs. Fifty-three percent give to support NRIOs. It is important to note that while it is probably not surprising that donors who support religious congregations allocate the majority of their charitable giving to organizations with religious ties (80%), they often support NRIOs too. The flip-side is true as well. Even donors making gifts for non-religious purposes often find their charitable giving going to organizations with religious ties.

The religious identity of organizations and the motivations of individual donors are much more complex than often understood, and are likewise essential for fundraisers to investigate, whether their nonprofit considers itself religious or not.

From Institutions to Individuals

As noted above, religiosity (measured through belonging, behaving, and believing) is a significant predictor of giving to all sectors. Those who report that religion is very important or somewhat important give more to congregations, RIOs, as well as NRIOs than those who claim religion is not very or not at all important. The same is true for attendance at religious services as well as affiliation (identifying as religious over simply spiritual). While a higher level of individual religiosity leads to higher rates of giving to both religious and non-religious organizations, the preponderance of giving is tied to congregations and RIOs (McKitrick, Landrew, Ottoni-Wilhelm, & Hayat, 2013).

These predictors hold true across religious traditions. When the *Connected to Give* study segmented Americans into the five broad religious traditions they were able to study (black Protestant, evangelical Protestant, Jewish, mainline Protestant, Roman Catholic), they saw these groups giving at remarkably similar rates to one another among congregations, RIOs, and NRIOs as shown in Figure 12.2. The only exception being that Jews gave at lower rates to congregations (McKitrick, Landrew, Ottoni-Wilhelm, & Hayat, 2013).

Within these broader religious families, however, some religious traditions give a higher percentage as a share of total income than others. In this study, looking at the narrower definition of religious giving primarily as giving to congregations, Mormons far outdistanced other groups (5.6%), followed by Pentecostals (2.9%), non-denominational Protestants (2.6%), and Baptists (2.0%). While the

FIGURE 12.2. PERCENTAGE OF AMERICANS WHO GIVE TO ALL TYPES OF ORGANIZATIONS BY RELIGIOUS TRADITION.

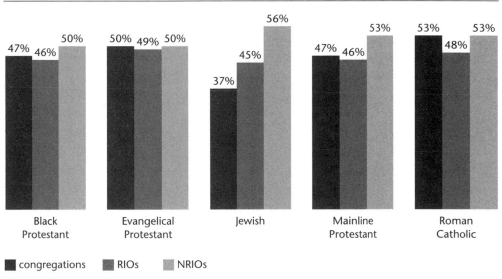

Source: McKitrick, Melanie, J. Shawn Landres, Mark Ottoni-Wilhelm and Amir Hayat. 2013. *Connected to Give: Faith Communities.* Los Angeles: Jumpstart.

distinctions among groups is important, maybe even more telling is the percentage of actual giving by religious practitioners in comparison to what is sometimes presumed from religious teachings. Among Judeo-Christian traditions that often speak of a biblical tithe (a tenth) of one's income as one model for giving, we see that only 2.7% of all American households give 10% to religious organizations, and the average even among the highest giving tradition, Mormons, falls well short of a traditional tithe (Rooney, 2010).

In this case, religious Americans are on par with other Americans. While the data are not equivalent, University of Notre Dame sociologist Christian Smith has estimated that among all American households, 2.6% give away 10% or more of their income; 3.1% give away between 5 and 10% while 9% give between 2 to 5%. Smith summarizes that over 86% give away less than 2% or more (Smith and Davidson, 2014). Giving to religious institutions (whether defined narrowly or more broadly) makes up by far the largest percentage of charitable giving. Likewise, a majority of all donors are compelled to give partly out of their religious motivations. This is true across a broad spectrum of religious traditions, gender, cultures, and class. Even as the contexts of religious giving may be changing for both donors and recipients, it does not appear that religion is losing significance as a factor in donor motivations. Understanding the religious motivations and contexts of your particular donors and organization should be an important tool in the toolbox of all fundraisers.

Making Sense of Religious Motivations

Giving has been at the heart of most religious traditions. The teachings of these traditions have remained foundational in how religious followers often understand the how and why of their giving. These traditions, however, do not all understand philanthropy in the same way. Attending to the language that various religious traditions use in framing their giving is important to engage donors and their religious motivations.

Judaism In the Hebrew Scriptures, the word *tzedakah* reflects the Jewish understanding of charitable giving. From the root word meaning justice, *tzedakah* is often framed as a practice of giving in order to help the poor and to rectify social imbalance. It is fueled more by a sense of justice than compassionate charity. From the Scriptures, it is considered a *mitzvah*, or commandment and obligation that Jews follow. Today many Jews also use the phrase *tikkun olam* to describe their charitable giving. Often translated "to repair or fix the world," this phrase has been adopted by many religious as well as secular philanthropic causes to describe the dedication of time, energy, and resources to improve the lot of others. It has developed resonance far beyond the Jewish community itself.

Roughly 40% of American Jews belong to a synagogue or temple where most donate through a system of annual dues. And while 23% of American Jewish giving is focused on congregations, another 39% is tied to other Jewish non-profits that work to sustain cultural identity, provide social services, healthcare, education, etc … Most Jewish communities of significant size are serviced by a Jewish federation that operates as an umbrella organization for receiving and distributing philanthropy. Another 39% of Jewish giving, however, is concentrated on non-Jewish organizations. Since Judaism is not only a religious movement but also a cultural identity, Judaism is as diverse as any American religious tradition, and the motivations and recipients of their philanthropy are equally so (Jacobs, 2009).

Christianity   Like Judaism, Christianity has a long and complex history with giving. In many Christian traditions still today, followers look to the Hebrew Bible (Christians often refer to the text as the Old Testament) for a biblical precedent of the tithe (giving one-tenth of an individual's income to God). Some see this giving as directed first to the church and additional offerings beyond it, while others consider other religious or secular donations as a part of this ten percent. Yet, as we have already noted above, only a small percent of Christians give a tithe. In the New Testament, Jesus talked of giving not only a tithe (10%) but challenged followers to give far beyond it. For instance, the Christian monastic tradition has seen men and women take vows of poverty to give themselves fully to the work of their faith.

Other language is also prominent within the Christian community. Stewardship is often used to talk about being a faithful steward of one's possessions that have been entrusted to individuals by God. As stewardship language has been employed by corporate and secular non-profits as well, however, some religious communities are uncertain how best to distinguish the term in their contexts. Employing one's resources to participate with God's work in the world is another consistent aspect of Christian theology. Responding in gratitude to God's generosity to humanity is also popular language prominent in appeals. While some see a tithe as an obligation or command from God, most Christian and Christian communities operate out of free will offerings. Appeals for weekly, monthly, annual, or special gifts with a variety of languages above operate as standard even though there is a wide diversity of approaches and responses.

Islam   One of the five pillars of Islam, *zakat* (literally to grow in purity), is an annual payment of 2.5% of one's assets, more an obligatory act decreed by God rather than a simple choice of charity. With specific aims for the poor, *zakat* is understood as a return of wealth and a right of the poor. *Zakat* has eight particular categories of worthy recipients and a special offering is often given before breaking the month-long fast of Ramadan.

Islam also has a long history of giving beyond the required *zakat*. *Sadaqah* (akin to the Jewish root *tzedakah*, justice) is giving beyond *zakat* as an act of loving to neighbors and beyond. *Waqfs* are specific types of endowment gifts initiated by the prophet Muhammad to establish schools, mosques, shrines, and other institutions (Mattson, 2010).

Like all religious traditions, debates commence on whether to apply charitable giving to local or global contexts; within the religious community specifically or to others in need. While Muslims have a long history of giving, it is important to recognize the particular importance of *zakat* in the religious practice of many Muslims and realize that attesting to the appropriateness of one's gift to meet the requirements of *zakat* is necessary for nonprofits that engage many Muslim donors.

Hinduism and Buddhism   While these two East Asian traditions have long and distinct histories, their philanthropic impulses are similar in contrast to the three Abrahamic traditions discussed above. In both traditions, *dāna* refers to charity or giving alms. It is a central aspect of the practice of both faiths, but it does not connote the same sense of obligation as scriptural mandates within Islam or Judaism. By giving away material possessions one accumulates spiritual merit. Donors give alms to the poor as well more specifically to those who have chosen a life of poverty (Brahmins who are tied to a life of study in Hinduism or Buddhist monks who shun most possessions). In contrast to other traditions, the intent of one's gift as well as the worthiness of the recipient is extremely important. If one gives out of the wrong motives, he may undermine the merit of his gift. At the same time, the gift must be given without attachment. For many, giving the gift is freeing oneself from material possessions. Therefore, nonprofits who are keen on reporting back achieved outcomes and proper accountability may meet with less interest from a Buddhist donor who may distance himself from his gift (Ilchman, Queen, and Katz, 1998).

As in all these traditions, these brief summaries demonstrate the long histories of these religions and the centrality of faithful giving as evident in their foundations, Scriptures, and practice. Yet, these are living traditions. Understandings continue to evolve over time. Multiple interpretations exist within the broad net of each tradition. And particular followers of these religious traditions are each unique. While it would be a mistake to discount the power these religious traditions play in shaping many people's charitable giving, for most they do not hold absolute sway. Other factors such as gender, ethnicity, culture, and generation explored elsewhere in this book are all well worth exploring. Each individual is a complex mix of motivations and circumstances.

Other Motivations for Religious Giving

People may give for different reasons, but we know that giving is relational. What many religious people share in common is the motivation to give in order to be in right relationship with God, a religious leader, a religious community, or the wider world. According to scholar Jim Hudnut-Buemler (2007), there are four kinds of motivations that shape religious giving:

1. Giving to achieve reciprocity with God – Some prosperity theologies propose that if you give, God will bless you with more money, but others give out of this motivation simply believing that giving is one way to achieve a closer or personal relationship with God.
2. Giving to achieve reciprocity with a particular religious group – This type of giving may reflect donors' desire to do their fair share in a community, or rather be recognized or elevated into a position of institutional leadership.
3. Giving as an extension of the self – This type of giving is a reflection of people's passions. They believe in or identify with a cause, or they may want to honor or extend institutions that have been a source of blessing to them.
4. Giving as an act of thankfulness or altruism – People give to commemorate and celebrate a family or life event, or to honor the memory of a friend or relative.

Obstacles to Religious Giving

While faith is often a tremendous asset for charitable giving, there are certain obstacles that have been identified that limit the generosity of many religious donors. The first is wealth insecurity. While sometimes actual, often a lack of financial resources to give is a perception over a reality. Many religious traditions serve as a tool to stress a proper understanding of one's possessions that combats forces of materialism and consumerism that can enable faithful giving. The second obstacle is often giving illiteracy. Many people of faith are confused or unconcerned as to what is a standard of generosity within their religious tradition. The third obstacle is "comfortable guilt." Many are content to give just enough to assuage their conscience of feelings that they should give more (Snell and Vaidyanathan, 2011).

Conclusion

Much of faith-based fundraising has focused more on the religious institutions rather than the donor. Yet, it is clear that it the donors' social networks, motivations, beliefs, and passions that most influence religious giving. Faith-based organizations must turn their attention away from their own immediate needs in order to cultivate donor relationships. Non faith-based institutions should do the same. Both should be willing to engage the values and religious foundations that shape donors. Questions of faith and giving are not chiefly about money, rather they are about 1) relationships; 2) vision; 3) trust; 4) and faith formation. Fundraisers should focus not only on the vision and accountability of an organization and its leadership, but religious donors also care about relationships with your institution, broader religious communities, and ultimately with a higher power. Attending to their faith, and cultivating not only their philanthropic capacities but also their faith motivations is an important long-term strategy for building deep relationships with donors that share a passion for your mission.

Entering the donors' new world, fundraisers should attend to donors' philanthropic autobiographies. As donors are considering a gift, many are asking questions such as: What is the meaning and purpose of life? What does it mean to live well? How will I be remembered? They are also asking what foundational experiences shaped their desire to be generous or to participate in your mission. For many, religion and spirituality are significant factors in answering these questions. At appropriate times, fundraisers in long-term relationships with donors often find themselves engaged in these formative conversations. Not shying away from them, but helping to unpack their meaning is an important part of the work that we do. While the institutions, forms of giving, and motivations may change, faith will continue to be a significant factor in philanthropy. Fundraisers cannot afford to avoid paying attention.

Discussion Questions

1) How would you define faith and giving?
2) How might the notion of religions as living traditions impact your own understanding of faith and philanthropy in your own work as a fundraiser?
3) How does your organization view faith as a part of its mission or how do you as a fundraiser include understandings of religion into your development work?
4) Explain the paradigm shift in religious giving. What other future shifts do you anticipate?
5) Compare and contrast giving in the religious traditions covered in this chapter.

CHAPTER THIRTEEN

ETHNIC DIVERSITY AND GIVING

By Una Osili and Sarah King

There is a great deal of interest among fundraisers and philanthropists in understanding how growing diversity in the United States will impact the non-profit sector. Several observers have noted that there is a need to adapt strategies and tactics in order to meet the needs of donors who represent increasingly diverse ethnic and racial backgrounds, cultural traditions, and experiences. Some researchers and practitioners have argued that greater diversity within communities can expand the scale and scope of the U.S. nonprofit sector while others have argued that increasing diversity may reduce the willingness of individuals to give to collective initiatives. In this chapter, you will learn:

- The definition and scope of diversity.
- Research on ethnic diversity and philanthropy.
- The role of immigration and philanthropy.
- Approaches to fundraising through diversity.

The rise in ethnic diversity will likely influence the philanthropic landscape in U.S. communities – now and in the future. In this chapter, we examine current and projected trends for the growth in U.S. ethnic and racial diversity. Recent data suggest that over two-thirds of Americans give in any given year (Indiana University Center on Philanthropy, 2009b). Several authors have emphasized that philanthropy is a central aspect of civic and economic life for Americans of diverse backgrounds. In analyzing the distinct traditions of African Americans, Native Americans, Asian Americans, and Latinos, Joseph (1995) emphasizes that philanthropy is a central value within America's minority groups. Vehicles for expression of philanthropy do matter, however, as traditions and priorities differ. Minority populations, soon to be the majority by 2044, have made significant contributions to the way in which philanthropy is defined in the United States, and will likely continue to shape American philanthropy over time.

More recently, the term "diversity" has expanded beyond race and ethnicity to all aspects of human difference. Nonprofit organizations who seek to enhance diversity in programming and donor outreach, as well as internally among staff and other stakeholders, have more resources and tools than they may have had in the past. New research in philanthropy has increasingly sought to evaluate fundraising appeals focused on ethnically diverse groups (Bryan, 2008). Organizations such as the W.K. Kellogg Foundation and the Rockefeller Foundation are energizing this movement by supporting new initiatives that promote diversity in the non-profit sector. Embracing diversity in fundraising begins with an institutional com-mitment to inclusivity. Leadership involvement is often critical for sustained imple-mentation of best practices (Chao, 2008). By re-evaluating traditional approaches to fundraising and tailoring these approaches to align with donor interests and values, fundraisers have the capacity to meet goals of diversity and inclusivity.

Defining Diversity

Defining diversity in a rapidly changing U.S. social and economic context presents some challenges. The commonly used phrase, "fundraising in diverse communi-ties," often found in titles of books and articles, may be less relevant in today's complex fundraising landscape. Perhaps it would be more relevant to emphasize "fundraising across, within, among, for, or with" diverse communities, because fundraising often implies cross-cultural fundraising in order to benefit various pop-ulation groups.

The Council on Foundations defines diversity as "encompassing the breadth and depth of human difference" (Rockefeller Philanthropy Advisors, 2012, p. 5). Originally used to refer to ethnic or racial groups, the concept of diversity now extends to all "forms of human expression" (Bryan, 2008; Rockefeller Philanthropy Advisors, 2012, p. 5). For example, recent studies on diversity focus on the follow-ing groups: the LGBT community and "people with disabilities, the economically disadvantaged, and rural communities" (Bryan, 2008). For the fundraising profes-sional, particularly those in higher education, consideration of diverse voices is a growing aspect of fundraising activity. Increasingly, many fundraisers understand that to approach a relationship and solicitation solely from their own cultural perspective may not be sufficient, as they may need to work across a range of traditions and experiences to achieve campaign goals (Rovner, 2015).

An additional concern is the use of relevant terminology when discussing ethnically diverse populations and philanthropy. Should correct designation for these populations be people of color, minorities, or ethnic groups? And is the correct terminology African American or Black, Hispanic or Latino, Asian American and/or Pacific Islander (U.S. Census Bureau, 2013)? Given the changing terminology, fundraisers and practitioners may need to better understand the preferences of their distinct communities and how these preferences evolve over time.

An important component in discussions of diversity is the role of recent immigrants in shaping the philanthropic environment. Immigrants represent one in eight people in the U.S. population and account for one in six of employed individuals (Immigration Policy Center, 2014). In some cases, ethnically diverse populations would prefer to be identified by their actual country of origin, or their source of national orientation. Mexicans or Mexican Americans, for example, would rather be distinctive than grouped into an overall designation (Taylor et al., 2012). For the purposes of this chapter, the following guidelines will be used.

To identify population groups that are often called minorities or similar terms, we will use people of ethnically diverse populations. Although preferences differ vastly among people of ethnically diverse populations as to specific nomenclature, for purposes of clarity and ease the following will be used, sometimes interchangeably (based on terminology found in current literature):

- African American or Black
- Hispanic or Latin
- Asian American or Asian/Pacific Islander
- Native American

In this chapter, we focus our attention on four major ethnic groups. We do, however, acknowledge that African Americans, Asian Americans, Hispanics, and Native Americans have been isolated from much of the broader mainstream philanthropic discussions and therefore have created their own philanthropic structures and practices. The structures and practices differ somewhat from each other as much as they differ from the majority in the United States, but there are also some similarities across the various groups. Philanthropy is a valued approach to addressing social issues across ethnic groups. Priorities and traditions for charitable giving will vary, however.

In general, fundraising professionals may need to increase their knowledge and understanding of diverse groups. There may be several models when fundraising from minority groups (Anft, 2002). Compounding the challenges is the fact that ethnic groups have been stereotyped as receivers, not givers, of charity (Newman, 2002). The following discussion of ethnically diverse population groups' philanthropy will help dispel myths and improve understanding of the practice of philanthropy.

Census Data on U.S. Ethnic Diversity

According to the 2010 U.S. Census, approximately 36.3 percent of the population currently belongs to a racial or ethnic minority group. In 2010, non-Hispanic whites were the majority group in the United States, comprising 63.7 percent of the population (U.S. Census Bureau, 2012a). By 2060, non-Hispanic whites will account for 44 percent of the population (U.S. Census Bureau, 2014). The 2010 census also presents a portrait of a changing racial and ethnic landscape with Hispanics accounting for 16.3 percent, African Americans accounting for 12.6 percent, and Native Americans making up 0.9 percent of the nation. It is also interesting to note that multiracial and other groups comprised 1.7 percent of the total population (U.S. Census Bureau, 2012c). The census data also projects that United States is expected to become a "majority–minority" nation by 2044. From 2012 to 2060, the Hispanic and Asian American populations are projected to more than double, with the African American population increasing steadily from 41.2 million to 61.8 million. Multicultural populations are expected to triple in size from 8 million in 2014 to 26 million in 2060 (U.S. Census Bureau, 2014).

Beyond overall numbers, of growing interest to fundraisers and nonprofit leaders is the overall economic and social characteristics of various groups within the U.S. population. We note that, with the exception of Asian Americans, the average income of ethnic and racial groups still lags below the national average of $49,445 (U.S. Census Bureau, 2012c). This gap continues to persist. In 1972 and in 2012, the household income of whites was 1.7 times that of the African American income. The income gap has widened in Hispanic households compared with white households from 1.3 in 1972 to 1.5 in 2012 (Fry, 2013).

Despite significant differences in income and wealth across race and ethnicity, educational attainment has risen at varying rates across all ethnic groups from 1999–2000 to 2009–2010. For example, African Americans and Hispanic students experienced a significant increase in the number of college degrees awarded. The number of bachelor's degrees awarded to African American and Hispanic students increased by 53 percent and 87 percent, respectively, during this period. Master's degrees earned by African Americans and Hispanics more than doubled

TABLE 13.1. U.S. CENSUS DATA BY ETHNICITY IN 2010.

Ethnicity	Percentage of Total U.S. Population (%)	Median Annual Household Income	Median Age (years)	Percentage Living in Poverty (%)
White/non-Hispanics	63.7	$54,620	39.0	9.9
Hispanics	16.3	$37,759	27.0	26.6
African Americans	12.6	$32,068	32.0	27.4
Asian Americans	4.8	$64,308	35.1	12.1
Native Americans	0.9	$35,062	29.0	28.4
Other (single or multiracial)	1.7		19.1	

Note: Adapted from 2010 U.S. Census by U.S. Census Bureau, 2011a.

from 1999–2000 to 2009–2010. Doctoral degrees awarded to Hispanic and African Americans increased by 60 and 47 percent, respectively. The number of degrees awarded to Asian Americans and Native Americans also increased across degree levels (U.S. Department of Education, 2012).

We also note differences in age and household composition by race and ethnicity. The median age of ethnic and racial populations was lower than the overall U.S. median age of 37 years, according to the 2010 U.S. Census. The median age of non-Hispanic whites is about 2 years greater than the national median, while Asian Americans have a median age of 35.1 years – approximately 2 years less than the total median age. African Americans follow with a median age of 32 years while Native Americans and Hispanics have median ages under 30 years to 28 years and 27 years, respectively. The multiracial population's median age is almost half the total median age at 19.1 years. From 2010 to 2060, median age across racial and ethnic groups is projected to increase and more closely approach the national median age at varying rates (U.S. Census Bureau, 2014). Table 13.1 illustrates ethnic diversity in the United States.

Research on Ethnic Diversity and Giving

Research based on data from the Philanthropy Panel Study (PPS), a module in the Panel Study of Income Dynamics (PSID), provides an opportunity to look anew at the implications of an increasingly diverse donor base. Using genealogical sampling, resulting data represent the largest one-time study of philanthropy in the United States and provide a unique opportunity to study the impact of ethnic diversity on charitable giving at the household level.

The data set contains a rich set of economic and sociodemographic variables including racial and ethnic background, migration and labor market experience, and household composition. In addition, it is important to note that the PPS data also contains high-quality data on income and wealth, which are typically unavailable within existing data sets on philanthropic behavior, allowing us to control for the household's economic resources.

In our analysis, we include several household characteristics, such as age of household head, age squared, marital status, gender, educational attainment, race and ethnic origin, family size, unemployment, immigrant status, and household income. To account for regional variation in charitable giving, we classify households into six geographic regions based on their state of residence.

We also fully exploit the rich set of income and wealth measures in order to capture the household's economic position. As permanent income tends to have a larger effect on charitable behavior than transitory income sources (Auten, Holger Sieg, and Clotfelter, 2002), we have also examined several measures of a household's economic position.

An initial analysis may suggest that ethnic and racial identity exerts a major influence on philanthropic behavior. In particular, Asian American households give to charity at the highest rate (71.1 percent) and have the highest average donation ($2,898), followed by nonminority donor households that give at a rate of 66.5 percent and have an average donation of $2,483. A lower percentage of African American (45.0 percent) and Hispanic households (45.1 percent) give to charitable causes and average total donation amounts for these households are less than half of the average donations of Asian American households. It is important that these initial statistics do not account for differences in income, education, wealth, and socioeconomic conditions.

However, although the initial PPS data shows lower giving incidence and amounts given for households headed by an African American or Hispanic as compared to a nonminority head, this difference does not hold up when we include controls for education, income, and wealth. When we account for education, income, wealth, and other demographic variables, a household having an African American and/or Hispanic household head is not significantly different either in incidence of giving or total amount given when compared to other ethnic and racial groups.

PPS data show that informal giving, or noninstitutional giving, is greater in minority households compared to nonminority households when we do not account for differences in income, wealth, and socioeconomic conditions. However, when we adjust for income, wealth, and demographic variables, we do not find significant differences in informal giving. Tables 13.2 to 13.4 illustrate the dynamics of philanthropy and ethnicity.

TABLE 13.2. OVERALL GIVING RATE BY HEAD OF HOUSEHOLD'S ETHNICITY.

Ethnicity	Giving Rate (%)	Average Total Donation
Nonminority head	66.5	$2,438
Hispanic head	45.1	$1,141
African American head	45.0	$1,316
Asian American head	71.1	$2,898
Other race head	60.0	$2,460

TABLE 13.3. INFORMAL GIVING INCIDENCE BY HEAD OF HOUSEHOLD'S ETHNICITY.

Ethnicity	Informal Giving Incidence (%)
Nonminority head	11.8
Hispanic head	12.6
African American head	12.8
Asian American head	13.3
Other race head	15.1

Related Studies

Existing research suggests that gender, income, education, and occupational status can influence giving and volunteering. Studies such as Rooney et al. (2005) examine the effect of ethnicity on philanthropy, while controlling for other variables. They utilized methodologies that rely "on the memories of respondents" and found no differences when comparing nonminority groups to minority groups in both the probability of giving and the amount given. Framing of the prompts affects the response of the participant, suggesting that there may be differences in the way in which ethnic groups respond to social interactions or even in exhibiting philanthropic behaviors.

Blackbaud's *Diversity in Giving* (Rovner, 2015) survey finds that donor habits and priorities do indeed differ subtly among ethnic groups surveyed. For example, 45 percent of Hispanics and 50 percent of African Americans prioritize giving to places of worship, compared with 34 percent of Asian Americans. Response vehicles also differ. African Americans and Hispanics tend to value giving more spontaneously, while Asian Americans are more likely to research and plan before giving

TABLE 13.4. DEMOGRAPHIC DATA BY HEAD OF HOUSEHOLD'S ETHNICITY.

Ethnicity	Age	Female	Total Family Income	Total Wealth	No College	Some College	Bachelors	Advanced Degree
Nonminority head	53	29.20%	$76,780	$277,510	40.30%	23.90%	20.10%	12.50%
Hispanic head	46	26.70%	$53,433	$51,949	64.70%	16.70%	6.80%	6.40%
African American head	48	49.80%	$44,328	$28,913	56.50%	26.30%	9.00%	5.10%
Asian American head	52	24.30%	$90,589	$334,932	20.70%	10.60%	33.90%	20.20%
Other race head	52	19.60%	$70,814	$247,570	37.90%	21.30%	23.90%	12.00%

to a cause. Values, such as the importance of giving, and indicators of giving, such as faith, are widely exhibited across all ethnic groups. Social networks also influence philanthropic decisions. Requests for support from friends and family tend to take precedence over organizational requests for 49 percent of Asian Americans. Personal engagement is valued as 28 percent of African Americans and 22 percent of Hispanics say that they have made a donation to a canvasser on the street, compared with 18 percent of the overall donor population. Giving through direct response channels, such as direct mail, lags behind the overall donor universe. The study emphasizes the under-representation of African American and Hispanic groups in the overall donor population. Asian American engagement is consistent with the overall Asian population, however (Rovner, 2015).

Ethnic Diversity's Impact on Charitable Giving

Ethnic diversity challenges the way in which we advance philanthropy. In an increasingly diverse United States, we must consider all forms of human generosity and the ways in which we provide opportunities for philanthropy. Ethnicity does not determine donors' likelihood of giving or the amount they will give (Rooney et al., 2005). However, ethnicity can influence the way in which donors think about philanthropy and their giving priorities. The PPS data indicate that although a greater amount of ethnic diversity within a community tends to have a negative impact on household giving to collective purposes in today's diverse communities, ethnic diversity can increase the probability of contributions and total amount contributed as more diverse groups form their own organizations – and as the size and scope of the nonprofit sector increases.

It is generally thought that the three main reasons that account for what may be a negative relationship between diversity and a low rate of giving are the difficulty of agreeing on communitywide objectives, the tendency to keep giving within a specific ethnic group, and the high "transaction costs" – such as time spent breaking down language barriers and building trust – among different groups. Fundraisers have struggled with these challenges in attracting donors, leading to under-representation of African American and Hispanic groups in the donor population. For example, 20 percent of African American donors and 18 percent of Latino donors (compared with 9 percent of overall donors) say that they would support more nonprofits if they were asked more often and 21 percent of Latinos stated they would support more nonprofits if they knew how (compared with 10 percent of overall donors) (Rovner, 2015). To overcome such challenges, fundraisers and nonprofit sector leaders can strive to recognize each of the distinct groups within their communities to "forge a community identity as well as celebrating differences."

Identity-based philanthropy, defined as a "growing movement to democratize philanthropy by activating and organizing its practice in marginalized communities," is one method utilized to support these minority donor populations (W.K. Kellogg Foundation, 2012). The movement challenges the gap that exists between the under-represented and over-represented in philanthropic contributions to mainstream institutions and promotes visibility of the multitude of ways in which ethnic groups express generosity. By leveraging resources through diverse fundraising vehicles, identity-based philanthropy also empowers marginalized populations with "knowledge, enthusiasm, expertise, activism, and pride" (W.K. Kellogg Foundation, 2012).

Informal Giving

For many ethnically diverse populations, philanthropy is seen in the broadest sense – gifts of time, talent, and treasure – and revolves around family, church, and education. Giving behavior may be highly influenced by leaders – religious, community, professional, social, and family. Informal giving has been an important aspect of philanthropy that persists within specific ethnic communities. There may be distrust for traditional nonprofits and direct support to extended family members may be important. Caretaking responsibilities may be assumed by families rather than government, private, or nonprofit groups. From sheltering a neighbor in need to contributions to a grassroots movement, giving generously through noninstitutional means may be a valued approach to philanthropy within diverse communities.

The Role of Immigration

An important issue in understanding ethnic diversity now and in the future is the impact of immigration on U.S. philanthropy. In 2010, 12.9 percent of the U.S. population was foreign-born. Over half of all foreign-born individuals are from Latin America, with 55 percent of these individuals born in Mexico. Asian immigrants follow – comprising 28 percent of the foreign-born population – while 12 percent come from Europe, 4 percent are from Africa, and 2.6 percent are from other regions. The immigrant population is estimated to reach 78 million (or 19 percent of the total U.S. population) by 2050 (U.S. Census Bureau, 2012b).

One important point for nonprofit leaders and practitioners is the geographic variation in the foreign-born population across the United States. Based on the most recent census data, population varies by state. California (27 percent), New York (22 percent), and New Jersey (21 percent) rank the highest percentages in

TABLE 13.5. ORIGIN OF THE FOREIGN-BORN POPULATION IN 2010.

Country of Origin	Percentage of Total Foreign-Born Population (%)
Africa	4.0
Asia	28.2
Europe	12.1
Latin America and the Caribbean	53.1
Other	2.6

Note: Adapted from 2010 U.S. Census by U.S. Census Bureau, 2012b.

TABLE 13.6. HOUSEHOLD INCOME BY NATIVITY OF HOUSEHOLDER.

Householder Origin	Median Annual Household Income	Percentage Living in Poverty (%)
Native-born	$50,288	14.4
Foreign-born	$43,750	19.9
Naturalized citizen	$52,642	11.3
Not a citizen	$36,401	26.7

Note: Adapted from 2010 U.S. Census by U.S. Census Bureau, 2012b.

foreign-born populations, with more than half of all immigrants in the United States residing in these states. States such as Texas, Nevada, and Florida also exceed the national average of 12.9 percent, while states in the midwest, with the exception of Illinois, tend to have foreign-born populations that are less than eight percent (U.S. Census Bureau, 2012b). Data about current U.S. immigrant origins, based on the 2010 Census, are illustrated in Tables 13.5 and 13.6.

Immigration and Philanthropy

Similar to earlier waves of U.S. immigrants, more recent immigrants bring traditions, religions, and cultures and have the potential to contribute to America's philanthropic institutions (Jackson et al., 2012). "Government tax rates, the importance of religion, whether 'unofficial' giving to family and social contacts is widely practiced, and a nation's wealth" can influence the way in which generosity is expressed (Osili and Du, 2003). Immigrants to the United States are often shaped by philanthropic practices in their country of origin and may be resistant to adopting the "United States' model of institutional philanthropy" (Osili and Du, 2003).

Foreign-born individuals who have resided in the United States for 10 years or less tend to exhibit lower rates of volunteerism and formal charitable giving – suggesting that cultural philanthropic traditions, social networks, and residential segregation may influence participation (Osili and Du, 2003). After 10 years, this effect lessens and immigrants tend to engage in charitable giving that is more aligned with American philanthropic practices (Osili and Du, 2003). Immigrants who have migrated from countries with similar philanthropic institutions to the United States may assimilate at faster rates than immigrants coming from countries with dissimilar traditions (Jackson et al., 2012). Considering diverse forms of philanthropic activity by informal and formal means, immigrant households do not significantly differ overall from native households in charitable giving, after controlling for household variables such as permanent income (Osili and Du, 2003; Aldrich, 2011).

Charitable giving traditions vary across immigrant populations. Informal philanthropy to extended family and mutual aid societies is a common practice. Motivated by social networks and sometimes reciprocity, immigrants are 10 percent more likely to send private transfers or remittances to individuals living outside the household, particularly to those living in countries of origin. In 2014, remittances to developing countries were estimated to amount to $583 billion, making these private transfer networks vital to developing countries. This figure is a lower estimate, not including in-kind gifts and other forms of generosity (Osili and Du, 2003; The World Bank, 2015). Social relationships are strongly influential in determining values and priorities. Aldrich (2011) suggests ways in which fundraisers can effectively invite immigrants to participate in philanthropy:

- *Provide access to volunteering opportunities.* Volunteering is a primary way in which immigrants become engaged in philanthropy. Make sure that your organization provides volunteer opportunities that are welcoming to immigrants and reach out to immigrants so that they know that these opportunities exist and so that they feel welcome to participate.
- *Identify philanthropic projects that appeal to immigrants' interests.* Work with your immigrant supporters to create win–win opportunities that help them achieve their philanthropic vision through your organization's programs.
- *Use social networks to build trust and engagement.* Use the importance of relationships and extended family and social groups to create a critical mass among your immigrant supporters.
- *Invite immigrants into your organization's leadership.* Show how your organization values your immigrant constituencies by including them in decision-making groups, such as board committees, task forces, and staff.

- *Ask them to share their philanthropic traditions.* Engage in conversations about philanthropy, giving, and volunteering so that native-born and immigrant supporters can both benefit from a richer understanding of each other's heritage of philanthropy.
- *Invite them to give.* Let them know that they are valued members of your organization by inviting immigrant constituents to give just as you would any other supporter.

Embracing Diversity in Fundraising

Today nonprofit institutions are increasingly embracing diversity as a mission and organizational value. Guided by principles and practices in emerging literature, such as that of W.K. Kellogg Foundation's *Cultures of Giving* initiative, organizations are promoting identity-based philanthropy – leveraging resources, diversifying support, and empowering ethnically diverse communities to elevate social change. As of 2012, identity-based funds distributed nearly $400 million per year – much of these funds raised by ethnically diverse populations (W.K. Kellogg Foundation, 2012). These institutions increasingly seek to access the economic growth and power of Hispanics, African Americans, Asian Americans, and other diverse population groups. For example, nonprofit organizations are strengthening their internal and external strategies by hosting forums and affinity groups to promote inclusion in outreach efforts to ethnically diverse communities (United Way, 2013). For many organizations, enhancing their ability to reach diverse groups is a critical component of building and managing credible, comprehensive fundraising programs.

At the same time, diversity may present some challenge to fundraisers. Ethnically diverse groups may be associated with identifiable, distinct, and significant philanthropic characteristics and traits. Therefore, fundraisers find that in order to be successful, they must tailor their fundraising appeals to the prospective donors' customs and sensibilities. In commenting on the new rules for engaging ethnically diverse donors, Carson said, "Fundraising in the 21st century will require a differentiated approach tailored to the interests, values, and traditions of the many rather than a one-size-fits-all approach based on the interests, values, and traditions of white Americans" (Rovner, 2015, p. 3).

Newman (2002) points out that the traditional donor pyramid works well for organizations that raise most of their charitable gifts from white donors but that it is not applicable for many cultures because of its hierarchical nature and the element of time involved in the donor development process. Newman presents a continuum of philanthropy that begins with families concerned with survival and basic needs, moving to those who help others who have less, and concluding with people who will invest in their communities and institutions to accomplish common and visionary goals. The continuum, therefore, as it moves from left to right, involves the labels of "survive," "help," and "invest" (Newman, 2002).

A review of the literature in fundraising among ethnically diverse populations indicates that traditional fundraising principles have to be adapted to changing donor populations. The fundraising professional needs to consider variations on donor approaches, including one-on-one solicitation, direct mail, use of the Internet, and telephone solicitation. Dissemination of information and knowledge sharing, through practices such as workshops, will help inform prospective donors and partners on models for impacting social issues (Jackson et al., 2012). Prospect research strategies must be redefined to capture information that is relevant and suitable to diverse donor identification and cultivation. Volunteers representing various ethnic groups will need to be recruited and trained.

Perhaps prior to modifying or enhancing fundraising strategies and practices, however, is for organizations to commit to diversity, both internally and among constituents and donors, to modify the organizational mission so that it reflects this commitment, and to provide any necessary training or programs that create awareness of diversity issues. To accomplish this, an organization must have top-level leadership support as well as diversity in its ranks. A needs statement should be crafted that identifies the organization's status regarding diversity, its willingness to embrace diversity, and how diversity issues fit into the organization framework. Identity-based affinity groups can advise on outreach in diverse communities. From there, best practices can be developed through study and research, and a transformational program established. Examining constituency networks can help fundraisers better understand the role and potential of philanthropy in ethnically diverse communities. Strategies that have demonstrated success for diversifying staff and the donor pool include internship and fellowship programs, and diversity funds (Chao, 2008).

Conclusion

Given the fact that growth rates among non-white and Latino populations are projected to far outpace growth rates for the majority white population, there is a growing recognition of implications of diversity for communities throughout the United States (U.S. Census Bureau, 2012a). This fact provides organizations with new opportunities to understand and interact with rich differences in languages, values, and cultural practices.

Research on diversity shows that fundraisers need to diversify strategies to meet the unique interests and priorities of donors. However, embracing diversity extends beyond fundraising among ethnically diverse constituents, and also in promoting diverse voices at the core of the organization. A growing literature suggests that equitable representation among internal and external stakeholders is a priority for many nonprofit institutions. With more tools and resources, fundraisers can seek to engage diverse voices in order to build a more comprehensive understanding of an increasingly diverse population.

Discussion Questions

1) Why should fundraisers be concerned about ethnicity and philanthropy?
2) List three ways traditional fundraising approaches might be changed to appeal to different ethnic groups.
3) How does immigration impact fundraising?
4) How might the typical donor pyramid be reshaped for different ethnic groups?

CHAPTER FOURTEEN

GENERATIONAL DIFFERENCES IN GIVING

By Amy N. Thayer and Derrick Feldmann

As fundraisers look to the future of giving and volunteering, perhaps no other factor is as important as a consideration of the ways in which generational differences will affect the philanthropic landscape. Research related to differences in giving among the generations show pronounced differences in preferences and identities between individuals born before 1964 and those born since then. These differences are important for a number of reasons, including the need for nonprofit organizations to engage the younger generations in their activities *now* so that Generation X and Millennials will transition into the core group of donors as the population ages. The giving and volunteering patterns of people born since 1964 will become increasingly important for charitable organizations in coming decades, and those involved in fundraising will need to take into account numerous factors important to Generation X and Millennials. Diversity in engagement strategies and types of donations solicited, rethinking the role of the workplace, and new ways of describing how gifts achieve impact are just some items for consideration.

Generations and Giving Patterns

The parameters for defining when a particular generation starts and ends are nonstandardized, and nearly every generational investigation indicates there is flexibility around the boundary years selected. To discuss charitable giving among the four most recent generations, the following terms, boundaries, and descriptions are presented for the following age cohorts:

- Before Boomers/Matures: born 1945 or earlier.

    The Before Boomers/Matures were born during the Great Depression and grew up during a time when television, telephones, home appliances, and automobiles were being mass produced. Familial structures often included extended family and social relationships were developed within the schools, communities of faith, and neighborhood associations. This generation is commonly characterized by their loyalty, hard work, devotion to work, respect for authority, and working towards the common good.

- Boomers: born 1946 to 1964.

    The Boomers are a generation distinguished by Post World War II affluence, civil rights movements for women, homosexuals, and racial/ethnic minorities, the exploration of space, the Cold War, and the Vietnam War. While they were predominantly reared in nuclear families, television and peer groups were important elements in the Boomers' cultural and social development. This generation is typified by a sense of security that allowed for the exploration of new and innovative ideas and the protestation of inequalities. Additionally, Boomers are characterized as hopeful and optimistic and as valuing youth, material wealth, and health.

- Generation X: born 1965 to 1980 (some end this generation in 1976).

    Generation X is a cohort signified by the post-civil rights movement and during the time of both the Watergate scandal and the Vietnam War. This generation was the first to grow up with significantly high rates of divorced parents, thus receiving social support and interaction mostly from their peers and mass media. Generation X appreciates balance in their life – that is, they value meaningful work that offers an appropriate salary, but are equally concerned about securing opportunities for free time and to have fun. This generation eagerly adopted technology like the personal computer and the Internet, and they have only known diversity and equality to be the norm.

- Millennials: born 1980 to 2000 (some start this generation in 1977 and end it in the 1990s).

    The Millennials are the most educated, technologically advanced, and racially/ethnically diverse generation in history. This group has never known the world without advanced technology such as microwave ovens, personal computers, and the World Wide Web, which therefore has increased their procurement of global information and their cultivation of international relationships.

They place importance upon a healthy and active body and are described as fiercely loyal to family and friends. The Millennials are often characterized as exemplifying the work ethic of the Baby Boomers while using the technological acumen of Generation X.

Household Income and Generation

Boomers accounted for the largest number of households (44 million) in the United States in 2009. Boomers also have the largest number of households (19.3 million) with incomes above $75,000. The next largest group is Generation X, which has 34.3 million households, of which 11.5 million have incomes of $75,000 or more. Next are the Baby Boomers, with a total of 24.4 million households, with 5.9 million having incomes of $75,000 or more. Finally, Millennials, the youngest generational cohort, account for approximately 11.2 million households, with only 2.1 million realizing incomes of $75,000 or more (Demographics Now, 2010).

Generation X and Millennials account for 13.6 million households with incomes of $75,000 or more – twice as many as the 5.9 million Before Boomer households in this income range and almost two-thirds of the number of Boomer households at this income level. Additionally, recent research has estimated Generation X and Millennials are positioned to inherit nearly $40 trillion in the near future – which could be donated to charity (21/64 and Dorothy A. Johnson Center for Philanthropy, 2013). The future of charitable giving clearly lies with Generation X and the Millennials, who are now or will soon be entering peak earning years, assuming greater leadership roles, and controlling large sums of money, which will include charitable dollars.

The Effect of Cohort and Lifecycle Effects on Giving

When fundraisers look at distinctions in giving among the generations, they should consider the difference between *cohort* effects and *lifecycle* effects. A cohort effect is characteristic of people in the group throughout their lives. For example, if people who lived through the economic scarcity of the Great Depression have had their attitudes toward money and philanthropy permanently affected as a result, that is a cohort effect. A lifecycle effect changes as individuals age. An example would be a young person who is more generous in her forties than she was in her twenties because as she ages, she has more disposable income to devote to philanthropy, and perhaps her values and priorities change with age. Continued research asking the same questions over time will help answer these and other questions about lifecycle and cohort effects on charitable giving and volunteering.

Although a number of factors are known to be associated with giving (e.g., income, household wealth, education level, marital status, number of children in the household, and employment status), it is clear there are still distinct differences in giving between Generation X and Millennials and the older Before Boomer and Boomer generations. Millennials and Generation X demonstrate a lower rate of giving and lower dollar amounts given than either the Boomers or Before Boomers. A recent study released by Blackbaud and Edge Research indicates approximately the same percentage of Millennials and Generation X report giving charitably. However, while Generation X donates less money than Boomers and Before Boomers, the amount they donate is more than one and one half times the amount Millennials give (Rovner, 2013).

It is not yet known if the differences in giving between Millennials and the older generations are a result of the cohort effect or the lifecycle effect. Lower rates of giving by Generation X combined with lower rates of giving and lower amounts of giving by Millennials may be indicative of the decreased engagement of individuals in these generations with religious institutions when compared to Boomers and Before Boomers. In 2013 an estimated $105.53 billion – the largest portion of charitable dollars – or 31 percent of the overall total of charitable giving was contributed to religious organizations (The Lilly Family School of Philanthropy, *Giving USA*, 2014a); according to the Jumpstart and Indiana University Lilly Family School of Philanthropy study, *Connected to Give: Faith Communities*, over half (55 percent) of Americans indicate that their faith is an important influence in their charitable giving decisions and that nearly three-fourths (73 percent) of all charitable gifts by Americans is allocated to religiously associated organizations. Nevertheless, more Millennials (29 percent) and Generation X (21 percent) report being unaffiliated with a religion than either Boomers (16 percent) or Before Boomers (9 percent) (Pew Research Center, 2014).

Financial security is also a significant factor impacting the number and amount of charitable contributions; therefore, another plausible explanation for the divergence in giving by generations is the economic climate faced by the Millennials, in particular, as they entered both post-secondary institutions and the job market. Realizing lower levels of income and wealth in addition to higher rates of poverty, unemployment, and educational loan debt than any of the three older generations did at the same point in their lifecycle, 71 percent of Millennials report encountering a more challenging financial environment than that of their parents' generation when they were young (Pew Research Center, 2014). Clearly, economic standing may have strong implications for giving, but so too do each generation's distinct values, preferences, and behaviors for giving.

Giving Profiles by Generation

This section presents detailed information about how each generation gives, including the number and percentage who give, average annual gift total, and number of charities supported. Data are for 2013 and are from the Blackbaud and Edge Research study (Rovner, 2013). Also included are insights about which causes are most important to each of the generations, how they engage with the primary charitable organizations they support, and what channels of transaction they use. Data are derived from the Blackbaud and Edge Research study (Rovner, 2013) and the Convio and Edge Research study (Bhagat, Loeb, and Rovner, 2010), each of which surveyed a representative sample of between 1,000 and 1,500 charitable donors.

Shared Giving Characteristics of All Generations

Giving by individuals in 2013 was estimated to total $240.60 billion – 72 percent of total giving (*Giving USA*, 2014). Table 14.1 illustrates specific giving characteristics by generation as reported in the Blackbaud and Edge Research study (Rovner, 2013). Boomers comprise the largest group of donors, although the majority in each generation gives. While Millennials give the lowest average annual gift and support the fewest charities, they also plan to increase both the financial gifts donated as well as the number of charities supported, more than any other generation.

Causes The top charitable causes supported by all generations are similar when donors select them from a list, as in the Blackbaud and Edge Research study, results of which are summarized in Table 14.2. Across the generations the top five charitable causes that individuals were likely to support were local social service, place of worship, health charities, children's charities, and education. Although each generation shares interest in the first four causes, albeit with different priorities, there is variance in the fifth selected cause by generation (Rovner, 2013).

Engagement The principal form of engagement with a donor's primary charity across all generations was providing monetary donations, followed by donating goods, visiting the charity's website, and volunteering (summarized in Table 14.3). However, differences were present between the older generations who perceived that monetary donations made the greatest difference for the charity and the younger generations who reported they believed they could make the most

TABLE 14.1. GIVING STATISTICS FOR ALL UNITED STATES GENERATIONS (2013).

Generation	Number of Donors	Percentage Making Charitable Gifts	Average Annual Gift	Future Dollar Amount of Charitable Giving Will Increase	Number of Charities Supported	Will Support Additional Charities in the Future	Percentage Making Charitable Gifts More than Once a Year
Before Boomers	27.1 million	88%	$1,367	10%	6.2	4%	45%
Boomers	51.0 million	72%	$1,212	10%	4.5	2%	47%
Generation X	39.5 million	59%	$732	18%	3.9	6%	50%
Millennials	32.8 million	60%	$481	21%	3.3	13%	41%

Source: The Next Generation of American Giving: The Charitable Giving Habits of Generations Y, X, Baby Boomers, and Matures, Blackbaud and Edge Research, authored by Mark Rovner.

TABLE 14.2. TOP CHARITABLE CAUSES FOR ALL UNITED STATES GENERATIONS (2013).

Generation	1	2	3	4	5
All Generations	Local Social Service (44%)	Place of Worship (41%)	Health Charities (39%)	Children's Charities (34%)	Education (29%)
Before Boomers	Place of Worship (46%)	Local Social Service (37%)	Health Charities (23%)	Troops/ Veterans (22%)	Education and Children's Charities (20%)
Boomers	Place of Worship (38%)	Local Social Service (36%)	Children's Charities (22%)	Health Charities (19%)	Animal Rescue/ Protection (18%)
Generation X	Place of Worship (36%)	Local Social Service (29%)	Children's Charities (28%)	Health Charities (24%)	Animal Rescue/ Protection (21%)
Millennials	Children's Charities (29%)	Place of Worship (22%)	Health Charities (20%)	Local Social Service (19%)	Education (17%)

Source: The Next Generation of American Giving: The Charitable Giving Habits of Generations Y, X, Baby Boomers, and Matures, Blackbaud and Edge Research, authored by Mark Rovner.

TABLE 14.3. HOW DONORS ENGAGE WITH TOP CHARITY FOR ALL UNITED STATES GENERATIONS (2010).

Generation	Donations Directly to Charity	Donate Goods (Clothing, Food)	Visit Charity's Website	Volunteer
All Generations	68%	28%	23%	13%
Before Boomers	81%	23%	13%	7%
Boomers	76%	30%	20%	11%
Generation X	66%	30%	23%	17%
Millennials	50%	26%	34%	14%

Source: The Next Generation of American Giving: A Study on the Multichannel Preferences, and Charitable Habits, of Generation Y, Generation X, Baby Boomers, and Matures, Convio and Edge Research, authored by Vinay Bhagat, Pam Loeb, and Mark Rovner.

TABLE 14.4. DONORS' TRANSACTION/GIVING CHANNELS FOR ALL UNITED STATES GENERATIONS (2010).

Generation	Checkout Donations	Purchase of Proceeds	Online Donation	Pledge	Honor/ Tribute Gift	Mailed Check/ Credit Card
All Generations	50%	40%	39%	35%	32%	32%
Before Boomers	44%	36%	27%	38%	42%	52%
Boomers	53%	41%	42%	39%	42%	40%
Generation X	51%	42%	40%	39%	24%	22%
Millennials	52%	39%	47%	22%	17%	10%

Source: The Next Generation of American Giving: The Charitable Giving Habits of Generations Y, X, Baby Boomers, and Matures, Blackbaud and Edge Research, authored by Mark Rovner.

difference for the charity by spreading the word, fundraising for the charity, and volunteering (Bhagat, Loeb, and Rovner, 2010).

Transaction/Giving Channels This term refers to the ways in which individuals made donations to charities. Checkout donations, purchase of proceeds, and online donations were the top three donation points across the generations. The three younger generations selected these channels as the top three transaction types, but with different priorities. Only Before Boomers selected primary channels differently (Rovner, 2013). These findings are presented in Table 14.4.

The differences in likelihood to support a specific cause, the ways in which individuals from distinct generations choose to engage with organizations, and the channels through which they donate are important considerations when fundraisers are determining how to effectively involve members of each generation in giving. The distinctive giving characteristics, causes supported, engagement, and transaction channels of each generation are explored in the following sections.

Before Boomers

People born before 1945 are now retired or are planning to phase out of their active professional lives. Many will continue to work either part-time or as consultants. People in this generation have been important contributors to nonprofit organizations for decades, through their volunteer work, board and committee service, and financial support. They report having strong feelings of loyalty to charities they have supported in the past.

Giving Characteristics Approximately 26 percent of all monetary donations come from the 27.1 million (or 88 percent) of Before Boomer donors. This generation contributes the highest average annual gift ($1,367) and supports the most number of charities (6.2) among the generations. Before Boomers' giving looks to remain stable in the near future with only 10 percent indicating they will increase the amount of their giving and 4 percent reporting they will support additional charities in the coming years (Rovner, 2013).

Causes   Nearly half (46 percent) of Before Boomers rank place of worship as their top charitable cause followed by local social service (37 percent), which is similar to the priorities of Boomers and Generation X. However, nearly a quarter (23 percent) of Before Boomers, like Millennials, report that health charities are a third priority. Before Boomers are unique from any of the other groups in that they support troops/veterans (22 percent), perhaps signaling a cohort effect (Rovner, 2013).

Engagement.   Most Before Boomers (81 percent) became engaged with their top charity by donating money and fewest in this group became involved by volunteering with the charity (7 percent). Although these responses emulate the engagement trend across generations, these percentages are extreme when compared to any of the other generations (Bhagat, Loeb, and Rovner, 2010). Further, when indicating ways they believed they could make the most difference with a charity, more Before Boomers selected volunteering (24 percent) than Boomers (20 percent). Far fewer Before Boomers report spreading the word (8 percent) as a way to make the most difference in a charity than any of the other generations (Rovner, 2013).

Transaction/Giving Channels   Unlike any other generation, most Before Boomers – more than half – give to charity by mailed check/credit card (52 percent). Moreover, Before Boomers were the least likely to give by making online donations (27 percent). Equal percentages of Before Boomers and Boomers give to charities via an honor/tribute gift (42 percent), although Boomers rank this mechanism as their second highest channel, tied with online donations, and Before Boomers rank it third (Rovner, 2013).

Boomers

Arguably the most studied generation to date, Boomers have long been the focus of marketers and are still a dominant economic force in the United States and internationally.

Giving Characteristics   Boomers are responsible for 40 percent of all monetary donations, which come from the 51.0 million (or 72 percent) of donors in this generational cohort. Boomers contribute the second highest average annual gift ($1,212) and support the second most number of charities (4.5) among the generations. Like the generation preceding them, Boomers' giving looks to remain stable in the near future, with 10 percent indicating they will increase the amount of their giving and only 2 percent reporting they will support additional charities in the coming years (Rovner, 2013).

Causes   Similar to the generations before and after them, most Boomers (38 percent) rank place of worship as the primary cause to which they give, followed closely by local social service (36 percent). Conversely, the remaining three priorities mirror Generation X: children's charities (22 percent), health charities (19 percent), and animal rescue/protection (18 percent). In fact, Boomers' top five priorities are identical to Generation X.

Engagement   More than three-fourths of Boomers (76 percent) became engaged with their top charity by donating money. Like Generation X, 30 percent of Boomers provided goods to organizations as a means of engagement, a higher percentage than either Before Boomers (23 percent) or Millennials (26 percent) (Bhagat, Loeb, and Rovner, 2010). Finally, more Boomers than any other generation indicated they would engage in fundraising activities (7 percent) to make the most difference with a charity. Conversely, no Boomers (0 percent) reported that they could make the most difference with a charity by advocacy efforts, which is lower than any other generation (Rovner, 2013).

Transaction/Giving Channels   Most Boomers, like Generation X and Millennials, give to charity by checkout donations (53 percent). Boomers were equally as likely to give by donating online (42 percent) or providing an honor/tribute gift (42 percent). Finally, comparable proportions of Boomers and Generation X gave via pledge (39 percent), which was slightly higher than Before Boomers (38 percent) and much higher than the 22 percent of Millennials (Rovner, 2013).

Generation X

Despite having fewer members than the Boomer or Millennial generations, this generation has become one of the major creative economic forces in recent decades. Generation X has distinguished itself through its interest in nontraditional ways to give back, including social entrepreneurship.

Giving Characteristics   Approximately 20 percent of all monetary donations come from the 39.5 million (or 59 percent) of Generation X donors. This generation contributes less money and to fewer charities than either the Before Boomers or Boomers, but more than Millennials, with an average annual gift of \$732 and support of 3.9 charities. However, only 18 percent of Generation X report they will increase the amount of their giving and 6 percent indicate they will support additional charities in the coming years, both of which are less/fewer than Millennials (Rovner, 2013).

Causes   Generation X, similar to the Millennials in many ways, also demonstrates likeness to Boomers in their prioritization of the top five causes they support. Like Boomers, Generation X ranks place of worship (36 percent) and local social service (29 percent) as first and second priorities, albeit both at lower percentages than Boomers. The remaining three causes also mirror Boomers' selections: children's charities (28 percent), health charities (24 percent), and animal protection/rescue (21 percent), although these percentages are higher than reported by Boomers.

Engagement   Two-thirds (66 percent) of Generation X become engaged with their top charity through direct donations, and less than a third (30 percent) do so through goods donations. Surprisingly, less than a quarter (23 percent) of Generation X, compared to 34 percent of Millennials, engage with their primary charity through website visits (Bhagat, Loeb, and Rovner, 2010). Although Generation X demonstrates a clear distinction between pathways to engage with charities, when reporting the ways they could make the most difference with a charity, this generation selected donating money (36 percent) and volunteering (31 percent) at nearly equal rates (Rovner, 2013).

Transaction/Giving Channels   Generation X closely mirrors Millennials in the rankings of ways they give in that Generation X is most likely to give through checkout donations (51 percent) and least likely to give by mailed check/credit card (22 percent). However, while Generation X ranks giving online (40 percent) as their third most likely way to give, nearly half (47 percent) of Millennials give online, their second ranked preferred method of giving. Moreover, while both Generation X and Millennials rank pledges as the third most likely way to give, a much higher proportion of Generation X (39 percent) than Millennials (22 percent) give in that way (Rovner, 2013).

Millennials

By some estimates, there are 80 million Millennials; other estimates put the number of Millennials even higher. However, note that the definition of this generation can include people born in 2000, so many in this group are still years away from adulthood. The oldest Millennials turned 35 in 2015.

Giving Characteristics   Nearly 11 percent of all monetary donations come from the 60 percent, or 32.8 million, Millennial donors. This group donates the lowest average annual gift ($481) and supports the fewest number of charities (3.3) among the generations. However, over one-fifth (21 percent) indicate they will increase the dollar amount of their donations in the future and 13 percent reveal they will support additional charities in the future – much higher percentages than any of the other generations (Rovner, 2013). Not much data exist about earlier generations' giving patterns when they were in their late teens and early twenties, so it is difficult to know whether the lower amounts here are cohort or lifecycle effects.

Causes   Millennials, unlike their elder generations, did not rank place of worship as their top charitable cause. Instead, Millennials ranked children's charities (29 percent) as the most likely recipient of their charitable dollars, followed by place of worship (22 percent) and health charities (20 percent). Local social service charities (19 percent) were Millennials' fourth ranked cause to which they would likely make a donation, in contrast to the older generations, who all selected it as a second priority (Rovner, 2013). These findings support other research suggesting that Millennials are more interested in supporting causes that help people and not institutions (Millennial Impact Report, 2013).

Engagement   Although members of this generation, like the three generations before them, most frequently became engaged with their top charity by donating money (50 percent), far more Millennials (34 percent) than Generation X (23 percent), Boomers (20 percent), or Before Boomers (13 percent) engaged with a charity through the organization's website (Bhagat, Loeb, and Rovner, 2010). Further, when indicating ways they believed they could make the most difference with a charity, more Millennials selected volunteering (30 percent) over donating money (25 percent). Nearly the same percentage of Generation X also selected volunteering (31 percent), although it was not their number one choice (Rovner, 2013).

Transaction/Giving Channels   Like Boomers and Generation X, most Millennials participate in checkout donations (52 percent) as a means to give to charity. However, Millennials were more likely to give by making online donations (47 percent) than any other generation, and far less likely to make a pledge (22 percent), honor/tribute gift (17 percent), or mailed check/credit card (10 percent) as transaction/giving channels than all of the other generations (Rovner, 2013).

This finding suggests that Millennials are perhaps more immediate with their giving and more technologically savvy in the channels through which they give.

Engaging the Next Generation of Donors

As the data suggest, younger generations are supporting charitable causes, although not yet at the rates of their predecessors. Historically, each generation builds wealth and interest in certain causes based upon education and their experience with causes. The question for debate is how will that happen given a new generation's approach to volunteerism and giving. Based upon the Millennial Impact Report, a comprehensive analysis of more than 30,000 Millennials, it is clear fundraisers need to be mindful of new approaches and understand the motivation, interests, and perspectives of the following trends (2014).

Events: The First Fundraising Experience

The first philanthropic experience of Millennials is event style fundraising. This approach to fundraising has remained a dominant entry point for this generation as 63 percent of Millennials raised money through event style fundraising and more than 50 percent of them supported a friend at an event fundraiser (Millennial Impact Report, 2013). Most Millennials have grown up with fundraisers at schools and while at college experienced events to raise money for their club or organization's activities. Therefore, the event-based model and fundraising efforts were already part of their cause and nonprofit sector experience. Fundraisers need to be mindful of this trend and look at events to inspire interest and participation by Millennials and their peers.

Millennials Engage with Causes to Help Others, Not Institutions

Friends and peers motivate a Millennial's passion for a specific cause, not necessarily an institution or organization. This level of cause or charitable involvement is inspired by how the Millennial can cause change or help change someone's (beneficiary) life for the better. Ultimately, they want to support a cause, help other people, and become part of a community (digital and in-person) that is equally excited and eager to make a difference. This interest in issue-based fundraising inspires the generation to give. Millennials are also most likely to donate to a nonprofit when they feel inspired and the organization is able to stimulate their personal interests through peers and digital marketing for the cause (Millennial Impact Report,

2010). Fundraisers have historically focused on the institution's brand first. The Millennial approach is a change where the individual is attracted to the cause issue rather than the institution. Fundraisers need to look at changing the solicitation message to build a relationship between the individual and the beneficiary through image, video, and an authentic case for support.

Millennials Prefer Smaller Actions before Fully Committing to a Cause

In addition to events, the majority of Millennial donors seem to enter a cause by completing smaller actions rather than making a long-term commitment. Millennials are more motivated to "Like" a Facebook page, share a video, or attend an event before participating in higher states of engagement. However, the stronger their relationship with an organization, the more likely they are to give larger gifts over time. Millennials' interactions with nonprofit organizations are more impulsive and immediate. When inspired, they will act quickly – from small donations to short volunteer stints – provided that the opportunities are present and the barriers to entry are low. This results in smaller amounts of giving to multiple organizations rather than a giving focus on a small group of recipients. Fundraisers must organize messaging and create clear calls to actions that help Millennials express their support for the issue the organization addresses. A continuum of engagement that builds upon these small actions, leading to solicitations, will help the individual grow passive interest into support for the cause.

Millennials Treat Their Time, Money, and Assets as Having Equal Value

Millennials see assets related to time, money, skills, etc., as having equal value when giving to a cause. Interestingly, research shows that Millennials consistently view both their network and their voice as two additional types of assets they can offer organizations. Aided by technology, an individual who donates his or her voice may still give skills, time, and money, and then go beyond these actions to advocacy. Donating one's social network involves capitalizing on professional and personal relationships to expose others to a cause. Fundraisers need to design additional campaigns targeting all Millennial assets to strengthen the relationship between the individual and the institution (Millennial Impact Report, 2013). Using these asset campaigns prior to solicitations will also increase awareness and interest in supporting the cause, resulting in higher response rates.

The Workplace is an Influential Place

The workplace has become an institution of inspiration and passion for most Millennials. Millennials are looking to blend their personal and professional interests and perform cause work such as charitable giving, volunteering, etc. on behalf of a nonprofit organization throughout the day. Therefore, it is no surprise that Millennials actively engage in cause-based initiatives in the workplace.

Corporate social responsibility, volunteerism, and workplace giving programs matter to Millennials when looking at employment options. While only 39 percent of Millennials said the company discussed cause work during the interview process, those that did influenced the Millennial by that discussion. In fact, of the Millennials who heard about cause work during the interview, 55 percent said the company's involvement with causes assisted in persuading them to take the job. Female employees, in particular, were influenced by cause work in the interview (63 percent), compared to 45 percent of male employees (Millennial Impact Report, 2014).

Not surprisingly, Millennials who already volunteered with and donated to nonprofits were much more likely to care about and research a company's involvement with causes. For example, 52 percent of employees who had volunteered 4 to 10 hours and 55 percent of employees who had volunteered 10 to 20 hours in the past month were interested in their company's cause work during the job search, while only 26 percent of employees who hadn't volunteered at all in the past month were interested in their company's cause work during the job search. Similarly, 46 percent of employees who donated more than $1,000 in 2013 and 37 percent of employees who donated $50 to $100 were interested in their company's cause work during the job search, compared to 27 percent of employees who hadn't donated at all, yet were interested in their company's cause work during the job search (Millennial Impact Report, 2014).

Fundraisers should look to companies that encourage active cause engagement at the workplace. Using company time to express cause interest will continue to increase given the recent research. Therefore, fundraisers should create partnerships that allow these employees to advocate, self-organize, and create peer fundraising campaigns for the organization at the workplace. Once such partnerships have been established, fundraisers need to provide the resources, messaging, and solicitation tools that allow the employee to be successful and build upon their interest in the organization's cause.

Conclusion

Engaging the generations in philanthropy, particularly the new donors of the Generation X and Millennial groups, means identifying ways to share in a sense of excitement and purpose about a charitable cause. It also means providing multiple ways for people to engage with organizations that support causes of interest and being willing to adopt new approaches and ideas for fundraising and in building a community of supporters.

Discussion Questions

1) Do you think the differences in the generations' approaches to philanthropy, and charitable giving specifically, are a result of cohort or lifecycle effects? Why?
2) In what ways can fundraisers empower members of each generation to reach their full potential in creating lasting change through philanthropic endeavors?
3) Based on their unique approaches to philanthropy, how will Generation X and Millennials effectively transmit prosocial values to their children?
4) Given that Generation X and Millennials stand to inherit a significant amount of money, what steps (and in what ways) should nonprofit organizations take now to cultivate ongoing and authentic relationships with this group of future, albeit powerful, charitable donors?

CHAPTER FIFTEEN

UNDERSTANDING HIGH NET WORTH DONORS

By Patrick Rooney and Una Osili

High-profile donors and the efforts of philanthropists such as Bill and Melinda Gates, Oprah Winfrey, Mark Zuckerburg, Warren Buffett, George Soros, and Ted Turner, among others, have generated a renewed interest in the idea of the wealthy giving away large portions of their fortunes to charitable causes. Beginning with Andrew Carnegie, the wealthy have historically contributed generously to various philanthropic causes. This chapter reviews the literature on giving by high net worth individuals and identifies implications for fundraisers, practitioners, and nonprofit leaders. Key questions include:

- Who gives? (What percentage of high net worth individuals donate to charity?)
- How much do they give? (How do factors like income and wealth affect the amount donated to charity by high net worth households?)
- To what purposes? (What subsectors benefit most from high net worth individuals' contributions?)
- What are the regional variations in high net worth giving?
- In what ways do "mega-gifts" ($50 million or more) differ from other forms of high net worth giving?

Other questions have to do with public policy and how laws related to charitable deductions and estate taxation impact high net worth individuals' decisions to give. These questions are all significant in furthering our understanding of the dynamics that influence the gifts of wealthy donors.

Patterns of Giving

Most studies of giving by high net worth individuals have found that the wealthy are very likely to give, with 95 percent or more reporting that they contribute to charitable causes (Bankers Trust Private Banking, 2000; U.S. Trust, 2002; Spectrem Group, 2002; Indiana University, 2010). By comparison, according to the Philanthropy Panel Study, a module of the Panel Study on Income Dynamics (PSID) conducted by the University of Michigan, about 65 percent of the United States general population as a whole contributed to charity in 2007, as shown in Figure 15.1.

Most research suggests that the wealthy give substantially more than the general populace. The disproportionate share of total charitable dollars that high net

FIGURE 15.1. PERCENTAGE OF HIGH NET WORTH HOUSEHOLDS WHO GAVE TO CHARITY IN 2009, 2011, AND 2013, COMPARED TO THE U.S. GENERAL POPULATION (%).

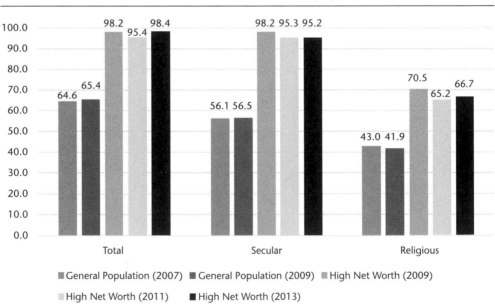

Note: Source for the U.S. general population are the Philanthropy Panel Study 2007, 2009 waves, the latest year available. High net worth figures are for 2009, 2011, and 2013 giving and are based on the Bank of America Merrill Lynch (BAML) Study of High Net Worth Philanthropy.
*The difference between general population and high net worth results was found to be statistically significant.

worth individuals contribute is significant. Studies suggest that a very small percentage of the population is responsible for a comparatively large portion of charitable giving. For example, in 2000, 0.4 percent of families had incomes of $1 million or greater, yet they accounted for 16 percent of charitable dollars (Schervish and Havens, 2003)

One of the most intriguing questions related to high net worth philanthropy is how changes in income and wealth affect giving. In a comprehensive article on patterns of giving among high net worth individuals, Steuerle (1987) found that for those earning higher than the median income, charitable donations tended to increase with income. The author also identifies a threshold of $500,000 in net worth as the point at which charitable bequests begin to increase commensurate with increasing wealth, but concludes that net worth in and of itself is not a good predictor of lifetime charitable giving. Havens, O'Herlihy, and Schervish (2006) noted that giving as a percentage of income was fairly constant at about 2.3 percent among the 98 percent of households that earned less than $300,000, and that above the $300,000 level, giving increased to an average of 4.4 percent of income. Though inconsistent measures of wealth and income make a comparison across different studies difficult, there do appear to be some differences in the patterns of giving between average donors and wealthy donors.

Several surveys examine contributions as a percentage of income and consistently find that a majority of donors contribute less than 5 percent of income, regardless of their level of income (INDEPENDENT SECTOR, 2001; U.S. Trust, 2002). However, another survey found that of clients who requested philanthropic offerings in their portfolios, high net worth individuals contributed 7.6 percent of their wealth in 2006, while ultra-high net worth individuals (those who have assets in excess of $30 million) contributed at least 10 percent of their wealth (Merrill Lynch and Capgemini, 2007). Similarly, the recent 2014 U.S. Trust Study of High Net Worth Philanthropy found that high net worth households gave about 8 percent of their income in 2013 (Indiana University, 2014).

Finally, the source of a donor's wealth has been found to have an impact on how much the donor contributes. The Bank of America Merrill Lynch (BAML) and U.S. Trust Studies of High Net Worth Philanthropy (Indiana University, 2010, 2012, and 2014) show that despite a decline in giving between 2007 and 2009, those donors whose wealth comes from a family or start-up business tend to be generous, giving an average of $110,000 in 2009. This number fell from a 2007 average of $270,000, as did the disparity between giving based on the source of wealth. In fact, those who earned their wealth primarily from investment and asset growth achieved near parity with those who gained their wealth from family or start-up businesses. Among the lowest average giving groups in 2009 were those who earned their wealth from real estate and those who earned their wealth from professional success. The approach to measuring a donor's wealth was revised in the 2014 survey and those findings overwhelmingly suggest that high net worth donors' charitable funds come from inheritance or family wealth.

Volunteering by High Net Worth Individuals

In addition to contributing money, about 75 percent of high net worth individuals surveyed report volunteering their time in 2013, giving an average of 195 hours. Based on an estimated value of $23.07 per volunteer hour (INDEPENDENT SECTOR, 2014), 195 hours amounts to $4,500 in contributed value. High net worth individuals were most likely to volunteer to serve on a board in 2013, with 45.7 percent reporting service to this type of organization. Volunteering at social/community service organizations, event planning, and fundraising followed, with 45.4 percent, 38.6 percent, and 38.5 percent of respondents, respectively, reporting volunteering for each type of activity. The study also finds that the number of volunteer hours and giving tend to be highly correlated (Indiana University, 2014).

High net worth individuals often possess specific skills and traits that add value to an organization, such as business or leadership experience, which can lead to service on boards and advisory committees. These individuals have often reached their peak earning years and have experience that lends itself to important roles within an organization. Volunteers, particularly those who serve in more specialized capacities, such as board members or professional consultants, also tend to contribute more to organizations than those who donate money or assets solely and those who volunteer in a more general role (Indiana University, 2008a, 2010, 2012, 2014).

Giving Vehicles

Some research, including Steuerle's (1987) and Joulfaian's (2000) studies of tax returns and the BAML Studies of High Net Worth Philanthropy, have focused on the strategies and methods that high net worth individuals use to donate money, and finds that, in general, those with high net worth prefer to contribute more out of their estates than out of lifetime income. Of the fraction of donor resources that are contributed during life, high net worth donors show a high likelihood of using a number of vehicles for giving, rather than giving directly to an individual or an organization. Auten, Clotfelter, and Schmalbeck (2000) provide an excellent overview of many of these vehicles, including private foundations and split-interest trusts, analyzing the tax implications for each. In many cases, high net worth individuals are able to receive more advantageous tax treatment through the use of a charitable remainder trust or other giving vehicle than by simply selling an asset, particularly when the size of a contribution exceeds the limit for deductibility.

Steuerle (1987) found strong evidence to suggest that high net worth individuals are likely to make larger gifts through bequests than they do annually during life. He explains that donors might be likely to give from liquid assets during their lifetime, while wealth in the form of corporate stock and real estate is less likely to be donated during life. A more recent study by Joulfaian (2000) finds that the largest contributions came through bequests. In the ten years before death, wealthy individuals donated an average of $3.1 million and at death their charitable bequests averaged $8.4 million. For those estates valued at more than $100 million, charitable bequests accounted for 78 percent of their total gifts during the ten years studied. These data confirm Steuerle's earlier finding that high net worth individuals are more likely to give from their wealth rather than annual income.

Figure 15.2 uses data from the U.S. Department of the Treasury to demonstrate the percentage of estates that contain provisions for bequests to various subsector organizations. Aside from donations to giving vehicles such as foundations (labeled below as "philanthropy/voluntarism"), the largest share (14 percent) of

FIGURE 15.2. PERCENTAGE OF ESTATES WITH A CHARITABLE BEQUEST BY TYPE OF RECIPIENT ORGANIZATION.

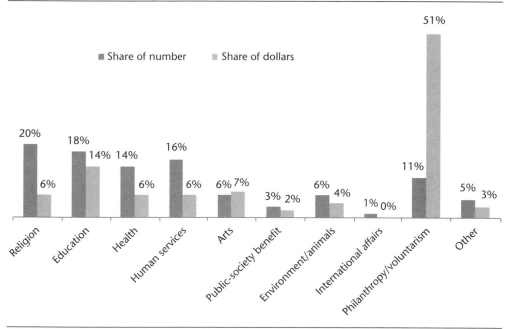

Source: Giving USA 2009, analysis provided by U.S. Department of the Treasury, 2009.

these bequest dollars are designated for educational organizations. This is consistent with other sources that show high net worth individuals are more likely to contribute to educational institutions than average donors, a claim that is supported by research on the recipients of contributions from high net worth donors, to be discussed later.

The 2014 U.S. Trust Study of High Net Worth Philanthropy finds that in 2,013 respondents contributed an average of $130,697 to a giving vehicle such as a private foundation, fund, or trust. Additionally, over 15.6 percent reported having an endowment fund with a specific charitable organization and 14.5 percent reported giving to a community foundation through a donor-advised fund. Nearly half (46 percent) of respondents reported having a charitable provision in their will. Among those respondents who had or would consider establishing a particular giving vehicle, maximizing charitable deductions was ranked among the top three reasons for all five types of vehicles examined. Avoiding capital gains, estate, or gift taxes was also a frequently cited reason for several of the types of giving vehicles. Schervish and Havens (2001) also found a propensity among high net worth donors to use vehicles of philanthropy rather than giving directly, with the largest share of charitable dollars (63 percent) going to trusts, gift funds, and foundations rather than directly to charitable organizations. An interesting area for additional research involves the reasons for this propensity, which could include issues of trust and confidence, tax considerations, and control of the grantmaking mission of the organization.

Where High Net Worth Donors Give

High net worth individuals are distinct from those of the general population in the specific subsectors to which they contribute charitable support. Several academic studies and convenience sample surveys find that high net worth donors are more likely than the general population to give to educational institutions, and while the potential for tax benefits does influence the decision to give, the specific cause or organization is a more important factor. The source of a donor's wealth also appears to have an impact on where contributions are made. Several studies have found that high net worth donors value personal connection to and relationship with a cause or organization, and one report suggests that charities have the opportunity to access an untapped pool of resources from high net worth donors if they can connect their goals and values to those of donors effectively. Figure 15.3 shows the distribution of high net worth giving among the various subsectors, using data from the 2014 and 2012 Studies of High Net Worth Philanthropy reports (Indiana University, 2012, 2014).

FIGURE 15.3. DISTRIBUTION OF HIGH NET WORTH GIVING BY SUBSECTOR, 2009 (%).

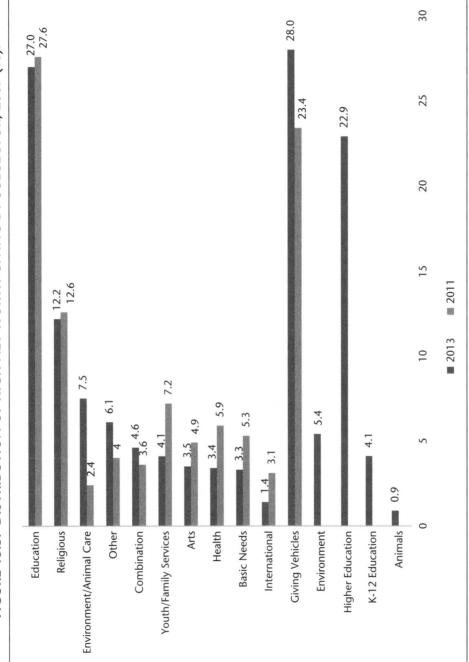

Note: Combined organizations include *United Way, United Jewish Appeal,* and *Catholic Charities. Giving Vehicles* represents gifts to private foundations, charitable trusts, or donor-advised funds.

Several studies indicate the wealthy give more to education, arts, and political/advocacy organizations than do households in the general population (HNW Inc., 2000; U.S. Trust, 2007). Havens, O'Herlihy and Schervish (2006) find that high net worth donors give the largest percentage of their total charitable contributions to education, followed by religion and human services. This contrasts with donors in the general population, who give a larger percentage of total donations to religious organizations than to any other subsector. Figure 15.4 shows the percentage of high net worth households who gave to charitable subsectors in 2007, 2009, 2011, and 2013.

Donor Motivations and Constraints

A consistent finding in various studies is that high net worth donors are cited as wanting to "give back" to the community. Other motivating factors include making a difference in the world, feeling strongly about a cause or an organization, feeling financially secure, and receiving tax benefits (HNW Inc., 2000; Citigroup, 2002; Schervish, 2007; Indiana University, 2014).

Religion is a factor in many high net worth households, with two-thirds of donors reporting contributions to religious causes in 2014, despite only 40.1 percent reporting that religious beliefs are an important motivating factor in their giving (Indiana University, 2014). Other research suggests that religious donors may show more consistency in their philanthropy. Helms and Thornton (2008) find that, among donors at all income levels, nonreligious donors giving to secular causes were more sensitive to tax rates and income compared to religious donors.

Another intriguing pattern among high net worth donors is the transmission of philanthropic values to younger generations. The 2014 BAML Study of High Net Worth Philanthropy finds that 58.7 percent of high net worth donors report having at least one family tradition of philanthropy, and 54.7 percent report using their own personal or family network's philanthropic efforts to educate their children about giving. Schervish (2007) found that high net worth donors identify transmission of values to children as a motivating factor in their giving. Researchers have also found that peer influence was an important factor for donors.

Ostrower (1995) notes that some donors use philanthropy as either an entrée to or a demonstration of high social standing, one reason why high net worth individuals are more likely than average donors to contribute to educational and cultural institutions, which are perceived as being more elite. In some cases, the desire to have one's name and identity outlive the donor was an additional motivation for giving by bequest. Although Ostrower found that more than half of the people she interviewed planned to do most of their giving during their lifetimes, among

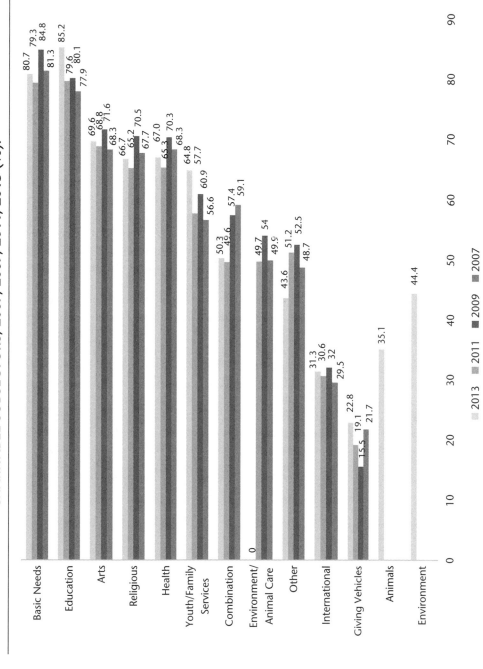

FIGURE 15.4. PERCENTAGE OF HIGH NET WORTH HOUSEHOLDS WHO GAVE TO DIFFERENT CHARITABLE SUBSECTORS, 2007, 2009, 2011, 2013 (%).

■ 2013 ■ 2011 ■ 2009 ■ 2007

Subsector	2013	2011	2009	2007
Basic Needs	80.7	79.3	84.8	81.3
Education	85.2	79.6	80.1	77.9
Arts	69.6	68.8	71.6	68.3
Religious	66.7	65.2	70.5	67.7
Health	67.0	65.3	70.3	68.3
Youth/Family Services	64.8	57.7	60.9	56.6
Combination	50.3	49.6	57.4	59.1
Environment/Animal Care	0	49.7	54	49.9
Other	43.6	51.2	52.5	48.7
International	31.3	30.6	32	29.5
Giving Vehicles	22.8	19.1	15.5	21.7
Animals	35.1			
Environment	44.4			

Source: 2014 U.S. Trust Study of High Net Worth Philanthropy, researched and written by the Indiana University Lilly Family School of Philanthropy.

those donors who planned to include a charitable bequest in their estate plans, an important motivation is the ability to connect to an institution for which the donor feels some passion. Sargeant, Ford, and West (2005) support this conclusion, stating that "where giving makes a donor feel good about themselves and where there is a family connection to the cause, it would appear that individual bonds to the organization are strengthened" (p. 5).

Sargeant, Ford, and West (2005) also found that a prospective donor's trust in an organization and its ability to impact the selected cause can be a strong motivating factor for giving. The authors note that "trust appears to be significantly affected by the performance of the charity and its communication." Additionally, "trust is created when a nonprofit is perceived to have had an impact on the cause and by maintaining appropriate communications with the donor" (Sargeant, Ford, and West, 2005). The development of a personal connection to an organization or cause, coupled with trust in the organization's ability to make an impact, can have an enormous effect on giving. The nonprofit sector enjoys a comparatively high level of trust it receives from high net worth individuals. The 2014 U.S. Trust Study of High Net Worth Philanthropy (Indiana University, 2014) finds that 91.6 percent of respondents have "some confidence" or a "great deal of confidence" in nonprofit organizations and their ability to solve societal and global problems. This is higher than the level of confidence placed in businesses and government at all levels.

Karlan and List (2007) examine the effect of donor matching and found that revenue per solicitation increases by 19 percent and the probability that an individual donates increases by 22 percent when match money is available. This increase occurs only when the match is at a rate of $1:$1. Increasing the ratio to $2:$1 and even $3:$1 has no additional impact on the donor. These findings support the notion that potential donors are more likely to contribute if they perceive an additional incentive, but the findings look only at average donors, not specifically at the effect such matching incentives have on high net worth donors or very large gifts.

Constraints on Donors

There are also a number of factors that dampen high net worth donors' giving. High net worth donors tend to have expectations of the organizations to which they donate, both in terms of how the organization behaves toward potential donors and how they operate. In one study (Indiana University, 2006), respondents indicated four categories that would induce them to give more: (1) improved perceptions of operations, especially efficiency, with the most frequent choice being "less spent on administration"; (2) greater personal financial capacity; (3) more information available about nonprofit and giving options; and (4) personal preferences about time allocation and information-sharing. The 2014 U.S. Trust Study of High Net Worth Philanthropy (Indiana University, 2014) found almost 80 percent of respondents reporting they give to an organization if they know it operates with sound business practices. Some donors cite being asked too often and being asked for an inappropriate amount as reasons they would stop supporting an organization (Indiana University, 2014; Hope Consulting, 2010).

Policy Issues

Of interest to fundraisers and nonprofits is the effect of tax policy on giving levels. The Filer Commission noted that U.S. tax policy has traditionally served to encourage charitable giving by reducing the tax liabilities of those who give.

Several studies have found that among high net worth donors, tax benefits did have some impact on the decision to give, but were less important than other factors (Citigroup, 2002; U.S. Trust, 2002). Another study found that more wealthy people (34 percent) valued tax benefits than respondents in the general population (11 percent) (HNW Inc., 2000).

Empirical research shows that tax policies have a considerable effect on the high net worth donors from whom a large percentage of total charitable contributions derive. Data from the 2014 BAML Study of High Net Worth Philanthropy expands on the discussion of the effect of tax policy on the likelihood of high net worth donors to give. When asked how their giving would change if there were no tax deductions for donations, 50.4 percent of respondents in 2014 said they would decrease their contributions either somewhat or dramatically. This contrasts with 2007, when only 47 percent of respondents reported that they would decrease donations. The study also finds that less than half of respondents (47.5 percent) would leave the same amount to charity if the estate tax were permanently repealed and 48.7 percent would increase their contributions to some degree. Figures 15.5 and 15.6 illustrate the potential implications of changes in tax policy for high net worth philanthropy, based on data from the 2006, 2010, and 2014 BAML Study of High Net Worth Philanthropy reports. These figures demonstrate that although high net worth donors rank tax considerations lower than other motivating factors in their impact on the decision to give, changes in the level of tax benefits for charitable contributions could potentially have a significant impact on the amounts that high net worth donors give.

Auten, et al., (2002) examines the effects of changes in tax policy in the 1980s both through economic models and analysis of 1989 income tax returns. The author notes that two major tax bills (one in 1981 and a second in 1986) cut the

FIGURE 15.5. CHANGE IN GIVING IF INCOME TAX DEDUCTIONS FOR DONATIONS WERE ELIMINATED, 2005, 2007 AND 2009 (%).

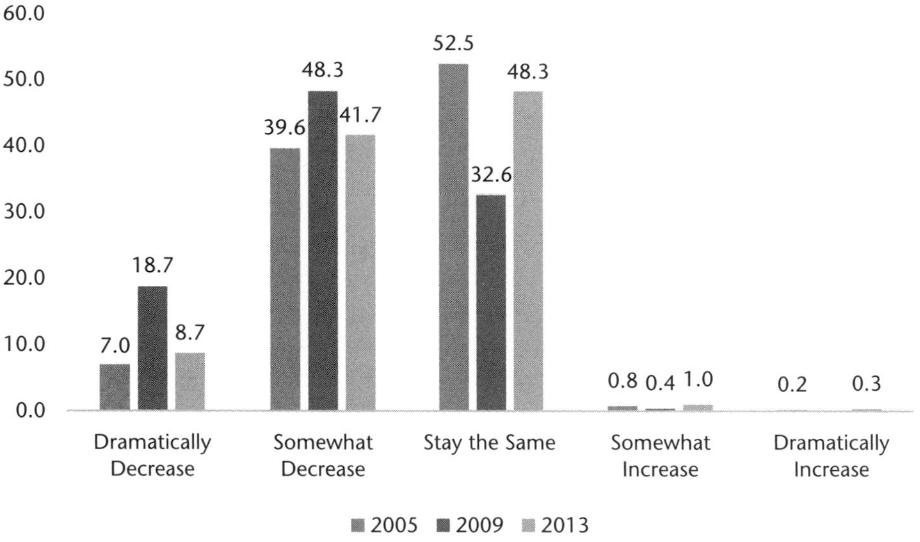

Source: Indiana University, 2006, 2010, 2014 Bank of America Merrill Lynch Study of High Net Worth Philanthropy.

top marginal tax rates significantly, increasing the cost of making charitable contributions for those taxpayers who itemize their deductions. He finds that, consistent with economic models that predict such a decrease, charitable contributions among wealthy taxpayers declined following the changes in tax laws. Auten points out that the models were not (and cannot be) perfect predictors of behavior that is largely influenced by noneconomic factors. However, his analysis suggests that changes in tax policies, especially significant reductions in rates among the highest tax brackets, have a substantial effect on charitable contributions by the wealthy, and subsequently on the organizations that rely on these donations (Clotfelter, 1990).

Implications for Fundraisers

Giving by high net worth households grows exponentially with both income and wealth. As income and wealth doubles and doubles again, giving tended to increase even faster. Moreover, the sources of wealth and income seem to matter. It looks like from both current and prior years that those who created a significant share of

FIGURE 15.6. CHANGE IN ESTATE PLANS IF THE ESTATE TAX WERE PERMANENTLY ELIMINATED, 2005, 2007 AND 2009 (%).

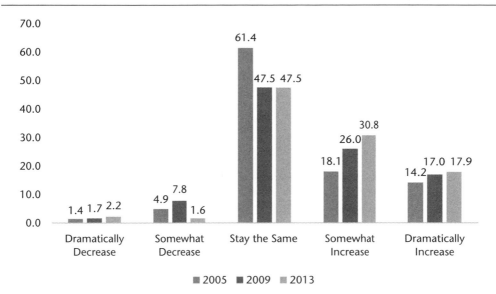

■ 2005   ■ 2009   ■ 2013

Source: Indiana University, 2006, 2010, 2014 Bank of America Merrill Lynch Study of High Net Worth Philanthropy.

their wealth from entrepreneurial activities gave more than other high net worth households. Those who inherited a significant share of their wealth usually came in at the second highest levels of giving. Perhaps both of these groups are the most motivated to "give back" to society.

A small number of gifts, but the biggest gifts by far, go to create or enhance the asset base of family foundations. While individual charities may prefer to receive these gifts directly, such gifts do create a permanent commitment to philanthropy and will pay out at least 5 percent of the asset base for many years or in perpetuity (depending on the structure, etc.). Education is the second largest share of the number of gifts (trailing only religion) and the second largest share of the dollars given (trailing only foundations). Clearly, high net worth households appreciate their alma maters and reward them generously when they become wealthy. With respect to the share of the dollars given, there is an approximate tie for third place between the arts, health, human services, and religion. While a relatively large number of high net worth donors make gifts to help the needy, relatively few of the gift dollars go to help the needy.

Another implication of this research is that while high net worth households do not give because of the tax deduction, they may alter how much they give, when they give, and how they give based on the tax implications. Most high net worth households said that they would not change their annual giving if the tax deduction were eliminated entirely, and most of the rest would decrease their giving "somewhat." Similarly, most or nearly so would keep their charitable bequest, giving the same if the estate tax were permanently eliminated. However, most of the remaining households said that they would increase their bequest gifts "somewhat" if the estate tax were eliminated. This suggests that in the absence of the estate tax, they would increase their giving to their heirs and to their favorite charities. While charitable bequests grew in 2010 when the estate tax was temporarily eliminated from 2009, the bequest giving levels were conspicuously lower than they were for several years before that. David Joulfaian's (2000) research suggests that elimination of the estate tax would likely be associated with a large drop in bequest giving.

High net worth donors are highly motivated by the impact a gift can have and that their gift can "make a difference." Charities need to be able to articulate with data and/or case studies (stories) of their organization's success and their impact. Similarly, volunteering is an important part of philanthropy, and we found that high net worth households, who volunteer, give much more on average than those who do not volunteer, and that the level of giving grew as the level of volunteering increased. Charities need to engage donors as volunteers effectively, which means investing in volunteer coordinators and listening to your donors and volunteers about how they would most like to help your charity as volunteers.

Not everything about understanding individual donors can be understood from existing research. For example, what are the similarities and differences among the "typical high net worth households" and the "typical ultra-high net worth households" (e.g., $50 million or more in net worth, excluding their principal residence)? At what points on the income and wealth scales do households start making larger and/or permanent commitments to philanthropy through their foundations? At what point do high net worth households start making "large" gifts to charities? When do they move from $1,000 gifts to $100,000 gifts and then to gifts of $1 million or more? Fundraisers no doubt would like to know how, when, and why donors make decisions about the tax consequences, the timing, and the risk-return tradeoff both for themselves and the potential recipient organization(s) in considering contributing large gifts during life and/or at death.

Discussion Questions

1) Choose a subsector (education, religion, etc.) and discuss the implications of current findings about the giving patterns of the wealthy for that subsector.

2) Discuss several ways in which wealthy donors differ from the general population of donors.

3) Why should one be cautious in using data like that contained in this chapter with a prospective donor?

4) Discuss four motivations the wealthy have for making a gift and how those motivations can be helpful in fundraising.

5) How important is a trust to wealthy donors?

CHAPTER SIXTEEN

GLOBAL AND CROSS-CULTURAL FUNDRAISING

By Lilya Wagner

After completing this chapter, you will be able to:

1. Understand the extent of fundraising around the world and the reasons for this proliferation.
2. Implement information about differences in how various populations view generosity and what traditions and cultural effects influence these views.
3. Apply information about cultural differences when planning donor invitations to give, and abandon the idea that "one size fits all" in philanthropy.
4. Appreciate the layer of diversity that enriches both the personal and the philanthropic outreach of causes and organizations.
5. Provide information that will influence and motivate further study into specific areas of diversity and philanthropy.

The old adage, "there's nothing new under the sun," has rarely been more true than when discussing global philanthropy or the international perspectives and aspects of fundraising because generosity and sharing of resources have existed throughout time immemorial. Conversely, all too often United States fundraising professionals and their teams continue to function under this same premise, "there's nothing new under the sun," and while acknowledging that cultural differences exist, continue to raise funds with a "business as usual" mentality and practice.

This chapter will address how philanthropy and fundraising have proliferated globally while building on distinctive cultural, religious and societal traditions, differences, and behaviors. Traditional practices in individual countries have been augmented by the U.S. model for fundraising in many cases throughout the last several decades, and while the U.S. components often work well, some principles have to be modified and adapted to the individual cultural setting.

This is also true in considering the diversity of cultures in the United States and how these relate to philanthropy and fundraising. Awareness and information about the influences of countries of origin and therefore approaches to giving and asking for funds in the United States must be part of the fundraising professionals' knowledge base and shape professional practice. The culmination of accumulated knowledge coupled with experience in cross-cultural philanthropy and fundraising results in the culturally proficient professional, one who understands the benefits of cultural proficiency and engagement both for him or herself as well as the organization.

Global Perspectives on Philanthropy and Fundraising

Philanthropy is as ancient as human existence. On a global scale, virtually all nations and cultures have traditions of giving. The editors of *Philanthropy in the World's Traditions* (1998, p. x) stated that "philanthropy was not a free-floating activity separated from the complex elements of the societies in which it resided, but was influenced, indeed structured, by the specificity of particular cultures." As a recognized practice, philanthropy was written about in historical records of the Greeks and Romans as well as specifically addressed in many religious tomes such as the Bible and the Koran. The concepts of sharing wealth, of giving to others, of asking for funds, were prevalent in many cultures and societies. Generosity was discussed and practiced by early Christians, was part of the Arab/Islamic set of beliefs, and even existed in pagan times and cultures. Philanthropy in its broadest sense was not inhibited or constrained by distinct cultures, geographic areas, or religions, but ways of practicing philanthropy differed distinctly in the cultures and geographic areas of the world, and were often shaped by religion.

As a formalized and recognized practice, however, the roots of philanthropy and fundraising are distinctly in the United States. For the purposes of this chapter, recognizing that formal fundraising in a professional sense was largely a U.S. development, while building on the various influences of those brought by immigrants from all parts of the world, is sufficient. The development of fundraising as a profession in the United States will be discussed elsewhere in this volume, and will serve as an enhancement for this chapter's content.

Understanding philanthropy as a global practice is essential for two reasons. First, civil society organizations (CSOs) or nongovernmental organizations (NGOs), as nonprofits are known in much of the world outside the United States, have played a critical role in the shaping of local civil society because of the shifting social and political developments, and frequently this progress has been supported and accomplished through philanthropy. Events of the last 25 years, perhaps best seen during the post-Soviet era and the developing democracies in many parts of the world, have caused citizens to push for more self-expression and freedom of expression, for the opportunity to voluntarily gather together for common vision and goals, and for the aid of those in the poorer segments of society. Civil society provides a powerful means for mobilizing such citizen participation. As a consequence, national boundaries are not as important as international cooperation and collaboration, as well as cross-national understanding and collegiality.

During the final decades of the twentieth century the U.S. model became one that was sought after and emulated in many parts of the world. These decades saw a great shift in the social and political geography of the world, which created both an opportunity and a need for citizens to become increasingly involved in the political and social lives of their communities, countries, and the world. The growth and development of civil society organizations provided a powerful means for mobilizing such citizen participation. Beginning in the 1990s the role of governments was measurably reduced because of the emergence of new democratic cultures, technological advances in communications, and the inability of many governments to keep up with even basic services to its populations. Therefore there was a rapid development of NGOs that were service providers while also acting as advocates for reform. Along with the emergence of civil society organizations came attention on philanthropy, whether as a renewed and regenerated concept or as a new endeavor based on related traditions. The consequence of this confluence of events and circumstances was that the practice of fundraising grew dramatically around the globe.

Leading experts in the globalization of foundations and philanthropic giving (Anheier and Daly, 2005, p. 174) explain, "Global philanthropy has expanded and become a supporter of civil society organizations in many parts of the world." Indeed, "Transnational philanthropy has been and can remain a major force for improving the lives of millions of people worldwide, particularly in regions that are underdeveloped economically and are socially and politically fragile" (Anheier and Daly, 2005, p. 174). In recent years, philanthropists in many parts of the world have rivaled the giving by wealthy individuals in the United States. As a feature article in *Newsweek* (Carmichael 2007, p. 51), pointed out, "inspired individuals can take on and conquer some of the world's biggest problems." Couple this with giving from many other parts of the world as philanthropy is taking hold in action and not just rhetoric or tradition, there is evidence that global philanthropy is working and continuing to develop.

The *World Giving Index 2010* prepared by the Charities Aid Foundation explains and summarizes charitable behavior globally: "Charitable behavior differs immensely across the globe. An act that is considered charitable in one country may be seen as a regular, everyday, activity in another" (p. 31). The report clearly shows how countries have their own charitable strengths and weaknesses, and how in some places the growth of civil society has been impeded by war, famine, and other external factors that make philanthropy difficult. The high level of detail in the report explains qualities that appear to affect philanthropy and volunteering, and yet acknowledges that some cultures are more amenable to philanthropic action than others, while at the same time not passing judgment on those that score lower, for whatever reason, in their analysis of giving data.

In short, the growth of philanthropy in most parts of the world has become organized, with experience and advice crossing borders as funders – individuals, corporate, foundations, even governments – seek to ensure that their giving is effective. The idea of promoting civil society through philanthropy, of bringing people together, is attractive everywhere from Slovakia to Brazil.

Global Development of Fundraising

Philanthropy has grown globally partially due to the spread of democracy and capitalism, but it has also been spurred by technological advances that promote global and cross-border understanding, growing wealth and positive peer pressure to be philanthropic, disasters and traumatic events that call attention to the benefits and outcomes of giving, and an increasing number of nonprofit organizations (NPOs) or nongovernmental organizations (NGOs). Transnational government aid has also helped in focusing on the positive results of generosity, although this is not necessarily visible in some countries where only a few benefit. Nevertheless, philanthropy has become, to put it into the vernacular, popular in many places in the world.

We who are fundraising professionals can grow in collegiality across the globe when we realize that philanthropy in some form or other is present in every culture around the world and many countries have developed structures for organized fundraising. Often what those who contact U.S. resources seek is the process for integrating fundraising into the administrative structure of nonprofit organizations, for recognizing and respecting philanthropic traditions in a culture and country, and for building a total development program that includes practices such as major gifts, use of volunteers, and personal solicitation. Therefore, fundraising as a profession is enriched by its proliferation and adaptation across nations and cultures, awareness of cultural issues, sensitivity toward differences, and the expression of a genuine appreciation of our international fundraising professionals' efforts and achievements.

However, international philanthropy can also be complex because even in established democracies, charitable organizations are at times different from those in the United States. This is even more true in fragile, emerging civil societies. Therefore cultural differences as well as foreign legal and political environments must be considered when the U.S. model of fundraising is applied. International charities are looking to American experts in large part because the United States has a long-established tradition of raising money from private sources. Penelope Cagney (2013) explained this relationship well when she said: "we have the opportunity to consciously participate in the world-wide evolution of our profession and, in doing so, shape a tomorrow in which all fundraisers have the support they need to function effectively and ethically on behalf of the important missions they serve and where our profession is understood and respected everywhere."

As the U.S. model is considered by many countries, it becomes clear that many philanthropic fundraising principles are universally adaptable while at the same time they must be culturally and situationally appropriate. Within universality of principles and generalizations about fundraising, differences and similarities between the U.S. and international fundraising should be noted. It is useful for the fundraising practitioner to know which concepts and principles of fundraising can be universally applied and are adaptable. A few of these are:

- The need and art of making a strong, compelling case for funding, and expressing this case in differing ways to different markets are concepts understood everywhere.
- Donor motivations, when discussed as part of both training and practice, are surprisingly universal. Some differences do exist, but the desire to help others is often a motivation that can be aroused or tapped.
- International fund raisers also understand the need to research and know the potential markets, the application of the exchange relationship in determining why a donor might give, and diversity in funding sources.

On the other hand, there are differences in principles and practice that international colleagues must deal with and U.S. professionals should respect. Tactics that work for U.S. fundraisers at home may not necessarily always translate abroad.

- The matter of professional compensation can provide challenges. For example, working for a commission can be an ethical dilemma in some cultures while acceptable in others.
- Prospective donor research becomes difficult in some places because of lack of research resources as well as prevailing attitudes toward privacy. Consider as examples the still-lingering hostility among Germans for those who build dossiers on prospective donors and the impact of nearly 50 years of KGB activity in the former Soviet Union.
- Board responsibility is uneven in many countries and the idea of board members seeking funds is often an unacceptable or at least unwelcome concept.
- Tax deductibility and the concept of planned gifts do not exist in many nations.

Understanding international NGOs and fundraising aids comprehension of what is happening in the culturally diverse world inside the borders of the United States. Understanding cultural influences on giving on a global scale helps create an understanding of what is happening in our local communities. In addition, as we have already discussed, but it bears repeating, philanthropy and the securing of funds to benefit others is an ancient practice and America represents only a portion of this rich history. Although we in the United States have perfected many fundraising techniques and have much to offer in terms of sharing our expertise, we also have much to learn. International understanding enriches the global community of fundraising practitioners; we are part of a global system.

Cultural Influences and Fundraising in the United States

An article in *Harvard Business Review* stated, "The culture in which a person is born – the home culture – plays a key role in shaping his or her identity. No matter where people end up living, they retain a sense of themselves ... Even if they wish to forget their ancestry, the society to which they have moved – the host culture – tends to make that difficult because it views them as different and as newcomers, even pretenders" (Kumar and Steenkamp, 2013). Therefore immigrants have two challenges that, admittedly, lessen the longer they are in the host country. The first is to maintain their cultural distinctiveness while living in a foreign society. The second is affiliating themselves with the host culture and assimilating. Another author explains some of the challenges presented by these situations when those in the host country interact with immigrants, particularly first and second generation newcomers: "it's all too common to rely on clichés, stereotyping people from different cultures on just one or two dimensions ... This can lead to oversimplified and erroneous assumptions" (Meyer, 2014).

While providing advice to corporations in "Crossing the Divide," a writer in *The Economist* (2013) stated, "Coping with cultural differences is becoming a valued skill. The advance of globalization … means that companies have to deal with business and consumers from a wider range of backgrounds." The article continues with examples of cross-cultural challenges as well as successes in practice, pointing out that sometimes companies embrace these complex differences to their advantage and the benefit of consumers, yet sometimes they become more ethnocentric and nationalistic.

Consequently, given these perspectives and cautions from the corporate sector, a conclusion presented in "Contextual Intelligence" (Khanna, 2014) is that management practices – and we can extrapolate the same for fundraising practices – don't always travel well across borders because economic development, education, language and culture vary widely from place to place. The author, Tarun Khanna, suggests that professionals, whether in business or the nonprofit sector, have to develop contextual intelligence, to recognize what we need to know versus what we don't know and adapt to different situations, environments, and peoples.

For the fundraising professional, perhaps the above can be summed up by an article in *Newsweek* on "How to be Invisible." In it, travel writer Seth Stevenson (2010) wrote, "The joy of travel, is to let different cultures seep into your identity. It's not to bring your own culture with you so you can inflict it on the native populace." Perhaps this is the best advice as fundraisers look to diversify their donor outreach to various cultures in the United States – a practice that not only enriches our organizations but ourselves – and reach across transnational borders as well.

Implementing Fundraising Principles Across Cultures

A *Chronicle of Philanthropy* (Hall, 2010) headline written a few years ago proclaimed, "Wanted: Fundraisers whose entrepreneurial spirit, cross-cultural knowledge, and analytical abilities match their skills in building strong personal ties to donors." That need on the part of nonprofits and NGOs is still prevalent today. As Henry Ramos (n.d.) wrote in the conclusion of an article "Harnessing the Still Untapped Potential of Diverse Donors," "professional nonprofit fundraisers must begin to better understand and act on the dynamics and meaning of these impending changes in the social and charitable landscape. Failure to do so will risk important nonprofit groups falling behind in their resourcing and relevance to the communities they will be increasingly serving."

At times fundraisers are either overwhelmed or intimidated by the complexity of cultures and the implications for fundraising as they survey the potential donors in their community or among their constituents. Admittedly, if one begins to consider the plethora of cultural aspects such as traditions, behaviors, religious implications of a particular population group, it may seem to be daunting. However, it doesn't need to be this way. An example of how to move from awareness to proficiency in fundraising from various cultural groups can be adapted from a corporate perspective. Global leaders, who the authors of the *Harvard Business Review* article call the global elite, are those who have the ability to create value by helping their organizations adopt a global perspective. They suggest the following steps for acquiring a global outlook (Unruh and Cabrera, 2013).

1. Learn by thinking. Develop a broad outlook by thinking globally, moving beyond your frame of mind to unfamiliar territory.
2. Observe, ask questions, and do not assume you know the answers.
3. Study, both through formal education and via all the other means available today, such as literature, websites, webinars, foreign films, and many other means.
4. Keep an open mind and heart. Understand that differences are not value statements but just that – differences. Welcome new experiences. Develop empathy.
5. Learn by doing, by forging relationships, and by attending events.
6. Begin locally and work with others. Seek opportunities to mingle, join, and collaborate with people from other cultures.
7. Go international, even if it is venturing to a club event or a church service held by a culture other than your own.
8. In summary, "successful global leaders take risks by putting themselves in unfamiliar situations and challenging their mental models."

Using the above as both a model and a guide, the following steps may be helpful for the fundraising professional when expanding outreach to nontraditional donors of a nonprofit.

A first step in culturally sensitive fundraising is to become aware of a particular culture. Talk with community leaders, develop an advisory group or council, show a genuine interest, read background material such as information on the country of origin, and be a listening learner.

Second, involve key people from the selected cultural group in the activities of the organization. Invite people to events or give special tours. Find out if there is research on the giving amounts and habits, preferences, and practices and study this information. Much information is now available about giving by diverse populations and is quite easily accessible.

Third, test your fundraising outreach strategies on the key people whom you have invited to be involved in some way. Do not assume without checking on their preferences and behaviors. Evaluate the outcomes of this testing step and modify your campaigns accordingly.

Fourth, as you build your knowledge base and expertise, branch out even more and learn about the diversity within multicultural population groups. For example, while initially it may be useful to consider what particular philanthropic traits Hispanics have in common, begin to identify the philanthropic nature of Mexicans versus Peruvians. Continue to be involved with diverse communities yourself and encourage volunteers to work across cultures.

Fifth, integrate diverse strategies into your overall fundraising program gradually, ensuring that all your population groups are as appropriately approached as possible. This would include women's giving and proceeding to how women in various cultures might give, giving by generations or how long a donor has been in the United States, and differences by country or geographic area.

While it would be impossible within the confines of this chapter to delineate the cultural traits of the myriad of cultural groups represented in the United States, some generalizations of what a fundraiser may observe when laying a foundation for cultural awareness may be useful. As a recognized expert in cultural intelligence wrote (Peterson, 2004), "Generalizations ... are quite different from stereotypes (and more reliable). With generations, we look at a large number of people and we draw certain conclusions. ... There are exceptions to every rule but generalizations that come from research and from the insights of informed international cultural experts and professionals allow us to paint a fairly accurate picture of how people in a given country are likely (but never guaranteed) to operate."

1. There are three stages of giving in most population groups. The first is *survival*, sharing among social and economic peers, within an ethnic group, and building a new home and community in America. The second is *helping*, when financial stability is reached, giving to the less fortunate. The third is *investing*, going beyond responding and moving to a long-term vision of helping the community.
2. Philanthropy often begins with the nuclear family, which presents the groundwork for developing philanthropic habits and practices. Then it reaches the extended family and fictive kin. Finally, giving may extend to the broader community.
3. Religion often plays a significant role in developing the habit of giving, in inculcating expectations of generosity, and in promising blessings of giving. Virtually all religions promote and teach philanthropic values, although with differing emphases.
4. Special occasions are often a platform for giving and volunteering.
5. The concept of not giving to strangers is prevalent in many cases.

6. Traditional, mainstream nonprofits are often shunned and there is at times some distrust of these due to previous less-than-positive experiences.
7. Philanthropy may be practiced extensively but not always in ways recognized by nonprofits and the IRS.
8. For many cultures, philanthropy is viewed in the broadest sense – gifts of time, talent, and treasure combined or given individually – and revolve around family, church, and education.
9. Level of immediate need is important. Long-term support, such as planned giving, is not often a priority.
10. Most cultural groups are influenced by leaders – community, religious, professional, social, and family.
11. Much giving is focused outside of the United States without regard to tax benefits.
12. Reciprocity is an accepted concept. As has often been advised, "serve before you ask." Also, helping those in ways they themselves were helped often motivates cultural groups.

These are some of the most prevalent generalizations, providing a basic foundation for acquiring far more information about specific cultural groups. At the same time, some caveats are recommended. These include a reminder that lumping together all subcultures into a culture may skew the view, such as Asian Americans, but such an action may provide, at the least, a beginning point for understanding individual cultures. Language use is important. Knowing how various cultures wish to be identified (e.g., Hispanic versus Latino) is also highly recommended.

Acquiring cultural proficiency is a privilege, a responsibility, and a pleasure. It need not be a chore but can develop in a step-wise progression, as advised by a leading expert in cultural studies, Michael Winkelman (2005).

• Ethnocentric – ignorance of and dislike of other groups.
• Contact – initial learning leading to development or withdrawal.
• Awareness – recognition of the importance of cultural differences.
• Acceptance – appreciation of differences.
• Sensitivity – capable of culturally appropriate behaviors.
• Competence – works effectively with other cultures.
• Proficiency – capable of teaching cultural competence to others.

Winkelman (2005) further defined the four sectors of achieving cultural competence.

• Personal, including cultural self-awareness, personal management, and cross-cultural adaptation skills.

- Cognitive, including knowledge of cultural systems and beliefs and their impacts on behavior.
- Interpersonal, particularly knowledge of intercultural process dynamics and cross-cultural skills.
- Professional skills in intercultural relations, relevant to specific activities.

Culturally proficient professionals make it their responsibility to be aware of, respect, and communicate across global, cultural, and subcultural lines. Our demographics are changing vastly and rapidly. The savvy professional will realize the need to broaden the definition of philanthropy to include traditions, preferences, and ways of giving by diverse populations and not attempt to function under the comfortable "one size fits all" mentality. To ignore or remain unaware of the rich and varied giving traditions of the many population groups in North America is not only unwise but leaves our fundraising practice and ourselves as professionals incomplete and unbalanced.

Conclusion

Without a doubt, cultures and subcultures shape how people do and will relate to philanthropy. Culturally specific groups and populations will engage in philanthropy as their preferences are respected and understood. There are significant and numerous changes in how philanthropy is done globally and in North America. True, resistance to cultural understanding crops up periodically and is a two-way street in our global community, but the challenge is to be savvy and embrace changes for ultimate benefit to ourselves as professionals as well as our organizations. Becoming a culturally proficient fundraiser means that we are able to add more understanding to our donor outreach and therefore engage in better and best practices.

Discussion Questions

1) Since giving and asking have been part of the history of humankind, why might the U.S. model be the preferred avenue for developing successful fundraising in another country?
2) What pitfalls are there in adapting the U.S. model? What beneficial aspects can be seen in using this model?

3) Even today, fundraisers tend to raise funds via strategies that seem to reflect a "one size fits all" mentality. Why might this be detrimental to a fundraising program and what can a fundraiser do to overcome this mentality?

4) Describe your progression from developing awareness of another culture and its philanthropic traditions and behaviors to proficiency in interacting with that culture and its donors.

PART THREE

STRUCTURING YOUR FUNDRAISING

CHAPTER SEVENTEEN

THE TOTAL DEVELOPMENT PLAN BUILT ON THE ANNUAL GIVING PROGRAM

By Timothy L. Seiler

A fter completing this chapter, you will be able to:

1. Identify the components of an integrated total development plan.
2. Explain the primary purposes of each fundraising component in the total development plan.
3. Define the annual giving program as the key to the other components.
4. Enumerate several key functions of the annual giving program.

As development and fundraising have become more formalized and professionalized, practitioners and volunteers alike have become more cognizant of the disciplined, systematic process that effective fundraising follows. Donors and prospective donors, too, have become more aware of the heightened level of conscious activity on the part of nonprofits to engage them more fully and intimately in the activities of the nonprofit.

The growing seriousness with which nonprofits and fundraising staff and volunteers take fundraising is seen clearly in two venues: the increase in the amount of continuing education and professional development and the increase in academic programs in nonprofit management and development in colleges and universities. For example, when The Fund Raising School moved from California to Indiana in 1987 to become part of Indiana University, there were approximately

600 participants a year attending about a dozen courses offered in cities around the United States. Now, approximately 4,500 to 5,000 participants per year attend courses in cities in the United States and around the world or enroll in courses online. The number of nonprofit academic programs in colleges and universities has likewise blossomed during this same period. In 2012, Indiana University established the first School of Philanthropy in the world. A university in China soon followed by establishing its own school of philanthropy.

This growth reflects the maturity of nonprofits and their growing understanding of the complexity of building and sustaining a disciplined fundraising program. Nonprofit boards and staff realize more acutely that relying on fundraising special events and direct mail – or social media – will leave them short of the funds required to sustain their programs and operating at a level below their potential. Nonprofit organizations and nongovernmental organizations around the world are discovering that fundraising success year after year calls for a fully integrated comprehensive plan that develops and nurtures a diversified funding base built on a variety of committed constituencies.

The Total Development Plan: Planning, Communication, and Fundraising

This chapter reflects on the components of the integrated development plan or the total development plan and suggests a model for building and sustaining effective fundraising and achieving excellence in fundraising.

Development as an organizational process involves fundraising but is more than fundraising. Development is growth of mission and includes planning, communications, and fundraising.

Planning calls for vision and leadership. It means setting the direction for the future by answering these questions (and is also addressed in Chapter 4):

Who are we?

What distinguishes us from our competition?

What do we want to accomplish?

How will we reach our goals?

How do we hold ourselves accountable?

The answers to these questions address mission, goals, objectives, programs, evaluation, and stewardship. Answering the questions provides a core script for communications. Effective communications programs include not only dissemination of information but also a means for interaction with constituencies. Good communications programs seek to engage constituencies in substantive exchange of ideas, allowing a forum for constituencies to articulate their interests and desires to the nonprofit. The best communications programs in the most effective development plans seek to nurture in-depth relationships with constituencies. They provide opportunities for constituencies to understand the organization's case for support, to endorse the case, and to become involved in the active articulation of the case.

Effective communications plans invite constituencies to join in sharing their own dreams and vision for how they can participate in fulfilling the mission of the nonprofit. Communications plans help cultivate relationships between prospective donors and the organization. They provide a means for involvement in the life of the organization.

Fundraising is an essential component of a development plan, and it often is the ultimate goal of the overall plan. Fundraising, however, is more than just asking for money. Effective fundraising includes identifying the most qualified prospective donors by focusing on their linkage to the organization and their interest in its work as well as their ability to make gifts. Fundraising involves the development of a relationship between prospective donors and the organization, a relationship fostered by mutual values and shared interests. As the organization makes its case, and as prospective donors realize how their own interests are met by the work of the organization, fundraising becomes a process of the mutual fulfillment of the donors' and the organization's needs.

Fundraising Programs

Historically, organizational financial needs have fallen into these categories: ongoing program support, special purpose needs, capital needs, and endowment needs. The fundraising programs for raising the needed funds have been the annual giving program (sometimes called the annual fund), special gifts, capital campaign, and planned giving; the latter three are explained more fully in other chapters in the book. This model is still relevant today, although one modification seems to be a renaming of the special gifts program as a major gifts program. This is especially true in large fundraising programs most often found in colleges and universities, hospitals and medical centers, and large mainstream arts organizations, such as metropolitan opera organizations, art museums, and urban theatre organizations. However, even small to mid-size organizations recognize the value of a focused major gifts effort. Major gifts programs are often the natural outgrowth of successful capital campaigns and are a means of continuing the higher level of

FIGURE 17.1. THE FOUR-LEGGED STOOL OF FUNDRAISING.

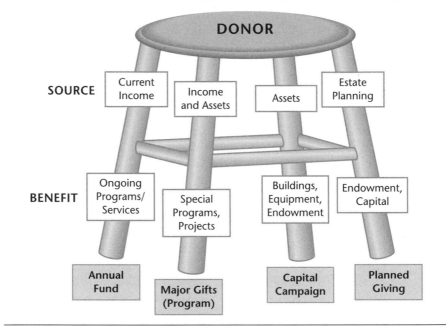

Source: The Fund Raising School, 2009b, p. II-6.

giving established during the capital campaign. A total fundraising program might be illustrated with a diagram such as a four-legged stool, shown in Figure 17.1.

The annual fund, or a regular yearly fundraising effort, regardless of what it is called, is still the foundation of all successful fundraising. Donors contribute to the yearly fundraising effort to support current, ongoing programs to fulfill the organization's mission. The ongoing programs are the organization's way of addressing the larger needs of the community. The programs provide solutions to the problems the donor and the organization agrcc nccd to be addressed.

The annual fundraising program also serves to bond a large number of donors to the organization through recurring gifts. As donors develop a history of giving they grow more interested in and involved with the success of the organization. This base of regular givers becomes the most likely core group of donors for other fundraising programs such as major gifts, capital gifts, and planned gifts.

While the special gift in response to a special need or opportunity is still a part of a total development program, the more likely formalization of this type of program/gift is the major gift. Major gifts are part of all fundraising campaigns – annual, capital, and endowment – and they are also a program. That is, it has become a common model for organizations to maintain a major gifts program inside or in addition to its annual fund. The major gift is one that is larger than the typical gift to the annual fund, raising the sights of the donor and bonding the donor even more closely to the organization. Typically, donors who make major gifts begin by making modest but regular gifts on an annual basis.

Capital campaigns meet the organization's needs for increasing its own assets, often physical, such as renovating facilities, building new facilities, or acquiring land for expansion. Capital campaigns also support program development and expansion, and, increasingly, they support endowment. The comprehensive capital campaigns today have included all components of the integrated fundraising plan: an increase in annual support, capital needs (including buildings and programs), and endowment.

Because capital campaigns seek very large gifts, donors typically make their gifts from their own asset base. Their gifts will generally be pledged over a period of years, typically the number of years of the campaign itself.

In the mega-campaigns today, capital campaigns have lasted five to seven years, with some continuing for as long as ten years, although some professional association guidelines suggest a limit of seven years. In these larger campaigns it has not been uncommon for donors to make multiple gifts or to extend their pledges.

Planned giving has been one of the most exciting growth areas in fundraising in recent years. Planned gifts, by definition, are gifts that are made in the present but whose value to the organization usually occurs at a later time, generally at the death of the donor or a surviving beneficiary. The most common forms of planned gifts are charitable bequests, charitable gift annuities, and charitable trusts. Other types of planned gifts are life estates, insurance, and bargain sales. In the past couple of decades, as employee pension plans accelerated in value, qualified pension plans became an exciting planned gift option for many donors.

While some planned gift instruments are highly sophisticated and technical and may be beyond the capacity of smaller nonprofits to manage, charitable bequests are the simplest form of planned gifts. Every nonprofit seeking to build a totally integrated development plan should be involved in planned giving at least through wills and bequests.

One of the conventional models of fundraising is the donor pyramid, demonstrating the typical process of how organizations manage the fundraising process of donor involvement from annual gifts to special/major gifts, to the capital gift, and ultimately to the planned gift (see Figure 17.2). The pyramid shows graphically how an organization generally employs various fundraising strategies to engage

FIGURE 17.2. DONOR PYRAMID OF FUNDRAISING STRATEGIES.

Source: The Fund Raising School, 2009b, p. IV-8.

prospective donors and donors to build relationships over time. The process begins with the use of less personal fundraising strategies – to engage what is usually an entry-level gift – and moves to more personal strategies and to more personal involvement. The less personal strategies build the broad base of donors, and as donors deepen their involvement, they make larger gifts. As the pyramid narrows from the wide base, fewer donors are making larger gifts. While there will be an occasional exception – a donor's first gift as a capital gift – this model still has validity today. Its primary value is in demonstrating the interrelatedness of all the components of the integrated development plan. Effective fundraising recognizes how the components are interdependent and manages the process of developing the components as mutually reinforcing.

With these models in mind, the four-legged stool and the donor pyramid, the rest of this chapter expands on the idea of the annual giving program – the annual fund – as the foundation upon which the other components are built.

The First Leg: The Annual Giving Program

The annual giving program is the lifeblood of the organization's gift income. Its purpose is to seek gifts on a recurring basis – at least once a year – to fund the ongoing programs and service needs of the organization. In some larger organizations, annual giving, or the annual fund, provides additional discretionary funds for special initiatives. Whether for ongoing programmatic support or for special needs/opportunities, annual gifts are often unrestricted, to be used at the discretion of the leadership of the organization. As mentioned earlier, gifts to the annual fund come from all sources: individuals, corporations, foundations, associations, and civic clubs (such as Lions, Kiwanis, Rotary, and so on).

Besides funding programs and services the annual giving program is central to building and expanding a broad base of donors. A key strategy is to strengthen the bond between donors and the organization by inviting the renewal of the gift and for some donors an increase in the size of their gifts. This deepening involvement solidifies the exchange relationship and lays the groundwork for future fundraising and giving activities, such as major gifts, capital gifts, and planned gifts.

Yet another key function of the annual giving program is to maintain in the community an awareness and appreciation of the organization's value and the quality of its programs and services. The annual giving program puts the organization "on trial" on a yearly basis. This effort compels validation and revalidation of the organization's mission, goals, and objectives, and tests its accountability and stewardship (see Chapter 31, "Stewardship and Accountability").

The annual giving program, or the annual fund, is much more than a fundraising effort. It is a systematic testing of the relevance and validity of the organization's case for support, a validation of the program and special needs of the organization, and an outreach effort to identify, inform, and involve multiple constituencies in the work of the organization.

A robust annual giving program is essential for a nonprofit organization.

Conclusion

The total development plan, fully integrated, is becoming the norm for sustainable fundraising. Organizations that limit themselves to lower-end activities such as special events, direct mail, email, and social media, deprive themselves of the opportunity for high-impact major gifts – Hodge's gifts of significance (see Chapter 18) – or the institution-changing capital or planned gift. Fundraising that proceeds with pride in mission, boldly inviting large gifts, will raise more money through a total development plan than through hit-and-miss appeals designed only to keep the doors open or to "fund the budget."

The totally integrated development program recognizes the giving patterns of the majority of donors. The annual fund builds a large base of loyal donors who give repeatedly year after year. Their deepening commitment makes them likely donors of special gifts in addition to their annual gifts. The total development program builds on the annual fund and special/major gifts programs for the occasional capital campaign, which expands the asset base of the organization. A carefully coordinated orchestration of all the components of the integrated program realizes that the ultimate gifts made through planned giving usually come from donors who have participated in the earlier stages of the program. This wisdom about fundraising has been substantiated through Paul Schervish's work, which found that major donors develop a philanthropic identification with the organization through "communities of participation" (Schervish, 1997). These are the very structures that the total development program fosters.

Other chapters in this book on major gifts (Chapter 18), capital campaigns (Chapter 19), and planned giving (Chapter 20) address the strengths of each discrete fundraising program. Each leg of the fundraising stool plays a strategic role in the life of the organization's fundraising. The overall program, when it is fully integrated and carefully coordinated and managed, positions the organization to conduct and manage fundraising at the most effective level.

The power and the efficacy of the total development plan lie in bringing to bear the essential elements for long-term fundraising success. These include market-oriented programs and services; well-informed constituencies capable of and willing to serve the mission; a well-defined workable plan that can be monitored, evaluated, and adapted; dedicated leadership by staff, board, and other volunteers willing to work, to give, and to ask others to give; and a high level of accountability and prudent stewardship.

These elements, properly managed, with disciplined attention to the demands of organized fundraising, will carry the organization to higher levels of effectiveness. The total development plan will raise funds necessary for program support, special needs, capital needs, and long-term endowment needs. The total development plan demands commitment to hard work. It requires investment of time, energy, and financial resources. Its returns are high.

Discussion Questions

1) How does your organization engage constituents in the various steps of the total development process?

2) In which of the components of the total development plan is your organization most effective? In which do you need to improve?
3) How effective is your organization's annual fundraising effort? How can it be expanded and/or made more effective?
4) Describe how your organization communicates with constituents at the different steps in the total development program.

CHAPTER EIGHTEEN

MAJOR GIFTS

By James M. Hodge

Nonprofit organizations, large and small, rely heavily on major gifts to reach annual fund objectives as well as to ensure the success of capital campaigns. The Rosso model of a total development program depends on personal solicitation of major gifts to complete a benefactor pyramid. The definitions of a major gift vary as greatly as the institutions themselves. One thing is certain: major gifts are inspired gifts that have a significant impact on the development program and the institution. Such gifts make it possible to launch new program initiatives, transform the physical plant, and endow vital components of nonprofit organizations. Defining major gifts by their size alone is insufficient to characterize the role they play in an organization's vitality. One group's definition may be $1,000 while another's may be $100,000. Frequently, major gifts are defined as gifts that constitute 1 to 5 percent (or more) of the number of gifts to an annual fund drive goal or 50 to 75 percent of the total dollars given to a capital campaign. In recent years there have been significant shifts in the old adage that 80 percent of contributions come from 20 percent of the benefactors. In some organizations 95 percent of contributions come from 5 percent of the benefactors. This trend of supporting the importance of major gifts is likely to continue as recent studies demonstrate that more and more of America's wealth is concentrated in fewer and fewer individuals' hands.

In this chapter you will learn about:

- The varying definitions of major gifts.
- How development officers can be agents of change.
- The stages of solicitation of major gifts.
- What works and does not work in obtaining gifts of significance.
- Values-based inquiry.
- The art of invitation.

Defining Major Gifts

Gifts of significance come in many forms. They may be substantial cash contributions, gifts of appreciated securities, or in-kind gifts such as contributions of valuable art or tangible personal property. Often major gifts are in the form of multi-year pledges given outright or through planned giving vehicles such as bequests, charitable trusts, or gift annuities. Regardless of the form they take, gifts of significance most often arise from benefactors who have contributed several "step gifts" or loyalty gifts over a period of time. Charitable step gifts are often smaller initial gifts made by a benefactor to increase their understanding of a nonprofit organization and allow the benefactor to test the efficiency and effectiveness of the organization. More and more major gifts are blended in nature and include requests for annual gifts for the organization's operating funds with an estate commitment of 20 times the annual gift to endow and sustain the annual gift in perpetuity. Hank Rosso's philosophy was that every benefactor, regardless of gift size, was a prospective benefactor for a gift at a higher level.

Leaders in the field of development have posited models of gifting, leading to major or ultimate gifts. Perhaps one of the best examples is that espoused by David Dunlop (2000). Dunlop classifies gifts as "annual," "special/capital," and "ultimate." His work details the size, frequency, types, and characteristics of gifts on a continuum. In this model, major gifts are 10 to 25 times larger than the annual gift. They are infrequently requested and require considerable thought on the part of the benefactor prior to confirming a commitment. These and other similar models of major gifts presented by Dunlop give form and context to the work of major gift officers.

Although most major gift models focus on the sizes, types, and purposes of major gifts, a new or perhaps renewed paradigm of major gifts is emerging in the philanthropic literature as well as in the practice of development. These models involve ever-deepening relationships between the development officer and the benefactor, as well as between the benefactor's values and the institution's

EXHIBIT 18.1. STAGES OF TRANSFORMING PHILANTHROPY.

Transational Stage: Giving	Transitional Stage: Naming	Transformational Stage: Changing
Ask and give	Give and name	Partner and change
Smaller gifts	Major gifts	Gift of significance
More frequent	Less frequent	Rare
Acquaintances	Friends	Soul mates

mission. Such models consider how the value systems of donors overlap with the core values and mission of the organization. These are the models and stages of transforming philanthropy (see Exhibit 18.1). The theory behind such models is based on the "why of giving" far more than the "how of giving." This is a clear shift from transactional fundraising to relational, benefactor-centric fundraising. Gifts of significance are given to organizations that earn the trust and confidence of benefactors. As Eric Uslander observed, "Trust matters most for those activities that signify the greatest commitment to your community: donating money and especially giving time" (2002, p. 133). Covey (2006) noted that "Trust is a function of two things: character and competence. Character includes your integrity, your motive, your intent with people. Competence includes your capabilities, your skills, your results, your track record. And both are vital" (p. 30). Authentic, ethical advancement professionals working in effective organizations compel philanthropically minded individuals to invest in, partner with, and commit to meaningful contributions to worthy organizations. In this way trust is both a social and a business lubricant. High-trust businesses earn better ROIs, and high-trust nonprofits raise more money.

Relationship-based models of philanthropy require development officers to be "agents of change," as articulated by Sheldon Garber in a thoughtful essay (1993). As agents of change, or "intrapreneurs," development officers are charged with articulating the institutional mission, finding its most contagious messengers, discerning the core values of prospective major benefactors through a values-based inquiry, and developing a deeper sense of the role and meaning of philanthropy in a well-examined life.

Regardless of the model of philanthropy, there are a few essential aspects to the work of major gift fundraisers. Development officers, often working with volunteers, explore both the philanthropic nature and the *financial* capacity of prospective benefactors and the *inclination* those benefactors may have to make a gift to their specific organization. Determining a benefactor's capacity requires the development officer to explore indices of wealth from public records, be familiar with their gifts to other nonprofits, garner information from volunteers who know the prospective benefactor, and draw conclusions based on interactions with the benefactors themselves. Larger advancement offices have full-time staff whose job it is to search databases and other sources of wealth to determine the financial capacity of prospective benefactors. (Using this information in the fundraising process is explored more fully in Chapter 7.) With or without such research staff, it is imperative that the development officer garner all possible knowledge about prospective benefactors before strategizing and formulating an invitation to give. Fortunately, in this age of information, and with powerful search engines such as Google, this research has been more readily available to all in the profession.

Arthur Frantzreb (1991), in describing benefactor research, states the necessity to understand the "interests, concerns, hobbies and eccentricities; education; family history, spouse and children; experience in the nonprofit world; residences; civic, social and fraternal positions; and religion" of potential major benefactors (p. 120). This information serves as a basis for evaluating a benefactor's financial capacity and inclination to make a major gift. Paul Schervish, in his studies of the wealthy, has postulated that the truly wealthy have the advantage of satisfying all their comfort needs in life and that often such individuals no longer have to expend energies on accumulating wealth. Rather than focusing on asset accumulation needs, the truly wealthy, those with abundance, can explore ways their resources can have a meaningful impact on the world (Schervish, O'Herlihy, and Havens, 2001, pp. 3–4). These individuals have the capacity to make a discernable impact on an organization, a community, or a cause. Such benefactors can make a difference in the world and truly leave a legacy of compassionate, impactful change through philanthropic gifts. In a sense, this is a way to transform money into meaning in the lives of philanthropists. To inspire gifts of significance, one must cultivate relationships with individuals passionate about improving the lives of others and who can commit significant resources. Mere indices of wealth capacity alone do not suffice to guarantee the procurement of major gifts. Both the inclination to make the world a better place and a focused passion for the organization are required for the realization of a major gift. Instead of merely chasing money, development officers and volunteers must be cognizant of signs of wealth, yet place equal emphasis on those individuals with a charitable nature and a passion for their cause.

Who are the natural partners for one's organization? First and foremost are present contributors to the nonprofit. Major gifts generally come from individuals who already embrace the institution's mission and case for support. Other potential major benefactors are committed volunteers who are governing board or committee members, the nonprofit's constituencies (alumni, former campers, members, and so on), and philanthropically minded individuals in the community. The 2014 U.S. Trust *Study of High Net Worth Philanthropy* (Indiana University, Lilly Family School of Philanthropy) showed that volunteers gave 75 percent more to nonprofits than those who did not volunteer. Earlier studies have found that individuals who are traditionally religious or spiritual are more likely to use philanthropy to vote their values and to find meaning in their lives (INDEPENDENT SECTOR, 2002b). Major gift programs must focus more time and attention on the *communities of the committed*, who believe in the organization and wish to propel it to new levels of service, efficiency, or effectiveness.

Utilizing benefactor wealth research and screening tools as well as referrals from board members, volunteers, and major donors, development officers create lists of individuals with the capacity to make a difference in the organization. It is then the development officer's responsibility to create an engagement strategy and inspire individuals to participate in the life of the organization. For it is through genuine engagement in the experiences of the nonprofit and the impact your organization has on those who they serve that vital social equity increases between individuals and organizations, resulting in philanthropic gifts of significance.

Numerous models describing stages in the solicitation of major gifts have been postulated over the years. The Fund Raising School (2009) uses an eight-step model (see Exhibit 18.2). As donors are involved deeply in the life of the nonprofit organization, they develop an "ownership position" in the good that is done through the organization. As donors increase their "social equity share" in the institution and see their personal values overlap with the institution's mission, more and more significant gifts are made to further the cause. Benefactors no longer will accept being merely "deep pockets" but rather yearn for and require authentic experiences with the organizations they support. According to experts, "People tend to perceive as authentic that which is done exceptionally well, executed individually and extraordinarily by someone demonstrating human care; not unfeelingly or disingenuously performed" (Gilmore and Pine, 2007, p. 49).

EXHIBIT 18.2. MAJOR GIFTS: THE EIGHT-STEP SOLICITATION PROCESS.

1. Identification
2. Qualification
3. Development of Strategy
4. Cultivation
5. Solicitation and Negotiation
6. Acknowledgment
7. Stewardship
8. Renewal

Source: The Fund Raising School, 2009.

How does the development officer engage potential benefactors in the mission of the organization? Once natural partners are identified, it is through authentic relationship building that the development officers promote major investments. Inviting donors to volunteer on important committees, raise funds, share their expertise, and serve on the governing boards are some of the most common ways of building ownership. Potential major benefactors are in constant demand and volunteer burnout is rampant, but a surefire way to propel an organization in the arena of major gifts is to authentically involve donors in the mission of the non-profit. Perhaps the highest form of reverence we can demonstrate to donors is to genuinely ask their opinions and, equally important, to seriously consider those opinions as they may impact the institution's mission and core values.

It is also instructive to note why fundraisers fail or why donors refuse to make major gifts to nonprofits. Sturtevant (1997) identified the most common reasons that major gifts fail to materialize: institutional leaders and development officers neglect to establish basic trust between the organization and the nonprofit's mission, vision, and services; nonprofit leaders do not help donors connect with the institution and serve the benefactor's interests and needs; and fundraisers fail to instill a sense of urgency for the request. Major benefactors do not make major gifts because of a mismatch of interests between donor and institution, a premature request before the donor was ready to give, a failure to ask for a specific amount, being asked too many times by the organization or by competing nonprofits, and a lack of connection between the solicitor of the gift and the donor. Major benefactors have experienced disingenuous encounters with nonprofits and rarely continue relationships with organizations whose only interest is in their money. A Canadian study in 2011 found three main reasons individuals failed to commit a contribution. The first was an offensive tone or approach to the solicitation followed by frequency of requests or multiple requests from the same organization (Redbird, 2011). Likewise, the 2014 U.S. Trust *Study of High Net Worth Philanthropy* also found that the reason major benefactors stopped giving was the frequency of being asked as well as a view that the nonprofit was not effective in their work.

The wealthy, like all of us, are tired of being manipulated to make gifts. The proper stance to take in relationship-based philanthropy is not to manipulate but to inspire, not to push someone to make a "transaction-based" gift but rather to make the mission and its work so real and important as to compel or "pull" a donor to make a gift. As Tom Morris said in his book *If Aristotle Ran General Motors* (1997), "Pull is the lure of an attractive goal or a strongly desired good, recognized by Plato and Aristotle as well as by many other great thinkers of the past … embodying a valued ideal. It attracts us and calls us to put forward our greatest efforts. The greater the ideal, the greater the power it can have in our lives" (p. 63). A master key question professionals should always ask themselves is: Are we telling, selling, or compelling in our work with philanthropists? This is especially important when working with Generation X or Millennials who do not want to be *told or sold anything*.

What Works in Major Gift Fundraising

Fortunately, in the past several years, practitioners in the field of philanthropy and professors in our nation's universities have begun to explore more deeply why benefactors make major gifts and why donors say they do not make gifts. This donor-centered research is both welcomed and instructive. *The Seven Faces of Philanthropy* (Prince and File, 1994) categorizes wealthy donors into seven motivational types. This important work emphasizes understanding the interests, concerns, needs, and motivations of wealthy individuals toward the role of philanthropy in their lives. Developing an understanding of benefactors' motivations, the development professional can strategize how to meaningfully involve prospective benefactors in the work of the nonprofit. Cluster analysis by Prince and File revealed four important donor segments: "affiliators," who look for social and business linkages through nonprofit activities; "pragmatists," who see personal financial advantages through support of nonprofits; "dynasts," who are heirs to family affluence and to the tradition of philanthropy; and "repayers," who want to reciprocate benefits they or someone close to them received from a nonprofit.

Some benefactors make major gifts because of a sense of obligation to the nonprofit, the greater community, or the world. Gifts of significance, however, arise out of the true interests, values, and passions of the prospective benefactor (see Figure 18.1). Regardless of the particular motivation for giving, the role of the

FIGURE 18.1. VALUES OVERLAP.

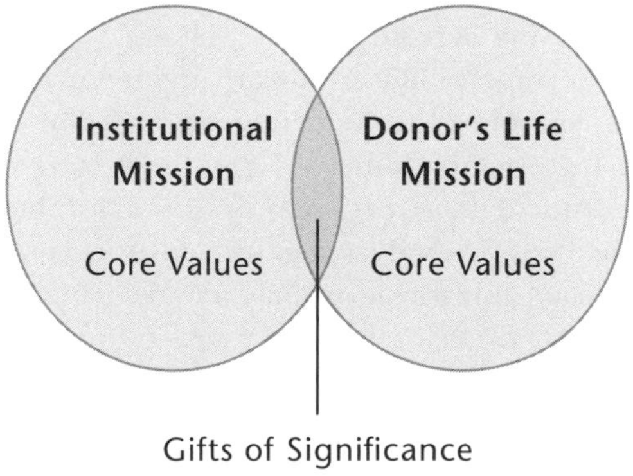

Gifts of Significance

major gift officer is to engage the donor in the important work of the nonprofit and deepen the benefactor's involvement in the organization's mission and value systems.

Inquiring and Inspiring

Given the anecdotal findings of professionals in the development field and the recent research of social scientists, we are better prepared to understand the motivation of major donors. The next question confronting nonprofits is how we best position our institutions and our prospective benefactors for success in the area of major gifts. Hank Rosso (1991) put it best when he said, "Fund raising is the gentle art of teaching people the joy of giving." He long understood and practiced the idea of "transformational philanthropy." He knew that major gift work was the result of relationship building, and, like Sheldon Garber, he understood the need for development officers to be agents of change in the lives of their organizations and benefactors.

What skills, then, do development professionals working in the area of major gifts need to succeed? Clearly, they require strong communication skills to help them understand the values and motivations of potential major benefactors and to articulate the institution's mission, and they must have the creativity and passion to inspire the benefactor to action. Being a successful major gift officer and volunteer fund raiser does not require having all the answers about the prospective benefactor, but it does require that the development professionals and volunteers know all the right questions to ask of both the institution and the donor.

The following are some key questions the major gift officer must ask of the institution:

- Is our mission relevant, important, effective, and compellingly articulated?
- Can we use outcome measurements to determine if we are advancing the mission? Can we measure impact?
- What is our responsibility to steward and report to our benefactors?
- How can we better involve volunteers and donors in the good that is done through our organization?
- Who best articulates our mission and vision for the future?
- Who would be a natural partner with a particular benefactor?
- Who is responsible for developing and deepening the relationship with a specific benefactor?

Every nonprofit must identify the "vision master," a leader who brings the mission to life for benefactors. Just as important, each institution must identify the staff members with the skills to transform vision to action, to make things happen so as to advance the mission through definable steps and acts. Finally, the major gift officers must be primarily responsible to advance the relationship between the prospective benefactor and the institution. This is where benefactor and institutional values overlap and the "dance of philanthropy" is performed. Some institutions discover that the vision master is primarily the organization's president or chair of the board of directors. For other nonprofits, there will be many hands in the work of inspiring major gifts. It is wise to have multiple links between the nonprofit and the benefactor. This prevents reliance on a few people to raise major gifts. That can be devastating when and if the major players leave the nonprofit. Malcolm Gladwell, in his book *The Tipping Point* (2000), speaks of the need for both "sticky" messages and "contagious" messengers in order for ideas and innovations to take hold. The "sticky" message is the institution's most compelling articulation of its primary mission or cause. In order to attract the new, more engaged philanthropist, it is the development officer's duty to discover from within or without their organization those contagious people who can bring mission and impact alive for benefactors.

There are questions major gift officers must ask themselves as well. To paraphrase Robert Payton (1988, p. 74), who posed the most piercing questions of all. Do we as professionals work for philanthropy or off philanthropy? Why are we doing this important work? For major gift work is less of a job and more of a calling. Development professionals are not selling products; they are promoting visions and possibilities for the betterment of humankind. This is serious work, which must be taken seriously by the professionals engaged in it. It is not a vendor–vendee relationship but rather a genuine partnership we inspire with our benefactors. O'Neill (1993) saw development professionals as moral trainers. Major gift officers are indeed moral trainers whose work is about ethical inspiration (Rosso's "teaching the joy of giving"). Hence one must ask: Are we serving as role models of philanthropy? Are we making important philanthropic gifts ourselves? Do we serve as "soul models" of well-examined lives? And perhaps most important of all: Are we devoted to helping individuals find meaning in their lives through acts of philanthropy? Many prospective major benefactors know how to accumulate "means" but not "meaning" in their lives. One way of looking at major gift work is that development officers, volunteers, and donors are on a long walk together to find meaning in life. Meaning can be found through philanthropy.

As important as it is to be an agent of change through professional introspection and probing the mission and values of the institution, the great work of development is done through exploring a benefactor's values in an atmosphere of trust. Using a process Dunlop (2000) refers to as "nurturing inquiry," major gift officers ask defining value questions of donors. The classic work by Kübler-Ross (1969) on death and dying teaches that, on their deathbeds, individuals do not measure the value of their lives by their net worth or accumulations; rather they measure their life's meaning based on whether they were their authentic selves in life, if they made a difference in the world, and left a lasting legacy. It seems apparent that through philanthropy, development officers and volunteers can help donors provide meaningful answers to both lifelong and deathbed questions. This makes the essence of major gift work "helping people arrive before they depart!" This requires encouraging benefactors to transform from role models in business to soul models in philanthropy. By asking important questions, we help individuals transform from motivations that are mostly intrinsic to extrinsic, from self-centered to other-centered, and from independent to interdependent. Transforming major gift work is all about changing "me-centeredness" to "we-centeredness."

Questions of Value   Prior to elucidating some of the key value questions, it is important to understand guidelines for values-based inquiry. Before one asks important questions regarding values, it is necessary to establish an atmosphere of trust. Two essential components for an atmosphere of trust are permissions and protections. These are assurances to the donors that before we probe core values, we will seek their permission to enter a deeper relationship. Beyel (1997, p. 52) calls it "philanthropic informed consent." This is a discovery process whereby the development officer and the donor engage in a moral and ethical dialogue. This may be as simple as asking permission to inquire about closely held values, but more often it is an intuitive process, much like knowing when it is safe to ask an acquaintance a question we would normally ask a close friend. The second important way of establishing trust is to ensure that any information divulged will remain private and confidential. This means that the development officer must guard all confidential information and never share that information with the donor's family, friends, or colleagues. Care must be taken about what should be put in visit reports.

Some key donor questions include these: What values do you hold most dear? Who has inspired you in your life and your work? How does one make a difference in the world? What is your legacy in the world today or in the world of tomorrow? To whom are you grateful? Can you finish your legacy alone? How much is enough money to leave heirs? Is there ever too much money to leave to heirs? What is the most satisfying philanthropic gift you have made and why? Which one of the nonprofits you support does the best job of keeping you involved in its mission? What kinds of reports do you want and expect as stewardship for your major gift? How do you prefer to be invited to make a charitable gift? These are only a few samples of key questions the major gift officer must ask while developing a relationship with each benefactor. The questions are asked at appropriate stages in the relationship.

They are meant to be stretching questions but can seem impertinent or assertive if they come too early in a relationship.

Building an Ownership Position   The most important role for the major gift officer is to forge a close relationship between a donor and the nonprofit, including its volunteers. One important method in relationship building is philanthropic storytelling, inspiring the benefactor by telling the great things that others have done to advance the organization's mission through philanthropy. Storytelling allows the development officer to comfortably make maps for donors to follow with their own personal gifts. A part of the cultivation and relationship-building process is to invite the donor to make an investment or step gifts to the organization, as discussed earlier in the chapter. It is important to ask for these smaller gifts, as they allow the donor to open a window into the nonprofit and provide the nonprofit with the opportunity to further involve the donor through meaningful stewardship and appropriate recognition. Invitations for such early investments allow the development officer to determine if the proposal harmonizes with the donor's core values. However, rather than asking merely for any "starting gift," it is paramount to consider what sort of gift will further involve the donor in the nonprofit and might naturally lead to new and greater commitments. The major gift officer should ask, "Does this proposal have the potential to grow into more meaningful and impactful gifts by the donors?" A step annual gift request for a partial academic scholarship can lead to further requests to provide full scholarships and eventually investments to endow that scholarship in perpetuity or, perhaps through an estate gift, to name the academic unit wherein the scholarship lies.

Although step gifts are common ways to encourage major gifts, it is not unheard of for a first gift to a nonprofit to be a major gift. Development officers and volunteers must be alert to those unique individuals who can quickly catch a vision and make major initial gifts to the nonprofit. This is especially true with gifts from younger entrepreneurs, as seen recently through billion-dollar gifts from the founders of Google and Facebook. The information age and the technology it has sparked have made billionaires out of 30 year olds, and they are asking themselves earlier and earlier about the social responsibility of their wealth. Many of these gifts are inspired by older mentors such as Bill and Melinda Gates and Warren Buffett through the Giving Pledge and remarkable conversations led by thought leaders in Silicon Valley. In anticipation of buyouts of their companies or their businesses going public, they gift stock to organizations that inspire them.

The Invitation   Most of the strategic work of our profession is done prior to drafting a proposal or asking for a gift. Donor values have been explored, appropriate gift levels have been considered and related directly to the impact that the gift will have, and the proposal team has been carefully selected and has rehearsed the solicitation in detail. The major gift officer must ask several questions. Have we come to know this donor sufficiently? Has this donor been involved meaningfully in the work of our organization? Is this an appropriate time for this request? Are we requesting a respectful amount and considering what gift vehicle and appropriate asset would be best for the benefactors to give? Will the project or the gift purpose resonate with the benefactor? Is this the inspiring team to set a vision and make the request?

In setting up a specific meeting to discuss a proposal, it is important that the potential benefactors know that the purpose of the visit is to invite their philan-thropic support for an important organizational project. This avoids fundraising by stealth or surprise and is the respectful thing to do. In some cases, saying, "We are excited to share a compelling vision and a big idea that we believe will inspire you," is sufficient to let the prospective benefactor know that a request will be made of him or her. The question "Would you be open to hearing about a big idea that we believe could have a profoundly positive impact on our community?' is a powerful way to request a meeting.

Other important questions should be strategized by the major gift officer and those participating in a gift solicitation. Where will the major gift proposal be made? The site should be chosen with the donor's needs and comfort in mind. Usually it is at the donor's home or place of business. Sometimes it takes place at the nonprofit, particularly if the request requires a tour or on-site demonstration of how the donor's gift will impact the work of the nonprofit. Public settings such as restaurants for major gift solicitations can be disastrous. Privacy and protection can never be guaranteed in such a setting. A waiter may interrupt or stumble just as the proposal reaches its apex, spoiling both mood and decorum. It may be best to ask the benefactor where they would like to hold such a meeting.

Regardless of the setting, the major gift officer must be sure to consider: Who will be in attendance from the benefactor's side of the equation? Are all the deci-sion makers at the table, or is this a meeting with the potential benefactor alone? Eventually all the appropriate leaders of the organization, the donor and spouse and family, and legal and financial advisers, as appropriate, may have to be on board. The proposal itself must be clear and include the gift amount, project goals and means of measuring the achievement of those goals, recognition options for the gift, and a plan for reporting or stewardship after the gift is made. A pre-proposal rehearsal will make certain that at the right time the right person makes the right request. Part of a good rehearsal session before a major request is to brain-storm potential benefactor questions, to have ready the answers to those questions, and to determine who precisely is responsible for answering those questions about the proposal at hand. The worst possible scenario is for a potential benefactor to ask an important or unanticipated question and to be met with hesitation as to who should address that question. Many times volunteers prefer to tell the stories of their passion for the cause and describe the project but feel more comfortable if a member of the organization actually makes the ask for a specific amount of money. "We are requesting your consideration of a leadership gift of (*specific amount*), which will be the catalyst for making this project a reality" is only one tried and true way of making the ask itself.

The more significant the gift, the more important it is to present a well-designed proposal as a leave-behind for the donor and their advisors. Many philanthropists, and particularly entrepreneurs, are visual learners. Charts, graphs, colorful illustrations, and/or very brief videos (less than two minutes) are essential to catch and keep their attention. Telling stories about how their gift will change lives and the use of metaphors and examples that can unlock complex concepts should be embedded in the proposal. Visually appealing proposals have literally been created as "road maps" or "blueprints" for the benefactor to follow during discussions. Advancement professionals, writers, and designers should ask themselves if a proposal could be creatively captured in one slide or illustration.

Stewardship and Recognition Once a gift commitment is entered into, the process of stewardship begins (consult Chapter 31). To ensure that there is no "donor regret," to steal a term from the for-profit world, the organization must immediately thank the donor and plan strategic and meaningful stewardship that engages the benefactor in the impact of their gift. Thank-you letters from scholarship recipients, financial reports, lab tours, photos, web cams and web sites documenting construction projects, and personal visits with progress reports are simply the best ways to strengthen donor ties to the nonprofit. Stewardship is both ethical and essential following receipt of major gifts, and it is the smart thing to do to encourage future investments from the benefactor. Major benefactors drift away from organizations that fail to demonstrate the impact of their gifts.

Benefactor recognition is another way to link benefactors with the nonprofit. "How would you and your family like us to acknowledge your generous gift?" is an appropriate inquiry. Recognition should be as personal as possible, reflective of the uniqueness of the nonprofit and the gift, and appropriate to the size and importance of the contribution. Most major benefactors do not need more generic plaques, paperweights, or assorted other "trinkets," but they always appreciate meaningful "recognition" that is unique, personal, links them emotionally with the organization, and reinforces the significance of their contribution. Other major donors in waiting will examine how your institution respectfully recognizes and stewards gifts of significance.

3

Managing the Major Gift Process

Whether a major gift officer heads a one-person shop or is a part of a large and complex major gift team, the key to major gift success is an organized system for the identification, engagement, and solicitation of potential major benefactors. The literature is rife with examples of how to manage the major gift process. Successful programs can be managed using simple index cards or sophisticated software programs. Exhibit 18.3 provides a guide for managing the major gift process. Regardless of the format, every institution must identify the top 25 to 100 or 5 to 10 percent of the institutional donor base, for potential major donors whose philanthropy can have a significant impact on the organization.

Once identified, each donor benefactor should be assigned an individual file. Files should be developed with respect for the donor and include only information that is pertinent to the relationship and the potential major gift. This information will be useful in determining what types of nonprofit projects will resonate with the donor's value systems. Private and potentially embarrassing information about a donor has no place in these files. A good guide is only to include information, notes, or comments from benefactor visits that could be read over your shoulder by the benefactor him/herself without embarrassment. Files should also include the names of natural partners who are centers of influence in the donor's life. Vital is information about regular meetings with institutional leaders to discuss the benefactor, his or her deepening involvement in the nonprofit, a realistic potential gift amount, and details of any projects of great potential interest. All encounters, engagements, and experiences with the benefactor should be appropriately documented, for these relationships are a result of the alignment of the institution and the donor, and they do not belong solely to development officers who manage the relationships.

Specific ways to further the donor's involvement and interests can then be documented. Essential to the management process is the appointment of the relationship manager, the person responsible for advancing and documenting the relationship. Many management plans set metrics for specific numbers of personal visits with potential major benefactors, the number of proposals presented, and total dollars raised each year. However, it is not the frequency of the encounters that is important but rather how deep an impact the development officer or other institution leaders and volunteers have on a donor's sense of belonging to the nonprofit. Visit numbers are less important than meaningful encounters with predetermined objectives that increase the donor's "equity share" in the nonprofit. We must fashion metrics based on the deepening of relationships as well as the number of donor contacts.

EXHIBIT 18.3. DEVELOPING A STRATEGY FOR THE MAJOR GIFT PROCESS.

Benefactor Biographic Information
- Name, address, phone numbers
- Family information, marital status, children
- Degrees, interests and hobbies
- Governing board and committee memberships
- Interest areas for potential major gifts
- Other pertinent publicly known information

Financial Information
What is known about the prospective benefactor's financial information and ability to make a major gift?
- Public information on stock and real estate ownership
- Previous gifts to the organization and other charities
- Other pertinent public financial information

Linkages
- Who are the individuals, staff, and volunteers closest to the prospective benefactor?
- Who are the donor's natural partners?

Strategy
- Who should be involved in the relationship building, proposal development, and the request?
- For what specific purpose is the gift being sought?
- What is the proposed gift amount?
- Who will present the proposal?
- When will it be presented?
- What specific steps or next actions must be accomplished before a proposal can be made? By whom? By when?
- Are there any roadblocks to this proposal, and if so, who can remove them?
- What coaching, rehearsals, or strategy planning sessions will be necessary?

Specific Next Steps
- Set up a reminder system, manual or computerized, to monitor next steps and for revision of strategies as appropriate.
- Determine what actions should be taken, by whom, and by when.

The Philanthropic Road Ahead

Much has transpired in the world of philanthropy since the publication of *Achieving Excellence in Fundraising, Third Edition*. Research led by the Lilly Family School of Philanthropy has revealed important evidence about who are the most generous people in the world. As Greg Dees was quoted in the book *Philanthrocapitalism*, "Philanthropy today is best defined more broadly than giving money away, as mobilizing and deploying private resources, including money, time, social capital and expertise, to improve the world in which we live" (Bishop and Green, 2008, p. 49).

The first lesson to be learned in major gift work is to scan your institution's database for the entrepreneurs in your midst. This movement has been led by the words and the works of powerful exemplars of philanthropy and the positive impacts they have had in the world. Bill Gates, Warren Buffett, Bono, Muhammad Yunus, Steve Case, and many, many others are questioning the traditional "give, name, and go away style of philanthropy" that was more common in decades past. According to Bishop and Green, "One of the key elements of philanthrocapitalism is an obsession with ensuring that money is put to good use" (2008, p. 69). They go on to say that Mario Morino, founder of Venture Philanthropy Partners (VPP), "agrees that being businesslike as a philanthropist, which he favors, is not the same thing as treating nonprofits as if they were businesses. The social sector, he says he has learned, is far more dependent on relationships than systems" (p. 91). There are indeed economic norms associated with business while our field is grounded on social norms. The new "engaged philanthropist," however, expects that nonprofits look at and learn from the business world to gain efficiencies, learn to model new programs, replicate those models, and then scale them. These hypomanic, passionate, and results-driven philanthropreneurs will not tolerate nonprofit "business" as usual. They expect we will work as hard at doing good with their gifts as they worked to earn the money in the first place. They bring to the table their creative minds, their intense curiosity, their experience, and their contacts. They are attracted to new ways of doing social good and are willing to participate in venture philanthropy to change our way of serving the world, try new models, tinker with delivery systems, and quickly reinvest in success. They also know the value of leverage in their gifts and simply expect more from us.

There is a new landscape of philanthropy evolving in the past decade or more and spreading rapidly around the globe. It is what I call the "philanthropy to business continuum," which can be found in Figure 18.2. This new business approach to philanthropy appears to include the questioning of gifts of endowments to organizations. When philanthropists are making 10, 20, 30 percent or more investing their own money, the thought of giving endowments that yield 4–6 percent is uninspiring. Additionally, some philanthropreneurs think of endowments as *perpetuating the past* for the organization rather than funding new models that drive the nonprofit into the future.

As moral trainers, relationship managers, agents of change, and provocateurs, we are fully equipped to ethically inspire these game-changing philanthropists. We are accustomed to working with business-minded individuals; we know what

FIGURE 18.2. PHILANTHROPY TO BUSINESS SPECTRUM.

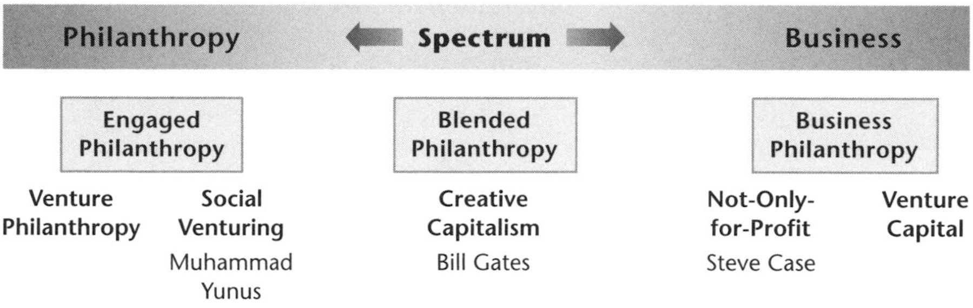

Philanthropy	← Spectrum →	Business

Engaged Philanthropy	Blended Philanthropy	Business Philanthropy

Venture Philanthropy	Social Venturing	Creative Capitalism	Not-Only-for-Profit	Venture Capital
	Muhammad Yunus	Bill Gates	Steve Case	

motivates them. We are well positioned to lead dialogues within our organizations as to how to navigate these engaged benefactors. The new future of our work, as beautifully articulated in the book *Forces for Good* (Crutchfield and Grant, 2008), emphasizes that our work ahead will be all about collaboration not competition. The next stage of our work will be to explore the environment searching for opportunities for collaborations between countries, companies, nonprofits, and philanthropists. Sectors are both bending and blending, requiring us to co-create the future with our best allies and philanthropists.

Conclusion

Some specific techniques of major gift work have been explored in this chapter, along with ways to approach and manage the major gift process, but when all is said and done, it is still the spirit behind the major gift process that determines its success. If, as major gift officers, we operated on the "push" or "scolding" model of development (Schervish, 2000b, pp. 2–3) we will have neither long-term success in the field nor satisfaction in our work (see Exhibit 18.4). It is through Schervish's "discernment model" that we respect donor wishes in the fund-raising process. If we compete with other nonprofits for perceived limited charitable dollars, we will look like avaricious children squabbling over a parent's estate. We should adopt a "supply-side" approach to philanthropy and not a "scarcity model," as good philanthropic work is like the rising tide that lifts all ships and spirits. Schervish (2000b) helps us do just that with his idea of "supply-side philanthropy." This elegant theory postulates that it is not through competition for an illusionary and limited "pie of philanthropy" but rather through inspiring individuals toward gifts of significance that the true growth of philanthropy will occur. This theory implies that the only

EXHIBIT 18.4. THE SCOLDING AND DISCERNMENT MODELS.

Scolding Model	Discernment Model
You are not giving • Enough • To the right causes • At the right time • In the right way	Is there something • You want to do with your wealth • That fulfills the needs of others • That you can do more efficiently and more effectively than government or commerce, and • That expresses your gratitude, brings you satisfaction, and actualizes your identification with the fate of others?

Source: Paul G. Schervish, "The Spiritual Horizons of Philanthropy," in E. R. Tempel and D. F. Burlingame (eds.), *Understanding the Needs of Donors.* New Directions for Philanthropic Fundraising, no. 29. Copyright © 2000 John Wiley & Sons, Inc. This material is used by permission of John Wiley & Sons, Inc.

limits to philanthropy are those that we impose on ourselves and our institutions through misinformed notions of this important work and the transforming effect philanthropy can have on the lives of our benefactors. The 2014 U.S. Trust *Study of High Net Worth Philanthropy* said it best when it concluded, "Nonprofit organizations that understand what savvy donors value and respect, who carefully steward their gifts, and demonstrate that they are making a meaningful difference through wise and transparent use of resources can develop enduring partnerships with donors that achieve a shared vision."

Discussion Questions

1) How are major gifts generally defined within organizations and what kind of impact can they have on annual fund or capital campaign fund raising success?
2) Define "capacity and inclination" as those terms relate to major gift fund raising.
3) Explain the difference between "transactional and relational" fund raising approaches and why the latter is more effective in raising major gifts.
4) List three reasons why major benefactors make gifts to organizations and three reasons why they stop making major gifts.
5) What does the author mean by "sticky messages and contagious messengers" related to major gifts?
6) What are three or four key questions one should ask before presenting a proposal for a major gift?

CHAPTER NINETEEN

CAPITAL CAMPAIGNS

By Aaron Conley

In the first edition of this book, Henry Rosso (1991) personally authored the chapter "Asset Building Through Capital Fund Raising," which provided a thorough study of the necessary components for a successful campaign. His basic principles are still relevant today. In particular, his 12-step readiness test remains a valuable tool any organization should undertake before embarking on a campaign, especially if it is their first.

Over the past two decades, campaigns have taken on even greater importance for nonprofit organizations. While major universities draw the most attention with campaign goals that have crossed into the multibillion dollar range, campaigns have become familiar – and likely expected – among all organizations in the non-profit sector. Agencies providing basic human services, arts and culture organizations, churches, and even public K-12 schools have all ventured into campaigns with increasing frequency. This chapter covers:

- The history and definition of various types of campaigns.
- The essential steps in planning and managing a campaign.
- How to kick off and conclude a campaign.
- The important role of determining impact and demonstrating stewardship.
- A successful campaign through a case study.

Defining Today's Campaign

The introduction of the modern-day campaign dates back to 1905 when Charles Sumner Ward of Chicago was retained to help the YMCA in Washington, DC, raise funds for a new building (Cutlip, 1965). Shortly thereafter, the University of Pittsburgh retained him to apply what became known as the "Ward method" to help manage a $3 million campaign. The fundamentals introduced by Ward included a publicly announced dollar goal and a defined time period within which these funds were to be raised. These fundamentals persisted throughout the following century and remain just as relevant today.

As campaigns have become more common throughout the nonprofit sector, a substantial body of literature has been generated on the mechanics of a successful campaign. The second and third editions of this book both include an outstanding chapter on campaigns, authored by Robert Pierpont (Tempel, 2003; Tempel, Seiler, and Aldrich, 2011). Kent Dove's second edition of *Conducting a Successful Capital Campaign* (2000) has become an industry standard and higher education benefited from the publication of *Leading the Campaign: Advancing Colleges and Universities* (Worth, 2010).

This chapter addresses many of the same basic structures of a campaign discussed in these and other publications. Prior to this, however, it is important to note that the term "capital campaign" has persisted into today's lexicon, rather incorrectly, to refer to something other than its historical context. Multiyear campaigns that sought to raise money for an organization's capital purposes, mainly buildings but also endowment in support of the organization's programs, have traditionally carried the capital campaign label.

Today's campaigns have evolved in most cases to include all funds raised for all purposes, which carries a more appropriate label of "comprehensive" campaign. As noted by Worth (2010, p. 5), this is especially true of colleges and universities where multiple projects and initiatives can be pursued under the umbrella of a single campus-wide campaign. These efforts may include capital projects such as new buildings or renovations, but also include targeted goals to enhance student scholarships, increase endowed chairs for faculty, and strengthen support for libraries, student activities, and other special programs. The comprehensive campaign label also effectively describes efforts by hospitals, art museums, symphony orchestras, public libraries, and other similar organizations that concurrently raise private support for capital projects along with current program needs under the same campaign effort.

For organizations that do not undertake comprehensive campaigns, or for those that do but are in the period between the end of one and the start of another, it has become common to pursue smaller and shorter campaigns with outcomes that are more narrowly defined. Dove calls these "single-purpose campaigns" (2000, p. 18), which may raise money for a building, a specific endowment fund, or other isolated objectives. He also provides a useful definition for "sub-campaigns" (p. 19), which exist as part of an organization's continuous major gift program and allow for smaller initiatives that are in concert with overall institutional strategies.

Fundamental Structure of a Campaign

Rosso's basic definition of a campaign is still valid today, where he described it as an "… intensive function designed to raise a specified sum of money within a defined time period to meet the varied asset-building needs of the organization" (1991, p. 80). Even though new technologies have greatly influenced the ways we communicate with and solicit prospective donors, a campaign still retains a core structure not unfamiliar to those conducted throughout the past century.

Figure 19.1 illustrates the key phases of a campaign, along with critical steps to be taken within each phase. Note the way two of the phases – Pre-Campaign Planning and Stewardship and Campaign Impact – fall outside the formal boundaries of the campaign's beginning and end. Too often, these phases are passed over too quickly, jeopardizing the success of not just the current campaign but future ones as well.

Pre-Campaign Planning

Campaigns are undertaken to raise the resources necessary to address a need or collection of needs. All too often the "need" is driven by the organization. "We need a building" or "we need scholarships" or similar statements are behind the genesis of many campaigns. The pre-campaign planning phase is critical to begin orienting everyone – organization executives and board members, fundraising staff, and key volunteers – to begin thinking about the campaign from both the organization's perspective and that of the donors.

Campaign plans should be predicated on an organization's strategic plan. Nonprofit organizations exist to serve some critical societal need, and the way in which they address this need should be clearly articulated through this documented plan. Those organizations either too resistant or complacent to develop a strategic plan should, as a minimum, have a "statement of strategic direction" that

FIGURE 19.1. PHASES OF A CAMPAIGN.

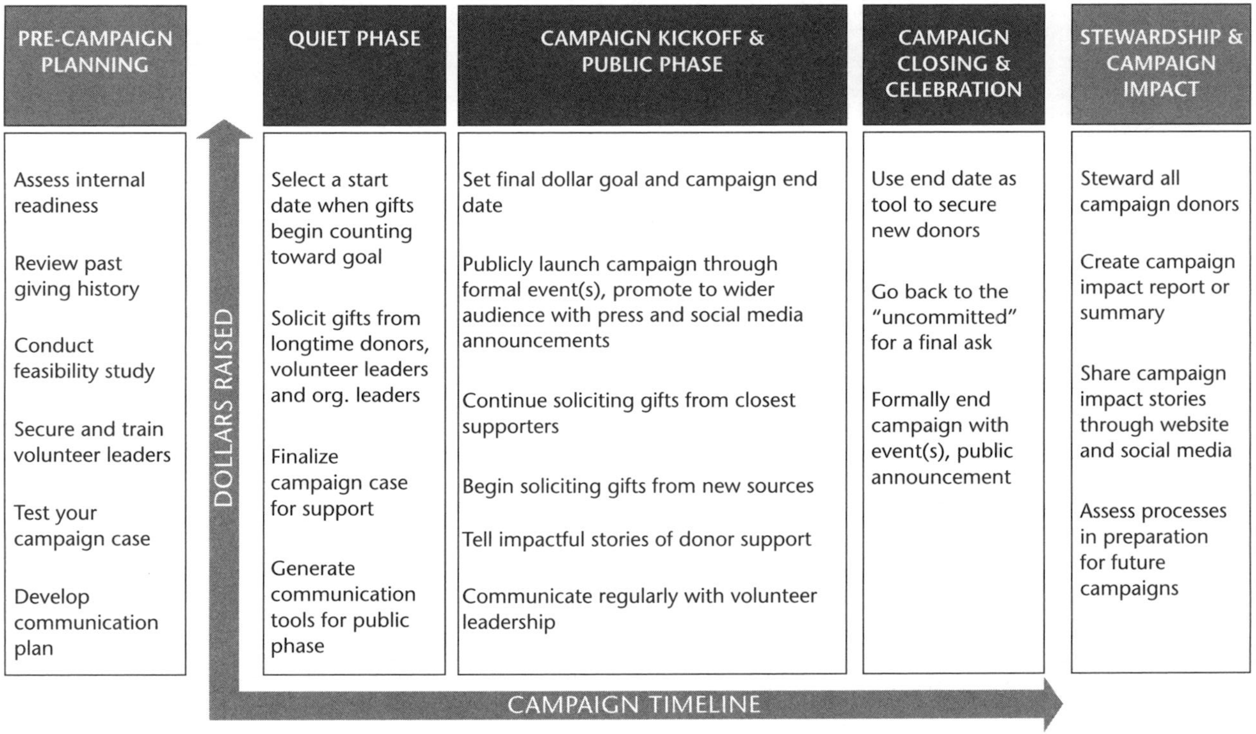

PRE-CAMPAIGN PLANNING	QUIET PHASE	CAMPAIGN KICKOFF & PUBLIC PHASE	CAMPAIGN CLOSING & CELEBRATION	STEWARDSHIP & CAMPAIGN IMPACT
Assess internal readiness	Select a start date when gifts begin counting toward goal	Set final dollar goal and campaign end date	Use end date as tool to secure new donors	Steward all campaign donors
Review past giving history	Solicit gifts from longtime donors, volunteer leaders and org. leaders	Publicly launch campaign through formal event(s), promote to wider audience with press and social media announcements	Go back to the "uncommitted" for a final ask	Create campaign impact report or summary
Conduct feasibility study	Finalize campaign case for support	Continue soliciting gifts from closest supporters	Formally end campaign with event(s), public announcement	Share campaign impact stories through website and social media
Secure and train volunteer leaders	Generate communication tools for public phase	Begin soliciting gifts from new sources		Assess processes in preparation for future campaigns
Test your campaign case		Tell impactful stories of donor support		
Develop communication plan		Communicate regularly with volunteer leadership		

DOLLARS RAISED

CAMPAIGN TIMELINE

246

provides some degree of the organization's identity and vision for how they will make a positive impact in the future (O'Brien, 2005).

Utilizing the strategic plan (or alternative document), an organization can then begin to craft a compelling case statement, which articulates to prospective supporters how a campaign will better empower them to fulfill the critical need(s) they exist to serve. A case statement will likely go through several iterations during this early phase, as the process forces everyone to think critically about the organization's mission, structure, and current effectiveness in delivering their particular services or activities.

The development of the case is typically just one component of a larger feasibility study conducted prior to the initiation of a campaign. This study helps an organization determine if they are prepared to undertake the rigor of an ambitious, multiyear campaign. Organizations can be assisted through a feasibility study with the services of a fundraising consultant.

Consultants can perform many key planning steps that may be beyond the expertise or capacity of a nonprofit organization. Maxwell (2011, p. 377) identifies these services as:

- Auditing the organization's current staffing and fundraising results.
- Developing the case for support (drawn from the strategic plan).
- Testing the case with current and potential major gift donors.
- Screening the organization's donor list to identify prospective major gift donors.
- Assessing the strength of the organization's communications methods for informing potential donors.
- Identifying and training volunteer leadership.
- Recommending the preferred strategies for the fundraising plan.
- Managing the overall effort.

One of the most critical outcomes of the feasibility study is not just a projected campaign dollar goal, but a realistic assessment of the organization's potential donor base and whether enough prospective donors exist to reach the goal. Failure to invest in this step during the pre-campaign planning phase represents one of the most common causes of unsuccessful campaign experiences.

The outcome of this exercise is commonly presented in the visual form of a campaign pyramid, a gift range chart, or a similarly named illustration that breaks down the campaign dollars needed by segments of donors. The methodology for this exercise has historically been referred to as the 80/20 rule, where it could be expected that 80 percent of the dollars raised during the campaign will come from just 20 percent of the donors. See Table 19.1 for a sample gift range chart illustrating a $10 million campaign and the projected number of donors needed at major gift levels.

TABLE 19.1. SAMPLE GIFT RANGE CHART: $10 MILLION GOAL—FIVE-YEAR PLEDGES.

Type of Gift	Number of Pledges	Number of Prospects	Pledge Size	Total for Size	Cumulative Total	Percentage of Goal
Lead Gift	1	5	$1,000,000+	$1,000,000	$1,000,000	47.5%
	1	5	750,000–999,999	750,000	1,750,000	
	3	15	500,000–749,999	1,500,000	3,250,000	
	6	30	250,000–499,999	1,500,000	4,750,000	
Major Gifts	12	48	100,000–249,999	1,400,000	6,150,000	39.5%
	24	96	50,000–99,999	1,300,000	7,450,000	
	50	100	25,000–49,999	1,250,000	8,700,000	
Special Gifts	70	210	10,000–24,999	700,000	9,400,000	12%
	100	300	5,000–9,999	500,000	9,900,000	
General Gifts	All others	Many	Under 5,000	100,000	10,000,000	

Numerous resources can also be found on the Web to assist in calculating gift range charts. Organizations should take particular care in crafting their projections based on the knowledge of their own history of past major gifts and the depth of prospective donors at each level. For example, if a recommended top gift of $5 million is needed for a $25 million campaign and the organization has no history of receiving gifts that size, nor any possible donors to solicit at that level, then consideration should be given to emphasizing more gifts below $5 million. A $25 million goal may still be feasible, but with the understanding that far more potential donors will be needed who may give between $1 million and $2 million.

Quiet Phase

This phase of the campaign, which is also commonly referred to as the "nucleus" or "silent" phase, commences when an organization selects the date in which gifts begin counting toward the campaign goal. This date is generally known only to the organization's administrative leadership and governing board, key volunteers and major donors, fundraising staff and other related audiences. Through the completion of the feasibility study during the prior phase, a potential dollar goal or range should be broadly accepted among the campaign's leadership, with the understanding that a final target does not yet have to be established.

Even though gifts have begun counting toward the campaign, this phase still entails substantial planning activity that must be completed prior to the next phase. Foremost among these remaining planning efforts is finalizing the campaign case for support. As this phase begins, it presents a valuable opportunity to assess whether the campaign has an effective and compelling case for support. During this phase, organizations should be approaching their closest long-time supporters and asking not just for a gift commitment, but also for their candid reaction to the case for support. Organizations should be prepared for suggestions and possible criticism, and react in a way that acknowledges the feedback of their donors constructively and leads to positive refinements in the case statement.

This process also directly contributes to helping finalize the campaign's communication plan. During the pre-campaign planning phase, this plan should have begun to take shape through discussions on how the organization would communicate with donors and potential donors throughout the course of the campaign. Communication plans are largely defined by the budget resources that can be committed, as costs must be closely examined related to creating web sites, videos, print materials such as campaign brochures and newsletters, and Internet-based communications including e-mail, e-newsletters, and social media strategies that generate greater public awareness.

The final and most critical steps of the quiet phase are reaching consensus on the dollar goal to be announced, and the end date by which the campaign should achieve this goal. Comprehensive campaigns generally have multiple components, in which each smaller goal collectively adds up to the overall campaign goal. This is especially the case in higher education, where a university's overall campaign goal may be comprised of individual goals for each school or college, major units such as athletics and the library, and special initiatives such as scholarship programs, community engagement activities, or special presidential initiatives.

There is no exact time period a quiet phase should encompass, but it should allow enough time to determine if the dollar goal presented in the feasibility study is proving to be realistic. If little or no support is being realized for a given goal, the quiet phase provides the opportunity to reassess whether the proposed dollar goal should be revised downward or the campaign time period should be lengthened before launching the public phase.

Campaign Kickoff and Public Phase

The next phase of the campaign represents the most visible and exciting stage. It can also be the most time-intensive and stressful on staff and volunteers as the organization publicly commits to a specific dollar goal to be raised by a fixed deadline.

While this phase formally begins with a highly visible event or series of events, several key steps must take place just prior to the campaign kickoff. Foremost among them is an assessment of gifts raised to-date and the remaining prospect pool to be solicited in the time left before the campaign's announced end date. Most organizations will begin the public phase of a campaign if they have raised 50 percent or more of the goal during the quiet phase. Commencing the public phase with less, such as 25 to 35 percent, may give the impression of a campaign lacking momentum, while launching with more, such as 65 to 75 percent of the goal already raised, may leave potential donors feeling success is within reach and their support may not be needed.

Another key process that should be followed up to this point is Rosso's "sequential solicitation" (1991, p. 92). Solicitations for campaign support should start with prospective donors at the top of the gift range chart and work down to those in the smaller gift range. By the time the public phase of the campaign begins, the organization should have solicited as many of the top prospects as possible.

Rosso also advocated an inside-out approach in addition to top-down. Before the public phase begins, all individuals directly tied to the organization should have made their own campaign commitment. This includes gifts from the administrative leadership, governing board, staff, and others who are intimately involved in the campaign planning process. Only after all these internal constituents have given should an organization begin looking outward. This combination of "top down and inside out" should be a guiding operational principle throughout the course of any campaign.

Campaign Closing and Celebration

As a campaign draws closer to its announced end date, two valuable opportunities will be presented to the organization's fundraising staff and volunteers. First, the impending end date presents the chance to encourage new donors to be part of a successful effort. Using the sports cliché, "everybody supports a winner," this emphasis on participation with a gift at any level can be invaluable in expanding the donor base and thereby improving the chances for larger future campaigns.

The other opportunity a campaign's end brings is to go back to the "uncommitted" one final time. Every organization will have a number of individuals who they believed would be an early supporter of their campaign but, for whatever reason, declined or deferred a commitment. For those who never gave an outright rejection to a campaign ask, this closing stage presents a final chance to go back and summarize the campaign's successes and make one final ask. Even if these individuals were among the most highly rated prospects for the campaign, a gift of any amount at this final stage should be just as welcomed and appreciated as a major gift at the campaign's beginning.

The final and most visible activity of this phase is typically a formal closing event or ceremony to announce the overall dollar amount raised and key priorities that the campaign helped address. While the accomplishment of a dollar goal should be acknowledged, more emphasis should be placed on the donors themselves. A campaign closing presents a wonderful and valuable opportunity to demonstrate that a college, museum, symphony, or other organization does not undertake a campaign simply to raise money. The greater accomplishment of a campaign is found in making that connection between a donor's passion and an organization's need.

Stewardship and Campaign Impact

The closure and celebration of a campaign may indicate to donors that this effort has ended, but a number of critical follow-through activities should be undertaken to position the organization for future campaign success. This stage, like the pre-campaign planning stage, can often be overlooked or given too little attention since it falls outside the formal boundaries of a campaign.

First and foremost, a successful campaign will present exciting new opportunities to steward both long-time donors as well as new supporters. The biggest challenge an organization will likely face during this post-campaign phase is determining how to steward a base of donors that should have expanded significantly.

Wherever possible, there is no substitute for personal stewardship. An organization's executive leadership should commit the time to personally visit as many campaign donors as possible for the sole purpose of expressing thanks. This not only includes the largest campaign donors but those new donors who show promise for long-term engagement and continued future support.

Other stewardship strategies can provide this personal element while reaching far greater numbers of donors. Some of these suggestions include the following:

- Small group events, such as a gathering of the campaign's volunteer leadership or donors who gave above a specified level.
- Publications such as an impact report that summarizes the campaign, the programs or facilities it supported, and the donors who gave.
- Digital communications that can be shared via e-mail and on the organization's web site, including the aforementioned impact report as well as videos and e-newsletters.
- For historical purposes, permanent signage acknowledging the years of the campaign, the amount raised, and the campaign's impact. Space permitting, this display could also highlight names of volunteer leadership, major donors, or other key figures.

The overall stewardship goal to accomplish in this final phase of a campaign is to make every donor feel their gift made a difference in two distinct ways. They should feel they helped support the particular need, program, or effort the campaign was intended to address. They should also feel that their gift, regardless of size, was invaluable in achieving the dollar goal set to be overcome within the announced time frame.

Lastly, a comprehensive internal review and evaluation of the campaign can yield helpful insight to inform the planning effort of future campaigns. During the course of a campaign, internal operational matters can easily be overlooked as so much of the organization's emphasis is outwardly focused on securing gifts. A post-campaign assessment exercise should address such questions as:

- Did we effectively manage the increase in gift volume with timely processing and acknowledgments?
- Were we able to provide adequate and timely research information to staff and volunteers on prospective donors?
- Could major gift proposals be drafted, reviewed, and approved more quickly?

- Was the process effective for scheduling time for the president to meet with donors or speak at events?
- Are there ways to improve processes that support our front-line development staff, such as arranging travel and reimbursing expenses?
- Did staff and volunteers feel adequately informed on campaign progress?

Operational matters such as these should obviously be addressed as they arise, but the pace and demands of a campaign can easily result in these issues being pushed into the background. Conducting a post-campaign assessment gives the entire organizational team the opportunity to weigh in on what worked and what didn't. Bringing in a consultant or skilled process evaluation expert to lead this exercise can help position an organization for an even greater future campaign experience.

Campaign Case Study

The following case study of a successful campaign at the University of Texas at Dallas is intended to provide a tangible illustration of the campaign phases as outlined in Figure 19.1. The author served as the vice president for development and alumni relations at UT Dallas and led the planning and execution of this first comprehensive campaign in the university's history.

Institutional Background

UT Dallas traces its origins to the early 1960s when the founders of Texas Instruments Inc. purchased 1,000 acres of cotton fields in Richardson, Texas, to establish their own research institute. They chose to donate their Graduate Research Center of the Southwest to the state of Texas in 1969, thereby creating UT Dallas and a new member of The University of Texas System.

The institution initially offered only Master's and PhD programs, primarily in the physical sciences and later in management. Undergraduate transfers at the junior or senior levels were allowed in 1975, but the first class of freshmen students were not enrolled until 1990. The university's first residence hall opened in 2009, and four additional halls were added over the next four years.

Given the institution's history as a predominantly graduate-level school offering evening programs, little tradition was built for engaging alumni or seeking donor support beyond Texas Instruments and a small number of local individuals, companies, and foundations.

Pre-Campaign Planning   In 2008, UT Dallas engaged the consulting firm of Bentz, Whaley, Flessner (BWF) to conduct a campaign feasibility study. BWF conducted interviews in early 2009 with university leadership, major donors, and local company executives, including many who were not supporters of the university.

BWF provided their initial campaign recommendation to the university's leadership in August 2009, which was presented in October to the Development Board, the university's top volunteer leadership organization. However, it was decided by the university that the quiet phase would commence on September 1, 2009 and all gifts and pledges from that date forward would count toward the campaign goal.

This was decided because the state of Texas had authorized a matching gift program to encourage gifts for research purposes to UT Dallas and six other public "emerging research universities" in the state, including UT Arlington, UT El Paso, UT San Antonio, University of North Texas, University of Houston, and Texas Tech University. Gifts eligible for matching had to be designated to chairs or professorships for faculty, fellowships for graduate students, or support for research programs. This program, called the Texas Research Incentive Program, or TRIP, went into effect on September 1, 2009 (Hacker, 2009).

Even though UT Dallas had a limited history of philanthropic support and previously averaged annual private support of $5 million to $15 million, BWF and university leadership believed the introduction of TRIP provided a unique and timely stimulus to justify an ambitious campaign goal. BWF presented a final recommendation to pursue a six-year campaign with a goal range of $150 million to $200 million.

Quiet Phase   The introduction of TRIP did indeed result in numerous major gifts to UT Dallas, and the first year of the quiet phase resulted in a record $40.6 million in overall gifts and pledges to the university. In their campaign recommendation, BWF indicated at least $35 million in each of the first two years of the campaign would need to be raised to safely pursue their recommended range of $150 million to $200 million. The second year of the campaign resulted in another record giving year, with a total of $55.2 million.

During the first two years of the quiet phase, a number of critical activities were undertaken to prepare for the public launch of the campaign. Many of these follow Rosso's "top down and inside out" principles and included:

- Solicitations of the university's few but long-time major gift donors.
- Multiyear campaign commitments by the university's president and leadership cabinet.
- Creation of a University Campaign Council, resulting in four honorary campaign co-chairs, four chairs, and 14 council members.

- Three "campaign clinics" for the development staff, deans and department chairs, volunteers, and other key individuals who would benefit from these one-day training sessions.
- Hiring of Snavely Associates, a communications consultant to develop the case statement, campaign theme and logo, brochures, and web site.

Another key exercise during the quiet phase was finalizing a gift range chart to help predict and project the number of major gifts needed. Following the record first year campaign total, the university leadership began to narrow BWF's initial goal range and timeline down to a target of $200 million by December 31, 2014. To help the campaign leadership understand and visualize what would be needed to accomplish this goal, a campaign pyramid illustration was developed (see Figure 19.2).

FIGURE 19.2. CAMPAIGN GIFT CHART RANGE.

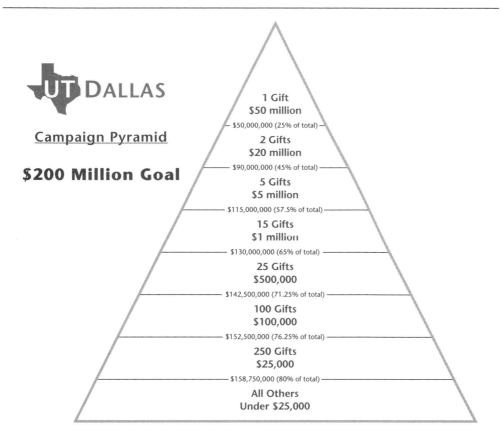

This tool was utilized throughout the course of the entire campaign, both internally and with the University Campaign Council. Progress would be shown in the number of gifts that had been received within each of the top levels. A top gift of $50 million was never realized during the campaign, making this tool even more effective in demonstrating the importance of raising more gifts at the lower levels. This approach worked, as a total of 45 gifts of $1 million and above were raised during the campaign, including seven gifts of $10 million or more. By comparison, UT Dallas received just nine gifts of $1 million or more in the five years prior to the campaign.

Campaign Kickoff and Public Phase   The public phase of the campaign was announced on March 29, 2012 through two major events. A large tent was erected on campus and utilized for a lunch event that day where the entire university community of students, faculty, and staff was invited. Later that evening, a private dinner was held for major donors, campaign volunteers, university leadership, and other special guests.

These events provided the opportunity to announce the campaign theme of "Realize the Vision: The Campaign for Tier One and Beyond." They also helped promote the campaign goal of $200 million by December 31, 2014; progress to-date of $110 million had already been raised. Brochures for the schools and units with a campaign goal were available at these events, and the campaign web site went live the following day.

Throughout the remainder of the public phase, a number of key activities took place that helped continue the momentum of the kickoff and building of greater public awareness. Some of these activities included:

- A brief e-newsletter to the University Campaign Council and Development Board with routine updates on campaign progress and upcoming events.
- Quarterly campaign progress charts for the deans of each school and heads of other units with a specific campaign goal.
- A campaign newsletter, *Momentum*, mailed twice annually to all UT Dallas alumni and nonalumni donors and friends. The publication was also distributed via e-mail and available on the campaign web site.
- A new *Annual Report to Donors*, started in 2013.
- A new stewardship event, *Celebration of Support*, held every fall for members of new donor recognition societies created in 2010.

Following Rosso's "top down and inside out" process, major gift solicitations moved further down into the middle range of gifts needed, and outward to engage new potential donors. One of the most effective tools for building a stronger base of middle-range gifts from new donors was through a new unrestricted endowment vehicle called Opportunity Funds (University of Texas at Dallas, 2015). Donors could designate an unrestricted endowment to any school or unit for a minimum gift of $10,000. Nearly 100 of these funds were established during the campaign.

Campaign Closing and Celebration   The campaign ended on December 31, 2014 with more than $270 million in total support raised. A campaign celebration took place on October 29 with an evening reception, music, and fireworks open to the entire campus and the public. It was hoped that holding the celebration a few months prior to the official close would encourage new donors to be part of this historic effort, and help encourage the "uncommitted" who had been approached earlier in the campaign.

In addition to accomplishing an ambitious dollar goal, the campaign addressed the critical need to strengthen the university's endowment. The number of individual funds comprising the endowment at the beginning of the campaign was 169. Five years later, the total was 409. These 240 new endowed funds also helped increase the endowment's market value from $195 million to $381 million.

Stewardship and Campaign Impact   The unprecedented support for this campaign gave UT Dallas a valuable opportunity to begin building the same type of philanthropic tradition that many private colleges and universities have cultivated over more than a century. The introduction of new stewardship tools during the campaign, including donor recognition societies, donor appreciation events, and new publications, has provided UT Dallas with numerous vehicles to continue conveying messages on the importance of private support.

Another positive but less visible campaign outcome was the realization among deans, faculty and staff, and volunteers that UT Dallas can successfully undertake a major comprehensive campaign. Few of these constituencies had prior fundraising experience, but this first campaign provided a greater level of comfort and confidence in their ability to raise private support in the future, regardless of whether or not it is under campaign circumstances.

Discussion Questions

1) Discuss the difference between a capital campaign and a comprehensive campaign.
2) Discuss four elements of the test for readiness. Why are they important to the success of a campaign?

3) Construct a gift range chart for a $4 million campaign.
4) What is meant by "top down" and "inside out" and why are these concepts important to a successful campaign?
5) Discuss two aspect of the case study that contributed to the success of the campaign.

CHAPTER TWENTY

ESTABLISHING A PLANNED GIVING PROGRAM

By Dean Regenovich

After completing this chapter, you will be able to:

1. Recognize key donor motivations for making planned gifts.
2. Articulate the importance of an organization's strategic plan in establishing and conducting a planned giving program.
3. Describe the primary roles of the board and staff in adopting and managing a planned giving program.
4. Differentiate among various planned giving instruments, including those that are of current value to the organization, those that are of future value to the organization, and those that provide income to the donor.
5. List several key characteristics of likely planned gift prospective donors.
6. Describe several ways to promote the concept of planned giving to the organization's constituency.

In today's philanthropic environment, individuals rely on various charitable instruments – bequests, beneficiary designations, charitable gift annuities, and charitable trusts – to fulfill their philanthropic and financial objectives. These giving arrangements are typically referred to as "planned gifts," for they require thoughtful and focused planning on the part of the donor, oftentimes the donor's family, and the donor's professional financial advisors (estate planning attorney, tax accountant, certified financial planner, certified life underwriter, etc.). It was not until the mid-1970s that charities began integrating planned giving programs into their comprehensive development plans. Initially, most of the efforts were focused on the establishment and marketing of wills and charitable bequests, which continues to be the cornerstone of most successful planned giving programs. The fact that bequests are revocable, thereby allowing donors the ability to make changes at any time during their lifetime, is the primary factor that makes it the most popular planned giving option. *Giving USA* (2015) reports that of the $358.38 billion contributed in 2014, bequests accounted for $28.13 billion, accounting for 8 percent of all contributions made.

The Internal Revenue Service has populated the Internal Revenue Code with various tax provisions designed to encourage philanthropy. Donors are entitled to a charitable income tax deduction for outright gifts of cash and property. The deduction for gifts of property is equal to the property's current fair market value, thereby making appreciated assets a logical choice for some donors. If donors make gifts using irrevocable instruments such as charitable gift annuities or charitable remainder trusts, they will not be entitled to a charitable income tax deduction for the full value of the asset transferred because of the financial benefit they are receiving in exchange for the gift, namely a stream of income that will be paid back to the donor over his lifetime.

Another potential tax benefit that a donor can derive from making a gift is the avoidance of the capital gains tax. Capital gains tax is triggered when an individual sells an asset for a price that is higher than the purchase price. The capital gains tax is levied on the gain on the sale, which is calculated by deducting the original purchase price from the sales price. It is a common giving strategy for a donor to make an outright gift using an appreciated asset, which the charity then sells free of capital gains tax because of its tax exempt status. Not only is the capital gains tax completely avoided, but the donor will receive a charitable income tax deduction equal to the fair market value of the property on the date of the gift.

A third potential tax benefit a donor can realize as a result of his or her gift is the partial avoidance, or complete elimination, of estate and gift tax. A very small percentage of donors will be subject to estate tax at their death since the estate tax applies only to estates that are valued at over $5.43 million. The exemption amount typically changes each year and has gradually increased from $5 million in 2011 to $5.43 million in 2015. Estate and gift tax rates are similar to income tax rates in that they are progressive taxes whereby the percentage of the estate tax increases as the value of the estate over the exemption level increases. In 2015, the highest estate and gift tax rate is 40 percent, but that percentage is subject to change as a result of new tax legislation.

The philanthropic community – donors, professional financial advisors, and charitable organizations – are increasingly taking advantage of the aforementioned tax incentives and accompanying charitable estate planning instruments to enhance the number and size of gifts. An aging donor population and an unprecedented growth in asset values has further strengthened the attractiveness of charitable estate planning instruments such as the charitable remainder trust and charitable gift annuity. In addition to offering potential income, capital gains, and estate and gift tax benefits, these vehicles can be used to generate a new stream of income for the donor and/or an income beneficiary named by the donor.

Organizations have responded to the increased interest in charitable estate gifts by hiring development professionals who have a solid understanding of the various planned giving vehicles and an ability to articulate such benefits to donors and professional financial advisors. Many major gift officers do not come from a technical background nor have they achieved a high level of expertise, but they have developed of level of knowledge that allows them to spot planned giving opportunities and know when to enlist the help of the technical experts to assist in working with donors and their advisors. Some charities have the resources to hire development professionals who focus primarily on planned gifts. Many of these individuals have a legal, accounting, or financial planning background and thus are well versed on the technical aspects of the various planned giving instruments. Other charities, primarily because of budgetary constraints, do not have a dedicated planned giving staff and instead rely on volunteers and friends of the organization who are willing to provide training and assist on a case by case basis. Although a formal background in the legal, tax, or financial planning areas is not a prerequisite to becoming a successful planned giving officer, a professional designation such as a JD, CPA, or CFP oftentimes gives the planned giving officer instant credibility with donors and professional financial advisors.

It is important to recognize that planned giving should play an integral role in all major gift programs regardless of an organization's size, mission, age, budget, in-house expertise, or prior fundraising success. Hank Rosso, the founder of The Fund Raising School, decades ago issued a challenge to all nonprofit organizations that they work toward a total development program that included planned giving. His challenge has become even more relevant in today's competitive philanthropic environment. This chapter is designed to assist you in determining the level of planned giving activity appropriate for *your* organization and give you a general understanding of the techniques and instruments that are commonly used in planned giving. The level of sophistication of your charity's planned giving program should not be a cause for concern, especially if you are in the initial stages of implementing a program. Most planned giving programs are built piecemeal, with layers added over time as the development program grows and matures. This chapter will also touch on the marketing of planned gifts and the process of identifying viable planned giving prospective donors.

Institutional Readiness

Not all charities are in a position to implement a comprehensive planned giving program. In fact, most small to mid-size charities, particularly relatively new organizations, do not have the financial resources and personnel to allow for a comprehensive planned giving program that includes not only expectancies such as bequests, life insurance, and retirement plan/IRA designations, but also life income arrangements such as charitable gift annuities and charitable remainder trusts. What is important to recognize is that despite the age of an organization and the limitation on resources, all organizations can, and should, begin implementing a planned giving program that can be enhanced over time. The primary focus for charities interested in starting a new planned giving program should be on expectancies for they are easy to explain, easy to understand, can be secured with little or no out-of-pocket expense, and are popular with donors because they are revocable.

The Organization and Staff

The first order of business is to ensure that a thorough strategic plan exists before deciding on the level and sophistication of the planned giving program. Consider the following self-analysis. Does the organization have a strategic plan that outlines goals and objectives for the next 3 to 10 years? Is the mission statement clear and does it accurately depict the organization as it exists today? Is there a case statement that clearly and concisely describes what the organization does, why the services provided are important to the community, and how those services will be delivered? If the organization's mission and case statement are unclear, the planned giving program will most likely experience limited success. Is there an annual fund in place that has a track record of securing unrestricted annual gifts? Many of your top planned giving prospective donors could come from your annual fund.

Since many planned gifts benefit the nonprofit organization at some future date (thus the term "deferred gift"), donors must be comfortable with the stability and permanence of the organization. How long has the organization existed? Is it likely that the organization will be in existence 30 years from now to receive the planned gift? Is the organization's overall development effort growing or shrinking? Is there staff continuity, both administrative and fundraising? These are some of the questions donors will ask before contemplating a planned gift, particularly since planned gifts are typically larger in dollar amount than annual fund gifts.

Before making a planned gift, some donors may also be interested in the financial stability of the organization. Does the organization have the capacity to satisfy current operating expenses? Does the organization have a history of balancing its budget? Will the organization be a responsible steward of their gift? Does the organization have the financial staff to account for and invest the gift properly? Will the organization ultimately use the gift in accordance with the donor's wishes? Donors are demanding greater accountability as to how their gift will be invested and used; thus organizations must be prepared to provide financial reports and annual reports outlining the organization's overall financial performance. Donors who establish endowments for a specific purpose may also demand regular updates on the performance of their fund. Many charities prepare gift agreements when a new endowment account is created, which outlines the criteria by which the fund will be administered in perpetuity. Such agreements are typically signed by the donor, the CEO of the organization, and, if in an academic setting, the Dean of the school that will benefit from the gift. Although such agreements are not legally binding, they provide the donor with a certain level of assurance that the charity is committed to using the gift in perpetuity in the manner agreed to when the gift agreement was signed.

People give to people. Planned gifts typically come from donors who know and trust the organization. Attaining this level of comfort typically requires the development of close personal relationships with individuals over time. Thus, many planned gifts come from donors who have been supporting the organization for a period of time. Some of your best planned gift prospective donors may be annual fund donors who have been giving consistently to the annual fund regardless of the dollar level of those gifts. Oftentimes, a donor's planned gift will be much larger than the outright donations he made over his lifetime. To be successful in planned giving, organizations must have knowledgeable development staffs with a thorough understanding of the organization's mission and programs, and a point person who has the technical knowledge to assess a particular donor's giving options based on his or her philanthropic and financial objectives, and can clearly articulate those options to the donor.

Board Commitment

The board must be fully supportive of short- and long-term benefits of a planned giving program in order to achieve the results desired. They must understand the role planned giving plays in ensuring the long-term growth and stability of the organization through deferred gifts and short-term opportunities it provides to engage and involve donors. Additionally, the board must be willing to assist the development department with the planned giving program by taking an active role in the identification, cultivation, and, in some instances, solicitation of planned giving prospective donors. Sometimes it will require the influence of a board member to open a door to a planned gift prospective donor that the development officer may never reach.

Before considering a planned giving program, the board must first understand the goals and objectives of the program and how it fits into the overall development plan. How will planned gifts benefit both the organization and the donor? A brief seminar for the board, which addresses the various planned giving options and the specific benefits afforded by each option, might be helpful in explaining how planned giving complements the organization's existing development efforts. It is not uncommon for boards to develop a mindset that planned gifts will detract from the annual fund and current giving, when in fact it has been repeatedly proven that a healthy planned giving program enhances current annual gifts. Bringing in an outside consultant or a third party professional financial advisor to make the case for the merits of a planned giving program is helpful. Sometimes boards must hear this message from an impartial third party instead of the organization itself before they become convinced that a planned giving program is vital to the long-term growth and stability of the organization.

There is no better way to start a planned giving program than by securing planned gift commitments from current and former board members. This should be done by conducting personal visits with each board member, rather than making an impersonal broad appeal to the entire board. Due to the sensitive nature of the information surrounding planned gifts, individuals are oftentimes not inclined to discuss their planned gift intentions in front of others. There is no better way for the board to demonstrate the importance of a planned gift than for them to make their own personal planned gift commitments. Leadership gifts from the board will provide the momentum needed to secure planned gifts from others outside the organization.

The board must be willing to provide the financial resources necessary to begin implementing a planned giving program. An effective program will be built around the development of long-term personal relationships with donors. This is a labor intensive process, which may require adding a development professional(s) to the staff whose primary responsibility is to spend time outside the office cultivating close personal relationships with prospective donors. Marketing the planned giving program will also require additional financial resources. It is not imperative that an organization purchase new print materials to market planned giving opportunities. Be creative and explore ways to incorporate planned giving messages into existing publications such as the annual report, annual fund solicitations, website content, and hard copy mailings such as newsletters and brochures.

Since most planned gifts generally come from donors who have had a long-term relationship with the organization, the board must recognize that new planned giving programs are not likely to generate immediate results. These gifts will take time and require ongoing discussions. Some planned gifts may occur immediately, while others may take a lifetime to finalize. As is true with most gifts, the donor ultimately decides when the time is right to make the planned gift. For that reason, when evaluating the progress of a planned giving program, particularly one that is relatively new, the metrics should be more heavily weighted to the number of substantive personal contacts made by the development officer, rather than the actual dollars realized. As the planned giving program matures, the metrics will then place more emphasis on the actual dollars realized each year. You will have developed a fully mature planned giving program when the organization begins receiving a steady flow of realized gifts coming from estates and irrevocable arrangements. In summary, the board can provide leadership to the planned giving program by:

- Publicly endorsing the merits of planned gifts.
- Identifying and cultivating prospective donors.
- Introducing development staff to prospective donors.
- Assisting in the solicitation of planned gifts.

By properly educating the board at the outset and using their time judiciously throughout the process, you are likely to find that most Board members will vigorously endorse and support the planned giving program. Along the way, be sure to publicize completed planned gifts and provide the Board with regular updates on the gifts documented and dollars realized.

The Planned Giving Professional

Due to budget constraints and limited human capital, many charities are not in a position to hire a full-time development professional whose sole responsibility is planned giving. Therefore, it is common for many organizations to begin their planned giving program by marketing the more basic planned giving opportunities, such as bequests, retirement plan/IRA designations, life insurance, and gifts of appreciated assets. They can then grow the program over time to include irrevocable arrangements such as charitable gift annuities and charitable remainder trusts. Simultaneously, the organization must look for opportunities to train its development officers on the basics of planned giving. There are a variety of on-line and live sessions available, ranging from one-hour sessions that cover specific topics to full-week sessions that cover the full menu of charitable giving opportunities in detail. The level of training offered to development officers should be made on a case-by-case basis, taking into account prior exposure to financial matters, the number of years served as a development officer, and their willingness to learn more information to become more effective major gift fundraisers.

How an organization prepares to respond to planned giving inquiries from individuals can be handled in a variety of ways. First, the organization can assign that responsibility to a development officer whose sole responsibility is to raise money – preferably a major gifts officer – who should be trained to identify planned giving opportunities. There are inherent limitations with this approach since it will take a period of time before the development officer becomes conversant with planned giving options. However, he or she can at the very least gather information from the donor and follow up with answers shortly thereafter.

A second option is to build a network of "friends" who have experience working in charitable estate planning. These "friends" could come from a variety of professions including estate planning attorneys, certified public accountants, certified financial planners, bank trust officers, certified life underwriters, stock brokers, etc. Although these professionals can provide the organization with the technical support necessary to respond to specific planned giving inquiries, it is likely not feasible to expect them to be part of the ongoing cultivation team because of the demands on their schedule and the need for the organization to be the key stakeholder in the relationship with the donor. Professional advisors are best suited to handle the technical functions, such as drafting planned giving instruments, accompanying the development professional on a personal visit to explain gift illustrations, developing strategies, answering questions posed by the donor or the donor's advisor, and assisting in the review of planned giving marketing materials.

A third option, and one that is not feasible for some organizations because of budget constraints, is to hire a development professional whose primary responsibility is planned giving. This person may or may not have previous development experience as a major or planned gift officer and will need to learn on the job. A growing number of planned giving officers are coming from the for-profit world. Estate planning attorneys, accountants, bank trust officers, and financial planners have moved from the for-profit sector to the not-for-profit sector either because of the desire to make a career change or to serve an organization they have a passion for.

Although it is not imperative that the planned giving officer has had formal training, legal or otherwise, it is advantageous if that individual has some familiarity with financial issues. Some of the best planned giving professionals have come from nontechnical backgrounds and have learned the technical aspects of planned giving through self-study, attending seminars, and practical hands-on training. The desire to learn is of critical importance.

What attributes should a nonprofit organization look for when hiring a planned giving officer? The following characteristics merit attention:

- *Good interpersonal relationship skills.* The ideal planned giving officer has the ability to develop meaningful personal relationships with donors.
- *Proactive.* An effective planned giving officer must spend a significant time outside the office developing personal relationships with donors, rather than being consumed with in-office administrative details. Approximately 30 to 60 percent of a planned giving officer's time should be spent outside the office cultivating donors and professional financial advisors. Most planned gift donors will not come to you – it is up to you to find them and initiate the discussion. The good news is that they are likely to be individuals already supporting your organization.
- *Simplicity, understanding and listening skills.* Individuals skilled in articulating the technical aspects of planned giving with simplicity and understanding are likely to be successful. This same skill is also important when training the development staff, the board, and volunteers. Of equal importance is actively listening to what your donors are telling you.
- *Thirst for knowledge.* The tax laws surrounding planned giving are fluid; thus an effective planned giving officer must be diligent about staying abreast of tax law changes and case law developments that impact charitable gift planning.
- *Articulate the mission and programs with clarity.* Although the planned giving officer is responsible for explaining the technical aspects of planned giving and identifying the donor's financial objectives, that individual must also be able to clearly articulate the organization's mission and programs.

Policies and Guidelines

Before embarking on a planned giving program, board approved written policies and guidelines governing the development program should be adopted. It is highly recommended that board approval be a prerequisite to the implementation of such policies and guidelines. Once approved by the board, development personnel, volunteers, and donors are subject to the parameters contained in the document, thereby allowing the planned giving program to move forward with clarity as to the process that must be adhered to when dealing with specific assets and charitable instruments. Clear and concise written policies and guidelines also help protect development officers from potentially awkward situations where donors feel the development officer is not accommodating their wishes.

The following is a list of issues charities should consider addressing in their policies and guidelines:

1. Will the organization offer charitable gift annuities? How will payout rates be determined? What is the minimum age of the annuitant(s)? What is the minimum gift amount needed to establish a gift annuity? What types of property will be accepted?
2. Will the organization serve as trustee of charitable remainder trusts and/or charitable lead trusts? If not, is it the donor's responsibility to secure a trustee and attorney to draft the trust document? If the organization will serve as trustee, what is the minimum charitable remainder interest they must have?
3. Will the organization administer charitable gift annuities internally? If not, who will serve as the outside third-party administrator?
4. What minimum dollar amounts and minimum age requirements should be established for each of the planned giving instruments? What is the minimum gift amount the organization is willing to accept for a charitable gift annuity? What is the minimum gift amount the organization is willing to accept for it to serve as trustee of a charitable remainder trust or charitable lead trust? Are there minimum age requirements that the income beneficiaries must satisfy before the organization will enter into a charitable gift annuity contract with the donor? Are there minimum age requirements the income beneficiaries must satisfy before the organization can serve as trustee of a charitable remainder trust?
5. Who in the organization has the authority to accept gifts of real estate? What are the procedures that must be followed when considering a gift of real estate such as a site visit analysis, environmental review, and title search? Is board approval required before real estate is accepted?
6. Who in the organization has the authority to accept gifts of closely held stock? What is the process that must be followed when considering a gift of closely held stock?
7. Who in the organization is authorized to negotiate the terms of a planned giving instrument, such as the payout rate on a charitable gift annuity? Who in the organization must approve the contract before it is executed?
8. Who in the organization has the authority to sign the planned giving document on behalf of the organization?

The following are guidelines the charity may want to consider incorporating into a policies and guidelines document, but please note that the numbers and percentages ultimately used may vary from one organization to the next, and are not intended to suggest that they should be followed uniformly by all charities:

1. *Percentage payout rate on charitable remainder trusts.* The percentage payout rate on charitable remainder trusts must be at least 5 percent but shall not exceed 50 percent.
2. *Minimum age requirements and funding levels for charitable remainder trusts.* If the organization is willing to serve as trustee, the minimum age of an income beneficiary should be 55. The minimum funding level should be $100,000.
3. *Percentage payout on charitable gift annuities.* It should be the organization's general practice to use the gift annuity rates established by the American Council on Gift Annuities.
4. *Minimum age requirements and funding levels for charitable gift annuities.* The minimum age of an income beneficiary should be 55. The minimum funding level should be $10,000.
5. *Trustee.* Most organizations should not serve as a trustee of charitable remainder trusts and charitable lead trusts. The donor is responsible for selecting a trustee.
6. *Real estate and closely held stock.* All proposed gifts of real estate and closely held stock must be approved by a committee of the board before accepted.
7. *Donor-centered philanthropy.* All arrangements entered into with donors should always have the donor's best interests in mind, provided the terms of the arrangement do not violate the organization's policies and guidelines.
8. *Legal counsel.* Donors should be advised to consult with legal counsel or a financial advisor before executing a planned giving instrument with the organization.
9. *Confidentiality.* All information about a donor or named income beneficiaries including names, ages, gift amounts, net worth, etc., should be kept strictly confidential unless permission is obtained from the donor to release such information.

The Planned Gift Options

Planned giving generally involves one of three methods – current outright gifts, expectancies, and deferred gifts. A common misnomer among development officers is that all planned gifts are "deferred gifts." In reality, some planned gifts provide immediate benefits to the nonprofit organization as a result of thoughtful planning involving a partial or complete outright gift to the charity. It is common today for many major gifts to be structured in a "blended" fashion, meaning that they have both a current outright gift component and a deferred gift component.

This affords the donor the opportunity to experience the importance of his or her gift during his or her lifetime and the added bonus of knowing that further funding will occur at their death. In all instances, how the gift is structured should be done with the donor's philanthropic and financial objectives at the forefront.

Current Outright Gifts   Gifts of appreciated assets such as real property, securities, and tangible and intangible property, although given for the current use and enjoyment of a charity, generally fall within the definition of a "planned gift." These gifts are generally made jointly by spouses because of the dollar amount and the fact that they require significant contemplation and planning, unlike annual fund gifts, which are oftentimes made spontaneously in response to a mail appeal and without spousal consent.

Real Property   The largest single component of the average estate is real property. This alone makes it imperative that charities be prepared to discuss this option with donors and develop a process by which a potential gift of real estate is evaluated. The Survey of Consumer Finances 2009 indicates that real estate accounts for 23 percent of the assets of the top 1 percent of the wealthy, and 43 percent of the assets of the top 10 percent of the wealthy.

Gifts of real property can take several forms including, but not limited to, personal residences, vacation homes, commercial property (office building, condominiums, etc.), farmland, and commercially developable property. Because real property can carry with it risks and expenses, charities should establish procedures and guidelines to ensure that such expenses and risks are commensurate with the value of the gift.

The process of evaluating gifts of real estate may involve a host of professionals such as the Office of Gift Planning, the Office of Business and Financial Services, the Chief Financial Officer, and the General Counsel. Generally, the Office of Gift Planning obtains and provides all necessary information to the group for review to make a determination of whether to accept the proposed gift. Many charities also require that a formal gift agreement be prepared and accompanied by the following information:

1. Gift of Real Property Information Sheet. This form incorporates an environmental checklist with financial information about the property including mortgages, restrictions, covenants, liens, easements, and other encumbrances. In addition, documentation may be required to ensure that the property is free from title defects or encumbrances.

2. Site visit analysis. Before a charity accepts a proposed gift of real property, the CEO, or his or her designee, should visually inspect the real property and analyze the following:
   a. Market conditions for resale or the ultimate disposition of the property.
   b. The condition of any improvements located on the property.
   c. Current and potential zoning, land use, and concurrency issues.
   d. Any costs associated with preparing and listing the property for resale.
3. Findings from an environmental review. An environmental review should be performed on every potential gift of real property prior to acceptance. If the initial environmental review indicates areas of significant concern an additional investigation, including a Phase I, Phase II, or Phase III audit may be required.
4. Qualified independent appraisal. The IRS requires that the donor obtain a qualified independent appraisal if the value of the real property is over $5,000 and the donor wishes to claim a charitable deduction.
5. Title Information. Before accepting a gift of real property the charity should obtain a general warranty deed, a title search and title insurance, an owner's affidavit, and a survey.

Securities   Securities, particularly stocks and bonds, are often used as gift assets by donors to fund gift plans. There are two primary types of stock used for giving purposes, publicly traded stock and closely held stock. Charities generally prefer gifts of publicly traded stock since such stock can be immediately liquidated and the proceeds used to support the charity's mission. Publicly traded stock is also simple to convey and can be transferred through a broker from the donor to the charity in a seamless transaction. Closely held stock, on the other hand, may present liquidity issues thereby requiring the charity to retain the stock until a third party buyer is found. The charity may be at least partially liable for any liabilities arising during the period they own the stock, thereby causing some charities to be very thorough and deliberate before accepting such gifts.

Securities that have appreciated in value are especially beneficial to the donor. If a donor were to sell stock that appreciated in value after it was purchased, the donor would have to pay a capital gains tax on a portion of that sale. However, if instead of selling the stock, the donor gives the stock to the charity, the capital gains tax is avoided and the donor is entitled to a charitable income tax deduction equal to the full current fair market value of the property.

Gifts-in-Kind: Tangible Personal Property and Intangible Personal Property
Tangible personal property is property, other than real property, whose value is derived from its physical existence. Tangible personal property includes, but is

not limited to, artwork, antiques, automobiles, boats, books, technology, hardware, home furnishings, appliances, office and other equipment, and personal items.

Intangible personal property is property, other than real property, whose value stems from intangible elements rather than physical or tangible elements. Examples of intangible personal property include stock, patents, copyrights, licenses, and computer software.

Generally, a charity may consider accepting a gift of tangible or intangible personal property only if it can use the property in a manner related to its mission or, after a thorough review, determines that the property is readily marketable.

Gifts of Services   Gifts of services are donations of professional or personal services that are not allowable by the IRS as a charitable contribution. For instance, artists may deduct only the cost of materials and supplies purchased for artwork they create and donate and not the time they spend creating the artwork. Although gifts of services are not tax deductible, some charities accept such gifts for recognition purposes if it supports the charity's mission. Generally, the charity will not issue a tax receipt for gifts of services, but an appropriate gift acknowledgement letter may be sent.

Some charities require the donor to complete a Gift-in-Kind/Gift of Services Acceptance Form prior to accepting the gift. This form typically includes relevant contact information such as name, address, e-mail and phone number, a description of the property, donor assigned gift value, and an indication of whether the property is a gift-in-kind, vehicle, or a gift of services.

Charitable Lead Trust   A charitable lead trust is a trust that pays current annual income to at least one qualified charitable organization for a period measured by a fixed term of years, the lives of one or more individuals, or a combination of the two. When the trust ends, the trust assets are paid to the grantor or one or more noncharitable beneficiaries named in the trust instrument. The annual income payment made by the trust is comparable to an outright gift of cash, for the charity is free to use the cash immediately, subject to any restrictions placed on the gift by the donor. There are four basic types of charitable lead trusts: (1) qualified reversionary grantor trust; (2) qualified nonreversionary grantor trust; (3) qualified nonreversionary nongrantor trust; and (4) nonqualifed reversionary nongrantory trust. Each type of trust produces a different tax benefit, thus the one ultimately selected should be determined by the donor's financial and philanthropic objectives.

Charitable lead trusts are one of the most sophisticated planned giving instruments; thus the donor should seek the assistance of an experienced estate planning attorney before executing such a trust. Charitable lead trusts are generally

Exhibit 20.1. CHARITABLE LEAD TRUST.

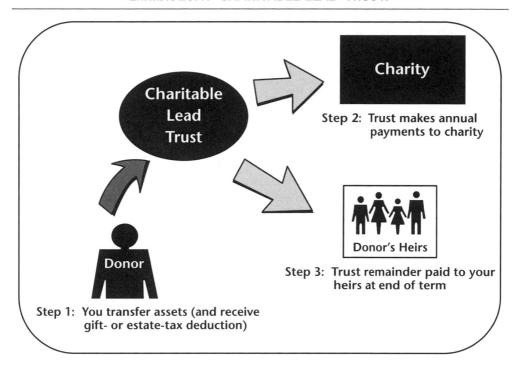

utilized by high net worth individuals seeking to minimize or avoid estate and gift tax; therefore, they are useful only to that small percentage of individuals over the annual estate tax exemption amount, which in 2015 is $5.43 million per individual (see Exhibit 20.1).

Expectancies An expectancy is a promise by a donor to make a gift to a charity at some future date, however, that promise may be revoked any time prior to the donor's death. Thus, it is called an expectancy because the charity is expecting to receive the gift at some future date, but ultimately may not receive it if the donor changes his or her mind prior to death. Since expectancies are not considered a completed gift because they are revocable prior to death, the donor does not enjoy the benefit of a charitable income tax deduction when the expectancy provision is created. However, since the donor retains the ability to revoke the gift, coupled with the fact that the asset is retained by the donor until death, most planned gifts take the form of an expectancy. The most common types of expectancies are bequests, retirement plan/IRA designations, and life insurance designations.

Bequests Bequests are the backbone of all planned giving programs and, historically have been the most popular planned giving method utilized by donors. According the *Giving USA* 2015, bequests accounted for 8% of all gifts made in 2014. They are popular with donors because they are easy to understand, relatively easy to establish, and can be revoked any time before death. They also provide donors with the peace of mind knowing that they retain ownership and control of these assets during their lifetime, and have the ability to access these assets for their personal use should they encounter unforeseen expenses such as medical or nursing home costs. Bequests are also popular with charities because they are easy to explain to donors, require very little cost to market, and, once in place, they are rarely revoked.

The bequest itself is a written statement in a donor's will directing that specific assets, or a percentage of the estate, will be transferred to charity at the donor's death. Since many individuals choose to transfer their assets at death by will, and since bequests can be established for any dollar amount, nonprofit organizations should consider marketing bequests to their entire constituency, regardless of age and net worth. If there is one giving opportunity worthy of marketing to an entire constituency, it is the bequest. Charities who do nothing more than regularly market bequests by including sample will language in their communications will have implemented the cornerstone of most planned giving programs. Charities who have marketed bequests over an extended period of time are now reaping the benefits of these anticipated gifts, and a majority of these gifts satisfy the charity's definition of a major gift.

Retirement Plans and IRAs A second type of expectancy growing in popularity among donors is the designation of a charity as a beneficiary of a retirement plan or IRA. The two largest holdings of the average individual are vested retirement funds and the equity in their home. According to the Investment Company Institute, retirement assets of all types totaled \$23 trillion as of March 31, 2014. Furthermore, according to the Federal Reserve, total household financial assets as of March 31, 2014 were \$54.7 trillion. Thus, retirement assets account for nearly 35% of all household financial assets.

Like the bequest, retirement plan designations are easy to understand, easy to transfer (a legal document is not needed, only the beneficiary designation form provided by the plan administrator), and revocable, thereby allowing the donor to change his or her mind any time before death. Gifts of retirement plans may be made during the donor's lifetime, but because the donor will have to pay an income tax on the withdrawal, it is generally not advisable. The one exception applies in situations where the retirement plan owner reaches $70\frac{1}{2}$ years old, and therefore must withdraw at least a required minimum distribution from the retirement plan

TABLE 20.1. UNIFORM LIFETIME DISTRIBUTION.

Age	Minimum Withdrawal	Age	Minimum Withdrawal	Age	Minimum Withdrawal
70	3.65%	80	5.35%	90	8.77%
71	3.77%	81	5.59%	91	9.26%
72	3.91%	82	5.85%	92	9.80%
73	4.05%	83	6.14%	93	10.42%
74	4.20%	84	6.45%	94	10.99%
75	4.37%	85	6.76%	95	11.63%
76	4.55%	86	7.09%	96	12.35%
77	4.72%	87	7.46%	97	13.16%
78	4.93%	88	7.87%	98	14.08%
79	5.13%	89	8.33%	99	14.93%

each year. In those cases, it may make sense for the donor to make the withdrawal and donate that amount to charity, for the charitable income tax deduction may come close to eliminating the income tax on the withdrawal. The percentage of retirement assets that must be withdrawn each year increase gradually with the plan owner's age according to Table 20.1.

In most cases, it is more tax efficient for the donor to make a charitable gift of his or her retirement plan at their death. That is because the gift is subject neither to income nor estate tax. The charity will not have to pay income tax at the time of the transfer because it is a tax-exempt entity, and the amount of the transfer will not be subject to estate tax because of the unlimited estate tax charitable deduction.

Donors seeking to distribute their estate assets between heirs and charity are better advised to give appreciated stock and real estate to heirs and make charities the beneficiary of all or a portion of their retirement plan. The heirs will receive a stepped-up basis in the stock and real estate and thus be taxed only on the gain that occurs between the time they receive the asset and sell it. In contrast, if they receive the retirement plan assets instead, they will be required to pay income tax on every dollar of retirement funds they receive, in the year they receive them. Table 20.2 illustrates the tax ramifications of leaving a retirement plan to heirs versus leaving a retirement plan to charity.

Life Insurance A third type of expectancy, life insurance, is used by some donors because it affords them the opportunity to make a potentially sizeable gift for a minimal outlay of cash each year in the form of premiums. Donors may make a gift of an existing policy, either fully or partially paid, or purchase a new policy and make annual payments on the policy. Similar to retirement plan designations,

TABLE 20.2. GIFT OF QUALIFIED RETIREMENT PLAN.

	Gift to Heirs	Gift to Charity
Assume a final balance	$250,000	$250,000
Less Income Tax "Income in respect of decedent" (up to 39.6%)	99,000	0
Net Estate/Gift Value	151,000	250,000
Less Estate Tax (up to 40%)	60,400	
Net Disposable Balance	90,600	250,000

Note: $250,000 gift provision could cost as little as $89,375.

the proposed gift to charity is accomplished by naming the charity as a beneficiary of the policy on the beneficiary designation form provided by the life insurance company. No other legal documentation is needed to effectuate the transfer. Upon the donor's death, the charity will receive all, or a portion of, the proceeds from the policy. The donor is entitled to a charitable income tax deduction equal to the cash surrender value of the policy, and any future premiums paid, only if the charity is named as both the owner and beneficiary of the policy. Simply naming a charity owner, or beneficiary, will not entitle the donor to a current charitable income tax deduction.

Deferred Gifts Deferred gifts are irrevocable transfers of cash or property not available for the charity's use and enjoyment until some future time, typically the death of the donor. Because the transfer is irrevocable, the gift is deemed complete at the time of the transfer, thereby entitling the donor to a current charitable income tax deduction. The charity receives no current benefit from the gift; however, a triggering event, typically the death of the donor, will cause the charity's interest to come to fruition. The most prevalent types of deferred gift arrangements, both of which offer income to the donor or a beneficiary designated by the donor, are charitable gift annuities and charitable remainder trusts. Since deferred gifts are irrevocable, they are not nearly as common as revocable gifts, but the amount of the deferred gift usually results in a major gift to the charity.

A charitable gift annuity is a simple contract between the donor and the charity whereby the donor makes an irrevocable transfer of cash or property to the charity (see Exhibit 20.2). In return for the contributed property, the charity promises to make fixed annuity payments to one or two life annuitants. Payments can begin immediately or can be deferred for a period determined by the donor and set forth in the annuity contract. The payment period can be measured by one annuitant's life (which is the donor in most cases) or by the lives of two joint and survivor

Exhibit 20.2. CHARITABLE GIFT ANNUITY.

Step 1: You give the charity a gift of cash or property (and receive an income-tax deduction)

Step 2: The charity makes fixed payments to you and/or another beneficiary starting now

Step 3: Remainder to charity

annuitants (usually the husband and wife). Charitable gift annuities are not issued for a fixed term of years.

The donor need not be a life income beneficiary of the gift annuity – payments can be made to elderly parents, children, or other loved ones. The payout rate offered by the charity will depend on the number of income beneficiaries (two is the maximum) and their ages. Most charities offer annuity rates as suggested by The American Council on Gift Annuities. These suggested rates are based on the assumption that, if followed, the charity will realize a 50 percent actuarial residuum from the annuity. The rates are based on current mortality studies, prevailing and projected investment returns, and projected administrative costs.

Many charities offer charitable gift annuities since they are easy to explain, require minimal administrative time and expense to implement and administer, and allow a donor to make a gift at a relatively low level. Many charities establish a minimum funding level of $10,000 for charitable gift annuities, but have the ability to establish lower funding levels as they see fit. Charitable gift annuities are attractive to donors interested in making a gift to charity but might not be able to do so because of limited financial resources. The gift annuity allows such donors to make a current gift to charity and in return receive a fixed stream of income for their lifetime.

Charitable gift annuities are regulated by state law; thus charities must be aware of the laws in the state where they are doing business, in addition to the laws of the states in which the gift annuitant donors are domiciled. The first step in implementing a charitable gift annuity program is satisfying the state's registration requirements. The second step is determining who will administer the gift annuity program. Will it be done in-house or outsourced to a third party such as a bank, accounting firm, or private company qualified to administer such plans? Charitable gift annuity administration includes mailing the donor's check for the proper amount on a timely basis, and issuing a Form 1099 to the donor at year end, which reports the amount of the payment that must be reported as taxable income. Failure to satisfy these requirements on a timely basis can have a negative effect on a charity's donor relations program. It is not uncommon for donors having a positive experience with the first charitable gift annuity they create to enter into additional charitable gift annuity contracts with the same charity.

Charitable Remainder Trusts   A charitable remainder trust is an irrevocable trust in which the donor transfers cash or property to a trustee and, in return, the donor and/or other individuals named by the donor as income beneficiaries receive income at least annually for life or for a term of years (see Exhibit 20.3). When the trust terminates, the remaining trust principal is distributed to at least one or more qualified charities. This type of trust might be attractive to donors who need an income for life or for a particular time period, have a desire to liquidate highly appreciated assets free of capital gains tax, or have a need to shelter assets from estate tax because they are above the estate tax exemption level.

Donors who wish to create a charitable remainder trust must choose between the charitable remainder annuity trust or the charitable remainder unitrust. The principal difference between the two is the way in which income is distributed. The other primary difference is that annuity trusts do not allow for additional contributions once funded, while unitrusts allow for additional contributions at any time.

Charitable remainder annuity trusts pay an annual sum certain (which is not less than 5 percent of the initial fair market value of all property placed in the trust) to one or more persons ("income beneficiaries") for a term of years (not to exceed 20) or for the life or lives of the income beneficiaries. The annuity amount paid to the income beneficiaries may be stated as a fixed percentage of the initial fair market value of the property placed in the trust or it may be stated as a fixed sum. For example, assume a donor transfers $100,000 to an annuity trust with a payout rate of 5 percent, payable for the life of the income beneficiary. The named

Exhibit 20.3. CHARITABLE REMAINDER TRUST.

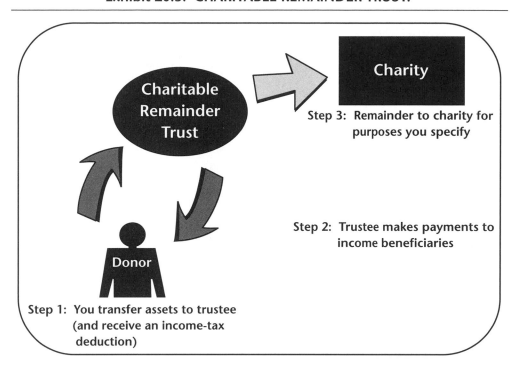

income beneficiary will receive $5,000 annually until his or her death. The entire remaining trust principal will then be distributed to the named charitable remainder beneficiary. Annuity trusts are generally favored by donors who are interested in receiving a fixed income rather than fluctuating income payments. For this reason, donors with a conservative investment philosophy tend to favor annuity trusts.

Charitable remainder unitrusts pay a fixed percentage (not less than 5 percent) of the net fair market value of the trust assets, valued annually, to one or more persons ("income beneficiaries") for a term of years (not to exceed 20) or for the life or lives of the income beneficiaries. The variable payment structure is the primary difference between the unitrust and the annuity trust. The unitrust is favored by donors who need income for life or for a particular time period and who desire a rise in income as the value of the trust increases. However, such donors must be in a position to tolerate some investment risk and possible downward fluctuations in income in years when the trust principal decreases. For example, assume a donor transfers $100,000 to a unitrust with a payout rate of 5 percent, payable for the life of the income beneficiary. The named income beneficiary will receive $5,000 in the first year. However, income payments may vary in subsequent years. If in the second year the trust principal grows in value to $110,000, the income beneficiary will receive $5,500 (5 percent of the new revalued trust principal of $110,000), thereby enjoying the benefit from the appreciation experienced by the trust. Conversely, if in the second year, the trust principal drops in value to $90,000, the income beneficiary will receive only $4,500 (5 percent of the new revalued trust principal of $90,000). Market volatility will have a direct impact on the income payments received each year by the income beneficiary. Thus, aggressive, entrepreneurial-minded donors who can tolerate investment risk tend to favor the unitrust.

With both trusts, the IRS requires that the payout percentage provided for in the trust document must be at least 5 percent but not in excess of 50 percent. Although this allows for a broad range of payout rates, most charitable remainder trusts provide for a payout percentage ranging from 5 to 10 percent depending on the number of income beneficiaries and their ages. If the charity is not the trustee of the trust (and many charities are not willing to assume that legal fiduciary responsibility), the donor is free to establish the payout percentage (assuming the 10 percent test is satisfied). However, charities who are willing to serve as trustee do have a voice in determining the payout percentage.

Marketing Planned Gifts

Developing a planned giving program internally among staff, volunteers, and the board is the first step in implementing a planned giving program, but the charity must then think about how it will effectively market the program to its constituency. Careful thought must be given as to how the charity will communicate these giving opportunities to current and prospective donors. Determining how each planned giving opportunity is marketed, and to whom, will be critical to the overall effectiveness of the planned giving program.

For organizations just getting started in planned giving, it is unrealistic to expect that a comprehensive program offering every available planned giving opportunity must be rolled out in a vacuum. Many organizations develop planned giving programs on a piecemeal basis, first introducing the revocable arrangements such as bequests, retirement plan/IRA designations, and life insurance designations, and then adding irrevocable arrangements such as charitable gift annuities and charitable remainder trusts at a later time after they have experience success with the revocable arrangements. If an organization is not prepared to respond to inquiries concerning the more technical instruments such as charitable remainder trusts, then it is probably not a good idea to market that option until later. Make sure your backyard is in order before proceeding. Donors must be left with the impression that the organization is capable of answering questions accurately and has the ability to clearly articulate the benefits of a particular opportunity to donors and/or professional financial advisors.

Not every available planned giving opportunity should be marketed to an organization's entire constituency. In some instances, it may be prudent to market a particular giving method to the entire constituency (such as bequests and retirement plan designations), but other giving methods may appeal only to a narrow segment of the constituency (such as charitable remainder trusts) and, therefore, marketed in a targeted fashion to that group alone. Age, family situations (living spouse, children, grandchildren, etc.), career success, prior giving history, level of affluence, and prior involvement with the organization are some of the factors to consider when determining which gift opportunities should be marketed to a particular donor.

The essence of a successful planned giving marketing program is to educate and inform the organization's constituency about the various giving opportunities available to help one accomplish his or her philanthropic and financial objectives. Effectively communicating to prospective donors that the organization has added planned giving to the overall fundraising program sends the message that the organization is planning for the future and committed to building and growing the organization. Many donors choose to restrict their planned gifts for endowment purposes, which ensures that the gift will perpetuate itself since only a portion of the principal is spent and the excess earnings reinvested in the fund. It is not common for donors to direct their planned gifts for unrestricted purposes or to current operating expenses. For this reason, charities must be prepared to share with donors the full menu of endowment opportunities and funding priorities.

Print Materials

The development of print materials may be the first step in disseminating planned giving opportunities to an organization's constituency. Print materials may include planned giving brochures, planned giving newsletters, planned giving inserts, planned giving ads, stand-alone mailings made up of a cover letter and accompanying illustrations, and the integration of planned giving messages throughout all facets of the organization's communication pieces including annual fund appeals.

Planned giving brochures and newsletters are commonly used by organizations to market planned giving opportunities. There are two basic approaches to consider with brochures. The first is the creation of a comprehensive brochure containing a brief explanation of each available planned giving opportunity – bequests, retirement plan designations, charitable gift annuities, etc. These brochures tend to be widely distributed since they cover all available planned giving opportunities, from the most basic, bequests, to the most sophisticated, charitable lead trusts. An all-inclusive brochure may be particularly attractive to organizations with a limited budget since design and printing expenses will be kept to a minimum.

The second approach is the creation of a series of planned giving brochures, each describing in detail a particular planned giving method. For example, individual brochures may be created for "Bequests," "Charitable Gift Annuities," "Retirement Plan and IRA Designations," "Charitable Remainder Trusts," etc. These brochures are typically not intended for widespread distribution, but rather are available to share with donors on a limited basis during personal visits or when a donor expresses an interest in a particular giving method.

Regardless of which approach is used, there are a number of companies who offer copy-ready generic brochures, which can be purchased and imprinted with the organization's name and logo. Many of these companies also give the nonprofit organization the ability to custom-tailor the generic brochure and incorporate photos, stories, and mission-related information specific to the organization. Weaving organizational information into the generic text is the preferable approach for it affords an organization the ability to produce a brochure with a look and message consistent with other communication pieces.

Some organizations assume the task of preparing the entire planned brochure in-house. There is merit to this approach in that the brochure is completely written and produced by individuals who work for the organization, and therefore know its mission best. However, before embarking on a project of this magnitude, an organization should ask itself, "Do we have the capacity and technical expertise in-house to produce an effective brochure which is technically sound, conveys a clear and understandable message to our constituency and can be produced in a timely fashion?" Since planned giving relies heavily on relationship building, an organization may conclude that their planned giving officer's time is better spent out of the office developing these relationships with key donors, rather than behind a desk preparing brochures.

Each brochure should contain a reply device, giving donors an opportunity to request additional information, indicate they have already included the organization in their will or estate plan, request an illustration, or request a personal visit from the planned giving officer. Donors who take the time to respond to mailings are prime planned gift prospective donors and should be contacted immediately to gather additional information and schedule a personal visit.

Planned giving newsletters sent on a periodic basis (quarterly, semi-annually, annually) is another way to market planned giving opportunities to an organization's constituency. Each newsletter can focus on a specific planned gift instrument and contain a donor testimonial about a donor who has utilized that particular method to benefit the organization. Some nonprofit organizations have been successful in securing newsletter sponsors, such as law firms or banks, who are willing to underwrite the cost of producing the newsletter in exchange for placing the firm's name on the newsletter. Newsletters typically lend themselves to widespread distribution – all donors of record, volunteers, professional financial advisors, etc. – for the cost-per-newsletter drops significantly once a certain level is produced.

One-page planned giving inserts that accompany annual fund appeals and ads in existing organizational publications are cost-effective ways to communicate with a broad base of the organization's constituency. For instance, if a university regularly sends an alumni magazine to its constituency, an ad inside the magazine highlighting the opportunity to support the organization through a bequest or charitable gift annuity may resonate with some readers and prompt them to self-identify as planned giving prospective donors.

Integration with Annual Appeals

Nonprofit organizations interested in marketing planned giving opportunities to their constituency should first consider reviewing existing communications to find ways to incorporate planned giving messages into these communications. This should be the most cost-effective way to begin the marketing effort, particularly for organizations with limited budgets who do not possess the financial resources to produce newsletters and brochures. This could be something as basic as including language on annual appeal slips, which give donors the opportunity to check boxes indicating they have already included the organization in their will or estate plan, requesting additional information about a particular planned giving method, or requesting a personal visit from the organization to discuss.

Stand-Alone Mailings

For the cost of a postage stamp, stand-alone mailings using a cover letter and accompanying illustration highlighting a specific planned giving instrument is another cost-effective marketing strategy. For example, mailing sample bequest language accompanied by a cover letter signed by a key board member, volunteer, or leader within the organization, extolling the importance of bequests to the long-term viability of the organization, can be done with minimal time and expense.

Revocable planned giving methods, such as bequests, retirement plan/IRA designations, and life insurance designations are typically marketed to a broader base of donors than are irrevocable arrangements, such as charitable gift annuities and charitable remainder trusts. Donors tend to gravitate to revocable arrangements because they are easy to understand, implemented with minimal effort, designated for any dollar amount, and allow donors to change their minds any time before death. Since revocable arrangements appeal to a narrower segment of the constituency, consider segmenting marketing messages based on age, level of affluence, prior giving history, involvement with the organization, or some combination of these factors.

Seminars

Planned giving seminars are an excellent way for an organization to educate its constituency about the various planned giving opportunities and create an awareness that the organization is ready to discuss and assist donors in facilitating such gifts. Seminars can be designed for a variety of audiences such as donors, volunteers, board members, faculty, and professional financial advisors.

The audience will dictate the level of technical content presented at the seminar. It is important to make donor and volunteer seminars concise and understandable. This may be the first opportunity for donors or volunteers to learn about these gift instruments, so it is important they leave the seminar with a clear understanding of the topics presented, as opposed to feeling confused and overwhelmed. Donor and volunteer seminars should avoid presentations involving in-depth technical discussions. Discussions about bequests, retirement plan/IRA designations, life insurance designations, charitable gift annuities, and in some cases charitable remainder trusts, are best suited for these types of seminars. Securing a well-respected professional advisor within the community to serve as presenter will lend credibility to the program, but first make sure this individual has the ability to present the material in an understandable fashion to an unsophisticated audience.

Seminars for professional financial advisors, on the other hand, should be more technically oriented. Many, but not all, professional advisors understand the basics of planned giving, so it is generally safe to provide a thorough discussion of the various instruments delving into the income, capital gains and estate and gift tax issues, as well as related estate planning issues. Offering continuing education credit may make the seminar particularly attractive to an advisor and help ensure a solid turnout.

Personal Visits

Although newsletters, brochures, ads, and seminars are useful ways to market planned gifts, nothing takes the place of personal visits. A marketing program that relies primarily on print materials and overlooks the importance of the personal visits will have limited success. When an individual responds to a mailing or calls requesting information, it is imperative that the charitable organization follow-up in a timely fashion. The donor may lose interest if the organization is slow to respond. Most planned gifts occur as the result of a long personal relationship with the donor so organizations should always be looking for ways to engage and involve the donor on a personal level. Letters, e-mails, and telephone calls are not substitutes for personal visits, but rather should be used to complement the visits. Depending on one's job responsibilities beyond fundraising, all development officers should set goals for conducting a certain number of personal donor visits per month. In the early stages of a planned giving program, it may be more realistic to measure a planned giving officer's progress on the number of personal visits made, rather than the number of planned gift arrangements closed or dollars raised.

Planned Giving Recognition Society

The primary reason for creating a planned giving recognition society is to identify individuals who have already included the organization in their will or estate plan. Donors may neglect to notify the organization that it has been included as a beneficiary in the estate plan. Such omissions are sometimes intentional, but in other instances the donor simply fails to think about notifying the organization. Creating a planned giving recognition society and marketing it to the organization's constituency creates a heightened awareness among individuals that the organization is interested in learning about their future plans to benefit the organization. It also provides an opportunity to begin building personal relationships with the donors and engage them in a meaningful way.

The charitable organization establishes which planned gift arrangements qualify one for membership in the society. Many organizations make membership all-inclusive, in that all of the various planned giving arrangements qualify one for membership, regardless of the dollar amount and the ability to revoke. Some organizations require the donor to provide a copy of the legal document that references the donor's gift, while others are comfortable taking donors at their word and merely ask for a written statement from the donor summarizing the gift arrangement.

Planned giving recognition society brochures explaining that the society exists, the organization's mission, a brief description of the planned gift methods that qualify one for membership, a roster of current planned gift donors, and an explanation of what action must be taken to become a member are sometimes created to help market the society. These brochures are typically sent to planned gift donors of record, board members and volunteers, annual fund donors, and professional financial advisors.

An annual event exclusively for society members, such as a luncheon or dinner, is used by some organizations as a way to thank members for their participation. Most planned gift donors do not expect organizations to bestow them with tangible objects such as plaques, paperweights, etc. In fact, some donors are adamant that the organization refrain from using gift dollars for anything other than activities and programs that directly support the mission of the organization.

Identification of Prospective Donors

Planned giving prospective donors come from all ages (young and old), levels of affluence, family situations (married, single, multiple children, childless, etc.), philanthropic objectives (capital, endowment, operating), and financial objectives (increased income, income tax savings, capital gains tax savings, estate and gift tax savings). It is a mistake to pigeonhole planned giving prospective donors into a narrowly defined set of characteristics. Sometimes planned gifts are made by donors you least expect, so it is important not to overlook anyone in your constituent population because of particular characteristics. With that said, where do you begin? Some organizations begin the identification process by analyzing individuals who are currently on the radar screen, namely, those individuals who have previously made planned gift commitments to the organization or are supporting the organization on a regular basis through annual fund commitments. Do not feel as though the process of identifying planned gift prospective donors must begin by identifying "new" prospective donors with no previous gift history. It is more likely than not, that those individuals who become planned gift donors have a history of previous giving and involvement with the organization.

Current Planned Gift Donors

Begin by identifying individuals who already have planned gift commitments in place. Perhaps they have named the organization as a beneficiary in a will, retirement plan, or life insurance policy. As discussed previously, a donor has no obligation to notify an organization that it has been included as a beneficiary. For that reason, some organizations create planned giving recognition societies because they provide an opportunity for donors to notify the organization that a planned gift commitment is already in place. Once current planned gift donors are identified, it is the planned giving officer's responsibility to contact those donors, thank them for their commitments, and attempt to begin building personal relationships with those donors. Not only will this provide an opportunity to obtain details about their planned gift, but it may also provide an opportunity to convert revocable arrangements, like bequests, into irrevocable commitments.

Annual Fund Donors

Next, look at donors who have participated in the organization's annual fund. In particular, look at the number of years they have participated. Donors who have made annual fund gifts for each of the last ten years, or eight out of the last ten years, are sending a message that they are committed to the organization and willing to support it on a consistent basis. These same donors may also be interested in learning how they can support the organization in a more significant way, either during their lifetime or at death. Because some planned gift arrangements offer income to the donor in return for their gift, in addition to providing various tax benefits, some donors may reason that they are capable of making a gift they did not think was otherwise possible, or making a gift at a level that is much higher than they ever expected.

Board, Volunteers, and Staff

Then look at individuals who have a history of direct involvement with the organization. These individuals may be former or current board members, volunteers, administrative and professional staff, donors, and community leaders. The "linkage" to the organization exists, or did exist at one time – it is the planned giving officer's responsibility to determine if the "ability" and "interest" are present. Keep in mind that most individuals have a variety of charitable interests; thus, even if the "interest" in the organization is not at the highest possible level, an individual may still be interested in supporting the organization, particularly through an estate plan arrangement, which does not require a current outlay of cash or assets. Not all planned giving prospective donors will have a high net worth. There will be individuals of moderate wealth who are willing to entertain the idea of making a current transfer to an organization in return for a stream of income, or are willing to include an organization as a beneficiary in a will, retirement plan, or life insurance policy. In addition, do not overlook donors who fall below certain annual giving levels, such as $500 or more. Some individuals, no matter how committed to an organization, may not make a significant commitment during their lifetime because of conservative financial views and/or require the peace of mind that they will have sufficient assets available if confronted with unforeseen emergencies such as major medical expenses. However, these same individuals may be willing to make a significant gift to the organization, at death, through one of the various planned giving methods.

Professional Financial Advisors

Networking with professional financial advisors, particularly those practicing in your community, can sometimes lead an organization to new prospective donors and help you identify professionals who might be willing to lend advice with specific planned giving opportunities. Clients sometimes look to their professional advisors, such as attorneys, accountants, financial planners, and bank trust officers, for advice in satisfying philanthropic objectives. Many financial advisors actively promote philanthropy as part of their client's overall financial plan, particularly if the client is likely to lose ownership and control over a certain percentage of assets at death based on their current situation. If structured properly, some charitable estate plans can allow an individual to redirect dollars that would have otherwise been lost to the government in the form of taxes to their favorite charities. The plan allows them to retain control over the assets they leave behind, so they can determine how their hard-earned dollars are spent rather than paying tax to the government.

Some organizations choose to formalize their network of financial advisors by creating a planned giving committee, which meets periodically to create gift acceptance policies, review prospective donor lists, prepare articles for planned giving newsletters, and learn about the organization's mission. You will find that some professional advisors are eager to learn more about an organization's mission, the programs it offers, and the people it serves. By creating opportunities for advisors to come to an organization's site and observe firsthand how the organization is serving the community may leave an indelible mark on the advisor and cause him or her to think about the organization when discussing philanthropic opportunities with clients.

Conclusion

A successful planned giving program must be carefully planned to meet each organization's specific needs. Commitment from institutional leadership (the board and CEO) is critical. As gift planners, it is our job to address the donor's philanthropic and financial objectives and build the gift plan around meeting those objectives. Never lose sight of the significance of your organization's mission to the donor. Planned gifts are rarely made based strictly on tax and estate planning considerations. A belief in the organization's mission is generally the driving force behind most planned gifts. Once a donor has decided your organization merits his or her support, strategizing as to how the gift should be structured to maximize available tax benefits should be done in conjunction with the donor's professional financial advisor, planned giving experts within the organization, and/or friends of the organization who are willing to share their time and expertise to help complete the gift.

Similar to successful major gift programs, successful planned giving programs are based on the ability to develop meaningful relationships with your constituency and identify how a gift to your organization can help donors satisfy their philanthropic and financial objectives. People give to people with causes. Understanding your donor's motivations and objectives – which is accomplished primarily through personal contacts and relationship-building – is far more important than understanding the technical nuances of planned giving. However, you must also be committed to understanding the basics about the various planned giving instruments. Commit to developing meaningful relationships with your top prospective donors, increase your knowledge about the various planned giving instruments, and recognize that most planned gifts require a team effort comprised of multiple individuals who understand their role and that of the others involved. Success will follow.

Discussion Questions

1) What are the primary benefits of planned giving to donors? To nonprofit organizations?
2) For smaller nonprofit organizations or those with limited capacity, what is the best way to begin a planned giving program?
3) Discuss how the board can be most supportive of a planned giving program.
4) How would you assess your organization's readiness and capacity to begin a planned giving program or to expand a current program?
5) Develop a profile of current and prospective donors who are the strongest candidates for a planned gift to your organization.

PART FOUR

MANAGING THE FUNDRAISING PROCESS

CHAPTER TWENTY-ONE

MANAGEMENT AND LEADERSHIP IN FUNDRAISING

By Elizabeth A. Elkas

After completing this chapter, you will be able to:

1. Appreciate the complexities of managing a fundraising program.
2. Apply the critical steps of the management matrix to fundraising.
3. Recognize the traits of an effective fundraising leader.
4. Articulate how fundraising leaders provide leadership to the nonprofit organization.
5. Recognize ways fundraising leaders manage conflicting views of how to fundraise.

Search online for material on the subjects of management and leadership and the results cascade in like a tsunami. One could scroll through more than 75,000 titles, each offering steps to success in a variety of disciplines. While literature on these topics is plentiful, comparatively little has been written on the subject of leadership in fundraising; this is likely due to the fact that the field is still emerging as a recognized professional career path.

In this chapter, we will consider the topics of management and leadership in fundraising; however, there are no secrets, codes, or one-minute solutions to be found here. The concepts are straightforward, pragmatic, time-intensive, and, at times, repetitive, but that does not necessarily mean they are easy to accomplish.

What they will provide the reader with is a way to contemplate these vital functions and to begin to understand how one successfully manages, how one successfully leads, and how one accomplishes these characteristics with commitment, vitality, transparency, and accountability over the long term for the health of the nonprofit and its people.

Today a number of critical issues face fundraising managers and leaders, including:

- Continuing to attract effective, engaged, and generous board members.
- Raising more money in a changing and competitive environment.
- Handling the critical demand for more services to meet the organization's needs.
- Making time to hear what board members, staff, and constituents are saying.
- Recognizing the increased speed of just about everything, including expectations.
- Ensuring that your organization can serve the needs of today and tomorrow.

Fundraising Managers and Their Responsibilities

Given the pressures of time, money, and management, skilled fundraising professionals are needed now more than ever. Arguably, the most important strength is the leader's belief in the mission of the nonprofit's work coupled with the ability to inspire others to champion the cause. Not satisfied with the status quo, fundraising leaders are change makers – they see ahead to what the organization could accomplish to fulfill its mission and set a path toward attaining it. They are influencers in the best sense of the word as they draw upon their communication skills to share their vision for the future.

A fundraising leader serves as a mentor, a careful and thoughtful listener. She or he possesses integrity and is trustworthy and fair in providing feedback and counsel, and someone who can be entrusted with confidential information. Without micromanaging, the fundraising leader communicates regularly with the board and staff, and is adept at presenting the case for support with influence and conviction. Ever enthusiastic, this individual possesses an earnest commitment to see the possibilities, to invest the time to plan and execute the strategy, to develop stretch goals, and works toward reaching them. Moreover, such individuals are proud to be known as fundraising professionals who abide by an ethical code demonstrated through work and actions.

Managing the fundraising process is complex. To keep people and programs on track and moving toward desired goals, it is essential to have a system in place that standardizes the process and measures outcomes so the leader knows what works, what doesn't, and where to direct future energies.

Meeting the Challenge Through Basic Management Functions

The Fund Raising School's management process is comprised of six separate building blocks. When stacked next to one another they form a useful structure for planning, implementing, and assessing the fundraising program. The building blocks are: analysis, planning, execution, control, evaluation, and professional ethics. The results from each block are compiled into a comprehensive document that provides an in-depth look into the overall viability of the fundraising program and points to opportunities for future directions. Oftentimes we talk about skills related to relationship building as the "art" of fundraising. This section leans toward the "science" of fundraising, drawing from assessments and measurements. Of course, it is the happy convergence of the art and science of fundraising where committed people and their missions thrive and excel.

Analysis   The management process begins with a measurement of the organization's resources. Resources may include areas such as staff, budget, space, and programs. An in-depth analysis answers the question, "Where are we today?" It is also helpful to conduct a SWOT (strengths, weaknesses, opportunities, threats) appraisal to determine the non-profit's "holes" and the work that needs to be done to address them. This is not something that is done in an afternoon. It takes the investment of time from the right people who are knowledgeable of the organization's resources and programs.

Planning   Good plans come from good planning; therefore, the *process* of planning is key. Sloppy plans, overly ambitious plans, and "wing-and-a-prayer" plans are of little use to fundraising managers. Organizations that do no planning, or very little planning, suffer from unclear or unrealistic expectations from the board, staff, donors, and volunteers. The reality is that too little planning leads to mistrust, apathy, missed opportunities, and lost time. Conversely, too much planning paralyzes people who may fear making a mistake. Flexibility is key so people can feel empowered to develop a plan and adjust it as the process evolves.

Written plans should be developed and updated at least annually. This is referred to as *strategic planning* (covering the next six to twelve months). A *long-range plan* (generally one to five years or more) may be updated annually for maximum benefit to keep the document current and relevant. All who are important to decision-making roles should be invited to participate during the course of the planning process. This includes the CEO, the board, the fundraising board, staff, major donors, constituents, and volunteers, whose input is incorporated into the plan, not simply tacked on as an afterthought or addendum.

Execution   Just as an orchestra conductor lifts a baton to signal for the musicians to start playing, the fundraising leader signals to the board, staff, and volunteers when it is time to put the plan into action by assigning responsibilities. After all the hard work and investment of time to develop the plan, people will naturally be enthusiastic and excited to see it spring to life. Copies of the document should be given to all key stakeholders, including the staff members who will be called upon to carry out many of the initiatives. Time management is essential for seeing the plan take shape. It is a good idea for the fundraising leader to check in regularly with staff, board members, and volunteers to ensure their understanding and ownership of the process. Without doing so, they may head in the wrong direction or misunderstand the goals or assignment.

Control   Control ensures that all of the hard work, creativity, and many hours that went into the plan bear fruit. As the word implies, control is designed to manage and measure standards that have been set by the leader and other stakeholders. It is the effective implementation of systems and guidelines – measuring both people and paper – to establish standards within the organization. For example, after a donor's gift is received, control ensures that the organization is accountable and has followed through with its established processes to deposit the gift, properly record the gift, follow-up with the donor in an appropriate and timely manner, and direct the gift as designated by the donor.

Evaluation   Fundraising leaders and managers need to regularly ask themselves: Are we accomplishing what we set out to do? How well is it working? Do board members, volunteers, and staff understand and support the direction we are taking? How do our gift dollars and donor numbers compare to the same time last year? These are tough questions to ask ourselves. While not always comfortable to do, evaluation is the process of taking a hard look at the numbers in the control category to assess strengths and weaknesses. For example, if the Fall direct mail appeal fell short of realizing its goal compared to last year's results, it is prudent to review all of the mailing elements, including the messaging, the signer, the time of year mailed, the package content, and the response vehicle, and consider external factors that could have influenced the response rate, such as the state of the economy.

Professional Ethics   Through actions, words, and deeds, the fundraising leader demonstrates professionalism to all, including the organization's CEO, board, staff, volunteers, and the community at large. Such leaders are regularly faced with judgment decisions that draw upon their personal standards as well as those of the organization. The pressure to secure major gifts in today's marketplace is intense and seems to grow more so with each passing year. This challenge could cause nonprofits to compromise their standards by accepting a gift that is expedient rather than ethical. The fundraising leader needs to determine what is acceptable so as not to hurt the organization or the donor. "The practice of gift seeking is justified when it exalts the contributor, not the gift seeker" (Rosso, 1991, p. 7). Before publically announcing the start of a capital campaign, a volunteer may press to solicit a leadership level gift from a longtime donor who recently suffered a medical illness and is cognitively compromised. It is the job of the fundraising leader to provide counsel to the energetic volunteer so as not to exert undue pressure or guilt on the donor. This is the kind of ethical behavior that nonprofits seek in their leaders. Such leaders are highly regarded for their integrity, care, and concern for maintaining excellent relationships with all, including donors.

Fundraising Staffing

Regardless of the nonprofit's size, the hiring of staff is a big investment and a critically important management function, both financially and strategically. As with any job, fundraisers want to know exactly what their supervisors expect of them and how they may excel at the job. That makes a well-thought-out job description invaluable, and it should be part of the office records. It is helpful to share the job description with candidates during the interview process and, likewise, make it available for all staff to see, thereby promoting transparency and full understanding of the new employee's role. Well-crafted job descriptions give staff members a sense of the magnitude and responsibility of their positions and serve as a measuring stick for future performance reviews and professional growth. If the organization currently has other fundraising staff members on the board, they are an excellent group of people to include in the interview process, given their familiarity with the organization.

Professional Staff Responsibilities   Although fundraisers are hired primarily to raise money, at times the purpose of their job is reshaped by their managers, who direct them to take on additional duties to meet the organization's needs. Clear communication here is the key. To stay focused and on target, it is helpful for the

TABLE 21.1. THE MANAGEMENT MATRIX.

What must be managed	Analysis	Planning	Execution	Control	Evaluation	Professional Ethics
Institutional Readiness (Internal and External) Case Communications Constituents Stewardship	***Example: Case*** Review all elements including the mission, goals, objectives and services. Where are we today and where are we going?	Determine the number of key people and constituents to include in the process. Create a timeline for writing and testing.	Present the case to the board and key donors. Distribute it to all relevant audiences.	Implement standards to ensure the case addresses all important aspects. Modify as necessary.	Does it effectively address "what we do" as an organization? Is it compelling and does it get people excited?	Does the case document accurately and fairly encompass our mission as a positive, committed organization?
Human Resources Staff Boards Committees Campaign Leadership Volunteers	***Example: Staff*** Assess the number and effectiveness of current staff. Will more staff be needed to reach the goals?	Outline the specifics of staff positions and determine how many people are required. Review budget and space needs.	Advertise, conduct interviews, check references, involve the board members and key leaders in meeting finalists.	Ensure that existing procedures and reporting mechanisms are effective; modify if necessary.	Do we have the right people and the right number of people? Are they deployed for maximum benefit? What have they accomplished?	Is the organization making effective use of resources spent on staff? Does the staff represent the organization with professionalism?

Markets	Example: Individuals					
Individuals Corporations Foundations Government Coordinating Agencies Associations	Review our list of individual donors and prospects. Why did they give? What stopped others from giving?	Meet with the board, staff and volunteers to help expand and refine prospect lists. Develop strategies to engage prospects.	Deploy programs to engage and involve individuals in the life of the organization.	Are we effectively meeting the needs of individuals through our mission? Steward gifts and continue to involve donors.	Do individuals understand and support our mission through their gifts and volunteerism?	Is the organization committed to enhancing meaningful relationships that engage individuals to become more involved?

Vehicles	Example: Annual Fund					
Annual Fund Capital Campaign Major Gifts Endowment Planned Giving	Assess last year's results, determine current needs.	Work with the board and staff to determine priorities, messaging, design, materials and strategic approaches.	Solicit the board, donors and other key constituents at appropriate levels.	Determine the measures and systems in place to review the annual fund.	Assess dollars, the number of gifts and feedback. Was it a success? What could be improved?	Is the annual fund managed with integrity and a commitment to serve the needs of the organization?

Strategies	Example: Direct Mail					
Direct Mail Internet Phone Solicitation Personal Solicitation Proposals Events	Consider how direct mail fits into our overall plan? What observations do we have from the past?	Determine the structure, strategy and timeline; refine prospect pool; select writer and craft compelling content driven message.	Segment and customize lists. Ensure the piece is error-free and professional looking. Drop on time.	Follow-up and follow through. Respond with positive, personalized acknowledgments within 24–48 hours.	Did the mailing go well? Measure results: how much was raised and what was the cost to raise a dollar? What improvements can be made?	Does the organization's strategy for direct mail reflect it in a favorable light?

Other

Source: The Fund Raising School, 2009, pp. 111–114.

fundraising manager to present written expectations and an agreed upon time frame in which the fundraiser may accomplish them. Of course, the staff member should also be encouraged to ask appropriate follow-up questions to make sure he or she understands the assignments.

Many, if not most, nonprofits have established specific ambitious goals for the number and type (identification, cultivation, solicitation, and so on) of contacts per month and year as well as target goals for current and planned gift dollars to be raised, and a minimum number of proposals to be presented. The objective here is to make the goals competitive and ambitious to keep the fundraising team excited and focused rather than feeling overwhelmed and fearful of not making a monthly contact quota. The number of contacts must be developed with input from the manager, keeping in mind the organization's maturity, donor base, staff size, and prospective donor pool. For example, a large, established nonprofit may expect major gift fundraisers to carry a portfolio of 150–175 or more qualified prospective donors, each of whom has a gift potential of $50,000 or more over the next five years. The manager may expect the gift officer to make anywhere from 30 to 40 meaningful donor contacts per month. Gift officers assigned to solicit principal gifts would have far fewer assigned prospective donors but the dollar potential of gifts would be significantly larger. At the other end of the spectrum, a new, small nonprofit may hire a single part-time fundraiser to lead its $60,000 annual fund campaign. Of course the number of viable, qualified prospective donors would likely be smaller, as would the solicitation amounts. It is extremely helpful, yet too often neglected in small shops, to determine reasonable goals for the number of contacts and gift amount ranges for development staff. Working together to establish long- and short-term goals is a helpful management tool for building the program.

Staff Retention   One of the most challenging issues for fundraising managers is staff retention. All too frequently, fundraising professionals leave one job for another and their departure can cause serious problems for the nonprofit. The financial and emotional costs of recruiting and training new staff are high, from hundreds to many thousands of dollars. Add to that the loss of unrealized income for the organization during the time the position is open and a staff departure could cost the opportunity to secure important gifts. Time is also a critical element since it typically takes many months for a new major gift officer to be proficient at building relationships and soliciting gifts, and that is added to the time it takes to advertise the position and select the new individual.

Many nonprofits are in a tug-of-war for talent, particularly for those fundraisers with major gifts experience. As such, some competing organizations are prepared to offer eye-popping packages to entice these individuals to their doorstep.

Other fundraisers feel that they will never have the opportunity to move up in the nonprofit, so for them the solution is to jump to another job. For others, the pressures are too hard and the goals unrealistic. The simple fact is this – if the staff member is talented and shows promise, it is oftentimes wise for fundraising leaders to retain the individual, particularly senior staff members who have built meaningful and productive relationships with key donors. Are there ways to respond to competing offers, even if a dollar for dollar match is not available? Yes, in many instances there are. Examples include giving a higher level of staff recognition, offering flexible work hours, and working to make the work environment a comfortable, congenial place, and, perhaps most importantly, setting realistic goals where talent can excel. Keep in mind an oftentimes under-recognized pool of potential staffers – those who currently serve in other capacities within the organization. These individuals may possess familiarity with many of the donors, an understanding of internal systems and goals, and an enthusiastic dedication to the mission. With the proper fundraising training, they can develop into a capable, committed fundraising staff.

Periodic staff evaluations allow for a time to discuss the fundraiser's successes, strengths, and opportunities for the future. Like all professionals, fundraisers seek genuine understanding and appreciation for a job well done and look for opportunities for growth and promotion within the organization. The fundraising manager's job is to listen and hear the staff's current desires and look ahead to meet future needs. The payoff will be a gratified and productive team of professionals who want to invest their future in the organization because they can see a meaningful place for themselves there.

Leadership Principles for Fundraisers

The first part of this chapter addresses *managing* the fundraising program. Now we shift gears to focus specifically on *leading* the fundraising program. True, fundraising managers may realize success without being leaders, but all effective fundraising leaders must be competent fundraising managers. This section addresses traits and best practices of leadership, and why and how these individuals are so important to the vibrancy and health of nonprofits.

Some contend that leaders are born, not made – perhaps it is true, perhaps otherwise. Each of us can point to a mentor we have known during our childhood or adult years. Maybe it was a coach, a teacher, a relative, or a boss. Those engaged with the nonprofit sector are no different. Someone in a leadership role took the time to encourage another to look at life a bit differently – an integral step for making the future better and stronger. The strength of our sector includes a commitment to replenish leaders from our ranks. It is the beauty of what we do – we pass our skills forward.

How Leadership Looks in the Organization

For a fundraising manager to effectively lead, followers must follow. As simple as the statement seems, it carries a lot of weight.

There are two well-recognized styles of leadership in our culture: *positional leadership* and *tactical leadership*. Most organizations are structured for positional leadership; for example, a corporate chairman and even those in leadership positions on our nonprofit boards, such as the CEO or board chair, are regarded as positional leaders. By virtue of a person's position within an organization, others are aware of his or her post as the person in charge. The other well-recognized type of leadership style is that of *tactical leadership*, most often equated with military leaders, coaches, and politicians. They are leaders who rally a brigade group or a team toward a specific objective aimed at defeating an opponent, thereby laying claim to victory.

One may consider an additional type of leadership style that is suited to the nonprofit sector: that of a "collaborative leader," as described by David D. Chrislip and Carl E. Larson in their work entitled *Collaborative Leadership: How Citizens and Civic Leaders Make a Difference* (1994). Collaborative leaders recognize that ownership is shared; therefore, the more people on board working toward a goal, the more successful they will be in serving the broader purpose for which the organization exists.

To lead by collaboration, it is vitally important that the individual be regarded as a leader by the nonprofit CEO, board chair, volunteers, donors, and staff. It enables the leader to implement a workable plan for success, and count on others to help realize a mutual goal. Without such recognition from all parties, the organization may lack focus and direction, experience diminished enthusiasm by board members and volunteers, and see donor dollars drop off.

In other words, the successful fundraising leader is not just a leader to the development staff, but a leader for the entire organization! Part of the leader's job is to fully understand the inner workings of the organization so as to effectively communicate it externally to prospective donors and inwardly to the staff. On the other hand, the job also includes educating leaders and staff throughout the organization about fundraising so everyone understands its importance and how it can be ethically achieved. That being said, fundraising leaders are comfortable in their own skin and they recognize the importance of their place in the organization. They are not driven by pretense, self-aggrandizement, or the constant need to be front and center.

Development Leader's Traits   So how does one inspire a diverse group of individuals? Certainly, there is no simple answer, but effective leaders typically are able to master certain skills. A brochure from The American Society of Association Executives lists the seven skills needed for effective leaders (Bethel, 1993). Each of the skills detailed below lends itself to the characteristics and attributes seen in many exceptional fundraising leaders.

Servant Leadership   Fundraising leaders serve to make a positive difference. They see the unique talents and potential in people and enjoy helping them grow. Consummate professionals, they possess an altruistic spirit and positive outlook, and are transparent in their words and actions. They give generously of their time and resources and thank others for doing the same. These confident leaders make it gratifying and enjoyable for others to be involved.

Creating and Communicating a Vision   Communicating a compelling vision and encouraging the organization to think beyond itself are hallmarks of fundraising leaders. They have the ability to negotiate challenges and solicit gifts with success; likewise they are excellent listeners and consider the viewpoints of others. Such individuals grow the nonprofit with an eye on today and the future.

Promoting and Initiating Change   Recognizing the need to take strategic risks, fundraising leaders see opportunities for continuous improvement. They bridge the gap between needs and resources so the organization does not become isolated or irrelevant. When changes in the environment do occur, they respond with adaptability and flexibility.

Building Partnerships   Fundraising leaders see the power of working as a team and achieving goals together. They are natural nurturers and go out of their way to build leadership skills in others. Likewise, they encourage new outlooks and partnerships, even with competitors, and recognize the importance of taking risks.

Valuing Diversity   Knowing that inclusivity makes organizations stronger, fundraising leaders value diversity and what it brings to the nonprofit through new talents and ideas. They advocate for diversity geographically, demographically and societally, and take pride in positioning their organization as leaders.

Managing Information and Technology   Technology utilizes the power of measurements and controls that result in voluminous amounts of information. Wise fundraising leaders are mindful of keeping a balance between the human elements and quantitative elements.

Achieving Balance   There is joy in seeing others learn and thrive as they accomplish their goals. Fundraising leaders relish this feeling and are gratified to help the organizations succeed. They also understand the constant internal and external pressures of the job and the limitations of time. They work hard to achieve a balance for themselves and their staff.

Leading by Example

Asking for and securing large gifts is a prime role of the fundraising leader. He or she must have the ability to engage prospective donors in meaningful discussions about a shared vision. It is important to understand why a donor wants to give and what is motivating their action, whether the gift amount is $5,000 or $5 million. Likewise, a fundraiser needs to be able to earnestly ask what is *preventing* a donor from making a gift or committing to a larger gift. Of course, the donor may have numerous questions that need to be addressed before any commitment is made.

Building trust and respecting a donor's expectation of responsible stewardship are paramount. Without trust, the donor may be convinced the fundraiser is more concerned about "landing the gift" than helping the nonprofit make positive change in the community. Clearly, receiving leadership level gifts with integrity and commitment is the lifeblood of making many good things happen for the nonprofit. Without the ability to secure gifts, the leader is simply a figurehead who may look good online, in press releases, or on the speaking circuit, but is ineffectual in helping the organization reach its potential.

Hand in hand with good communication is the ability to build meaningful relationships based on accountability and transparency. Let me underscore this point. Without accountability and integrity to the process, fundraising leaders would be unable to effectively connect with board members, the CEO, donors, and volunteers – the very people that give life to our organizations. "Accountability is not just a buzzword of the last decade. Accountability has become an essential concept for nonprofit organizations viability and success in the twenty-first century" writes Gene Tempel (Tempel, Seiler and Aldrich, 2011, p. 339).

As the chief steward of the organization, a fundraising leader wants to do the best job he or she can in order to successfully grow people and programs. Sometimes, though, competing ideas arise from the board. The leader needs the strength to listen to what is being said and give it full consideration. If he or she feels such ideas are not helpful, the leader must be able to stand up to board members who wish to sidetrack, shift, or even derail, established plans that the group has worked hard to prepare. For example, such competing voices may offer up expedient or easy ways to reach a capital campaign goal that are poorly conceived. The fundraising leader needs to consider all information, address concerns, and make a balanced decision based on policies and experience respectfully so all can continue to work productively.

Effective fundraising leaders recognize their ability to communicate and to listen carefully. Realizing they are not the only ones with new ideas, they listen to other points of view, effectively address questions, and publicly recognize others for good ideas. They use language with clarity to deliver powerful messages, both verbally and in writing, and they possess the ability to convey compelling stories that capture people's imaginations.

Conclusion

Managing and leading the fundraising program demands an investment of head and heart. Characteristics include a strong vision for the organization's future, superb communication skills, and an unwavering belief in the mission. It also takes determination, good humor, and, more than anything, a plan of action. In this day of nonprofit boards demanding (as well as wanting and needing) ever increasing dollars to serve an escalating number of constituents, fundraising leaders have a lot riding on their shoulders. Rather than allow themselves to be tugged off course by the urgent rather than the important, they are wise to strategically manage the fundraising process. This process gives fundraising leaders a way to analyze, conduct, track, and evaluate sequential planning that considers all stakeholders and the numerous functions that need to be managed. It also enables them to articulate the plan for a sustainable future, knowing that the right level of resources can be identified and achieved. It also brings about ambitious yet achievable goal setting. Best of all, it leads to a vigorous group of committed people – the board, staff, donors, and volunteers – who stretch to realize more and larger gifts, thereby advancing the mission.

Discussion Questions

1) What is the Management Matrix? How can it help a fundraising leader perform his or her job better?

2) Name traits and characteristics of an effective fundraising leader. How do these traits benefit the organization?

3) Fundraising leaders have an incredible opportunity to grow the leadership skills among their staff, Board, and volunteers. What are some specific examples of how they may nurture leadership skills in others?

4) What are ways in which a fundraising leader may handle competing ideas from the fundraising Board members who disagree with one another?

CHAPTER TWENTY-TWO

ORGANIZATIONAL DEVELOPMENT FOR FUNDRAISING

By Eugene R. Tempel and Lehn Benjamin

Fundraising is an active management process that is built on organizational strengths. Fundraising fails because of organizational vulnerabilities. Hank said, "You can raise a lot more money through organized fund raising than you can through disorganized fund raising." Public perceptions about whether an institution is well organized have a great deal to do with fundraising success. This chapter examines the various organizational factors that are necessary for an organization to succeed in raising philanthropic dollars.

This chapter covers the following:

- Organizational responsiveness as a foundation for fundraising.
- Essential aspects of institutional readiness for fundraising:
  - Planning.
  - Human resources.
  - Sources of support.
  - Fundraising vehicles.
- The importance of organizational effectiveness and accountability.

Essential Foundations for Philanthropy

Often an effort to provide for the public good begins with a single individual acting on his or her own. Others might be drawn in to help support the effort with time or talent or money. Success might lead to organized voluntary association or, ultimately, to the formation of a nonprofit organization, eligible to receive philanthropic contributions qualifying for the U.S. Federal Charitable gift deduction by the Internal Revenue Service. It is through these formal organizations (meeting the requirements of 501 (c)(3) of the Internal Revenue Code or being organized as a church) that most philanthropic gifts are made. A nonprofit organization is able to engage volunteers and raise philanthropic dollars based on organizational strengths that reflect its understanding of the external environment and internal preparedness and readiness that make fundraising possible.

Many experts say that organizations must have a culture of philanthropy. Most mean that the responsibility for fundraising must be accepted by board members, organizational leadership, and staff in addition to fundraisers. At the heart of a culture of philanthropy is a belief in philanthropy as a legitimate source of support. That belief rests on the case for support. The case for support is expressed in external or public terms.

For an organization to be successful in fundraising, it must be connected to its external environment. It must understand the changing needs of that environment and its ability to respond to the organization's need for human and financial resources to remain functional. The organization must have management structures in place that interpret its mission in relation to changing external needs. An organizational tendency toward an "open system" relative to the external environment enhances its fundraising ability.

For nonprofit organizations to be successful in the twenty-first century, they must operate as open systems (Katz and Kahn, 1978), understanding that they are interdependent with their external environment, even if they are highly institutionalized with values that appeal to a narrow base of supporters. Research indicates that philanthropic giving is closely related to growth of the economy (*Giving USA*, 2009). Changing needs in society call for adaptations by nonprofit organizations and so do changing donor preferences.

Nonprofit organizations have a natural tendency to become "closed systems." The attempt to build endowments reflects that tendency. A fully endowed nonprofit organization can become a closed system irrelevant to changes in the common good and vulnerable to decline. Organizational leadership must help organizations focus on the external environment.

In the 25 years since the first edition of *Achieving Excellence in Fund Raising*, nonprofit organizations have begun functioning more as open systems. Professional management, calls for transparency and accountability, changing donor behavior, public policy, and scholarship on best practices have all been responsible. For example, higher education institutions functioned as though they could shape and control their outside environments, which began to end 20 years ago. The intense marketing programs that colleges and universities have in place today indicate they have come down from "the ivory tower," a tag that indicated they were out of touch with the real world. Many higher education institutions have developed elaborate feedback systems to determine student preferences, developed new services and programs to respond, and sophisticated advertising and communications and incentive programs to recruit students they want.

When organizations desire or require a broad base of support or seek wider influence, they must be managed as "open systems." Open-system theory assumes that organizations are not independent of their external environments, but that they have impact on, and are affected by, their environments. According to the open-system theory, organizations depend upon a hospitable and supportive environment for supplies of human, fiscal, and material resources, as well as for consumption of goods and services.

To function successfully as open systems, organizations must monitor continually the environment and either adapt to changes or attempt to change inhospitable elements in the environment. Organizations that fail to adapt or fail to influence the environment eventually produce unwanted goods or unneeded services and lose their ability to attract vital resources.

Fundraising success depends on an organization's ability to adapt to surrounding conditions. A nonprofit organization exists to provide services for which there is a public or societal need, often on a small or local level. If that need is otherwise met, then the organization's rationale for existence disappears. If it continues to provide staff and programs to fill the outdated need, then it will be viewed as wasteful, inefficient, and unresponsive. Its sources of support will diminish, and it will be forced to close. For example, the Young Men's Christian Association (YMCA) was established in the nineteenth century in response to the need for a healthy Christian environment for young men who moved from rural areas to the cities for jobs. Had the YMCA not adapted to a new environment by abandoning its "hotel" business when that migration ended and shifted to filling other needs in the urban environment, it might not exist today. Similarly, the March of Dimes was founded in 1938 as the National Foundation for Infantile Paralysis, largely through the efforts of President Franklin D. Roosevelt. When a vaccine for polio was developed and the disease eliminated, the organization lost its rationale for existence. In this case, the organization found another health problem, children's birth defects, that required solution and which allowed it to adapt to other social needs.

Responding to changes in the environment is not as simple as meeting current needs. Organizations that respond to changing needs by altering dramatically their own institutional value systems also risk their future. If traditional contributors fail to support an old institution in its newest efforts, then their contributions may be lost before a new support base is established. For example, consider a small Roman

Catholic liberal arts college built on the tradition of providing a well-rounded education based on Catholic values in a highly personal environment. The college might respond to declining enrollments by orienting itself toward meeting needs for continuing education in local workplaces. The college risks losing completely its traditional student base, however, as well as its existing alumni support. The college may gain an expanded new student body and obtain private dollars from the community, but it will be a different institution with different potentials for fundraising.

Kotler has made significant contributions by adapting marketing principles from business to nonprofit organizations (Andreasen and Kotler, 2008). He devised a scale that described an organization's orientation in one of three ways: 1) unresponsive, 2) casually responsive, or 3) fully responsive. Unresponsive organizations function as closed systems, as bureaucracies. They do not encourage customers to submit inquiries, complaints, or suggestion; they do not determine customer satisfaction or needs or train staff to be customer oriented. The casually responsive organization begins to look externally in its planning. It encourages its constituents to provide feedback and periodically measures constituent satisfaction. The fully responsive organization shares the characteristics of the casually responsive organization but it also tries to improve its services based on new needs and preferences and prepares its staff to be customer oriented.

Many nonprofit organizations cannot and should not become fully responsive to the market in order to enhance their fundraising. They must remain in harmony with the values and mission upon which they were founded. Organizations with strong internal value systems that give rise to their missions should become highly responsive by actively involving their clients and potential contributors in the organization's affairs. Fundraising success depends upon the sensitive inclusion of potential supporters in the life and spirit of the organization.

Kotler comes to the same conclusion (Andreasen and Kotler, 2008): "If a manager wishes the organization to be wholly customer-driven, he or she must directly confront the often unspoken fear that this type of marketing orientation will ultimately cause artists, surgeons, librarians, museum directors, and other nonprofit professionals to bend their professional standards and integrity to 'please the masses'."

Nonprofit organizations today are vulnerable to concepts of social entrepreneurship and market orientation. Donors often push nonprofits toward operating more market-based services, using a business model, with a focus on the bottom line. Some nonprofit organizations have had to deal with external pressures to balance bottom line interests of donors and board members with top line mission orientation.

Some organizations are setting up market-based services that reflect the mission to generate income to support the basic mission. Other organizations are able to generate revenue in excess of expenses with some market-based services (i.e., web site design services offered by a technical training program, childcare services offered by a family shelter). However, this does not mean that there are additional needs to fulfill basic mission programs that provide a basis for fundraising.

Although nonprofit organizations do not exist to generate profits, their long-term survival depends to some extent on good business practices. Nonprofits that develop surplus income protect themselves from fluctuations in client fees and fundraising levels. Surplus revenue also assures contributors that the organization has a secure future. Organizations that strive to provide the most effective services with the fewest resources are the most likely to generate surpluses. Organizations that are viewed as effective *and* efficient also have the best opportunity to attract philanthropic dollars. How well a nonprofit organization is managed also has an impact on its ability to raise money.

Accountability is a major force in nonprofit organizations today. Accountability encompasses not only how well a nonprofit is managed but also how well a nonprofit communicates its management and outcomes to its constituents. It is an organizational strength for a nonprofit organization to hold itself accountable to demonstrate good stewardship to its constituents.

Business techniques might be useful in managing nonprofit fundraising. However, the values and beliefs that give rise to these organizations often lead them necessarily to defy good business marketing practices. New service initiatives that abandon a mission to enhance revenue production can harm philanthropic efforts. When unpopular causes must be pursued, if the organization is to remain faithful to the requirements of its mission, then it must defy marketing information in favor of its mission.

Sometimes, fidelity to a mission leads to conflict with sources of support. A conservative funding source might hesitate to support an organization that is serving a controversial cause because its employees, customers, or stockholders might object. Organizations that understand and manage this complexity put themselves in a position of strength when raising funds.

Fundraising is an effective test of organizational viability. As such, fundraising can become the catalyst for organization renewal and commitment. To be successful in fundraising, the organization must be viewed by potential supporters as responsive in its delivery of quality services. These services must be provided in an effective and efficient manner to constituents. Potential supporters must understand and accept the value systems that affect these services. An organization that lacks internal meaning has no basis for stimulating philanthropy.

By managing tensions between responsiveness to changing environmental factors and its mission an organization can enhance its strengths and minimize its vulnerabilities. A simple SWOT analysis (Strengths, Weaknesses, Opportunities, Threats) will enable an organization to conduct and know better how to succeed with its fundraising (Kearns, 1996). SWOT analysis can help an organization build on its strengths, minimize its weaknesses, and deal with opportunities and threats in its external environment. SWOT analysis can help an organization focus on its strengths and reduce its vulnerabilities in institutional readiness, human resource, markets, vehicles, and management, the factors that are essential to successful fundraising.

Institutional Readiness

The premise of this chapter is that effective fundraising is built upon organizational strengths and that organizational weaknesses and vulnerabilities can undermine fundraising efforts. With this in mind, an organization preparing itself for fundraising must analyze its strengths and weaknesses and provide an inventory of those resources that are essential for successful fundraising.

Fundraising based on the strengths of the organization assumes a dignity that flows from those strengths, obviating any need on the part of staff or volunteers to apologize for the solicitation process. Fundraising based on values and mission is a meaningful part of philanthropy. To take its case for philanthropic support to the public, the organization must have prepared itself internally to focus on its strengths and deal with its weaknesses.

An essential readiness element is the institutional plan. The plan attests to the stability and to the future of the organization correctly based on an assessment of current and future social and human needs within the scope of the organization's mission. One of the greatest strengths that the plan can bring to the fundraising process is the affirmation that the organization is confident of its future and empowered by its vision for a better society.

An effective plan must go beyond a description of programs. Programs must be drafted in economic terms if they are to provide a suitable foundation for fundraising. The plan must project annual income and expense requirements for each program, both those in existence and those planned for the future. Equally, the plan should identify special purpose, capital, and endowment needs that are anticipated during the designated period. The organization is strongest when the prospective donor can accept the validity of the income and expense projections relative to past accomplishments and future program delivery. If financial accountability through the planning process can demonstrate efficient use of resources for effective programs, then good stewardship has begun.

The financial plan should go beyond ordinary income and expense projections. It should state the amounts that must be raised for current program support through the annual fund; the amounts required for special projects, some immediate and urgent, others deferrable, and the amounts required for capital projects; and endowment and cash-reserve requirements of the organization. This comprehensive financial analysis, with its realistic assessment of anticipated revenue and gift production, forces careful evaluation of program proposals and responsible decisions when priorities are set.

Before the planning process can be initiated, the process itself should undergo scrutiny from the professional staff and volunteers of the organization to determine the extent to which it has involved the organization's primary constituency. The sensitive and responsive plan involves the professional staff and volunteers from the governing board as the plan's architects. Both groups must commit themselves to implement the plan and to evaluate it on a continuing basis or the organization will be vulnerable during the fundraising process. The organization can benefit by creating among the constituents "ownership" in the plan. This can be done by inviting leaders within the constituency to become part of the planning activity. The more affirmation there is of the organization's mission through planning, the better the chances of winning the constituency's endorsement when the plan is finished. The plan will give substance to the various programs that have been devised to respond to the designated human and societal needs. From these program descriptions can be drawn the four, five, or more of the most salient and exciting expressions that will animate the case.

Human Resources

The first human resource strength in institutional readiness is the governing board. A thoughtfully structured, involved, and dedicated board of trustees is a symbol of responsible governance and an asset to the fundraising process. A passive, uninvolved, and disinterested board is a weakness that organizations must address.

It is essential that board members be involved actively in planning, from the beginning delineation of the planning format, through the periodic review, and as part of the final acceptance of the plan with its definitions of program and financial priorities. By accepting the plan, board members accept the responsibility to give and to ask others to give in proper measure against the financial needs. This is board engagement at its best. Finally, the board members must have integrity and credibility with the community, serving as the organization's first point of accountability to the public and as stewards of the public trust.

The board has a direct responsibility to press for the success of the organization's fundraising programs. To accomplish this, the board should include a fundraising or a development committee as a standing committee. This committee should include in its membership those board members who have the strongest interest in the organization's mission and whose linkage with the community helps initiate fundraising. This committee should meet regularly and actively develop, implement, and evaluate fundraising plans. Committee membership can be extended to those non-board members who would be willing to give, ask, and work as advocates of the organization.

The second point of strength in human resources is the professional staff: the chief executive officer (CEO), individuals responsible for managing programs and finances, and the fundraising staff. The nonprofit entity's viability depends upon long-term delivery of quality services that the public perceives as needed. This focuses attention on the CEO and the program staff. Filled with capable people, these positions provide an organizational strength. The CEO is a key strength in the fundraising process as a link to engage the board and to represent the organization in engaging donors and prospects. The CEO also sets the stage for organizational support of fundraising. Lack of CEO understanding, involvement, and support is a key weakness that must be addressed.

For long-term fundraising to succeed, it requires the attention of someone who is competent to plan, organize, and manage the fundraising process. Fundraising management positions vary by organization as to the amount of time and the level of professionalism allotted to the task, and range from volunteer to minimal part-time to full-time with a multiple-member professional staff, often a function of organizational age and size. The fundraising position of an organization is enhanced if it has full-time professional staff members at the helm who are dedicated to involving board members, other volunteers, and administrative, program, and support staffs to assist in the fundraising process.

The governing board and CEO must be prepared to become involved in fundraising. Board members must accept ownership of the organization and support it financially as a necessary first step in establishing institutional readiness. The final assessment of readiness is to determine the ability of board members, fundraising professionals, the CEO and key staff members to come together as a development team. There must be an understanding of and a commitment to the concept that successful fundraising depends upon the active participation of board members, the CEO, and key staff members on the team, both in the development and organization of fundraising programs and in asking for gifts.

Acceptance of this concept by all is essential to the fundraising process. Under the definition of this process, the fundraising staff will provide the management services for the fundraising program. The volunteers will provide the linkage and the leverage to the gift-making potential of the community. A properly developed governing board, volunteer and professional staff members represent a necessary strength for undertaking fundraising.

Sources of Support

Philanthropic funds originate in general areas of the economy, referred to as "gift sources" or "gift markets." The five gift sources for fundraising activities are individuals, corporations, foundations, associations, and government. To some extent, every nonprofit organization has potential supporters among these markets. Opportunities for fundraising come from recognizing the potential for support among specific subsectors of each market. Proper prospect-development practices will make it possible to identify, cultivate, and solicit prospective donors within each subsector.

Government funds are *not* philanthropic funds, but it is important to recognize that government funding has become a larger rather than a smaller source of revenue for nonprofit organizations, especially in some subsectors. A slowed economy is likely to impact continued growth of government funding and make it challenging, especially for small neighborhood organizations and church and para-church activities that provide neighborhood services.

The second decade of the twenty-first century sees a continued change of gift markets to those from which organizations sought funds at the beginning of the last decade of the twentieth century. Foundations have continued to be an important source of funds; corporations take a more strategic approach and continue to be impacted by a slowed economy; individuals are more likely to be interested in program-related projects that allow them to express their own values and interests, many with private foundations to make their giving more formal. Understanding the values, interests, and needs of donors has always been important to fundraising, but it is even more important to funding success today. Patience with loyal donors facing a more uncertain economic future, increasing health care costs, and diminished assets is key to success.

Organizations today must have specific information about the prospect's interests and linkages, and the ability and willingness to give. By accepting this basic principle of fundraising, the practitioner can understand that the organization will approach fundraising markets from its strongest position when it involves its board members, non-board volunteers, and staff members in identifying, understanding, engaging, and soliciting potential contributors from any of the gift sources.

Fundraising Vehicles

A nonprofit organization maximizes its potential for philanthropic support it if utilizes the full array of fundraising vehicles in a total development program. These include annual giving, special gifts, major gifts, the capital campaign, and planned giving. The organization's fundraising plan must take into account the human and financial resources it can commit to different fundraising activities. Today that includes use of a website for solicitation and acceptance of gifts and taking advantage of the various "e-philanthropy" and social networking opportunities available to it.

Organizations that depend too heavily on the annual fund through direct mail, telephone, and special events fundraising are vulnerable to high fundraising costs. Organizations that are dependent on one or two large individual, corporate, or foundation sources are vulnerable to the changing interests and funding capacities of these sources. The more comprehensive the fundraising plan is in utilizing all the fundraising vehicles available to approach the full scope of funding sources, the stronger it will be.

For small nonprofit organizations, this can be a challenge, especially with major and planned gifts. However, every organization can encourage bequests or giving through wills and use volunteer or pro bono consultants or a local community foundation to help with special opportunities for other types of planned gifts.

Management

Most experts agree that nonprofit organizations are more professionally managed today than they were a decade ago. However, a Kellogg Foundation initiative, called Knowledge Management in Nonprofit Management Education, for the first decade of the twenty-first century is based on the evidence that professional talent is not uniformly distributed throughout the nonprofit sector. There is, however, some acceptance of the notion that even unsophisticated nonprofits are fairly efficient in the use of funds and effective in providing good services (Drucker, 1990).

Poor management or perceived poor management is a deficiency that leaves a nonprofit organization vulnerable to failure in fundraising. Sound management staff and processes are an organizational strength upon which successful fundraising can be built.

The most successful organizations will have a management team of volunteers, administrators, program managers, and fundraising managers who operate the organizations to some extent as an open system. This management team will involve its various constituents – clients, donors, trustees, volunteers, vendors, the community, and its own staff – in continued analysis and planning before executing programs and exercising management control over its programs. The successful organization will involve the same constituents in evaluating its programs as the management process of analysis, planning, execution, control, and evaluation begins another cycle.

Fundraising is a management process. It is based on the strength of an organization's programs to fulfill the organization's mission. Therefore, the organization must be well managed. Transparency and accountability are the focus of management today. Organizations must illustrate to the public that they are good stewards of contributed funds and that the organization's programs are making a difference. In the strongest organizations, the fundraising manager has persuaded the board of trustees and the CEO to dedicate significant portions of their time and energies to the fundraising effort of the organization.

Fundraising involves engaging constituents with the organization and helping them identify with organizational values and missions. It requires a comprehensive view of client constituencies, volunteers, advocates, and those who are prospective contributors. Fundraising demands the mastery of professional technical skills that are required for fundraising and the ethical values that foster and protect philanthropy. It includes the management of planning and other efforts that precede many of society's voluntary actions for the public good.

Organizational Effectiveness and Accountability

Donors have long been concerned that nonprofits use their resources wisely, but the demand for evidence of effectiveness has escalated in the last 20 years. This demand for evidence of effectiveness has been fueled by the growth in the number of nonprofits globally and the more central role they are playing in solving social problems. Funders and donors want to know about the social return on their investment. Some funders are investing in social impact bonds, while still other donors are asking nonprofits whether they are using evidence-based practices. More importantly, nonprofit managers recognize that getting regular feedback on how they are doing is essential for the people or cause they are dedicated to. Nonprofits that do not learn how to systematically collect evidence of effectiveness and use that evidence to make improvements will be left behind.

However, as many fundraisers know, this is not easy. Organizations often lack the capacity or resources to do this well and often find that some things are simply difficult to measure. So what can nonprofits do? Collect regular and useful feedback from the people they seek to serve, impact, or engage. Most nonprofits, even the smallest organizations, have the capacity to ask one question: Did we treat you well? Then, depending on whether a nonprofit is an arts organization, an environmental group, or a social service agency, one can ask a second or third question. For example: Did we help you? Did we provide an experience you enjoyed? Did you learn something new? Nonprofits can build from there. Ideally, staff measures of effectiveness are clearly linked to desired program outcomes and then those program outcomes are linked to organizational outcomes. This cascade of outcomes, as it is often called, helps nonprofit leaders manage for greater effectiveness.

What is the role of the fundraiser? Fundraisers will likely face questions from potential and existing donors about the impact of the nonprofit. This requires being knowledgeable about measurement approaches and trends, but more importantly it requires understanding the data that the nonprofit collects and being transparent about what it does and does not represent. Too often there is a tendency to inflate nonprofit results or only talk about success stories. Fundraisers miss two critical opportunities here. First, they miss the chance to demonstrate that their nonprofit is a learning organization. Organizations make mistakes; they sometimes fail to provide an effective service. What matters is how they are changing as a result. This is more likely to impress donors than simply selective success stories. Second, they miss the chance to talk about the data management systems needed to support effective practice. Many nonprofits lack effective data management systems, hobbling together results in a piecemeal fashion to produce reports. Fundraisers are in a critical position of helping donors understand the infrastructure necessary to support effectiveness. In the end, fundraising is much easier if the nonprofit organization is effective. An effective nonprofit is not one that always gets it right, but rather is one that is data driven and striving for greater impact for those it ultimately seeks to benefit.

Conclusion

Fundraising success or failure is often related to organizational dynamics rather than fundraising strategies. Successful fundraising is built on strengths. Fundraising often fails because of organizational weaknesses or vulnerabilities.

First, to be successful in fundraising, organizations must operate as "open systems" while being true to their mission. Understanding the dynamics of the external environment whose gift support is sought is a key organizational strength. A sound plan for the future, developed with the involvement of key constituents, is an organizational strength in fundraising. It is also essential to have the CEO and the board involved in the process. Finally, the organization must have a communication plan through which it holds itself accountable to the public.

If organizations operate as "closed systems," focused internally with no plan for the future based on external needs, they are vulnerable to decline and failure in fundraising. Simply doing good work is no longer sufficient to ensure long-term success. More sophisticated donors and funders today are holding organizations to higher standards of accountability. Doing so demands professional management approaches that lead to institutional readiness for fundraising.

Discussion Questions

1) How do "open" and "closed" systems impact fundraising?
2) Describe organizational planning as it relates to fundraising.
3) Why is it important to identify potential sources of support and the best ways to approach them in fundraising?
4) Discuss how organizations can measure effectiveness even if they lack resources for formal evaluations.

CHAPTER TWENTY-THREE

BUDGETING FOR AND EVALUATING FUNDRAISING PERFORMANCE

By James M. Greenfield and Melissa S. Brown

Budget preparations often begin three to six months prior to the fiscal year end. Nonprofit staff assess program and service priorities for the coming year, review current revenue sources and expense reports, and estimate the resources needed to continue its programs and meet new service demands within the organization's fiscal capabilities.

Some organizations receive significant amounts of revenue from public participation such as ticket sales for performing arts organizations, tuition and grants for colleges and universities, insurance reimbursement and patient payments for hospitals, and so on. Such program service revenue can also include contracts for services, whether with governments or other payers. Organizations without program service revenue, including houses of worship and many social service agencies, typically rely extensively on gifts, grants, and contributions for their annual operating revenues. In this chapter you will gain an understanding of the fundraising plan, a program budget, how to evaluate fundraising performance, how to set fundraising goals, and finally how to measure success.

Development, as with other organization operating units, will evaluate the departmental status and prepare budget plans for the next fiscal year. These preparations follow an established fiscal regimen within the nonprofit's accounting or budget software program. Ideally, that program tracks expenses in summary categories such as staff salaries and benefits and direct costs such as postage, printing, travel, and more (see Table 23.1). Many of these software programs also follow the

TABLE 23.1. THE DEPARTMENT BUDGET WORKSHEET.

The combination of direct costs (program expense) with office operations (indirect costs) represents the true and complete budget required for fundraising. Preparation of the budget for the year should be based on an analysis of both prior years' expenses and individual program results.

	Current Fiscal Year		Next Fiscal Year
	Budget	**Actual**	**Budget Estimate**
A. Administration/Salaries			
Director of Development	$	$	$
Professional Staff	$	$	$
Office Support Staff	$	$	$
Part-Time Workers	$	$	$
Temporary Workers	$	$	$
Sub-Total	$	$	$
Fringe Benefits (%)	$	$	$
Pay Increases (%)	$	$	$
TOTAL:	$	$	$
B. Office Operations			
Office Supplies	$	$	$
Telephone Charges	$	$	$
Telephone Equipment	$	$	$
Rental Equipment	$	$	$
List Fees	$	$	$
Postage Fees	$	$	$
Printing Costs	$	$	$
Books/Periodicals	$	$	$
Travel (trips)	$	$	$
Travel (local)	$	$	$
Entertainment	$	$	$
Awards/Plaques	$	$	$
Dues/Memberships	$	$	$
Professional Development	$	$	$
Insurance	$	$	$
Office Rental	$	$	$
New Equipment	$	$	$
Equipment Maintenance	$	$	$
Consultant Fees	$	$	$
Services Purchased	$	$	$
Other	$	$	$
Sub-Total	$	$	$
C. Budget Summary (A + B)	$	$	$

Excerpted : AFP Fundamentals of Fundraising Course ©Association of Fundraising Professionals, 2010 list of routine expenses used in filing an Annual Information Return (consult IRS Form 990, Part I, page 10).

A budget for fundraising is also an investment and should realistically reflect anticipated fundraising returns, based on amounts raised in prior years. There are no rules about the ratio of investment to the amount raised (return on investment) because solicitation programs vary greatly. A given organization's capacity to raise funds will depend on its access to revenue sources, image and reputation, history of support, and leadership, plus the fundraising staff and budget size. Research shows, for example, that organizations that rely entirely on volunteer fundraising have a more difficult time reaching their fundraising goals than do organizations of comparable size that have at least one full-time fundraising professional (Nonprofit Research Collaborative, 2012, p. 12).

The Budget is a Plan

A fundraising budget is a fiscal plan. It is derived from the organization's strategic plans and guided by prior results, both income and expenses, in order to support programs that benefit the community directly. A fundraising budget can and ought to be a multiyear investment strategy with an expected growth capacity and long-term rate of return that at least exceeds \$1 for every dollar invested, and might reach \$6, \$10, or even \$20 return for every \$1 invested. As such, fundraising budgets are unlike most other operating areas that are expense activities or cost centers. Fundraising is guided by expectations of its "profitability," that it will generate more than it costs.

Budgeting for fundraising is a fiscal strategy with specific revenue goals linked with the organization's most urgent service delivery or mission-focused priorities. The charitable use of funds raised is often linked to previous donor interests or donor preferences, which animates the fundraising plan, revenue goals, and specific fundraising activities.

Three necessary ingredients support preparation of a new fundraising budget. Essential questions start with: What can the organization do with funds raised? What revenues can the organization expect? Then lastly, how can fundraisers use their insights into organizational funding priorities matched with donor interests to estimate gift, grants, and contributions to help the organization meet its mission-driven goals?

Start with the organization's program and service priorities for the coming fiscal year along with their estimated expenses. Follow with an analysis of *all* revenue sources available to meet these anticipated program and service expenses. Third, based on these first two components, prepare realistic estimates of fundraising revenue based in part on prior giving and in part on a sense of donors' interests in program and service funding priorities.

After discussion about realistic fundraising revenue forecasts and the most urgent priorities, fundraising executives and organization executive team members can prepare estimates as fundraising goals that might be realized. The fundraising executive will have a plan that includes solicitation activities and the budget required to secure these revenues. These three essential components – organizational priorities, revenue sources, and gift forecasts based on prior year fundraising results, combined with the fundraiser's knowledge of current donor interests – guide the organization's leadership in setting new fundraising goals and objectives.

Fundraising results from prior years, as presented in month-by-month standard gift reports, can be an invaluable resource when setting fundraising goals and objectives. Exhibits 23.1, 23.2, and 23.3 illustrate sources of gifts, purposes or uses of funds raised, and solicitation methods used to produce these results. Each is discussed further in the section on Program Budgeting. These summary data, aided by analysis of results from prior years, allow the organization to forecast future results with reliability and to guard against unrealistic expectations. If your organization does not use these categories, consider checking the reporting standards and guidelines suggested by the Council for Aid and Support of Education or the Association for Healthcare Philanthropy. Such guidelines are particularly important for tracking deferred gifts.

EXHIBIT 23.1. GIFT REPORT ON SOURCES OF GIFTS RECEIVED.

Sources of Gifts	Number of Gifts	Gift Income	Average Gift Size
Trustees/Directors	15	$28,500	$1,900
Staff & employees	235	19,650	84
New donors (acquisition)	625	18,950	30
Prior donors (renewed)	690	59,635	86
Corporations	22	106,500	4,840
Foundations	28	185,000	6,607
Associations/societies	4	30,000	7,500
Bequests/estates	2	100,000	50,000
Unsolicited gifts	39	9,500	244
Other gifts received	9	3,500	389
Total:	1,799	$561,235	$312

EXHIBIT 23.2. GIFT REPORT ON PURPOSES OR USES OF GIFTS RECEIVED.

Purpose or Uses of Gifts Received	Number of Gifts	Gift Income	Average Gift Size
Unrestricted funds	658	$101,850	$155
Temporarily restricted funds			
Programs/services purposes	345	129,457	375
Capital/equipment purposes	165	50,500	306
Education/training purposes	240	45,000	118
Research/study purposes	118	63,800	541
Client financial needs purposes	114	18,600	163
Staff/employee purposes	22	8,500	386
Other restricted purposes	120	8,028	67
Subtotal:	1,782	$434,235	$244
Permanently restricted funds			
Unrestricted endowment	6	$45,000	$7,500
Restricted endowment	11	90,500	8,227
Subtotal	17	$135,500	$7,971
Grand total	1,799	$561,235	$312

EXHIBIT 23.3. GIFT REPORT OF SOLICITATION ACTIVITIES AND RESULTS BY METHOD.

Solicitation Activities	Number of Gifts	Gift Income	Average Gift Size
Annual Giving Programs			
Direct mail (acquisition)	456	$10,050	$22
Direct mail (renewal)	408	25,855	63
Membership associations ($100)	319	31,900	100
Activities, benefits, special events	380	40,800	107
Donor clubs and support group	125	31,250	250
Organizations ($250)			
Associations/societies	4	10,000	2,500
Volunteer-led personal solicitation	55	19,880	362
Subtotal	1,747	$169,735	$97

(Continued)

EXHIBIT 23.3. (CONTINUED).

Solicitation Activities	Number of Gifts	Gift Income	Average Gift Size
Major Giving Programs			
Corporations	22	$106,500	$4,840
Foundations	28	185,000	6,607
Capital campaigns	-0-	-0-	-0-
Bequests/estate gifts	2	100,000	50,000
Subtotal	52	$391,500	$7,529
Grand total	1,799	$561,235	$312

Once completed, a fundraising budget plan, accompanied by estimated gift revenues, is submitted as part of the organization's overall budget plan. After internal reviews and adjustments, the plan becomes the board-approved organizational budget plan for the next fiscal year.

Program Budgeting

The next task is to translate fiscal preparations into an active fundraising strategy, typically in the form of a written plan with a defined schedule of public solicitation activities guided by the annual "Case for Support." Throughout the year, an organization may solicit funds using a variety of fundraising methods and techniques. These solicitations will match approved program and service priorities. Each method generates results and month-by-month reports, as shown in Exhibits 23.1, 23.2, and 23.3, aid in monitoring budget expenses and estimated revenues.

To illustrate, prior years' results in Exhibit 23.1 reveals two bequests valued at $100,000 as part of $561,235 total revenue. Estimating bequests at a similar level again is unwise and $461,235 is the more accurate baseline figure to use in forecasting future results. Exhibit 23.1 also does not reflect any solicitations still in progress, such as major gift cultivations or grant applications awaiting approval, both of which required expenses in the current fiscal year. Multiyear reports can aid in establishing more reliable trending data for forecasting purposes.

Exhibit 23.2 offers another illustration of forecasting guidance. These separate uses show how the public responded to previous solicitation appeals, an indication of giving preferences. It also offers insights into possible strengths and weaknesses when funding priority changes and may signal the amount of effort required to engage the public in new priority needs. Research shows that donors' generosity is linked to their ability to direct their gifts toward specific areas of operation. Donors often prefer to give based on their interests. While organizations prefer unrestricted gifts, an organization can raise more overall by offering contributors flexibility to direct funds to current priorities (Eckel, Herberish, and Meer, 2014).

Exhibit 23.3 illustrates how individual solicitation methods perform separately from who gives and where they direct their funds. Average gift size is a helpful detail here, especially when compared with prior year information. Over time, both improved results and lagging returns can be spotted early and acted upon. An important indicator of fundraising effectiveness is numbers of donors and the extent to which those donors remain "loyal" to your organization by giving repeatedly over time (Sargeant, 2001a, b). Money follows people, not the other way around.

Budgets prepared based on these three reports plus comparable prior year results will illustrate how each solicitation method is performing as part of a multiyear fund development strategy. These exhibits will also display new audiences added from recruiting donors in Exhibit 23.1 using social media, changes in donor preferences in response to new funding priorities in Exhibit 23.2, and new or extra solicitation methods and their results in Exhibit 23.3.

These routine reports do not include fundraising expenses. Determining costs at the solicitation level is usually impossible. Instead, expense records are kept at a summary level (i.e., all mailing costs for direct mail, event invitations, thank you letters, meeting notices, newsletters, etc., are reported together as "postage"). At the summary level, the organization should consider labor costs for staff and benefits along with direct and indirect expenses for solicitations along with gift processing, gift reporting, volunteer training, meeting support, prospect research, and more. With summary or "bottom-line" data, an organization can review the cost–benefit of its entire fundraising program to be sure it is generating a positive return on investment (ROI).

Fundraising managers have responsibility for creating budgets that reflect all costs for fundraising, which include activities for "back office" support (gift processing, for example). However, not all fundraising staff spend 100 percent of their time fundraising. Some time is part of overall organizational development, including staff meetings or other activities. Some fundraising staff also have responsibility for marketing, communication, volunteer administration, and other functions that are not direct fundraising expenses.

Software that supports financial reporting for nonprofits is usually built with the IRS Form 990 in mind. Under those rules, expenses fall into three broad categories: program and services; administration and general; and fundraising (see IRS Form 990, Part I, page 10). Because a portion of fundraising expense appears on the IRS Form 990 as "administration and general," that form and the software generating it are not a good measure of the true cost of fundraising. To calculate the cost–benefit ratio for contributions some fundraising departments run "shadow systems" to track fundraising costs and reconcile that system with the nonprofit's overall accounting system on a regular basis.

Finally, budgets for fundraising compete with essential operating expenses needed for charitable programs and services that have first priority in meeting current mission objectives. As a result, fundraising budgets often receive minimal support with maximum expectations. According to industry reports, "The reality is that most institutions aren't spending enough on fundraising because their leaders fear public criticism or donor backlash. We need to talk instead of why organizations are under-investing in themselves. That's the real challenge" (Jaschik, 2005, p. 31).

Summary Budget Request with Estimated Net Revenue

The summary budget for fundraising should be prepared along with estimated total revenue (see Exhibit 23.4). New and previous donors will give different amounts this year compared with last. However, past history is valuable for estimating gift revenue alongside the budget request, as it offers a reasonable comparison for budget review using performance data. The addition of three previous years of results also demonstrates overall program growth. Adding expenses to this review also displays levels of effectiveness and efficiency achieved in terms of net revenue, cost of fundraising, and return on investment.

EXHIBIT 23.4. SUMMARY BUDGET REQUEST WITH ESTIMATED EXPENSE AND NET REVENUE.

	Previous Year 2013	Last Year 2014	Current Fiscal Year 2015	Coming Fiscal Year 2016
Expenses				
Labor costs	$66,009	$67,989	$70,029	$72,129
Non-labor costs	50,541	52,056	53,619	55,227
Total budget	$116,550	$120,045	$123,648	$127,356
Gift Revenue				
Gross revenue	$448,765	$507,855	$561,235	$611,235
Less expenses	116,550	120,045	123,648	127,356
Net revenue	$332,215	$387,810	$437,587	$483,879
Performance Evaluation				
Cost of fundraising	$0.26	$0.24	$0.22	$0.21
Return on investment	285%	323%	354%	380%

Fundraising Performance Evaluation

For decades, fundraising performance has been measured by two simple criteria: "How much did you raise?" and "How much did it cost?" These two are essential components, yet judgments based only on a cost–benefit ratio can be misleading since it offers no details on solicitation activities and their results, such as documented in the previous exhibits. Further, there is no national standard for a cost–benefit measurement of fundraising. Organizations also should be cautious about comparative analysis of their fundraising performance with other nonprofits, including between like organizations in the same community or geographic area. Such assessments can be counterproductive and lead to misinterpretations and incorrect assumptions. Why? These other nonprofits are not using the same solicitation methods to the same audiences for the same purposes at the same time and nor do they have the same donors, volunteer solicitors, priority of needs, or history of service to the community.

In the absence of uniform guidelines for fundraising performance, several "charity watchdogs" have created their own evaluation criteria to report nonprofit performance. These include a system of stars used by Charity Navigator (www.charitynavigator.org); a "grade" from the American Institute of Philanthropy (www.charitywatch.org) in its *Charity Rating Guide and Watchdog Report*; or a "completeness rating" from Guidestar.org, based on the amount of information provided on the IRS Form 990 and to the site itself (Hopkins, 2002, p. 446).

In today's quest for greater accountability, nonprofit organizations need to address their own performance in terms of measurable outcomes from their best use of revenues received from all sources. They also need to quantify their programs and services as defined benefits delivered back to the public consistent with their mission, vision, and value statements. Judgments based on a ratio of fundraising costs to funds raised are a wholly inadequate analysis of the organization's own performance. Economics scholars Steinberg and Morris (2010, p. 89) explain: "The ratio of costs to donations is idiosyncratic for each charity, so no one-size-fits-all constraints will be helpful. Some charities will be forced to spend too little on fundraising, hindering their ability to pursue their charitable mission. Other more popular charities can comply despite wasteful practices. More fundamentally, the efficiency with which a charity passes through and applies donations to its mission is unrelated to the cost ratio. The cost ratio reflects average behavior, rather than the behavior resulting from an increase in giving, and pass through rates depend on the latter."

Another independent evaluator is the Better Business Bureau Wise Giving Alliance (2014). The BBB, considered the "Good Housekeeping Seal of Approval" for nonprofits, is neither a watchdog nor a "rating agency" but conducts voluntary charity reviews for many of the larger nonprofits engaged in national and global fundraising. Charitable organizations can meet or not a 20-point "Standards for Charity Accountability" in four broad areas: Governance and Oversight; Measuring Effectiveness; Finances; and Fundraising and Informational Materials. Two criteria are linked to fundraising expenses, Standards 8 and 9, as follows:

"8. Spend at least 65% of its total expenses on program activities.

9. Spend no more than 35% of related contributions on fundraising."

Much of the public information about charities is available on IRS Form 990. All registered nonprofits with gross receipts of $200,000 or more, except religious organizations, are required to file the most extensive version of a Form 990 annually. The IRS Form 990 provides detailed disclosure of financial details along with governance operations. Two main depositories are available for public access to these annual IRS Form 990 returns, GuideStar (www.guidestar.org) and the National Center for Charitable Statistics (www.nccs.org) housed at The Urban Institute. These sources are not watchdogs but provide Internet access to actual IRS Form 990 returns. Both data sites also allow charities to post their own information, including details to generalized impact questions, and more. In 2014 Guidestar announced an effort to compile nonprofit organizations' self-reports about impact. Note that a shift from financial accountability to mission accountability is likely to be partially a result of observations such as the following: "However, the widespread availability of the information necessary to do these kinds of calculations has driven people to make giving decisions based exclusively on the measurement and evaluation of fundraising revenues and costs. To some donors, the cause matters less than the ability of the organizations to demonstrate that it is a good steward of the money that the public entrusts to it. In turn, organizations begin to control their public *financial* face so that it projects the kind of image that attracts donors and grant makers while keeping watchdogs, regulators, and the bad press at bay" (Hager, 2004).

Nonprofits must plan to be as transparent as possible about their finances and mission achievement. Many nonprofits exhibit copies of IRS Form 990 on their website along with their annual audit statement and annual report, in the spirit of added accountability, transparency, and full disclosure. This can facilitate relationship building as candidates for larger (and even smaller) gifts investigate nonprofit organizations to determine their worthiness before investing personal assets of any size.

Fundraising Goals and Objectives

Not every nonprofit organization can mount the full array of traditional solicitation activities. Newer and smaller agencies with start-up fundraising programs begin with traditional annual giving methods to acquire and engage donors along with selective corporate and foundation grantseeking. These annual programs are designed to build a base of reliable contributors, a process that requires a minimal investment of three to five years to achieve consistent levels of productivity as shown by experience. Annual donors in time can become candidates for major gifts and estate planning opportunities provided the agency engages them continuously in positive relationships beyond a once-a-year gift solicitation.

Funding priorities can and do change each year and some flexibility is required in setting or assigning overall fundraising goals and objectives. External revenue sources can also reduce their gifts and grants, resulting in revenues falling below expectations. The recent economic recession was a time when donors of all types either reduced, redirected, or discontinued their financial support. Only after a perceived recovery and a more positive outlook have they returned to their comfort levels in giving. *Giving USA* (2014) reported that total giving in 2013 neared – but did not surpass – the all-time high of 2007. Another result of the 2007–2009 recession was consumption of reserve funds that need to be rebuilt. Lastly, a valuable benefit from this recession is increased appreciation by nonprofits of the true value of current donors, with the result that more time and resources have begun to be directed toward stewardship of donors, providing avenues for donors to have active relationships with their favorite nonprofits.

Budget cycles also are driven by institutional priorities, which also can and do change. An example is funding needs for new buildings, new or replacement equipment, rebuilding of endowments, or all three in a major, multiyear capital campaign. Current fundraising goals must be adjusted for major capital priorities that will also require additional staff and operating costs beyond existing budget levels, while maintaining budgets for annual solicitation activities that must be continued. Another example is some organizations' increased focus on major gift solicitation, which is a more intense effort that requires greater preparation, added staff, and participation by nonprofit leaders and volunteers to succeed.

Benchmarks, Online Performance, and Fundraising Effectiveness

Fundraising analysis is moving from cost–benefit analysis to industry-wide benchmarks for nonprofit operating results and other performance information. The public is interested in quantitative and qualitative data about program outcomes to validate gift investments, often prior to making their gift or grant decision. "What did you do with my money?" is the new question and answers must document a nonprofit's accountability with actual performance data, termed by some as the "impact" achieved in measurable public benefits.

Benchmarks and dashboard metrics are useful tools for fundraising results analysis. Three indicators identified by The Association for Healthcare Philanthropy (AHP) (www.ahp.org) are return on investment (ROI), cost to raise a dollar (CTRD), and net fundraising returns (NFR). AHP annually identifies performance benchmarks based on hospital fundraising results. AHP's "Standards for Reporting and Communicating Effectiveness in Healthcare Philanthropy" (2012) defines the following three metrics:

- ROI – A key measure that represents the financial return on each dollar spent raising funds during the reporting year. It is also the inverse of the CTRD metric. ROI is an indicator of fundraising *effectiveness*, illustrating the amount applied toward the bottom line in relation to the cost. ROI is the product of dividing gross funds raised by total fundraising expenses.
- CTRD – A key measure of fundraising *efficiency*, providing an abbreviated look at the total amount spent to raise each dollar in support of the organization's mission. It is the product achieved by dividing fundraising expenses by gross funds raised during the reporting year.
- Net fundraising returns – An important metric that reflects bottom-line fundraising returns in support of the organization's mission. It is commonly described as the "what" that accompanies the "how" provided by CTRD and ROI. It is the product achieved by subtracting fundraising expenses from gross fundraising revenues from production.

AHP also has identified several factors that influence total dollars raised, namely fundraising budget, staff size, staff tenure and compensation, and a focus on major gifts (Association for Healthcare Philanthropy, 2014).

In 2006, The Association of Fundraising Professionals (AFP) began the "Fundraising Effectiveness Project" (FEP) in partnership with The Urban Institute and participating donor software firms (www.afpnet.org/FEP). This project helps nonprofit organizations measure their fundraising "fitness" and maximize their annual growth in giving, or "GIG." FEP focuses on effectiveness rather than efficiency and offers free Excel worksheets to encourage organizations to evaluate their own performance, including gain (loss) statistics, and growth in giving data (see Exhibit 23.5). Organizations can use the FEP Fitness Test to measure their own fundraising gains and losses from year to year, donor retention rates, and gift-size statistics compared to other similar organizations

---

EXHIBIT 23.5. INTERPRETING AFP'S FEP AND GIG REPORTS.

The transition from a focus on fundraising cost to fundraising effectiveness reveals solid results in the overall fund development program. Tracking donors and their repeat giving illustrates their loyalty as well as reliable gift income. As shown in the sample gain/loss report for 2010 below, attention to donor stewardship produced a 28.3 percent in upgraded giving for 27.2 percent of gift revenue and signals an added capacity exists. Those 414 donors who gave less (36.7 percent) could likely benefit from increased attention, especially since their gifts account for 36.7 percent of all revenue received in 2010. Lastly, the overall renewal rate of 59.4 percent is encouraging but is offset by 920 lapsed donors (40.6 percent) along with their $180,126 in lost gift revenue.

Gain/Loss Report

Gain/Loss	2010 Donors	Donor Percent	2010 Gifts	Gift Percent
Category	Number of donors		Amount of gifts	
Gave same	293	12.9%	$61,136	9.2%
Upgraded	641	23.2%	$181,338	27.2%
Downgraded	414	18.3%	$245,298	36.7%
Subtotal	1,348	59.4%	$487,772	73.0%
Lapsed	920	40.6%	$180,126	27.0%
Total	2,268	100.0%	$667,898	100.0%

Gift Size Analysis

If gift ranges are added to donor retention analysis it will show overall gains and losses by gift size and demonstrates the value of attention to these more generous donors. The overall donor retention rate of 59 percent and above and between 73 percent and 87 percent among repeat $5,000 and up donors also indicates the potential for added revenue from individualized major gift cultivation.

(Continued)

EXHIBIT 23.5. (CONTINUED).

Donor Retention Analysis for 2012
Using Gift Transaction Data by Giving Level/Range

Retention Performance	All Donors	Giving Level/Range				
		Under $100	$100 to $249	$250 to $999	$1,000 to $4,999	$5,000 and Up
New donor retention rate	35%	20%	43%	75%	70%	50%
Repeat donor retention rate	76%	54%	73%	88%	91%	87%
Overall donor retention rate	59%	31%	62%	86%	87%	79%
Donor gains (new and repeat)	1,159	647	351	134	20	7
Donor losses (new and repeat)	920	541	268	89	16	6

Growth in Giving

Regular reports prepared from in-office donor records software using AFP's FEP and GIG worksheets (www.afpnet.org/FEP) allows leadership and fundraising staff to monitor solicitation results and to respond with adjustments within the fiscal year in order to achieve assigned funding goals and objectives. Further, adding gift data from prior years illustrates overall growth in giving (GIG) results.

Overall 3-Year "Growth in Giving" Analysis
From 2009 through 2011

	Results 2 years Ago 2009	Results Last Year 2010	Rate of Growth Last Year	Results This year 2011	Rate of Growth This Year	3-Year Cumulative Growth
All donors	1,833	2,268	24%	2,507	11%	37%
Gross revenue	$581,172	$667,898	15%	$818,249	23%	41%
Average gift size	$317	$294	-7%	$326	11%	3%

Note: When comparing your organization's 3-year GIG analysis with online reports, please realize that the online results change with each imported set of data. Thousands of organizations work through their donor software to share donor-anonymous information to create benchmarks for Fundraising Fitness Test and Growth in Giving analyses. For more about the Fundraising Effectiveness Project and Growth in Giving analysis, see www.afpfep.org.

Return on Investment

Growth in giving is the direct result of continued investment in the fundraising program. All the above examples illustrate solid results in acquiring new donors and retaining current donors (37 percent over three years) with a cumulative 41 percent increase in gift revenues. Lastly, average gifts above $250 demonstrate reliable revenues along with success in active communications to encourage donor's engagement in the cause.

Several metrics for social media as a communication outlet and as a fundraising vehicle are available to assist with fundraising evaluation (see the discussion on social media metrics in Chapter 29). Metrics matter, in this domain as in others. According to one expert: "Good metrics is based on a clear understanding of what is being measured and the ability to apply those findings to the decision-making process. ... Start with the core metrics. Expand over time and begin to test different scenarios with different audience groups. Share your results internally and with other nonprofit organizations. Focus on lessons learned and how to improve results by turning raw data into useful information" (MacLaughlin, 2010, p. 128).

In summary, good metrics require recordkeeping and careful assignment of costs and results by fundraising activity. The effort will be repaid at the beginning of the next budget cycle, when the fundraising manager will have reports and information to support projected revenue and estimated fundraising expenses to help the organization meet its mission.

Conclusion

Budgeting is not an exact science. It represents a well-prepared fiscal plan that includes estimated revenues and expenses needed to carry out the organization's mission. Fundraising budgets also include forecasts of gift revenues to result from well-planned, well-executed solicitation activities. During the fiscal year, accounting reports monitor expenses incurred and gift reports show contributions received. Combined these reveal progress toward estimated budgeted revenues and expenses.

Fundraising staff need to become proficient managers of both budgeting and goal setting as well as interpreters of results achieved from effective and efficient use of their budgets. The critical "bottom-line" value of contributions is the good works it funds, not its fundraising cost.

It is increasingly important how contributions are used by the organization, which is accountable for its application exclusively for community benefits. This is the same public who provided the generous funds received; they deserve clear evidence of its best use through quantitative and qualitative reports of benefits received by those served. Solid answers to "What did you do with my money?" are highly valued by contributors and reinforce the bond of trust so essential to their continued public support.

CHAPTER TWENTY-FOUR

MARKETING AND COMMUNICATIONS FOR FUNDRAISING

By Margaret M. Maxwell and Sean Dunlavy

One of Hank Rosso's most classic and lasting definitions is the simple but elegant phrasing he used to describe fundraising itself: the "gentle art of teaching people the joy of giving." In that simple definition, Rosso, perhaps unwittingly, went so far as to suggest a brand for fundraising: an art that is kind, gentle, and focused on teaching about human joy and gifts. Facilitating that art – making it possible – is the work of marketing in a fundraising environment.

In his "Philosophy of Fund Raising," Rosso also stressed the concept of exchange that underwrites giving. "Gift making is based on a voluntary exchange," he said. "The contributor offers a value to the nonprofit organization.... In accepting the gift, it is incumbent upon the organization to return a value to the donor" (Rosso, 1991, p. 5). The best thinkers and teachers in fundraising and marketing agree with Rosso on this primary principle: our work begins and ends with exchange.

This chapter focuses on the two-way exchange between an organization and its donors. Marketing for an organization's fundraising focuses on facilitating and consummating changes. This chapter covers:

- The role and rationale for marketing in nonprofit organizations.
- The planning process for marketing related to fundraising.
- Ways in which marketing for fundraising can be conducted.

- Communications as part of the marketing cycle and budgeting.
- Management of an ongoing marketing program, including ethical practices.

Toward an Understanding of Marketing

Marketing facilitates, eases, and assists in one primary function: to make possible an exchange of items of value. A donor brings a gift, a donation, a contribution, or some item of value. It may be cash, a treasured art collection, used clothing, or a commitment of time and talent as a volunteer. In return, the organization brings gratitude, appreciation, a sense of affiliation, and tax benefits to exchange with the donor.

This concept of exchange is at the core of every contemporary definition of marketing. The American Marketing Association (AMA) defines marketing as the process for "creating, communicating, delivering, and exchanging offerings" that have value for customers, clients, partners, and society at large.

To Philip Kotler, the concept of exchange is central to marketing. "Through exchanges, social units – individuals, small groups, institutions, whole nations – attain the inputs they need. By offering something attractive, they acquire what they need in return. Since both parties agree to the exchange, both see themselves as better off after the exchange" (Kotler and Fox, 1995, p. 6).

Historic Role of Marketing for Nonprofits

Perhaps because so much of fundraising practice focuses on communication and relationship building, marketing's role in a fundraising environment has not always been clear. In the corporate world, marketing was traditionally intermingled with sales. In the nonprofit sector, marketing commonly competes with such donor-focused activities as alumni events or donor appreciation initiatives. There has also been considerable confusion between marketing and promotion, which, indeed, is only one aspect of markcting.

Kotler was one of the seminal influences in the expansion of marketing to nonprofits. Kotler stated, "I share a lot of the responsibility for the broadened use of the term marketing. In 1969, we claimed that marketing can be used not only by profit-making organizations but also by nonprofit organizations such as museums, churches, charities… that want to attract clients, volunteers, and funds" (Kotler and Andreason, 1996, p. 7).

As marketing was adopted in the nonprofit sector, the traditional four P's of marketing – product, price, place, and promotion – began to undergo adaptation.

Human services and social causes replaced traditional products with increased subjectivity and emotion. Price was measured in noneconomic indicators, such as time, commitment, and advocacy.

Concepts intrinsic to marketing are at the core of good fundraising: identifying and understanding needs and wants, targeting and segmentation, an organization's brand and positioning, and effective communication. Marketing initiatives ideally facilitate exchanges that are at the very heart of fundraising.

The Marketing Cycle

Marketing is as a process, an ongoing and continuous cycle, with marketing goals met and adjusted along the way. Analysis begins with looking at the services a nonprofit organization delivers. Effective analysis can require modifications to the service, requiring new communication and delivery modes. In an organization that is truly market-responsive, the cycle is ongoing, as illustrated in Figure 24.1.

David Packard, founder of Hewlett-Packard, argued, "Marketing is far too important to leave to the marketing department." In a fundraising organization, marketing needs to be an organizational mindset, which causes everyone internally to look at the organization from an outsider's perspective. Having a marketing mindset helps the organization with strategic planning and analysis, fundraising program development, and effective communications with both active and

FIGURE 24.1. THE MARKETING CYCLE FOR NONPROFIT ORGANIZATIONS.

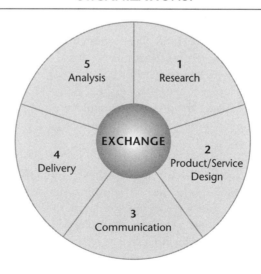

prospective donors. Ideally, market sensitivity helps an organization shape attitudes, awareness, and actions that positively impact the organization's fundraising results and, thus, mission fulfillment.

Practitioners argue that to be most effective, management of the marketing cycle must be a nonprofit executive priority. However, small organizations often find it is difficult to focus on the marketplace because there is no one on the staff who has the responsibility for seeking market input and then implementing any changes suggested by constituents. (In these cases, establishing a volunteer committee that can advise the organization may be better than having no marketing focus at all.) Larger nonprofit organizations can more reasonably seek to have a fully integrated, cohesive marketing department that has a seat at the senior management table.

The Marketing Plan

To become marketing-oriented, a fundraising organization should start with creating a marketing plan, which includes six traditional steps:

- Conduct a broad and unbiased **situation analysis** of your organization and the environment in which it operates. Itemize the forces that impact the organization's effectiveness, analyze resources, conduct an SWOT analysis (strengths, weaknesses, opportunities, and threats), and describe and profile the donor and client markets.
- Define the organization's marketing **objectives**, the broad outcomes being sought, in ranked order. Ensure the objectives are SMART (specific, measurable, achievable, realistic, and timely) and stated clearly and concisely. For example, an annual fund objective might be: *to retain 60 percent or more of first-time donors in the fiscal year following their first gift.*
- Choose the **strategies** that will help the organization achieve your objectives. Strategies are general statements that describe what must be done to meet the objectives. Using the previous example, if an organization wants to retain 60% of first-time donors in the following fiscal year, the best strategy may be: *to educate first-time donors about how their money was used before asking them to renew their gift.*
- Develop **tactics** that will lead to the accomplishment of the strategies. Complete with a time schedule and specific assignments for staff and volunteers, the list of tactics can serve as the development department's work plan. Continuing with the donor retention example, some tactics related to educating first-time donors could include: *send first-time donors quarterly print or e-newsletters; invite them to a tour or event that showcases the impact of their gift; engage them as a program*

volunteer; or ensure they get a special "thank you" phone call from a volunteer or board member in addition to a written gift acknowledgement.

- Set a **budget** for the tactics. Organizations should be realistic and obtain quotes for services, production, and distribution so you have a good perspective of what investment will be required to achieve success.

- Define **controls,** review processes, and identify metrics that will help assess whether the organization is making progress toward its overall objectives. In the retention strategies and tactics outlined above, controls could include: *incorporate web analytic tools to determine whether newsletters are being opened; track who attends events, becomes a volunteer, or receives a thank-you phone call from a volunteer.* As solicitation efforts occur throughout the year, the fundraiser can adjust the marketing plan, if necessary, to focus on the tactics that are proving to be most successful in reaching the overall objective of renewing at least 60 percent of first-time donors.

The Role of Market Research in Fundraising

Market research takes the guesswork out of fundraising. It substitutes knowledge and data for assumptions, hunches, folklore, and urban legend. It can help achieve efficiency and increase fundraising success. It will minimize risk in decision making and planning by helping determine where energies and resources should be invested.

Fundraising market research is about gathering, recording, and analyzing data that helps an organization become more knowledgeable about and responsive to its donors. Research can be as simple as putting together a demographic profile: Where do the organization's donors live? What are their ages and education levels? How much do they earn and where are they employed? How many children do they have and how old are they? Research can also be complex as a psychosocial analysis of how donors trust an organization's brand and identity. Between those two poles, there are a thousand stops along the way.

Market Research and Donor Data

The distinction between market research and researching an organization's in-house donor base is significant. Most organizations have the ability to access a database that records a tremendous amount of helpful information for the fundraiser. In addition to the basics — Who are the donors? How much have they given? What are their addresses, phone numbers, and e-mail addresses? The database ideally permits the organization to segment donors into subgroups of similar types, maintain a giving history for each donor, assess giving capability, and record additional information gleaned through donor conversations.

Market research, on the other hand, is focused on gathering external information that can help an organization facilitate effective fundraising planning and donor communication. It provides a perspective about the organization's donors and documents the effectiveness of different fundraising and communication strategies. It also assists fundraisers by providing the means to test and evaluate creative communication strategies long before they are refined and sent to donors.

Organizations can learn much through market research: What words and phrases best resonate with donors? Do they understand and have empathy with the organization's mission? Who are the organization's competitors for the donor's annual gift? Is e-mail, social media, or print the preferred communication channel for the organization's donors? Did the donor read the annual report? What kinds of photo images best communicate the organization's work? What news sources do the donors trust? What obstacles does the organization face in increasing the size of an annual gift? How does an economic downturn affect how donors feel about giving to the organization?

The list of "like to know" topics about donors can quickly grow and become unwieldy if the organization is not careful. Especially as an organization first embraces a marketing mindset, there can be a tremendous appetite for information. It is not uncommon, for example, to hear managers say, "It sure would be interesting to know if...." The marketing manager's task here is a quick rejoinder, "Interesting, yes, but not actionable for us now." The difference between "nice to know" and actionable research – information upon which plans, objectives, strategies and tactics can be built – is crucial and must not be minimized.

Setting Market Research Agendas

An organization's market research agenda is developed after donor markets are segmented and prioritized in the marketing plan. For most nonprofits, market segments include a mix of current, former, and prospective donors.

However, each donor market segment can have subgroups within it that may also be important. For example, the "current donor" market may include these subgroups:

- First-time donors
- $1,000 and above donors
- Donors who pledge
- Donors who give as a result of a specific strategy (direct mail, e-mail, website, social media, etc.)

To set a research agenda, the fundraiser must decide what needs to be known to effectively ask for a gift, steward the gift, and renew the gift. For example, if one of the priority markets is comprised of donors who pledge online, it will be helpful and actionable to know how these donors want to receive pledge reminders and how frequently they want to be reminded. Do they prefer the reminders to come through e-mail or a letter? A postcard or a brochure? Traditionally, organizations have answered these questions by making broad assumptions or guesses. Today's savvy nonprofit marketer instead says, "Let's go ask the donor."

Methods of Market Research

Market research can be either quantitative or qualitative, and both types are valuable to fundraisers. Quantitative research, which focuses on generating an appropriate number of responses in order to make generalized statements of fact, is often gathered through surveys and web analytic inquiries. A well-crafted quantitative market research study, for example, can help a fundraiser say with reasonable certainty, "80% of our donors are unsure of the value of unrestricted giving to our organization."

Qualitative market research is more concerned with subjective factors such as expressions, feelings, and emotions and is often gathered through focus groups or individual interviews. Questions posed through qualitative research are open-ended rather than yes/no, which means the results are difficult (if not impossible) to quantify with certainty. However, if an organization conducts multiple focus groups and/or individual interviews and hears the same feedback being shared, some generalizations can be drawn. A qualitative study might, for example, produce conclusions such as, "First-time donors perceive our newer programs as being more relevant to the community than our legacy programming, which is why they became involved. They'd like to know more about the impact these programs have before they consider giving again." It might also provide an organization with some of the compelling words or imagery that may end up in a case statement.

Primary and Secondary Research

Primary market research is original research done specifically for a certain market and focused on a particular organization's specific, immediate information needs. However, some nonprofit organizations may not have the resources to either conduct or buy their own primary research, which may lead them to explore secondary research resources. Secondary research is drawn from information that is gathered by some other organization for its own purposes, although the research findings might provide insights that are informative to other organizations as well.

For example, national trade and professional associations, local chambers of commerce, community libraries, online discussion groups, business development agencies, and state and federal government offices provide a wealth of data about demographics, giving trends, effective communication strategies, and a host of other issues that can sometimes satisfy a nonprofit's need for information. (The major caveat about using secondary research is to ensure the information comes from a credible resource.)

Types of Market Research Tools for Fundraisers

The types of market research that might be helpful in an organization's planning are listed here, along with a representative question that each type might answer.

Brand Testing: How is our organization perceived by our donors and clients?

Concept Testing: Will this idea work with our donors?

Copy Testing: Does this copy communicate and is it memorable?

Donor Satisfaction Studies: What do donors like and dislike about the events we sponsor?

Focus Groups: How do first-time donors evaluate our proposed ad campaign and how does that differ from repeat donor perceptions?

In-Person or Telephone Interviews: Is "leaving a legacy" a goal for our donors?

Campaign Planning Studies: How compelling is our case for support?

Mall Intercept: What does the person on the street think about holiday giving this year?

Mystery or Secret Shopping: How easy is it to make an online gift to one of our competitors and how does that compare to our web capabilities?

Online Panels: Do our donors understand our mission?

Segmentation Studies: Into what subgroups can our donors be divided?

Surveys: Who are our competitors and what do they do better than we do?

Website Analytics: What sections of our website do people visit and how much time do they spend there?

Web Intelligence Review: What are people saying online about us?

There is not one single "best way" to do market research with donors. In the end, the research tool(s) selected must match with the nonprofit's personality as well as the informational needs of the organization, the time available to the nonprofit to gather, analyze, and act on the data, and the organizational resources available to conduct various types of research. What is necessary, however, is that the organization recognizes that making "guesses" about donors is much less effective than basing decisions on real information.

Sophistication of Market Research

As market research has become an increasingly significant tool in the nonprofit sector, some organizations, with the very best intentions, are pursuing research agendas in "amateurish" ways. A word of warning is appropriate.

Research, by definition, must be sophisticated enough to be objective, reliable, and valid. Without professional guidance, there is the possibility of unwittingly making significant errors in research design, implementation, or analysis. Research with fatal flaws, such as an incorrect sample size, a built-in bias that impacts objectivity, or a measure of something other than intended, will not only fail to provide answers but can substantially harm the organization's reputation and community standing.

Realizing this challenge, nonprofit organizations may need to be creative about soliciting, purchasing, or bartering professional assistance to ensure that the end results are worthwhile. For example, a local college or university marketing program or a board member whose personal (or corporate) expertise is in marketing might be tapped to provide lower-cost (or free) assistance in designing the research process. If the organization cannot obtain the type of marketing counsel that will provide a reasonable confidence of success, it may be better to utilize discussion groups and dialogues to gain feedback and input.

Communication: Building Awareness and Motivating Action

Nonprofit organizations that want to maximize their contributed income need a coherent and executable development plan. Development plans need a viable communications strategy that helps the organization to carry out its mission, according to the policies it has set, and to serve the constituencies it has identified.

Effective communication plans deliver relevant messages to identified recipients using chosen media to obtain a predetermined action. In planning a communication strategy, the following critical questions should be considered:

- What is the desired message?
- Who will receive this message?

- What action is desired?
- How will the message be delivered?

Communicating Messages with a Purpose

There are two types of communication messages: those intended to influence attitudes and those intended to influence actions. Often communications intended to influence attitudes are based on public or media relations activities. These might include news releases, speeches, board and community presentations, and special events.

Communications intended to influence actions are generally based on advertising and promotional initiatives. These might include collateral material, newsletters, websites, advertisements, direct mail, and print and electronic solicitations with specific calls to action.

In fundraising, crafting, testing, revising, distribution, and analysis of these influential messages must be centralized and integrated. This assures that all marketing tools, approaches, and resources can be used to maximize impact on donors and prospective donors, as well as other significant constituents. In building awareness, there is little room for uncoordinated and inconsistent messaging.

Planning a Communications Campaign

A formalized market research program of collecting, organizing, and assessing data about primary markets helps fundraisers build awareness through marketing communications. Four steps in planning depend upon accurate and timely knowledge about the markets the organization is attempting to reach.

Defining the Market   Determining the recipients of the message is the most important part of the development communications strategy. Organizations should be as specific, focused, and as segmented as resources will allow. Rather than a scattered approach, hoping all messages and all words will reach all donors, development communications should target the segment that holds the most promise for return. Identifying the recipients for specific sets of messages is commonly done through rating and evaluating prospects.

Defining the Message   The goal of any communication is to generate action. The goal is to be as concise, clear, and direct as possible. Each communication message should have a defined and intended purpose and result. A personalized, one-off proposal to a donor will have the greatest impact, and at the right level of request that kind of focused messaging is proper. It is critical to understand the desired actions organizations want recipients to take before sending the message.

Testing Messages Online focus groups have increased the ability to pre-test message, colors, design, and text used prior to production. Do donors understand the iconic photography being used? Do they prefer black and white to full color? Do the messages look organized and economical or expensive and lavish?

Defining the Media The next step is to choose the media that will offer the greatest access at the best cost. Harmony between the organization and the media selected is important. Hot air balloons may reach a certain segment of the market on a fall afternoon, but what does it say about the organization? An executive director may be very skilled at Twitter, but is tweeting right for the organization's audience? When choosing media, organizations should remember what Marshall McLuhan, the famed social critic and one of the first fathers of the electronic age, said: "The medium is the message."

Media Selection

Adequate space does not allow an evaluation of all the media available in marketing strategies for fundraising. From the medium of print to the latest social media, interactive web sites, web banners, and instant messaging, the list is long. In evaluating media, the fundraising communicator should be sure to measure the return on investment (ROI). Assessing the cost, the number of people in the "audience," and the measurable outcome of the communication strategy will allow an organization to assess if the predetermined goal was achieved. This kind of specificity in reporting requires tracking and recording. With web sites, evaluating ROI has been greatly enhanced with such tools as Google Analytics, permitting organizations to track visits to their website, how long they visit, and how they navigate once there.

Marketing researchers should select media intrinsic to the process and work closely with media buyers. The team ideally includes a researcher who knows and understands the market and the market's preferences, creative strategists who craft and design effective messaging, media experts who buy time and space to distribute the message, and analysts who can measure success.

Affordability of electronic communication is complex. Many nonprofit managers still contend that e-mail is free. Indeed, depending upon the volume of e-mail distributed, the cost is low, much lower than direct mail and print advertising impressions. However, media decisions must also take into account that e-mails from nonprofits may have "hit a wall" in terms of market penetration and effectiveness.

Currently, e-mail marketing metrics (www.mailermailer.com) says that the average nonprofit can count on approximately 17 percent of its e-mail recipients to open their e-mail. Of that, only 2 percent are likely to click-through to the intended message. To properly estimate the cost of e-mail, these open/click-through rates need to be used rather than audience size figures. This more honest evaluation substantially increases the per-unit cost for e-mails.

The Creative Work: Themes and Technique

The adventure begins when a creative staff is together for that first brainstorm session. There is much advice on working with creative people, including many books and articles such as *Working with Creative People in 12 Steps* (Sterling, 2005) and *5 Reasons Creatives Hate Working for You* (Collin, 2009). "Nonsense" is what a good marketing manager will say. Give the "creatives" good direction, good resources, and good freedom and let them do what they do best: communicate.

Start with a common understanding of what the donor wants and needs to hear at various junctures in their relationship with the organization. With this understanding, writers and designers can craft and deliver stories and profiles with the facts and feelings about giving gifts.

Donors generally want to hear about the impact of their gifts, so there needs to be creative techniques to tell the stories of a nonprofit's fundraising priorities and programs. An article recently told the story of a gifted sculpture from the sculpture's perspective. Rather than hearing the words from a donor or a development officer, the sculpture itself noted its new surroundings and commented on the reaction of visitors when they walked past.

Marketing managers must respect the creative minds that can conceive and implement new themes and techniques for telling age-old stories. Is the sometimes noisy, disorganized, and frequent brainstorming that the creative team wants to do worth the effort? Yes, when it results in telling stories of gifts that have great impact and that also accomplish the donor's original intent.

Communication Budget and Schedule   Organizations need to determine the amount of staff time it will take and how much money will be needed to carry out the communication strategy. Development communication strategies cannot be carried out successfully unless there is a budget.

Developing a schedule for executing the components of the development communications strategy – and then sticking to it – is critical. Communication has to be given the same respect and attention to detail that every other aspect of fundraising gets.

Other Communication Issues   Branding, message repetition, production quality, viral marketing, graphic design, copywriting and editing, internal communications, social media, donor honor rolls, annual reports, web site design, and vendor relationships must be considered in crafting a strategic marketing communications plan. Information about those topics not fully covered here is readily available online.

Gaining exposure to successful marketing and advertising agency shops and enrolling in workshops and seminars are two other ways in which the manager can quickly learn techniques and best practices for nonprofit fundraising communications. There are also highly respected consulting firms who specialize in marketing for nonprofits and who can assist with the development of communication strategies and marketing assessments.

Trust and Responsibility: An Ethical Framework

The Association of Fundraising Professionals (AFP) Code of Ethical Principles and Standards of Professional Practice calls for integrity, honesty, truthfulness, and obligation to safeguard the public trust. It addresses professional fundraisers who serve the ideal of philanthropy. For marketing managers linked to fundraising organizations, there is another call to the highest form of responsibility and trust that is documented by the American Marketing Association (AMA). The organization's website (www.marketingpower.com) identifies these ethical norms for marketers:

- Do no harm.
- Foster trust in the marketing system.
- Embrace ethical values.

The ethical values called for by AMA are:

- Honesty: Be forthright in dealings with customers and stakeholders.
- Responsibility: Accept the consequences of marketing decisions and strategies.
- Fairness: Balance justly the needs of the buyer with the interests of the seller.
- Respect: Acknowledge the basic human dignity of all.
- Transparency: Create a spirit of openness in marketing operations;
- Citizenship: Fulfill the economic, legal, philanthropic, and societal responsibilities that serve stakeholders.

Conclusion

Marketing for a fundraising organization focuses on facilitating and consummating exchanges: items of value for items of value. Central to marketing activity in the nonprofit sector are three tasks:

- Analyzing the environment in which an organization conducts its business and defining opportunities and threats facing the organization.
- Crafting the objectives, strategies, and tactics by which the organization will choose to understand, prioritize, and communicate with its many markets about its fundraising priorities.
- Establishing a budget and management controls to monitor progress toward the achievement of marketing goals.

Fully functional and respected marketing as a nonprofit management tool fulfills tasks at the core of fundraising success: it will call attention to an organization and find the right words, phrases, images, and themes that translate that organization and its mission to a host of different market segments. It measures and understands how the organization is perceived and how those perceptions are changing over time. It increases awareness, builds consistent and memorable messages, and promotes an identity and brand for the organization. Most significantly, it advances the "gentle art of teaching people the joy of giving."

Discussion Questions

1) What is the role of market research in helping an organization determine how Kotler's "exchange" concept applies to its fundraising program?
2) How can qualitative and quantitative research be used effectively in developing each of the six steps of the marketing plan?
3) What are some open-ended questions that could help an organization assess its brand connections with current donors?
4) What types of newsletters should be developed to support an organization's fundraising efforts?
5) What elements of an organization's web site would let a prospective donor know that there is a well-functioning development program?
6) How should an organization evaluate the success of its development communication efforts?

CHAPTER TWENTY-FIVE

SELECTING AND WORKING WITH FUNDRAISING CONSULTANTS

By Margaret M. Maxwell

Human talent is the lifeblood of any nonprofit organization. Board members, other types of volunteers, and staff bring a broad range of experiences to their work on behalf of the clients served by the organization. However, when venturing into new areas – whether in direct service delivery or in developing the organization's capacity to sustain itself – organizations often find that they need to bring new skills to the table. Hiring consultants can provide a valuable and cost-effective solution for the organization to gain needed skills in a timely fashion.

This chapter covers:

- The different ways consultants can assist with fundraising.
- How consultants can assist with institutional readiness, campaign planning, and program implementation.
- How to locate and engage consultants.
- Tips for developing expectations, contracts, and relationships with consultants.

While many types of consultants work with nonprofit organizations, fundraising consultants in particular offer a wide range of services connected with building organizational capacity to deliver the mission in effective ways. From planning and coaching services focused on helping boards and executive leadership envision the organization's future (including the structure and leadership required to carry it out) to more focused fundraising planning for annual or capital campaigns or planned giving programs to tactical services to implement specific pieces of the fundraising effort, consultants are deeply involved in helping nonprofit organizations fulfill their missions. They are often valued for bringing an outside perspective that helps an organization see its options more clearly, making recommendations (based on research and/or best practices) that can help establish future direction, developing board or staff competencies through training or coaching, and bringing needed technical expertise to the organization.

Because of the variety of ways fundraising consultants interact with nonprofit organizations, it makes sense to examine the areas individually in order to understand the issues related to each in greater depth.

Institutional Readiness

Fundamental to an organization's ability to achieve fundraising success is its ability to plan effectively for its future. Donors – especially those willing to invest significantly in an organization by making a major gift – want to understand how the organization will adapt and change its programs in order to remain relevant to shifting circumstances in the local community and broader society. They want to understand how the organization identifies critical needs and develops programs that have a significant impact. They want to understand the challenges the organization faces in remaining relevant. They want to know that the people involved in carrying out the organization's work – both board and staff – are skilled and that they are organized in effective ways.

Current research indicates that some donors also want very specific information about the organization's finances. They may also be looking for new ways to engage with the organization as a volunteer and a donor, which may present some challenges to an organization as it envisions how to develop its program for the future.

While nonprofit organizations usually are highly effective at developing and delivering programs, they sometimes are not so good at developing strategic plans that inspire donors and volunteers by describing a preferred future, one based on research and planning. While board members may bring the required skill set to lead a strategic planning process, they oftentimes prefer to be fully engaged in the process as a participant rather than as the "neutral facilitator."

This confluence of circumstances can be the impetus for an organization to bring in a consultant to facilitate the planning process. While some consultants specialize in strategic planning, fundraising consultants also often provide this service because of the strong tie between strategic planning and the case for support. The consultant may conduct qualitative and/or quantitative research as a backdrop to the planning process and lead the board and staff leadership through a series of conversations focused on re-examining the organization's mission, laying out the vision for the future, and describing the programs that will help carry out the vision. Assistance in putting together the business plan to identify projected revenues and costs may also be provided. Finally, the consultant may be the one to draft the plan for the board and staff to discuss further and adopt.

Many nonprofit organizations conduct strategic planning on a regular basis – every three to five years, for example – although some use an event such as the arrival of new executive leadership as the impetus. Some organizations also use the planning process as a way of educating the board about the mission of the organization and their unique role as board members in safeguarding and stewarding its work. Fundraising consultants may be engaged to assist the organization in either of these activities (finding new executive leadership, such as the chief executive officer or the chief development officer, or conducting board training).

Campaign Planning

An organization's strategic plan is used to develop its annual fundraising plans but potentially may also be used as the basis for a capital campaign or planned giving program, particularly if the strategic plan suggests the organization should pursue significantly different directions for its future. Consultants are widely associated with planning for these types of fundraising initiatives, particularly capital campaigns.

Fundraising planning (whether for annual, capital, or planned giving programs) can involve a variety of services, including auditing the organization's current staffing and fundraising results, developing the case for support (drawn from the strategic plan), testing the case with current and potential major gift donors, screening the organization's donor list to identify prospective major gift donors, assessing the strength of the organization's communications methods for informing potential donors, identifying and training volunteer leadership, recommending the preferred strategies for the fundraising plan, and managing the overall effort. Even if consultants are engaged to play some or all of the roles described above, however, it is essential to remember that staff (including the CEO) and board members also play key roles in any campaign's success. The consultant and the organization's executive leadership and board leadership must be in agreement about the overall fundraising plan and also have a clear delineation of the responsibilities each has for carrying out the work.

Program Implementation

Organizations may have the capability to develop well-thought-out fundraising plans, but lack the in-house skill set (or time) to carry out a particular piece of the plan. In an annual fund, for example, boosting the results from a moribund direct mail solicitation effort may require outside expertise from a specialist in this area. Similarly, launching a new special event – even if volunteers are involved in planning and staffing it – may require the services of an event planner. Special event planners are sometimes expected to generate event sponsorships and create invitations as well as handle all of the details of setting up, tearing down, and cleaning up after the event itself. At other times, they may be engaged to carry out just a piece of the overall event (linen and décor selection and rentals for a dinner, for example).

For both annual funds and capital campaigns, many organizations use consultants to research potential funding sources and write proposals to institutional funders or government agencies. While the proposals may also be written by the in-house staff that are responsible for developing and carrying out the program to be funded, experienced consultants can add great value by helping the organization craft a proposal that stands out because of its clear language.

Communicating with constituents – through newsletters, social media, websites, or other means – is another area where consultants frequently assist nonprofit organizations. The consultant may be engaged to develop the communications strategy to connect with donors as well as to create the design and messages for specific communications pieces and platforms.

For any of these and other types of specific services, organizations have options for how to engage consultants. Some consultants bring a particular skill (such as direct mail or social media program design), and may be engaged to work with staff and/or other consultants to carry out that specific aspect of the fundraising program. Another option for organizations that need a range of services is to engage a full-service fundraising firm that can provide both planning and implementation services. For these types of longer-term or more comprehensive services, board members may be involved with staff in the consultant selection process as well as in the implementation of the planning process or the work that flows from it.

Finding and Engaging Consultants

Clearly, the range of ways that fundraising consultants are involved with nonprofit organizations varies widely, which means that engaging the right consultant to match the organization's needs is essential if the organization is to use its time and money wisely. The single most important thing an organization can do to ensure a successful consulting engagement is to be very clear up-front about why a consultant is needed. Both board and staff need to discuss and agree on the scope of work, the expected outcomes, and the timetable for the work.

Ideally, an internal team should be established to oversee the consultant engagement process, especially if the financial outlay for fees and expenses is expected to be significant in comparison to the development department's budget. Both board and staff members or staff alone may serve on the committee, depending on the scope of work for the consultant. Board members, for example, are usually very involved in selecting counsel for capital campaigns. Because board members will be working closely with the consultant, seeking their counsel in the selection process is critical. However, the board is generally much less involved in selecting consultants who merely bring technical expertise to the staff (e.g., direct mail production, special event logistics, or web design services). Some of the activities described in the Program Implementation section of this chapter may not warrant a committee at all; the process can instead be supervised by the appropriate staff member.

However the consultant engagement group is configured, the work assignment must include establishing the selection criteria for potential consultants. Some of the inherent issues in identifying these criteria include the importance of geographic proximity (local versus regional or national consultants), the size of firm (solo practitioner versus full-service firm), and whether the organization expects existing staff to develop new skills as a byproduct of the consulting engagement.

After reaching internal agreement about the type of services needed, the type of consultant firm that can best provide those services and the consultant selection process, the organization should identify potential consultants or consulting firms that have the expertise to do the required work. Sources for finding consultant names include the Giving Institute, (formerly the American Association of Fund Raising Counsel) and the Association of Fundraising Professionals (AFP). Depending on the type of organization, other professional organizations, such as the Association for Healthcare Philanthropy (AHP), the Association of Professional Researchers for Advancement (APRA), the Partnershp in Philanthropic Planning (formerly the National Committee on Planned Giving or NCPG), the Council for the Advancement and Support of Education (CASE), or other professional colleagues in the organization's particular field or community may be helpful in identifying potential names. Once a list is generated, however, it behooves an organization to narrow it somewhat by talking with professional colleagues about their experiences in working with the identified consultants and with the potential consultants themselves about their interest and ability to commit to the desired timetable.

The next step in the process is to generate a Request for Proposal (RFP) that outlines the scope of work and timetable as well as pertinent background information about the organization. Examples of pertinent information include the major directions articulated in the strategic plan, a brief description of the current fundraising program (including staffing), any challenges that the organization is facing in expanding its donor base or its overall program, positive or negative perceptions of the organization among the media or with specific donor segments, and a brief description of the governing board and its role in fundraising.

In addition, the RFP should also outline the types of information the organization expects to receive back in a proposal from the consultant and the format in which it is to be presented. It is entirely reasonable to expect consultants to outline the process they will use to conduct the requested work, a description of previous relevant engagements (ones that presented similar challenges), and references (including contact information) of organizations for which the consultant has recently conducted similar work. Other specific information, such as the amount of funds raised compared to the goal in campaigns the consultant has worked with previously, may also be requested. In addition, the organization should ask for the consultant to outline the timetable and fee, plus any incidental expenses (such as travel, duplicating, design work or other special services) not covered by the fee. (Ideally, the consultant will be able to provide an estimate of the total reimbursable expenses the organization should expect to pay.) The consultant should also identify the fee payment schedule, ideally tying it to deliverable work products throughout the engagement. Finally, the RFP should include the proposal deadline and an organizational contact person, in case the consultant has additional questions.

Before determining how broadly to disseminate the RFP, the organization should keep in mind the relative scope of work. An infrequent endeavor, such as a capital campaign that may go on over several years at a significant fee, may warrant casting the net for potential consultants more broadly than finding someone to write a single proposal. Both the consultants (who put together the proposals) and the volunteers and staff (who must read through and evaluate them) appreciate having their time respected, which suggests that the goal of the RFP process is not to generate a large quantity of proposals. Rather, the process should generate proposals only from qualified consultants who possess the skills and attributes being sought by the selection committee. In addition, the process should ensure that the nonprofit organization provides enough information about itself for the potential consultants to feel comfortable with the starting point for the proposed engagement.

Once the proposals are submitted, the internal committee should read through them and determine which consultants will be interviewed in person. In addition, the group should determine the questions to ask during the interviews and the process for "scoring" responses. As with hiring any new staff member, the main purpose for the in-person interview is to assess how well the personality and skill set of the candidate will fit the needs of the organization and the team that is already in place. In other words, the organization is seeking the elusive "chemistry" that will enable a positive outcome for the organization's fundraising program. Thus, the in-person interviews are generally focused on the "fit" with the potential consultant. Is their work style compatible with the organizational culture? How flexible are they in adapting their preferred systems and tools to the needs of the organization? Is the person being interviewed the actual person the organization will be working with? Do they have a strong commitment to the ethical practice of fundraising? How will they help develop staff and board skills so that the organization is able to carry on successfully without them at the conclusion of the engagement? How will the process they propose produce the results the organization needs? Do the timetables mesh?

Contracts as a Relationship-Building Tool

Any time a new individual is introduced into an organization – whether as a staff member, board member, volunteer, or consultant – the dynamics of the team within the organization will change. Even the best team relationships sometimes are complicated, and it behooves a nonprofit organization to do everything possible to ensure that hiring a consultant becomes a positive decision for the organization and its relationships with constituents. In order to ensure the best possible outcome, there are several issues that should be addressed in the contract between the organization and the consultant.

Either party can draft the contract, but both must ensure that it spells out in as much detail as possible the scope of work, timetable, fees, and billing schedule that will guide the consultant's work. Inherent in any contract is the assumption that both parties – organization and consultant – are engaged in a true partnership and that both are thus obligated to perform work that advances the overall engagement. The organization must in a timely fashion supply the consultant with any background information the consultant requests about the organization. Depending on the type of engagement, examples could include the strategic plan, fundraising plan, donation reports, fundraising and organizational budgets, bylaws, architectural renderings, board meeting minutes, development committee meeting minutes, etc. (While not common, some organizations may ask a consultant to sign a Confidentiality Agreement prior to releasing what is considered proprietary information.)

The organization also must commit to a decision-making process and timetable that advances the overall timetable for the scheduled work. For example, even though committees are often involved in reviewing their work, consultants usually expect to have a single point of decision-making contact established in the contract so that there can be clear direction coming out of group discussions where sometimes conflicting opinions are expressed.

Similarly, the contract should outline the consultant's deliverables, tying payments to the successful completion of each milestone. The contract also should contain a "back door" – a way for either party to end the agreement with appropriate notice and compensation for completed work. From the organization's perspective, the impetus for ending a consulting agreement can be driven by nondelivery of work at agreed-upon milestones or a bad "fit" between the organization and the consultant. From the consultant's perspective, the back-door clause might also be triggered by the same sense of "bad fit." In addition, the consultant may move to end the engagement if the organization does not provide payment at specified milestones or if the board and/or staff have pre-conceived expectations for the engagement's outcome and are unwilling to accept differing information or recommendations from the consultant.

Another issue to be addressed in the contract is ownership of the "work product." Oftentimes consultants bring to the engagement certain terminology, formats, templates, or other tools that they believe are proprietary. In some cases, these same types of work products might be developed in the course of the consulting engagement with the organization. The contract should spell out clearly who has the rights to use this work in the future.

In addition to a strong contract, it is important for an organization to have realistic expectations about the type of work that a fundraising consultant can actually do. For example, if the organization does not have a strong, compelling case for support, no fundraising consultant can magically create one by stringing together "pretty words." While the consultant can suggest the types of things that should be done in order to enhance the case, there must be a commitment from the board and staff to implement these changes if the case is to be strengthened.

Similarly, a consultant cannot manage a campaign without board and organizational leadership involvement. In effective engagements, the consultant is considered a vital member of the team, not someone for the organization to outsource its work to. The consultant should also not be expected to solicit gifts, although they may accompany volunteers or staff on solicitation calls. (It is very important that the relationships developed through any fundraising campaign remain between the organization and the donor, rather than between the consultant and the donor.) Finally, codes of ethics from every professional fundraising association dictate that a consultant should never work on a commission or percentage basis.

Conclusion

Fundraising consultants bring valuable expertise to nonprofit organizations, especially when the skills needed by the organization are not readily available on the staff or board. They also bring an outsider's perspective and can confirm and validate current programs and ideas, challenge the organization's leadership to build on what already exists, and share new ideas for how to improve fundraising success. By bringing a structure and rigor to the fundraising process, they can keep the organization on schedule to achieve the results it seeks. Finally, they can help build the organization's staff and volunteer skills through training, followed immediately by the opportunity to "practice" under their mentorship.

Consultants can be valuable members of the organization's fundraising team. Managing consultant relationships with some of the ideas presented here can help an organization grow its capacity to be successful with both raising more money and engaging constituents more deeply in its mission and work.

Discussion Questions

1) Identify some of the considerations that are critical to executing a successful contract with a consultant.
2) What are some ways an organization can ensure that it has done the appropriate due diligence in hiring a consultant?
3) Identify examples of some of the ways that consultants are used in fundraising.
4) What issues should board members consider in engaging a consultant to assist with fundraising?

PART FIVE

THE ART OF SOLICITATION

CHAPTER TWENTY-SIX

PERSONAL SOLICITATION

By Genevieve G. Shaker

After completing this chapter, you will be able to:

1. Identify several donor motivations for charitable giving.
2. Explain strategies for identifying major gift prospective donors.
3. Develop a cultivation plan leading to gift solicitation.
4. Describe the process of personal gift solicitation.
5. Appreciate the role of professionalism in fundraising.

One evening, the dean and chief development officer of Indiana University's Kelley School of Business took alumnus James R. Hodge to dinner (Sullivan, 2014). It was a culminating, climactic moment. Over the course of the evening, they asked Mr. Hodge to make a $15 million naming gift for the school's new building. It was the beginning of a structured conversation that lasted several months and yet actually was only the midpoint of a long-standing relationship that had begun much earlier. Not the first meeting with Mr. Hodge, it was the result of thoughtful, patient preparation by a fundraising team whose efforts were rewarded when Mr. Hodge agreed to make the gift.

Without careful preparation and thought, the outcome of the conversations with Mr. Hodge could have been much different. Preceded by many interactions over time, the face-to-face and in-person meeting with Mr. Hodge represents the framework for the preferred setting for solicitation of significant gifts. According to fundraising practice and literature (Kelly, 1998; Sargeant and Jay, 2014), in-person contact is essential for large gifts, reaffirmed by the proven donor pyramid of fundraising strategies as shown in the Donor Pyramid described in chapter 17. Personal contact is considered *the* way to work with capital and planned gift donors like Mr. Hodge (although there are certainly donors in the current information age who are quite comfortable making serious commitments via email, phone, and even text).

An age-old fundraising adage agreed upon by scholars and practitioners alike (Kelly, 1998, Sargeant and Jay, 2014) reminds us that the majority of gift dollars will come from a small minority of donors, as the gift range chart found in Chapter 19 illustrates. Typically, a few lead gifts make up a minimum of 80% of the total goal in capital campaigns. It is these gifts that make or break a fundraising campaign.

A successful request for support—large or small—requires the fundraiser to know her organization, herself, and her donor(s) by working through the following dimensions of personal solicitation: (1) the psychology of asking for money, (2) the identification and strategic cultivation of the prospective donor, and (3) the solicitation and invitation to give (Lilly Family School of Philanthropy, 2015). To this list, we might add a fourth dimension, understanding a duty to the profession.

Knowing Yourself: The Psychology of Asking for Money and the Professionalism of Fundraising

To be effective and uninhibited in making proposals to donors and in responding to their questions, fundraising professionals must address their own response to American (and increasingly other cultures') societal taboos regarding money (Lilly Family School of Philanthropy, 2015). In the United States, individual wealth is a private matter. Money is not a topic for "polite conversation," even within one's family and often despite the advice of financial advisers to the contrary. Asking for money, therefore, can appear rude. By coming to terms with their own personal attitudes about money and by recognizing its inherent value as a *means* to achieving donor goals while enhancing the public good, fundraisers can form an authentic and reflective approach to solicitation.

Ultimately, it is the charitable purpose of the request that will drive gift conversations. Booker T. Washington, a prominent educator and seasoned fundraiser for Tuskegee College in the 1800s, explained his approach: "…I think the main thing is for one to grow to the point where [he] completely forgets himself; that is, to lose [himself] in a great cause." (Jackson, 2008, p. 318).

Philanthropy enables donors to express their values and address societal problems, create the best kind of community and world (by their measure), and live "a good life" (Gunderman, 2009; Payton and Moody, 2008). It allows them to transmit these values to their children, to make a difference, to give back, to create a legacy—and to follow any number of personal priorities (Lilly Family School of Philanthropy, 2010). Research has shown that giving and volunteering make people feel good—the aptly-named "warm glow" evoked by philanthropy. They are motivated by a wide range of purposes, from the "altruistic" (and "other-oriented") to the self-oriented (Konrath, 2014; Smith and Davidson, 2014).

Although personal solicitation is based on meeting the donor's needs and goals, the ethical fundraiser is a professional with a duty to both the profession itself (as reflected in such attributes as a commitment to being prepared, to understanding and acknowledging the expectations for ethical behavior, to serving the greater public good, and so forth) and to the organization she represents. Consequently, as the representative of the organization, the fundraiser needs to understand and honor the mission, vision and values of the organization and to be the bridge between the values and goals of the donor and those of the organization—forgetting herself, as Washington advises, and remembering the broader social purpose at hand.

On occasion, the fit or match between donor and organization may not align, and then it is the challenging and difficult duty of the fundraiser to help redirect the donor's interests to another organization that is more suitable or gracefully to break off relations in order to preserve the integrity of the organization and the fundraiser herself. This is the one occasion when the fundraiser cannot forget or lose herself, but must act as a responsible steward of both donor and intended recipient. Part of the fundraiser's duty in knowing herself is also to recognize when values do not align, possibly losing a gift in the process.

Knowing Your Donor: Strategic Cultivation

Gift conversations can take place quickly over a few weeks or even multiple decades. Each process is unique and requires fundraising professionals to apply a personalized approach based on relational philanthropy (supply-side philanthropy), which takes its cues from the donor rather than demand-side philanthropy, which prioritizes the organization's transactional needs such as campaign timelines or fiscal years (Schervish, 2000). Built on the relational model, personal solicitation will be more successful if it considers the donor at every step while adhering to the mission and values of the organization seeking the gift.

Although most relationships depend on individual and personal contact of a central fundraiser with a donor, organizations typically structure their solicitations as team efforts so that more than one person is involved in the relationship and can fill in or take over as circumstances may change. Based on a lead solicitor's contacts, each fundraising team focuses on building cumulative interactions that keep the donor at the forefront, without losing track of organizational mission (Burke, 2003). This balance is more likely to be rewarded with mutually satisfying results when taken up intentionally. And it is more likely to be successful when anticipated and planned instead of created hastily in response to an unexpected development.

Identifying your best prospective donors

With giving at any level, the first step is to discover your constituent group—who are your likely donors? Individuals' *linkage* to the organization, *ability* to give, and *interest* in the organizational mission (often cited as LAI) provide a classic model for identification of potential donors (Lilly Family School of Philanthropy, 2015). The most probable prospective donors for major, capital, and planned gifts are among an organization's existing donor population. The LAI, therefore, can be "reapplied" with tighter criteria and heightened thoughtfulness as an approach to sifting through a donor database. In addition to fundraiser and staff (or volunteer) knowledge about individual prospective donors, research is the central avenue for gathering information about a donor's LAI at a given moment.

Research staff who may never meet the prospective donor, volunteers who wish to remain anonymous, and fellow fundraisers who have only transactional interactions with the prospective donor may comprise the solicitation team. Mr. Hodge likely never knew (beforehand and perhaps afterward) just how many people engaged in matching his interests with those of the school, nor would he have been aware of team discussions of the possibility of the gift and clarifications within the organization about the match of values and mutual interests.

Managing the strategy and building a relationship

In developing the cultivation process and determining the best request to meet both the donor's interests and the organization's needs, the fundraiser gathers an array of information about the donor *and* her own organization. Fundraisers need to look at their own institutions critically and objectively, as a potential investor would, and not assume that the donor shares their knowledge or warm feelings. The Fund Raising School (Lilly Family School of Philanthropy, 2015) offers a set of questions, enhanced here, as tools for the cultivation:

- What are the donor's interests, values, and passion, specific to your organization?
- What are the donor's current financial commitments, personally and philanthropically?
- What is the desired purpose and impact of the gift?
- Is the gift a priority for the organization? How will it support the mission?
- What are the long-term implications for the organization in using these funds to accomplish the goal?
- Does the gift provide enough resources for the organization to deliver the impact the donor envisions?
- Who will be involved in the solicitation—from the organization and from the donor's life?
- What assets will the donor use to create the gift? In what form and when? What gift instruments can the organization provide and support?
- Is the organization the best fit for what the donor wants to achieve with the gift, and how can this be demonstrated effectively?
- What are the donor's preferences for involvement with the organization (and gift) and how does this affect the gift and stewardship?

The use of these questions (or other devices like them) is strategic, but the discovery process is artful.

Listening is a critical skill in determining the donor's heartfelt priorities and how those hopes can (or cannot) be brought to life within a particular organization. From disciplined listening, the fundraiser will discover where to steer the conversation, items to revisit along the way, and degree of alignment of donor intent with organizational need. At the same time, the donor will be learning about the organization and forming opinions about what it does and how it works; the better the donor knows the organization, the more likely the philanthropic match will be "right" and lasting (Siegal and Yancey, 2003).

Strategic conversations may take place in person, by phone, through email, and personally at special events—most often carefully conceived as moments of engagement and interaction. The conversations may include key staff members, volunteers, friends or family, senior organizational officials, or service recipients (such as students or clients), carefully chosen to facilitate particular topics or experiences. The conversations may relate to broader contextual factors of interest, to accomplishments of organizational outcomes, or to donor experiences in relation to organizational mission.

Shaping donor experiences is both intentional and imaginative, with adaption and flexibility fostered through sufficient analysis and preparation to accommodate the unexpected. A key consideration, therefore, should be the bonding of the donor and the organization (its leadership, staff, and/or volunteers), not solely between the donor and the lead gift officer (Cluff, 2009). The donor's schedule and preferences should drive the cultivation; nevertheless, the fundraiser is expected to move the dialogue forward and to judge the time to ask for a gift, taking into consideration the donor's capacity and proclivity to give, based on research and prior interactions.

The moment for the gift conversation most effectively occurs when the fundraiser knows the donor's philanthropic vision, priorities, and circumstances well enough to make an appropriate request and has the interpersonal knowledge necessary to choose the suitable timing, approach, place, and format for the meeting. It is well worth noting that opportunity and happenstance can require working "off-plan" or ahead of the anticipated schedule—rather than allowing such moments to pass by. An ability to recognize the best timing for gift solicitations becomes an instinct informed by experience and preparation and building on adaptability, flexibility, and originality as key characteristics of gift officers (Cluff, 2009).

Knowing When and What to Ask: The Invitation to Make a Gift

The basic constructs of meeting with a donor have changed little since John D. Rockefeller's (1933) advice to fundraisers:

"... know your subject: Be so sold on it yourself that you can convincingly present its claims in the fewest possible words. A letter may well precede an interview, but personal contact is the most effective. Know as much as you can about the man to whom you go: Give him a general idea as to the contributions being made by others in his group, and ... suggest in a gracious and tactful way what you would be glad to have him give, leaving it entirely to him to decide what he shall give. Be kindly and considerate. Thus will you get closest to a man's heart and his pocketbook."

While the modern fundraising professional is likely to be bolder in shaping the request than Rockefeller advocates, her decisions and behaviors still stem from listening to the donor and knowing the cause at hand. As Rockefeller advocates, the fundraiser will be prepared, gracious, kind, tactful, succinct, considerate, and, most of all believe in the request's charitable purpose. These general recommendations go hand in hand with a reasoned and thoughtful plan of action.

Planning and conceptualizing the invitation to give Laying the groundwork for a solicitation requires a significant amount of time, but more thought may be needed than even the most cautious strategist might estimate. Where and when should the conversation take place? Is a meal the right kind of moment and how does the intent of the donation reflect the setting? Is the donor a morning person or evening person? Who should be involved in the meeting? How can the invitation for the meeting be structured to respect the donor but ensure that the "right" people are present to achieve a desired result? Is there a detail—probably insignificant in itself—that shows how carefully the fundraiser has listened and paid attention to the donor's interests and life story?

There is no end to such questions and the thought behind them. Just as each situation is as different as the donor, so must be the thought process, planning, and self-questioning of the fundraiser. And so must be the fundraiser's capacity to adapt from following a plan, no matter how well conceived.

Shaping and preparing the solicitation team As noted, in most cases, a major gift invitation will be a team effort. The influence of peer donors, for example, has been shown to be important in demonstrating to potential donors their own capacity to make gifts as well as the effectiveness of philanthropy in furthering their values (Shaker, 2013). This may be relevant for strategic cultivation or the solicitation conversation itself or it may also transpire beyond the cycle described here in a way that transcends fundraising planning or strategy. In Mr. Hodge's case, planned giving officers with legal and tax information were available to support ongoing discussion. The utilization of carefully chosen individuals—during, but also before and after the request—can signal the request's importance, can provide a peer perspective, and can validate the request's centrality to organizational mission.

Using an internal planning document or template and completing it in conversation with organizational stakeholders (including the solicitation team and perhaps other staff) will formalize knowledge into expectations, build on (and develop) co-worker expertise, and ensure team buy-in and understanding with this tool. Most established organizations with years of experience in fundraising have created templates for recording and assessing donor meetings; while examples are available, the best templates are those that evolve based on the organization's own experience and its ability to use the information it collects.

A team rehearsal and a specific plan designed for each meeting provides opportunity to align with the participating individuals' strengths. The gift officer will prepare her colleagues to be active listeners and conversationalists, sensitive interpersonal communicators in the context of philanthropy. She will remember that coaching, guidance, and practice may be needed for her colleagues. Even for experienced staff colleagues, the stereotype of fundraiser salesmanship may need to be overcome. Professionalism marked by preparation, a commitment to ethical conduct, and a genuine belief in the cause of the organization can eliminate most worries.

When full preparation is not possible, facilitating a conversation among the staff (in organizations large enough to have staff) that lays out expectations and that brainstorms possible donor questions is essential. If soliciting a gift individually without staff support, the fundraiser can develop a plan by projecting the kind of discussion that might have occurred if staff were present. With experience, fundraisers can be quite adept at role-playing and taking the parts of their absent (or even nonexistent) colleagues.

The Solicitation Meeting

The steps described in this section follow naturally from the preparations described above, but they can still be difficult to implement well. Experienced fundraisers know that success in personal solicitation comes through asking and asking often. Practicing the craft (and reflecting on that practice) will build confidence, skill, and grace in what can be unpredictable conversations. The strategizing conversations with staff build poise and self-assuredness, especially as colleagues reinforce the fundraiser's own role as leader and spokesperson for the organization. Again, this roadmap, based on The Fund Raising School curriculum, is not the one for *every* gift conversation with *every* donor. However, it provides a foundational approach on which to build and refine.

Open the Meeting with a Plan

Upon arrival, begin by building rapport as one would in any polite conversation, greeting the prospective donor(s) and gauging the correct tone and pace. Inquiring about family, for example, may be a good opening—but this depends on the situation and is an example of where prior knowledge is important. Even small details that reflect interest in the donor will help build trust and confidence; an uninformed comment or unintentional blunder can end a promising discussion even before it begins. The next step is to develop the context for the particular conversation, thanking the donor for past support or involvement with the organization, reviewing what the donor means to the organization, and expressing appreciation for the opportunity to meet. Gauge how things are going – for example, if the team learns that the donor has just experienced a loss in the family, business issue, or the like, adaptation to the plan may be necessary. Then provide a reminder of the meeting purpose and plan to move in quickly from that point. Be attentive to achieving the pre-determined objective and utilizing the precious time together. Requests should be made earlier rather than later in the conversation. Respect the time allotted for the meeting.

Involve the Donor

The next phase is to engage the donor in talking—asking questions, reminiscing, or even correcting comments from the fundraiser. Talk about what has been learned about the donor's priorities and values from the cultivation process and research, listening carefully and adjusting the direction of the conversation based on the donor's reactions. Revisit key moments in that process, using the donor's own words and important donor and organization moments.

Be sincere, respectful, and authentic. Be succinct, keeping in mind that the donor's time is valuable and that some donors may appreciate a shorter grounding discussion. Watch the donor's body language and make adaptations as appropriate.

Make the Request

If this is still the "right" meeting, ask for the gift, describing the purpose, amount, and benefits for the organization and donor as well as the desired timeframe. To the extent possible, describe how the organization will assess results and be accountable for the gift. Be direct, confident, and positive—persuade the donor with conviction and passion about the cause, need, and/or values. Remember that this moment is not a surprise but, by this point, likely an expectation.

Pause and wait for the answer in silence. Give the donor space to think and respond. Be an engaged listener, maintaining eye contact. The temptation to fill the silence and speak will be strong—if not for the fundraiser, then for others on the solicitation team. Resist the desire to fill the vacuum of silence and give control of the conversation to the donor.

Donors will respond to gift requests in any number of ways. Assume a response of "no" or "not now" or "that's not exactly what I care most about," and be prepared to ask questions to learn more about these statements. Even in the best case scenario, when the donor says "yes" or "I could be interested in that" or "tell me more," additional discussion will be necessary before the gift comes to fruition. Remember that asking is only the midpoint to a successful gift.

Engaging in Discussion

Sophisticated donors, including many younger donors, are increasingly likely to be concerned with supporting outcomes-driven philanthropic purposes and hands-on involvement with their gifts (21/64 and Dorothy A. Johnson Center for Philanthropy, 2013). Contemporary donors are developing giving plans, participating in giving circles, considering innovative "venture" giving approaches, discussing concepts like "social return on investing," reading philanthropic literature, and working with advisors—all of which are making a larger proportion into increasingly savvy philanthropists with deeper understandings of the nonprofit sector and of their own priorities and standards within it.

Regardless of these relatively new approaches, all donors will be interested in results and impact from their giving. Be prepared to describe what the impact will be—and especially how you or the actual stewards of the gift will be able to report impact. This need not be a formal plan for "assessment" but it should indicate that you and the organization have thought about the need to show results and be accountable for the gift in ways responsive to donor interests.

Do not be surprised if the donor has done her own research, perhaps finding information about your organization or the mission it serves online or turning to one or more of the charity "rating" organizations. Fundraisers need to know more about how the organization is represented—and perceived—through media than a potential donor and be ready to address both positive and negative representations honestly and fairly.

As the donor is considering the request, further information will probably be required about avenues for making the gift. The donor almost certainly will desire some adjustment to aspects of the purpose or gift criteria, even after everything may appear settled. Be prepared to provide options on the funding and also to negotiate specific details that may come up. Do not lower the amount of the gift, keeping in mind that the figure was predetermined through careful thought, research, and analysis to meet both the organizational purpose and to achieve the donor's desired impact. If Mr. Hodge had offered $5 million instead of the $15 million, for example, the gift would have become different than the original proposal. Be ready to discuss alternate giving opportunities better aligned with the donor's core interests or financial situation.

The Close

Finish by thanking the donor for engaging in the conversation, no matter the outcome. Discuss next steps and establish a plan that suits the donor. For affirmative conversations, a next step might be another follow-up meeting between the donor and team members who can address legal, accounting, or tax issues.

For a redirected or rejected request, a next step might be a follow-up activity of another kind with the organization, a return to the conversation at an agreed upon future date, a referral to another part of the organization (if it is large), or even a suggestion of another organization that better aligns with the donor's wishes. Do not be afraid to help the donor meet her real needs, even if your organization is not the best means.

In either context, the fundraiser should call, write, or email the donor within the next day. Gratitude for the donor's time and attention is an important part of cultivation and solicitation, but it is also stewardship. Communicating periodically with the donor about progress in implementing the plan is essential.

Beyond Solicitation: The Fundraiser as Professional

In making the case for donor-centered fundraisers, Burke (2003) references, in priority order, the following central responsibilities: (1) cultivating the philanthropic spirit and encouraging giving to the nonprofit sector as a whole for the good of society, (2) advocating for donors, and (3) building philanthropic support for one's own organization. For most fundraising professionals, the third attribute will understandably seem the most pressing and real. In the long term, however, concern for the first two guidelines will better serve the practitioner, the organization, the donor, and society. This framework fosters high ethical standards and an abiding recognition that the donor's purpose and the organization's mission are about creating a better society. Accepting the importance—even priority—of the first two responsibilities is key to self-identification as a professional.

Giving away money is a serious matter even if the gift is relatively small; proportionate to the capacity to give, one donor's small gift may be more of a sacrifice than a wealthier person's much larger gift. The fundraising professional is an advisor and advocate for the donor during this process, helping her navigate the organization's needs, hopes, and policies—in tandem with the support donors receive from family members, wealth advisors, lawyers, or accountants.

Fundraising requires self-assurance and a certainty of purpose, made strong by the knowledge that donors want to share their resources for worthy causes—but guided by a duty to honor the donor's wishes first and foremost. The university officials guiding Mr. Hodge could be certain that what they were proposing would benefit thousands of students in compelling ways over many years and this knowledge enabled better stewardship of Mr. Hodge's gift.

Conclusion

To ask for money is to contribute to society as a whole. It is a privilege and a vocation that requires a high level of integrity, sensitivity, creativity, and preparation.

As giving brings joy to the donor, the donor's joy and society's benefit bring great gratification to the fundraising professional.

Discussion Questions

1) When you think about asking a person for money, in person and out loud, how do you feel? What are the roots of these feelings?
2) What techniques will you use to determine appropriate timing and approach for the invitation to give?
3) How can concern for a donor's interests be infused throughout the solicitation process and in a way that maintains organizational purpose?
4) What words and messages are suitable for the invitation to give? Practice a three-to-five sentence request for support and remaining silent for 30-60 seconds afterward.

CHAPTER TWENTY-SEVEN

DIRECT RESPONSE

By Deborah L. Eschenbacher

After completing this chapter, you will be able to:

1. Explain the role direct response plays in building a broad base of prospective donors to your organization.
2. Demonstrate how to maximize return on investment in direct response fundraising by utilizing direct mail and e-solicitation to support one another.
3. Describe common elements of effective direct response vehicles and how to incorporate them in successful appeals.
4. Justify the value of testing appeals to specific audience segments and how to measure success.
5. Explain the legal requirements regarding registering nonprofits in each state in which your organization does direct response fundraising.

Critical funding needed to support the work of nonprofit organizations is dependent upon sustainable annual revenue generated by a variety of annual fundraising vehicles. These fundraising vehicles generate primarily unrestricted annual revenue in the form of smaller, repeatable and potentially upgradable gifts. Through direct response vehicles, organizations present multiple opportunities for donors to give at different times in different ways during the year. In addition to generating primarily unrestricted revenue to support operations, programs, and services, direct response vehicles generate a steady stream of prospective donors on whom organizations will build the rest of their fundraising programs. In addition, direct response vehicles identify and provide a means of acquiring donors for the purpose of further qualification and cultivation for higher-level giving through repeat and upgraded giving strategies. These strategies allow the organization to test the potential for major gifts and planned giving. They provide a platform for educating the general public as well as the organization's constituencies about current programs and services, reporting outcomes, sharing special stories, and building a positive and trusted public image.

Additionally, when multiple direct response vehicles are used to support one another and become part of a larger, more comprehensive effort, the result is more effective and efficient fundraising. Solid direct response fundraising, which constantly tests and analyzes information gathered from donors' responses, is the basis of every strong fundraising program.

The term "direct response" covers a variety of vehicles designed to elicit action on the part of the prospective donor. Among those vehicles are direct mail, e-solicitation, social media, mobile giving, online tools, display ads, telemarketing, radio and television, insert media, and out-of-home advertising. This chapter focuses on direct mail and e-solicitation.

Applying Direct Mail Principles to Other Direct Response Fundraising

Historically, direct mail has been one of the most traditional and recognizable ways for organizations to ensure annual contact with donors. The growing and ever-changing possibilities that e-solicitation and social media offer cause many to argue that securing donations through direct mail is a thing of the past. However, for nonprofits with a wide geographic distribution of prospective donors, direct mail is often the most successful way to reach them, as current donors' given street addresses are easier to obtain than electronic addresses. Direct mail is often the key to communicating with all or specific segments of an organization's constituency and donor base on an annual basis.

Direct mail has continually provided the most metrics-driven method of testing messages, refining audience segmentation, and upgrading giving. Direct mail fundraising has been well measured and the principles that have made it successful over the years have been well documented. It seems prudent to utilize these years of experience and the wealth of information gathered as fundraisers expand their efforts in the area of e-solicitation. Guiding principles for direct mail fundraising easily apply to all direct response fundraising.

The following principles of direct response fundraising are adapted from James Greenfield (2002). Direct response fundraising:

1. Should raise funds in a cost-efficient manner.
2. Can dramatically increase the number of donors to an organization.
3. Can broaden an organization's visibility and make it more recognizable.
4. Can identify substantial prospects for capital or planned giving campaigns.
5. Can identify new volunteers for an organization.
6. Reaches the great majority of those an organization wishes to contact in the way the organization wants to contact them.
7. Can take advantage of current events because it can be formulated and implemented in a very short time period.
8. Requires continual management and monitoring by an organization's development team.
9. Provides immediate gratification.
10. Requires less staff time to implement than phone-a-thons or in-person calls.
11. Gives an organization a full opportunity to tell its complete story.
12. Can be individualized/personalized and segmented to appeal to a specific audience.
13. Should be looked upon as a continuing program to upgrade donors.
14. Provides an easy follow-up advantage in solicitation.

Direct Mail as a Template for Other Direct Response Fundraising

Years of developing and refining direct mail appeals have demonstrated that successful direct response fundraising depends upon testing and analysis, planning, innovation, and steady revenue growth. Understanding what is involved in accomplishing this will prove helpful when an organization expands its fundraising to incorporate other direct response fundraising vehicles.

Accurate Prospective Donor Lists and Segmentation

Lists must be appropriately segmented – first, according to broad screening criteria and, later, by more in-depth information as it is collected. An internal database management system, designed to collect and track comprehensive donor information and giving history, is essential. Accuracy and consistency in recording information and coding will provide optimal results for analyzing data. This database must be kept current and maintained with maximum continuity by a dedicated data manager (part-time or full-time, according to the size of the organization) who can provide comprehensive reports for analysis and planning purposes. Selective direct response lists that focus on key constituencies/segments will continue to evolve and grow over time.

The Fund Raising School (2015) at the Indiana University Lilly Family School of Philanthropy lists the best prospective donors as:

- People who share an interest in your mission or goals.
- People who match current donor profiles. May include age, sex, income level, geography, family composition, education level, political affiliation, and profession.
- People who already donate to nonprofit causes. (Remember: not everyone is your donor.)
- People who are mail-responsive or e-solicitation responsive, including those who shop online or by catalog.

Direct Mail Donor Categories

The following donor categories are often used in segmenting direct mail solicitations.

Current Donors   These are an organization's most responsive donors. They have already demonstrated that they know enough about the organization to have made a gift in the current year. It is important that in subsequent solicitations an organization should try to learn more about these donors' giving preferences by testing additional areas to support and work toward encouraging them to repeat and upgrade their gifts.

Occasional Donors   These are donors who gave last year or in earlier years but have not given this year or in the most recent year(s). Also among the more responsive of an organization's donors, they often need an additional reminder to give in the current year. Because they have made a previous gift, they have most likely been receiving a newsletter and/or other materials designed to keep them informed about the organization. Acknowledgement and appreciation of past giving is important to remind such donors how important their ongoing support is to the organization. Recognition of past giving and a message that says the organization has missed them, coupled with a specific giving opportunity, is the most effective way to re-engage occasional donors.

Nondonors These are prospective donors with potential for becoming donors. At this early stage, little is known about them except that they have met some identification criteria (have been recommended by friends of the organization, support organizations that have similar values and serve similar needs, etc.). These prospective donors have the lowest return rate, but are worth testing to determine potential for support.

Planning: Frequency and Timing of Solicitations

An annual fundraising plan must be developed with careful attention to providing year-round revenue that will support the ongoing work of the organization. Planning will include a determination of the role direct response will have in an organization's overall annual fundraising plans, ensure that realistic goals are set, and that timelines for preparation, mailing and response are considered. A comprehensive and well-balanced plan will be based on the analysis of previous fundraising history, goals, and results. It will routinely include multiple solicitations, some general in nature and others tailored to specific constituencies/segments – all conducted at well-timed intervals throughout the year and implemented in an intentional manner. The plan must be flexible enough to take into consideration additional solicitation opportunities directly relating to something of timely or immediate significance/need (commemorations or celebrations, new or expanded programs, etc.) as they arise. October through December is recognized as one of the most productive times of the year for many organizations' direct response appeals. End-of-the-year appeals are designed to capitalize on donors' philanthropic holiday spirit and provide a final chance to make year-end tax deductible gifts. In order of most to least productive, other timeframes for giving are March to June, January to March and July to September (Greenfield, 2002). All direct response efforts throughout the year must be coordinated with all other organizational fundraising and mass communication activities. Each activity reinforces the other and can be positioned to take advantage of peaks in an organization's visibility as well as provide cross-promotional support for other programs or fundraising.

Elements of Direct Mail and Application to e-Solicitation

The successful time-tested elements of direct mail solicitation transfer easily to e-solicitation and provide a platform on which to build a successful electronic fundraising program. It is important to remember that subtle changes in elements can effect a difference in giving. Like direct mail, e-solicitation relies on constant testing for improvement. Test elements of e-solicitation against one another for effectiveness with different constituencies/segments and analyze the results.

Carrier Envelope   The amount of thought or time an organization has invested in creating the "perfect" solicitation message and supporting materials does not matter if the envelope or e-solicitation is not opened by the intended prospective donor. The *carrier envelope or electronic message delivery format* needs to be appealing so that it encourages the recipient to open it.

For *direct mail*, this means that the size and color of the envelope will be taken into consideration, as will the type of postage, recipient's address, return address and any additional message that will be printed on the envelope. The *envelope* size and color must match the design of the solicitation so that a complete "look" will be presented. Attention to the possibility of special *postage* requirements to accommodate the size and weight of all pieces in the solicitation package will need to be considered as this will directly affect mailing costs. Postage options include First Class stamps, Nonprofit stamps, and Metered or Permit Imprint Indicia. It is generally understood that First Class and Nonprofit stamps are preferred. The *prospective donor's name and address* must be accurate. If an organization's database is not maintained by continually collecting and verifying up-to-date and accurate addresses, direct mail solicitations will never reach prospective donors. When prospective donors first look at an envelope, it will be easy for them to lose interest if the address contains mistakes in title or spelling or lacks proper respect by using a nickname or assuming that members of a couple wish to be addressed, for example, as Mr. and Mrs. rather than by first names or vice versa. If the organization opts to use an address label instead of printing the address on the envelope, the label must be affixed evenly. If the organization uses a window envelope, it is critical that the materials are designed to line up with the window so that the recipient's address may be easily read. The *return address* may be placed in the traditional upper left-hand corner on the front of the envelope or on the back flap. It may contain the organization's name and address or simply the address alone. Incorporating the logo on the carrier envelope often boosts the organization's visual recognition, which is a benefit of ongoing branding efforts. If a specific solicitation utilizes the name of a recognizable public figure, it may be appropriate to include that name in the return address as well. Equally as important as affixing an address label evenly on an envelope is affixing a return address label evenly on an envelope if the return address is not printed directly on to the envelope. Frequently an organization will print a one- or two-line message (or banner) on the envelope to encourage the recipient to look inside.

For *e-solicitation*, three things will influence whether the prospective donor will open the solicitation. The first is ensuring the accuracy of the *electronic address*. If the organization does not continually collect and verify the accuracy of electronic addresses, solicitations will never reach recipients. The second is the *address of the sender*. Too often, the name of an individual employee of the organization appears as the sender and, not recognizing the name or that the employee is part of the sending organization, prospective donors ignore or delete electronic messages. Just like the organization's permanent return address that is used in direct mail, all electronic communications should originate from the same electronic sender and address – the name of the organization and its central electronic address. This is the electronic address that should be utilized for all official communications that originate from an organization. The third is the subject line, which is the space provided for stating the *purpose of the message.* This is the place to create headlines that will grab attention and compel recipients to open electronic messages of solicitation and general communication. Over time, an organization can develop a style of creatively stating the purpose of its electronic messages and gain a loyal following that enjoys hearing from them.

The Letter/Message   A successful solicitation is dependent upon the effectiveness of the design and the compelling content of the message. An appropriate salutation, an engaging design, and effective communication of needs in an easily readable manner will result in more effective solicitations.

Design influences how quickly and easily the recipient will be able to read the content and understand what is being requested. Effective use of paragraph length, indentation, white space, font selection, point size, boldface, italics, numbers, bullets, and color all add to the way the design helps move the reader through the copy. Additionally, the use of photos, video links, etc., will add life to the message and provide a unique way for an organization to feature activities and demonstrate impact.

In both direct mail and e-solicitation, the *salutation* sets the tone for the rest of the message. The choice of whether the salutation is formal or informal is at the discretion of the organization, but it must always be correct. Ongoing data collection and maintenance of the database will ensure that the correct salutation will be known and available for use. Sometimes a general salutation is necessary and appropriate ("Dear Friend," etc.), but it is always more desirable to personalize the salutation. Understanding exactly how a prospective donor wishes to be addressed and not taking liberties with names or titles will go a long way in setting the stage for the rest of the solicitation.

The *message* must be carefully written so that it communicates interesting and timely information, conveys the compelling nature of the solicitation, creates a sense of urgency, reflects the culture of the organization, and demonstrates an understanding of the intended audience's interests and motivations to give. Utilize the organization's Case for Support to provide continuity in all messaging and, when possible, demonstrate how the organization is meeting community needs by featuring people who have benefited from or are currently receiving services. For some organizations and audiences, it may be entirely appropriate to write multiple pages filled with stories, but, for others, one page filled with information-laden bullet points may be best. Testimonials provided by recipients of services, experts in a specific field, or, occasionally, by celebrities can help describe the organization and its work in a very personal way. Following the "needs message" is the request for gift support. Always specific, the request states exactly what type of support is sought (suggested giving amounts, upgrade giving suggestions, designation(s), timing) and benefits, if any. If there is a time-critical need for funding, it is imperative that the message creates a sense of urgency. This may vary from disaster relief to meeting a "matching gift" challenge timeline. Often urgent funding requests lend themselves to repeated contacts over a short period of time. This allows prospective donors to see the collective progress toward a goal and provides a way to demonstrate how each individual gift helps.

The end of the letter is as important as the beginning. Whose *signature* the organization chooses to close with should add value to the message. Often organizations use the "default signature" of the Executive Director/CEO/Development Director. Although these may be appropriate in certain circumstances, an organization would do well to explore others whose endorsement may have more influence in motivating individuals to give. Those with recognizable names, such as community leaders, local/regional/national celebrities, recipients of services, key volunteer leadership, organization founders, etc., should be considered.

Not to be overlooked is the importance of the *PS*. The PS is the final opportunity for the organization to provide a brief emotional appeal and state a call to action. Donors report they often skip to the end of solicitation letters and look at the PS for a recap and instructions regarding how to give. As with all written representation of an organization, it cannot be emphasized enough how important it is to proofread for accuracy of spelling and grammar.

Additional *materials* are often enclosed (direct mail) or attached (electronic solicitation) in direct response fundraising. These may include some type of involvement device such as surveys or requests for additional information. Being intentional about which supplemental materials to include as well as the rationale and ultimate use of information requested will ensure that the organization does not waste time or financial resources.

Response Mechanism   The response or reply mechanism is the final element of the direct response package. For traditional direct mail, a reply form/card and a return envelope will be enclosed in the carrier envelope along with the letter and any supplemental materials. Budget considerations and testing of best results for response returns will help determine whether to pre-pay postage (stamped envelope or Business Reply Envelope) or request the donor to provide postage. Donors want to know that the organization will actually receive the response; the street address of the organization is preferable for the location where the response will be sent rather than a post office box. Responses sent to out-of-state addresses or fulfillment centers send a negative message about how important and/or urgent the donor's gift is to the organization. Direct mail and electronic solicitations both rely on clearly worded reply devices that guide the donor through the process of making the gift. Whether printed or electronic, the response/reply will be created to match the giving levels suggested in the content of the letter and will provide options for the financial transaction.

Donor Retention, Renewal, and Upgrade Strategies

Generating sustainable annual revenue and creating opportunities to learn more about donors and their giving preferences are key to successful direct response programs. This requires the utilization of strategies focused on retaining donors and upgrading gifts. Communicating with donors at times other than solicitations as well as inviting them to engage in person or online provide donors with opportunities to learn about the organization and understand its need for support. Building long-term donor–organization relationships prepares donors for future solicitations. Upgrade strategies may include the use of matching gifts/challenge gifts, multiyear pledges, monthly giving (electronic fund transfer), membership programs with options to give additional charitable donations, gift clubs, national "giving days," or solicitations preceded or followed by a personal telephone call.

Among the added benefits that will result from the combination of donor relations, communications, and renewal solicitations are (Greenfield, 2002, p. 117):

1. Prior donors are the best prospective donors for other gifts as well as renewed annual gifts.
2. At least 50 percent of prior donors should repeat their gifts in the same amount.
3. As many as 15 percent of prior donors will increase if asked.
4. After second renewal (third gift), the donor is likely to remain faithful for from five to seven more years.
5. Renewal donors will give from five to eight times more money than new, first-time donors.
6. After five years, renewal donors will provide 80 percent of the money raised each year.

Measuring Success

These well-established criteria for measuring the success of direct response fundraising enable organizations to determine the success of each individual appeal as well as to make comparisons between similar appeals made at the same timeframe in different calendar years. Collect and analyze the following data points:

- Number of pieces sent (the list)
- Number of respondents who sent donations
- Percentage of total list who sent donations
- Number and percent of pieces returned as undeliverable
- Average gift size
- Gross revenue received
- Total direct costs
- Net revenue (gross revenue minus total direct costs)
- Cost per dollar raised (expenses divided by gross revenue)
- Return on investment (gross revenue divided by expenses)
- Number of respondents requesting additional information and/or seeking additional engagement with organization
- Timely gift processing and acknowledgement

State Charitable Registration and Reporting Requirements

In order to maintain nonprofit status, organizations are legally required to comply with state and federal laws that affect fundraising activities. This impacts direct response fundraising to the extent that organizations are engaged in interstate solicitations. Individual state registration requirements, charitable fundraising regulations, and compliance with nonprofit statutory requirements vary from state to state. The National Association of State Charity Officials (NASCO) is the national group of state offices with responsibilities for regulating charities (see Chapter 35 for a discussion of the laws governing fundraising).

NASCO's Charleston Principles and guidelines for Internet and social media solicitations are especially important documents to consult. Because the consequences of noncompliance can seriously impact an organization's ability to raise funds in a specific state and the costs of noncompliance can be substantial, this cannot be ignored. It can be a time-consuming process to file and meet the reporting requirements for all states on an annual basis. Legal practices with specialized services designed to help organizations meet these legal requirements can provide an alternative to managing this in-house.

Case Study: Combining Direct Response Vehicles for Maximum Effectiveness

Combining two or more direct response vehicles to support an appeal will often lead to increased effectiveness. A case study of an effective appeal utilizing direct mail and e-solicitation follows.

In 1993, an East Coast preparatory school received a transformational gift from a prominent Class of 1927 alumnus. This alumnus remained connected to the school over the years and made a gift of $25 during the school's first annual fund campaign in 1945. Twenty years later, in 2013, the school's annual fund direct mail appeal featured the original ledger sheet on which that gift was recorded. In its succinct narrative, the school emphasized the tradition of giving to the annual fund, stated its case for support for unrestricted annual gifts and featured photos of today's campus and students. The easy-to-follow response form offered a full complement of gift club levels, gave an opportunity for donors to indicate a company matching gift program, provided information regarding how to give online, requested updated donor information, and ended with a final Thank You that emphasized how vital unrestricted gifts are to the future of students and the school. An alumni challenge followed in the form of an e-solicitation encouraging alumni to give to the annual fund in honor of the 20th anniversary. Sent by an alumnus of the Class of 1993, the year in which the transformational gift was given, the e-solicitation focused on a special and time-sensitive giving opportunity. It showed a photo of the alumnus, then in his final year at the school, engaged in conversation with the transformational gift donor at a luncheon in 1993. The 1993 alumnus issued a challenge stating that if 100 alumni made gifts to the annual fund within the following 24 hours, he would personally match those gifts up to a generous set amount. This e-solicitation provided a large "give now" button so the recipients could make their gifts immediately on the school's website.

Conclusion

Recognizing the importance of a well-planned and well-implemented direct response program and dedicating the time as well as the financial and human resources necessary to develop it is a sound investment for an organization. The result is steady growth of primarily unrestricted annual revenue, opportunities to build and enhance an organization's public image, and the continued expansion of a prospective donor base that will provide a pipeline for identifying, qualifying, and cultivating higher-level giving. Additionally, when several direct response vehicles are utilized to strengthen one another, the results are multiplied.

Discussion Questions

1) Compare and contrast the elements of an effective direct mail solicitation with the elements of an effective e-solicitation.
2) What staffing needs must be satisfied within the organization in order to fully prepare and implement a comprehensive year-round direct response program? In what way might it be appropriate to incorporate the volunteers in direct response fundraising?
3) How could an organization maximize the impact of direct response solicitation by utilizing a combination of direct mail and e-solicitation?
4) Are there other annual fundraising activities (e.g., special events, etc.) that could benefit from being partnered with a direct response vehicle?

CHAPTER TWENTY-EIGHT

TELEPHONE SOLICITATION AND STEWARDSHIP

By Sarah K. Nathan

As fundraisers, we engage givers and receivers in creative and meaningful ways that enable nonprofit organizations to fulfill their mission on behalf of donors (Clohesy, 2003). Although telephone fundraising is often considered the most difficult, it is key to the traditional annual giving role of developing a broad donor base from which major gift and gift planning prospects can be cultivated over a period of years or decades. Therefore, designing a telephone program that meaningfully engages donors is essential.

This chapter covers:

- The role that telephone solicitation plays in a total development program.
- The challenges of and opportunities for using the telephone in fundraising.
- The steps to establishing a telephone program or reviewing a current one.
- The options for managing telephone programs.
- How to use the telephone for stewardship.

Since at least the 1990s, fundraisers have worried about the challenges posed by home answering machines, call waiting, and caller ID. Add the permanence of mobile phones and ubiquity of smart phones and it is easy to see that the environment for telephone fundraising is changing rapidly. Today, 50 percent of American adults aged 18 to 44 use only mobile phones. Even in a "mostly wireless home" with a landline, one-third of individuals receive all or most of their calls on a mobile phone (Blumberg and Luke, 2014). At the same time, donors' transaction preferences are in flux. According to one survey, giving by phone is the least popular. Only 10% percent of donors gave by phone in 2013 (Burke, 2014) and yet, despite the many challenges, telephone solicitation remains an essential component of a comprehensive development program.

In particular, a well-designed telephone fundraising program plays an essential role in maximizing the effectiveness of any comprehensive annual giving program, as described in Chapter 17. Telephone solicitation supports the following objectives of annual giving:

Educate the organization's constituency. The personal interaction between a well-trained caller and a prospect allows an organization to test and personalize messaging across multiple constituent segments, personalize the case for support based on individual and real time prospect interaction, and immediately overcome both anticipated and unexpected objections.

Acquire, renew, and upgrade donors. Because well-developed telephone solicitation programs allow for high-volume personal solicitation, donor acquisition and renewal rates far exceed direct mail or e-solicitation results. Furthermore, the personal and interactive negotiation inherent in phone solicitation facilitates upgrading a donor's gift amount.

Establish donor giving habits. A well-planned and executed annual phone campaign can penetrate deeply into an organization's constituency and facilitate regular giving across the donor base. Conducted on an annual basis, a phone campaign is vital to creating and sustaining a culture of regular giving.

Provide donor stewardship. Whether using volunteers or paid callers, the power of a live and personal thank you is unparalleled. Stewardship is explored further later in this chapter.

Develop prospective donors for major gifts and gift planning. Additionally, with proper planning, training, and care, the modern comprehensive telephone solicitation program can be leveraged to facilitate leadership gift solicitation and gift planning.

Because telephone solicitation fulfills these five objectives and provides other benefits, it can serve as the foundation upon which comprehensive development programs are built. Following are key concepts to take into consideration in developing an excellent telephone solicitation program.

Planning

Whether a phone campaign lasts a few weeks or is in operation 12 months a year, extensive planning is necessary to maximize results. While there is no one right way to implement a phone campaign, there are key issues to take into consideration and significant decisions to be made during the planning phase of any successful campaign.

Legislation and Regulation

Laws related to telemarketing are being introduced regularly at both the state and federal level. While charities are generally exempt from the core elements of such legislation, it is important to remain knowledgeable of the changing regulatory landscape. Though charities are legally permitted greater latitude in the use of telemarketing, it is wise to operate within industry standards including calling between the hours of 8 a.m. and 9 p.m. and honoring requests to be added to an organization's internal do not call list.

Additionally, other regulations exist related to telemarketing such as Payment Card Industry (PCI) standards that govern the manner in which credit/debit card payment information is processed. As a result, it is important to consult with the attorney general's office in the states you plan to solicit or otherwise seek legal counsel before implementing any phone solicitation program.

Data

Complete and accurate data are essential to telephone solicitation. Some specific areas are critical to a successful program. At the most basic level, contact information is needed – name and phone number, but ideally home and business address as well. All efforts should be made to capture cell phone numbers and to distinguish this information from landline numbers in your database. Prior gift history is also essential for call planning purposes so that previous support can be properly acknowledged and the current solicitation can be appropriately structured.

Beyond these essential data, it is ideal to maintain information related to spouse and family, volunteer involvement, predictive modeling, and wealth screening. In general, the more data points you maintain in your database, the more strategically and personally you can segment your calling to develop the most personal relationship possible between your organization and its donor base and maximize giving.

Budget

Budget resources must always be balanced appropriately across the various functions of a development program. Likewise, developing a balanced approach to the various aspects of phone solicitation is critical to creating and maintaining success. The various elements of the program include donor renewal, lapsed donor reactivation, nondonor acquisition, pre-call e-mails or postcards, pledge reminder calls and mailings, and thank you calls. It is important to plan how you will allocate your budget across the options.

In budget planning, be sure to consider the short-term and long-term implications of such decisions. Short-term returns often drive budget allocation decisions, but the long-term impact of annual giving should be based on a multiyear view of return on investment. New donor acquisition is a critical component of any annual giving program, but is also the most costly. It is not unusual for the direct cost to raise a dollar ratio to exceed 1:1 in nondonor segments if only measured within a given 12 month period. However, with careful stewardship and deliberate donor retention programming, the three to five year cumulative giving of newly acquired donors will far exceed the initial budget outlay needed to acquire their support. This benefit increases when one considers the total lifetime giving of new donors. Without consistent investment in new donor acquisition, an organization's donor base will stagnate and shrink over time, limiting its fundraising potential.

Use of Volunteer or Paid Callers

Twenty-five percent of American volunteers are engaged in fundraising efforts and it is well documented that volunteers are almost twice as likely to contribute as other donors (Corporation for National and Community Service, 2014). Whether to use volunteer or paid callers can be driven by budget, organizational culture, and availability of ample committed volunteers. However, it can also be driven by an organization's primary objectives. There are clear advantages and disadvantages to both approaches. Even in well-staffed organizations that choose to use paid callers, it is wise to think creatively about how volunteers can be engaged in solicitation and stewardship.

Volunteer calling provides an opportunity to engage a large number of supporters in an activity that directly benefits the organization. These volunteers see the direct impact of their efforts, learn about the organization's mission, and take greater ownership in the organization. While not every volunteer is interested in making direct solicitations, there are ample clerical duties associated with a phone campaign that engage volunteers. A volunteer phone campaign not only provides a means to raise needed funds but also presents an opportunity to engage and energize volunteers.

On the other hand, volunteer callers are not necessarily well suited for organizations that count on their phone campaign to maximize contacts made and dollars raised. Organizations with large donor bases, complex segmentation needs, and an extended calling schedule will likely turn to paid callers to meet these needs. With paid callers, staff can be more selective in the screening and hiring process. More extensive training and higher levels of accountability can be implemented as well. Finally, paid callers that underperform can be terminated. These factors maximize the efficiency and effectiveness of a phone program.

Call Automation

Automation presents an opportunity to increase program efficiency in large calling programs. There are a variety of automated systems with a wide array of functionality and price tags. Good systems properly implemented drive efficiency by automatically dialing the phone, adjusting solicitation levels to match prospect giving history, presenting detailed prospect information, scheduling call backs as needed, securely processing credit card gifts, and much more. Automated systems also increase efficiency when customizable reports can be generated nightly and on demand. The selection of an automated system requires research and discussion with peers who have experience with such systems. Many systems are good but not necessarily good for your organization. Take the time to find the best fit for your particular needs.

Use of a Consultant

Using a consultant to manage part or the entire phone program is a significant decision and one that should be made in the context of an organization's overall development philosophy. For some organizations, a consultant can greatly increase the efficiency of an existing phone program or provide an easy way to begin a new one. It can also free up the time of current in-house staff to concentrate on other aspects of the development program. Other organizations have extensive in-house phone campaign experience and can effectively manage their program, tightly control their message, and take advantage of opportunities to leverage volunteer involvement. Other organizations choose a blended approach by retaining an in-house phone campaign function to address certain segments and outsourcing other segments to a consultant. In the end, the right decision is dependent upon the organization's circumstances, experience, and comfort level.

In choosing a consultant, it is important to conduct extensive research. The number of companies, and the breadth of services these companies offer, has greatly expanded. This growth has created a buyer's market and has also added considerable complexity to the process of finding a company that is both reputable and a suitable fit for a given program's needs. It is critical to interview a number of companies and interview their current and past clients.

Selection is only the first step. One needs to work with the consultant before, during, and after the campaign to devise segmentation strategies, provide information for script development and caller training, ensure proper and consistent messaging, track campaign progress, handle prospect comments and questions, and other issues related to the campaign. A successful consultant/client relationship depends on a shared understanding of expectations and regular communication between both parties.

Strategy and Segmentation

Strategy and segmentation are driven by many factors, not including the size of the prospect base and the desired number of contacts to be made within that prospect base. For some institutions, segmentation may be as simple as calling a segment of former donors during the annual calendar year campaign. More complex institutions may have more than 1,000 individual segments called throughout the course of a 12 month, continuous campaign.

A regular review of strategy and segmentation can yield significant results. Year to year performance depends on revision to past successful segmentation plans to adapt to changing characteristics of an organization's constituents. Analysis of segment performance guides changes and provides strong indicators of opportunities to expand calling, add new segments, and increase the initial solicitation amounts or, where performance results dictate the need to revise messaging, call at a different time of year, reduce initial solicitation amounts, or cease calling all together. Constant monitoring of segment results allows small adjustments to maximize performance during a campaign and make fundamental adjustments to future campaign strategy based upon a greater volume of past performance data.

Anatomy of the Call

Fundamental to any successful phone campaign is the call itself. While every call is a dynamic interaction between caller and prospect, well-trained callers ensure that each call contains the following key elements.

Training

Time spent training callers, whether volunteer or paid, is time well spent. Training may be an hour or several, but should include plenty of time for callers to practice building rapport, negotiating a gift, and handling objections through role play.

Pre-call Planning

This portion of the call should not be lengthy, but it is critical to a successful solicitation. A pre-call review of the prospect's name, place of residence, and giving history is critical to preparing the caller.

Introduction

The first seconds of the call are critical to setting the stage for a successful call and by building a positive relationship between the caller and the prospect. Confidence, professionalism, and enthusiasm are essential to a strong introduction. The introduction includes who the caller is and why he or she is calling. Also before the solicitation is made, the caller can ask for important demographic information – mailing address, e-mail address, cell phone or landline number confirmation, employer and business information. This early stage of the call is also critical to building a positive rapport between the caller and the prospect and establishing an understanding with the prospect that this is not a telemarketing call but rather a contact on behalf of an institution seeking support to advance a worthy cause.

The Case for Support

A caller has limited time to complete all elements of the call, so the case for support must be concise, convincing, and relevant to the prospect. The caller must articulate the organization's mission, why that mission matters, and the impact a gift makes in advancing that mission. Advanced training helps ensure callers are prepared to convey the case of support confidently and convincingly. Both volunteers and paid telemarketing professionals must understand and believe in the worthiness of the organization's mission to present powerfully this phase of the call.

The Solicitation

There are many benefits to a call that are not related to directly asking for support, but solicitation is the central reason for making the call. As in other phases, the caller must be confident, professional, and enthusiastic. Callers should be deliberate in the tone of their voice and the phrasing used when making the solicitation and be assumptive to the extent appropriate. For example, there is a significant difference between a solicitation phrased as, "Would you have any interest in giving $500?" and "It would be great if you could commit to a gift of $500 tonight! You can put your gift to work immediately by using your credit card." Often, the difference between a pledge and a no pledge is word choice and enthusiasm.

It is also critical that callers follow the organization's prescribed solicitation structure. The most common response to any solicitation is "no." Therefore, a sound strategy uses multiple solicitations throughout the call. Callers must be prepared for initial rejection and the objections prospects will present. An important aspect of this phase of the call is to be appropriately, and tactfully, persistent in overcoming these objections by listening and demonstrating genuine concern for the prospect's objection and then to present reasons for giving that will resonate with him or her based on the feedback provided. Each organization must determine the level of persistence with which it is comfortable, but it is not uncommon to include three or four separate solicitations in a single call. This is consistent with Hank Rosso's notion of accepting no only after four or five attempts to deal with objections.

Also, it is best to determine a specific amount for each solicitation. For prospects with prior giving history to the organization, it is common to determine the solicitation amount based on some multiple of the last gift amount. For example, if the prospect's last gift was $50 then the first suggested pledge amount may be ten times that amount, or $500. Starting with a suggested pledge amount that is significantly higher than the previous gift amount provides the prospect the opportunity to contemplate a gift amount greater than what they might have considered previously. Additionally, in the event that the initial suggested gift amount is higher than the prospect is interested in supporting, it provides significant opportunities to continue the conversation, provide other compelling reasons to give, and discuss subsequently lower gift levels that may still be an increase over the prior gift amount. For prospects with no giving history or other significant data point upon which to base an ask amount, you can create a static structure $500 for the first solicitation, $250 for the second ask, $100 for the third ask, and $50 for the fourth ask.

Another approach to determining gift amounts is the use of social information. Research from experimental psychology suggests that social information, that is, knowing what others have given, helps individuals set their own expectations for giving and understanding of what is an appropriate amount (Shang and Croson, 2009). In particular, "upward social information" may even increase giving. In one study, when donors were presented with the first gift amount in the 90th percentile of gifts (i.e., significantly higher than the average gift), giving went up by 12 percent for new donors and these new donors were twice as likely to give again the next year than other new donors who had not been presented the social information (Shang and Croson, 2009). While the upward social information did not impact renewing donors, who likely already have a sense of expectations, consider what a 12 percent increase in giving would equal for your organization!

The Close

The end of the call is a critical time, regardless of whether the prospect has made a pledge or not. It provides your organization's last impression on the prospect. If a pledge has been made, this is an important opportunity to secure it immediately though a credit card, capture matching gift information related to the prospect's corporate employer, confirm demographic information, and, most importantly, to thank the prospect. If a pledge has not been made, it is important to end the call on a positive note and encourage the prospect to consider support at some time in the future. Under all circumstances, the close serves as the last opportunity to ensure that the relationship between the prospect and the organization is positive.

Campaign Management

Performance measures and data points can be tracked throughout the course of a phone campaign. Some call center managers focus on creating new and more complicated statistics and view analysis as a rewarding challenge to the position. Others focus narrowly on one or two statistics – perhaps total dollars pledged and pledge rate. Regardless of the approach, it is important to define priority outcomes and then focus on the statistics that help achieve those outcomes.

Total dollars and donors often serve as the bottom line outcome for a phone campaign. However, more specific measures can be critical to achieving larger objectives. The following are metrics to help manage campaigns.

Record Count

The most fundamental element of phone program success is the record count, so maximizing the number of records with accurate phone numbers on file should be a constant emphasis. Success in this area depends on regular record updates and data cleaning. Much of this work can be done internally through proper record keeping using regular contact with constituents. Vendors also provide various data management services.

In addition to the integrity of the data in your database, it is also important that the record count is scrutinized to check the accuracy of the data selection used to populate your call segments. This should be well thought out when developing the data selections, but should also be checked in terms of record counts produced from those data selections. Comparing record counts across a number of prior years will serve as a useful way to spot check the accuracy of the record counts you have selected for each calling segment.

Completion Percentage (Total Completes/Total Records)   Completion percentage measures how deeply you are penetrating the prospect base. It is reasonable to expect that you can complete 75–80 percent of any given segment, and it is critical that you do so in order to maximize the depth of solicitations made to the donor base. The more complete you call each segment, the more solicitations you can make and thus the more money that can be raised.

Pledge Rate (Total Pledges/Total Contacts)   This measurement tends to dominate the focus of many phone program managers. Determined by calculating the total number of contacts (all pledges plus all refusals) and dividing by the total number of pledges, the pledge rate will drive your ability to grow the number of donors to and total dollars raised for the organization.

Average Pledge (Total Dollars Pledged/Total Pledges)   The average pledge is another core measurement for most programs. The average pledge provides a financial measure and is also a key indicator of callers' skills in negotiating a pledge that maximizes gift support. A declining average pledge can mean that callers are skipping solicitation levels or that the solicitation ladder is not structured properly. A matching gift component incorporated into each call can greatly increase your average pledge as well as total dollars raised, so many programs will track the matching gift rate separately.

Fulfillment Percentage (Total Dollars Fulfilled/Total Dollars Pledged)   Most phone programs report pledges, but it is essential to focus on the fulfillment of those pledges. The fulfillment percentage should be tracked regularly in terms of both total dollars and number of pledges. A key related statistic is the percentage of pledges fulfilled during the call with a credit or debit card. Credit card payments should be emphasized in the close of any pledge. Successful programs should expect 30 percent or more of phone pledges fulfilled through credit cards. Credit card pledges are so critical that many programs monitor this statistic separately.

A low or declining pledge fulfillment percentage should prompt an analysis of a pledge reminder and the stewardship process and prompt discussions related to call quality and solicitation amounts. Because fulfillment elements are "behind the scenes," constant monitoring of this statistic is critical to success.

Completes/Contacts per Hour (Total Completes or Contacts/Total Calling Hours)   The number of completions and contacts made in an hour is an important efficiency metric and should apply to individual caller performance, specific segments, and for the program as a whole. Completions made per hour is critical to help determine the productivity of the staff and program, and also to aid in performance projections.

Dollars per Completion (Total Dollars/Total Completions)   Dollars per completion is the most important statistic for a program. It provides an instant assessment of the three most significant elements of your program: donors (pledge rate), dollars (average pledge), and data quality (contact percentage). This statistic can be measured for an overall program, but is important at the segment level as well. For organizations with many segmentation possibilities but a finite budget, dollars per contact is an important way to determine which segments will return the best direct results. This statistic provides an instant snapshot of the health of the program and should be monitored constantly.

Stewardship

As defined in Chapter 31, stewardship is both the managerial and ethical process by which donors' funds are acknowledged and used by the recipient organization. Indeed, stewardship should be part of all aspects of the fundraising process and should be a goal of any phone campaign. Even the most basic phone campaign involves significant resources and infrastructure, and should be utilized to maximize donor stewardship activities.

However, opportunities to elevate stewardship efforts through the phone program may not be obvious. Asking callers to sign personally thank you cards between calls and incorporating thank you segments into your call schedule are two common ways to add personalized stewardship.

Donors' preference for tangible recognition – such as plaques and other tchotchkes – is declining while the desire for more meaningful recognition remains (Burke, 2014). Among the most valued recognition donors ask for is a personal thank you phone call. A short-term, telephone stewardship campaign is an excellent opportunity to involve the highest-level volunteers: the organization's board members. In one study of donors, 90 percent of respondents indicated they would give again if they received a thank you by phone from a board member. Practicing good stewardship is inherently worthwhile, but is also an easy way to reduce donor attrition. In the same study, two-thirds of respondents said they would likely give more if they received such a thank you phone call (Burke, 2003).

Leveraging the Full Capacity of a Phone Program

With increasing demands on annual giving programs, it is important to look beyond the traditional role of a phone solicitation program. In addition to the above, consider the full extent to which a phone program can improve the organization's fundraising efforts. Successful organizations are constantly trying and testing new ideas (Berkshire, 2012). Consider the following:

> *Second solicitation program.* Donors who have made a gift earlier in the year can be solicited again later in the year. With a deliberate approach and continuous stewardship, a healthy second solicitation program can yield pledge rates of 60 percent or higher with average gifts that are comparable or even higher than found in the initial solicitation.
>
> *Leadership annual giving calls.* While phone programs are often used to secure smaller gifts, donors with greater capacity to give can be approached through a phone solicitation for larger gifts. This type of program requires special caller selection and training.
>
> *Wealth screening and predictive modeling.* Much data analysis can be completed in-house with varying levels of sophistication. However, organizations able to invest resources into professional wealth screening and predictive modeling can incorporate these into the phone program. This information will add precision to segmentation strategy, suggested solicitation amounts, and other elements of the phone campaign.
>
> *Gift planning discovery calls.* Organizations that have an existing gift planning operation can consider adding a phone component to aid their discovery efforts. Several vendors offer this service, but some organizations are adding this element to their in-house phone campaign as well. Because gift planning is a particularly complicated element for even the most sophisticated organization, adding this element to the phone program requires deliberate planning.

Conclusion

A well-planned phone solicitation program can serve as the foundation of the annual giving efforts and add great value to the total development program. Phone solicitation continues to evolve in the midst of an ever changing philanthropic and legal landscape. This constant state of evolution presents challenges but also a great opportunity to continue advancing support for your organization. Successful programs are vigilant in monitoring the various elements of the program and persistent in seeking outside input from peers and other professionals. By using these approaches, the program will continue to be a vital element in helping individuals make the world a better place through support of the organization.

Discussion Questions

1) How is telephone fundraising integrated into your organization's comprehensive development program? Where are opportunities to strengthen efforts?

2) What are the advantages and disadvantages of a telephone fundraising campaign?

3) In what ways can telephone fundraising support an organization's annual fund and stewardship efforts?

4) What considerations should be made before outsourcing an organization's telephone fundraising campaign?

CHAPTER TWENTY-NINE

DIGITAL FUNDRAISING

By Jeff Stanger

After completing this chapter, you will be able to:

1. Explain how "permission" is an asset that impacts fundraising online and offline.
2. Set clear, measurable goals for digital fundraising.
3. Describe how websites, social media, e-mail, and mobile fundraising are dependent upon each other and require an integrated approach.
4. Argue that the best practices in fundraising are true regardless of the social platform.
5. Respond appropriately to negative comments on social platforms.

In the last 15 years, social media has caused a transformation to our culture, our politics, and our fundraising. We have seen companies like Facebook go from a campus student directory to a publicly traded company valued at over $1 billion. Twitter has changed the way news is broken and the press release has given way to the 140-character tweet. YouTube reports that its users upload 300 hours of video every minute. Meanwhile, threaded through all the social platforms is an e-commerce and digital advertising strategy to capture your dollars, your attention, or your vote. In the 2012 presidential election, the Obama campaign reported raising $690 million online (Scherer, 2012). Last year, American nonprofits raised $2 billion dollars online (MacLaughlin, 2015).

Throughout the history of social media, the one constant has been change. When the last edition of this book was written, MySpace was a large player in the social media world. Since then, it has become more of a punch line. Pinterest, Snapchat, and Instagram were not even on the radar when we last published. Now, they have their own unique niches for social content. In light of the constant change, this chapter offers what we believe to be fundamental truths that transcend platforms. It is critically important to understand digital fundraising and social media in their proper context and to apply sound fundraising principles when using these tools.

As we mentioned earlier, American nonprofits raised $2 billion dollars online last year. It is important to note that the Blackbaud 2014 study cited above indicates that online giving was up 8.9 percent while overall giving increased by only 2.1 percent. This has implications as we see giving trends and preferences starting to shift. As more and more Americans become comfortable with doing business and donating online, nonprofits need to employ best practices to ensure they are providing a safe, secure, and mobile friendly way for donors to carry out their philanthropic goals online.

Permission

Any discussion about social media, e-mail marketing, or digital fundraising must begin with the concept of permission. Permission is the single most important asset we have in fundraising. In many ways, permission is the first gift a donor gives us.

Donations of time, talent, or treasure do not occur until we have permission to have conversations and share our case for support. This is true both online and offline. When someone follows us on Facebook, we have permission to show up in his or her newsfeed. When someone gives us his or her physical mail address, we have permission to send mail appeals.

So if the gift of permission makes a fan or follower to some extent a donor, how do we treat him or her? How do we cultivate him or her? How do we turn the gift of permission into a gift of cash? Consider approaching a possible donor in the same way we would a major gift donor. It is generally accepted in the field that the typical major gift takes 6–18 months to cultivate. To do so takes a long commitment of time on the part of your major gift officer. It not only takes a long amount of time, but it takes consistent communications.

It is the same with social media and digital strategy. Your organization must commit to a long-term strategy of consistent communications. There cannot be long gaps when you do not post to your social channels. You must serve up a menu of relevant, informing, and inspiring content to your social followers. There must also be a strategy behind the content you share and a consistency or integration throughout all the social platforms you use and your offline efforts as well.

Three Goals

So what should our online strategy be? This question has been a challenge for nonprofits of all sizes. Most of the conventional wisdom surrounding social media is that it is ineffective for actual fundraising. Many experts believe it to be mostly comprised of platforms that friends raise rather than fundraise. As such, your goals should be tied up in things like "engagement" and "reach."

How do we measure those things? Sure, Facebook can tell us how many people were reached by the event photo you shared yesterday, but what does that mean? How do you measure the actions that are relevant to your organization's bottom line by measuring Reach?

The answer is: you don't. You can't. The truth is, I cannot walk into my CEO or Development Director's office and tell him or her anything meaningful about the "Reach" of that photo. That is why a completely different measuring paradigm is recommended. Design your messaging and measuring around three very specific, very measurable goals: e-mail signups, volunteers, and monthly givers.

Why these three? First, all of them are measurable. All of them are very clear and specific. All of them have, at their heart, outcomes that directly impact the bottom line of an organization, and all of them are very easy to explain to your boss, your board, and your constituents.

First, let us look at e-mail. Despite claims to the contrary, e-mail is not dead. Consider these statistics:

- 95 percent of consumers use e-mail and 91 percent check it once a day. (That is still more than Facebook.) (Lacy, 2013)
- There are 3.25 times more e-mail accounts than social media accounts. (Radicati, 2013)
- Last year, marketers reported e-mail delivered more new customers than Facebook and Twitter. (Aufreiter, Boudet, and Weng, 2014)
- 42 percent of heavy social media users still check their e-mail a minimum of 4 times per day. (Connolly, 2011)
- 75 percent of social media users say that e-mail is the best way for brands to communicate with them. (TowerData, 2013)

Integrating e-mail with your social media is still the best way to maximize your brand online. E-mail is a higher level of permission than a follower or fan because

TABLE 29.1. VALUE OF VOLUNTEERS RECRUITED BY SOCIAL MEDIA.

Volunteers Recruited via Social Media in 2014	Total Volunteer Hours They Performed	Total Volunteer Value
75	1500	$34,605

I can build a profile of you and send you much more targeted communications than I could just posting to Facebook and Twitter. So the idea here is to regularly post calls-to-action via your social channels (Facebook, Twitter, etc.) to sign up for your e-mail list.

Next, let us look at volunteers. According to the Corporation for National and Community Service, the average value of a volunteer hour is $23.07. By tracking the volunteers you recruit via social media and tracking their volunteer hours, you can create a simple and easy to understand value of those social media efforts, such as the example shown in Table 29.1.

It is not just volunteer hours that have value. We know that eight out of ten people who volunteer give to charity – twice the rate of people who do not volunteer (Corporation for National and Community Service, 2014). By tracking the donations made by volunteers you recruit via social media, your organization can further build a clear picture of the true return on investment (ROI) for your social media efforts. Again, we do this by a strategy of regular, intentional calls-to-action to encourage people to volunteer.

Finally, we look at monthly giving. Monthly giving programs are an excellent way to even out your annual giving. They also provide a less expensive way to fundraise since cultivating the relationship with an existing donor is less costly than recruiting a new donor. However, there are more compelling reasons to take a fresh look at monthly givers. First, we know that donor renewal rates can be pretty dismal. Last year, the average was around 75 percent attrition for American nonprofits, yet we know from research that monthly givers renew at around 60 percent or better (Blackbaud, 2014).

Better yet, monthly givers tend to give to an additional two–three appeals per year. They have a lifetime value that is twice that of once a year givers. Looking at the long term, monthly givers are the most likely in your donor base to give both a major gift and/or a planned gift. With that in mind, the cultivation of monthly givers is critical, not just for annual fund stability but also for future giving. Once again, the strategy we recommend is to consistently post calls-to-action to your social media and e-mail subscribers to join your monthly giving program. Like the other two goals, this is easy to measure and easy to report.

In summary, these three goals give you an easy to understand framework and content strategy. They are easy to report and easy to track. They will not completely replace all your messaging. You will still report the events, milestones, and other things you post now to social media. However, there will be an intentional mix of messages containing calls-to-action for these three goals. Committing to these for the long term will help you succeed regardless of the platform because they can be adapted to whichever social channel you feel reaches the audience you want to attract.

Web Sites

It is important to note that all the shininess of the newest social platform cannot replace the significance of your web page. This is still the hub that you want fans and followers to visit for more information and to take action.

Your homepage is the front lobby of your organization's presence on the web. It must be welcoming, easy to use, and provide visitors with the information they seek – and fast. You have only a few seconds to engage them before they click on something else. It helps to look at what makes a good landing page and how to avoid common mistakes. As a fundraising professional, this will help you evaluate your organization's website for maximum effectiveness and give you the confidence to ask the right questions of your web design vendor.

Another compelling reason it is so important to have a well-designed and easy to use homepage is how it influences giving offline. A survey of donor behavior revealed that 49 percent of midlevel and major donors will visit a nonprofit's website before making a giving decision. Of those major donors, 18 percent will visit the website to make a second gift (The Wired Wealthy, 2008). Are you making it easy for them to do so?

The Charitable Giving Report mentioned earlier reported that American non-profits received between 6.5 and 18 percent of their donations online in 2012 (depending on the sector). That number has been steadily increasing each year and experts predict that this number will top 50 percent by the year 2020. As online donations increase, we expect some types of giving to decline and others become more intertwined with your online message. In 2012, online giving grew an average of 10.7 percent across the sector.

However, it is important to remember what web sites can and cannot do. When designed well, a nonprofit web site is uniquely efficient for attracting new donors and creating impulse giving opportunities. They are not as effective at facilitating donor relationships for the long term. However, you can use social networking tools, e-mail newsletters, and RSS subscriptions to grow donor loyalty.

Keeping in mind that your website at its most basic function is a tool to attract and retain donors, it is imperative that your site speaks clearly and concisely to visitors. It must be easy to navigate and easy to understand. It is also important that you understand your donor base. There is *no* cookie cutter approach to nonprofit website design. Some organizations need to convey large amounts of information. A magazine format site might better serve them. Others may be volunteer driven and require social networking tools or a higher degree of interactivity.

Blogging

Where do blogs fit into the social media landscape? Think of the blog as your content hub. Blog posts of 300 to 500 words can be easily be repurposed in ways that save you time. This is particularly important if you are wearing multiple hats and are pressed for time. Here is an example of how a blog can save you time.

Imagine you have created a blog post and have included an image. You can pull two quotes from the post and schedule them on Twitter. The image and the headline of the article can be shared on Facebook (with the link back of course) and the image and link can be shared on Pinterest and Instagram. Finally, the post can be shared in the "News" section of your web site. You may not be using all of these platforms, and that's okay. The point is that one blog post was leveraged into seven different messages online. Add the image and a blurb from the post to your next newsletter and that is eight different messages from one post!

Blogging Tips

Blogs are written in a conversational style. The language is easily digestible with paragraphs and sentences that are short. The typical web user has a short attention span. Therefore, long complex sentences will not hold the reader. You have to be concise and conversational. One of the big mistakes nonprofits make is using inside jargon. Avoid this at all costs. Assume your reader knows very little about your organization.

Be a unique character. Encourage the person writing your blog to let the personality of the organization shine through. More importantly, look for who will benefit most from the content you have to share and write to that person. Finally, make sure you are always relating back to your mission and case statement.

Another key way to grow your blog's readership is to make it search engine friendly. The easiest way to do this is to think of *five keywords* that are easily associated with your organization. For example, if you are running a shelter, you might use the following keywords: homeless, shelter, hunger, your city, and your organization's name. Have the person writing your blog post these key words near his or her computer. When they go to write a post, they should aim to use 2–3 of these words each time. Soon, when people search in your area for these terms, your organization will be closer to the top results.

Basics Tips for Blogging

- ☑ Write in a conversational style.
- ☑ Be brief while including relevant content.
- ☑ Encourage comments and discussion.
- ☑ Link to other blogs, sources, articles.
- ☑ Include pictures.
- ☑ Set a blogging policy for your organization with clear boundaries and objectives.

Along with the daily short posts you will be doing, you should also add the occasional "pillar post" to the mix. Pillar Posts are longer posts that contain timeless, original, and unique information. They are centered on one particular topic and offer deeper insight or expertise on that subject. Pillar Posts attract links from other bloggers, are bookmarked more frequently, and are forwarded to more people than regular posts.

E-mail

We spoke about e-mail earlier in the three goals section. Now we want to share more about how to use e-mail effectively. With the rise of social media, it is often easy to forget the importance of e-mail to communicate with volunteers and donors as well as being a tool to raise money. Recently, a study of donor behavior revealed some surprising insights into the relationship between e-mail, direct mail, social media, and giving.

The Convio Online Benchmark Study

In March 2012, Convio surveyed a wide cross-section of nonprofits in order to learn more about trends in giving and how they relate to e-mail (Bhagat, McCarthy, and Snyder, 2012). Here are some of the key findings:

1. Smaller organizations grew the fastest in 2011. Of those surveyed with less than 10,000 e-mail addresses, giving grew online by 26 percent and the number of gifts by 32 percent.
2. The median donation size grew to $93.67.
3. Sustainer giving programs grew by 38 percent in 2011.
4. Nonprofit e-mail files grew by 17 percent in 2011.
5. Website traffic grew by 11 percent in 2011, but registration rates dropped to 1.9 percent from 2.1 percent the previous year.

At this point, we want to dive into a problem that we see in many organizations. They may have a nice web site and may be doing well on Facebook, but their e-mail files are stagnant. When taking a closer look, it is often the case that organizations are not placing a prominent sign-up button on their site, or not regularly reminding fans/followers to sign up. This is a wasted opportunity. It is important to remember that deeper conversations and more specific solicitations come from the e-mails we send. Keep registration (a permission asset) a high priority.

What Did the Convio Study Reveal about Younger Donors?

1. Members of Generation Y tend to be less loyal to an organization.
2. They do have a strong desire to help others and are more likely to raise awareness among their friends and social networks about causes they support.
3. Of those respondents under 30, 37 percent had forwarded a message about a charity (e-mail, Facebook post, or Tweet) to a friend in the past month.
4. Direct mail can still have an impact: 43 percent of Generation X and 26 percent of Generation Y members gave via direct mail.
5. By comparison, 35 percent of Generation X had given via a charity web site and 29 percent of Generation Y members gave online.
6. One of the most surprising stats came across all age groups surveyed: 52 percent of all donors had given at a supermarket or retail store. That might explain the continued success of The Salvation Army's Red Kettle program or the Girl Scouts Cookie sales.

Some of the advantages to e-mail include reaching more people for less money than you could offline. A report by the Direct Marketers Association states that e-mail returned $48 for every $1 invested. It does require more attention to permission than you might do offline. The idea of the prospecting mailing does not apply online – that is called Spam and it can have dire consequences for your organization.

In a down economy, e-mail is particularly effective in helping you reduce costs and gather information. If your ratio of physical mail addresses to e-mail addresses is high, you may be able to reduce costs by replacing a physical appeal with an online appeal. You can also use e-mail to keep top donors informed or reward brand loyalty with freebies or coupons.

To have a successful e-mail campaign, you have to have e-mail addresses. You will need to build your e-mail database and this takes time and focused effort. Start by making it very easy for visitors to your web site to give you their e-mail addresses. Make the sign-up button easy to find and use language that adds a sense of community to the experience. Invite them to join the cause.

You will also want to consider multiple ways for people to join your e-mail list. Add it to your e-mail signature. Include it on written forms your volunteers fill out. Offer the opportunity at events. Another good idea is to set up polls or contests online where visitors give their e-mails. Finally, always include a "Forward to a Friend" link in your e-mails so your donors can spread the word.

Additional Tips for Your E-mail Campaign

1. Make it mobile friendly. Make it mobile friendly. Then make it mobile friendly. Okay, maybe I got carried away, but e-mail marketers report between 53 and 66 percent of all e-mails were opened on mobile devices last year (smart phones and tablets). That rate keeps going up so make sure you are using an e-mail delivery platform that makes reading via mobile an enjoyable experience.

2. Keep it readable and simple. Do not include too many pictures or graphics and use quality fonts.

3. If you have a long story to tell, consider sending only an excerpt and linking to the full story on your web site. You can also provide a link to a hosted version of the e-mail as well.

4. Use a catchy subject line. The subject line is just like the headline of a newspaper article. If it does not grab you, you will not read the story. According to the Convince and Convert study via Salesforce.com, 33 percent of people open e-mails based on the headline alone! Your subject line matters!!!

5. Send e-mails only to people who have given you permission! It is also a good idea to remind them how you got their information and why they are receiving the message.

6. Encourage list members to add you to their e-mail address list. This will help you avoid their bulk e-mail folder and can increase the likelihood that images open properly.

7. Use the tools of your particular e-mail provider or software to personalize the message as much as possible.

8. Always include an opt-out link and a valid physical address.
9. Commit to replying to e-mails! This sounds obvious, but you really need to think through who in your organization will answer responses. Make sure the reply-to address is valid and do not use autoresponders.
10. Test, Measure, Rinse, Repeat! Share your results with your team and strategize on how to improve.
11. Send a test e-mail to your team first. This can help you avoid many headaches.
12. Be consistent. This works only if you send consistent e-mails to people who have given you permission.
13. Handle spam complaints and unsubscribe requests immediately. This will keep you from becoming blacklisted.
14. Avoid sending e-mails on Mondays and Friday afternoons. Most e-mails are deleted on Monday mornings.
15. Create opportunities to connect with your online supporters in the real world! Invite them to volunteer, take a tour, or come to a special event. This is where the real payoff to online marketing and fundraising occurs.
16. Excess punctuation and Caps Lock can send you to the junk folder.
17. Do not send attachments.

The E-mail Welcome Series

Another great way to improve donor retention is to create a carefully planned donor welcome series of e-mails to deploy after a first online gift is made. When a new donor makes a gift, we recommend the following plan:

1. An immediate confirmation of the gift with a thank you.
2. About a week later, send a welcome e-mail that further thanks them, reminds them of the mission, and say how their gift will be used.
3. Continue the welcome series of e-mails with either 2–3 follow-ups spaced 2–3 weeks apart.
4. At the appropriate time (after a program is completed, a campaign has ended, etc.), send a "Look what you've done" e-mail. This lets the donor know that his or her gift is appreciated and has been stewarded well. Be as specific as you can about how much impact a gift of their particular amount may have meant.
5. Continue regular communications.

The importance of such reinforcement cannot be overstated. American non-profits do a dismal job of donor retention. Online and off, donor retention is hovering between 25 and 29 percent. In one study of donors who were asked why they had not made a second gift, 9 percent could not recall making the first gift (Sargeant, 2001a). Whose fault is that? Hint: it is not the donor's fault!

E-newsletters

Taking the e-mail communication one step further, you can create an e-newsletter. An e-newsletter can help you save money and keep donors and volunteers informed. Here are some tips for creating a quality e-newsletter:

1. Be consistent. If you say you are going to e-mail monthly, then stick to it.
2. Include links to your web site, longer versions of stories, and a call to action.
3. Use headers and footers that clearly brand your organization.
4. Include an unsubscribe option.
5. Keep the content concise, with short paragraphs and only 4–5 items.
6. Develop a conversational voice for the newsletter.
7. Test the e-mail before sending to your entire list.
8. Segment your list for better results (e.g., by age, gender, cause, etc.).
9. Consider linking to group pages so the discussion can continue.
10. Do not include attachments.

Facebook

To be effective on Facebook or any other form of social media, you have to remember the word "social." This is not just about us. It is about the audience and what they want. In fact, maybe we should not even be using the word "audience" any more. Katya Andresen, author of *Robin Hood Marketing* (2006), has taken the phrase "The People Formerly Known as the Audience," originally coined by NYU's Jay Rosen, and stated clearly how it relates to social media.

The people formerly known as the audience:

1. Don't want to listen. They want to speak.
2. Don't want to passively receive information. They want to interact.
3. Don't want to consume content. They want to create it.

Her assessment is spot on. Organizations that see Facebook as a place to just throw up another online brochure are not going to see their expectations match their results. We have to commit to engaging donors and letting them take part in our organization. Do we encourage our fans to post on our Facebook walls? Do we encourage them to upload photos and videos? Our fans want to interact, to speak, and to create.

Slacktivism　In recent years, fundraisers and industry pundits have used the terms "slacktivism" or "click through philanthropy" to describe a particular online behavior. Using Facebook for an example, imagine you have suggested I be a fan of a particular cause. I check it out and notice that five of my friends have become a fan of this page. Not wanting to be left out or look like I am not a concerned citizen, I become a fan.

However, my motivation was not linkage, ability, interest; it was that I did not want to look like the one person in my circle of friends who does not care about the particular cause. Because my motivation is not connected to the organization's mission, I am likely to ignore the messages that appear in my newsfeed from this organization. Worse yet, I might block the messages, but remain a fan. That way when people look at my interests, they still see I am a concerned citizen. That is slacktivism and it often accounts for some of the reasons that organizations do not feel their expectations for social media are meeting up with their actual results.

Pages and Groups   Facebook offers two ways you can interact with people beyond the individual page. Groups and Pages offer different ways to interact with your constituents. Groups are a great way to communicate with volunteers and manage discussions within your organization. Pages also allow for more customization and give you the option to measure traffic.

Once you have created a Page for your organization, you can run ads on Facebook. The advantage of advertising on Facebook is that you can focus your audience in ways that would be much more expensive to recreate in the physical world. Imagine being able to send a message to everyone in Indianapolis who is female, between the ages of 21 and 45, loves cats, and graduated from college. You would pay lots of money to get that mailing list (if it exists!). However, with Facebook ads, you can place ads on the profiles of just that audience. You can set a daily budget for your ads and pay via cost per click or cost per thousand impressions.

There are three types of ads to be aware of on Facebook. Engagement ads direct people to sites on Facebook, not external sites. Therefore, an engagement ad is used to get people to "Like" your page or to engage in a contest or promotion you are running on Facebook. Sponsored stories are ads that run in the newsfeed or alongside an action that someone has taken on your page. For example, if I interact with your page, a sponsored story might show up on my friend's newsfeed that I liked, commented, or took some action on your page. In a sense, I have become an endorser of your page to all my friends. Finally, you can place ads that go to an external site, like your home page or a landing page.

Facebook's Timeline   Timeline was officially rolled out for nonprofits on March 30, 2012 and over the past 3 years it continues to be tweaked, updated, or mutilated depending on your point of view. The most important thing to remember is Facebook is constantly changing it, so stay abreast of the recent changes. Many organizations have found the new format to be useful in telling their story while others have struggled to keep up with the changes. The following pages illustrate the key features in this update and give you some ideas on how to make it work best for you.

The Cover Image   Use an image that tells your story and draws people in to learn more. Capture volunteers or staff in action. The image takes up a lot of space, so it will be the focal point when people arrive at your page. It is okay to use a collage of images, but think about picking shots that show iconic images of your organization or somehow incorporate your logo. The size of the cover image is 851 × 315 pixels. The size of the profile (avatar) image is 180 × 180 pixels.

Pay-to-Play   Most of what you have just read over the past few pages has been rendered irrelevant by Facebook's increasing adherence to the Pay-to-Play model. What that means is Facebook has been turning the screws on businesses and organizations who have built large fan bases by forcing them to pay for ads in order to reach their audiences.

So why did we cover that info you may ask? First, it is important to know what the best practices are and have been for cultivating your audience while they are on your page. Second, there is a pushback from large companies who have spent years building their Facebook fans to have some of the Timeline restrictions turned back. As of this writing, it is hard to say who will win out, but we want you to be prepared for both scenarios and that is why we have kept the previous sections.

Going forward, the most important thing to note is that only a small percentage of your fans will see your posts. You must use ads to get the most important messages out to a higher percentage of your fans or to get those messages in front of new fans. In that way, Facebook has become just another advertising channel and less of a true social media site. However, it is still incredibly inexpensive to advertise on Facebook and so much easier than a printed ad to focus on the demographics you want.

How Do I Manage It All?

By now you might be thinking, how can I manage Twitter and Facebook with all of the other things that I have to do for my organization? Look for tools like Hootsuite, Tweetdeck, and Sprout Social. These applications allow you to manage multiple social media feeds. After you sign up, you can connect your Facebook profile, your organization's Facebook fan pages, all of your Twitter accounts (if you have more than one), and even your LinkedIn profile.

Best of all, you can schedule messages. For example, when you are coming up to a busy time of year you could schedule event announcements, calls for volunteers, and reminders weeks or months in advance. These platforms also allow you to manage lists and view statistical data on your various accounts. Most of these have free and paid options, so be sure to read the details to find the option that is best for you.

Crowdfunding

Crowdfunding has grown into a huge fundraising force for both nonprofit organizations and for-profit start-ups. There are a variety of platforms you can use like Crowdrise, GoFundMe, Kickstarter, etc. The basic idea is that small amounts of money are raised from a large group of people through digital means. They work best when they are focused on a specific goal, have a clear case for support, empower and inspire people to become brand ambassadors, and sometimes include rewards/perks for different giving levels. (At this time there is not enough good data on how this impacts nonprofit giving. It certainly has a positive impact on for-profit campaigns).

The most important thing to remember is that your fundraising principles should not go out of the window when you do a Crowdfunding Campaign. If you do not have a compelling case for support and a solid existing base of donors who are willing and excited to engage in peer-to-peer fundraising on your behalf, the campaign will not be effective. Thus, the keys to Crowdfunding success have less to do with digital strategy than with being an organization that is well organized and able to tell its story well.

Regulations

It is important to note that online fundraising has grown faster than many organizations' understanding of the laws governing it. Each state has different laws regarding solicitations and fundraising practices and since online fundraising goes beyond the borders of your state, you may need to be in compliance with the rules of other states. To make it easier to wade through these regulations, the National Association of State Charity Officials (NASCO) created the Charleston Principles, a document meant to serve as a guide and resource for charities to determine where and when they must register. It is highly recommended that you read through the document yourself. However, we have summarized some key points here.

First, even if you use a third party fundraising platform or portal to solicit and process payments, and that party is registered, you may still need to register in most states. This is because the organization that is soliciting the gift (you) must be registered and not the one collecting (your vendor). Second, most states require you to register if you are soliciting in their state, even if you are not based there. Finally, the Charleston Principles are guidelines and not legally definitive. What that means is, just because your organization falls within the guidelines, it does not mean that state regulations will define your organization in the same way. Therefore, it is best to consult an attorney or request information from any state from which you receive donations.

Responding to Critics

A great quote from Chris Anderson, author of *The Long Tail* (2008, p. 99), states, "For a generation of customers used to doing their buying research via search engine, a company's brand is not what the company says it is, but what Google says it is." Word of mouth and customer reviews are given more weight than traditional advertising. That is why you need to be aware of how your nonprofit is being perceived in the vast online world.

Some organizations have employees who have no other function than to monitor blogs, forums, and chat rooms for mentions of their brand. That is probably unrealistic for most nonprofits, but you can use tools to monitor your brand's image. One simple way is to use Google Alerts. Simply sign up (it is free), enter the keywords you want to monitor (your name, your cause, etc.), and Google will send regular e-mails with web page and blog mentions of your phrases.

A great way to dialogue with your supporters is through blog comments and forums. What do you do if the comments go negative? How do you stop a flame post (a comment written out of anger or meanness) from turning into a full-blown PR nightmare?

First, act quickly. If the comment warrants a response, give a sincere, transparent response. Is the person voicing a legitimate concern or pointing out a true weakness in your organization? If so, acknowledge it and share how you will overcome the problem. This is an opportunity to win significant goodwill if handled properly. You cannot please everyone, but you can treat people with respect and listen to their concerns.

Resist the urge to delete the comment if it is on your blog (unless it is vulgar or offensive to your audience). Instead, use the interaction with the individual to show your transparency and reinforce your commitment to mission.

Policies

Finally, it is important to have policies in place that define how your organization will engage online. Be sure to include things such as:

1. A definition of your goals and principles.
2. Social Media Roles. Who will be responsible for what content?
3. What you will and won't share online.
4. What will be your monitoring policy?
5. How will you respond to critics/comments?
6. Definitions of privacy, permissions, and copyright/attribution guidelines.
7. A definition of professional conduct expected by all who contribute.

Setting these policies in advance will help you avoid many of the pitfalls that unprepared organizations can face. If you want to see a sample policy, many organizations share them online, so Googling a sample policy is your best bet.

Conclusion

Social media and digital fundraising will continue to evolve. Since it changes so rapidly, it is important to hold firm to foundational principles while keeping abreast of the changing landscape. At its essence, it is simply another tool for sharing your case for support. Share your case clearly and compellingly and you can succeed. Set goals for your organization that are clear and concise (like our examples above) and you can raise money via social media.

Discussion Questions

1) How would you rate your organization's web site for usability? Is it easy to navigate? Can people find what you do and what you do with their donations quickly?
2) How does your organization measure return on investment for social media?
3) How would you deploy the three goals using your current social media platforms?
4) Does your organization promote monthly giving? Do you go beyond having it as an option on your donation form (a giving club for example)?
5) How do you respond to negative comments? Does your organization have a policy in place?

CHAPTER THIRTY

SPECIAL EVENTS

By Roberta L. Donahue and Caitlin Deranek Stewart

After completing this chapter, you will be able to:

1. Explain special events as a tool for donor cultivation.
2. Describe how special events are an effective way to engage board, management, staff, and other volunteers in a specific type of fundraising.
3. Argue the importance of special events as a reinforcement of the connection between the organization's mission and event participants.
4. Explain the significance of clearly defined goals and desired outcomes beyond dollars raised.
5. Describe what special events can bring to a diverse fundraising plan.

The Association of Fundraising Professionals' *Fundraising Dictionary* defines a special event as "a function designed to attract and involve people in an organization or cause." Where in this definition does it say anything about raising money? Yet, there is a perception that events are a quick and easy way to do just that. Experience has shown, however, that events are neither quick nor easy and research indicates that most events, when reviewed as stand-alone fundraising vehicles, are not cost effective when considering the staff and volunteer time invested and can even be loss leaders (Indiana University Center on Philanthropy Philanthropic Giving Index, December 2009). Why do people insist that events are essential to success?

As it turns out, events are neither a panacea nor a curse. They are merely one tool to assist donors as they build a meaningful relationship with a cause.

Three key aspects of a fundraiser's work are cultivation, which seeks to engage and grow the interest and involvement of a donor; solicitation, in which a donor is asked for a gift; and stewardship, in which the relationship with the donor is further strengthened through acknowledging the donor's gift and informing the donor of its impact. Special events are best viewed through these same lenses. Too often, events are seen only as solicitation tools and, frequently, as a passive solicitation or one with little or no mission-driven focus. Fundraisers can identify new measures of success if they use special events as a strategic means of building and strengthening donor relationships.

Cultivation Events

The goal of a cultivation event is "to engage and maintain the interest and involvement of a donor, prospective donor or volunteer with an organization's people, programs and plans" (Association of Fundraising Professionals, *AFP Fundraising Dictionary*, 2003, p. 35). It is interesting how well the definition of an event fits with this understanding of cultivation. Optimizing cultivation requires integrating strategies at all levels of the organization and customizing opportunities for different types of donor.

New prospective donors are on a fact-finding mission when they attend an event for a charity to which they do not currently contribute. Any number of factors may have drawn them to the event:

- An appealing activity such as golf
- A personal invitation from a friend
- An honored guest or speaker who may have interest for them
- A location that they desire to visit

While these reasons may have brought prospective donors to the event, the ultimate goal of the activity is to engage him or her in the cause being supported and ignite a passion to take action whether as a volunteer or donor. If a prospect had a wonderful time but cannot remember how the organization makes a difference, one might liken the event to an artistic commercial that sticks in the mind but the product just cannot be remembered. What portion of a cultivation event should engage the attendee in the work of the organization? The organization must carefully design the cultivation aspect to ensure that it is engaging and people-focused, and then complete prompt personal follow-up with each attendee. Cultivation events for former and current donors are focused on re-energizing the bond to the mission that exists or once existed. It is the opportunity for former and current donors to share with others why they got involved with the organization and what difference they can make through their involvement, including their charitable gifts. Organizations planning cultivation events must strive to reaffirm attendees with their important work. If the purpose is to strengthen the relationship to the mission, what was in place to encourage that process?

Here is how one nonprofit addressed that issue. As part of a dinner/auction, the organization had a small wooden box at each place setting. Prior to beginning dinner, the host asked each guest to open the box. Inside was a wish from one of the clients (in this case, the service recipient) of the nonprofit. Each guest was asked to read his or her client's request aloud. The prospective donors, who had come to the event only to hear the speaker, were introduced to eight lives that the nonprofit was working to change. Those current and former donors were reminded, in a very personal way, why they had become involved with the organization. During the dinner, much of the conversation centered on the dreams of the clients and personal experiences with the organization.

Solicitation Events

Solicitation events are those events that result in someone asking the guests for "a contribution of money, resources, a service or opinion" (Association of Fundraising Professionals, *AFP Fundraising Dictionary*, 2003, p. 111). Research has shown that the most effective way to raise money is face-to-face, so one might think that solicitation events can be very effective. Indeed, they certainly can be, if they are approached with the same general principles that apply to personal, face-to-face solicitation.

The event must include a social time for exchange of pleasantries. This time allows attendees to get comfortable and to focus on the organization and the mission. Because donors seek positive feedback from other donors or trusted friends, this time can be crucial and must be well orchestrated. The organization's leaders, especially volunteers, play an important role in meeting, greeting, and introducing guests to one another. This inclusion leads to the *involvement* phase of the event. Hosts share their own stories and invite others to do the same. Questions such as, "Did you hear about?" or "Have you heard about the difference the ABC program has made?" invite participation with the organization's mission. Hosts must be prepared to share information or know where the answers can be found at the event. Staff and hosts must be clearly identified.

It is during the *presentation* that an event really differs from the one-to-one solicitation. Visual aids, expert witnesses, and those who have benefitted from the organization accentuate the need for financial support and embody the results of a gift. However, there must be an opportunity for prospective donors to engage and ask questions. This must be orchestrated to enhance success. Hosts can be strategically placed to lead discussions and answer questions prompted by the presentation.

With these steps completed effectively, most attendees will be ready, and even expect, to be asked for a financial commitment. Many will be anxious to hear how they can be involved, having witnessed the difference they can make. The challenge is determining the right amount to solicit from each attendee. There is a variety of ways this can be resolved:

- Each prospective donor is given a customized pledge card with the prospective donor's name and a suggested amount.
- The host recommends a range of gifts that is appropriate for the group around the table. This works well when prospective donors are grouped by capacity.
- A suggested minimum gift may be presented by the featured speaker or another trusted representative of the organization.

In each case, the host also completes the response device and collects the responses of those with whom the host is working.

Another approach combines the best of events and face-to-face solicitations. The donors join others for the presentation and the excitement of the event, but a face-to-face solicitation occurs before the end of the event or follows the event in a very timely fashion. For this approach, donors must be carefully matched with a designated solicitor already identified based on mutual experience or relationship. This is a particularly good approach for capital or endowment campaigns.

Stewardship Events

Stewardship is "the process whereby an organization seeks to be worthy of continued philanthropic support including the acknowledgment of gifts, donor recognition, honoring of donor intent, prudent investment of gifts, and the effective and efficient use of funds to further the mission of the organization" (Association of Fundraising Professionals, *AFP Fundraising Dictionary*, 2003, p. 113). In other words, stewardship events are an opportunity to demonstrate to donors the prudent and impactful use of their financial contributions.

Stewardship events are about the donor, not about the organization. According to Penelope Burke's *Donor Focused Fundraising* (2003), donors report the most attractive things about donor recognition events:

- Learning more about the charity's work (28 percent).
- Seeing others who support the same cause (20 percent).
- Socializing and networking with other guests (19 percent).

That donors want to learn more about the good work the organization is doing should be no surprise. Donors may be viewed as investors or stakeholders, eager to learn how their contributions or investments make a difference. They want to understand the outcome of the nonprofit's work. They want to build on the personal connection that has developed. Attendees will share stories, learn new aspects of programs and hear testimonials that are part of casual conversation. Donors find it reassuring to be in the company of peers who are also committed to a cause. Just being at an event with others interested in the mission builds community.

Consider the excitement and feeling of community created by alumni events and homecoming activities for universities or watch the excitement in the eyes of a donor who meets the student his or her scholarship helped. Stewardship events are critical to building and growing the donor's belief in the mission.

Engagement of Staff

What is the effect of events on the staff? Are they helping to build a community within the nonprofit's staff? In any organization, depending on the approach, special events can be seen as either a rallying point or an unwelcome distraction that diverts energy and resources away from the mission.

Seven key elements contribute to a successful event experience for donors or prospective donors (The Fund Raising School, 2009):

- Clear purpose for the event
- Recognized organizational need
- Invitation to participate from others
- Unique opportunities
- Connection
- Tradition
- Value

What if we apply those same elements to the internal event participants (board, management, staff, and volunteers)?

Clear Event Purpose

Integrated events clearly define what is to be accomplished for all levels of the fundraising team. Team members know the expected outcomes and recognize that this is the logical way to accomplish the goal of the event.

Recognized Organizational Need

What does the organization need from the event? Internally, there may appear to be an easy answer to this question: "money." However, that may not be the real answer. As stated earlier, events do not necessarily generate substantial money. The need may have to do with something other than solicitation – it may instead be cultivation or stewardship. Based on this realization, with all the members of the leadership team in agreement, special events can be woven into the entire fabric of a donor-focused fundraising plan. Fundraisers can plan their strategies for their donors around the internal need.

Invitation to Participate from Others

Rather than taking for granted that all hands are on board, the invitation to participate can go a long way to build the fundraising team and beyond. Encouraging team members to view events as an extension of their own areas of expertise, whether that is an annual fund, major gifts, planned giving, or even programming, can place the opportunities presented by events in a new light.

Unique Opportunities

Events provide unique opportunities for interaction with donors and prospective donors. Carefully orchestrated introductions and guided conversations can enable the staff members or volunteer to learn more about the donor and gain new insights into donor interests. Post-event activities should be designed in a way that continues to build the community feeling and must be included in the original event plan. Team members can weave these post-event steps into their overall fundraising plans and establish these expectations as part of early planning.

What happens post-event? The obvious tasks include thank you notes to volunteers, sponsors, and others involved in creating a successful event, but that is just the beginning. There should be a debriefing of those involved in the inner circle of the event as well as event summaries from hosts, board members, and other key volunteers engaged in conversations with donors and prospective donors throughout the evening.

Donor records will reveal that many of the same donors will attend events. This raises the question: what about the other donors? They share the same commitment to the mission and may even send a gift with their RSVP but do not attend. What could be the problem? Maybe they simply do not care for special events and simply would not enjoy attending. An astute development person needs to take these preferences into account when working with donors.

If the development officer feels that the donor would be excited about the programmatic portion of the event, perhaps the speeches, the testimonials from those served and other aspects could be brought to the donor in another fashion. This provides another opportunity to be donor-focused. Asking donors about their event preferences can stretch an event into other venues. Perhaps they would be more comfortable in a smaller gathering. A video presentation of the original program can be brought to the donors and their friends.

Connection

Events can reinforce the connection donors have to the mission in ways that staff alone cannot. Personal stories of experiences, benefits, and histories with the organization draw others closer to the case for support. In a social setting with peers, the prospective donor or current donor may be more open to engaging in a way that deepens the attendee's knowledge and commitment.

To facilitate and maximize the connection, hosts need guidance. They can seek pertinent and critical information that may be missing from a prospective donor's profile. Through casual conversation, a host can learn values, family history, and other involvements. To be effective, however, the host must know where to steer the conversation. A report to staff, either verbal or written, helps to make sure that the information gets into the prospective donor's file.

What traits might you look for in a host? The answer is simpler than one might think for they are the traits of a good volunteer:

- Active supporter
- Effective advocate for the cause
- Reliable and dedicated
- Connected and respected
- Has the time to help plan and attend the event
- Willing to identify, cultivate, and ask prospective donors to attend the event
- Represents the organization without appearing to have a vested interest
- Willing to make a gift at the event, if required

Tradition

A strong tradition of philanthropy is a valuable asset to any organization. Special events can be a part of that tradition, but tradition is not the only reason to continue an event. Staff will appreciate a traditional event if they are aware of the current benefits and how the ongoing tradition contributes to their success as fundraisers and to the success of the organization's mission. "Because we've always done it" is not a reason to continue to plan an event and each event should be considered with a critical eye before planning to do it again.

Value

Is there a more effective/efficient way to accomplish the organization's goal besides hosting an event? If the answer is no, internal staff should see the value of proceeding. With the other key elements of a successful event clearly presented to the staff, the value to personal and organizational work will be clear.

The value will be reinforced if a review of *hard* and *soft* goals is conducted in a timely fashion and shared with the team and leadership, including volunteer leadership. The evaluation should be based on the original event plan and on the benefits to other fundraising activities. These points of discussion might include the following factors:

- Did the annual fund acquire more possible contacts?
- Did the major gift officers feel that donors were brought closer to the case for support?
- Were relationships strengthened?
- Were financial goals met?
- Was the investment of time by staff and volunteers well spent?
- Do board, management staff, and volunteers still believe that this event is the most effective/efficient way to accomplish the goal?

Integrated Events

What makes integrated events different from other events? The difference between integrated events and events that happen in a vacuum can be seen from the earliest planning stage. As a part of annual and strategic planning, dates, times, locations, themes, audiences, and objectives for events must be reviewed and endorsed by the development team defined by The Fund Raising School (2009):

- Chairman of the Board
- Executive Director
- Chief Financial Officer
- Development Director
- Chairman of the Development Committee

So what might this mean to an organization? For teams that view development as a holistic and donor-centered calling, events become avenues to accomplish the mission with the support of the team and volunteers. There should be no surprises at such events. The integrated special event is clearly recognized, along with other strategies, for what it can bring to the entire fundraising plan. It is one more tool all team members can use to evaluate and determine how the event best helps reach fundraising goals.

For organizations struggling with competitive cultures and tight budgets, events may mean resources expended that would have been more productive as part of another solicitation process, with the result being lost opportunities. As fundraising has become more sophisticated, many nonprofit organizations are experiencing interteam competition, silos, and territorialism concerning donors.

One or more of these dynamics may be in play if:

- Development team members refer to donors as "ours."
- Donors are "protected" or "shielded" from invitations.
- Major gift officers work with their prospective donors in a vacuum.
- Principals of corporations are viewed as "hands off" for annual fund solicitation.
- There is a feeling of unhealthy competition between different fundraising teams or within teams themselves.

If one of these dynamics appears in a fundraising department, there is a good chance that there are others, even though they may not be blatant. The result will be poor staff morale, which is very detrimental to the donors, especially those donors transitioning to a major gift. Coming together for an event, reviewing the audience and accomplishing the goals as a team can help to rebuild the morale and, with further work, reinforce bonds among the team.

Critical Factors for Event Success

There are a number of factors that must be considered by the planning team to ensure an event has the desired effect. From beginning to end, each event must be carefully crafted to meet a specific set of goals built in conjunction with the desires and needs of the nonprofit's constituents. The elements to be considered include:

- *A clear plan for internal communication.* Staff buy-in for an event is crucial and is best built by clear communication on the potential impact and benefit of the event from the planning team. By keeping gift officers and others informed of the details of who is attending, the messaging being shared, and the quality of the logistics, there is a much higher likelihood that they will find the event valuable, volunteer their time to make it better, and encourage those constituents with whom they have relationships to participate.

- *A strongly built invitation list.* Events are made or broken on guest lists. Making sure that all individuals who should be included are and those that have expressly stated that they would not like to be included are not helps build goodwill while avoiding hurt feelings. The planning group should consider the type of constituent to be included, such as donors, prospective donors, clients, and volunteers. If a special guest is being honored at the event, that individual should also be given the opportunity to add his or her special guests to the list.

- *Logistics.* The planners of any event must carefully consider logistical elements such as venue, timing, and menu. An exciting and classy venue can be a draw for attendees but at the same time must not give the impression that the organization has funds to burn. The timing of the event, both in terms of time of year and time of day, can make a large difference as well. Ensure that your event is not scheduled on a religious or other holiday and avoid other major conflicts such as another popular local event. Planners must also consider whether introducing multiple revenue sources makes sense for any given event. Options include:
  - Asking for cash donations to sponsor a table or other item.
  - Whether an event should be free to attend or have a ticket cost.
  - General event sponsorship, including in-kind donations.
  - Selling branded merchandise on site.

- *A compelling message.* In their book, *Made to Stick: Why Some Ideas Survive and Others Die,* Chip and Dan Heath (2007) claim that a compelling message must be simple, unexpected, concrete, credible, and emotional. To inspire action from event attendees, one of the most significant points must be a carefully designed message on the importance of the organization's mission and work. Balancing an emotionally compelling case with direct, actionable steps that attendees can take to help alleviate the problem will increase response and make follow-up that much easier. Planners must also consider who should deliver the message and, if included, complete the solicitation.

- *A contingency plan.* There are always unplanned happenings at events. These can range from minor issues such as a loud party in the next room disrupting the program to major issues like a featured speaker being snowed out and unable to make the event entirely. Weather, low participation, food allergies, and a large number of no-shows are all possible concerns that must be addressed. A well-planned event will take all of these factors into account before the event and will have back-up plans already in place before the big day arrives. On the day of the event, it is essential that one staff person is designated as the decision maker who will handle any unforeseen changes. This avoids having to consult multiple people before a quick, responsive solution can be enacted.
- *A follow-up plan.* After an event, the development professionals and other leadership of an organization have a unique opportunity to reach out to attendees and build on the momentum created. Techniques range from sending photographs taken at the event to sending recorded programs to interested individuals who were unable to attend. Thoughtful, personal follow-up can contribute to strengthening the relationship of donors to the organization and lead to increased donations.

Conclusion

Many of the tasks of a leader as set out in John W. Gardner's treatise, *On Leadership* (1990), clearly apply to building a successful, integrated event, both internally and externally. The leader must be able to:

- Explain the purpose.
- Envision the goals.
- Affirm the value.
- Motivate staff and volunteers.
- Manage all aspects of the event.
- Achieve a workable level of unity internally and externally.
- Serve as a symbol of ethical fundraising.
- Provide for a review that allows for renewal.

All of this will result in an event that helps staff at all levels reach the ultimate in successful fundraising – getting all the "right things" in place that lead to a gift that reflects the values of the donor and meets the needs of the community served by the organization: the *right* person asking the *right* prospective donor for the *right* gift for the *right* program at the *right* time and in the *right* way.

Discussion Questions

1) When is an event the correct vehicle for fundraising? When should you as the fundraiser or nonprofit leader push back on the idea planning of an event?
2) How do you develop a thoughtful and integrated event? Who should be consulted and what decisions need to be made?
3) How should cultivation, solicitation, and stewardship events differ? Which factors should change and which should remain the same?
4) As a fundraiser, the follow-up after an event can be just as important, if not more so, as the event itself. How would the plan differ for follow-up with an individual just learning about the organization versus a major gift prospective donor?
5) What factors might make you consider either cancelling or dramatically changing a traditional event? Under what circumstances would this type of change be necessary?

PART SIX

INVOLVING VOLUNTEERS

CHAPTER THIRTY-ONE

STEWARDSHIP AND ACCOUNTABILITY

By: Eugene R. Tempel and Timothy L. Seiler

This chapter is about the concepts of stewardship and accountability and their importance to the management and leadership of a successful fundraising program. This chapter will help you:

- Understand the current focus on transparency and accountability and the organization's responsibility for building trust and confidence.
- Understand the concept of stewardship and how it applies to unrestricted funds, restricted funds, and endowment funds.
- How to develop concepts of responsibility for endowment funds.
- How to use gift clubs for stewardship and accountability.
- How to report on use of funds to donors and the public.

Ask any nonprofit executive, including fundraising executives, and they will tell you that transparency and accountability are the key issues in relating to donors. How does the organization hold itself accountable for the funds that have been provided to it to accomplish a public benefit? In the 2014 Study of High Net Worth Households respondents indicated they would give more only if they knew the funds had the desired impact. Transparency and accountability help build trust and confidence. Trust is the stock and trade of philanthropy. Trust in non-profit board members, executives, and fundraising staff is critical for successful fundraising. Many studies have shown that trust is directly related to whether people are willing to give and how much they give (Light, 2008).

Stewardship is the foundation for holding ourselves accountable. Reporting is the foundation for transparency. Stewardship is the wise use of resources. Stewardship is "… being responsible for something valuable on behalf of someone who has entered it into our care" (Conway, 2003, p. 432). The first stewardship task of nonprofit organizations is to maintain the trust in their role as servants to the public good, demonstrated through steadfast faithfulness to their philanthropic mission, their very *raison d'etre*. Stewardship is holding gifts in trust (hence, trustee) for the public good; serious regard for this trust is the soul of stewardship (Conway, 2003).

To understand the concept of stewardship we must understand the root of the word. The steward was the master of the household, the administrator, the chief operating officer who used resources wisely according to the master's wishes. Today in philanthropy nonprofit organizations must use the resources of donors wisely. Fundraising executives must help assure wise use of donors' resources.

Many today apply the concept of stewardship to donors. Fundraisers are not "stewards" of donors. Donors are not "resources" to be used wisely. As this chapter discusses, making certain donors' gifts are used wisely, used for intended purposes, managed well in endowments, have an impact, and all this communicated to donors through various ways, is stewardship.

Organizations today receive a lower percentage of gifts unrestricted than they did a decade ago. However, those who make unrestricted gifts deserve stewardship over their gifts. They have a right (see the Donor Bill of Rights in Chapter 34) to hear from the organization how their gifts were used or how they made a difference. Donors who make, often smaller, unrestricted gifts, should be viewed as special donors to the organization. Even if unrestricted gifts were used for utilities and maintenance, an honest report to donors who made unrestricted gifts about what the maintenance and utility costs for the year were and how unrestricted gifts made it possible for the organization to pay these costs and continue to provide the services, is good stewardship.

When donors make restricted gifts, the organization agrees to act as trustee to carry out the purposes for which the gift was solicited or for which the gift was intended. Fundraisers have a shared ethical obligation with other leaders at organizations to make sure that the intentions are honored. This is more than an ethical obligation outlined in codes of ethics and the Donor Bill of Rights, it is a legal obligation. Reporting to donors that the funds were used as intended and the accomplishments achieved with the gift or gifts is good stewardship practice.

Often fundraisers are involved in major gifts solicitation for special projects or endowments. Special stewardship efforts are called for to make certain the funds are used as intended and the outcomes of the gift reported to the donor, including inviting donors to see firsthand the results of their gifts. At the major gifts level donors might fund an entire program. It is important that fundraisers and others in the organization do not over promise an outcome and impact and that they then report accurately on program development, demonstrating impact.

Fundraisers often do not concern themselves with the organization's endowment performance. But they must. The organization's long-term endowment performance and the strategies it has for managing endowments going forward is an essential stewardship aspect in building trust and confidence. Donors must be able to believe with confidence that funds they entrust to the organization for perpetuity or for long periods of time into the future have reasonable prospects of holding their value and increasing over time. Most organizations invest their funds prudently with moderate risk, using investment advisors who will help the endowment perform to near the peaks of various indicators, but above the low points of those indicators as well. Communicating clearly to potential donors and creating understanding of expectations is the first step in stewardship of endowments.

New funds are typically added to endowments by donors from their assets using a variety of planned gift structures available to them (see Chapter 20). Organizations must make only reasonable promises about donor income and benefits from such structures as charitable gift annuities, charitable remainder trusts, and charitable lead trusts. Fundraising executives can protect the donor and the organization by making certain that donors have independent legal counsel on all major transactions.

As discussed in Chapter 34, promise-keeping is one of the ethical values. And it is critical for stewardship of endowment. Promise-keeping has three aspects fundraisers must assure simultaneously. First are promises made to donors about their income and tax benefits. Second are promises about past performance of the organization's endowed funds and reasonable expectations for the future. Third are promises related to the program or programs (or the organization overall if the endowment purpose is unrestricted) that will be funded by proceeds from the endowment, including the organization's payout policy related to endowments. Stewardship needs to account for all those aspects. Donors must have reports from organizations on all three. Transparency and accountability call for honesty even when funds may not perform as well one year as they did the previous one. Funds made available to a restricted program are one part of stewardship, but, as with advice on other aspects of organizational performance in this and other chapters, reporting on the outcomes and impacts made possible through the funds is the other.

Gift Clubs

Fundraisers typically think of gift clubs as donor recognition groups, but they are much more than that. They are first ways in which organizations can demonstrate stewardship and accountability. Paul Schervish in his work on philanthropic identification outlines various factors necessary for individuals to see themselves in those being benefitted and provide philanthropy to come to their aid (1997). Most important among the eight factors he cited was what he called "communities of participation." Communities of participation are opportunities for individuals to come together with people with shared values to accomplish a greater good. Gift clubs provide the perfect opportunity to engage donors thematically with the organization and each other. Engagement can range from special newsletters, web portals to special gatherings. The Fundraising Cycle and the Total Development Program (see Chapter 17) assume that every donor is a prospective donor for another gift and larger gifts over time. Gift clubs provide an opportunity to demonstrate good stewardship, the impact that gifts have made, report on new gifts made, success of the organization generally, and more closely engage donors with the organization. Gift clubs also provide a great form of donor recognition. They respond to donors' interests in coming together with others to accomplish something larger than they can accomplish themselves (see Chapter 15 on high net worth donors).

Gift clubs can be organized around any aspect of the organization's donor base. Good stewardship demands that the activities of the gift club relate to organizational purposes accomplished by the donors. And it argues for choosing names that relate to the organizational mission.

A time-tested gift club has been related to annual gifts of $1000. But the past 25 years have eroded the purchasing power of $1000 to $552.41 today (Bureau of Labor Statistics, 2015). Setting the level should take into consideration the organization's gift amounts, the number of donors who make gifts at various levels, and concrete accomplishments that can be related to gift amounts. For example, $1000 donors could belong to a club that provides first generation scholarships or free passes for children from lower socio-economic families to attend a theatre or visit a museum or the zoo, or shelter for a number of homeless families for two-week periods. The gift club provides donor recognition, but more importantly it provides an opportunity to demonstrate good stewardship to a community of those who support the organization.

Similarly, gift clubs can be organized around special gifts made on an annual basis or even major gifts made through special campaigns. Donors making gifts of $25,000 annually might each sponsor some important aspect of the organization's work. These could range from scholarships at a private school or college or university to a musician in the orchestra or the meals for Thanksgiving dinner at a homeless shelter. A special club allows those significantly engaged and supporting the organization to come together with each other, provide feedback to the organization, and learn more specifically about how their funds have been used, and their impact on beneficiaries.

Two other special gift clubs can be organized for those who have made endowment gifts through current transfers or through one of the several annuity or trust mechanisms allowed by law and through estate gifts. Again, the first aspect most fundraising executives see is the donor recognition aspect. And indeed all gift clubs provide an opportunity to say thanks, express appreciation, and recognize donors at different levels. But gift clubs for those two groups provide an opportunity for the special stewardship efforts they require. Donors who have income interests from planned gifts can be provided information about the performance of the funds invested for their benefit. The organization can also provide them information about the number of new donors and amount of funds represented by their gifts as well as funds that have become available for the organization's use and what those funds are accomplishing. It is also an opportunity to bring together individuals who support the organization in a unique and specific way. Often organizations take for granted those who have made estate commitments. Those donors should be celebrated too. Since donors who make significant estate gifts may be annual donors at smaller amounts, we can demonstrate stewardship of their larger but unrealized gifts by illustrating the impact that estate gifts have on the organization, memorializing donors when their estate gifts are realized, and by providing opportunity for estate donors to engage with the organization and each other.

Reporting

Perhaps the longest and most universally used form of demonstrating stewardship by reporting is the annual report. Typically, the annual report is a statement of all income and expenses. It can be oriented to a variety of supporters by including a section on major outcomes and impacts. It can include success stores featuring the impact on individual clients or beneficiaries. It can include a special section on philanthropy, reporting briefly on gift club numbers and activities and projects funded or supported by gift clubs. With the prevalence of digital commitments, today the annual report has become more sophisticated and delivered through email or websites and through such social media as Facebook. It can now include video messages that bring the letter from the CEO or Board Chair to life. Similarly, success stories can now feature clients or beneficiaries on video. Additionally, reporting from the organization can now be quarterly, monthly, even weekly, using digital reporting. YouTube and cell phone cameras make video reporting less expensive. Special reports to gift club donors can also be done digitally with special messages from board members, organization leadership, or clients and beneficiaries.

In the digital era organizations should not forget the impact that a personal letter can have. Personalized reports to donors at a pre-determined level can be very effective. These can focus on accomplishments of gift club donors or the impact that a donor's major gift for a special project has had on the organization and its ability to deliver services, and on those being served. Those who are most deeply engaged with the organization entrust the organization with larger gifts. Donors who make larger gifts can trust the organization to be good stewards of those resources. Special stewardship report to these donors can be accomplished through personal letters.

Those who have made endowment gifts have a right to know how the organization has managed and been a good steward of the endowment. Overall, endowment results generally measured over a five-year and one-year period can tell the story. But reports illustrating the endowment performance and the payout for program use of an individual account are best practice for major gift donors. The more specifically donors can see the impact of their gifts and the organization's management of this gift the higher level of trust the donor develops in the organization's stewardship.

Organizations that spend over $750,000 of federal funds in a single year are required by the IRS to have annual outside audits (National Council of Nonprofits, 2015). Many other organizations do so as well. Audits should be made public in an effort at transparency, to hold the organization accountable, and as another way to demonstrate good stewardship. When the organization receives a "clean" letter in an audit, this should be made known to help build trust and confidence. If the audit letter has recommendations for improvement, or findings that must be addressed, revealing the shortcomings and outlining the organization's response, a plan for dealing with concerns, and a report on steps taken demonstrate good stewardship.

Organizations with budgets over $50,000 are required to file electronically a form 990 with the Internal Revenue Service on an annual basis (IRS, 2015). An organization's 990 is publicly available through GuideStar. However, the information on GuideStar is generally a year old and it requires donors and the public search for a particular organization. Organizations have an opportunity for demonstrating transparency and practicing good stewardship by making their 990 available as soon as it is officially approved and filed with the IRS.

Most organizations today have a website. The website is not only a great way to help clients and beneficiaries find services, it is also one of the organization's most significant stewardship tools. Websites provide an opportunity for transparency.

The audit and the Form 990 can be posted on the website. The annual report can be posted on the website. The website can make available to the public and donors a dashboard of key indicators for progress and success. It can tell stories of impact. Board and staff directories allow the public and donors to access the organization and understand who holds the future of the organization and its mission in trust.

Websites can also host portals for board members, donor stewardship clubs, or other groups where special and restricted access may help create greater engagement and enhanced stewardship reporting.

Conclusion

Being accountable means that an organization is able to give account – of its adherence to mission and of its appropriate use of resources, especially those which are contributed philanthropically. Accountability is the first step towards stewardship, "honoring what has been given to us" with gratitude and grace (Block, 1993, 22). The Fund Raising School defines stewardship as the "guiding principle in philanthropic fundraising ... the philosophy and means by which an institution exercises ethical accountability in the use of contributed resources ... and a donor exercises responsibility in the voluntary use of resources" (2015, p. 129). This definition suggests that donors share a responsibility to make informed decisions about resources (stewardship). Fundraisers have a responsibility to help donors through a process of discovery of how they might use resources prudently for philanthropic purposes. Paul Schervish (2000) describes this process as one of discernment, or inclination. The fundraiser's role is to pose to the philanthropist the right questions:

- What would you like to do with your resources?
- That is important to do for others?
- That will give you a sense of fulfillment and express your gratitude?

In making the case for support for the organization, the fundraiser might add: How can we help?

Such a discernment process joins philanthropist and fundraiser in a mutually fulfilling relationship that is an example of how fundraising is servant to philanthropy and how fundraising is the gentle art of teaching the joy of giving – the highest form of stewardship (Rosso, 1991).

Discussion Questions

1) Discuss stewardship in the context of donor intent.
2) What is the important distinction between stewardship of a donor's gifts and stewardship of the donor?
3) What role can gift clubs play in stewardship?
4) How can an organization's website be used in stewardship?
5) What is the role of stewardship related to endowments?

CHAPTER THIRTY-TWO

ENGAGING THE BOARD IN FUNDRAISING

By Eugene R. Tempel and Timothy L. Seiler

"Fundraising Begins with the Board"

Henry A. Rosso

This chapter is based on the notion that board engagement is essential to organizational success in fundraising. It focuses on Henry "Hank" Rosso's adage that "fundraising begins with the board." Through understanding this chapter you should be able to do the following:

- Discuss the rationale for board engagement in fundraising.
- Develop concepts for engaging board members in various fundraising activities.
- Understand what value board members bring to fundraising.
- How to develop concepts for recruiting new board members, engaging existing board members, and orienting and training board members to engage in fundraising.
- How to support board members in fundraising.
- How to develop accountability and commitment as well as celebrate successes.

The Roles and Responsibilities of Board Members

Board members are entrusted with the legal and stewardship responsibilities of philanthropic organizations. Their specific responsibilities include:

1. Legal
2. Stewardship of mission
3. Stewardship of resources
4. Self-renewal

In carrying out their responsibilities board members assure that the organization complies with all applicable laws and regulations, managing its finances, compensating staff, and filing its reports. This is the first aspect of trust building.

Self-renewal is the final responsibility of boards of philanthropic organizations. They must take stock of their own composition, commitment, and performance given the needs of the organization.

Stewardship of mission and stewardship of resources create the rationale for board engagement in fundraising. Stewardship of mission is the responsibility to ensure that the organization's mission is viable in changing times. It gives rise to strategic planning. It is the foundation for the concept that the board member represents the organization to the community in building trust. It also requires board members to represent the larger community to the organization in ongoing planning. This representation is critical to building trust. A recent study (Perry, 2015) found that Americans have more confidence in their local charities than in charities overall. Stewardship of resources is the responsibility to ensure adequate financial resources to carry out the organization's mission. It means securing, managing, and deploying funds. It means assuring that funds are expended for the purposes for which they were given. It means managing endowment funds responsibly. It means involvement in fundraising.

Involvement in fundraising does not mean only being involved in soliciting gifts. In fact, engaging in a variety of these fundraising tasks is often good "training" for board members who are new to fundraising.

The 2015 report from BoardSource, *Leading with Intent: A National Index of Nonprofit Board Practices*, indicates an improvement in Board giving over the past 20 years from 60 to 85 percent. However, it indicates that there is still discomfort with fundraising. On identifying donors, meeting donors, and asking donors, 56 percent, 60 percent, and 51 percent of board members, respectively, indicated they are comfortable, but on the same three practices, 20 percent, 27 percent, and 43 percent, respectively, said they are not comfortable.

Engaging in Fundraising

The first level of involvement in fundraising is planning for fundraising. Board members must ask questions that ensure that the fundraising strategies and tactics employed by the organization are based on reliable data, good intuition, and sound practices. These questions may include:

- Are fundraising plans based on solid research and data? What missed opportunities could be captured? What obstacles stand in the way of success?
- Will the approach being suggested appeal to the organization's key donors?
- If a campaign is being considered, has a test of feasibility been conducted?
- Is the organization prepared to implement its fundraising plans and committed to achieving greater success?

Boards must play an active and inquiring role in developing and vetting organizational fundraising plans so that the organization has the benefit not only of the knowledge of its professional fundraising staff but also of its volunteer leadership in crafting its fundraising strategies.

Every fundraising effort, whether it is for annual operations or for multiple years and hundreds of millions of dollars, should be discussed, understood, and approved by the board. The board must be confident that the fundraising effort has been well planned and that the goal, the volunteer leadership, the main strategic elements, and the cost have all been tailored to fit the organization's goals and needs.

This is important to create ownership by the board of the organization's fundraising. When board members are asked to approve a fundraising effort, they are also being asked to support it both with personal gifts and through their ongoing efforts to help the organization raise funds. When board members vote to approve a fundraising plan in which they have been actively consulted and engaged, they own the plan.

Board members should receive regular updates on recent gift totals, indicators of overall success, timelines, and milestones, so they can give informed advice and take action to help ensure success. Reviewing and interpreting gift results and assisting in crafting solicitation strategies for selected individuals are only two of the many ways in which board members can and should be actively engaged in fundraising.

The following list highlights (Tempel, 2004, p. 19) ways for board members to be involved in the fundraising process (in order of direct involvement):

- Make a personal contribution.
- Write thank you notes for gift acknowledgement.

- Participate in strategic and development planning.
- Add names to mailing lists.
- Write personal notes on solicitation letters.
- Introduce potential donors to members of the organization.
- Write a support letter to a government agency, foundation, or corporation.
- Seek out donations for a special event or help plan a special event.
- Cultivate relationships with potential donors.
- Make a solicitation call with other volunteers and/or board members.

The process of planning for and soliciting gifts has many components. Perhaps next to fundraising planning the easiest way for board members to become engaged in fundraising is by thanking donors. From writing handwritten notes to making phone calls to signing letters and adding a PS, this important aspect of fundraising often helps board members understand and become comfortable with fundraising.

Board members can also be involved in signing solicitation letters to selected groups and individuals. They can host events for potential donors, from receptions in their home to luncheons and receptions at the organization so potential donors can learn more about the organization and fundraising staff can follow up.

They can also assist the organization with donor identification, qualification, and engagement strategies for selected prospects. Through their social and business networks, they are very likely to know persons who have the capacity to be generous and who might be interested in learning more about the organization. Fundraisers must help boards understand that prospective donor identification and qualification are part of the fundraising process. Fundraisers should also ask the board to participate in donor-rating sessions or peer-screening sessions during which they help identify which prospective donors might be interested in making a gift and an appropriate gift range. Traditionally asking board members to discuss potential donors and prospects with fundraising staff is associated with campaigns and early stage campaign planning. However, asking board members to participate in this process on an ongoing basis is good practice.

In addition to hosting events for multiple individuals, board members can assist in fundraising by helping develop and implement cultivation strategies to engage individuals, typically major gift prospects, more closely with the organization. Cultivation of prospective donors takes board members another step closer to engagement in solicitations. Through cultivating prospective donors, board members help to build relationships upon which successful fundraising depends, and they have the opportunity to recall how they were drawn closer to the organization before they became donors and board members. It is rewarding for board members to see how their personal giving, encouragement, and quiet endorsement of an organization can encourage others to do the same. Even more fulfilling for a board member is to watch others make a transformational gift to the organization that improves their lives and the lives of those the organization serves.

It is important for the board members to coordinate with fundraising staff. The best results occur when fundraising staff have worked with the board member to create an appropriate context for introducing the prospective donor to the organization. A close partnership between the board member and fundraising staff makes the engagement of a new prospective donor more enjoyable and successful.

Finally, boards can be effective in personal solicitation. Engaging boards in all aspects of fundraising discussed above will help introduce board members to personal solicitation. It is essential for board members who become engaged in solicitation to have embraced the organization's mission, its case for support, its fundraising plan, and to have made a generous gift themselves. It is important for fundraising staff to educate board members about the solicitation process for inviting a prospective donor to consider joining them in supporting the organization based on the case for support. Experienced board members who embrace their fundraising responsibilities know that soliciting a gift is a powerful moment with the donor. During this moment, board members are authentic, opening themselves and their values to prospective donors by asking them to join in making gifts to test their generosity to important work they support. Because of the importance of the work and the moment, board members who are committed to their fundraising responsibilities rarely give up at the first rejection or hard question, doing everything they can to make the donor understand that he or she is engaged in an honest discussion that is focused first on realizing change in the world through the organization and second on the funds necessary to make that happen. Fundraising staff can help board members understand the process and encourage them in solicitation efforts by emphasizing a solicitation approach that has integrity, avoids surprising the potential donor by securing his or her permission to ask first, and creates an atmosphere in which the donor and the solicitation team can have the type of discussion that honors mutual respect of the solicitation process. However, board members should not engage in any serious gift discussions with donors unless fundraising staff are fully aware, involved, supportive, and willing to help. Effective solicitation is a partnership between board members and fundraising staff.

What Board Members Bring to Fundraising

Board members serve as advocates for the organization. They can provide testimony to the public at large about the importance of mission and the role of philanthropy in fulfilling the mission based on their close knowledge of the organization, their stewardship of the organization, and their own generous support of the organization. Board members must say with conviction that they believe in and support philanthropy and its power to fulfill its mission. Board members can share their reasons for giving with others, allow themselves to be listed as donors, and tell part of their own story of philanthropic engagement with the organization in a public forum, in the organization's newsletter, or through solicitation of other donors. The impact on others of hearing why a board member is motivated to make a generous gift has a positive effect on others giving and on the organization.

Board members are viewed as leaders in giving to the organization. They have peer status with many of the organization's major donors and major gift prospects. What they signal through their giving is noticed by peers: donors and constituencies assume that board members have the closest inside knowledge of the organization. They assume board members are knowledgeable about organizational needs and that board members are sincere when they say the organization deserves private gift support. However, they must demonstrate integrity by giving generously so their words and action reinforce one another.

Board members serve as advocates; they serve as examples. They bring their own philanthropy to bear on all fundraising efforts perhaps more generously because they are board members. They serve as peers of many of the leading donors and prospects. They can provide knowledge about donors and prospects and the fundraising environment. They bring relationships. They can open doors and through peer status, they can solicit gifts.

Fundraising staff have high expectations of board members, but board members have high expectations of staff too. Board members expect fundraising staff to support their engagement in fundraising. They expect fundraising staff to make appointments and carry out follow-up tasks. They expect staff to have deep knowledge of organizational projects and programs just as staff expect board members to have deep knowledge about the community and prospects. Board members expect staff to prepare them for solicitation calls. They expect staff to treat their time with respect and they expect staff not to exploit relationships in soliciting gifts.

Recruiting Board Members

Organizations must recruit all volunteers, but especially board members, from a position of strength based on the mission and case for support rather than apologetically. Recruiting board members is like fundraising in that the case for support is the rationale for the invitation and the invitation includes philanthropic generosity to the organization.

Recruitment of board members typically begins with an analysis of board strengths and weaknesses, and particular needs the board may have – skills, demographics, geographic distribution, or because of the organizational dynamics of the time. By using a grid such as the one in Figure 32.1, the governance committee, committee on the board, nominating committee, or whatever structure the board is utilizing for self-renewal and self-perpetuation can have a snapshot of the board and its key characteristics and determine its highest priorities. A board may be focused on demographics such as age, gender, or ethnicity; it may be focused on a geographic distribution; and it may have special needs in legal, scientific, communications, financial, marketing or administrative specialties. However, it must always consider what role a prospective board member can play in fundraising and it must always consider the prospective donor's interest in the mission and generosity in supporting it. (Generosity is a measure of philanthropy against one's ability to give as opposed to a simple amount.)

In recruiting new board members three things are necessary: (1) the organization's mission and general case for support, (2) the particular strengths that the board member brings to the organization, and (3) a brief document outlining duties, responsibilities, and expectations. This document should make clear general board and individual member expectations. One expectation must be that the individual will make a generous gift and participate in fundraising at one or more levels (see Exhibit 32.1).

Board members must receive appropriate orientation and training if they are to be effective in fundraising (BoardSource, 2012a). Even when board members have been effective in fundraising as board members for other organizations, we should not assume that they will automatically be effective for their next board assignment.

Orientation might begin during recruitment when the mission and case for support for the organization is the basis for recruitment. Additionally, the orientation should include an introduction to the organization's programs, budget, finances, and philanthropy required to support them. Training should include a review of the roles of philanthropy in general and the specific role that philanthropy plays in the organization. It should include an introduction to the dynamics of asking for and making gifts (see Chapter 4 on A Case for Support). Training should include an introduction to the solicitation exercise outlined in Chapter 26. Board members will often say they are reluctant to become involved in personal solicitation because they do not know how to ask for gifts. Providing training, having them practice, and reviewing roles and responsibilities with a board member before specific fundraising calls will help reduce the reluctance to move from less personal to more personal approaches.

FIGURE 32.1. BOARD COMPOSITION GRID.

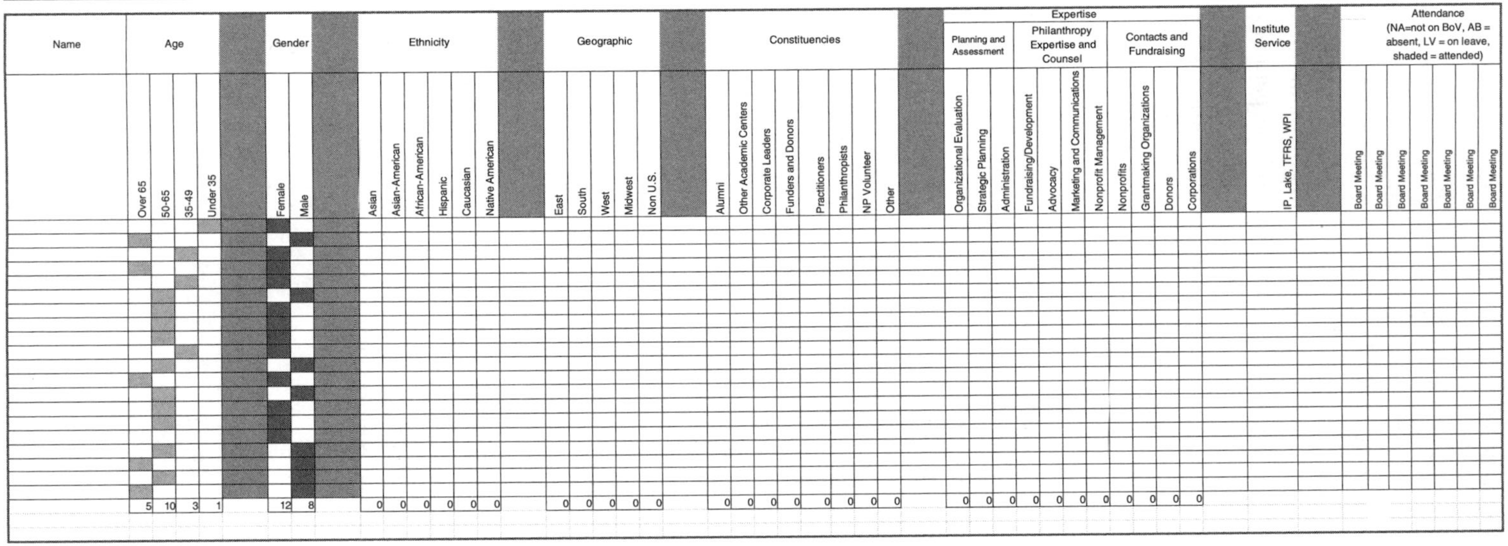

Name	Age				Gender		Ethnicity						Geographic					Constituencies									Planning and Assessment			Philanthropy Expertise and Counsel			Expertise		Contacts and Fundraising				Institute Service	Attendance (NA=not on BoV, AB = absent, LV = on leave, shaded = attended)							
	Under 35	35–49	50–65	Over 65	Male	Female	Asian	Asian-American	African-American	Hispanic	Caucasian	Native American	East	South	West	Midwest	Non U.S.	Alumni	Other Academic Centers	Corporate Leaders	Funders and Donors	Practitioners	Philanthropists	NP Volunteer	Other	Organizational Evaluation	Strategic Planning	Administration	Fundraising/Development	Advocacy	Marketing and Communications	Nonprofit Management	Nonprofits	Grantmaking Organizations	Donors	Corporations	IP, Lake, TFRS, WPI	Board Meeting	Board Meeting	Board Meeting	Board Meeting	Board Meeting	Board Meeting	Board Meeting	Board Meeting
	1	3	10	5	8	12	0	0	0	0	0	0	0	0	0	0	0	0	0	0	0	0	0	0	0	0	0	0	0	0	0	0	0	0	0	0									

EXHIBIT 32.1. SAMPLE BOARD AGREEMENT LETTER.

Organization Name

For Fiscal Year 2016–2017

Responsibilities of the Board   The Board of Directors is legally responsible for the work of the organization. Directors will act in a close advisory and advocacy role with the Organization's Executive Director and other executive staff.

The Board shall have the following collective responsibilities:

The Board of Directors furthers the mission and objectives of the organization by all available means, with emphasis upon public relations and financial assistance, through encouraging gifts, grants, donations, and bequests.

- To recommend policies related to the development and renewal of the mission of the organization.
- To ensure the ongoing strategic planning and evaluation of the programs of the organization.
- To serve as ambassadors on behalf of the organization, representing key constituents to the organization and representing the organization to its constituents.
- To secure adequate financial resources and ensure stewardship of the organization's resources.
- To evaluate its own composition and performance and recommend new members for the Board.
- To serve as a think tank to generate new ideas for application of the organization's wide array of capabilities.

Individual Responsibilities of Directors

Each member of the Board of Directors will be expected to serve on one or more committees, to participate fully in the work of the Board, and to attend two Board meetings annually, unless excused by the Chair of the Board. International members are expected to attend one out of two in-person meetings of the Board.

Additionally, the Board of Directors will be expected to:
- Take an active role in the organization's strategic planning process.
- Ensure that the case for support is strong by reviewing the organization's mission and goals with the staff.

(Continued)

EXHIBIT 32.1. (CONTINUED).

- Participate in the evaluation of the organization's work and the performance of the Executive Director.
- Provide an external resource for advice and counsel to the organization's Executive Director and key staff.
- Provide a resource for significant, relevant contacts who can assist the organization in pursuit of its mission.
- Assist with the formulation of policies and procedures related to major gift solicitation and recognition.
- Provide advice and active assistance in planning, cultivation, and solicitation phases of the organization's fundraising activities.
- Make annual and campaign gifts commensurate within their donative capacity.

I have read the collective and individual responsibilities of members of the Board of Directors and pledge to fulfill them to the best of my abilities.

_____
                                Board Member
        Date

_____

Board members must be supported in doing fundraising work from signing thank you notes to doing face-to-face solicitation. A good exercise is to ask a board member how staff can support them in fundraising. They will say things like: respect their time, offer support, behave in a professional manner, and have a deep knowledge of the organization.

Often when staff complain that they cannot get board members involved in fundraising, they have not considered the potential that they may be at fault because they do not support board members in this work. Expecting board members (or any volunteers) to undertake fundraising for the organization on their own, even from a position of strength, armed with the case for support and given training, is unrealistic. Without staff support their attention is focused on professional and personal lives. Staff must focus board members on fundraising and support them.

Organizations begin to create a culture of support when they see board members as valuable members of the organization's fundraising team. Board members, other volunteers, organizational leadership, and fundraising staff all have roles to play, often jointly, in achieving fundraising success. Organizations must use planning sessions to help board members prepare for fundraising work, whether it is sending personal appeal letters, or preparing for a face-to-face solicitation.

Developing commitment to engagement in fundraising begins in the recruitment of board members. An open discussion of the expectations of individual members, including an expectation that they support the organization generously and become engaged in fundraising is essential. Using a "job description," as discussed earlier in this chapter, makes it clear that this is part of the expectations. A letter of commitment, like the example presented in Exhibit 32.1, signed by board members annually is a renewal of commitment to live up to those expectations.

Annual self-evaluations by boards can help develop accountability. Research on evaluations in a variety of settings finds that self-evaluation often is more severe than evaluations performed by others. When board members are not fulfilling their commitments to fundraising (or other commitments for that matter), it is the chair of the board or the chair of either the governance or development committee who will have a conversation with the board member about living up to commitments. Board members who cannot commit to engaging in fundraising in one of several ways as outlined earlier in this chapter should consider resigning. It is important that discussions about issues related to a board member's engagement in fundraising be conducted by a board leader who is fully engaged, not a staff person.

It is important to celebrate successes. Board meetings should report on success in fundraising and provide positive feedback and recognition for individual board member successes. Development committees can celebrate successes while they focus on the work ahead in fundraising. Special events to thank board members (and other volunteers) for their work in fundraising can be held on an annual basis. Board engagement in fundraising should not be taken for granted; it is important for staff of the organization and the development committee of the board, if one exists, to express appreciation. Celebrating success in fundraising provides role models and positive encouragement for those who have been less engaged or less successful.

Conclusion

This chapter reviews the critical issue of engaging the board in fundraising. Organizational leaders, including fundraising executives, understand the value that a fully engaged board brings to the fundraising process, but often fall short of developing a board that is fully engaged in fundraising. This chapter helps you to understand how to engage board members successfully for fundraising. It covers the roles and duties of board members and the rationale for engaging board members in fundraising. It covers the variety of ways board members can assist in fundraising and the value they bring to the process. It focuses on the all-important topics of recruiting from a position of strength, orienting and training board members in fundraising, and supporting them in their work. Finally, it focuses on commitment and accountability and celebrating successes.

Discussion Questions

1) How would you explain the importance and rationale for engaging board members in fundraising?
2) What are the essential ingredients for recruiting board members to engage in fundraising?
3) How would you design an orientation and training program to engage board members in fundraising?
4) In what ways might an organization hold board members accountable in fundraising?
5) How might an organization celebrate success in fundraising?

CHAPTER THIRTY-THREE

VOLUNTEER MANAGEMENT

By Tyrone McKinley Freeman and Elena Hermanson

Historically, the value of American volunteerism in society has been greatly underestimated and not fully recognized for its overall contributions (Ellis and Noyes, 1990). From colonial times to the present, volunteerism and civic engagement have been important threads in the fabric of American life. Because of their passion and commitment to the cause, volunteers add special value to fundraising efforts. Professional fundraisers should make every effort, wherever possible, to conceptualize meaningful volunteer involvement in their fundraising programs and execute deliberate processes for achieving successful volunteer participation. Doing so will produce considerable returns that will move organizations closer to achieving their overall goals in raising money to meet important social needs and building community among their constituents.

In this chapter you will gain information of volunteer rates and the various types of volunteering, international contexts, why volunteers are motivated to participate, the strategic value of volunteers in the organization's fundraising program, and an eight-step model of volunteer engagement.

Volunteer Rates and Activities

Volunteering is a vital and important form of philanthropy in the United States. In 2013, nearly 63 million Americans (or 25 percent of the adult population) formally volunteered for nonprofit organizations, contributing nearly 8 billion hours of service worth more than $173 billion in labor (Corporation for National and Community Service, 2015). Even during the preceding six years, which included the worst economic recession in recent history, that volunteer rate remained relatively stable as Americans gave up many things to weather the times – including some of their charitable giving – but mostly held on to their volunteering.

On this side of the recession, volunteering continues to thrive in varied forms, including those that leverage technology to make volunteering accessible to willing and able participants interested in serving regardless of their physical location. While traditional forms of volunteerism remain popular and dominant, they have been joined by other forms such as microvolunteering – brief service assignments that can be completed in time increments ranging from a few minutes to a few hours – and virtual volunteering (or e-volunteering) – service contributions facilitated by and made through social media and other internet platforms (see Chapter 29 for the use of social media in fundraising). Although some forms of Internet-enabled volunteerism have been pejoratively labeled "slacktivism," because they require less commitment from people or differ greatly from the common face-to-face forms of engagement, technology has overcome the traditional constraints of time and geography to grant both organizations and individuals alike great flexibility in how they connect through volunteerism.

In addition to the evolving approaches to formal volunteering, informal volunteering, defined as providing assistance to individuals outside one's household such as neighbors or friends, thrives (Lee and Brudney, 2012). In 2013, 138 million Americans helped their friends and neighbors by providing support for childcare, housesitting, and purchasing needed items (Corporation for National and Community Service, 2015). This informal volunteering is important because it emerges out of and enhances the social ties and relationships between individuals and families at the community level. Such local engagement contributes to the overall civic health of a community and represents a significant pool of prospective volunteers that fundraisers should consider and cultivate (Lee and Brudney, 2012). However, no matter the form of volunteerism, the core remains the same: individuals continue to find value and meaning in giving service to others and causes they deem worthy, and successful fundraising operations create ways to engage such people.

This idea is important because just as philanthropic giving is a values-based exchange between donors and recipient organizations, volunteerism, too, reflects the values and commitments of those who engage in it. People give to and volunteer for organizations that they connect with or that mean something particular to them. It is no accident that the top three types of organizations that Americans give the most money to support – religious, educational, and human services – are also the top three types of organizations for which they volunteer (*Giving USA 2014*, 2014; Corporation for National and Community Service, 2015).

Research from The Corporation for National and Community Service has repeatedly confirmed the connection between giving and volunteering. In 2013, 79 percent of American volunteers made donations to charitable organizations, whereas only 40 percent of those who did not volunteer made charitable donations (Corporation for National and Community Service, 2015). Additionally, fundraising remains the number one activity volunteers report engaging in when they serve, followed by collection and distribution of food, general labor, and tutoring or teaching.

International Contexts of Volunteering

Volunteerism, however, is not just an American phenomenon. In 2013, 44 percent of Canadians over the age of 15 formally volunteered for nonprofit organizations to the tune of 1.96 billion hours (Turcotte, 2015). While this volunteer rate has declined slightly in recent years, the number of hours given has remained stable. Further, the relationship between giving and volunteering in Canada appears strong as the provinces with the highest rates of giving tend to share the higher rates of volunteering as well. According to Volunteering Australia, 19.4 percent of Australians volunteered their time to organizations, and most of their services were rendered in the areas of sports, religion, and social welfare (2015). In terms of informal volunteering, just under 12 percent of Australians reported helping others outside their families suffering from illness or managing disabilities while more than 30 percent reported caring for the children of friends and neighbors (2015). Beyond North America and Australia, significant volunteer levels and practices have been observed in parts of Asia, across sub-Saharan Africa, and in South America. The Gallup Organization has identified volunteering rates ranging from between 2 percent and 48 percent of the populations of 130 countries, and informal helping rates ranging from between 21 percent and 81 percent (English, 2011). Additionally, the United Nations has acknowledged the positive local, national, and global impact of volunteerism, both formal and informal, and has taken steps in recent years to encourage international conversations about volunteerism and better measurement and tracking of volunteer activities around the world (United Nations Volunteer, 2015). Clearly, volunteerism is a global phenomenon, and fundraisers play a vital role in connecting volunteer resources with local community needs.

Volunteer Motivations and Advantages

As fundraisers, we must keep this in mind as we manage volunteers in various aspects of our mission. While having responsibilities for volunteer management (as distinguished from working with the board) can sometimes feel like a distraction from the work of fundraising, it is actually critical for meeting your annual and strategic goals.

Before we attempt to manage volunteers, we must understand them and what they bring to our fundraising. People volunteer for a variety of reasons, including those related to valuing particular organizational missions, wanting to learn and enhance themselves, interacting with and relating to others, developing employable skills, and escaping from or coping with difficult life experiences (Musick and Wilson, 2008). Many volunteers have altruistic desires to help others by being available through service to make a difference or to support causes that will have a particular impact on community life. Some people volunteer in order to develop themselves as individuals or professionals by utilizing special knowledge or skills they possess in service to important causes. Volunteerism is also a way in which individuals can acquire new skills, gain valuable work-related experiences, and develop networking opportunities that may lead to employment or promotion. In fact, recent research has shown that unemployed volunteers had a significantly higher probability of gaining employment than unemployed nonvolunteers (Corporation for National and Community Service, 2015). Many professionals also volunteer as a part of their transition from work to retirement, and retirees often increase their volunteer commitments to fill portions of their newly available time. Still others volunteer out of a need for camaraderie or a sense of belonging to a community. They seek engagement in their community and in the lives of others in ways that add meaning to their lives and provide a sense of being useful and helpful to others. As a generation, Millennials seem to have a penchant for volunteerism, perhaps because of the community service requirements of their K-12 schooling or their evolving concern for the social conditions of the world, and, of course, one of the top motivations for volunteering is being asked to serve. None of these motivations are mutually exclusive. Indeed, volunteers often have a collage of motivations animating their service and all should be valued and respected as integral to the success of your mission and fundraising efforts.

When properly harnessed, your volunteers' motivations can yield important advantages for successful fundraising in your organization. Volunteers can enrich an organization by injecting passion and energy into the daily work. As representatives of the community, volunteers also serve as ambassadors and can help build goodwill for your organization. Volunteers also bring unique blends of skills and talents that can enhance your organization's work and impact. They also possess material resources and personal and professional contacts that can greatly add to your fundraising efforts. No one can vouch for your organization's relevance, value, and success like a volunteer and, as professional fundraisers, we should make every effort to involve them in our charge to secure the necessary resources to meet community needs.

The Strategic Value and Role of Volunteers

Volunteers play an important role in successful fundraising. As volunteers – that is, people who are not paid for their work on behalf of your nonprofit – they represent an internalization of the organization's values. In many ways they embody your mission and can serve as powerful advocates of its validity and impact precisely because they are not financially compensated for their service and have no vested financial interest. Volunteers have their own lives, their own jobs, and many other responsibilities and obligations related to family, work, and community. The fact that they choose to serve your organization speaks highly of your work and should be utilized to support your fundraising.

Volunteers provide important linkages to donors and prospective donors. Remembering the principle of Linkage Interest Ability (from Chapter 3), which states that the greatest potential for a gift exists when a prospective donor has a linkage or connection to your organization, an interest in your cause, and the ability to give at the desired level, volunteers can help make such connections and discern donor interests and giving capacities through their personal and professional social networks. Volunteers are essential for successful prospect research because they live out in the community amongst your donors and can help you make critical assessments of their likelihood for giving and help you build meaningful and lasting relationships with them.

Volunteers can also serve as bell-weathers for gauging your local community's needs and responsiveness to particular cases for support and fundraising campaigns. Through their local involvement as citizens and neighbors they can provide insights that can help keep your fundraising activities fresh, updated, and effective.

Volunteers should also believe in philanthropic support and be donors to your organization. Given the previously discussed connection between volunteerism and philanthropic giving, as fundraisers, we would be remiss in our responsibilities if we did not give our volunteers an opportunity to financially support the organizations that they already energetically support through their time and talents in other ways. This is particularly true for those volunteers who support the fundraising program. Before they begin supporting your fundraising efforts, they must give. No one should solicit on behalf of your organization without giving themselves – staff, board, and general volunteers included.

Volunteers also provide strategic value in your planning and evaluation of fundraising activities. This is particularly evident when reviewing the Fundraising Cycle, which is not only a management model that will help you coordinate all activities but is also an educational tool for engaging volunteers in fundraising (see Chapter 3). This model has two explicit points of entry for volunteer involvement and activation, but you can truly engage volunteers at any point along the cycle. Certainly when examining the case for support, analyzing market requirements, defining and validating needs statements and objectives, volunteers can provide critical feedback against which to gauge your understanding, articulation, and presentation of community needs to your constituents. This process can be accomplished by engaging volunteers in focus groups or by circulating drafts of documents for their comments. When evaluating gift markets, selecting fundraising vehicles, identifying potential giving sources, and creating your fundraising and communications plans, volunteers can provide recommendations, contacts, creative ideas, and other valuable inputs for your planning and decision making processes. Their preparedness and willingness to participate in fundraising can dramatically extend the capability of your fundraising program, particularly if you are in a one-person or small shop. Finally, volunteers can be highly effective solicitors and relationship-builders as part of your fundraising. With proper training and support, they can help solicit gifts, demonstrate stewardship, and renew gifts through strategic and meaningful engagement with donors, both for donors they know personally as well as those they do not know personally. A volunteer can be a powerful witness and advocate for your organization when put before an individual donor, a foundation program officer, or corporate giving committee. They can provide the right blend of passion and energy to artfully convey the importance of your mission. This is particularly true for those volunteers who have personally benefited from your organization's programs and services. Determining how to create opportunities for them, in particular, to share their experiences and enthusiasm can help solidify donor relationships and illustrate your organization's impact and accountability in personal and direct ways that are nearly impossible for paid staff to accomplish. For these reasons and more, volunteers have been identified as a vital workforce for addressing the nonprofit sector's skills, manpower, and leadership gaps (Eisner et al., 2009). Therefore, when contemplating your many roles and responsibilities as a fundraiser in your organization, it is important to periodically stop and think about ways in which you can usefully and meaningfully engage volunteers in your work in order to be more effective and efficient in reaching your fundraising goals.

Steps for Successful Volunteer Involvement

As you think about how best to utilize volunteers in your fundraising program, there are eight steps for successful volunteer involvement to consider. The daily stresses of fundraising may sometimes make it difficult to do such planning and preparation. However, an initial investment of time and resources into these steps can save time, energy, and money later because you will have thoughtfully identified the intersection of needs between your organization and your volunteers, and created a process that continually supports their recruitment, training, engagement, and evaluation.

Determine the Organization's Needs

First, it is essential that you analyze the organization's volunteer needs. Volunteers can effectively serve in all aspects of a comprehensive fundraising program from direct mail, events, telethons, personal solicitation, planned giving, capital campaigns, and social media and communications (Lysakowski, 2005). So ask yourself which fundraising tasks need to be completed? How can volunteers help? How many volunteers will you need? What kind of knowledge, skills, energy, and time commitment will be necessary for the volunteers to experience success? Asking and answering these kinds of questions will help you best determine how to effectively use volunteers and how to provide meaningful experiences for them. Remember that volunteers want to be useful. Providing concrete, organized tasks that can be completed within the constraints of their availability are very important to properly engaging them and keeping them satisfied over the long term, especially in light of their many options for volunteering and the aforementioned turnover rate. After you assign roles and tasks for volunteers, you can create job descriptions that clearly delineate the assignments, requisite skills, knowledge, and time commitment for success. Doing so will help you consider the kind of individuals who may best fit your volunteer positions in terms of expertise, temperament, and availability. It will also help you clearly communicate volunteer opportunities and expectations for performance as well as consider the kinds of support you may need to provide as the fundraising professional managing volunteer involvement. It is also useful during this step to consider any legal protections, requirements, or other best practices that should guide your volunteer engagement and then develop and implement policies and procedures to operationalize them. For instance, youth organizations commonly require background security checks for volunteers who will interact with youth participants. Even if your organization may not need to take such a step, it is useful to think about other issues of concern that may impact your volunteers and prepare for them, such as privacy, confidentiality of donor records, and basic ethical practice.

Identify and Recruit Volunteers

With a clear understanding of the tasks to be completed, you can then begin the next two steps of identifying and recruiting volunteers for the positions. It is important to approach this process with the same due diligence given to the hiring for paid professional staff positions, particularly when seeking campaign chairs and others whose service and volunteer leadership will be critical to your overall success. To promote your volunteer opportunities, use word of mouth and social media amongst your organization's networks. There are also volunteer web sites such as www.volunteermatch.org that help connect volunteers with causes. There may be other volunteer matching networks in your community through your local United Way, community foundations, service clubs, youth organizations, and corporations that promote employee volunteerism. You may also have particular people in mind and may choose to begin a process of personally soliciting their involvement. This will likely be the case for key volunteer leadership positions essential to fundraising success, so give careful consideration to your prospects and approach them in dignified and respectful ways. As you interact with them, you must be prepared to make the case for why they are the best candidates for such service and how their particular blend of expertise, knowledge, skills, relationships, and reputation are appropriate for the tasks at hand. You will also want to provide volunteer candidates with sufficient time and opportunity to seriously consider their involvement and make thoughtful decisions about their commitment and participation.

Volunteer Orientation

Once your volunteers have agreed to participate, providing orientation and training is the next step for their successful involvement. Even in the case of seasoned volunteer leaders, we must take time to equip them with the basic knowledge necessary for success in their roles, whether it is general background information about the organization or the nuts and bolts of successful donor solicitation. A firm grounding in the organization's mission and operations is essential. You should never assume your volunteers are fully informed. Your orientation program can provide your volunteers with nuanced perspectives on your work and community impact. As it relates to fundraising, it is especially important for your volunteers to be versed in your organization's finances, programmatic needs, and the case for support so they can effectively and ethically interact with donors on your behalf. It will also be helpful to provide some sort of manual or online resource to which they can continually refer to enhance their understanding of your organization. After you have oriented them, it will be important to provide training that directly relates to the tasks they will perform. If they will interact with donors, then solicitation training may be in order. If they will be answering phones for the telethon, then your training will thoroughly review scripting, calling procedures, recording gifts, and using related technologies. Refer back to the job descriptions and create training opportunities that support the tasks to be completed. Also think about the time commitment necessary for training to be effective. Some tasks may only require a few hours of review and practice of particular procedures before volunteers actually begin their work. Other tasks may require extended periods of training that span several weeks to fully prepare them for service. It may also be necessary to employ the use of consultants, vendors or other volunteers in providing this training support. Clearly thinking about the training needs and the best modes of delivery will help you ensure successful entry experiences for your new volunteers and continuing satisfaction for your veteran volunteers. Lastly, do not forget the importance of motivation and inspiration. As you seek to equip your volunteers by engaging their minds and bodies through specific knowledge, procedures, and skills that will aid their completion of assignments, be sure to touch their hearts as well. Tap into their motivations and help them make connections between their tasks, your mission, and the difference being made in the lives of others and in the community. Demonstrate the value of their work. Help them catch your organizational vision of success. If possible, enable them to interact with program beneficiaries and participants or to otherwise observe your mission in action. Never miss an opportunity to reinforce your mission and connect your volunteers to it, and do not forget to provide ongoing training, validation, and support as necessary throughout the course of their volunteer assignments.

Ensure Meaningful Engagement

After properly orienting and training your volunteers, you can then involve them in the designated roles and tasks. It is critical to be direct and concrete in your assignments and to be mindful of their own interests and talents. For volunteers to find meaning in their service, they must feel connected to their work and capable of successfully serving in the prescribed activity. Finding the proper match between their personal profiles and your fundraising activities will be critical to their successful involvement and long-term engagement. Additionally, we must ever be cognizant of our volunteers' satisfaction with their service so they stay focused and committed to the work and we are successful in achieving our fundraising goals. This relates to the next step of using volunteers' time carefully. Volunteers have limitations on the amount of time and energy they can devote to your cause, so you must use their time wisely and never waste it with menial tasks that do not reflect the caliber of work described to them during the earlier recruitment, orientation, and training steps. Our goal should never be to keep them busy, but rather to meaningfully engage them in advancing the mission.

Evaluate Volunteers' Performance

The penultimate step to successful volunteer involvement in fundraising is evaluation of your volunteers' performance. We must take time to properly evaluate their performance for a variety of reasons. First, doing so demonstrates to our volunteers their importance to our mission and their intrinsic value to the organization. Second, evaluation provides useful and constructive feedback to enable volunteers to reflect upon and assess their contribution. Third, as professionals, we are accountable for the work done by our volunteers and we must be sure that work is indeed being completed in the proper manner so that overall goals and standards are met. Evaluation should be performed in accordance with standard practices and acceptable procedures that align with job descriptions and the information disseminated through orientation and training. It should be provided verbally and in written form and contain a mix of positive assessments of activities successfully completed and constructive critiques of activities that need improvement and development. For areas of concern, there should be specific recommendations for ways to improve, and training and support to facilitate the desired changes. When presented in such a fashion, evaluation provides an effective forum for redirecting the energies and efforts of volunteers who are not meeting expectations and giving them opportunities and support to improve their performance. For those who continue to struggle to meet expectations in spite of adequate support and constructive feedback, evaluation also provides a basis for ending a volunteer assignment and identifying a different mode of service or terminating the volunteer relationship altogether.

Recognize Volunteers

The eighth and final step in successful volunteer involvement is to provide recognition. Recognition may be public or private, formal or informal. Regardless of the form it takes, recognition is essential to supporting your volunteers, ensuring their satisfaction, and showing appreciation for their service. Given that volunteers operate from a variety of motivations for serving, as previously discussed, rewards can help fulfill some of their needs for acknowledgement and also celebrate models of successful and effective service. It is also important that recognition be provided through an appropriate vehicle that matches the service provided. First, of course, are the words, "Thank you." You should use them frequently and generously with your volunteers. Recognition can also be in the form of letters of appreciation, plaques and awards, media coverage, and acknowledgement at dinners or other events. Depending upon the organization, it may also be appropriate to provide small tokens of appreciation such as gift certificates, promotional items with organizational logos, or other representations of the mission. The key is to think about meaningful expressions of gratitude, appreciation, and support for the service rendered.

There are many reasons for involving volunteers in your organization's mission. The key to being successful in such involvement is being clear about organizational needs for volunteers, being prepared to receive volunteers and effectively use their time and talents toward the advancement of your mission, being direct about expectations and deliberate in matching volunteer talents and interests with organizational needs and opportunities, and being constructive in your evaluation and recognition of their service.

Volunteer Policies and Procedures

Volunteer policies and procedures are essential for supporting the eight-step model of volunteer engagement. They serve many functions within a nonprofit organization, such as: conveying organizational values, protecting all stakeholders, creating consistency, articulating organizational processes, and providing clear expectations for roles and responsibilities within volunteer management. Additionally, organizations' use of signed agreements can help manage legal or ethical dilemmas, and formal disciplinary and dismissal procedures can help an organization terminate or reassign a troublesome or ineffective volunteer, which is sometimes an unfortunate yet very real aspect of our work.

There are many questions to consider when developing volunteer policies and procedures for your nonprofit organization. Using the eight-step model of volunteer involvement can help guide your initial process. Ask yourself who the policies need to protect? Consider all stakeholders, including staff, volunteers, clients, and donors. Also ask yourself what kind of work will volunteers do? What expectations should the organization have for volunteers and their work? Will volunteers handle sensitive information or work with vulnerable populations? Using these questions to start a dialogue within your development office or organization can begin the process of articulating volunteer policies and procedures.

The types of specific volunteer policies needed may vary from organization to organization due to differences in mission, needs, culture, and constituents. However, general volunteer management policies to consider include those related to confidentiality, use of volunteers in events, conflict of interest, background checks, staff–volunteer relations, antidiscrimination and sexual harassment, as well as dismissal and disciplinary action. Increasingly, organizations need to consider policies to govern individual volunteers or independent groups of volunteers who seek to raise money, build public awareness, or otherwise advocate for them on their own apart from the formal structures and processes of the nonprofit organization. Such volunteers have been labeled "free agents," and can be valuable assets to your mission (Kanter and Fine, 2010). Traditionally, nonprofits may have ignored free agent volunteers because they were not formally affiliated with the organization and it was a sufficient task for them to keep up with the formal volunteers who were officially connected. In today's highly networked world, nonprofits are having to rethink how they interact with free agents in order to maximize their reach. Creating policies for this type of third-party volunteer can help establish parameters for how far they may go in representing your cause; making claims about your mission; raising money on your behalf; and using your logos, taglines, and other promotional material. The final step in policy development is to follow your organization's governance structure so that the board and its committees may thoughtfully consider, debate, and approve the volunteer management policies.

Volunteer management in fundraising can be very difficult at times, but creating policies and procedures allows staff to maintain organizational standards and provide a safe, consistent environment for volunteers. Such consistency and structure can lead to more fulfilling and positive volunteer experiences.

Volunteer Retention

The vast majority of volunteers continue their service annually; however, one-third of volunteers lapse in their service year to year (Corporation for National and Community Service, 2010). This turnover rate is very high, but, while we as fundraising professionals may not be able to control all of the factors that contribute to it, there are steps we can take to keep our volunteers happy and engaged. Research has shown that volunteers tend to end their involvement due to poor matches between their skills and available volunteer activities; inadequate acknowledgement and recognition practices; poor training and support; and inadequate leadership and supervision (Eisner et al., 2009). Each of these factors can be easily avoided by fundraising professionals who make the time to take care of their volunteers. Providing orientation, training, continuing support, evaluation, and recognition, as discussed above, are all critical elements of successful volunteer retention. Research shows that the more time volunteers spend in service, the more likely they are to continue serving (Corporation for National and Community Service, 2010). Therefore, we must diligently support and be attentive to our volunteers. In this way, our volunteer relationships are very much like our donor relationships. They require the same kind of nurturing, cultivation, and stewardship in order to be rewarding for volunteers and effective sources of labor for organizations.

Staff Driven versus Volunteer-Driven Fundraising Programs

As fundraising has become more professionalized and fundraising programs more institutionalized, a tendency has developed in certain institutions for staff-driven fundraising over volunteer-driven fundraising. It is fairly common in colleges and universities, hospitals, and cultural institutions to observe staff-driven fundraising programs in which paid professional staff conduct all aspects of fundraising with little or no apparent volunteer involvement in the process. There are numerous arguments in favor of such approaches, having to do with the efficient use of staff time in actual fundraising rather than volunteer management, and concerns over volunteer commitment and availability over extended periods, such as those marked by annual or capital campaigns. That said, even staff-driven institutions often find ways to meaningfully engage volunteers in their fundraising, whether formally through serving on campaign cabinets and advisory councils or informally through reviewing prospect lists and opening doors to donor contacts. Ultimately, it is up to each organization to determine the extent to which it will involve volunteers in fundraising. Certainly, all fundraising should begin and end with an organization's board of directors (see Chapter 32 for a discussion of the board's role in fundraising). Nothing can supplant the leadership and involvement of board volunteers in successful fundraising. However, as has been discussed in this chapter, non-board volunteers have much to offer fundraising programs and with adequate planning and deliberate execution, such volunteers can be successfully integrated into organizational fundraising.

Conclusion

Volunteers are essential for successful fundraising. Nonprofit organizations that do not find ways to meaningfully engage volunteers in their fundraising are missing major opportunities to strengthen ties with their donors, build their credibility, enhance their own community relations, and draw upon qualified talent to support their missions. Professional fundraisers should understand what motivates their volunteers so they can effectively steward the volunteer relationship to maximize volunteer service and satisfaction along with community impact. The eight-step model of volunteer involvement is a proven approach for matching volunteer skills and interests with organizational needs in fundraising. Hank Rosso believed that volunteers, both board and others, were essential to successful fundraising because of their lack of vested interest in organizations and the passion and enthusiasm they bring because organizational missions resonate with their deeply held values and personal priorities. Organizations that establish policies, processes, and procedures for regularly and effectively engaging volunteers in fundraising in meaningful ways will experience tremendous returns on their investment.

Discussion Questions

1) Why is it important to understand volunteer motivations? How can this information aid your organization in identifying, recruiting, and retaining volunteers?
2) What strategic value can volunteers provide to your organization? List three ways volunteers can uniquely contribute to your mission.
3) Which step in the eight steps for successful volunteer involvement do you believe to be the most challenging for your organization? Why and what steps can you take to address it?
4) What is your organization's volunteer retention rate? What does it reveal about your current volunteer management program?

PART SEVEN

ETHICS AND ACCOUNTABILITY

CHAPTER THIRTY-FOUR

ETHICS AND ACCOUNTABILITY

By Eugene R. Tempel

Why do the actions of a few impact so many? This is one of the key questions that resulted from the study of U.S. fundraisers (Duronio and Tempel, 1997). Fundraisers are concerned about the ethics of their colleagues. The answer to this question lies in public expectations of the nonprofit sector. Those working in the nonprofit sector are held to a higher level of trust than those in the for-profit sector. The Association for Fundraising Professionals (AFP) code of ethics (see Exhibit 34.1) challenges its members to accept responsibility, not only for their own behavior but the behavior of their institutions as well, in areas such as stewardship, accountability, and confidentiality.

As fundraising practitioners work toward professional status, both technical and ethical standards are essential. Most of this volume deals with the rationale for, and technical aspects of, fundraising. This chapter deals with the ethical aspects. The ethical practice of philanthropic fundraising is essential to both the continued development of philanthropy through increased public confidence and trust and the professionalization of fundraising as a field of practice.

This chapter covers the following:

• Role of ethics in professionalism.
• Standards and codes of ethics.
• Ethical values and competing goods.
• Identifying and solving ethical dilemmas.

EXHIBIT 34.1. ASSOCIATION OF FUNDRAISING PROFESSIONALS (AFP) CODE OF ETHICAL PRINCIPLES AND STANDARDS OF PROFESSIONAL PRACTICE.

Adopted 1964; amended September 2007

The Association of Fundraising Professionals (AFP) exists to foster the development and growth of fundraising professionals and the profession, to promote high ethical behavior in the fundraising profession, and to preserve and enhance philanthropy and volunteerism.

Members of AFP are motivated by an inner drive to improve the quality of life through the causes they serve. They serve the ideal of philanthropy, are committed to the preservation and enhancement of volunteerism, and hold stewardship of these concepts as the overriding direction of their professional life. They recognize their responsibility to ensure that needed resources are vigorously and ethically sought and that the intent of the donor is honestly fulfilled.

To these ends, AFP members, both individual and business, embrace certain values that they strive to uphold in performing their responsibilities for generating philanthropic support. AFP business members strive to promote and protect the work and mission of their client organizations.

AFP members, both individual and business, aspire to:

- Practice their profession with integrity, honesty, truthfulness, and adherence to the absolute obligation to safeguard the public trust.
- Act according to the highest goals and visions of their organizations, professions, clients, and consciences.
- Put philanthropic mission above personal gain.
- Inspire others through their own sense of dedication and high purpose.
- Improve their professional knowledge and skills, so that their performance will better serve others.
- Demonstrate concern for the interests and well-being of individuals affected by their actions.
- Value the privacy, freedom of choice, and interests of all those affected by their actions.
- Foster cultural diversity and pluralistic values and treat all people with dignity and respect.
- Affirm, through personal giving, a commitment to philanthropy and its role in society.
- Adhere to the spirit as well as the letter of all applicable laws and regulations.
- Advocate within their organizations adherence to all applicable laws and regulations.

- Avoid even the appearance of any criminal offense or professional misconduct.
- Bring credit to the fundraising profession by their public demeanor.
- Encourage colleagues to embrace and practice these ethical principles and standards.
- Be aware of the codes of ethics promulgated by other professional organizations that serve philanthropy.

Ethical Standards

Furthermore, while striving to act according to the above values, AFP members, both individual and business, agree to abide (and to ensure, to the best of their ability, that all members of their staff abide) by the AFP standards. Violation of the standards may subject the member to disciplinary sanctions, including expulsion, as provided in the AFP Ethics Enforcement Procedures.

Member Obligations

1. Members shall not engage in activities that harm the members' organizations, clients, or profession.
2. Members shall not engage in activities that conflict with their fiduciary, ethical, and legal obligations to their organizations, clients, or profession.
3. Members shall effectively disclose all potential and actual conflicts of interest; such disclosure does not preclude or imply ethical impropriety.
4. Members shall not exploit any relationship with a donor, prospect, volunteer, client, or employee for the benefit of the members or the members' organizations.
5. Members shall comply with all applicable local, state, provincial, and federal civil and criminal laws.
6. Members recognize their individual boundaries of competence and are forthcoming and truthful about their professional experience and qualifications and will represent their achievements accurately and without exaggeration.
7. Members shall present and supply products and/or services honestly and without misrepresentation and will clearly identify the details of those products, such as availability of the products and/or services and other factors that may affect the suitability of the products and/or services for donors, clients, or nonprofit organizations.
8. Members shall establish the nature and purpose of any contractual relationship at the outset and will be responsive and available to organizations and their employing organizations before, during, and after any sale of materials and/or services. Members will comply with all fair and reasonable obligations created by the contract.

(Continued)

EXHIBIT 34.1. (CONTINUED).

9. Members shall refrain from knowingly infringing the intellectual property rights of other parties at all times. Members shall address and rectify any inadvertent infringement that may occur.
10. Members shall protect the confidentiality of all privileged information relating to the provider/client relationships.
11. Members shall refrain from any activity designed to disparage competitors untruthfully.

Solicitation and Use of Philanthropic Funds

12. Members shall take care to ensure that all solicitation and communication materials are accurate and correctly reflect their organizations' mission and use of solicited funds.
13. Members shall take care to ensure that donors receive informed, accurate, and ethical advice about the value and tax implications of contributions.
14. Members shall take care to ensure that contributions are used in accordance with donors' intentions.
15. Members shall take care to ensure proper stewardship of all revenue sources, including timely reports on the use and management of such funds.
16. Members shall obtain explicit consent by donors before altering the conditions of financial transactions.

Presentation of Information

17. Members shall not disclose privileged or confidential information to unauthorized parties.
18. Members shall adhere to the principle that all donor and prospect information created by, or on behalf of, an organization or a client is the property of that organization or client and shall not be transferred or utilized except on behalf of that organization or client.
19. Members shall give donors and clients the opportunity to have their names removed from lists that are sold to, rented to, or exchanged with other organizations.
20. Members shall, when stating fundraising results, use accurate and consistent accounting methods that conform to the appropriate guidelines adopted by the American Institute of Certified Public Accountants (AICPA) for the type of organization involved. (In countries outside the United States a comparable authority should be utilized.)

Compensation and Contracts

21. Members shall not accept compensation or enter into a contract that is based on a percentage of contributions; nor shall members accept finder's fees or contingent fees. Business members must refrain from receiving compensation from third parties derived from products or services for a client without disclosing that third-party compensation to the client (for example, volume rebates from vendors to business members).
22. Members may accept performance-based compensation, such as bonuses, provided such bonuses are in accord with prevailing practices within the members' own organizations and are not based on a percentage of contributions.
23. Members shall neither offer nor accept payments or special considerations for the purpose of influencing the selection of products or services.
24. Members shall not pay finder's fees, commissions, or percentage compensation based on contributions, and shall take care to discourage their organizations from making such payments.
25. Any member receiving funds on behalf of a donor or client must meet the legal requirements for the disbursement of those funds. Any interest or income earned on the funds should be fully disclosed.

Source: Copyright © 1964, Association of Fundraising Professionals (AFP), all rights reserved. Reprinted with permission from the Association of Fundraising Professionals

Issues of Trust

America was in a crisis of trust during the end of the twentieth century. Only 57 percent of those surveyed in a national study indicated they trusted or trusted highly private higher education, the highest level of trust in any American institution. The numbers for healthcare were 39 percent, while private and community foundations were 31.6 percent. Only 15.8 percent indicated they trusted or trusted highly Congress (INDEPENDENT SECTOR, 1996). Since then, public confidence in nonprofit organizations remains low. According to a March 2008 study, 34 percent of Americans said they had "not too much" confidence in charities or "none at all." This lack of confidence seriously challenges "the sector's distinctiveness as a destination for giving and volunteering" (Light, 2008). A 2015 *Chronicle of Philanthropy* survey (Perry, 2015) found no change in this number with two-thirds of Americans indicating they have a great deal or a fair amount of confidence in charities. One hopeful note is that eighty percent indicated that charities "do a very good or somewhat good job of helping people" (Perry, 2015).

Scandals, stories of abuse, mismanagement, and waste, while sometimes sensationalized by the media, affect people's confidence in the nonprofit sector as a whole. Trust is the foundation upon which philanthropy is developed. Donors must "trust" and have confidence that when they contribute their funds to an organization they will be used wisely as promised. As was indicated in Chapter 22, today donors and the public demand transparency and accountability from organizations. Transparency and accountability and ethical behavior on the part of fundraisers and by their organizations build trust and support philanthropy.

Ethics and Professionalism

Ethics is one of the key elements in making a group of practitioners a profession. More than 25 years ago, Carbone focused on the concept of fundraising as a profession. He evaluated fundraising according to six criteria commonly accepted as essential to a profession: (1) autonomy, (2) systematic knowledge, (3) self-regulation, (4) commitment and identification, (5) altruism and dedication to service, and (6) ethics and sanctions (Carbone, 1989). Fundraisers have made significant progress toward securing a profession based on these six criteria. The majority of fundraisers are committed both to their organizations and to their careers. Fundraisers are more generous with their resources and time than other citizens. Fundraisers are concerned about the ethical behavior of other fundraisers (Duronio and Tempel, 1997). AFP has in place a process for sanctioning members who violate the code of ethics.

A profession is built upon the notion of service to others and the trust that comes from a commitment to place the interest of clients above self-interest. Pribbenow (1999) argues that, as a profession, fundraising must focus on serving the public good rather than attempting to define itself in terms related to other professions. Service to the public good ensures trust. Trust is built on the practitioner's performance with both technical and ethical proficiency.

There is a larger knowledge base to help us develop proficiency in both arenas. Scholars have attempted to assist fundraisers faced with ethical problems and ethical dilemmas. This includes David Smith, in his edited volume *Good Intentions: Moral Obstacles and Opportunities* (2005) and Janice Gow Pettey's practical guide entitled *Nonprofit Fundraising Strategy* (2013). Taken together, these resources provide a framework for dealing with the ethical questions faced by fundraisers and their nonprofit organizations.

Fundraising executives, leaders, and managers have a responsibility to be informed and to think carefully and critically about the ethical standards and ethical issues that are essential to the health of the nonprofit sector and philanthropy.

They also must be able to teach colleagues and donors about ethical issues. These issues are critical to the nonprofit organizations that carry out the work of the sector and to the fundraisers who help those organizations acquire their resources.

There are standards covered later in the chapter that can help guide us in ethical practice. However, most ethical issues are not as simple as a series of "do's and don'ts" that can be memorized and uniformly applied. Ethical issues require fundraisers to develop broad frameworks, principles through which best choices can be made. Robert Payton, former director of the Center on Philanthropy at Indiana University, said, "There are no ethical answers; there are only ethical questions." Therefore, practicing fundraisers aspiring to be professional in their work to enhance the public trust need to educate themselves about the ethical questions in their profession so they can make the best choices when confronted with them.

Ethical standards can help fundraisers decide initially on a number of issues that are clearly unethical. The Code of Ethics of the Association of Fundraising Professionals (see Exhibit 34.1) provides such guidance and so do the codes of the Association of Healthcare Philanthropy (see Exhibit 34.2), CASE and others. They provide excellent foundations for ethical practice, and adhering to them builds trust. However, they will not provide all the answers. Most decisions are not as simple as following rules. Therefore, fundraisers must prepare themselves to function in an ethical context, where concern for meeting public and professional expectations as fully as possible is always a primary focus.

EXHIBIT 34.2. AHP STATEMENT OF PROFESSIONAL STANDARDS AND CONDUCT.

All members shall comply with the Association's Statement of Professional Standards and Conduct:

Association for Healthcare Philanthropy members represent to the public, by personal example and conduct, both their employer and their profession. They have, therefore, a duty to faithfully adhere to the highest standards and conduct in:

I. Their promotion of the merits of their institutions and of excellence in health care generally, providing community leadership in cooperation with health, educational, cultural, and other organizations.

II. Their words and actions, embodying respect for truth, honesty, fairness, free inquiry, and the opinions of others, treating all with equality and dignity.

III. Their respect for all individuals without regard to race, color, sex, religion, national origin, disability, age, or any other characteristic protected by applicable law.

(Continued)

EXHIBIT 34.2. (CONTINUED).

IV. Their commitment to strive to increase professional and personal skills for improved service to their donors and institutions, to encourage and actively participate in career development for themselves and others whose roles include support for resource development functions, and to share freely their knowledge and experience with others as appropriate.

V. Their continuing effort and energy to pursue new ideas and modifications to improve conditions for, and benefits to, donors and their institution.

VI. Their avoidance of activities that might damage the reputation of any donor, their institution, any other resource development professional or the profession as a whole, or themselves, and to give full credit for the ideas, words, or images originated by others.

VII. Their respect for the rights of privacy of others and the confidentiality of information gained in the pursuit of their professional duties.

VIII. Their acceptance of a compensation method freely agreed upon and based on their institution's usual and customary compensation guidelines, which have been established and approved for general institutional use while always remembering that: any compensation agreement should fully reflect the standards of professional conduct; and antitrust laws in the United States prohibit limitation on compensation methods.

IX. Their respect for the law and professional ethics as a standard of personal conduct, with full adherence to the policies and procedures of their institution.

X. Their pledge to adhere to this Statement of Professional Standards and Conduct, and to encourage others to join them in observance of its guidelines.

Some years ago, when Robert Payton was still an executive with the Exxon Education Foundation, he asked fundraisers the question, "Do we live for philanthropy or do we live off philanthropy?" Professional fundraising executives must keep this question before them constantly. Personal gain is the first vulnerable point in public trust. Section 501(3)(c) of the Internal Revenue Code, which provides for the establishment of nonprofit organizations, defines criteria for those eligible for charitable contributions:

Corporations, and any community chest, fund, or foundation, organized and operated exclusively for religious, charitable, scientific, testing for public safety, literary, or educational purposes, or for the prevention of cruelty to children or animals, no part of the net earnings of which inures to the benefit of any private shareholder or individual, no substantial part of the activities of which is carrying on propaganda, or otherwise attempting, to influence legislation, and which does not participate in, or intervene in (including the publishing or distributing of statements), any political campaign on behalf of any candidate for public office.

Fundraising executives must be cognizant especially of the "nondistribution" clause: "no part of the net earnings of which inures to the benefit of any private shareholder or individual."

The nondistribution clause requires nonprofit organizations and those associated with them to commit themselves to the public good. It is the foundation for the establishment of trust between donors and organizations. Professional fundraising executives have a legal and ethical responsibility to make certain that all others associated with organizations do not benefit personally from the funds that are contributed to the organization.

This does not mean they should not be paid fairly and equitably for their work. It does mean that they do not accept commissions on gifts. It does mean that they do not accept personal gifts from donors. It does mean that salaries must be commensurate with public expectations. It does mean that board members should not have competitive advantage in bidding for business with the organization. So important is the nondistribution clause to the issue of trust that associations representing professionals and organizations in the nonprofit sector worked together to pass legislation known as "intermediate sanctions" to aid the sector in self-regulation and to provide the IRS with penalties it can impose for excessive benefit and inside dealing (INDEPENDENT SECTOR, 1998). The regulations for Intermediate Sanctions can be found on the INDEPENDENT SECTOR's website.

What distinguishes the professional from the technician may be trustworthiness. The professional is conscientious about putting the interests of the client first. Those who work on behalf of nonprofit organizations must have fidelity to their missions. They must earn the trust of the organizations that employ fundraisers. Finally, they have an obligation to understand the larger mission of the nonprofit sector, to understand the role of philanthropy generally, not just their own organization, because the donor and the organization function in the larger environment of the nonprofit or philanthropic sector. Understanding the mission of the sector helps them view philanthropy from the donor's perspective. Increasingly fundraisers are called upon to assist donors with philanthropy in ways other than to their own organizations (Tempel and Beem, 2002). A recent study of high net worth households by the Indiana University Lilly Family School of Philanthropy (2014) found again that nonprofit organizational staff are among the key advisors on philanthropy.

These issues of professionalism raise such broad questions as the following (The Fund Raising School, 2009):

- What is the role of trust in development fundraising professionals?
- What are the burdens placed on fundraising practitioners by the "non-distribution clause" in Section 501(c)(3) of the code?
- As fundraising practitioners, who is the client: the donor or the organization?
- In every transaction, what are the intents of the donor and what are the intents of the organization?
- How can fundraising professionals protect and maintain their integrity as "boundary spanners" between donors and organizations?
- How do fundraisers manage the tensions that arise when working for organizations who also assist donors to expand their philanthropy?

Approaches to Ethics

In some circumstances, these and other questions are easy to answer because there is a clear-cut, best choice. However, when there is conflict between two goods or the appearance of conflict between two goods, the questions become more difficult to answer as in the typical tainted money questions. If money obtained under less than honorable circumstances is offered for a worthy cause, should it be accepted? Does accepting it compromise the organization's integrity while it provides some public good? Does accepting it add legitimacy to the source of the money? Does denying it enhance your organization's integrity while denying fulfillment of some public need?

Payton's statement that there are only ethical questions echoes a number of other writers, Josephson (2002), Anderson (1996), Fischer (2000), who agree that ethics in fundraising is complex. Philosophers like Kant suggested that there were, in fact, right answers, but Kant's categorical imperative suggests that ethical theories and dilemmas are often difficult to assess at the level of practice.

Anderson (1996) refers to this approach as formalism, and formalism provides a beginning. In fact, some ethical matters can be decided based on standards such as codes of ethics. However, situations where there are competing goods require a more complex decision-making process. Both Josephson (2002) and Anderson (1996) refer to this as consequentialism. The question for fundraisers is "What will be best for the greatest number of constituents in the long run?" The ethical conflicts fundraisers face can be reconciled through sets of values, beliefs, and commitments against which they can judge their actions.

What lies behind ethics? This could be a set of values and beliefs that lead to trust in the decisions that are made and that lead to expectations about the actions of others. The Josephson Institute has surveyed more than 10,000 individuals to define the values that are important to an ethical or virtuous person. This experiment can be replicated with a group. Ask the group what they think are the attributes or characteristics of an ethical person. They will come up with a list similar to the ones below. *Making Ethical Decisions* (Josephson, 2002) is grounded in the advocacy of 10 major ethical values that form the basis for ethical decision making. Josephson's 10 values are:

1. Honesty
2. Integrity
3. Promise-keeping
4. Loyalty/fidelity
5. Fairness
6. Concern for others
7. Respect for others
8. Law-abidingness/civic duty
9. Pursuit of excellence
10. Personal accountability

Anderson (1996) developed a similar list:

1. Respect
   - Individual autonomy
   - Personal privacy
   - Non-maleficence
2. Beneficence
   - Public good
   - Charitable intent
3. Trust
   - Truth-telling
   - Promise-keeping
   - Accountability
   - Fairness
   - Fidelity of purpose

INDEPENDENT SECTOR (2002a) outlined nine commitments that mirror the ethical values listed by Anderson and Josephson. These commitments are proposed as essential to those who are associated with the nonprofit and philanthropic sectors.

- **Commitment beyond self** is at the core of a civil society.
- **Obedience to the laws**, including those governing tax-exempt philanthropic and voluntary organizations is a fundamental responsibility of stewardship.
- **Commitment beyond the law**, to obedience to the unenforceable, is the higher obligation of leaders of philanthropic and voluntary organizations.
- **Commitment to the public good** requires those who presume to serve the public good to assume a public trust.
- **Respect for the worth and dignity of individuals** is a special leadership responsibility of philanthropic and voluntary organizations.
- **Tolerance, diversity, and social justice** reflect the independent sector's rich heritage and the essential protections afforded it.
- **Accountability to the public** is a fundamental responsibility of public benefit organizations.
- **Openness and honesty** in reporting, fundraising, and relationships with all constituencies are essential behaviors for organizations that seek and use public or private funds and that purport to serve public purposes.
- **Prudent application of resources** is a concomitant of public trust.

INDEPENDENT SECTOR (2002a) proposes that those working in nonprofit public benefit organizations must integrate these nine commitments into their work. This certainly holds true for fundraising. Strengthening transparency, governance, and ethical standards are so important to the health of the nonprofit sector that INDEPENDENT SECTOR developed the *Principles of Good Governance and Ethical Practice* (2007). The report is freely available online and is an excellent resource for new organizations just getting started and for well-established organizations who want to evaluate and improve their current practices.

These values and commitments apply to the behavior of fundraisers and to the various codes of ethics included in the exhibits accompanying this chapter. In fact, when Peg Duronio asked participants in her study of fundraisers what they admired most about their ideal colleague, the overwhelming response was "integrity" (Duronio and Tempel, 1997).

Fundraisers must be honest in dealings with donors and organizations. Their behavior must be dependable and they must be true to their word. To earn integrity, they must carry out their work in ways that represent their organizations and colleagues best. They must keep the promises made to donors when their gifts were accepted. Fundraisers must be loyal to both the organization and the donor. Their negotiations must be fair to both the organization and the donor. Fundraisers must demonstrate concern for the donor as an individual or entity and have genuine respect for donors rather than envy their resources or view them as objects to be manipulated for gain.

Fundraisers must not only abide by the laws but demonstrate their own civic and philanthropic responsibility as well. They have a responsibility to be the best they can be as professionals and they must be personally accountable for their actions and the actions of their clients. All can agree to the set of obligations that Josephson's values promote, but it is conflict among these values that requires complex decision making.

Ethical Dilemmas

What does the professional fundraiser do (personal accountability) when the organization (loyalty–fidelity) decides to use funds given for one purpose by a donor (promise keeping, integrity, honesty) for another purpose? Josephson (2002) recommends three steps for considering ethical conflicts:

I. All decisions must take into account and reflect a concern for the interests and well-being of all shareholders.
II. Ethical values and principles *always* take precedence over nonethical ones.
III. It is ethically proper to violate an ethical principle only when it is CLEARLY NECESSARY TO ADVANCE ANOTHER TRUE ETHICAL PRINCIPLE, WHICH ACCORDING TO THE DECISION MAKER'S CONSCIENCE, WILL PRODUCE THE GREATEST BALANCE OF GOOD IN THE LONG RUN.

Fischer (2000) has outlined a similar approach. She poses questions around three broad themes: organizational mission, relationships, and personal integrity.

INDEPENDENT SECTOR (2002a) outlines three tiers of actions. First, some actions are clearly illegal. Decisions about these are very clear. Second, some things are clearly unethical. Decisions about these actions are also fairly easy to make, sometimes using codes of ethics. Third, there are what INDEPENDENT SECTOR calls ethical dilemmas. Decisions about ethical dilemmas resemble the Josephson Institute's model and also Anderson's discussion where there are competing goods or conflicting values.

INDEPENDENT SECTOR (2002a) recommends evaluating these choices in terms of the commitments beyond self. It provides examples of actions involving all three levels:

• Example of an illegal act. The organization's copying and fax machines are used routinely by a friendly candidate for public office. Why is this illegal?
• Example of unethical behavior. In lieu of salary, the staff director prefers receiving a percentage of all funds raised. Why is this unethical?

- Example of an ethical dilemma. The all-volunteer organization recognizes that hiring its first executive director will absorb all the money on hand and in sight. Half of the board argues that all the time and money will go to support the position with nothing left for programs and the other half says it is a necessary investment in future growth. What should they do?

Josephson's model provides us with a framework for getting to a best answer. The problem posed is not unlike a choice that fundraising executives confront on an annual basis. A new investment in fundraising leaves less money for programs. On the other hand, new investments in fundraising eventually produce additional dollars for programs (long-term/short-term dilemmas). Under what circumstances does the future potential outweigh the current loss? What other ethical values come into play when this decision is made? Who are the key stakeholders?

Applying Ethics in Fundraising

Robert Payton designed an ethics cube to outline the categories of ethical dilemmas that fundraisers face. The top and bottom of the ethics cube contain the words: "Individual" (here meaning the fundraiser) and "Organization," respectively. The four sides of the cube contain the words: "Competence," "Language," "Relations," and "Mission." These components are timeless.

The Individual and the Organization

The first ethical tension that fundraising executives must mediate is the potential conflict between themselves (as individuals) and their organizations. Fundraising executives must examine their motives constantly to make certain that they are not acting in their own self-interest but rather in the interests of the organization. "Do we live for or off philanthropy?"

At the same time, fundraising executives have a right to expect the organization to treat them as professionals. Issues of compensation, for example, arise from this tension. Fundraising executives have a right to expect fair and adequate compensation, in line with what others in the organization, and similar organizations, are paid. However, fundraising executives should not accept percentage compensation because it focuses their work on personal gain rather than organizational benefit (and donor interests). The "Intermediate Sanctions" codes of the IRS provides guidance determining fair compensation. The requirements are available on the INDEPENDENT SECTOR website.

Another tension arises when fundraisers face the question, "Who is the client?" Is the organization the client or is the donor the client? They must protect the interests of both. This heightens the tension between the fundraiser as an individual and the organization that employs him or her, a tension, as indicated earlier, that is likely to increase in the twenty-first century.

The client question is a serious one. Mediating between the donor and the organization is the most difficult role the fundraising executive must play. Grounding oneself in ethical values and understanding the tensions that accompany this relationship are important steps in becoming a fundraising professional. Fundraisers can best prepare themselves by understanding that both the donor and the organization have rights and interests. Fundraisers must first understand the boundaries, the parameters of the organization. They must also understand the boundaries of donors in general and the particular boundaries and interests of particular donors. Being honest with both the organization and the donor is the first step in mediating the interest of organizations and donors. Maintaining integrity and keeping promises are not possible without honesty about what is possible.

Competence

The concept of competence also applies to fundraising executives. Professionals must dedicate themselves to being as competent as they can possibly be (personal accountability). What are the ethical and technical standards that they must learn and implement to become competent professionals? Training to develop technical standards and academic study to help develop technical expertise are important. However, understanding ethical standards, developing ethical values, and applying standards and ethical values to decision making about ethical dilemmas in fundraising are essential. The concept of competence relates to both Josephson's values and INDEPENDENT SECTOR's commitments. Josephson's values of law abidingness/civic duty, pursuit of excellence and personal accountability apply here. The INDEPENDENT SECTOR values of obedience of the law, commitment beyond the law, accountability to the public, commitment to the public good, and prudent application of resources apply here.

Language

Language is an important aspect of fundraising. The ways fundraisers talk about their profession and the ways they discuss the process of fundraising and philanthropy from individuals, corporations, foundations, and others are important to the dignity of the processes. Donors are not "targets." The dignified process of inviting someone to make a gift is not "hitting them up." The materials about the organization must reflect the mission, intentions, and purposes of the organization. Case materials should not simply respond to donor interest with no intention of fulfilling donor interest once the gift is received. The Josephson Institute values of honesty and integrity are appropriate to the concept of language. The INDEPENDENT SECTOR commitment to openness and honesty applies to ethics in language.

Relationships

The fundraising process is about building relationships between donors and organizations. One of the key questions for a fundraiser is "Who owns the relationship?" Relationships that fundraisers have with donors exist only because of the organization. The organizations own the relationships. Who benefits from these relationships? Benefits should accrue only to the organization. The role of trust also is important here. The donor must be able to trust that the fundraising executive will not benefit personally from the relationship. The organization must also be able to trust that the relationship will remain with the organization if the executive leaves.

The Josephson Institute values of promise keeping, loyalty–fidelity, fairness, concern for others, and respect for others help create an ethics of relationships. The INDEPENDENT SECTOR commitments of respect for the worth and dignity of individuals, a commitment to tolerance and diversity and social justice, contribute to the ethics of relationships. The Rosso phrase often cited in this book, "Fundraising is the servant of philanthropy," applies here.

Mission

Fundraising begins with mission. Every organization has a responsibility to understand its rationale for existence as a nonprofit organization. Fundraising executives must understand the mission and use the mission as the means for bringing individuals, corporations, foundations, and others together with the organization based on mutual values and interests. Mission is directed to client needs. Mission is based upon the public good. Fundraisiers have a responsibility to help organizations be true to their missions. All fundraising must be based on mission. The Josephson Institute values of honesty and integrity are applicable here. INDEPENDENT SECTOR's commitment beyond self is an excellent measure for mission. Mission must be directed externally beyond those who are employed by the organization. INDEPENDENT SECTOR's commitment to the public good is the basis for the concept of mission and provides a basis for forming an ethical understanding of actions related to mission.

These six concepts provide a framework for bringing together the various aspects of ethical values introduced earlier in this chapter and applying them to the area of greatest tension for fundraisers.

This chapter opened with the notion that there are no ethical answers, only ethical questions. Fundraising professionals must develop an ability to make ethical decisions, to solve ethical dilemmas. However, there are some starting points. Every profession must have a set of ethical standards about which there are no questions. Fundraising executives might belong to several professional associations that provide guidance. A starting point for all fundraising executives is the Code of Ethics and Standards of Practice developed by the AFP. All members of AFP are asked to subscribe to both.

Another useful perspective for fundraising executives is the Donor Bill of Rights (see Exhibit 34.3). The relationships between donors and organizations create certain expectations. If fundraisers are to develop the public trust necessary to function as professionals they must have a guide to protect donor rights. AFP, CASE, AHP, the Giving Institute, and a number of other organizations have signed a commitment to a Donor Bill of Rights to remind members of the importance of respecting donors and their responsibilities to them. The sponsoring organizations encourage organizations to adopt the Donor Bill of Rights, to copy them, or to order additional copies from AFP to distribute to their staff and donors.

EXHIBIT 34.3. THE DONOR BILL OF RIGHTS.

Philanthropy is based on voluntary action for the common good. It is a tradition of giving and sharing that is primary to the quality of life. To ensure that philanthropy merits the respect and trust of the general public and that donors and prospective donors can have full confidence in the nonprofit organizations and causes they are asked to support, we declare that all donors have these rights:

 I. To be informed of the organization's mission, of the way the organization intends to use donated resources, and of its capacity to use donations effectively for their intended purposes.
 II. To be informed of the identity of those serving on the organization's governing board and to expect the board to exercise prudent judgment in its stewardship responsibilities.
 III. To have access to the organization's most recent financial statements.
 IV. To be assured their gifts will be used for the purposes for which they were given.
 V. To receive appropriate acknowledgement and recognition.
 VI. To be assured that information about their donation is handled with respect and with confidentiality to the extent provided by law.
 VII. To expect that all relationships with individuals representing organizations of interest to the donor will be professional in nature.

(Continued)

EXHIBIT 34.3. (CONTINUED).

VIII. To be informed whether those seeking donations are volunteers, employees of the organization or hired solicitors.

IX. To have the opportunity for their names to be deleted from mailing lists that an organization may intend to share.

X. To feel free to ask questions when making a donation and to receive prompt, truthful, and forthright answers.

The Donor Bill of Rights was created by the Association of Fundraising Professionals (AFP), the Association for Healthcare Philanthropy (AHP), the Council for Advancement and Support of Education (CASE), and the Giving Institute: Leading Consultants to Non-Profits. It has been endorsed by numerous organizations.

Conclusion

A U.S. News and World Report article two decades ago described fundraising as a "dance of deceit," where fundraisers and donors are less than honest with each other. Elliot (1991) provided us guidance on the concept of deception as applied to fundraising. Avoiding deception means telling the whole truth and not allowing either party to reach a conclusion because of something that has not been said. The image of a "dance of deceit" calls for an ethical response by fundraisers and their organizations. It calls also for fundraisers to educate others about the values that motivate philanthropy.

Transparency is the beginning of ethical behavior. Transparency means that organizations open their private organizational processes to public view because they serve the public good and as such they must accept responsibility for the public trust. Accountability means using funds as intended to accomplish a promised public good and reporting it to donors and the public honestly. Transparency and accountability create larger public involvement, create public understanding, and enhance public trust.

Discussion Questions

1) Tainted money is one of the most common ethical dilemmas that fundraisers will face. What are the issues and values that must be considered in either accepting or rejecting a gift? What is the fundraisers' role?

2) Who is the client? Is it the organization or the donor? How do you decide?

3) What impact can the Donor Bill of Rights have on an organization?

4) How can the AFP code of ethics guide fundraisers on the issue of knowledge about a donor that they have because of their tenure at another organization?

CHAPTER THIRTY-FIVE

THE LAW AND FUNDRAISING

By Philip M. Purcell

After completing this chapter, you will be able to:

1. Discern the sources and role of the law in prudent decision-making, governance, and ethical considerations.
2. Explain the legal duties of care, loyalty, and obedience relative to fundraising responsibilities of directors, trustees, and staff.
3. List legal issues for fundraising that emanate from state law such as the oversight role of the attorney general, enforcement of gift restrictions, charitable pledges, endowment management, fundraising registration, and regulation of consultants and solicitors.
4. Identify legal issues for fundraising that emanate from federal law such as completion of the IRS 990 form, distinctions between public benefit charities, member benefit organizations and private foundations, supporting organizations, donor advised funds, unrelated business income tax, tax benefits for charitable giving, and gift substantiation and disclosure.
5. Describe a variety of legal issues that impact fundraising relative to international philanthropy, donor privacy, and confidentiality.

Fundraising excellence requires adherence to both the letter and spirit of legal and ethical standards. The importance of the law in fundraising is evident by the attention given to charitable organizations and their fundraising practices by the United States Congress, Internal Revenue Service (IRS), state attorney general, nonprofit boards of directors, and donors. For example, the IRS commonly includes documented abuses in fundraising and management by tax exempt organizations or donors in its annual "Dirty Dozen" list of tax scams.

The law that governs fundraising is a complex partnership of federal and state statutes, administrative regulations, and judicial decisions. Of course, this law is dynamic and subject to change. Sources of current and accurate legal information include qualified legal counsel, independent auditors, updated reference works, consultants, and state or federal government offices (e.g., state attorney general or secretary of state, IRS).

Ethical standards of conduct have been promulgated by various associations representing the fundraising profession and charitable organizations, including the Association of Fundraising Professionals, Partnership for Philanthropic Planning, Association of Healthcare Philanthropy, Council for the Advancement and Support of Education, INDEPENDENT SECTOR, and the American Council on Gift Annuities. Furthermore, associations of for-profit advisors, such as attorneys, accountants, financial planners, and insurance professionals promote ethical standards of conduct. Common themes of all ethical standards, charitable and for profit, include protecting donor or client confidentiality, avoiding conflicts of interest, assuring fair and appropriate compensation, providing competent advice to donors and clients, and complying with all legal and ethical standards. This chapter will highlight the most significant aspects of this complex legal and ethical landscape to assure excellence in fundraising.

Prudent Decision Making

Many issues in the law of fundraising are not "black and white." Rather, legal and ethical dilemmas are not easily resolved by an examination of applicable standards. Resolution of a dilemma requires considerable discernment. First, all facts and circumstances must be accurately clarified and understood in detail. Next, the current laws and ethical standards that may apply to the situation must be identified and examined. Discussion must take place with all appropriate parties who may include staff, counsel, and other appropriate constituents of the charitable organization as circumstances warrant, such as fundraisers, staff leadership, board of directors, legal counsel and auditors, as well as volunteers, donors, and their professional advisors (e.g., legal counsel, accountant, financial advisor). Finally, a decision must be made, implemented, and monitored or modified for similar circumstances in the future.

Governance

The beginning point for prudent decision making in fundraising is effective *governance*, which in turn depends in part on the organizational structure. Pursuant to state law, charitable organizations may generally be an unincorporated association, nonprofit corporation, charitable trust, or other options such as a limited liability corporation. The governance structure of each is determined under applicable state law by articles of association, constitution or bylaws (for unincorporated associations), trust instruments and governing statutes (for charitable trusts), or articles of incorporation and bylaws (for nonprofit corporations) (Fishman and Schwarz, 2010). A nonprofit corporation is the most popular organizational format as it offers a valuable balance of limitation of liability for directors and an effective governance structure. Once organized pursuant to state law, a charitable organization may seek qualification for tax exemption by the IRS as a public charity (for public or mutual benefit) or as a private foundation (consult IRS Forms 1023, 1024, and IRS Publication 557, freely available at www.irs.gov).

Duty of Prudent Care The board of directors or trustees is ultimately responsible for the oversight of a nonprofit corporation, including the assurance of fundraising excellence. State law imposes three primary legal duties on nonprofit corporation boards of directors: prudent care, loyalty, and obedience (Fishman and Schwarz, 2010). The *duty of prudent care* requires directors to exercise their responsibilities in good faith and with the diligence and skill that a prudent person would under the same circumstances. This prudent care requires carefully made decisions relative to both expenses and revenues, including generation of revenue by fundraising. When exercising this prudent care, state law may allow directors to delegate some responsibility to board designated and controlled committees that may include nondirectors. Use of development, fundraising, campaign, and other committees to oversee fundraising is an excellent means to satisfy the duty of care responsibility. A helpful resource for planning and evaluating governance best practices is the INDEPENDENT SECTOR's *The Principles for Good Governance and Ethical Practices: A Guide for Charities and Foundations (*INDEPENDENT SECTOR, *2015)* and its companion workbook to assist an organization's compliance with 33 standards of best practice.

Conflicts of Interest The *duty of obedience* requires a nonprofit corporation to carry out its legally stated charitable mission. The *duty of loyalty* requires directors to avoid acting in any manner that may harm the nonprofit corporation or that may result in the directors' personal financial gain. While the duty of loyalty is imposed by state law, federal oversight is involved as well when charitable organizations apply for tax exempt status pursuant to Internal Revenue Code section 501(c)(3) and other Code sections, requiring submission of a copy of the corporate bylaws and attestation that a conflict of interest policy has been approved by the board of directors. For example, conflicts of interest can arise in the context of fundraising if charitable gifts are used to leverage financial contracts by the charitable organization with directors or with those who may have certain relationships with directors (e.g., family or business).

IRS Form 990 and Governance   The IRS annual Form 990 information return for larger organizations asks substantive questions relative to charitable organization governance. Information concerning the board of directors, conflict of interest policies, charitable gifts, and other data are now collected and subject to IRS review. The Form 990 also asks whether the board of directors has reviewed it. Board review of the 990 is an emerging best practice that is often accompanied by review of the annual financial audit by the board. Smaller organizations pursuant may submit a simple postcard or other form requiring less information (current versions of the Form 990 and instructions are available at www.irg.gov). Completed 990 forms are available for public inspection. Oversight of prudent governance and fundraising practices will increasingly be a shared responsibility of federal and state authorities.

State Law Considerations

Oversight of charitable organizations at the state level often rests with the state Attorney General. Other state offices with oversight depending on the state may include the Secretary of State (e.g., nonprofit incorporation and annual certification) and Department of Revenue (e.g., application for property, sales and other tax exemptions, charity gaming such as bingo). The Attorney General typically has the legal standing on behalf of the general public to bring a lawsuit in court or to impose other relief (e.g., injunctions, asset receiverships, replacement of directors or trustees) in cases where claims have been made by donors, whistleblowers, or the general public asserting that mismanagement, theft, or other abuse has occurred on behalf of a charitable organization.

Definition of a Gift and Donor Restrictions

State and federal courts have required both a subjective and objective test to determine the existence of a charitable gift. The subjective test requires that the donor's intent must be "disinterested generosity" to support a charitable mission. The objective test requires that the gift does not include any financial benefit or *quid pro quo* returned to the donor in exchange for the gift (*United States v. American Bar Endowment*, 1986). In addition, a donor cannot impose restrictions on a gift that inappropriately restrict the duty of care owed by the board of directors over the use of the gift (e.g., sale or investment of donated assets).

Charitable designations or restrictions by donors are permissible. For example, restrictions for specific charitable program support are typically designated as temporarily restricted assets pursuant to the Financial Accounting Standards Board (FASB), with approval by an independent auditor, until the restriction is fulfilled. Some gifts with restrictions such as charitable endowments may be listed as permanently restricted assets by FASB. However, there are limits to donor designations, especially when uses become impossible, impractical, or illegal to fulfill. For example, in such cases where a donor is deceased, most states provide statutory procedures for a charity to modify the designations of a gift so that it can be used. These procedures are outlined in state statutory and/or court case trust law such as the legal doctrines of *cy pres* and equitable deviation, as well as pursuant to the Uniform Prudent Management of Institutional Funds Act (UPMIFA) adopted by most states.

Charitable Pledges   Fundraising programs often encourage multiyear pledge commitments. While lawsuits to enforce charitable pledges are understandably rare, these commitments may be deemed enforceable contracts pursuant to state law, particularly in cases where the charitable organization has acted in reliance on the pledge (e.g., building construction begins in reliance on a major gift pledge). In addition, FASB requires charitable pledges to be booked as a receivable on the audited financial statement of the charitable organization. Donors with active pledges may be requested to confirm their commitment by the independent auditor. Furthermore, donors to donor advised funds and private foundations cannot have their personal pledges paid from the donor advised fund or private foundation.

Charitable Endowments   A fundraising goal of many charitable organizations is to establish charitable endowments for long-term financial support. Most states have adopted a version of the Uniform Prudent Management of Institutional Funds Act (UPMIFA) as the law governing endowments. A copy of the model UPMIFA statue and a current list of enacting states is available from the Uniform Law Commissioners at www.nccusl.org. Pursuant to UPMIFA and FASB accounting standards, an endowment is defined as a gift designated as permanently endowed by a donor, either in a communication from the donor (e.g., transmittal letter, signed endowment fund agreement) or in response to the marketing materials of the charitable organization (e.g., endowment campaign letters and brochures). Alternatively, a gift that is not restricted by the donor for endowment, but is treated as endowment by action of the board of directors, is deemed to be *quasi-endowment* pursuant to FASB standards. Quasi-endowments may be spent at any time by action of the board of directors.

A board of directors must approve policies for the prudent investment, spending, and fees applicable to its endowments. While private foundations are legally required to spend at least 5 percent of its assets each year (with some exceptions), a public charity endowment does not have a required spending rate. Pursuant to UPMIFA, it is the duty of the board of directors to spend or accumulate assets as it deems prudent, balancing the short-term need for funds with the long-term perpetual support from the endowment – often with a goal of generational equity.

State Fundraising Registration

Fundraising registration requirements differ from state to state. The National Association of State Charity Officials (NASCO) is an association of state offices charged with the oversight of charitable organizations and solicitation. NASCO (www.nasconet.org) offers a model charitable solicitation law, including a unified registration form that has been used or modified by some states. Some states exempt from registration those charitable organizations domiciled in the state and who use their own staff or volunteers to fundraise. However, charitable organizations located in other states may be required to register at least once or must provide an annual registration.

Internet Fundraising

Use of the Internet for fundraising has raised new issues and challenges for states that regulate fundraising. As a result, NASCO promulgated recommended guidelines for Internet fundraising called the Charleston Principles. A basic premise of the Charleston Principles is that although existing state laws govern charitable solicitations on the Internet, state jurisdiction to regulate fraud and other deceptive practices typically exists even if an organization is not required to register to fundraise in the state.

Fundraising Consultants and Solicitors

Instead of using full or part-time staff, many charities hire consultants and/or solicitors to assist fundraising activities. The regulations for consultants and solicitors vary from state to state. In many states, a fundraising consultant is defined as an independently contracted person or organization hired to advise and train the charitable organization on fundraising strategies – but not to directly solicit gifts. A fundraising solicitor is an independently contracted person or organization hired to directly solicit gifts. Many states require annual registration with the Attorney General or other state office by fundraising consultants and solicitors before conducting business. The registration may require provision of a copy of the consulting or solicitor contracts, disclosure of the fees paid, and verification as to whether the consultant or solicitor will have custody of donations.

Percentage Requirements Percentage limitations imposed by state law on fundraising costs are not permissible. Further, fundraising solicitors are not required to affirmatively disclose fundraising costs while making the solicitation. However, states may prosecute fraudulent practices in cases where donors and prospects are not accurately informed of how much of their gifts will be paid to the fundraising solicitors (Fishman and Schwarz, 2010).

Telemarketing Many states through the Attorney General or other office maintain "do not call" lists to prevent unwanted soliciting telephone calls. Some states exempt charitable organizations from the "do not call" list so long as the charitable organization uses its own full or part-time staff or volunteers to make the soliciting calls.

Federal Law Considerations

The Internal Revenue Code (IRC) permits two types of charitable organizations pursuant to IRC Section 501(c)(3): public benefit charities and private foundations. Generally speaking, a charitable organization is presumed to be a private foundation unless it proves on its annual IRS 990 information return that it is a public benefit charity instead. The distinction is very important since gifts to public charities provide greater tax benefits to donors. In addition, private foundations must comply with a number of very restrictive rules (consult Internal Revenue Code Section 4940). These restrictions exist because the private foundation allows a single donor (an individual, family, or corporation) to have significant control over the investments, grantmaking, or operating programs of the private foundation.

Donor Advised Funds

A donor advised fund (DAF) can be an attractive alternative to a private foundation. While DAFs have been popular for many years, the Pension Protection Act of 2006 provided the first legal definition and other requirements for DAFs. DAFs are held by public charities including local community foundations and "gift funds" initiated by financial firms such as the Fidelity Charitable Gift Fund that have a charitable mission allowing grants to other qualified charitable organizations. Gifts to DAFs qualify for the enhanced tax benefits of gifts to a public charity rather than a private foundation. Pursuant to a signed agreement, the donor retains a right to recommend grants from the DAF. However, the DAF donor does not have the legal right to control the distribution of the grants or the investment of the donated assets as with a private foundation. Rather, the board of directors of the charity sponsoring the DAF retains this ultimate legal control. Pledges of donors cannot be paid from DAFs nor may the DAF make a grant for the value of a *quid pro quo* received for a gift, such as the cost of the meal included with a fundraising dinner ticket purchase.

Types of Public Benefit Charities

The Internal Revenue Code allows for two general types of public charities distinguished by whether the organization must pass a "public support test" or not. The public support test is a complicated formula that must be annually completed on the IRS Form 990 information return. In general, the public support test requires that one-third of the total support of the organization must be derived from the public and not from one person or a small number of persons. An essential component of this public support includes fundraising revenue from a broad number of donors. The types of organizations that qualify as public benefit charities without the necessity of the public support test include churches, schools, hospitals, medical research organizations, state university foundations, and governmental units (Fishman and Schwarz, 2010).

Supporting Organizations

Another type of public benefit charity that is not required to satisfy the public support test is called a supporting organization. By design, supporting organizations are created to support the charitable mission of another public benefit charity, that is, the supported organization. There are three types of supporting organizations depending on the nature of the organizational relationship and control by the supported organization of the supporting organization (Fishman and Schwarz, 2010). From a fundraising perspective, supporting organizations can be very helpful in a number of special circumstances, such as accepting specific assets that may carry potential liability (e.g., real estate), accepting large gifts to avoid violation of the public support test by the supported organization, or as an "incubator" for a charitable program that may ultimately evolve into a public benefit charity.

Member Benefit Charities

Income of a qualified member benefit organization is not taxed, but gifts to these tax exempt organizations typically do not qualify the donor for an income tax charitable deduction. Member benefit charities include civic leagues, business leagues, chambers of commerce, real estate boards, social and recreational clubs, fraternal benefit societies or associations, credit unions, and veterans organizations. The income tax deduction is available for gifts to veterans organizations, fraternal societies for charitable purposes, and cemetery companies (Internal Revenue Code Section 170(c)(3)–(5)). Some member benefit charities partner with separately incorporated public benefit charities that serve as a charitable "foundation" to accept tax deductible gifts for qualified charitable purposes (e.g., a fraternal organization using a foundation to accept gifts for scholarships).

Unrelated Business Taxable Income

Tax exempt organizations do not normally pay income tax on their fundraising or other revenue. However, revenue generated by the organization from a trade or business that is regularly carried on and not substantially related to the charitable mission will be taxed as unrelated business taxable income (UBTI). Exceptions to UBTI include revenue generated from qualified sponsorship payments so long as the donor recognition provided to sponsors does not become advertising. Many charitable organizations utilize sponsorships to meet resource development goals. Advertising that does not qualify as sponsor recognition includes endorsements, an inducement to purchase, and/or messages containing qualitative or comparative language, price information, or other indications of savings or value. Other exceptions to UBTI include passive investment income on a charitable endowment, rental on real estate, and bingo game revenue (consult IRS Publication 598, "Tax on Unrelated Business Income of Exempt Organizations," for additional guidance).

Income Tax Benefits for Charitable Giving

The income tax charitable deduction was introduced in 1917 and the estate tax charitable deduction in 1921. The dollar amount of the charitable deduction depends on the asset(s) donated as well as the type of charitable organization recipient (Toce, 2010). Gifts of cash to public benefit charities (and private operating foundations) qualify for an income tax deduction of up to 50 percent of the donor's adjusted gross income (AGI). Any excess deduction may be carried over for up to the five following tax years, claiming as much deduction as possible each year. Gifts of cash to private nonoperating foundations qualify for a deduction of up to 30 percent of the donor's AGI, with five years of carry-over. Nonoperating private foundations do not directly manage charitable programs. On the other hand, operating private foundations receive the enhanced tax benefits available to publicly supported charities for gifts that support the charitable programs they operate.

Gifts of long-term (i.e., held for more than one year) appreciated property (e.g., stock, real estate) to public benefit charities (and operating foundations) qualify for a deduction for the fair market value of the property up to 30 percent of the donor's AGI with five years of carry-over. Gifts of any asset other than qualified appreciated stock to private nonoperating foundations qualify for a deduction for the value of the donor's cost basis in the asset up to 20 percent of the donor's AGI with five years of carry-over. The donor and charitable organization owe no capital gains tax if the appreciated property is later sold, regardless of whether the donee is a public charity or private foundation.

Gifts of short-term appreciated property and ordinary income property (e.g., inventory of a trade or business such as crops, life insurance contracts, an artwork by its creator) to a public benefit charity (and operating private foundation) qualify for a deduction for the cost basis in the property of up to 50 percent of the donor's AGI, and the same gift to a private nonoperating foundation allows a deduction for the cost basis up to 30 percent of AGI, with five years to carry over any excess deduction for each.

Gifts of tangible personal property (artwork, equipment, books, etc.) to a public charity, private operating or nonoperating foundation in cases where the donee organization does not use the donated property for a purpose related to its charitable mission will result in a deduction value for the cost basis of the property up to 50 percent of the donor's AGI if given to a public benefit charity or operating foundation and 20 percent of AGI if given to a non-operating foundation, with five years of carry-over for each.

Gift and Estate Tax Benefits for Charitable Giving

There are significant differences between the income, gift, and estate tax benefits for charitable giving. First, the gift and estate tax charitable deduction does not have percentage limits. Second, the income tax charitable deduction is available only for gifts to domestic organizations while the estate tax deduction is available to domestic and foreign organizations. Third, for estate tax purposes the donee must be a corporation, association, trust, or fraternal society whereas for income tax purposes the donee may also be a community chest, fund, or foundation. For gift tax purposes, the donees are the same as for the estate tax except that gift tax law also recognizes a community chest, fund, or foundation as a qualified donee without any requirement that it be in corporate form (see Internal Revenue Code Section 2522(a)).

Gift Substantiation and Disclosure

A donor cannot claim a tax deduction for any single contribution of $250 or more unless the donor obtains a contemporaneous, written acknowledgment of the contribution. An organization that does not acknowledge a contribution incurs no penalty, but, without a written acknowledgment, the donor cannot claim the tax deduction. Although it is a donor's responsibility to obtain a written acknowledgment, an organization can assist a donor by providing a timely, written statement containing the following information:

1. Name of organization.
2. Date of the contribution.
3. Amount of cash contribution.
4. Description (but not the value) of the non-cash contribution.
5. Statement that no goods or services were provided by the organization in return for the contribution, if that was the case.
6. Description and good faith estimate of the value of goods or services, if any, that an organization provided in return for the contribution.
7. Statement that goods or services, if any, that an organization provided in return for the contribution consisted entirely of intangible religious benefits, if that was the case.

There are no IRS forms for the acknowledgment. A donor should not attach the acknowledgment to his or her individual income tax return, but must retain it to substantiate the contribution. Recipient organizations typically send written acknowledgments to donors no later than January 31 of the year following the donation. For the written acknowledgment to be considered contemporaneous with the contribution, a donor must receive the acknowledgment by the earlier of: the date on which the donor actually files his or her individual federal income tax return for the year of the contribution or the due date (including extensions) of the return.

The acknowledgment must describe goods or services an organization provides in exchange for a contribution of $75 or more. It must also provide a good faith estimate of the value of such goods or services because a donor must generally reduce the amount of the contribution deduction by the fair market value of the goods and services provided by the organization. Goods or services include cash, property, services, benefits, or privileges. However, there are important exceptions for benefits considered to be tokens (insubstantial value), membership benefits, and intangible religious benefits. For a summary of the gift receipt rules, consult IRS Publication 1771, "Charitable Contributions – Substantiation and Disclosure Requirements."

Non-Cash Gifts

To claim an income tax charitable deduction for a non-cash gift (e.g., stock, real estate, artwork, equipment, software) requires the donor to complete IRS form 8283 (with an exception for gifts of small value), and to file this form with the income tax return. If the donor claims a deduction over $5,000, then a qualified and independent appraisal is required. A helpful resource for non-cash gift valuation is IRS Publication 561, "Determining the Value of Donated Property." If the donee charitable organization sells the donated non-cash property within three years of the gift, then it must file IRS form 8282 reporting the sale price with some exceptions such as for gifts of publicly traded stock. The IRS compares the sale price with the deduction value to determine if there may be an inappropriately inflated deduction. There are many special rules that prohibit or limit the amount of the charitable income tax deduction for certain gifts. For example, there is no income tax charitable deduction for volunteer time or services and no deduction for the loan of property. IRS Publication 526, "Charitable Contributions," is an excellent resource that reviews the tax rules for various types of gifts.

International Philanthropy

Philanthropy is increasingly global. Not surprisingly, the legal aspects of international fundraising – and the tax benefits for donors – can be quite complex. As a result of the 9/11 tragedy, a number of regulations, including lists of organizations linked to terrorism, were promulgated to assure that philanthropy was not assisting terrorist activities. The U.S. Department of Treasury offers the latest information on these regulations for donors and grantmakers. In general, only gifts to charitable organizations created under the laws of the United States – or gifts subject to tax treaties between the United States and select countries (e.g., Canada, Mexico, and Israel) – qualify for an income tax deduction. This rule does not apply to the estate tax charitable deduction. Of course, U.S. charities may use tax deductible donations for work related to its mission that may be fulfilled in other countries (e.g., church missions, Red Cross, "friends of" organizations). In addition, private foundations may make qualified grants (nontaxable expenditures) to foreign organizations so long as the private foundation satisfies an equivalency determination test or an expenditure responsibility test (Toce, 2010).

Donor Privacy and Confidentiality

All codes of ethical conduct in fundraising, as well as federal and state privacy laws, require the protection of donor privacy and confidentiality. State laws that allow access to public records may apply to donor records of organizations that receive tax revenue. Some public university foundation records have been deemed accessible by the public pursuant to state law. Other laws that may impact donor records include the Family Educational Rights and Privacy Act (FERPA) and the Health Insurance Portability and Accountability Act (HIPAA). Legal counsel should be consulted to determine the applicability of all laws and procedures for best practices to assure donor privacy and confidentiality.

Conclusion

Fundraising excellence requires adherence to both the letter and spirit of legal and ethical standards. Prudent management of charitable organizations requires careful attention to the "black and white" legal and ethical requirements for fundraising as well as making good decisions in cases where a dilemma is presented and a difficult decision must be made. Good decision making requires one to clarify the facts, understand the applicable legal and ethical standards, and make a reasonable decision. Evaluating and modifying one's decisions helps to continually improve fundraising practices. Achieving excellence in fundraising demands nothing less.

Discussion Questions

1) Do your directors, trustees, and/or staff engage in prudent decision making, governance, and ethical considerations relative to fundraising? Does your board follow the 33 principles of good governance promulgated by INDEPENDENT SECTOR?

2) Do your directors, trustees, and staff understand their legal duties of care, loyalty, and obedience relative to fundraising responsibilities? Does your board have an active committee tasked with oversight of fundraising? Does the organization have comprehensive gift acceptance policies approved by the board?

3) Are you familiar with the applicable laws of your state relative to the oversight role of the attorney general, enforcement of gift restrictions, enforcement and financial display of charitable pledges, endowment management, fundraising registration, and regulation of consultants and solicitors?

4) Are you familiar with the federal laws that govern fundraising? For example, does your board review the IRS 990 form with its questions and schedules that disclose fundraising-related information? What type of organization are you: public benefit charity, supporting organization, member benefit organization, or private foundation? If you are a public benefit charity, must you and do you pass the public support test? Do you hold or promote gifts to or from donor advised funds? Are you compliant with the associated rules of donor advised funds? Do you understand the tax benefits for donors from charitable giving? Do you comply with the rules for gift substantiation and disclosure?

5) Are you familiar with and do you comply with any applicable laws of international philanthropy, donor privacy, and confidentiality?

PART EIGHT

YOUR CAREER IN FUNDRAISING

CHAPTER THIRTY-SIX

FUNDRAISING AS A PROFESSION

By Eva E. Aldrich

While fundraising has long been a part of charitable endeavors, the professionalization of fundraising is a phenomenon of the late twentieth century and continues today. Scholarly consensus is that fundraising is still an emerging profession, with the further development of research and theory being vital to the profession's future. A review of key milestones in fundraising and key issues of the emerging professional can help illuminate how far fundraising as a profession has come – and how far it still needs to go.

This chapter covers:

• The history and evolution of organized fundraising.
• A discussion of the essential elements of a profession.
• The debate about the status of fundraising as a profession.
• The types and roles of credentials.
• The differences between certificates and certification.

Milestones in the Professionalization of Fundraising

In 1641, clergymen Hugh Peter, Thomas Weld, and William Hibbens left the Massachusetts Bay Colony to travel to England to seek funds to support Harvard College, thus earning a place in history as members of the "first systematic effort to raise money on this continent" (Cutlip, 1965, p. 3). While systematic, this effort was nonetheless ancillary to the participants' acknowledged professions as clergy. Fundraising would remain an ancillary activity rather than a professional pursuit until the middle of the nineteenth century, when the growing needs of the poor during the Industrial Revolution outstripped the ability of philanthropy to meet these needs face-to-face. Only then did fundraising begin to emerge as a distinctive discipline (Pribbenow, 1993).

By the end of the nineteenth century, major campaigns at institutions such as Johns Hopkins University and the University of Chicago (where Baptist clergy Frederick T. Gates and Thomas W. Goodspeed were instrumental to the effort's success) demonstrated the way in which major fundraising efforts were increasingly professional endeavors rather than volunteer-driven efforts (Pribbenow, 1993). The work of Lyman Pierce and Charles S. Ward for the YMCA is another instance of how professional organization had begun to transform fundraising practice. Their pioneering of "the mass campaign for small donations" revolutionized fundraising, effectively "democratizing philanthropy" and paving the way for other successful fundraising efforts based on a high volume of small contributions, such as the National Christmas Seals and March of Dimes (Hodgkinson, 2002, p. 397). By the time of World War I, the mass campaign was an established vehicle – and one that allowed the Red Cross to launch the country's first nationwide fundraising campaign, which succeeded in raising a remarkable $114 million in eight days in 1917 (Cutlip, 1965).

The end of the war saw the birth of the professional fundraising consultant. While several firms were created in that era, including Ward and Hill (Charles S. Ward was one of its founders) in 1919, Ketchum Inc. (then known as Ketchum Publicity) in 1919, and Marts and Lundy (a breakaway firm from Ward and Hill) in 1926 (Cutlip, 1965). The latter two firms are still in existence today.

One of the most successful firms of the era was John Price Jones, founded in 1919. Whereas previous generations of fundraisers had generally relied on personal qualities such as those recommended by Frederick T. Gates, who "exhorted himself and his followers to appeal only to the highest motives, to not flag when frustrated, and to canvas all day, everyday, rain or shine" (Pribbenow, 1993, p. 206), the firm of John Price Jones added "'scientific' and comprehensive" methods (p. 208). As Cutlip (1965) notes in discussing the methodology behind John Price Jones' fundraising efforts to help Harvard raise $14 million in 1918–1919, John Price Jones was the first to use a strategic public relations program and contemporary campaign committee structure. The discipline imposed by such a structure was a far cry from prior fundraising methodology, which relied on good fortune as much as good planning.

By the time of the Great Depression in the early 1930s, "fundraising had evolved into a legitimate profession" (Hodgkinson, 2002, p. 397). Partly in response to this, and partly as Cutlip (1965) contends to mounting competition and criticism of funding drives during the era's hard times, the American Association of Fund-Raising Counsel was formed in 1935. As Hodgkinson (2002) notes, since that time many more professional organizations for fundraisers have formed, including the Association of Fundraising Professionals (then the National Society of Fund Raising Executives) in 1960; the Association for Healthcare Philanthropy (1967); the Council for the Advancement and Support of Education (1974); and the National Committee for Planned Giving (1988).

The Fund Raising School, which has been noted as the "first formalized training program for fundraising professionals," was founded in 1974 by Hank Rosso, Joe Mixer, and Lyle Cook (Wagner, 2002, p. 34). The Fund Raising School is now a key program of the Indiana University Lilly Family School of Philanthropy.

Issues of Fundraising as an Emerging Profession

Despite the rapid growth of fundraising as a profession, a survey of literature suggests that fundraising continues to be widely regarded as an emerging rather than an established profession (Carbone, 1989; Bloland and Bornstein, 1990; Pribbenow, 1993; Duronio and Tempel, 1997; Bloland and Tempel, 2004; Levy, 2004; Chobot, 2004; Wagner, 2007). As Bloland and Bornstein (1990) observe, "fund raisers aspire to what professions and occupations generally seek: effectiveness and efficiency in the work, control over work and work jurisdiction, and recognition of the legitimacy of the work and those who perform it" (p. 69). Carbone (1997) goes further, asserting that there are three distinct approaches with discernible steps. First is the process approach, in which the profession is first designated as a full-time endeavor, followed by the establishment of specialized educational and training programs and an acknowledged professional association. Next is the power approach, in which the profession establishes market control through convincing the public that the services it performs are vital and not readily learned by a large number of people. Last is the structural–functional approach, which demands a base of theoretical and applied knowledge; professional autonomy in decision making; service to others; the acknowledgment of professional authority; the development of a distinctive professional culture; and societal recognition of the legitimacy of the profession.

Bloland and Tempel (2004) echo Carbone (1997) while offering a shorter list of commonly accepted characteristics of professions, including "a body of applicable expert knowledge with a theoretical base, acquired through a lengthy period of training (preferably in a university), a demonstrated devotion to service, an active professional association, a code of ethics, and a high level of control over credentialing and application of the work" (p. 6). However, they note that measuring the degree to which fundraising fulfills these traits as a profession can be challenging, as an examination of each of these areas demonstrates.

Expert Knowledge with a Theoretical Base

Bloland and Tempel (2004) note that "For a busy and successful fundraising professional, theory may seem obscure and hard to connect with practice. Yet theory that is generated through research is so significant that it is a major means for marking the difference between professions and nonprofessions" (pp. 11–12). Despite this, the fundraising profession and fundraisers in general seem to value the development of skills over the development and utilization of theoretical or research-based knowledge (Bloland and Bornstein, 1990). In part, this is due to the way in which fundraisers have traditionally been trained. In one study, 74 percent of respondents cited learning on the job as the way in which they learned fundraising; 43 percent cited non-degree professional development training; and less than 10 percent listed formal education (Tempel and Duronio, 1997). Many experienced fundraisers maintain that the primary qualifications for the profession are personal qualities such as those cited by Wood (1997), which include good skills in listening, negotiation, and communication. However, by having a solely skills-based conception of the profession, these individuals overlook the consideration that "Although the work of fundraising is shared with amateurs, with a theory and research base in the hands of professionals, the distinctions between professional and amateur can be more sharply drawn, and fund raising could have a greater ability to define and defend its work boundaries" (Bloland and Bornstein, 1990, p. 82).

As fundraising matures as a profession, formal education programs are on the rise – and in fact are seen as trailing demand (Cohen, 2007). The Nonprofit Academic Centers Council (NACC), which describes itself as "an international membership association comprised of academic centers or programs at accredited colleges and universities that focus on the study of nonprofit/nongovernmental organizations, voluntarism, and/or philanthropy," counts 46 institution of higher education among its members. Among other efforts, NACC has been instrumental in developing quality indicators for nonprofit academic centers (2006) as well as curricular guidelines for undergraduate and graduate study in nonprofit leadership, the nonprofit sector, and philanthropy (2007). It is interesting to note, however, that within NACC's curricular guidelines, the knowledge base for fundraising remains relatively broad. As an example, NACC's graduate study curricular guidelines contain only two entries under Section 10.0: Fundraising and Development. These are:

> 10.1 The various forms and structures in and through which organized philanthropy occurs
>
> 10.2 Components and elements that are part of a comprehensive fund development process (Nonprofit Academic Centers Council, 2007, p. 10)

It is helpful that these entries are not overly prescriptive in order to facilitate NACC's stated goal of attempting "to craft a set of guidelines that will be relevant in different cultural and institutional contexts" (Nonprofit Academic Centers Council, 2007, p. 5). However, this lack of specificity may also indicate how far fundraising must yet go before it is thoroughly embraced by the academy and successfully incorporated in an in-depth manner into some academic degree programs. It may also suggest why there continues to be a clear need for voluntary certification for fundraising professionals through a practitioner-based assessment such as the Certified Fund Raising Executive (CFRE) credential.

Academic programs and continuing education programs both play an important role in the professionalization of fundraising, and so does voluntary certification.

However, many fundraising professionals can become confused regarding the difference between educational programs (many of which offer a certificate of completion) and certification programs such as the CFRE (which is an accredited, independent third-party assessment of achievement). This is not to say that one is better than the other; rather, this simply points out that the process of becoming certified as a practitioner and the process of completing educational programs have different aims. In the case of the Certified Fund Raising Executive (CFRE) certification, what this means is that the CFRE credential is practice-based, measuring the knowledge needed in order to be able to apply best practice principles to real-life, work-related tasks and challenges faced by fundraising professionals. This differs from educational programs, the aim of which is primarily to expand the participant's base of knowledge. Another key difference between certification and educational programs is that certification is based on industry-wide standards formulated through a rigorous evaluation and testing process, whereas certificate programs (which can also be demanding) are more likely to have their standards of performance determined by the institution or instructor of record. CFRE International's description of the differences between achieving a certification such as the CFRE credential and educational programs (which may award a certificate of achievement) appears as Table 36.1.

TABLE 36.1. CERTIFICATION VERSUS CERTIFICATE.

Certification	Certificate
Results from an assessment process	Results from an educational process
For individuals	For individuals
Typically requires some amount of professional experience	For both newcomers and experienced professionals
Awarded by a third-party, standard-setting organization	Awarded by educational programs or institutions
Indicates mastery/competency as measured against a defensible set of standards, usually by application or exam	Indicates completion of a course or series of courses with specific focus; is different than a degree-granting program
Standards set through a defensible, industry-wide process (job analysis/role delineation) that results in an outline of required knowledge and skills	Course content set a variety of ways (faculty committee; dean; instructor; occasionally through defensible analysis of topic area)
Typically results in a designation to use after one's name (CFRE, ACFRE, FAHP, CPF, APRA, CAE); may result in a document to hang on the wall or keep in a wallet	Usually listed on a resume detailing education; may issue a document to hang on the wall
Has on-going requirements in order to maintain; holder must demonstrate he/she continues to meet requirements	Is the end result; demonstrates knowledge of course content at the end of a set period in time

Source: CFRE International, 2001

Certification, continuing education certificate programs, and academic programs and degrees all have a role to play in the ongoing growth of the fundraising professional. However, to make the most of the many opportunities in support of continued professional advancement, it is important for fundraisers to know and understand the differences among these complementary but distinctive activities. Certificate and academic programs advance knowledge within the profession and among fundraising professionals; certification builds the profession through setting industry-wide standards that help build trust in the profession and assure a fundamental level of knowledge and accomplishment among those who voluntarily certify. These complementary activities are vital for the ongoing strength of the fundraising profession, its practitioners, and the many nonprofit organizations they so ably serve.

A demonstrated devotion to service

Pribbenow (1999) agrees with Bloland and Bornstein (1990) that the claim of technical competence is insufficient as a claim to professionalism. According to

Pribbenow (1993), fundraising as a profession "suffers for its attempts to ground its knowledge-base in a contractual understanding of human relationships" and instead must be grounded in an ethic of service (p. 221). The typical fundraiser's understanding of the profession as a set of techniques and skills to be mastered "is important only if it is understood as part of the promotion of healthy relationships between institutions and their various friends and constituencies" (Pribbenow, 1993, p. 222). Pribbenow (1999) sees this "disconnection between knowledge and service" as a key problem and says that this disconnection explains why current efforts to professionalize fundraising further are "wrong-headed" (p. 34). He proposes that the next step in the evolution of fundraising as a profession is not to oppose the impulses of the amateur, whose pursuits are driven by love, and the professional, whose pursuits are driven by work, but rather to adopt a model whereby "love transforms work." In this way, the fundraiser's love of humankind and ethic of service to the community transforms the work of fundraising from a set of techniques into a powerful calling. This, says Pribbenow (1999), will rightly "define the profession of philanthropic fundraising in terms of its philanthropic dimension" (p. 42).

An Active Professional Association and a Code of Ethics

While having a code of ethics is one trait of professionalism, Bloland and Tempel (2004) point out that even this is problematic because "codes of ethics can be badly or well written. They may be too general or too specific, too stringent or too lax. They may miss the most significant measures of ethical behavior" (pp. 10–11). More importantly in terms of enforcement, the profession has not made it clear how to monitor ethics and standards, and what sanctions might be applied or how they might be enforced (Tempel and Duronio, 1997).

Despite this, perhaps the area in which fundraising has gained the most maturity as a profession is in the development of active professional associations and related codes of ethics. The fundraising profession possesses numerous professional associations worldwide, and increasingly there is mutual understanding and cooperation as fundraising associations around the globe are shaping fundraising as an international profession with a shared understanding of key ethical principles. A milestone in this effort was seen in 2006 with the development of the *International Statement of Ethical Principles in Fundraising*. This document was the culmination of a collaboration among fundraising associations in 30 countries that sought to articulate "an overarching statement of macrolevel principles that can unite all fundraisers" and transcend borders and cultures. The five universal principles of ethical fundraising that were identified were "honesty, respect, integrity, empathy, [and] transparency." From this, standards of practice were developed that include:

1. Fundraisers' responsibility regarding donations
2. Relationship with stakeholders
3. Responsibility for communications, marketing, and public information
4. Management reporting, finance, and fundraising costs
5. Payments and compensation
6. Compliance with national laws and fundraisers' responsibility regarding donations

As the creators of the document noted, "individual fundraisers will continue to subscribe to a particular local or national code of ethics, which will address key details and specific issues relevant to their region and code. The international statement…is flexible enough to accommodate political, cultural and legal differences" (n.p.).

Another way in which national fundraising associations are increasingly active and increasingly providing much-needed guidance to their members is through the development of professional pathway recommendations. As the variety of professional growth opportunities in fundraising rises to include continuing education, academic degrees, certification, and on-the-job learning/mentoring, fundraising professionals increasingly are seeking guidance regarding how to approach or sequence these opportunities in a way that makes sense for career success. Fundraising associations such as the Association of Fundraising Professionals, the Fundraising Institute Australia, the Fundraising Institute New Zealand, the Institute of Fundraising (United Kingdom), the Japan Fundraising Association, the European Fundraising Association, and others are all actively working to develop frameworks for professional growth and advancement that will assist their members in growing as effective, ethical fundraisers. Most, but not all, include the achievement of a voluntary credential and/or completion of a rigorous standardized curriculum in fundraising education as an important step in the professional development process.

Control over Credentialing

Chobot (2004) notes that "an initial stimulus for the creation of fundraising certification programs was a justification of fundraising as a profession" (p. 31). While credentialing is not necessary to practice the profession, and fundraisers have been known to debate among themselves the value of credentialing, they nonetheless have become a standard part of the fundraising profession. In his discussion of the comparative virtues of licensing, certification, certificates, and accreditation, he points out that credentialing programs make the case that credentials, such as the internationally recognized Certified Fund Raising Executive (CFRE) credential, have a distinct "return on investment" by providing the certificant with the benefits of professional acknowledgment, donor confidence, employment advantages, higher compensation, and a profession that is overall stronger (Chobot, 2004).

However, such benefits can sometimes be as much or more perceptual than actual. As Chobot (2004) points out, research supporting such claims is minimal to nonexistent, and while it would appear that certification would suggest a certain level of competence, what it documents in actuality is a baseline level of knowledge – two things that may be allied but are not equivalent. In fact, he reports that the most documentable correlation between the CFRE and professionalization is the fact that reported salaries for holders of the CFRE are consistently higher than those of noncredentialed professionals. This assertion is supported by results of the *AFP Compensation and Benefits Survey* (Association of Fundraising Professionals, 2014), which reports that individuals in the United States who hold the CFRE certification earn around $25,500 more annually than their noncertified peers, and those holding an advanced certification earn around $46,000 more than noncertified fundraisers annually (p. 22). Overall, however, Chobot concludes that what is most important about credentialing programs for fundraisers and the fundraising profession is the way such credentials have evolved to be "examplars of good fundraising practice" that have gained acceptance across the globe (p. 47).

Given the historic absence of ready access to academic degree programs in fundraising, it is easy to see that voluntary credentials have played an important role in building professionalism within fundraising. The accredited CFRE credential has served a further purpose in regularly researching and documenting the practitioner body of knowledge for fundraising as a profession through its periodic CFRE Job Analysis. A key piece of research that has informed the CFRE credential since its founding in 1981, the CFRE Job Analysis is an international survey of fundraising practice that is conducted every five years. It asks fundraising professionals the tasks they perform in doing their work, how often they perform the tasks, the importance of the tasks to fundraising success, and the knowledge used to perform the tasks. In 2014, the most recent CFRE Job Analysis study was completed. The research was conducted by a professional testing agency under the oversight of an international task force of fundraising subject matter experts who were senior practitioners holding the CFRE credential. Fundraising professionals in 10 countries were surveyed: Australia, Brazil, Canada, Germany, India, Japan, New Zealand, South Africa, the United Kingdom, and the United States. CFRE International's partners in distributing the survey were the Associação Brasiliera de Captadores de Recursos, Deutscher Fundraising Verband, European Fundraising Association, Fundraising Institute Australia, Fundraising Institute New Zealand, Fundraising Verband Austria, Institute of Fundraising, Japan Fundraising Association, Resource Alliance, and Southern African Institute of Fundraising. The results of the Job Analysis study confirm that fundraising is a global profession and that fundraising professionals consistently perform the same tasks, no matter their geographic area of practice. There was little difference between the mean ratings of respondents in different countries.

The results of the CFRE Job Analysis form the blueprint for the CFRE Test Content Outline. An updated CFRE Test Content Outline based on the results of the Job Analysis study appears as Table 36.2. This updated CFRE Test Content Outline will be used starting in 2016 as the blueprint for the CFRE exam. (More information about the CFRE credential, including application requirements and additional information about the exam, can be found on the CFRE International's web site at www.cfre.org.)

The reason that voluntary adoption of credentialing is particularly important for the fundraising profession has to do with the issue of professional autonomy. As Carbone (1997) points out, "Licensure is in some ways the enemy of autonomy since it is a mandate promulgated by civil authority, normally state governments" (p. 89). Not only is it an enemy of autonomy, licensure of fundraisers by government has other serious issues attached. Because fundraisers must have the public's trust, they must go beyond licensing, which is based on "meeting a minimal standard of competence" (Chobot, 2004). As Pribbenow (1993) points out, the "mutual relationship between the public and the voluntary sector is on a higher level of expectation; the public good requires public trust, and trust is a mutual relationship" (p. 229).

The Future of Fundraising as a Profession

The issues that Tempel and Duronio (1997) identified almost two decades ago as being key to the profession's future remain relevant today: turnover, attitudes toward asking for money, the feminization of the profession, and compensation. Turnover remains a challenge in the field, as the number of seasoned professionals lags behind demand, particularly in the arena of major gifts (Hall, 2007). Asking for money continues to be something that some fundraisers are loath to acknowledge for what it is, seeing it as the "dirty work" of an otherwise respectable career as a nonprofit professional (Bloland and Tempel, 2004; Tempel and Duronio, 1997). Women now constitute the majority of individuals in the profession, though they continue to occupy fewer positions of leadership and in terms of compensation make less money than their male counterparts (Tempel and Duronio, 1997); in fact, results of the *AFP Compensation and Benefits Survey* (Association of Fundraising Professionals, 2014) suggest that if the AFP sample is relatively representative

TABLE 36.2. CFRE TEST CONTENT OUTLINE – KNOWLEDGE DOMAINS AND TASKS. (EFFECTIVE 2016)

Domain 01: Current and Prospective Donor Research

Tasks

0101   Develop a list of prospective donors by identifying individuals, groups, and entities, such as foundations, corporations, and government agencies, with the linkage, ability, and interest to give in order to qualify prospective donors for further research and cultivation.

0102   Implement and utilize a secure data management system to ensure data privacy, store information on current and prospective donors, and enable segmented retrieval and analysis.

0103   Collect and analyze current and prospective donor information including demographics, psychographics, interests, values, motivations, culture, ability, giving and volunteer history, relationships, and linkages to select potential donors for particular projects and fundraising programs.

0104   Rate current and prospective donors on linkage, ability, and interest to prioritize and plan cultivation and solicitation.

0105   Communicate and validate relevant donor information with key organizational stakeholders to establish a plan of action for engagement, cultivation, solicitation, and stewardship.

Domain 02: Securing the Gift

Tasks

0201   Develop a case for support by involving stakeholders in order to communicate the rationale for supporting the organization's mission.

0202   Identify solicitation strategies and techniques appropriate to current and prospective donor groups.

0203   Develop and implement specific solicitation plans for the involvement of individual donors, donor groups, and/or entities.

0204   Prepare donor-focused solicitation communications in order to facilitate informed gift decisions.

0205   Ask for and secure gifts from current and prospective donors in order to generate financial support for the organization's mission.

Domain 03: Relationship Building

Tasks

0301   Initiate and strengthen relationships with constituents through systematic cultivation and stewardship plans designed to build trust in, and long-term commitment to, the organization.

0302   Develop and implement a comprehensive communications plan to inform constituents about the organization's mission, vision, values, financial and ethical practices, funding priorities, and gift opportunities.

0303   Promote a culture of philanthropy by broadening constituents' understanding of the value of giving.

0304   Acknowledge and recognize donor gifts and engagement in ways that are meaningful to donors and appropriate to the mission and values of the organization.

(Continued)

TABLE 36.2. (CONTINUED).

Domain 04: Volunteer Involvement

Tasks

0401   Identify organizational readiness and opportunities to engage volunteers.

0402   Create structured processes for the identification, recruitment, orientation, training, evaluation, recognition, retention, and succession of volunteers.

0403   Develop specific role descriptions and terms of commitment to empower and support volunteers and enhance their effectiveness.

0404   Engage various types of volunteers (for example, board, program, campaign) in the fundraising process to increase organizational capacity.

0405   Participate in recruiting experienced and diverse leadership on boards and/or committees to ensure these groups are representative of, and responsive to, the communities served.

Domain 05: Leadership and Management

Tasks

0501   Demonstrate leadership that advances fundraising practice.

0502   Advocate for and support a culture of philanthropy and the advancement of fundraising across the organization and its constituencies.

0503   Ensure that sound administrative and management policies and procedures are in place to support fundraising functions.

0504   Participate in the organization's strategic planning process to ensure the integration of fundraising and philanthropy.

0505   Design and implement short- and long-term fundraising plans and budgets to support the organization's strategic goals.

0506   Employ marketing and public relations principles and tools to support and grow fundraising programs.

0507   Conduct ongoing performance measurement and analysis of fundraising programs using accepted and appropriate standards and metrics in order to identify opportunities, resolve problems, and inform future planning.

0508   Recruit, train, and support staff by providing professional development opportunities and applying human resource principles to foster professionalism and a productive, team-oriented work environment.

0509   Utilize external services as needed to optimize the efforts of the fundraising function.

Domain 06: Ethics, Accountability, and Professionalism

Tasks

0601   Ensure that all fundraising activities and policies comply with ethical principles and legal standards and reflect the values of the organization and the community.

0602   Communicate principles of ethical fundraising to stakeholders to promote ethical practices and strengthen a culture of philanthropy.

0603   Promote ethical fundraising as a crucial component of philanthropy to strengthen the nonprofit sector and support the sector's role as a pillar of civil society.

0604   Clarify, implement, monitor, and honor donors' intent and instructions regarding the use of gifts.

0605   Ensure that allocations of donations are accurately documented in the organization's records.

0606   Report to constituents the sources, uses, impact, and management of donations to demonstrate transparency and enhance public trust in the organization.

0607   Participate as an active and contributing member of the fundraising profession through activities such as mentoring, continuing education, research, and membership in professional associations.

of the profession as a whole, that means that fundraisers are disproportionately white (89 percent) and female (75 percent), with women earning approximately $25,000 less per year than male fundraisers (p. 9). Compensation itself continues to be an issue for the profession, with parties having trouble deciding what the appropriate levels may be for fundraisers, who clearly are in demand but who operate within the cultural constraints of the nonprofit sector, where it is assumed that the satisfaction of mission-driven work helps make up for lower financial compensation levels (Duronio and Tempel, 1997). Wagner (2005) identifies another continuing challenge of the profession – that of "leading up", described as the need to "exercise leadership from whatever rank or position they [fundraisers] hold in order to motivate others" (p. 1). She goes on to assert that fundraisers are classic examples of Greenleaf's conception of the servant-leader, who are driven not by personal ambition but by a commitment to organizational mission and service (p. 97).

Increasingly, however, there is a great opportunity for fundraising professionals, and that is the international growth of the profession and the increasing cross-national understanding and agreement on core ethical principles and techniques of fundraising. The ability of the profession to build a truly global body of knowledge means that fundraising is an increasingly expanding and portable profession that is at the heart of shaping worldwide notions of philanthropy.

Conclusion

All in all, the profession of fundraising walks a tightrope. On one side is professionalization, with all its accompanying benefits, including the acknowledgment of expertise and respect from the wider society. On the other side is the ethic of service, which, as Pribbenow (1999) notes, harks back to the best aspects of amateurism, the love that drives mission. Ultimately, to flourish as a profession, fundraising must continue to grow the professional knowledge needed to elevate it from a set of techniques to a discipline possessing science to balance its traditional art. The knowledge that both practitioners and the academy bring to the table needs to be honored and integrated. As this is done, fundraisers – and the larger nonprofit sector – must continue to tell the story of the profession as one of public service and public trust. It is only in this way that, as The Fund Raising School phrases it, apology will be replaced with pride in fundraising, and that fundraising will truly solidify its place as a vital, appreciated aspect of the philanthropic enterprise.

Discussion Questions

1) What are the factors that define fundraising as a profession? Why is fundraising considered as an emerging profession?
2) What are the challenges and opportunities that exist for fundraising as a profession? As a career choice?
3) What options do fundraising professionals have to develop their knowledge and skills? How do these options contradict or complement each other?
4) What is the difference between certification and educational programs (which may offer a certificate of completion)?
5) What instances of commonality and/or cooperation exist within the fundraising profession globally? What does this mean for the future of the profession?

CHAPTER THIRTY-SEVEN

RESOURCES FOR STRENGTHENING FUNDRAISING

By Frances Huehls

As the fundraising profession has grown over the last 35 years, so too have resources – both academic and practical in nature – become increasingly available to fundraisers. This chapter is not an exhaustive treatment of organizations and publications and other resources that inform the nonprofit sector or even of fundraising, but rather a compilation of the resources that have consistently proved to be the most reliable – particularly in terms of quality. They tend to be mature resources that will continue to persist and inform us in some format –whether print, digital, or something that we cannot yet imagine – for some time to come.

What strengthens fundraising? Strong fundraisers, armed with the best available practices and research, are the foundation of strong fundraising. Some of the resources discussed in this chapter are clearly what would be seen as the realm of professional development. Others more directly strengthen informed practice. In order of appearance will be descriptions of the major associations and the services they provide, formal education opportunities, published resources, and major internet resources. The descriptive section is followed by an annotated list of all of the resources presented in this chapter.

Association Resources

Four major associations – the Association of Fundraising Professionals (AFP), the Council for Advancement and Support of Education (CASE), the Association for Healthcare Philanthropy (AHP), and the Association of Professional Researchers for Advancement (APRA) – all provide a multitude of services. As membership organizations, additional resources are available to those who join. All four sponsor conferences – United States, international, and web-based. In addition, there are options for training and workshops, such as CFRE certification preparation, career coaching, online conferencing, and webinars. AFP's public site provides access to the CFRE Resource Reading List. Special offerings include programming such as the AFP Leadership Academy and the AHP Madison Institute, an intensive program for health care development professionals. Each publishes a journal designed to promote best practices, in addition to having their own lines of specialized publications, such as the CASE *Matching Gifts* and the AFP Fund Development Series. Although their resource centers are restricted to members, the web sites of all of these organizations are rich with information that can be accessed by anyone interested in self-study. Finally, CASE, AFP, AHP, and APRA have moved beyond their own web sites, providing social networking opportunities through sites such as Facebook, LinkedIn, and Twitter.

Two additional membership organizations of note are the Giving Institute and the Partnership for Philanthropic Planning (formerly the National Committee on Planned Giving). The Giving Institute's membership numbers 45 fundraising consulting firms. In collaboration with The Lilly Family School of Philanthropy at Indiana University, the Institute publishes *Giving USA*, the annual compendium on sources and uses of philanthropic gifts. The Partnership for Philanthropic Planning has as its mission to assist donors and organizations in developing meaningful gift opportunities. The web site provides access to research and other resources for continuing education.

Options for Formal Education

For professionals who want the depth and breadth provided by formal education, there are a multitude of options available. By far the best source for locating educational opportunities that are offered through colleges and universities is the database developed and maintained by Roseanne Mirabella at Seton Hall University. This resource lists degree and non-degree programs, including opportunities to take classes online. The most current tabulation lists continuing education (non-degree) opportunities at 79 institutions. Many of these courses are offered through departments of continuing studies. The number of schools offering undergraduate coursework has grown to around 154, with around 33 percent of those having Nonprofit Leadership Alliance (formerly American Humanics) affiliation. The Nonprofit Leadership Alliance is a nonprofit organization that is dedicated to training entry-level nonprofit professionals through an experienced-based undergraduate curriculum that includes mastery of 10 core competencies. Those who complete the campus-based program are awarded the credential of Certified Nonprofit Professional. Post baccalaureate certificates and masters degrees are offered at more than 250 institutions, while 44 institutions offer doctoral programs. The academic home of these programs varies, ranging from schools of public affairs and business to liberal arts and social work. Close to 80 institutions offer some coursework online, either as a component of a degree or certificate program or as a non-credit offering. Some also offer "executive format" programs that are more accommodating to the schedule of working professionals.

Academic programs are typically broader than fundraising, including coursework such as law, economics, marketing, and ethics. The Nonprofit Academic Centers Council (NACC) is a membership organization of colleges and universities (currently 44) that offer coursework in nonprofit management. As part of its commitment to developing and maintaining high-quality academic programs, NACC has developed curricular guidelines for both undergraduate and graduate programs. Coursework in fundraising is recommended at both levels.

There are also non-academic options for formal coursework. Three such programs are The Fund Raising School (TFRS), the Grantsmanship Center, and the Association of Professional Researchers for Advancement (APRA). The Fund Raising School web-site lists the following offerings:

- Principles and Techniques of Fundraising (available online)
- Fundraising for Small Nonprofits
- Planned Giving (available online)
- Preparing Successful Grant Proposals (available online)
- Developing Annual Sustainability (available online)
- Managing the Capital Campaign
- Developing Major Gifts (available online)
- Faith and Fundraising
- Dynamics of Women's Giving
- Using Social Media in Fundraising (only online)

Although many are currently listed as being offered only at the home location in Indianapolis, some courses are also held in Chicago, Orlando, Minneapolis,

Dallas, Washington (DC), Nashville (TN), Burlington (MA), Tampa, Phoenix, and San Francisco. Customized workshops are available. TFRS also offers four additional courses leading to a Certificate in Nonprofit Executive Leadership.

The Grantsmanship Center in Los Angeles also offers customized training in addition to six regular courses:

- Grantsmanship Training
- Essential Grant Skills
- Research Proposal Workshop
- Competing for Federal Grants
- Grant Management Essentials
- Social Enterprise for Nonprofits

Detailed content analysis of each course is provided on the website. Courses – particularly Grantsmanship training – are taught at a variety of locations in the United States. The Grantsmanship Center also provides course follow-up support.

APRA offers online training opportunities in 10 topic areas – advanced research, campaigns, data analytics, healthcare, management and professional development, member and cause-related organizations, prospect identification, relationship management, research fundamentals, and industry trends. Their content can be delivered as online curriculum in the form of webcasts (APRA Online Curriculum), recorded sessions of past APRA International Conferences (APRA Conference On-Demand), or as commercial training for specific products or services (the Online Solutions Showcase). Their offerings can also be tailored for experience depending on the need for fundamentals, intermediate, or advanced training.

Published Resources

Academic Research

Fueling the wide range of academic programs is a rapidly growing body of research on fundraising and nonprofit marketing. Studies published in academic journals have proliferated since 2010, covering a wide range of topics including evaluation of fundraising, donor retention, the Internet and social media, branding, cause-related marketing, and relationship marketing. In addition, research is becoming focused on segments of the donor market such as ethnic and racial minorities, gender, and the LGBTQ community. This literature is important because it tests the validity of assumptions of best practice and develops theory. One hallmark of a profession is a body of theory around which a research conversation can develop. A short bibliography of recent books that go beyond reliance on best practices is included in the Resources section.

The journals publishing fundraising research fall primarily in the fields of business, economics, marketing, and nonprofit studies. Access can be found through private individual subscription or through academic libraries. Since privileges at academic libraries vary from institution to institution, fundraisers interested in this research should establish a relationship with a library in their area. Indexing services that provide the best access to this content include business sources such as *Business Source Premier* and *ABI/Inform*, as well as *Philanthropic Studies Index* (Indiana University) and *Google Scholar*. The latter two are available online to all users without charge. The four journals consistently publishing academic research on fundraising are the *International Journal of Nonprofit and Voluntary Sector Marketing*, *Nonprofit and Voluntary Sector Quarterly*, *Nonprofit Management and Leadership*, and the *Journal of Nonprofit and Public Sector Marketing*.

Focus on Practice

Many books on fundraising are based on best practices rather than research. As there is no shortage in numbers of titles to choose from, some discrimination is advised. Recommended reading lists can be found on many web sites including AFP, The Fund Raising School at Indiana University, CFRE International, and the Foundation Center. The best known experts in the field can be found as authors in the fundraising series published by Jossey-Bass, John Wiley & Sons Inc., and Routledge.

Numerous trade journals and newsletters are available. Many have a regional or local focus. On the national level, six in particular can be recommended for keeping abreast of news and best practices:

AHP Journal. The Journal of the Association of Healthcare Philanthropy focuses on resources for the health care industry including development programs, analysis of the philanthropic health care environment, and trends in the field.

Advancing Philanthropy. The Journal of the Association of Fundraising Professionals emphasizes practice-based information and tools for fundraising practitioners.

Chronicle of Philanthropy. Biweekly news of the nonprofit sector as well as listings of conferences, continuing education opportunities, available positions, and new publications.

Currents. The Journal of the Council for Advancement and Support of Education covers aspects of educational development including fundraising, marketing, and alumni relations.

Grassroots Fundraising Journal. The target audience is small- to medium-sized organizations; articles focus on legal issues, grassroots fundraising, case studies, and major donors.

Nonprofit Times. News and special reports including an annual salary survey and the NPT Top 100 Nonprofit Organizations.

Internet-Based Resources

Without question, the Internet makes a plethora of information available, whether it is accessible for free or for a subscription price. Four resources in particular are invaluable for informing practice and are tools that no fundraiser should be without.

The Guidestar database is the single largest source of information on individual nonprofit organizations. Participating nonprofits and subscribers have access to the information of 1.8 million nonprofit organizations registered with the IRS including extensive financial information and the Form 990. Using their advanced search engine, it is possible to create lists of comparable organizations using criteria such as the NTEE code, location, and assets. GuidestarPro subscribers can download data for analysis using a more extensive search engine. Guidestar also provides a basic version for the public at no charge and special versions for academic classroom use and libraries.

The Foundation Center (FC) is the top resource for information about foundations and grantmaking. To fulfill their mission of promoting transparency in foundation activity, FC engages in three major activities. The first is to report on foundation activity, which they accomplish through analyzing the information returns of private foundations (Form 990PF) and generating both special topic and statistical reports on grants and grantmakers. The IssueLab makes a vast body of foundation generated research available online. The Glasspockets initiative collects operating data from foundations to promote transparency in that part of the nonprofit sector. Much of this information is made publically available through the FC web site. Their second activity is the compilation of grant directories – both print and electronic. The *Foundation Directory* is by far the most comprehensive compilation of grant opportunities available. The third FC activity is public outreach and education. In addition to the massive amount of information on the web site, FC sponsors a Foundation Information Network that provides access to print and online grant information through public and academic libraries nationwide. An array of workshops is also available, primarily related to foundation fundraising that range from free online tutorials to full-day classroom training.

The Nonprofit Research Collaborative coordinates survey research on fundraising. Members of the collaborative include AFP, CFRE International, Campbell Rinker, Giving USA Foundation, the National Center for Charitable Statistics, and the Partnership for Philanthropic Planning. Through combining a number of survey efforts, the Collaborative can provide better benchmark and trend data on fundraising while reducing the amount of time nonprofits would need to spend completing surveys. The survey data, which is available on their website, provides answers about staffing, gifts, board giving, methodologies, goal achievement, types of donors, and social media in fundraising.

The Center on Nonprofits and Philanthropy at the Urban Institute is the home of the National Center for Charitable Statistics (NCCS). The NCCS is a clearing house for data on the nonprofit sector including charitable giving. Although perhaps not directly related to fundraising, the NCCS provides a backbone of context for fundraisers to understand the nonprofit sector. As previously mentioned, the NCCS is a partner in the Nonprofit Research Collaborative. The data that are publicly available through their site allow you to compare your organization against national benchmarks for financial activity and charitable giving.

Conclusion

Knowledge moves the fundraising profession forward and the information to craft that knowledge is available in many places and forms. If I have been successful, I have demonstrated that opportunities to strengthen the field have never been greater. Associations are strong and offer more formal and informal venues for education and professional networking than ever before. Opportunities for formal academic education are robust and continue to expand into new areas. At the same time, viable training options exist outside the academy. Publication is vigorous and academic research in the field is providing a welcome level of credibility to professional practice. Strong organizations like the Foundation Center are using technology to provide high-quality information to inform practice. It is impossible to know what the state of information resources will be when the next edition of this volume is published, but – for now – the state of resources to strengthen fundraising is sound.

Questions for Discussion

1) As the new and first director of development for a grassroots nonprofit organization, you quickly realize that training in donor development would help your devoted but small staff. You have no budget for this. What resources

are available at no cost that you could use to develop an in-house training program?

2) You are tasked with developing a self-study evaluation of fundraising by your organization. What resources are available that provide comparison data for fundraising, financial activity, and charitable giving that you can use as part of your analysis?

3) How can best practices in fundraising become more grounded in research? How can academics and practitioners collaborate to improve both research and practice to move the profession forward?

Organizations and Resources Referenced

Association of Professional Researchers for Advancement (APRA): international membership organization for professionals interested in research and relationship management; www.aprahome.org; 330 N. Wabash Ave., Suite 2000, Chicago, IL 60611, 312-321-5196.

Association for Healthcare Philanthropy (AHP): international membership organization representing development professionals in the health care field; http://www.ahp.org; 313 Park Ave., Suite 400, Falls Church, VA 22046; 703-532-6243.

Association of Fundraising Professionals (AFP): international membership organization dedicated to advocacy, education, certification, and fundraising research; www.afpnet.org; 4300 Wilson Blvd, Suite 300, Arlington, VA 22203; 703-684-0410.

Campbell Rinker: market research company that serves both specific clients and the nonprofit sector at large; http://www.campbellrinker.com; 25600 Rye Canyon Road, Suite 202, Valencia, CA 91355; 888-722-6723.

Center on Nonprofits and Philanthropy (Urban Institute): conducts and disseminates research on the role and impact of nonprofit organizations and philanthropy; http://urban.org/center/cnp/; 2100 M Street, NW, Washington, DC 20037; 202-833-7200.

Council for Advancement and Support of Education (CASE): international membership organization for educational institutions and their affiliated advancement professionals; www.case.org; 1307 New York Ave., N.W. Suite 1000; Washington, DC 20005-4701; 202-328-2273.

CFRE International: international provider of professional certification for fundraisers; http://www.cfre.org/contact.html; 300 N. Washington St., Suite 504, Alexandria, VA 22314, 703-820-5555.

Foundation Center: produces the Foundation Directory (print and electronic), the most comprehensive source for grant opportunities; wide range of educational programs; compiles and publishes information about foundation giving trends; supports a network of cooperating library collections in the United States and abroad; http://foundationcenter.org/; 79 Fifth Avenue/16th Street, New York, NY 10003-3076, 212-620-4230.

Giving Institute: membership organization for fundraising counsel; web site includes resource library of papers and presentations; Giving Institute Foundation published *Giving USA*, an annual compendium of sources and uses of philanthropic gifts; http://www.givinginstitute.org; 225 W. Wacker Drive, Chicago, IL 60606.

Grantsmanship Center: quasi-membership organization offering training workshops; www.tgci.com; 350 S. Bixel St., Suite 110, Los Angeles, CA 90017, 213-482-9860.

GuideStar: in-depth information for individual nonprofit organizations including finances, Form 990, board members, mission. GuideStar's goal is to promote transparency in the nonprofit sector and provide information for informed decision making and charitable giving; http://www.guidestar.org; locations in Williamsburg, VA (4801 Courthouse St., Suite 220), Washington, DC (1730 Pennsylvania Ave., NW, Suite 250), and San Francisco, CA (720 Market Street).

National Center for Charitable Statistics (NCCS): part of the Urban Institute, a clearinghouse of data on the nonprofit sector in the US; http://nccs.urban.org/; The Urban Institute, 2100 M Street, NW, 5th Floor, Washington, DC 20037; 866-518-3874.

Nonprofit Academic Centers Council (NACC): coalition of university-based academic programs offering formal coursework and degrees in nonprofit and philanthropic education; http://nonprofit-academic-centers-council.org/; 2121 Euclid Avenue, Cleveland, OH 44115, 216-687-9221.

Nonprofit Leadership Alliance: nonprofit organization that partners with academic institutions to offer an undergraduate curriculum that prepares students to enter management positions in nonprofit organizations; program focuses on curriculum that includes experiential education. http://www.nonprofitleadershipalliance.org; 1100 Walnut Street, Suite 1900, Kansas City, MO, 64106; 816-561-6415.

Nonprofit Management Education: Current offerings in university-based programs (Seton Hall University): most comprehensive listing of continuing education, online, undergraduate, and graduate (Masters and Doctoral) opportunities available through formal academic institutions; http://academic.shu.edu/npo/.

Nonprofit Research Collaborative: study charitable fundraising at organizations and the factors that influence success and growth; http://www.npresearch.org/; 530-690-5746.

Partnership for Philanthropic Planning: membership organization dedicated to assisting individuals and organizations in developing meaningful gift opportunities for both donors and recipients; http://www.pppnet.org; 233 McCrea Street, Suite 300, Indianapolis, IN 46225, 317-269-6274.

The Fund Raising School: affiliated with The Lilly Family School of Philanthropy at Indiana University; offers coursework in many areas of fundraising practice; http://www.philanthropy.iupui.edu/the-fund-raising-school; 550 W. North St., Suite 301, Indianapolis, IN 46202, 317-274-7063.

Indexing Sources

Due to the constantly changing nature of coverage of these products, a visit to the vendor or database site will provide more accurate information than reporting current statistics.
ABI/Inform. ProQuest LLC, Ann Arbor, MI.
Business Source Premier. Ebsco; www.ebsco.com.

Philanthropic Studies Index. Indiana University; http://cheever.ulib.iupui.edu/psipublicse arch/.

Google Scholar. www.scholar.google.com.

Academic and Trade Journals

Advancing Philanthropy. Arlington, VA: Association of Fundraising Professionals; bimonthly; practice based information and tools for fundraising practitioners; ISSN 1077-2545.

Chronicle of Philanthropy. Washington, DC; biweekly news of the nonprofit sector as well as listings of conferences, continuing education opportunities, available positions, and new publications; ISSN 1040-676x.

Currents. Washington, DC: Council for Advancement and Support of Education; monthly; articles cover aspects of educational development including fund raising, marketing, and alumni relations; ISSN 0748-478x.

Grassroots Fundraising Journal. Kim Klein; target audience is small- to medium-sized organizations; articles focus on legal issues, grassroots fund raising, case studies, and major donors; ISSN 0740-4832.

Healthcare Philanthropy. Journal of the Association for Healthcare Philanthropy; resource for healthcare development professionals; published semiannually; ISSN 2162-2493.

International Journal of Nonprofit and Voluntary Sector Marketing. John Wiley & Sons Inc.; quarterly; ISSN 1465-4520.

Journal of Nonprofit and Public Sector Marketing. Routledge; quarterly; ISSN 1049-5142.

Nonprofit and Voluntary Sector Quarterly. Sage Publications; quarterly; journal of ARNOVA: the Association for Research on Nonprofit Organizations and Voluntary Action; ISSN 0899-7640.

Nonprofit Management and Leadership. Jossey-Bass, Inc. quarterly; ISSN1048-6682.

NonProfit Times. NPT Publishing Group; 17 issues per year; news and special reports including an annual salary survey and the NPT Top 100 Nonprofit Organizations; ISSN 0896-5048.

A Sample of Books that Advance Research and Practice

Davis, E. 2012. *Fundraising and the Next Generation: Tools for Engaging the Next Generation of Philanthropists.* Hoboken, NJ: John Wiley & Sons, Inc.

Drezner, N. D. 2011. *Philanthropy and Fundraising in American Higher Education.* San Francisco, CA: Jossey-Bass.

Drezner, N. D. (ed.). 2013. *Expanding the Donor Base in Higher Education Engaging Non-traditional Donors.* New York: Routledge.

Drezner, N. D. and F. Huehls. 2014. *Fundraising and Institutional Advancement: Theory, Practice, and New Paradigms.* New York: Routledge.

Gasman, M. and N. Bowman. 2013. *Engaging Diverse College Alumni: The Essential Guide to Fundraising.* New York: Routledge.

Hunt, P. 2012. *Development for Academic Leaders: A Practical Guide for Fundraising Success.* San Francisco, CA: Jossey-Bass.

Pettey, J. G. (ed.). 2013. *Nonprofit Fundraising Strategy: A Guide to Ethical Decision Making and Regulation for Nonprofit Organizations.* Hoboken, NJ: John Wiley & Sons, Inc.

Polivy, D. K. 2014. *Donor Cultivation and the Donor Lifecycle Map: A New Framework for Fundraising.* Hoboken, NJ: John Wiley & Sons, Inc.

Sargeant, A. and E. Jay. 2014. *Fundraising Management: Analysis, Planning, and Practice.* New York: Routledge.

Thümler, E., N. Bögelein, A. Beller, and H. K. Anheier (eds.). 2014. *Philanthropy and Education: Strategies for Impact.* New York: Palgrave Macmillan.

W. K. Kellogg Foundation. 2012. *Cultures of Giving: Energizing and Expanding Philanthropy by and for Communities of Color.* Battle Creek, MI: W. K. Kellogg Foundation.

REFERENCES

21/64 and Dorothy A. Johnson Center for Philanthropy. 2013. *#NEXTGENDONORS: Respecting Legacy, Revolutionizing Philanthropy*. New York, NY. Retrieved from: www.nextgendonors.org/wp-nextgendonors/wp-content/uploads/next-gen-donors-brief.pdf.

Ableson, James L., T.M. Erickson, S.E. Mayer, J. Crocker, H. Briggs, N.L. Lopez-Duran, and I. Liberzon. 2014. "Brief Cognitive Intervention Can Modulate Neuroendocrine Stress Responses to the Trier Social Stress Test: Buffering Effects of a Compassionate Goal Orientation." *Psychoneuroendocrinology*, 44: 60–70.

Adelman, Carol, Yula Spantchak, Kacie Marano, and Jeremiah Norris. 2013. *2013 Index of Global Philanthropy and Remittances with a Special Report on Emerging Economies*. Washington, DC: Hudson Institute.

Aknin, Lara B., Elizabeth W. Dunn, and Michael I. Norton. 2012. "Happiness Runs in a Circular Motion: Evidence for a Positive Feedback Loop Between Prosocial Spending and Happiness." *Journal of Happiness Studies*, 13: 347–355.

Aknin, Lara B., Christopher P. Barrington-Leigh, Elizabeth W. Dunn, John F. Helliwell, Robert Biswas-Diener, Imelda Kemeza, Paul Nyende, Claire Ashton-James, Michael I. Norton. 2013. "Prosocial Spending and Well-Being: Cross-Cultural Evidence for a Psychological Universal." *Journal of Personality and Social Psychology*, 104: 635–652.

Aknin Lara B., Alice L. Fleerackers, and J. Kiley Hamlin. 2014. "Can Third-Party Observers Detect the Emotional Rewards of Generous Spending?" *The Journal of Positive Psychology*, 9(3): 198–203.

Alden, Lynn E. and Jennifer L. Trew. 2013. "If it Makes You Happy: Engaging in Kind Acts Increases Positive Affect in Socially Anxious Individuals." *Emotion*, 13(1): 64–75.

Aldrich, Eva E. 2011. *Giving USA 2011 Spotlight #2: Giving By Immigrants.* Chicago, IL: Giving USA Foundation.

Anderson, Albert. 1996. *Ethics for Fundraisers.* Indianapolis, IN: Indiana University Press.

Anderson, Chris. 2008. *The Long Tail: Why the Future of Business is Selling Less of More.* New York: Hyperion.

Andreasen, Alan R. 2009. "Cross-Sector Marketing Alliances: Partnerships, Sponsorships, and Cause-Related Marketing." In Joseph J. Cordes and C. Eugene Steuerle (eds.), *Nonprofits and Business.* Washington, DC: Urbana Institute Press.

Andreasen, Alan R. and Philip Kotler. 2008. *Strategic Marketing for Nonprofit Organizations,* 7th ed. Upper Saddle River, NJ: Pearson/Prentice Hall.

Andreoni, James, Eleanor Brown, and Isaac Rischall. 2003. "Charitable Giving by Married Couples: Who Decides and Why Does it Matter?" *The Journal of Human Resources,* 38(1): 111–133.

Andresen, Katya. 2006. *Robin Hood Marketing: Stealing Corporate Savvy to Sell Just Causes.* San Francisco, CA: Jossey-Bass.

Anft, Michael. 2002. "Tapping ethnic wealth: Charities Pursue Minority Giving as Incomes Rise Among Blacks, Hispanics, and other groups." *The Chronicle of Philanthropy,* January 10, 2002.

Anheier, Helmut K. and Siobhan Daly. 2005. "Philanthropic Foundations: A New Global Force?" In *Global Civil Society.* London: SAGE Publications Ltd.

Anik, Lalin, Lara B. Aknin, Michael I. Norton, and Elizabeth W. Dunn. 2009. "Feeling Good About Giving: The Benefits (and Costs) of Self-Interested Charitable Behavior." In *Harvard Business School Marketing Unit Working Paper No. 10-012.*

Association of Fundraising Professionals. 2003. *AFP Fundraising Dictionary.* Alexandria, VA: Association of Fundraising Professionals.

Association of Fundraising Professionals. 2006. *International Statement of Ethical Principles in Fundraising.* Association of Fundraising Professionals. http://www.afpnet.org/Ethics/IntlArticleDetail.cfm?itemnumber=3682.

Association of Fundraising Professionals. 2014. *AFP Compensation and Benefits Survey.* Arlington, VA: AFP Research. Available at www.afpnet.org/FEB.

Association for Healthcare Philanthropy. 2012. "AHP Standards for Reporting and Communicating Effectiveness in Health Care Philanthropy." Falls Church, VA: Association for Healthcare Philanthropy.

Association for Healthcare Philanthropy. 2014. "Two New Reports Confirm Number of Fundraisers, Staff Retention Key to Raising More Dollars, AHP Says." Accessed June 10, 2015: http://www.nonprofitpro.com/article/reports-confirm-number-fundraisers-staff-retention-key-raise-more/.

Aufreiter, Nora, Julien Boudet, and Vivian Weng. 2014. "Why Markerters Should Keep Sending You E-mails." McKinsey & Company. Available at http://www.mckinsey.com/insights/marketing_sales/why_marketers_should_keep_sending_you_emails.

Austin, James E. 2000. *The Collaboration Challenge.* San Francisco, CA: Jossey-Bass.

Auten, Gerald E., Charles T. Clotfelter, and R. L. Schmalbeck. 2000. "Taxes and Philanthropy Among the Wealthy." In Joel B. Slemrod (ed.), *Does Atlas Shrug? The Economic Consequences of Taxing the Rich,* pp. 392–424. Cambridge, MA: Harvard University Press.

Auten, Gerald E., Holger Sieg, and Charles T. Clotfelter. 2002. "Charitable Giving, Income, and Taxes: An Analysis of Panel Data." *American Economic Review,* 92(1): 371–382.

Badgett, M. V. Lee. 2001. *Money, Myths, and Change: The Economic Lives of Lesbians and Gay Men*. Chicago, IL: University of Chicago Press.

Badgett, M. V. Lee and Nancy Cunningham. 1998. *Creating Communities: Giving and Volunteering by Gay, Lesbian, Bisexual, and Transgender People*. New York, NY and Amherst, MA: Working Group on Funding Lesbian and Gay Issues and Institute for Gay and Lesbian Strategic Studies.

Badgett, M. V. Lee, Holning Lau, Brad Sears, and Deborah Ho. 2007. *Bias in the Workplace: Consistent Evidence of Sexual Orientation and Gender Identity Discrimination*. Los Angeles, CA: The Williams Institute.

Banaji, Mahzarin R. and Anthony Greenwald. 2013. *Blindspot: Hidden Biases of Good People*. New York: Random House.

Bankers Trust Private Banking. 2000. *Wealth with Responsibility/Study 2000*. Bankers Trust Private Banking.

Bell, Jeanne and Marla Cornelius. 2013. *Underdeveloped: A National Study of Challenges Facing Nonprofit Fundraising*. Oakland, CA: Compass Point and the Evelyn and Walter Hass, Jr. Fund.

Benson, Peter L. and Viola L. Catt. 1978. "Soliciting Charity Contributions: The Parlance of Asking for Money." *Journal of Applied Social Psychology*, 8: 84–95.

Berkshire, Jennifer C. 2012. "Charities Pick up New Ways of Reaching Elusive Donors by Phone." *The Chronicle of Philanthropy*, September 30, 2012.

Berkshire, Jennifer C. 2014. "Social-Service Group's Potential to Do More Inspires Donor to Give." *The Chronicle of Philanthropy*, October 23, 2014.

Bethel, Sheila Murray. 1993. *Beyond Management to Leadership: Designing the 21st Century Association*. Washington, DC: Foundation of the American Society of Association Executives.

Better Business Bureau Wise Giving Alliance. 2014. "How We Accredit Charities." Accessed December 30, 2014: http://www.give.org/for-charities/How-We-Accredit-Charities/.

Beyel, Joseph S. 1997. "Ethics and Major Gifts." In Dwight F. Burlingame and James M. Hodges (eds.), *Developing Major Gifts* pp. 49–59. San Francisco, CA: Jossey-Bass.

Bhagat, Vinay, Pam Loeb, and Mark Rovner. 2010. *The Next Generation of American Giving: A Study on the Multichannel Preferences and Charitable Habits of Generation Y, Generation X, Baby Boomers, and Matures*. Austin, TX: Convio and Edge Research.

Bhagat, Vinay, Dennis McCarthy and Bryan Snyder. 2012. "The Convio Online Marketing Nonprofit Benchmark Index Study." Austin, TX: Convio.

Bishop, Matthew and Michael Green. 2008. *Philanthrocapitalism*. New York: Bloomsbury Press.

Blackbaud. 2014. "Show the Love: Thoughtful Engagement to Retain Supporters." Accessed June 15, 2015: https://hello.blackbaud.com/1064_CORP_npExperts_DonorRetention_SharedAssets_RegistrationLP.html.

Block, Peter. 1993. *Stewardship: Choosing Service Over Self-Interest*. San Francisco, CA: Berrett-Koehler.

Bloland, Harland G. and Rita Bornstein. 1990. "Fundraising in Transition: The Professionalization of an Administrative Occupation." In *Taking Fund Raising Seriously: Papers Prepared for the Third Annual Symposium, Indiana University Center on Philanthropy, Indiana University-Purdue University Indianapolis*, June 6–8, 1990.

Bloland, Harland G. and Eugene R. Tempel. 2004. "Measuring Professionalism." In *New Directions for Philanthropic Fundraising*, No. 43, pp. 5–20. San Francisco, CA: Jossey-Bass.

Blumberg, Stephen J. and Julian V. Luke. 2014. "Wireless Substitution: Early Release of Estimates from the National Health Interview Survey." National Center for Health Statistics. Available from: http://www.cdc.gov/nchs/data/nhis/earlyrelease/wireless201412.pdf.

BoardSource. 2012a. *Nonprofit Board Answer Book: A Practical Guide for Board Members and Chief Executives*, 3rd ed. San Francisco, CA: Jossey-Bass.

BoardSource. 2012b. *Nonprofit Governance Index 2012.* Retrieved from: http://www.thenonprofitpartnership.org/files/board-source-governance-2012.pdf.

BoardSource. 2014. *Leading with Intent 2014: A National Index of Nonprofit Board Practices.* Retrieved from: https://www.boardsource.org/eweb/images/bds2012/Leading-with-intent-PV.pdf.

BoardSource. 2015. *Leading with Intent 2015: A National Index of Nonprofit Board Practices.* Washington, DC: BoardSource.

Bowersock, G. W. 2015. "Money and your Soul." *The New York Review of Books*, May 21, 2015.

Brogan, Chris. 2010. *Social Media 101: Tactics and Tips to Develop Your Business Online.* Hoboken, NJ: John Wiley & Sons, Inc.

Brown, Eleanor. 2006. "Married Couples' Charitable Giving: Who and Why." In Martha A. Taylor and Sondra Shaw-Hardy (eds.), *The Transformative Power of Women's Philanthropy*, pp. 69–80. San Francisco, CA: Wiley Periodicals Inc.

Brown, Eleanor and Patrick M. Rooney, P. 2008. "Proceedings from The Center on Philanthropy at Indiana University 20th Annual Symposium: Men, Women, X and Y: Generational and Gender Differences in Motivations for Giving." Indianapolis, IN: Unpublished report.

Brummelman, Eddie, Sander Thomaes, Stefanie A. Nelemansd, Bram Orobio de Castrob, Geertjan Overbeeka, and Brad J. Bushmane. 2015. "Origins of Narcissism in Children." *Proceedings of the National Academy of Sciences*, 112: 3659–3662.

Bryan, Brielle. 2008. *Diversity in Philanthropy.* Foundation Center. Retrieved from: http://foundationcenter.org/getstarted/topical/diversity_in_phil.pdf.

Bureau of Labor Statistics. 2015. "CPI Inflation Calculator." Accessed June 8, 2015: http://www.bls.gov/data/inflation_calculator.htm.

Burke, Penelope. 2003. *Donor Centered Fundraising: How to Hold on to Your Donors and Raise More Much More Money.* Chicago, IL: Cygnus Applied Research, Inc.

Burke, Penelope. 2014. *Donor Centered Leadership: What It Takes to Build a High Performance Fundraising Team.* Chicago, IL: Cygnus Applied Research, Inc.

Burlingame, Dwight F. 2003. "Corporate Giving and Fund Raising." In Eugene R. Tempel (ed.), *Achieving Excellence in Fund Raising*, 2nd ed., pp. 177–187. San Francisco, CA: Jossey-Bass.

Burlingame, Dwight F. and Dennis R. Young. 1996. *Corporate Philanthropy at the Crossroads.* Bloomington, IN: Indiana University Press.

Business Civic Leadership Center. 2008. *Corporate Community Investment Study.* Washington, DC: US Chamber of Commerce.

Cagney, Penelope. 2013. "The Global Fundraising Revolution." *Advancing Philanthropy*, Spring.

Callahan, David. 2015. "He May be Popular Now, But Darren Walker Has a Tough Message for the Nonprofit World." *Inside Philanthropy*, July 9, 2015.

Cam, Kelly. 2013. "Women in Leadership and Philanthropy." Presentation at the Council for Advancement and Support of Education and Women in Philanthropy Conference, Indianapolis, Indiana, November 3, 2013.

Campobasso, Laura and Dan Davis. 2001. *Reflections on Capacity Building*. Woodland Hills, CA: California Wellness Foundation.

Carbone, Robert F. 1989. *Fundraising as a Profession*. College Park, MD: Clearing House for Research on Fund Raising.

Carbone, Robert F. 1997. "Licensure and Credentialing as Professionalizing Elements." In *New Directions for Philanthropic Fundraising*, No. 15, pp. 83–96. San Francisco, CA: Jossey-Bass.

Carmichael, Mary. 2007. "A Shot of Hope." *Newsweek*, October 1, 2007.

Chance, Zoe and Michael I. Norton. 2015. *I Give, Therefore I Have: Giving and Subjective Wealth*. Unpublished manuscript.

Chao, Jessica, Julia Parshall, Desirée Amador, Meghna Shah, Armando Yañez. 2008. *Philanthropy in a Changing Society*. Rockefeller Philanthropy Advisors. Retrieved from: http://rockpa.org/document.doc?id=27.

Charities Aid Foundation. 2010. *The World Giving Index 2010*. Accessed June 11, 2015 https://www.cafonline.org/pdf/WorldGivingIndex28092010Print.pdf.

Chaves, Mark. 2004. *Congregations in America*. Cambridge, MA: Harvard University Press.

Chobot, Richard B. 2004. "Fundraising Credentialing." In *New Directions for Philanthropic Fundraising*, No. 43, pp. 31–50. San Francisco, CA: Jossey-Bass.

Choi, Namkee G. and Jinseok Kim. 2011. "The Effect of Time Volunteering and Charitable Donations in Later Life on Psychological Wellbeing." *Ageing and Society*, 31: 590–610.

Chrislip, David D. and Carl E. Larson. 1994. *Collaborative Leadership: How Citizens and Civic Leaders Make a Difference*. San Francisco, CA: Jossey-Bass.

Citigroup. 2002. *Among the Wealthy: Those Who Have It Give It Away*. Citigroup.

Clohesy, William W. 2003. "Fund-Raising and the Articulation of Common Goods." *Nonprofit and Voluntary Sector Quarterly* 32(1): 128–140.

Clotfelter, Charles T. 1990. *The Impact of Tax Reform on Charitable Giving: A 1989 Perspective* (Working Paper No. 3273). Cambridge, MA: National Bureau of Economic Research.

Cluff, Angela. 2009. "Dispelling the Myths about Major Donor Fundraising." *International Journal of Nonprofit and Voluntary Sector Marketing*, 14(4): 371–377.

Cohen, Todd. 2007. "Nonprofit Training Seen Trailing Demand." *Philanthropy Journal*, May 29, 2007.

Cohen, Janet, and Donna Red Wing. 2009. "Raising Heck and Raising Funds: A Conversation About Lesbian Philanthropy." Presentation at the annual AFP International Conference, New Orleans, Louisiana, March 29–April 1, 2009.

Collin, N. 2009. "5 Reasons Creatives Hate Working for You". http://ezinearticles.com/?5-Reasons-Creatives-Hate-Working-For-You-(And-What-To-Do-About-It)&id=3279820.

Committee Encouraging Corporate Philanthropy (CECP). 2008. *Giving in Numbers*. Washington, DC: Committee Encouraging Corporate Philanthropy

Cone Communications. 2013. *Social Impact Study: The Next Cause Evolution*. Boston, MA: Cone Communications.

Connolly, Lori. 2011. "*View from the Digital Inbox 2011*." Columbia, MD: Merkle, Inc.

Conway, Daniel. 2003. "Practicing Stewardship." In Eugene R. Tempel, *Achieving Excellence in Fund Raising*, 2nd ed., pp. 431–441. San Francisco, CA: Jossey-Bass.

Corporation for National and Community Service. 2010. "Volunteering in America Research Highlights." Retrieved January 10, 2010 from http://www.volunteeringinamerica.gov/.

Corporation for National and Community Service. 2014. "Volunteering and Civic Life in America." Accessed April 30, 2014: http://www.volunteeringinamerica.gov/infographic.cfm.

Corporation for National and Community Service. 2015. "Volunteering and Civic Engagement in the United States: Trends and Highlights Overview." Retrieved March 30, 2015 from http://www.volunteeringinamerica.gov/.

Covey, Stephen M. R. 2006. *The Speed of Trust.* New York: Free Press.

Crutchfield, Leslie R. and Heather McLeod Grant. 2008. *Forces for Good: The Six Practices of High-Impact Nonprofits.* San Francisco, CA: Jossey-Bass.

Cummins. 2009. *Sustainability Report: A Legacy of Dependability and Responsibility.* Indianapolis, IN: Cummins, Inc.

Cummins. 2014. *Living Our Values Through Our People, Products, and Practies: Sustainability Progress Report: 2013–2014.* Indianapolis, IN: Cummins, Inc.

Cunningham, Nancy. 2005. "Myth Versus Reality: State of the Lesbian, Gay, Bisexual, and Transgender Community and Philanthropy's response." In *State of Philanthropy 2004,* pp. 10–14. Washington, DC: National Committee for Responsible Philanthropy.

Cutlip, Scott M. 1965. *Fund Raising in the United States: Its Role in American Philanthropy.* New Brunswick, NJ: Rutgers University Press.

Daniels, Alex. 2015. "Foundation Heads Call on Peers to Publicize Diversity Data." *The Chronicle of Philanthropy,* June 29, 2015.

Danner, Deborah D., David A. Snowdon, and Wallace V. Friesen. 2001. "Positive Emotions in Early Life and Longevity: Findings from the Nun Study." *Journal of Personality and Social Psychology,* 80(5): 804–813.

Demographics Now. 2010. Table of the United States Population, Age by Sex Summary Report. http://www.demographicsnow.com, Jan 2010.

Dove, Kent E. 2000. *Conducting a Successful Capital Campaign,* 2nd ed. San Francisco: Jossey-Bass.

Drezner, Noah D. 2013. *Expanding the Donor Base in Higher Education: Engaging Non-Traditional Donors.* New York: Routledge.

Drucker, Peter F. 1990. *Managing the Non-profit Organization: Practices and Principles.* New York, NY: HarperCollins.

Dulin, Patrick L., J. Gavala, C. Stephens, M. Kostick, and J. McDonald. 2012. "Volunteering Predicts Happiness Among Older Maori and Non-Maori in the New Zealand Health, Work, and Retirement Longitudinal Study." *Aging and Mental Health,* 16: 617–624.

Dunlop, David. R. 2000. "Fundraising for the Largest Gift of a Lifetime: From Inspiring the Commitment to Receiving the Gift." Workshop at the Council for Advancement and Support of Education Conference (CASE), Charleston, SC, May 22–24, 2000.

Dunn, Elizabeth W., C.E. Ashton-James, M.D. Hanson, and L.B. Aknin. 2010. "On the Costs of Self-Interested Economic Behavior." *Journal of Health Psychology,* 15: 627–633.

Dunn, Elizabeth W., Lara B. Aknin, and Michael I. Norton. 2008. "Spending Money on Others Promotes Happiness." *Science,* 319: 1687–1688.

Duronio, Margart A. and Eugene R. Tempel. 1997. *Fund Raisers: Their Careers, Stories, Concerns, and Accomplishments.* San Francisco, CA: Jossey-Bass.

Eckel, Catherine, David Herberich and Jonathan Meer. 2014. "A Field Experiment on Directed Giving at a Public University." Accessed January 15, 2015: https://site.stanford.edu/sites/default/files/eckel_herberich_meer_directed_giving.pdf.

Eisner, David, Robert T. Grimm, Jr., Shannon Maynard and Susannah Washburn. 2009. "The New Volunteer Workforce." *Stanford Social Innovation Review*, Winter 32–37.

Elliot, D. 1991. "What Counts as Deception in Higher Education Development." In Dwight F. Burlingame and Lamont J. Hulse (eds.), *Taking Fund Raising Seriously*. San Francisco, CA: Jossey-Bass.

Ellis, Susan J. and Katherine H. Noyes. 1990. *By the People: A History of Americans as Volunteers*. San Francisco, CA: Jossey-Bass.

English, Cynthia. 2011. "Civic Engagement Highest in Developed Nations." Retrieved June 20, 2015 from http://www.gallup.com/poll/145589/civic-engagement-highest-developed-countries.aspx.

Fender, Stacy A. 2011. "Philanthropy in the Queer Community: A Review and Analysis of Available Research and Literature on Philanthropy Within the Queer Community from 1969 to 2009." MA thesis, Saint Mary's University of Minnesota.

Fischer, Marilyn. 2000. *Ethical Decision Making in Fund Raising*. New York: John Wiley & Sons, Inc.

Fishman, James J. and Stephen Schwarz. 2010. *Nonprofit Organizations*, 4th ed. New York: Foundation Press.

Flandez, Raymund. 2013. "As Wedding Bells Ring, Charities Seek Support from Newly Visible Same-Sex Couples." *Chronicle of Philanthropy*, May 19, 2013.

Fleishman, Joel L. 2007. *The Foundation: A Great American Secret*. New York: Public Affairs.

Foundation Center. 2014. *Key Facts on U.S. Foundations*. New York: Foundation Center.

Frantzreb, Arthur C. 1991. "Seeking Big Gifts." In Henry A. Rosso *Achieving Excellence in Fund Raising*, pp.117–129. San Francisco, CA: Jossey-Bass.

Fried, Linda P., M.C. Carlson, M. Freedman, K.D. Frick, T.A. Glass, J. Hill, S. McGill, G.W. Rebok, T. Seeman, J. Tielsch, B.A. Wasik, and S. Zeger. 2004. "A Social Model for Health Promotion for an Aging Population: Initial Evidence on the Experience Corps Model." *Journal of Urban Health*, 81(1): 64–78.

Friedman, Milton. 1970. "The Social Responsibility of Business is to Increase its Profits. *The New York Times Magazine*, September 13, 1970.

Fry, Richard. 2013. "Four Takeaways from Tuesday's Census Income and Poverty Release." Pew Research Center. Retrieved from: http://www.pewresearch.org/fact-tank/2013/09/18/four-takeaways-from-tuesdays-census-income-and-poverty-release/.

Galaskiewicz, Joseph and Michelle Sinclair Colman. 2006. "Collaboration between Corporations and Nonprofit Organizations." In W. W. Powell and R. Steinberg (eds.), *The Nonprofit Sector: A Research Handbook*, 2nd ed., pp. 180—204. New Haven, CT: Yale University Press.

Gallo, Marcia M. 2001. "Lesbian Giving – and Getting: Tending Radical Roots in an Era of Venture Philanthropy." *Journal of Lesbian Studies*, 5: 63–70.

Garber, Sheldon. 1993. "The Fund Raising Professional: An Agent for Change." Presentation at the International Conference for the Association of Healthcare Philanthropy, Chicago, IL, October 4, 1993.

Gardner, John W. 1990. *On Leadership*. New York: The Free Press.

Garvey, Jason C. and Noah D. Drezner. 2013a. "Advancement Staff and Alumni Advocates: Cultivating LGBTQ Alumni by Promoting Individual and Community Uplift." *Journal of Diversity in Higher Education*, 6(3): 199–218.

Garvey, Jason C. and Noah D. Drezner. 2013b. "Alumni Giving in the LGBTQ Communities: Queering Philanthropy." In Noah D. Drezner (ed.), *Expanding the Donor*

Base in Higher Education: Engaging Non-Traditional Donors, pp. 74–86. New York: Routledge.

Gates, Gary J. 2011. *How Many People are Lesbian, Gay, Bisexual, and Transgender?* Los Angeles, CA: The Williams Institute, UCLA School of Law.

Gates, Gary J. 2015. *Demographics of Married and Unmarried Same-Sex Couples: Analyses of the 2013 American Community Survey.* Los Angeles, CA: The Williams Institute, UCLA School of Law.

Gates, Gary J. and Frank Newport. 2012. "Special Report: 3.4% of U.S. Adults Identify as LGBT." *Gallup*, October 18, 2012. Available at: http://www.gallup.com/poll/158066/special-report-adults-identify-lgbt.aspx

Gilmore, James H. and B. Joseph Pine II. 2007. *Authenticity.* Boston, MA: Harvard Business School Press.

Giving USA: The Annual Report on Philanthropy for the year 2008. 2009. Chicago: Giving USA Foundation.

Giving USA: The Annual Report on Philanthropy for the year 2013. 2014. Chicago: Giving USA Foundation.

Giving USA: The Annual Report on Philanthropy for the year 2014. 2015. Chicago: Giving USA Foundation.

Gladwell, Malcolm. 2000. *The Tipping Point: How Little Things Can Make a Big Difference.* Boston, MA: Little, Brown and Company.

Gourville, John and V. Kasturi Rangan. 2004. "Valuing the Cause Marketing Relationship." *California Management Review*, 47(1), 38–56.

Gray, Kurt. 2010. "Moral Transformation: Good and Evil Turn the Weak into the Mighty." *Social Psychological and Personality Science*, 1(2): 253–258.

Greenfield, James M. 2002. *Fundraising Fundamentals: A Guide to Annual Giving for Professionals and Volunteers*, 2nd ed. New York: John Wiley & Sons, Inc.

Greenfield, Emily A. and Nadine F. Marks. 2004. "Formal Volunteering as a Protective Factor for Older Adults' Psychological Well-Being." *Journal of Gerontology*, 59B(5): S258–S264.

Gunderman, Richard. B. 2009. *We Make a Life by What We Give.* Bloomington, IN: Indiana University Press.

Hall, Holly. 2007. "Evaluating How Well a Fund Raiser Does in Luring Big Gifts." *Chronicle of Philanthropy*, October 1, 2007.

Hall, Holly. 2010. "People Skills No Longer Sufficient for Fund Raisers to Thrive." *The Chronicle of Philanthropy*, April 4.

Hacker, Holly K. 2009. "Seven Universities Raise Enough for 'Tier One'." *Dallas Morning News*, September 2, 2009.

Hager, Mark. 2004. "Exploring Measurement and Evaluation Effects in Fundraising." *New Directors in Philanthropic Fundraising*, no. 41. San Francisco: Jossey-Bass.

Harbaugh, William T., Ulrich Mayr, and Daniel R. Burghart. 2007. "Neural Responses to Taxation and Voluntary Giving Reveal Motives for Charitable Donations." *Science*, 316: 1622–1625. Oxford: Oxford University Pres.

Havens, John J. and Paul G. Schervish. 2001. "Wealth and Commonwealth: New Findings on Wherewithal and Philanthropy." *Nonprofit and Voluntary Sector Quarterly*, 5–25.

Havens, John J., Mary A. O'Herlihy, and Paul G. Schervish. 2006. "Charitable Giving: How Much, by Whom, to What, and How?" In Walter Powell and Richard Steinberg (eds.),

The Nonprofit Sector: A Research Handbook, pp. 542–567. New Haven, CT: Yale University Press.

Heath, Chip and Dan Heath. 2007. *Made to Stick: Why Some Ideas Survive and Others Die*. New York: Random House.

Helms, Sara and Jeremy P. Thornton. 2008. *The Influence of Religiosity on Charitable Behavior: A COPPS Investigation* (Working Paper). Birmingham, AL: Brock School of Business at Samford University.

Hirschfelder, Adam S. and Sabrain L. Reilly. 2007. "Rx: Volunteer, A Prescription for Healthy Aging." In Stephen G. Post (ed.), *Altruism and Health: Perspectives from Empirical Research*, pp. 116–140.

HNW Inc. 2000. *HNW Wealth Pulse: Wealth and Giving*. HNW Inc.

Ho, S. Shaun, S. Konrath, S. Brown, J.E. Swain. 2014. "Empathy and Stress Related Neural Responses in Maternal Decision Making." *Frontiers in Neuroscience*, 8: 152. doi: 10.3389/fnins.2014.00152.

Hodgkinson, Virginia. 2002. "Individual Volunteering and Giving." In Lester Salamon (ed.), *The State of Nonprofit America*. Washington, DC: Brookings Institution Press.

Hope Consulting. 2010. *Money for Good: The US Market for Impact Investments and Charitable Gifts from Individual Donors and Investors*. Hope Consulting.

Hopkins, Bruce R. 2002. *The Law of Fundraising*, 3rd ed. New York: John Wiley & Sons, Inc.

Horizons Foundation. 2008. *Building a New Tradition of LGBT Philanthropy*. San Francisco, CA: Horizons Foundation.

Huang, Yunhui. 2014. "Downward Social Comparison Increases Life-Satisfaction in the Giving and Volunteering Context." *Social Indicators Research*. doi: 10.1007/s11205-014-0849-6.

Hudnut-Beumler James. 2007. *In Pursuit of the Almighty's Dollar*. Chapel Hill, NC: University of North Carolina Press.

Hunter, K. I. and Margaret W. Linn. 1981. "Psychosocial Differences Between Elderly Volunteers and Non-Volunteers." *The International Journal of Aging and Human Development*, 12(3): 205–213.

IEG Sponsorship Report. 2009. IEG, LLC. www.sponsorship.com/iegsr.

Ilchman, Warren F., Stanley N. Katz, and Edward L. Queen. 1998. *Philanthropy in the World's Traditions*. Bloomington, IN: Indiana University Press.

Immigration Policy Center. 2014. *Strength in Diversity: The Economic and Political Power of Immigrants, Latinos, and Asians*. American Immigration Council. Retrieved from: http://www.immigrationpolicy.org/just-facts/strength-diversity-economic-and-political-power-immigrants-latinos-and-asians.

INDEPENDENT SECTOR. 1996. *Giving and Volunteering in the United States*. Washington, DC.

INDEPENDENT SECTOR. 1998. *Public Policy Update: Special Report*. Washington, DC.

INDEPENDENT SECTOR. 2001. *Giving and Volunteering in the United States*. Washington, DC.

INDEPENDENT SECTOR. 2002a. *Ethics and the Nation's Voluntary and Philanthropic Community: Obedience to the Unenforceable*. Washington, DC.

INDEPENDENT SECTOR. 2002b. *The New Nonprofit Almanac and Desk Reference*. Washington, DC.

INDEPENDENT SECTOR. 2007. *Principles of Good Governance and Ethical Practice*. Washington, DC.

INDEPENDENT SECTOR. 2014. *Value of Volunteer Time*. Retrieved April 22, 2015 from: http://independentsector.org/volunteer_time.

INDEPENDENT SECTOR. 2015. *Principles for Good Governance and Ethical Practice: A Guide for Charities and Foundations.* Washington, DC

Indiana University Center on Philanthropy. 2006. *Bank of America Study of High Net Worth Philanthropy: Portraits of Donors.* Indianapolis, IN: The Trustees of Indiana University.

Indiana University Center on Philanthropy. 2007. *Corporate Philanthropy: The Age of Integration.* Indianapolis, IN: The Trustees of Indiana University.

Indiana University Center on Philanthropy. 2008a. *Bank of America Study of High Net Worth Philanthropy.* Indianapolis, IN: The Trustees of Indiana University.

Indiana University Center on Philanthropy. 2008b. *An Analysis of Million Dollar Gifts (2000–2007).* Indianapolis, IN: The Trustees of Indiana University.

Indiana University Center on Philanthropy. 2008c.*Bank of America Study of High Net Worth Philanthropy: Portraits of Donors.* Indianapolis, IN: The Trustees of Indiana University.

Indiana University Center on Philanthropy. 2009a. *Philanthropic Giving Index: Summer 2009.* Indianapolis: The Trustees of Indiana University.

Indiana University Center on Philanthropy. 2009b. Overview of Overall Giving. Philanthropy Panel Study. Retrieved from: http://www.philanthropy.iupui.edu/files/research/2009ppskeyfindings.pdf.

Indiana University Center on Philanthropy. 2010. *Bank of America Merrill Lynch Study of High Net Worth Philanthropy.* Indianapolis, IN: The Trustees of Indiana University.

Indiana University Center on Philanthropy. 2011. *2011 Study of High Net Worth Women's Philanthropy and the Impact of Women's Giving Networks.* Indianapolis, IN: The Trustees of Indiana University.

Indiana University Center on Philanthropy. 2012. *Bank of America Merrill Lynch Study of High Net Worth Philanthropy.* Indianapolis, IN: The Trustees of Indiana University.

Indiana University Lilly Family School of Philanthropy. 2014. *The 2014 U.S. Trust Study of High Net-Worth Individuals.* Indianapolis, IN: The Trustees of Indiana University.

Indiana University Lilly Family School of Philanthropy. 2015. *The Philanthropy Outlook: 2015 & 2016.* Indianapolis, IN: The Trustees of Indiana University.

Indiana University The Fund Raising School. 2002. *Principles and Techniques of Fundraising.* Indianapolis, IN: The Trustees of Indiana University.

Indiana University The Fund Raising School. 2009. *Principles and Techniques of Fundraising.* Indianapolis, IN: The Trustees of Indiana University.

Indiana University The Fund Raising School. 2015. *Principles and Techniques of Fundraising: Study Guide.* Indianapolis, IN: The Fund Raising School.

Institute of Medicine. 2011. *The Health of Lesbian, Gay, Bisexual, and Transgender People: Building a Foundation for Better Understanding.* Washington, DC: National Academies Press.

Internal Revenue Service. 2007. *Female Top Wealth Holders by Size of Net Worth.* Retrieved from: http://www.irs.gov/uac/SOI-Tax-Stats-Female-Top-Wealthholders-by-Size-of-Net-Worth.

Internal Revenue Service. 2015. "Exempt Organization Annual Reporting Requirements – Overview." Accessed June 8, 2015: http://www.irs.gov/Charities-&-Non-Profits/Exempt-Organizations-Annual-Reporting-Requirements-Overview-Annual-Return-Filing-Exceptions.

Jackson, William J. 2008. *The Wisdom of Generosity: A Reader in American Philanthropy.* Waco, TX: Baylor University Press.

Jackson, Kenneth W. Alandra L. Washington, and Russell H. Jackson. 2012. "Strategies for Impacting Change in Communities of Color." *The Foundation Review,* 4(1): 54–67.

Jacobs, Jill. 2009. *There Shall Be No Needy: Pursuing Social Justice through Jewish Law and Tradition.* Woodstock, VT: Jewish Lights Publishing.

Jaschik, Scott. 2005. "Price Check." *CASE Currents,* January 4, 2005.

Joseph, James A. 1995. *Remaking America: How the Benevolent Traditions of Many Cultures Are Transforming Our National Life.* San Francisco, CA: Jossey-Bass.

Josephson, Michael S. 2002. *Making Ethical Decisions.* Marina Del Ray, CA: Joseph and Edna Josephson Institute on Ethics.

Joulfaian, David. 2000. *Charitable Giving in Life and Death* (Working Paper). University of Michigan Business School and Office of Tax Policy Research.

Kahana, Eva, T. Bhatta, L.D. Lovegreen, B. Kahana, E. Midlarsky. 2013. "Altruism, Helping, and Volunteering: Pathways to Well-Being in Late Life." *Journal of Aging and Health,* 25(1): 159–187.

Kanter, Beth and Allison Fine. 2010. *The Networked Nonprofit: Connecting with Social Media to Drive Change.* San Francisco, CA: Jossey-Bass.

Karlan, Dean and John A. List. 2007. "Does Price Matter in Charitable Giving? Evidence from a Large-Scale Natural Field Experiment." *American Economic Review,* 97(5): 1774–1793.

Katz, Daniel and Robert L. Kahn. 1978. *The Social Psychology of Organizations.* New York: John Wiley & Sons, Inc.

Kearns, Kevin P. 1996. *Managing for Accountability: Trust in Public and Nonprofit Organizations.* San Francisco, CA: Jossey-Bass.

Keidan, Charles, Tobias Jung and Cathy Pharoah. 2014. "Philanthropy Education in the UK and Continental Europe: Current Provision, Perceptions and Opportunities." Centre for Charitable Giving and Philanthropy, Cass Business School, City University London.

Kelly, Kathleen S. 1998. *Effective Fund-Raising Management.* Mahwah: Lawrence Erlbaum Associates.

Kendell, Kate and Ruth Herring. 2001. "Funding the National Center for Lesbian Rights." *Journal of Lesbian Studies,* 5(3): 95–103.

Khanna, Tarun. 2014. "Contextual Intelligence." *Harvard Business Review,* September 2014.

Koestner, Richard, Carol Franz, and Joel Weinberger. 1990. "The Family Origins of Empathic Concern: A 26-Year Longitudinal Study." *Journal of Personality and Social Psychology,* 58(4): 709–717.

Konrath, Sara. 2014. "The Power of Philanthropy and Volunteering." In *Wellbeing: A Complete Reference Guide, Interventions and Policies to Enhance Wellbeing,* Vol. 6, pp. 387–426. Hoboken, NJ: John Wiley & Sons, Inc.

Konrath, Sara, Andrea Fuhrel-Forbis, Alina Lou, and Stephanie Brown. 2012. "Motives for Volunteering Are Associated with Mortality Risk in Older Adults." *Health Psychology,* 31: 87–96.

Kotler, Philip and Alan R. Andreasen. 1996. *Strategic Marketing for Nonprofit Organizations,* 5th ed. Englewood Cliffs, NJ: Prentice Hall.

Kotler, Philip and Karen Fox. 1995. *Strategic Marketing for Educational Institutions,* 2nd ed. Englewood Cliffs, NJ: Prentice Hall.

Kubler-Ross, Elizabeth. 1969. *On Death and Dying.* New York: Simon and Schuster.

Kumar, Nirmalya and Jan-Benedict E. M. Steenkamp. 2013. "Diaspora Marketing." *Harvard Business Review,* October 2013.

Kumar, Santosh, Rocio Calvo, Mauricio Avendano, Kavita Sivaramakrishnan, and Lisa F. Berkmanb. 2012. "Social Support, Volunteering and Health Around the World: Cross-National Evidence from 139 Countries." *Social Science and Medicine* 74(5): 696–706.

Lacy, Kyle. 2013. "50 Email Marketing Tips and Stats for 2014." SalesForce. Available at http://www.exacttarget.com/blog/50-email-marketing-tips-and-stats-for-2014/.

Layous, Kristin, S. Katherine Nelson, Eva Oberle, Kimberly A. Schonert-Reichl, and Sonja Lyubomirsky. 2012. "Kindness Counts: Prompting Prosocial Behavior in Preadolescents Boosts Peer Acceptance and Well-Being." *PLoS ONE*, 7(12): e51380. doi: 10.1371/journal.pone.0051380.

Lee, Young-joo and Jeffrey Brudney. 2012."Participation in Formal and Informal Volunteering: Implications for Volunteer Recruitment." *Nonprofit Management and Leadership*, 23(2): 159–180.

Levinson, Kate. 2011. *Emotional Currency: A Woman's Guide to Building a Healthy Relationship with Money.* New York: Celestial Arts.

Levy, Jamie D. 2004. "The Growth of Fundraising: Framing the Impact of Research and Literature on Education and Training." In *New Directions for Philanthropic Fundraising*, No. 43, pp. 21–30. San Francisco, CA: Jossey-Bass.

Lewin, Tamar. 2000. "Couple Gives $2 Million for Gay Student Center." *The New York Times*, October 13, 2000.

LGBT Movement Advancement Project (MAP) and Services and Advocacy for Gay, Lesbian, Bisexual, and Transgender Elders (SAGE). 2010. *Improving the Lives of LGBT Older Adults.* Denver, CO and New York, NY: MAP and SAGE.

Li, Yunqing and Kenneth F. Ferraro. 2005. "Volunteering and Depression in Later Life: Social Benefit or Selection Process?" *Journal of Health and Social Behavior*, 46(1): 68–84.

Light, Paul C. 2008. "How Americans View Charities: A Report on Charitable Confidence, 2008." In *Issues in Governance Studies.* Washington, DC: Brookings.

Lipka, Michael. 2013. *What Surveys Say about Worship Attendance – And Why Some Stay Home.* Washington, DC: Pew Research Center.

Liu, Wendy and Jennifer Aaker. 2008. "The Happiness of Giving: The Time-Ask Effect." *Journal of Consumer Research*, 35: 543–557.

Lysakowski, Linda. 2005. *Nonprofit Essentials: Recruiting and Training Fundraising Volunteers.* Hoboken, NJ: John Wiley & Sons, Inc.

MacLaughlin, Steve. 2010. "Demystifying Online Metrics." In Ted Hart, James M. Greenfield, Steve MacLaughlin, and Philip H. Geier, Jr. (eds.), *Internet Management for Nonprofits: Strategies, Tools and Trade Secrets.* Hoboken, NJ: John Wiley & Sons, Inc.

MacLaughlin, Steve. 2015. *Charitable Giving Report: How Nonprofit Fundraising Performed in 2014.* Blackbaud, Inc.

Mattson, Ingrid. 2010. "Zakat in America: The Evolving Role of Islamic Charity in Community Cohesion," Lake Lecture. Indianapolis: Center on Philanthropy at Indiana University, Lake Institute on Faith and Giving.

Maxwell, Margret M. 2011. "Selecting and Working with Fundraising Consultants." In Eugene R. Tempel, Timothy L. Seiler, and Eva. A. Aldrich (eds.), *Achieving Excellence in Fund Raising*, 3rd ed., pp. 375–382. San Francisco, CA: Jossey-Bass.

McCarthy, Kathleen D. 2003. *American Creed: Philanthropy and the Rise of Civil Society, 1700–1865.* Chicago, IL: University of Chicago Press.

McDougle, Lindsey, Femida Handy, Sara Konrath, and Marlene Walk. 2013. "Health Outcomes and Volunteering: The Moderating Role of Religiosity." *Social Indicators Research*, 117: 1–15.

McKeever, Brice S. and Sarah L. Pettijohn. 2014. *The Nonprofit Sector in Brief 2014: Public Charities, Giving and Volunteering*. Washington, DC: National Center for Charitable Statistics at the Urban Institute.

McKitrick, Melanie, J. Shawn Landres, Mark Ottoni-Wilhelm, and Amir Hayat. 2013. *Connected to Give: Faith Communities*. Los Angeles, CA: Jumpstart.

McRobbie, Laurie B. 2013. "The Women's Philanthropy Council." In Michelle Minter and Patricia Jackson (eds.), *From Donor to Philanthropist: The Value of Donor Education in Creating Confident, Joyful Givers*, pp. 105–120. Washington, DC: CASE.

Meier, Stephan and Alois Stutzer. 2008. "Is Volunteering Rewarding in Itself?" *Economica*, 75(297): 39–59.

Merrill Lynch and Capgemini. 2007. *World Wealth Report 2007*. Merrill Lynch and Capgemini.

Mesch, Debra J. 2010. *Women Give 2010: New Research about Women and Giving*. Indianapolis, IN: Indiana University Lilly Family School of Philanthropy.

Mesch, Debra J. 2012. *Women Give 2012: New Research about Women and Giving*. Indianapolis, IN: Indiana University Lilly Family School of Philanthropy.

Mesch, Debra J. and Una Osili. 2014. *Women Give 2014: New Research on Women, Religion, and Philanthropy*. Indianapolis, IN: Indiana University Lilly Family School of Philanthropy.

Meyer, Erin. 2014. "Navigating the Cultural Minefield." *Harvard Business Review*, May 2014.

Millennial Impact Report. 2010. *A study of Millennial Giving and Engagement Habits*. Indianapolis, IN. Retrieved from: http://cdn.trustedpartner.com/docs/library/AchieveMCON2013/MD10%20Full%20Report.pdf.

Millennial Impact Report. 2013. *Connect, Involve, Give*. Indianapolis, IN. Retrieved from: http://cdn.trustedpartner.com/docs/library/AchieveMCON2013/Research%20Report/Millennial%20Impact%20Research.pdf.

Millennial Impact Report. 2014. *Inspiring the Next Generation Workforce*. Indianapolis, IN. Retrieved from: http://cdn.trustedpartner.com/docs/library/AchieveMCON2013/MIR_2014.pdf.

Miller, Neil. 2006. *Out of the Past*. New York, NY: Advocate Books.

Mirabella, Roseanne M. 2007. "University-Based Educational Programs in Nonprofit Management and Philanthropic Studies: A 10-Year Review and Projections of Future Trends." *Nonprofit and Voluntary Sector Quarterly*, 36(4 Suppl.): 11S–27S.

Mirabella, Roseanne M. 2015. "Nonprofit Management Education Current Offerings in University-Based Programs." Seton Hall University web site http://academic.shu.edu/npo/.

Mogilner, Cassie, Zoe Chance, and Michael I. Norton. 2012. "Giving Time Gives You Time." *Psychological Science*, 23(10): 1233–1238.

Mojza, Eva J., C. Lorenz, S. Sonnentag, and C. Binnewies. 2010. "Daily Recovery Experiences: The Role of Volunteer Work During Leisure Time." *Journal of Occupational Health Psychology*, 15(1): 60–74.

Moll, Jorge, Frank Krueger, Roland Zahn, Matteo Pardini, Ricardo de Oliveira-Souza, and Jordan Grafman. 2006. "Human Fronto-Mesolimbic Networks Guide Decisions about Charitable Donation." *Proceedings of the National Academy of Sciences*, 103(42): 15623–15628.

Morris, Tom. 1997. *If Aristotle Ran General Motors*. New York: Henry Holt and Company.

Movement Advancement Project. 2009. *LGBT Nonprofits and Their Funders in a Troubled Economy*. Denver, CO: Movement Advancement Project.

Musick, Marc A. and John Wilson. 2003. "Volunteering and Depression: The Role of Psychological and Social Resources in Different Age Groups." *Social Science and Medicine*, 56(2): 259–269.

Musick, Marc A. and John Wilson. 2008. *Volunteers: A Social Profile.* Bloomington, IN: Indiana University Press.

National Council of Nonprofits. 2015. "State Law Nonprofit Audit Requirements." Accessed June 8, 2015: https://www.councilofnonprofits.org/nonprofit-audit-guide/state-law-audit-requirements.

Newman, Diana. 2002. *Opening Doors: Pathways to Diverse Donors.* San Francisco, CA: Jossey-Bass.

Neyfakh, Leon. 2013. "Donor Advised Funds: Where Charity Goes to Wait." *The Boston Globe*, December 1, 2013.

Nonprofit Academic Centers Council. 2007. "Curricular Guidelines for Graduate Study in Nonprofit Leadership, the Nonprofit Sector and Philanthropy." Cleveland, OH: Nonprofit Academic Centers Council.

Nonprofit Research Collaborative. 2012. "Nonprofit Fundraising Survey for 2011 Year-End Results." Accessed January 26, 2015: http://npresearch.org/winter-2012.html.

Nonprofit Research Collaborative. 2014. "Nonprofit Fundraising Study Covering Charitable Receipts at Nonprofit Organizations in the United States and Canada in 2013." Accessed June 11, 2015 at http://www.afpnet.org/files/ContentDocuments/2014NRCWinter.pdf.

Norton, Michael I., Lalin Anik, Lara B. Aknin, Elizabeth W. Dunn, and Jordi Quoidbach. 2012. "Prosocial Incentives Increase Employee Satisfaction and Team Performance." Unpublished manuscript.

O'Brien, Carol L. 2005. "Thinking Beyond the Dollar Goal: A Campaign as Organizational Transformation." In *New Directions for Philanthropic Fundraising*, No. 47. San Francisco, CA: Jossey-Bass.

O'Connell, Martin and Sarah Feliz. 2011. "Same-Sex Couple Household Statistics from the 2012 Census." SEHSD Working Paper Number 2011-26. Retrieved from: https://www.census.gov/hhes/samesex/data/decennial.html.

O'Connor, Pauline. 2014. "The New Regulatory Regime for Social Enterprise in Canada: Potential Impacts on Nonprofit Growth and Sustainability." *Association of Fundraising Professionals.* Accessed June 4, 2015. http://afpdc.afpnet.org/International/fndnewsdetail.cfm?ItemNumber=24761.

O'Neill, Michael. 1993. "Fund Raising as an Ethical Act." *Advancing Philanthropy* 1: 30–35.

Osili, Una and Dan Du. 2003. *Immigrant Assimilation and Charitable Giving.* Retrieved from: http://www.philanthropy.iupui.edu/files/research/immigrant_assimilation_and_charitable_giving.pdf.

Ostrower, Francie. 1995. *Why the Wealthy Give: The Culture of Elite Philanthropy.* Princeton, NJ: Princeton University Press.

Otake, Keiko, Satoshi Shimai, Junko Tanaka-Matsumi, Kanako Otsui, and Barbara L. Fredrickson. 2006. "Happy People Become Happier Through Kindness: A Counting Kindness Intervention." *Journal of Happiness Studies*, 7(3): 361–375.

Payton, Robert L. 1988. *Philanthropy: Voluntary Action for the Public Good.* New York: American Council on Education/Macmillan.

Payton, Robert L. and Michael P. Moody. 2008. *Understanding Philanthropy: Its Meaning and Mission.* Bloomington, IN: Indiana University Press.

Perry, Suzanne. 2015. "1 in 3 Americans Lack Faith in Charities, Chronicle Poll Finds." *Chronicle of Philanthropy.* October 5.

Peterson, Brooks. 2004. *Cultural Intelligence.* Yarmouth, ME: Intercultural Press Inc.

Pettey, Janice Gow. 2013. *Nonprofit Fundraising Strategy: A Guide to Ethical Decision Making and Regulation for Nonprofit Organizations.* Hoboken, NJ: John Wiley & Sons, Inc.

Pew Research Center. 2014. *Millennials in Adulthood: Detached from Institutions, Networked with Friends.* Washington, DC Retrieved from: http://www.pewsocialtrends.org/files/2014/03/2014-03-07_generations-report-version-for-web.pdf.

Pew Research Center. 2015. *America's Changing Religious Landscape.* Washington, DC. Retrieved from: http://www.pewforum.org/files/2015/05/RLS-05-08-full-report.pdf.

Pine, B. Joseph II and James H. Gilmore. 1999. *The Experience Economy.* Boston: Harvard Business School Press.

Preston, Stephanie D. 2013. "The Origins of Altruism in Offspring Care." *Psychological Bulletin,* 139: 1305.

Pribbenow, Paul P. 1993. "Public Service: Renewing the Moral Meaning of Professions in America." Unpublished doctoral dissertation, University of Chicago, Divinity School, Chicago, IL.

Pribbenow, Paul P. 1999. "Love and Work: Rethinking Our Modes of Professions." In *New Directions for Philanthropic Fundraising,* No. 26, pp. 29–50. San Francisco, CA: Jossey-Bass.

Prince, Russ Alan and Karen Maru File. 1994. *The Seven Faces of Philanthropy: A New Approach to Cultivating Major Donors.* San Francisco, CA: Jossey-Bass.

Putnam, Robert D. and David E. Campbell. 2010. *American Grace: How Religion Divides and Unites Us.* New York: Simon & Schuster.

Quintana, Nico S., Josh Rosenthal, and Jeff Krehely. 2010. *On the Streets: The Federal Response to Gay and Transgender Homeless Youth.* Washington, DC: Center for American Progress.

Radicati, Sarah. 2013. "Email Statistics Report, 2013-2017." Palo Alto, CA: The Radicati Group, Inc.

Ramos, Henry. n.d. "Harnessing the Still Untapped Potential of Diverse Donors." *AFP Kaleidoscope.* Accessed June 11, 2015: http://www.afpnet.org/newsletters/k/Spring2013/harness.html.

Redbird. 2011. *Motivate and Convince: The Most Effective Tactics for Attracting Donors and Volunteers.* Accessed June 25, 2015: http://www.redbirdonline.com/sites/default/files/imce/motivate_and_convince.pdf.

Reker, Gary T., Edward J. Peacock, and Paul T.P. Wong. 1987. "Meaning and Purpose in Life and Well-Being: A Life-Span Perspective." *Journal of Gerontology,* 42(1): 44–49.

Reinhard, David A., Sara H. Konrath, William D. Lopez, and Heather G. Cameron. 2012. "Expensive Egos: Narcissistic Males Have Higher Cortisol." *PLoS ONE,* 7(1): e30858. doi: 10.1371/journal.pone.0030858.

Rockefeller, John D. 1933. "The Technique of Soliciting." Speech Delivered to the Citizens Family Welfare Committee, New York City.

Rockefeller Philanthropy Advisors. 2012. *Diversity, Inclusion and Effective Philanthropy.* Retrieved from: https://rockpa.org/document.doc?id=207.

Rooney, Patrick M. 2010. "Dispelling Common Beliefs about Giving to Religious Institutions in the United States." In David H. Smith (ed.), *Religious Giving: For Love of God,* pp. 1–27. Bloomington, IN: Indiana University Press.

Rooney, Patrick M., Eleanor Brown, and Debra J. Mesch. 2007. "Who Decides in Giving to Education? A Study of Charitable Giving by Married Couples." *International Journal of Educational Advancement*, 7(3): 229–242.

Rooney, Patrick M. and Sarah K. Nathan. 2011. "Contemporary Dynamics of Philanthropy." In Eugene R. Tempel, Timothy L. Seiler, and Eva A. Aldrich (eds.), *Achieving Excellence in Fundraising*, 3rd ed., pp. 117–124. San Francisco, CA: Jossey-Bass.

Rooney, Patrick M., Debra J. Mesch, William Chin, and Kathryn S. Steinberg. 2005. "The Effects of Race, Gender, and Survey Methodologies on Giving in the U.S." *Economic Letters*, 86: 173–180.

Rose, Sharon R. 1998. "A Study of Lesbian Philanthropy: Charitable Giving Patterns." MA thesis, University of San Francisco.

Rosso, Henry A. 1991. *Achieving Excellence in Fund Raising*. San Francisco, CA: Jossey-Bass.

Rovner, Mark. 2013. *The Next Generation of American Giving: The Charitable Habits of Generations Y, X, Baby Boomers, and Matures*. Charleston, SC: Blackbaud and Edge Research.

Rovner, Mark. 2015. *Diversity in Giving*. Blackbaud, Inc. Retrieved from: https://www.blackbaud.com/nonprofit-resources/diversity-in-giving.

Rudd, Melanie, Jennifer Aaker, and Michael I. Norton. 2014. "Getting the Most Out of Giving: Concretely Framing a Prosocial Goal Maximizes Happiness." *Journal of Experimental Social Psychology*, 54: 11–24.

Sacks, Eleanor W. 2014. *The Growing Importance of Community Foundations*. Indianapolis, IN: The Indiana University Lilly Family School of Philanthropy.

Sargeant, Adrian. 2001a. "Managing Donor Defection: Why Should Donors Stop Giving?" *New Directions for Philanthropic Fundraising*, 32.

Sargeant, Adrian. 2001b. "Relationship Fundraising: How to Keep Donors Loyal." *Nonprofit Management and Leadership*, 12(2): 177–192. San Francisco, CA: Wiley Periodicals, Inc.

Sargeant, Adrian, John B. Ford, and Douglas C. West. 2005. "Perceptual Determinants of Nonprofit Giving Behavior." *Journal of Business Research*, 59(2): 155–165.

Sargeant, Adrian and Elaine Jay. 2004. *Building Donor Loyalty: The Fundraiser's Guide to Increasing Lifetime Value*. San Francisco, CA: Jossey-Bass.

Sargeant, Adrian and Elaine Jay. 2014. *Fundraising Management: Analysis, Planning and Practice*. London and New York: Routledge.

Scheitle, Christopher. 2010. *Beyond the Congregation: The World of Christian Nonprofits*. New York: Oxford University Press.

Scherer, Michael. 2012. "Exclusive: Obama's 2012 Digital Fundraising Outperformed 2008." *Time*, November 15, 2012.

Schervish, Paul G. 1997. "Inclination, Obligation, and Association: What We Know and What We Need to Learn About Donor Motivation." In Dwight F. Burlingame (ed.), *Critical Issues in Fund Raising*. New York: John Wiley & Sons, Inc.

Schervish, Paul G. 2000a. "The Material Horizons of Philanthropy: New Directions for Money and Motives." In *New Directions for Philanthropic Fundraising*, p. 5–16. San Francisco, CA: Jossey-Bass.

Schervish, Paul G. 2000b. "The Spiritual Horizons of Philanthropy: New Directions for Money and Motives." In *New Directions for Philanthropic Fundraising*, p. 17–31. San Francisco, CA: Jossey-Bass.

Schervish, Paul G. 2007. "Why the Wealthy Give: Factors Which Mobilize Philanthropy Among High Net-Worth Individuals." In Adrian Sargeant and Walter Wymer (eds.), *The Routledge Companion to Nonprofit Marketing*, pp. 173–190. New York: Routledge.

Schervish, Paul G. and John J. Havens. 1997. "Social Participation and Charitable Giving: A Multivariate Analysis." *Voluntas*, 8(3): 235–260.

Schervish, Paul G. and John J. Havens. 2001. *Extended Report of the Wealth with Responsibility Study*. Chestnut Hill, MA: Social Welfare Research Institute, Boston College.

Schervish, Paul G. and John J. Havens. 2003. *New Findings on the Patterns of Wealth and Philanthropy*. Chestnut Hill, MA: Social Welfare Research Institute, Boston College.

Schervish, Paul G., Mary A. O'Herlihy, and John J. Havens. 2001. "The Spiritual Secret of Wealth: The Inner Dynamics by Which Fortune Engenders Care." Workshop presented at the Welfare Research Institute Conference, Boston, MA, September 20, 2001.

Schwartz, Carolyn E. and Rabbi Meir Sendor. 1999. "Helping Other Helps Oneself: Response Shift Effects in Peer Support." *Social Science and Medicine*, 48(11): 1563–1575.

Seiler, Timothy L. 2001. *Developing Your Case for Support*. San Francisco, CA: John Wiley & Sons, Inc.

Shaker, Genevieve. 2013. "The Generosity of the Professoriate: Faculty as Donors and Academic Citizens." *Metropolitan Universities*, 23(3): 5–25.

Shang, Jen and Rachel Croson. 2009. "A Field Experiment in Charitable Contribution: The Impact of Social Information on the Voluntary Provision of Public Goods." *The Economic Journal*, 119: 1422–1439.

Siegel, Dan and Jenny Yancey. 2003. *Philanthropy's Forgotten Resource? Engaging the Individual Donor: The State of Donor Education Today and a Leadership Agenda for the Road Ahead*. Mill Valley, CA: New Visions: Philanthropic Research and Development.

Smith, Hayden W. 1997. "If Not Corporate Philanthropy, Then What?" *New York Law School Law Review*, 41: 757–770.

Smith, David H. 2005. *Good Intentions: The Moral Responsibilities of Trusteeship*. Bloomington, IN: Indiana University Press.

Smith, Christian and Hilary Davidson. 2014. *The Paradox of Generosity: Giving We Receive, Grasping We Lose*. Oxford: Oxford University Press.

Smith, Christian, Michael O. Emerson, and Patricia Snell. 2008. *Passing the Plate: Why Americans Don't Give Away More Money*. New York: Oxford University Press.

Snell, Patricia and Brandon Vaidyanathan. 2011. "Motivations for and Obstacles to Religious Financial Giving." *Sociology of Religion*, 72(2): 189–211.

Spectrem Group. 2002. *Charitable Giving and the Ultra High Net Worth Household: Reaching the Wealthy Donor*. Spectrem Group.

Sprecher, Susan and Pamela C. Regan. 2002. "Liking Some Things (In Some People) More than Others: Partner Preferences in Romantic Relationships and Friendships." *Journal of Social and Personal Relationships*, 19(4): 463–481.

Steinberg, Richard and Debra Morris. 2010. "Ratio Discrimination in Charity Fundraising: The Inappropriate Use of Cost Ratios has Harmful Side-Effects." *Voluntary Sector Review*, 1(1): 77–95.

Sterling, M. 2005. *Working with Creative People in 12 Steps*. Southampton, Ont.: Chantry Island Publishing.

Steuerle, C. Eugene. 1987. *Charitable Giving Patterns of the Wealthy*. Washington, DC: Urban Institute.

Stevenson, Seth. 2010. "How to be Invisible." *Newsweek*, April 9, 2010.

Stukas, Arthur A., Russell Hoye, Matthew Nicholson, Kevin M. Brown and Laura Aisbett. 2014. "Motivations to Volunteer and their Associations with Volunteers' Well-Being." *Nonprofit and Voluntary Sector Quarterly.* doi: 10.1177/0899764014561122.

Sturtevant, William T. 1997. *The Artful Journey: Cultivating and Soliciting the Major Gift.* Chicago, IL: Bonus Books, Inc.

Sulek, Marty. 2010. "On the Classical Meaning of Philanthrôpía." *Nonprofit and Voluntary Sector Quarterly,* 39(3): 385–408.

Sullivan, Paul. 2014. "Giving Back to Your School in a Meaningful Way." *The New York Times,* October 10, 2014.

Taylor, Paul, Mark Hugo Lopez, Jessica Martínez, and Gabriel Velasco. 2012. "When Labels Don't Fit: Hispanics and Their Views of Identity." Pew Research Center. Retrieved from: http://www.pewhispanic.org/2012/04/04/ii-identity-pan-ethnicity-and-race/.

Tempel, Eugene R. 2003. *Achieving Excellence in Fund Raising,* 2nd ed. San Francisco, CA: Jossey-Bass.

Tempel, Eugene R. 2004. *Development Committee.* Washington, DC: BoardSource.

Tempel, Eugene R. 2008. "Bigger Isn't Always Better: The Importance of Small Gifts and Small Nonprofits." *Nonprofit Times,* June 15, 2008.

Tempel, Eugene R. and M. J. Beem. 2002. "The State of the Profession." In *New Strategies for Educational Fundraising.* Westport, CT: Praeger Publishers.

Tempel, Eugene R. and Margaret A. Duronio. 1997. "The Demographics and Experience of Fundraisers." In *New Directions for Philanthropic Fundraising,* No. 15, pp. 49–68. San Francisco, CA: Jossey-Bass.

Tempel, Eugene R., Timothy L. Seiler, and Eva A. Aldrich. 2011. *Achieving Excellence in Fundraising,* 3rd ed. San Francisco, CA: Jossey-Bass.

The Economist "Crossing the Divide: Why Culture Should be Cool." 2013. *The Economist,* October 12, 2013.

The Wired Wealthy: Using the Internet to Connect with Your Middle and Major Donors. 2008. Convio, Sea Change Strategies and Edge Research. Available at: http://seachangestrategies.com/scwp/wp-content/uploads/2014/03/wired-wealthy_final_32408.pdf.

The World Bank. 2015. "Remittances Growth to Slow Sharply in 2015, as Europe and Russia Stay Weak; Pick up Expected Next Year." Retrieved from: http://www.worldbank.org/en/news/press-release/2015/04/13/remittances-growth-to-slow-sharply-in-2015-as-europe-and-russia-stay-weak-pick-up-expected-next-year.

Tkach, Christopher Terrence. 2005. *Unlocking the Treasury of Human Kindness: Enduring Improvements in Mood, Happiness, and Self-Evaluations.* University of California, Riverside, Unpublished doctoral dissertation.

Toce, Joseph. 2010. *Tax Economics of Charitable Giving.* New York: Thomson-Reuters.

TowerData. 2013. "Social Media & Email Marketing Integration Part 1: The Business Case." Available at http://www.towerdata.com/blog/bid/118112/Social-Media-Email-Marketing-Integration-Part-1-The-Business-Case.

Tsvetkova, Milena and Michael W. Macy. 2014. "The Social Contagion of Generosity." *PLoS ONE,* 9(2): e87275. doi:10.1371/journal.pone.0087275.

Turcotte, Martin. 2015. *Volunteering and Charitable Giving in Canada.* Minister of Industry: Retrieved June 20, 2015 from: http://www.statcan.gc.ca/pub/89-652-x/89-652-x2015001-eng.pdf.

United Nations Volunteer. 2015. *State of the World's Volunteerism.* Retrieved June 20, 2015 from: http://www.volunteeractioncounts.org/en/swvr-2015.html.

United States v. American Bar Endowment. 1986. 477 U.S. 105.

United Way. 2013. "Heightening the Capacity of Our Nation." Retrieved from: https://secure.unitedway.org/page/-/Files/2013_DI_Annual_Report.pdf.

University of Texas at Dallas. 2015. "Opportunity Funds." Accessed June 8, 2015: http://www.utdallas.edu/opportunity.

Unruh, Gregory C. and Angel Cabrera. 2013. "Join the Global Elite." *Harvard Business Review,* May 2013.

Uslander, Eric M. 2002. *The Moral Foundations of Trust.* Cambridge, UK: Cambridge University Press.

U.S. Bureau of Labor Statistics. 2014. *Women in the Labor Force: A Databook.* BLS Report 1052. Retrieved from: http://www.bls.gov/opub/reports/cps/women-in-the-labor-force-a-databook-2014.pdf

U.S. Census Bureau. 2011a. *Income, Poverty and Health Insurance Coverage in the United States.* Washington, DC: Government Printing Office. Retrieved from: http://www.census.gov/newsroom/releases/archives/income_wealth/cb11-157.html.

U.S. Census Bureau. 2011b. *Facts for Features: American Indian and Alaska Native Heritage Month.* Washington, DC: Government Printing Office. Retrieved from: https://www.census.gov/newsroom/releases/archives/facts_for_features_special_editions/cb11-ff22.html.

U.S. Census Bureau. 2012a. *Overview of Race and Hispanic Origin: 2010.* Washington, DC: Government Printing Office. Retrieved from: http://www.census.gov/prod/cen2010/briefs/c2010br-02.pdf.

U.S. Census Bureau. 2012b. *The Foreign-Born Population in the United States: 2010.* Washington, DC: Government Printing Office. Retrieved from: http://www.census.gov/content/dam/Census/library/publications/2012/acs/acs-19.pdf.

U.S. Census Bureau. 2012c. *U.S. Census Bureau Projections Show a Slower Growing, Older, More Diverse Nation a Half Century from Now.* Washington, DC: Government Printing Office. Retrieved from: http://www.census.gov/newsroom/releases/archives/population/cb12-243.html.

U.S. Census Bureau. 2013. *About: Race.* Washington, DC: Government Printing Office. Retrieved from: https://www.census.gov/topics/population/race/about.html.

U.S. Census Bureau. 2014. *American FactFinder.* Washington, DC: Government Printing Office. Retrieved from: http://factfinder.census.gov/faces/tableservices/jsf/pages/productview.xhtml?src=bkmk.

U.S. Department of Education, National Center for Education Statistics. 2012. *The Condition of Education 2012* (NCES 2012-045), Indicator 47.

U.S. Trust. 2002. *Survey of Affluent Americans XXI.* U.S. Trust.

Van Willigen, Marike. 2000. "Differential Benefits of Volunteering Across the Life Course." *The Journals of Gerontology,* 55B(5): S308–S318.

Vespa, Jonathan, Jamie M. Lewis, and Rose M. Krieder. 2013. *America's Families and Living Arrangements: 2012.* United States Census Bureau. Retrieved from: http://www.census.gov/prod/2013pubs/p20-570.pdf.

Vohs, Kathleen D., Nicole L. Mead, and Miranda R. Goode. 2006. "The Psychological Consequences of Money." *Science,* 314: 1154–1156.

Volunteering Australia. 2015. *Key Facts and Statistics about Volunteering in Australia.* Retrieved June 20, 2015 from: http://www.volunteeringaustralia.org/wp-content/uploads/VA-Key-statistics-about-Australian-volunteering-16-April-20151.pdf.

Wagner, Lilya. 2002. *Careers in Fundraising.* New York: John Wiley & Sons, Inc.

Wagner, Lilya. 2005. *Leading Up: Transformational Leadership for Fundraisers.* New York: John Wiley & Sons, Inc.

Wagner, Lilya. 2007. "A Crossroads on the Path of Professionalism in Fundraising." *On Philanthropy*, September 17, 2007.

Walker, Julia Ingraham. 2006. *Major Gifts.* Hoboken, NJ: John Wiley & Sons, Inc.

Wang, Wendy, Kim Parker, and Paul Taylor. 2013. *Breadwinner Moms.* Washington, DC: Pre Research Center. Retrieved from: www.pewsocialtrends.org/2013/05/29/breadwinner-moms.

Wheeler, J. A., K. M. Gorey, and B. Greenblatt. 1998. "The Beneficial Effects of Volunteering for Older Volunteers and the People They Serve: A Meta-Analysis." *International Journal of Aging and Human Development*, 47(1): 69–79.

Wilhelm, Mark O., Eleanor Brown, Patrick M. Rooney, and Richard Steinberg. 2008. "The Intergenerational Transmission of Generosity." *Journal of Public Economics*, 92: 2146–2156.

Wilmington Trust/Campden Research Women and Wealth Survey. 2009. *The New Wealth Paradigm: How Affluent Women Are Taking Control of Their Futures.* Retrieved from: http://www.wilmingtontrust.com/repositories/wtc_sitecontent/PDF/new_wealth_paradigm.pdf.

Winkleman, Michael. 2005. *Cultural Awareness, Sensitivity and Competence.* Peosta, IA: Eddie Bowers Pub. Co.

Witter, Lisa and Lisa Chen. 2008. *The She Spot: Why Women are the Market for Changing the World and How to Reach Them.* San Francisco, CA: Berrett-Koehler Publishers, Inc.

W. K. Kellogg Foundation. 2012. *Cultures of Giving.* Retrieved from: http://www.latinocf.org/pdf/Cultures-of-Giving_Energizing-and-Expanding-Philanthropy-by-and-for-Communities-of-Color.pdf.

Wood, E. W. 1997. "Profiling Major Gifts Fundraisers: What Qualifies Them for Success." In *New Directions for Philanthropic Fundraising*, No. 15, pp. 5–15. San Francisco, CA: Jossey-Bass.

Worth, Michael J. 2010. *Leading the Campaign: Advancing Colleges and Universities.* Lanham, MD: Rowan & Littlefield.

INDEX